Lecture Notes in Computer Science 7763

Commenced Publication in 1973
Founding and Former Series Editors:
Gerhard Goos, Juris Hartmanis, and Jan van Leeuwen

T0224002

Mirosław Kutyłowski   Moti Yung (Eds.)

Information Security and Cryptology

8th International Conference, Inscrypt 2012
Beijing, China, November 28-30, 2012
Revised Selected Papers

 Springer

Volume Editors

Mirosław Kutyłowski
Wrocław University of Technology
Department of Fundamental Problems of Technology
Wybrzeże Wyspiańskiego 27, 50-370 Wrocław, Poland
E-mail: miroslaw.kutylowski@pwr.wroc.pl

Moti Yung
Columbia University and Google Inc.
Computer Science Department
Amsterdam Avenue 1214, New York, NY 10027, USA
E-mail: motiyung@gmail.com

ISSN 0302-9743   e-ISSN 1611-3349
ISBN 978-3-642-38518-6   e-ISBN 978-3-642-38519-3
DOI 10.1007/978-3-642-38519-3
Springer Heidelberg Dordrecht London New York

Library of Congress Control Number: 2013938367

CR Subject Classification (1998): K.6.5, E.3, E.4, F.2, D.4.6

LNCS Sublibrary: SL 4 – Security and Cryptology

Typesetting: Camera-ready by author, data conversion by Scientific Publishing Services, Chennai, India

Printed on acid-free paper

Springer is part of Springer Science+Business Media (www.springer.com)

Preface

These volume contains the proceedings of INSCRYPT 2012, the 8th China International Conference on Information Security and Cryptology, which was held in Beijing, November 28–30, 2012.

INSCRYPT 2012 was collaboratively organized by the State Key Laboratory of Information Security (SKLOIS) of the Chinese Academy of Sciences (CAS) and the Chinese Association for Cryptologic Research (CACR), in cooperation with the International Association of Cryptologic Research (IACR). It was partly supported by the Natural Science Foundation of China (NSFC) and the Institute of Information Engineering (IIE), Chinese Academy of Sciences (CAS).

The conference is a leading international meeting taking place in China devoted to the current research in cryptography and information security. The program of the conference consisted of sessions devoted to: Side Channel Attacks, Extractor and Secret Sharing, Public Key Cryptography, Block Ciphers, Stream Ciphers, New Constructions and Protocols. Besides contributed talks, the program contained invited talks by Jung Hee Cheon and Goichiro Hanaoka, as well as tutorials given by Mirosław Kutyłowski (Digital Electronic Identity Documents) and Junfeng Fan (Cryptographic Hardware: Design for Low Power, Low Area and Security Against Physical Attacks).

The international Program Committee of INSCRYPT 2012 evaluated 71 anonymous submissions from all over the world. Each submission was reviewed by at least four Program Committee members, who were supported by a number of external reviewers. After a strict evaluation process, 23 papers from Australia, P.R. China, Finland, France, Germany, Hong Kong, India, Israel, Japan, Malaysia, Russia, Singapore and Switzerland were selected for presentation during the conference.

We thank the authors of contributed papers, Program Committee members, external reviewers, and Organizing Committee (Dongdai, Lin, Rui Zhang, Zhijun Qiang, Yu Chen, Yao Lu, Fengjiao Yu) for their joint effort in making INSCRYPT 2012 happen. We further thank the EasyChair team for technical tools supporting the conference preparation and Kamil Kluczniak for technical assistance during preparation of this volume.

Mirosław Kutyłowski
Moti Yung

Organization

Program Committee

Martin Albrecht	UPMC Paris, France
Zhenfu Cao	SJTU, P.R. China
Bogdan Carbunar	Florida International University, USA
Liqun Chen	Hewlett-Packard Laboratories, UK
Zhong Chen	Peking University, P.R. China
Sherman S.M. Chow	University of Waterloo, Canada / CUHK, HK
Tassos Dimitriou	Athens Information Technology, Greece
Cunsheng Ding	Hong Kong University of Science and Technology, SAR China
Shlomi Dolev	Ben Gurion University of the Negev, Israel
Lei Hu	Chinese Academy of Sciences, P.R. China
Charanjit Jutla	IBM T.J. Watson Research Center, USA
Angelos Keromytis	Columbia University, USA
Kwangjo Kim	KAIST, Korea
Matthias Krause	Mannheim University, Germany
Miroslaw Kutylowski	Wroclaw University of Technology, Poland
Xuejia Lai	Shanghai Jiaotong University, P.R. China
Hui Li	Xidan University, P.R. China
Yingjiu Li	Singapore Management University, Singapore
Joseph Liu	Institute for Infocomm Research, Singapore
Peng Liu	The Pennsylvania State University, USA
Javier Lopez	University of Malaga, Spain
Mark Manulis	University of Surrey, UK
Krystian Matusiewicz	Intel Technology, Poland
Florian Mendel	KU Leuven, Belgium
Atsuko Miyaji	JAIST, Japan
Payman Mohassel	University of Calgary, Canada
Amir Moradi	Ruhr University Bochum, Germany
Yi Mu	University of Wollongong, Australia
Kaisa Nyberg	Aalto University, Finland
Claudio Orlandi	Aarhus University, Denmark
Kenneth Paterson	Royal Holloway, University of London, UK
Giuseppe Persiano	University of Salerno, Italy
Mariana Raykova	Columbia University, USA
Kouichi Sakurai	Kyushu University, Japan
Jun Shao	Zhejiang Gongshang University, P.R. China

Ron Steinfeld   Monash University, Australia
Wen-Guey Tzeng   National Chiao Tung University, Taiwan
Yevgeniy Vahlis   AT&T Labs, Security Research Center, USA
Wenling Wu   Institute of Software, Chinese Academy of
                           Sciences, Beijing, P.R. China
Adam Young   Cryptovirology Labs, USA
Moti Yung   Google & Columbia University, USA
Fangguo Zhang   Sun Yat-sen University, P.R. China
Yuliang Zheng   UNC Charlotte, USA
Hong-Sheng Zhou   University of Maryland, USA

Additional Reviewers

Armknecht, Frederik   Huang, Heqing
Asharov, Gilad   Huang, Jialin
Athanasopoulos, Elias   Huang, Xinyi
Au, Man Ho   Hubacek, Pavel
Blondeau, Céline   Hülsing, Andreas
Borghoff, Julia   Iovino, Vincenzo
Cai, Shaoying   Jovanovic, Philipp
Cao, Weiwei   Järvinen, Kimmo
Carlet, Claude   Kavun, Elif Bilge
Chakravarty,   Kemerlis, Vasileios P.
   Sambuddho   Kiyomoto, Shinsaku
Chen, Jiageng   Kontaxis, Georgios
Chen, Yu   Kopeetsky, Marina
Cichon, Jacek   Kourai, Kenichi
Clark, Jeremy   Kywe, Su Mon
De Caro, Angelo   Le, Dong
De Prisco, Roberto   Li, Jin
Deng, Tang   Li, Wei
Ding, Yi   Lu, Jiqiang
Enos, Graham   Lyubashevsky, Vadim
Fandina, Nova   Mikhalev, Vasily
Fernandez, Carmen   Mischke, Oliver
Forte, Andrea   Moyano, Francisco
Galdi, Clemente   Nad, Tomislav
Gong, Junqing   Nieto, Ana
Gopal, Vinodh   Nikova, Svetla
Gorbunov, Sergey   Nishide, Takashi
Guo, Fuchun   Omote, Kazumasa
Hakala, Risto   Pappas, Vasilis
Hamann, Matthias   Paul, Souradyuti
Han, Jinguang   Perret, Ludovic

Proctor, Gordon
Rios, Ruben
Rnjom, Sondre
Rosulek, Mike
Sadeghian, Saeed
Scafuro, Alessandra
Schläffer, Martin
Schmidt, Jörn-Marc
Shirase, Masaaki
Suzuki, Koutarou
Takahashi, Junko
Tang, Qiang
Tischhauser, Elmar

Wang, Guilin
Wang, Jun
Watson, Gaven
Wei, Puwen
Wichs, Daniel
Xiao, Gaoyao
Xie, Qi
Ximing, Li
Xu, Hong
Yan, Qiang
Yasuda, Takanori
Yasunaga, Kenji

Table of Contents

On the Multiple Fault Attacks on RSA Signatures with LSBs of Messages Unknown[*]

Lidong Han[1,2], Wei Wei[2], and Mingjie Liu[2,3]

[1] School of Information Science and Engineering,
Hangzhou Normal University, Hangzhou 310036, China
[2] Institute for Advanced Study,
Tsinghua University, Beijing 100084, China
[3] Beijing International Center for Mathematical Research,
Peking University, Beijing 100084, China

Abstract. In CHES 2009, Coron, Joux, Kizhvatov, Naccache and Paillier (CJKNP) introduced the multiple fault attack on RSA signatures with partially unknown messages. However, the complexity of their attack is exponential in the number of faulty signatures. At RSA 2010, this fault attack was improved, which runs in polynomial time in the number of faults. Both of the previous fault attacks deal with the general case. This paper considers the special situation that some least significant bits (LSBs) of messages are unknown. Because of this special case, our new multiple fault attack can handle a larger size of the unknown part of message. We provide two kinds of techniques to factor the RSA modulus N using the multiple faulty signatures. Comparisons between the previous attacks and the new attacks with a number of LSBs of the message unknown are given on the basis of the simulations.

Keywords: Fault Attacks, RSA Signatures, Least Significant Bits (LSBs), LLL Algorithm.

1 Introduction

RSA signature [13] invented by Rivest, Shamir and Adleman is the most popular digital signature scheme. To sign a message m, the signer first encodes m as $\mu(m)$ using the encoding function $\mu(\cdot)$, then computes $\rho = \mu(m)^d \mod N$, which is the signature of m. To verify the signature, the receiver checks whether $\rho^e = \mu(m) \mod N$ holds. A sophisticated way to speed up the signature generation is to exploit the Chinese Remainder Theorem (CRT). This is done by computing:

$$\rho_p = \mu(m)^{d_p} \mod p \text{ and } \rho_q = \mu(m)^{d_q} \mod q \tag{1}$$

where $d_p = d \pmod{p-1}$ and $d_q = d \pmod{q-1}$. We obtain the signature

$$\rho = \rho_p + p \cdot (p^{-1} \mod q) \cdot (\rho_q - \rho_p) \mod N$$

[*] Supported by the National Natural Science Foundation of China (Grant No.61133013) and the National Basic Research Program of China (Grant No. 2013CB834205).

M. Kutyłowski and M. Yung (Eds.): Inscrypt 2012, LNCS 7763, pp. 1–9, 2013.
© Springer-Verlag Berlin Heidelberg 2013

using CRT. Such an approach, called RSA-CRT, achieves the signing time that is approximately four times faster than signature using the standard RSA definition.

The first fault attack against RSA-CRT signature implementation was introduced by Boneh, DeMillo and Lipton [1] in 1997. In the fault attack, we assume the attacker has the ability to induce a fault when computing the signature by CRT and only one of the above computations (1) is faulty. Hence, if the encoding function $\mu(\cdot)$ is public, the RSA modulus N can be factored by computing the greatest common divisor GCD between $\rho^e - \mu(m)$ and N.

In ISO/IEC 9796-2 the encoding function is the form:

$$\mu(m) = 6A_{16}||m[1]||H(m)||BC_{16}$$

where $m = m[1]||m[2]$ is split into two parts. In [4], Coron, Joux, Kizhvatov, Naccache and Paillier (CJKNP) proposed several fault attacks against randomized version of ISO/IEC 9796-2 including the single fault attack and the multiple fault attack. The time complexity of the latter is exponential in the number of faulty signatures. Coron, Naccache and Tibouchi (CNT) [5] improved this multiple fault attack and applied it to EMV signature. The time complexity is polynomial in the number of faults.

Both previous attacks can be applied to the signatures with the unknown message part (UMP) in the middle. They didn't analyze the scenario that the UMP occurs in the least significant bits. For example, the 'stereotyped' message $m[1]$ is "On April 16, 2012, the secret key for this day is ... ". If the unknown part of this message is relatively long, both previous attacks are invalid.

Our main goal is to extend the bound of the UMP using the multiple faulty signatures. First, based on solving the simultaneous Diophantine approximation problem, the multiple fault attack can factor N if the size of the UMP is at most $N^{\frac{1}{2}-\frac{1}{2\ell}}$, where ℓ is the number of faulty signatures, while the previous bound in [5] is $N^{\frac{1}{2}-\frac{2}{\ell}}$. Although the attack is heuristic, it works well in practice and paradoxically becomes more efficient as the modulus bit-length increases. Furthermore, the bound of the unknown part of message $m[1]$ can be improved using a new lattice technique presented by Cohn and Heninger in [2]. We hope that our new attack can be helpful for users to design the signature schemes in smart cards.

The rest of this paper is organized as follows. Section 2 gives a simple description of ISO/IEC 9796-2, and recalls the results of the previous attacks. In section 3, we first describe a new multiple fault attack in a simple way when the unknown part of message is in a special place. Secondly, this fault attack is extended by Cohn-Heninger method. We will give some simulation results and compare the new attacks with the previous attacks in section 4.

2   ISO/IEC 9796-2 and Previous Attacks

2.1   ISO/OEC 9796-2 Standard

ISO/IEC 9796-2 is a special encoding function standardized by ISO, which allows partial or total message recovery [9,10]. The encoding function in ISO/IEC 9796-2 can be used with hash-functions $H(m)$ of diverse digest-size k_h. For the sake of simplicity, we suppose that k_h, the size of N (denoted by k) and the size of m are all multiples of 8. The ISO/IEC 9796-2 encoding function is:

$$\mu(m) = 6A_{16}||m[1]||H(m)||BC_{16}$$

where $m = m[1]||m[2]$ is split into two parts: $m[1]$ consists of $k - k_h - 16$ most significant bits of m and $m[2]$ represents the remaining bits of m. Recently, some attacks against ISO/IEC 9796-2 are proposed in [4,6,5].

2.2   Previous Fault Attacks

CJKNP Attack. In 2009, CJKNP described the fault attacks on a randomized version of ISO/IEC 9796-2 standard including the single fault attack and multiple fault attack in [4]. In their multiple attack, the message m is of the form

$$m[1] = \alpha||r||\alpha', \quad m[2] = \text{DATA}$$

where r is an unknown message part (UMP), α, α' are known and DATA is some known or unknown string.

Assume that the attacker can obtain many faulty signatures which satisfy that only one of two computations in (1) occurs error. After some optimal operations as in [4], one can get a set of equations:

$$a_i + bx_i + cy_i = 0 \quad \bmod p$$

where a_i, b and c are known and x_i, y_i are unknown and small. The goal is to compute the factor p of the RSA modulus. CJKNP show how to extend the Coppersmith's method [3] to these multiple polynomial equations similar to the method in [7]. It is concluded that, the bound tends asymptotically to $\frac{1}{2}$ when the number of faults ℓ approaches infinity. However, the complexity of the multiple fault attack is exponential in the number of the faulty signatures.

DNT Attack. In 2010, Coron, Naccache and Stern [5] improved the multiple fault attack, and the complexity is polynomial in the number of faulty signatures. We will simply introduce the CNT's attack.

Also assume the attacker can get a system of equations:

$$a_i + b \cdot x_i + c \cdot y_i = 0 \quad \bmod p$$

for $1 \leq i \leq \ell$, where a_i, b, c are known as in above subsection and ℓ is the number of faulty signatures.

Using the orthogonal lattice technique [12] and the LLL algorithm [11], one can obtain a short vector u, which indicates a two dimensional vector (α_0, β_0) in a lattice

$$L(c, p) = \{(\alpha, \beta) \in \mathbb{Z}^2 | \alpha + c\beta = 0 \quad \bmod p\}.$$

Many such vectors can yield another lattice that contains two important vectors, which can be used to compute the factor p. By the optimal analysis as in [5], the bound of the the UMP is $N^{\frac{1}{2} - \frac{2}{\ell}}$, where ℓ is the number of faulty signatures. The time complexity of the attack is polynomial in the number of faulty signatures.

3   Multiple Attacks against ISO/IEC 9796-2 with LSBs of Message Known

In this section, we analyze the multiple fault attack on the special probabilistic variant of ISO/IEC 9796 standard. That is to say, the UMP are some least significant bits of the message. This situation leads to a simpler multiple fault attack and the larger bit-size of the UMP. First, we use the method of solving the simultaneous Diophantine approximation problem to discuss the multiple fault attack. In the next subsection the multiple fault attack is extended by using the Cohn-Heninger technique.

3.1   Multiple Fault Attack under LSBs of Message Known

In the form of ISO/IEC 9796, we assume that some least significant bits of the message $m[1]$ are unknown. That is

$$m[1] = \alpha||r, \quad m[2] = \text{DATA}.$$

The size of unknown part r is denoted as k_r and the size of $m[1]$ is $k - k_h - 16$. The encoded message is then

$$\mu(m) = 6A_{16}||\alpha||r||H(\alpha||r||\text{DATA})||BC_{16}.$$

The total number of unknown bits in $\mu(m)$ is $k_r + k_h$, where k_h is denoted as the bit length of the hash function. Therefore, we can write

$$\mu(m) = s + r' \cdot 2^8$$

where $s = (6A_{16}||\alpha) \cdot 2^{k_r+k_h+8} + BC_{16}$ is a known value and $r' = r \cdot 2^{k_h} + H(m)$ is the UMP.

Suppose that the opponent possesses a faulty signature ρ such that

$$\rho^e = \mu(m) \mod p, \quad \rho^e \neq \mu(m) \mod q.$$

Therefore, we obtain

$$\rho^e = s + r' \cdot 2^8 \mod p.$$

This shows that $x_0 = r' = r \cdot 2^{k_h} + H(m)$ must be a solution of the equation

$$a + bx = 0 \mod p,$$

where $a := s - \rho^e \mod N, b := 2^8$ are known. Note that we can assume $b = 1$ by multiplying the equation by $b^{-1} \mod N$.

In the multiple fault attack, the attacker can obtain ℓ faulty signatures. Similar to the analysis described above, one has a collection of equations:

$$x_i + a_i = 0 \mod p, \quad \text{for } 1 \leq i \leq \ell \tag{2}$$

where a_i's are known and x_i's are unknown and small. Our goal is to recover the factor p.

In the following, we will adopt the technique of solving the simultaneous Diophantine approximation problem. Let X be a suitable bound such that $x_i \le X$ for all $i \le \ell$. We construct the lattice $\mathcal{L}$ spanned by the rows of the following matrix

$$M = \begin{pmatrix} X & a_1 & a_2 & \dots & a_\ell \\ & N & & & \\ & & N & & \\ & & & \ddots & \\ & & & & N \end{pmatrix}.$$

The dimension of the lattice $\mathcal{L}$ is $\ell + 1$ and the determinant of $\mathcal{L}$ is $N^\ell X$. From the Gaussian heuristic, the length of the smallest vector of the lattice $\mathcal{L}$ is roughly $\sqrt{\ell + 1} \cdot (N^\ell X)^{\frac{1}{\ell+1}}$. From (2), there exist integers k_i for all $i \le \ell$ satisfying $a_i + x_i = k_i \cdot p$. Therefore, in the lattice $\mathcal{L}$, we have the vector $(qX, qx_1, qx_2, \cdots, qx_\ell) = (q, -k_1, -k_2, \cdots, -k_\ell) \cdot M$. Its Euclidean norm is approximately bounded by $\sqrt{\ell + 1} \cdot qX$. If the bound is less than the heuristic shortest vector length, i.e., $qX \le (N^\ell X)^{\frac{1}{\ell+1}}$, it is very probable that the vector $(qX, qx_1, qx_2, \cdots, qx_\ell)$ in $\mathcal{L}$ is the shortest vector. Assuming $X = N^\delta$, the condition is equal to

$$\delta \le \frac{1}{2} - \frac{1}{2\ell}. \tag{3}$$

It means that, if all x_i's in equation (2) satisfy $x_i \le N^{\frac{1}{2} - \frac{1}{2\ell}}$, the shortest vector $\mathbf{v}$ is heuristically unique by Minkowski theorem. Applying the lattice basis reduction algorithm to a lattice of fixed dimension we obtain the shortest vector $\mathbf{v}$. This leads to factor N by computing the GCD of the first two components of $\mathbf{v}$.

From the inequality (3), it is easy to see that the new bound is better than the bound in [5]. We will give some comparisons by simulation test in the next section.

3.2 Extended Multiple Fault Attack by Cohn-Heninger Technique

In this subsection, instead of the simple method in above subsection, we will utilize the new technique by Cohn and Heninger in [2].

In detail, assume we have a set of equations each of which is in form of $x_i + a_i = 0 \mod p$ and r_i is the solution of each equation. Our goal is to find polynomials in forms of $h(r_1, r_2, ..., r_\ell) = 0$ over integers. From Howgrave-Graham theorem in [8], it is sufficient for h to satisfy the following conditions:

1. $h(r_1, r_2, ..., r_\ell) = 0 \mod p^k$.
2. $\|h(r_1, r_2, ..., r_\ell)\| < p^k / \sqrt{w}$, where $w = \deg(h)$.

For the first one, we will compute such modulo polynomials as the integer linear combination of products

$$(x_1 + a_1)^{i_1} \cdots (x_\ell + a_\ell)^{i_\ell} N^\kappa$$

where $i_1 + \cdots + i_\ell + \kappa \geq k$. To ensure $\|h(r_1, r_2, ..., r_\ell)\| < p^k/\sqrt{w}$, we require h has small coefficients. It can be achieved to reduce a lattice with entries of polynomial coefficients. Let X be an upper bound of r_i. Use the polynomials

$$(X_1 x_1 + a_1)^{i_1} \cdots (X_\ell x_\ell + a_\ell)^{i_\ell} N^\kappa$$

to construct the lattice $\mathcal{L}$, with $i_1 + \cdots + i_\ell + \kappa \leq t$ and $\ell = \max(k - \sum_j i_j, 0)$. The basis of the lattice consists of the ordering monomials and is an upper triangular matrix.

The dimension of $\mathcal{L}$ is

$$\dim\mathcal{L} = \binom{t+\ell}{\ell}$$

and the determinant is

$$\det \mathcal{L} = X^{\binom{t+\ell}{\ell}\frac{t\ell}{\ell+1}} N^{\binom{k+\ell}{\ell}\frac{k}{m+1}}$$

Applying a lattice reduction algorithm, we can get a reduced basis $v_1, v_2, ..., v_\ell$, such that

$$\|v_1\| \leq \cdots \leq \|v_\ell\| \leq 2^{\frac{\dim\mathcal{L}(\dim L - 1)}{4(\dim\mathcal{L}+1-\ell)}} (\det \mathcal{L})^{\frac{1}{\dim\mathcal{L}+1-\ell}} \tag{4}$$

If we require the right-hand side of the inequality (4) above is smaller than $p^k/\sqrt{\dim\mathcal{L}}$, from Howgrave-Graham theorem, then the polynomials h_i corresponding to $v_1, v_2, ..., v_\ell$ are equal to zero. Hence we can write it as

$$2^{\frac{\dim\mathcal{L}(\dim\mathcal{L}-1)}{4(\dim\mathcal{L}+1-\ell)}} (\det \mathcal{L})^{\frac{1}{\dim\mathcal{L}+1-\ell}} \leq p^k/\sqrt{\dim\mathcal{L}}$$

Neglecting all small terms, we have a asymptotical bound

$$(\det \mathcal{L})^{\frac{1}{\dim\mathcal{L}+1-\ell}} \leq N^{\frac{1}{2}k}$$

Substituting the values of $\det \mathcal{L}$ and $\dim\mathcal{L}$ and optimizing the value of t and k, under the assumption 1, we get the following theorem.

Assumption 1. *The resultant computations for the polynomials h_i yield nonzero polynomials.*

This assumption also indicates that all the polynomials h_i are algebraically independent. It needs to be pointed out that (most) attacks using Coppersmith techniques are heuristical, and experiments must be done for most cases to justify the assumption.

Theorem 1 (Cohn-Heninger [2]). *Given ℓ signatures $\rho_1, \rho_2, ..., \rho_\ell$ which are faulty signatures modulo p, and a bound X such that $|r_i| \leq X$ for all i, then the RSA modulus N can be factored, provided that $X < N^{\frac{1}{2} + \frac{1}{\ell}}$ and the assumption 1 holds.*

For $\ell = 1$, i.e., the attacker get only one faulty signature, the bound $X \leq N^{0.25}$ is the same as the one the single faulty attack in [4]. If $\ell = 2$, the dimension of the lattice is 36 by selecting $t = 7, k = 5$, and the bound is about $N^{0.31}$. For all $\ell > 1$, the new bound is better than the bound in subsection 3.2. However, the time complexity of this attack increases exponentially with the number ℓ.

4   Simulation Results

In this section we show some comparisons between the known attacks and our new attacks by simulation. We have simulated the fault attacks described above as follows. Firstly, we generate a correct $\rho_p = \mu(m)^d \mod p$ and a random $\rho_q \in \mathbb{Z}_q$, then using CRT compute a faulty signature ρ with a 160-bit hash function. Secondly, we compute $(\rho^e - s)2^{-8} \mod N$, where s is a known value as in section 3. We use the NTL library [14] LLL algorithm on a 2Ghz Intel notebook.

Notice that, in our simulation tests, we compare the new results with the previous attacks in [4,5] under the assumption that UMP locates in the lower-order bits, although the attacks in [4,5] can deal with the unknown bits in the middle.

Table 1. Comparison of new multiple-fault attacks and previous attacks in [5]

ℓ	$\gamma + \delta_{theory,new}$	$\gamma + \delta_{true,new}$	$\gamma + \delta_{theory,[5]}$	$\gamma + \delta_{true,[5]}$
2	0.250	0.247	-	-
3	0.333	0.329	-	-
4	0.375	0.372	-	-
8	0.437	0.434	0.250	0.214
10	0.450	0.447	0.300	0.280
14	0.464	0.461	0.357	0.330
25	0.480	0.478	0.420	0.400
70	0.492	0.488	0.471	0.450

From Table 1, for small $\ell \leq 4$, in our simulation results, the new attacks can work well while the previous attacks in [5] are invalid since the right-hand side of the bound $\delta < \frac{1}{2} - \frac{2}{\ell}$ is negative. Moreover, the asymptotic bound $\delta < \frac{1}{2} - \frac{1}{2\ell}$ in the new attacks seems more natural.

For large ℓ, the new attack has the asymptotic bound closer to $\frac{1}{2}$ than the former attacks, i.e., when $\ell = 70$, $k_r + k_h$ in [5] is 0.450 while it equals to 0.488 in our new attack. For a 1024-bit RSA modulus and a 160-bit hash value, the new attack can deal with the 340-bit UMP better than the 300-bit UMP in the previous attack. Therefore, the new attacks require less faulty signatures to reach the same bound. And the value $\gamma + \delta$ in the new results approaches to $\frac{1}{2}$ much faster.

From Table 1, another observation is that the difference between the theoretical bound and the test bound in the new attack is less than the difference in [5], e.g, the distance in our new attack is almost 0.03, however the distance provided by CNT is about 0.2.

In the extended multiple fault attack, the bound of unknown part is related to the parameters t, k. In the simulation test in Table 2, we compute the bound by different parameters for the same number of faulty signatures. For example, for $\ell = 3$, the bound is 0.343 by selecting $t = 5, k = 4$, while it becomes 0.360

Table 2. Extended Multiple-fault Attacks

ℓ	$\gamma + \delta$	t	k	w	time
2	0.310	7	5	36	15s
2	0.312	6	4	28	4s
3	0.325	4	3	33	10s
3	0.343	5	4	56	5min
3	0.360	8	6	165	3h
4	0.372	7	5	126	59min
4	0.385	6	4	210	10.3h

by choosing $t = 8, k = 6$. These two results are better than the result in second row in Table 1. But when $t = 4, k = 3$, the bound 0.325 is less than the second result in Table 1. The dimension of the lattice that we consider increases very fast with the parameters t, k, so the extended attack is efficient in practice only when ℓ is small.

5   Conclusion

This paper discusses an extended fault attack against a probabilistic version of ISO/IEC 9796-2. Instead of discussing the general case, we only argue a particular scene that some lower order bits of message are unknown. In the beginning, we use a very simple method of solving the simultaneous Diophantine approximation problem to give an analysis of the multiple fault attack. The bound obtained is better than in general case. Next, we apply the Cohn-Heninger technique to improve the bound of unknown part of message.

References

1. Boneh, D., DeMillo, R.A., Lipton, R.J.: On the Importance of Checking Cryptographic Protocols for Faults. Journal of Cryptology 14(2), 101–119 (2001)
2. Cohn, H., Heninger, N.: Approximate Common Divisiors Via Lattices. Cryptology ePrint Archive, Report 2011/437, http://eprint.iacr.org/2011/437
3. Coppersmith, D.: Small Solutions to Polynomial Equations, and Low Exponent Vulnerabilities. Journal of Cryptology 10(4), 233–260 (1997)
4. Coron, J.-S., Joux, A., Kizhvatov, I., Naccache, D., Paillier, P.: Fault Attacks on RSA Signatures with Partially Unknown Messages. In: Clavier, C., Gaj, K. (eds.) CHES 2009. LNCS, vol. 5747, pp. 444–456. Springer, Heidelberg (2009), Full version: eprint.iacr.org/2009/309
5. Coron, J.-S., Naccache, D., Tibouchi, M.: Fault Attacks Against EMV Signatures. In: Pieprzyk, J. (ed.) CT-RSA 2010. LNCS, vol. 5985, pp. 208–220. Springer, Heidelberg (2010)
6. Coron, J.-S., Naccache, D., Tibouchi, M., Weinmann, R.-P.: Practical Cryptanalysis of ISO/IEC 9796-2 and EMV Signatures. In: Halevi, S. (ed.) CRYPTO 2009. LNCS, vol. 5677, pp. 428–444. Springer, Heidelberg (2009)

7. Jochemsz, E., May, A.: A Strategy for Finding Roots of Multivariate Polynomials with New Applications in Attacking RSA Variants. In: Lai, X., Chen, K. (eds.) ASIACRYPT 2006. LNCS, vol. 4284, pp. 267–282. Springer, Heidelberg (2006)
8. Howgrave-Graham, N.: Approximate integer common divisors. In: Silverman, J.H. (ed.) CaLC 2001. LNCS, vol. 2146, pp. 51–66. Springer, Heidelberg (2001)
9. ISO/IEC 9796-2, Information Technology-Security Techniques-Digital Signature Schemes Giving Message Recovery-Part 2: Mechanisms Using a Hash-Funcion (1997)
10. ISO/IEC 9796-2: 2002 Information Technology Security Techniques-Digital Signature Schemes Giving Message Recovery-Part 2: Integer Factorization Based Mechanisms (2002)
11. Lenstra, A., Lenstra Jr., H., Lovász, L.: Factoring Polynomials with Rational Coefficients. Mathematische Annalen 261, 513–534 (1982)
12. Nguyen, P., Stern, J.: Cryptanalysis of a fast public key cryptosystem presented at SAC '97. In: Tavares, S., Meijer, H. (eds.) SAC 1998. LNCS, vol. 1556, pp. 213–218. Springer, Heidelberg (1999)
13. Rivest, R., Shamir, A., Adleman, L.: A Method for Obtaining Digital Signatures and Public Key Cryptosystems. Communications of the ACM, 120–126 (1978)
14. Shoup, V.: Number Theory C++ Library (NTL) version version 5.5.2, http://www.shoup.net/ntl/

Differential Fault Analysis of Twofish

Sk Subidh Ali and Debdeep Mukhopadhyay

Dept. of Computer Science and Engineering
Indian Institute of Technology Kharagpur, India
{subidh,debdeep}@cse.iitkgp.ernet.in

Abstract. In this paper we propose Differential Fault Analysis (DFA) of Twofish which was one of the five AES finalists. It uses the concept of key-dependent S-boxes and Pseudo-Hadamard Transform, which make the cipher secure against differential attack. Each S-box is dependent on key because of which the S-box is not known to the attacker. Therefore, the existing DFA techniques which use the differential properties of S-box are not directly applicable to Twofish. We propose DFA based on an approximation technique. The attack retrieves the secret key using around 320 pairs of fault-free and faulty ciphertexts with attack time complexity of 2^{40}. To the best of author's knowledge this is the first time a DFA attack is proposed on a cipher like Twofish which uses key-dependent S-box.

Keywords: AES, Twofish, Differential Fault Analysis, DFA, Fault Model.

1 Introduction

Modern day ciphers are constructed to save guard against known classical crypt-analysis techniques. But when these ciphers are implemented on hardware platforms such as smart cards, may leak information in the form of side-channels [1]. The attack which uses these implementation based weakness of the ciphers are known as side-channel cryptanalysis. There is another kind of attack which induces faults into the crypto-devices and then analyzes the faulty output of the cipher to ascertain the secret key. Fault based attacks were originally introduced in [2] to break the RSA crypto-system. Subsequently, a more strong form of the attack, known as Differential Fault Analysis (DFA), was proposed in [3]. DFA uses the concepts of conventional differential attack in context to fault attack. The first DFA was mounted on DES crypto-systems and the result showed that the secret key of DES can be retrieved by analysing 50 to 200 faulty ciphertexts generated from known but related plaintexts.

DFA gained significant attention in the research community when it was shown in [4], that faults can easily be injected in a crypto-chip using some less expensive devices like flashgun or laser pointer. Afterward, DFA was mounted against many crypto-systems like AES [5–12], Triple-DES [13], CLEFIA [14,15], IDEA [16], RSA [17–19]. In the same lines there is significant research in practical fault injection techniques. The recent results show that fault can also be

M. Kutyłowski and M. Yung (Eds.): Inscrypt 2012, LNCS 7763, pp. 10–28, 2013.

injected using glitches in the clock input line [20, 21], power glitch [22], under-powering [23, 24], laser beam [25] or electromagnetic radiations [26].

In this paper we investigate DFA on Twofish [27]. Twofish is a 128 bit symmetric block cipher. It supports key length of 128 bits, 192 bits, and 256 bits. Twofish was introduced by Schneier *et al.* as one of the AES candidates. The cipher was selected as one of the five AES finalist. Currently it is being used by many applications like PGP, SSH Tectia, Sentry NT/2000/XP, SQL 2000 DBA Toolkit [28]. Still there are hardly few reported attacks on Twofish. The designers claimed that impossible differential attack is possible up to 6-rounds of Twofish [29]. A Saturation attack was proposed on reduced round of Twofish (upto 7 round with full whitening and 8 rounds with pre-whitening) using upto 2^{127} plaintexts [30]. The observations made on the key-dependent S-boxes and the differential cryptanalysis performed in [31] claimed that 8-round Twofish can be attacked. Most recently, a truncated differential cryptanalysis of Twofish was shown in [32]. The authors have found out truncated differential for 12-rounds and 16-rounds, but a complete attack was not shown based on these results. State-of-the-art shows Twofish is secure against conventional cryptanalysis techniques and because of its design poses new challenges for cryptanalysis.

Literature shows no reported fault based analysis of the Twofish cipher. However, because of its rather uncharacteristic structure of key-dependent S-boxes, combination of integer modulo operations with XORs, they pose significant challenges to fault analysis as known methods of DFA on block ciphers do not directly apply. In this paper we propose DFA of Twofish based on approximation techniques. In this paper we targeted Twofish (with 128-bit key). The proposed attack uses 320 pairs of fault-free and faulty ciphertext and uniquely determines the secret key with attack time complexity 2^{40}. Apart from the specific objective of performing DFA on Twofish, it is also a case study to show that cipher structure has an impact on the robustness against DFA.

Organization

The paper is organized as follow: We start with Section 2, where we describe the preliminaries to this paper. In Section 3, we explain the motivations behind this work. Section 4 describes the proposed DFA method whereas the proposed DFA procedure is described in Section 5. The attack analysis and the detail experimental results are given in Section 6. Finally, we conclude in Section 7.

2 Preliminaries

2.1 Twofish

Twofish is a 128-bit symmetric key block cipher. It uses 16-round Feistel network with a bijective 'F' function. The cipher supports three different key lengths of 128, 192, and 256 bits. For brevity in this paper we only consider Twofish with 128 bits key. The structure of the cipher is shown in Figure 1. The 128 bit plaintext P is split into four 32-bit words $P_0, \ldots, P_3$ and XORed with the four words $K_0, \ldots, K_3$ of the whitening key (one rotated by 1 bit towards left) and followed by 16 rounds. Each round of the cipher, two most significant input words (one by rotating 8 bits towards left) are fed into the F function. Each F function consists of g function followed by Pseudo-Hadamard Transform (PHT) and key word addition. The g function consists of four byte-wide key-dependent S-boxes followed by linear mixing operation with the 4×4 MDS matrix. The two output words (one rotated by 1 bit towards right) of the F function are then XORed with the two least significant words of the round input. Here addition ($\boxplus$) defines the addition modulo 2^{32} operation.

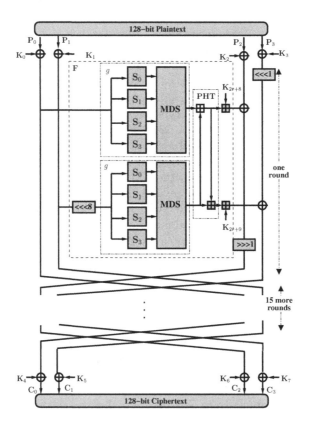

Fig. 1. Block diagram of Twofish

Pseudo-Hadamard Transform (PHT). It is a mixing operation. Given two inputs a and b, output of the PHT is defined as follows:

$$a' = a + b \ mod \ 2^{32}$$
$$b' = a + 2b \ mod \ 2^{32}$$

Key-Dependent S-Boxes. Twofish uses four key-dependent S-boxes. The four S-boxes use two 32 bits words Γ_0 and Γ_1 of the key material. The words are generated from the 128 bits Twofish key as follows:

$$\begin{pmatrix} \tau_{i,0} \\ \tau_{i,1} \\ \tau_{i,2} \\ \tau_{i,3} \end{pmatrix} = \begin{pmatrix} \cdots \cdots \\ \vdots\ RS\ \vdots \\ \cdots \cdots \end{pmatrix} \cdot \begin{pmatrix} k_{8i} \\ k_{8i+1} \\ k_{8i+2} \\ k_{8i+3} \\ k_{8i+4} \\ k_{8i+5} \\ k_{8i+6} \\ k_{8i+7} \end{pmatrix}$$

and,

$$\Gamma_i = \sum_{j=0}^{3} \tau_{i,j} \cdot 2^{8j}$$

where $i \in \{0,1\}$ and $k_0, \ldots, k_{15}$ are the 16 bytes of the key. The RS matrix is given as follows:

$$RS = \begin{pmatrix} 01\ A4\ 55\ 87\ 5A\ 58\ DB\ 9E \\ A4\ 56\ 82\ F3\ 1E\ C6\ 68\ E5 \\ 02\ A1\ FC\ C1\ 47\ AE\ 3D\ 19 \\ A4\ 55\ 87\ 5A\ 58\ DB\ 9E\ 03 \end{pmatrix}$$

The four S-boxes are generated as follows:

$$y_0 = q_1[q_0[q_0[x_0] \oplus \tau_{0,0}] \oplus \tau_{1,0}]$$
$$y_1 = q_0[q_0[q_1[x_1] \oplus \tau_{0,1}] \oplus \tau_{1,1}]$$
$$y_2 = q_1[q_1[q_0[x_2] \oplus \tau_{0,2}] \oplus \tau_{1,2}]$$
$$y_3 = q_0[q_1[q_1[x_3] \oplus \tau_{0,3}] \oplus \tau_{1,3}]$$

q_0 and q_1 are fixed 8-bit permutations and $X = \{x_0, \ldots, x_3\}$ and $Y = \{y_0, \ldots, y_3\}$ are the input and output words of the S-boxes, of dimension 8 bits each.

h-Function. h function plays an important role in Twofish cipher. The function is used in the key schedule as well as to derive the g function. Figure 2 shows an overview of the function. It takes the 32 bit input and a list $L = (L_0, L_1)$ of two 32-bit words and applies the S-box operation on the input where the list L, is used in reversed order. The S-box output is followed by a linear mixing operation with the MDS matrix. It can also be observed that the path of each 8 bits of the input in the function h can be visualized as application of either of the four S-boxes, $S_0, \ldots, S_3$ (as denoted by dotted line in Figure 2).

The MDS matrix is given as follows:

$$MDS = \begin{pmatrix} 01\ EF\ 5B\ 5B \\ 5B\ EF\ EF\ 01 \\ EF\ 5B\ 01\ EF \\ EF\ 01\ EF\ 5B \end{pmatrix}$$

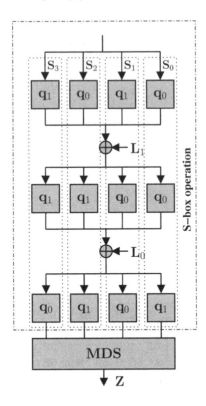

Fig. 2. The function h

Key Schedule. The key schedule provides the 40 expanded key words $K_0, \ldots,$ K_{39}; first 8 key words are used for whitening purpose and the rest of the 32 key words are used in 16 rounds. The initial 128 bits key is divided into four words $W_0, \ldots, W_3$. Then these words are again divided into two list W_e, W_o, where $W_e = (W_0, W_2)$ and $W_o = (W_1, W_3)$. The expanded key words are defined as follows:

$$\rho = 2^{24} + 2^{16} + 2^8 + 2^0$$
$$A_i = h(2i\rho, W_e)$$
$$B_i = ROL(h((2i+1)\rho, W_o), 8)$$
$$K_{2i} = (A_i + B_i) mod\ 2^{32}$$
$$K_{2i+1} = ROL((A_i + 2B_i) mod\ 2^{32}, 9)$$

where $i = 0, \ldots, 19$ and ROL is a rotation function that rotates its first argument towards left by the number of bits specified in the second argument. More details of the cipher can be found in [27].

2.2 Notation

In this section we define some parameters that we will use in rest of the paper.

$C = \{C_0, \ldots, C_3\}$: The 128 bit fault-free ciphertext, where $C_0 \ldots C_3$ are four eight byte words of the fault-free 128 bit ciphertext.

$C^* = \{C_0^*, \ldots, C_3^*\}$: The 128 bit faulty ciphertext. Here $C_0^* \ldots C_3^*$ are four eight byte words of the 128 bit faulty ciphertext.

$X_{(i)}$: refers the ith byte of the word X, where a word is of 4 bytes.

3 What Makes DFA on Twofish Different from Other Ciphers?

In order to understand why DFA on Twofish is different with respect to other studied ciphers, we first observe a generalized working of DFA on these reported cryptographic algorithms. DFA uses both the concept of differential attacks and fault attacks together. The attacker is expected to induce a fault into a particular round of encryption in-order to generate certain differences. Then following the differential characteristic, the attacker deduces some differential equations related to the input-output differential of the S-box. As the S-box is known to the attacker, therefore, he can get the input of the S-box using the difference distribution table which in turn gives the key.

Figure 3 shows the basic structure of r-round Simple Permutation Network (SPN) cipher with block length n-byte. The ith round consists of confusion layer S, and diffusion layer D^i, followed by an addition with the ith round key K^i. There is an addition with the whitening key WK at the beginning of the encryption called key-whitening phase. The confusion layer is generally provided by S-box operation which is a non-linear transformation. The diffusion layer is provided by some linear transformation like multiplication with MDS matrix followed by a rotation operation. Due to the diffusion operation the induced fault spreads to more number of bytes which depends on the branch number of the diffusion layer. For example in AES, inducing a single byte difference at the input of diffusion layer will spread to four bytes at the output as the branch number of the diffusion layer is five [33]. The attacker uses this property in-order to generate differential equations.

Suppose that a single byte fault is induced at the input of $(r-1)^{th}$ round and the corresponding difference at the input of D_{r-1} is α. If the branch number of the diffusion layer is b then the input byte-fault will spread to $b-1$ bytes $(\alpha_{\pi_0}, \ldots, \alpha_{\pi_{b-2}})$ at the output of D_{r-1}, where π denotes the transformation of the diffusion layer. Therefore, the attacker can represent this output bytes in terms of a pair of fault-free and faulty ciphertexts (C, C^*) as follows:

$$\alpha_{\pi_j} = S^{-1}(C_{\pi_j} \oplus K_{\pi_j}^r) \oplus S^{-1}(C_{\pi_j}^* \oplus K_{\pi_j}^r) \tag{1}$$

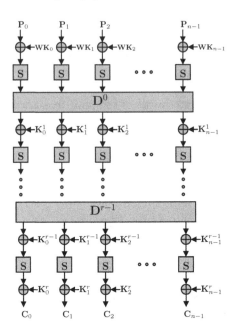

Fig. 3. Basic structure of SPN ciphers

where $j \in \{0, \ldots, b-2\}$ and S^{-1} represents the inverse of the S-box operation. Now the attacker knows the S-box input difference $C_{\pi_j} \oplus C^*_{\pi_j}$. From the difference distribution table he knows on average few values satisfy a chosen $(\alpha_{\pi_j}, C_{\pi_j} \oplus C^*_{\pi_j})$ pair. Further, because of the linear mapping in D_{r-1}, α_{π_j} depends linearly on α. Therefore, the attacker guesses the value of α and get the values of α_{π_j} i.e. the output differences. Using the input-output difference he retrieves the value $C_{\pi_j} \oplus K_{\pi_j}$ from the difference distribution table of the S-box. As C_{π_j} and $C^*_{\pi_j}$ is known to the attacker, hence he can retrieve the value of K_{π_j}. Because of the S-boxes in most of the modern day ciphers, the attacker can retrieve the entire b bytes of the key using two pair of fault-free and faulty ciphertexts [6].

Same technique is also applicable for ciphers based on Generalized Feistel Network [34]. Figure 4 shows the structure of a Feistel cipher highlighting the ith round. The input is divided into two parts X_i, and Z_i. The first part passes through the F after being XORed with key component, K_i. The output of F is XORed with the second part, Z_i and then is swapped. In most of the Feistel networks, the F function consists of key addition followed by an S-box operation.

In case of these ciphers, the attacker induces faults in such a way so that all the bytes of X in the last round, i.e. X_{r-1} gets corrupted. So, he can directly get the input-output difference of the S-boxes from the fault-free and the faulty ciphertext pair. Hence he can get the last round key using the difference distribution table of the S-box. Once the last round key is retrieved, he can do one round decryption and apply the technique again to get the penultimate round key. This technique is repeated until he gets sufficient amount of round keys from which he can retrieve the master key.

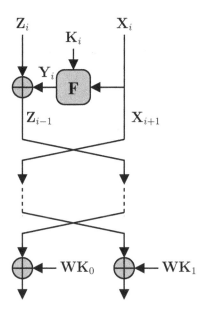

Fig. 4. Basic structure of Feistel ciphers

However, Twofish has significant difference from these structures. The first difference lies in the use of PHT operation in the F function. The PHT operation is specifically added to the design to protect the cipher against differential attacks [27]. Due to addition $mod\ 2^{32}$ operation in PHT, the difference does not pass through unchanged as in case of XOR operation. Therefore, it is impossible to obtain a suitable differential characteristic.

The second difference is in the round key addition. Unlike other Feistel ciphers, in Twofish the round key is added at the end of F function. As the addition is not at the input of S-box operation, therefore, even if the attacker retrieves the input-output difference pair of an S-box, he can not retrieve the key. Because, these differences are not directly related to the key as in case of SPN and Feistel ciphers shown above. Further, the round keys are applied by $mod\ 2^{32}$ addition.

The third and the major difference in Twofish cipher is in the use of key-dependent S-boxes. Each of the S-boxes use two bytes of the key material. Depending on the key material, there could be 2^{16} possibilities of each S-boxes. The attacker does not have the knowledge which S-box is being used. Hence he does not have the access to the difference distribution table of the corresponding S-box during the encryption.

In the next section we propose a DFA on Twofish which is based on approximation technique. In brief, we first target the key dependent S-boxes.

4   Proposed DFA Method

In this section we describe the method used to retrieve Twofish key. We show how to target the key-dependent S-boxes to the proposed DFA. We use approximation techniques to determine the differential characteristics of the cipher. Using these differential characteristics we attack the Twofish S-box key instead of attacking the round key which is generally done in case of known DFA on SPN and Feistel ciphers as discuss in Section 3.

4.1   Fault Model Used

For the DFA on Twofish we use popular single byte fault model. The single byte fault is induced at the input of last round. The single byte difference passes through corresponding S-box and then spreads to all four bytes of the MDS output. The PHT operation will mix the difference to the two output words of the F function.

The proposed fault model can be injected in hardware design of the cipher where an attacker can precisely determine the round operation and then using techniques like glitches in the clock input line [20, 21, 35], laser beam [4], or under-powering the device [22, 36], he can induce faults.

4.2   Attack Assumptions

We made the following assumption in our attack. For the sake of simplicity we first target the S-boxes in the first g function as depicted in Figure 6.

- We assume that the attacker has the ability to induce single byte faults at any particular byte of the inputs of F function.
- The attacker does not need to know the value of the faults.

4.3   Idea of the Proposed Attack

As discussed Twofish has two important components, the $mod\,2^{32}$ additions and key-dependent S-boxes. The proposed attack is based on two observations regarding these primitives. The first observation is the approximate differential property of the $mod\,2^{32}$ addition and the second observation is on the key-dependent S-boxes.

Approximate Differential of Modulo Addition. As Twofish uses $mod\,2^{32}$ addition, therefore, we can not directly get the input-output differential of an S-box from the fault-free and faulty ciphertexts. However, there is a probability that an XOR differential passes through the $mod\,2^{32}$ operation unchanged. If such probability is p, then it is expected that after $\frac{1}{p}$ faults, one can get at least one differential characteristic where the differential remain the same across the $mod\,2^{32}$ operation. The attacker can use this differential to get the input-output difference of the S-box.

Properties of Key-Dependent S-Box. Twofish uses key-dependent S-boxes, because of which it is difficult to obtain differential characteristics of the cipher which can be exploited for fault attacks. However, the S-box itself contains the key materials. Each of the S-boxes consists of two bytes of the key. It can be observed that given an input-output difference pair, all 2^{16} S-boxes are not equally likely. This implies that the robustness of the cipher against differential attack are not the same for all the keys. In fact, using multiple input-output differences we can reduce the possible choices of the S-box. Finally we can uniquely determine the S-box which corresponds to a unique pair of key bytes. Once we determine all the four S-boxes, we can get the eight bytes of the key material.

4.4   Twofish S-Box Analysis

Each of the four Twofish S-boxes can be considered as a function $S_{k_0,k_1}(x)$ of x, where k_0 and k_1 are the two bytes of the key material (Figure 5) . Depending on the values of k_0 and k_1 there could be 2^{16} such functions possible. Our objective is to determine the S-box based on the input-output difference. Given an input-output difference $(\Delta_{in}, \Delta_{out})$, we can write the following differential equation:

$$\Delta_{out} = S_{k_0,k_1}(x \oplus \Delta_{in}) \oplus S_{k_0,k_1}(x) \tag{2}$$

As per the Twofish specifications, each of the possible 2^{16} S-boxes poses good differential properties. For a given value of k_0, k_1, Δ_{in}, Δ_{out}, the above differential equation will have on average one solution of x. This implies, for a given value of $(\Delta_{in}, \Delta_{out})$ on average 2^{16} out of the 2^{24} values of the triplet $\{x, k_0, k_1\}$ will satisfy the above equation. Hence, one pair of input-output difference will reduce the search space of the triplet by 2^8. Therefore, on average we need three pairs of input-output difference to reduce the search space of the triplet to a unique value.

An exhaustive search is done to validate the above analysis. Results show that using single pair of input-output difference the search space of the triplet remains within a range of 2^{15} to 2^{16}. Using three pairs, in most of the cases the search space reduces to one whereas using four pairs the search space always reduces to one.

The results suggest that if the attacker is able to get four pairs of input-output difference of an S-box, he can uniquely determine the corresponding two key bytes and the input byte. Algorithm 1 summarizes the way to recover them.

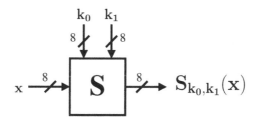

Fig. 5. Basic structure of one byte S-box

Algorithm 1. Deduce S-box key bytes k_0, k_1 and the input x

Input: $(\Delta_{in0}, \Delta_{out0}), (\Delta_{in1}, \Delta_{out1}),$
$\qquad\quad (\Delta_{in2}, \Delta_{out2}), (\Delta_{in3}, \Delta_{out3})$

Output: k_0, k_1 x

Solve the following simultaneous equations $\Delta_{out0} = S_{k_0,k_1}(x \oplus \Delta_{in0}) \oplus S_{k_0,k_1}(x)$
$\Delta_{out1} = S_{k_0,k_1}(x \oplus \Delta_{in1}) \oplus S_{k_0,k_1}(x)$
$\Delta_{out2} = S_{k_0,k_1}(x \oplus \Delta_{in2}) \oplus S_{k_0,k_1}(x)$
$\Delta_{out3} = S_{k_0,k_1}(x \oplus \Delta_{in3}) \oplus S_{k_0,k_1}(x)$
if k_0, k_1, and x are uniquely determined **then**
$\qquad$ **return** k_0 and k_1
end
else error

4.5 Determining the Approximate Differential of Modulo Addition

The PHT transformation was added in the design to thwart differential attack. The differential characteristic across the addition modulo 2^{32} is not the same as in case of XOR operation. There is a analysis on the differential properties of addition modulo 2^n given in [37,38]. However, in our case the required differential equation is different. We assume a single byte fault is induced at the first input of the F function. Figure 6 shows the flow of faults where the byte-fault is induced at the least significant byte of the first input word of the F function. The two input words of the two g functions are X_0 and X_1, and the corresponding output words are Y_0 and Y_1 respectively. Z_0 and Z_1 refer to the output words of the F function. The single byte fault is induced at the first byte of X_0 and the corresponding fault value is referred as f.

After the S-box operation f changes to f' and subsequently spreads to all four bytes of the MDS output. The difference at the output of the MDS is given by $\alpha = (5Bf'|5Bf'|EFf'|f')$ where 1, $5B$, EF, and EF are the elements of the first column of the MDS matrix in hexadecimal format. These four-byte fault value again changes to $\beta = (d|c|b|a)$ after the round key addition. Now, we would like to find the probability of $\alpha = \beta$, which means the difference across the PHT and key addition remain the same. The relation between α and β is given by following equation:

$$\beta = (Y_0 + Y_1 + K_{38}) \oplus ((Y_0 \oplus \alpha) + Y_1 + K_{38}) \qquad (3)$$

Now consider the operation: $S = Y_0 + Y_1 + K_{38}$ and $S' = Y_0 \oplus \alpha + Y_1 + K_{38}$. Substitute, $Y_1 + K_{38} = Y_1' \Rightarrow S = Y_0 + Y_1'$ and $S' = Y_0 \oplus \alpha + Y_1'$

The integer additions $y = x + k \bmod 2^{32}$ can be approximated as follows: $y[i] = x[i] \oplus k[i] \oplus k[i-1]$ with probability $\frac{3}{4}$ [39], where $y[i]$, $x[i]$, $k[i]$ represent the ith bit of y, x, and k.
$\Rightarrow S[i] = Y_0[i] \oplus Y_1'[i] \oplus Y_1'[i-1]$
and $S'[i] = Y_0[i] \oplus \alpha[i] \oplus Y_1'[i] \oplus Y_1'[i-1]$
Thus, $\beta[i] = S[i] \oplus S'[i] = \alpha[i]$ holds with probability $\frac{3}{4}$. It may be noted that $\beta[0] = \alpha[0]$ occurs with probability one. Therefore, α and β match in the first

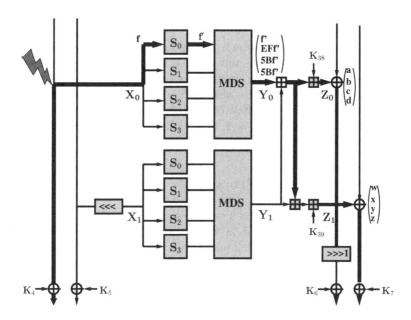

Fig. 6. Flow of single byte fault induced at the last round input

eight bits with probability $(3/4)^7 \approx 0.13$. In fact, we observe experimentally that for a random choice of Y_0, Y_1, K_{38}, and α, the probability[1] that α and β matches in the first byte is 0.13177.

This implies that if we induce ten random byte-faults at the input of the last round, there is a high chance that at least in one case the first byte (the least significant byte) of α and β matches. The value of β can be calculated from the fault-free and faulty ciphertexts. Therefore, if there is a hit in the first byte of α and β, then we can get the first byte of α from the fault-free and faulty ciphertexts. Therefore, we can get the input-output difference of the corresponding S-box. We call this input-output difference as exploitable input-output difference. The value of the first byte of α is f' when the byte-fault is induced at the first byte of X_0, as depicted in Figure 6.

From the MDS matrix we can also say that when the byte-fault is induced at the second, third, and fourth bytes, the value of the first byte of α will be $5Bf'$, EFf', and EFf' respectively where f' refers to the corresponding S-box output difference. From the above results we can say that in-order to get one exploitable input-output difference of an S-box, the attacker has to induce on average ten random byte-faults.

In-order to determine the S-box keys of the second g function we have to apply little different approach. In this case the fault is in second word of the F function. Therefore, in this case equation (3) will changed to

---

[1] We perform 100000 simulation. On an average in 13177 cases the match was found in the least significant byte of α and β .

$$\beta' = (Y_0 + 2Y_1 + K_{39}) \oplus (Y_0 \oplus 2(Y_1 \oplus \alpha') + K_{39}) \tag{4}$$

where α' and β' are the fault values corresponding to the second g function. It may be observed that here Y_1 and $Y_1 \oplus \alpha'$ are multiplied by 2. Therefore, in-order to get the first byte of α' from β' we have to test the cases when first byte of $(\beta' >>> 1)$ i.e. one bit right shift of β', matches with the first byte of α. This implies we have to consider first byte of $(\beta' >>> 1)$ as the possible output difference to the corresponding S-box. Rest of the analysis is the same as the of first g function.

5   The Proposed DFA Procedure

In this section we propose a DFA on Twofish using around 320 faulty ciphertexts. The proposed attack is described in three steps. In the first step the faulty ciphertexts are collected to get the input-output differences of the corresponding S-box. In the second step the two key bytes of each S-box is retrieved. In the third step the 128-bit Twofish key is recovered from the S-box key.

5.1   Getting the Input-Output Differences

For each of the S-box S_i where $0 \leq i \leq 3$, repeatedly induce byte-faults so that the faults affect the targeted S-box input. A list L_i is maintained corresponding to each S-box S_i. The lists will hold the input-output differences of the corresponding S-boxes. For j^{th} fault induction at the ith S-box, the input-output difference is extracted from the fault-free and faulty ciphertexts pair (C, C^*) as follows:

$$\Delta_{in_j} = C_{0(i)} \oplus C^*_{0(i)}$$
$$\Delta_{out_j} = ROL(C_{2(i)} \oplus C^*_{2(i)})$$
$$L_i[j] = \{\Delta_{in_j}, \Delta_{out_j}\}$$

Once we have the list of input-output differences, we can recover the S-box key using the differential properties of the S-box as explained in Section 4.4.

5.2   Retrieving the S-Box Key

It is already described in Section 4.4, that if the attacker is able to retrieve four input-output differences, he can uniquely determine the two key bytes of the S-box. However, in this regard the attacker has a list of input-output differences and it is not known which are the exploitable input-output differences. The attacker only expect that out of ten input-output differences there is at least one exploitable input-output difference. Therefore, he makes exhaustive search on all possible differences. In-order to do that he performs following three steps

Step 1. Choose any possible four input-output differences from L_i.

Step 2. Apply Algorithm 1 to the four input-output differences to determine corresponding S-box key. If the differences produce a pair of key bytes (k_0, k_1) and input x of corresponding S-box S_i, store it in the list SK_i.

Step 3. Repeat Step 1 and Step 2 for all possible four pairs of differences generated from the list L_i.

The attacker is expected to induce ten faults in-order to get one pair of exploitable input-output difference. Therefore, in-order to get four such input-output differences for a particular S-box, the attacker must induce at least forty faults. Therefore, L_i must contain at least forty input-output differences. From a set of forty elements one can choose four elements in $^{40}C_4$ ways. This implies, that the Step 1 and 2 is repeated for at least $^{40}C_4$ times. We get 2^8 hypotheses of (x', k_0, k_1) corresponding to each S-box.

The same technique is also followed to retrieve the S-box key from the second g function. Therefore, from two g functions we get two sets of values of each pair of S-box key bytes. We take the intersection of these two set based on the pair of key bytes and uniquely determine it . From, the unique pair of S-box key we also determine the S-box inputs x and x' corresponding to the two g functions. Following the same technique for all the S-boxes we uniquely determine the S-box key as well as the input to the F function.

5.3   Recovering Master Key

Now by applying the techniques shown in the previous section, we get the two input words X_0, and X_1 of the F function and the S-box key. We also know the ciphertexts. Therefore, using these two input words we can retrieve the two whitening keys K_4 and K_5, as $K_4 = X_0 \oplus C_0$ and $K_5 = X_1 \oplus C_1$, where C_0 and C_1 are the most significant two words of the ciphertext.

Again using X_0 and X_1 we get the two output words Y_0 and Y_1, of the F function. Now we can get following two relations of the two round keys K_{38} and K_{39},

$$\begin{aligned}
\beta &= (Y_0 + Y_1 + K_{38}) \oplus (Y_0 \oplus \alpha + Y_1 + K_{38}) \\
\beta' &= (Y_0 + 2Y_1 + K_{39}) \oplus (Y_0 + 2(Y_1 \oplus \alpha') + K_{39})
\end{aligned} \tag{5}$$

, where (α, β) and (α', β') correspond to any exploitable input-output differences we already determined while retrieving the S-box keys. By solving the above two equations we get the least significant 31 bits of K_{38} and K_{39} [16, §6.1]. we get total of four hypotheses of (K_{38}, K_{39}).

In-order to get the master key from the whitening keys and the round keys we use the Twofish key schedule. Using the key schedule we get the values of (A_2, B_2) from the value of (K_4, K_5). Similarly, we get the values of (A_{19}, B_{19}) from (K_{38}, K_{39}). If we see the h function in Figure 2 we observe it is an S-box operation followed by a MDS operation. Therefore, if we do inverse MDS operation on A_i we get the S-box output where W_e is the S-box key. The input to the S-box is the value $2i\rho$. Therefore, we know the input output pair of the S-box.

We have two values of A_i i.e. A_2, A_{19} and corresponding two input output pairs. Say, the two input output pairs of a particular eight bits S-box are (In_0, Out_0) and (In_1, Out_1). In-order to get the corresponding pair of S-box key we solve following two equations

$$Out_0 = S_{k_0, k_1}(In_0)$$
$$Out_1 = S_{k_0, k_1}(In_1) \tag{6}$$

Here k_0 and k_1 are the two S-box key bytes. The probability that a value of (k_0, k_1) satisfies the above two equations is $(\frac{1}{2^8})^2$. We have 2^{16} hypotheses of (k_0, k_1), of which only $\frac{2^{16}}{2^{16}} = 1$ is expected to satisfy the above two equations. We apply this technique to all the four S-boxes and determine the possible values of W_e.

It may be observed that we have four possible choices of A_2, A_{19} corresponding to four choices of K_{38}, K_{39}. As per the above analysis the expected number of value of W_e is four and rest will be discarded. We follow the same technique to determine the values of W_o from the four possible choices of B_2, B_{19}. By ordering the words of W_e and W_o we get the master key. This implies we will get $4 \times 4 = 16$ choices of master key. We have the plaintext, therefore, we can determine the exact master key out of the 16 choices.

6   Attack Analysis and Simulation Results

The attacker is expected to induce forty byte faults to retrieve the two key bytes of an S-box. However, from the fault-free and the faulty ciphertexts the attacker could not guess whether the pair of fault-free and the faulty ciphertexts lead to a exploitable input-output difference of the S-box. Therefore, he has to test all the faulty ciphertexts. In-order to do that he makes possible four input-output differences out of the forty differences generated from forty faulty ciphertexts. One can choose four out of forty elements in $^{40}C_4 = 91390 \approx 2^{16}$ possible ways. Therefore, the attacker will test Algorithm 1 for 2^{16} times. The time complexity of Algorithm 1 is 2^{24}, as the attacker has to try all possible values of x, k_0, and k_1. Therefore, for a particular S-box key recovery phase has a time complexity of $2^{16} \times 2^{24} = 2^{40}$.

For, a particular S-box the output difference is generated by inducing a difference to the input. The attacker only varies the input difference by inducing different faults at the input of the S-box. Therefore, the input x, to the S-box remains fixed. Only the input difference Δ_{in}, is varied. According to the differential properties of the S-box the input output difference mapping is one-to-one for a fixed input. Therefore, for a fixed input of an S-box, there are only 2^8 input-output differences possible. The input and output difference are two bytes which can have 2^{16} possible values. Therefore, the probability of one input-output difference satisfying an S-box with fixed input is $\frac{2^8}{2^{16}} = \frac{1}{2^8}$. Therefore, four such input-output differences satisfy the S-box with probability $\frac{1}{(2^8)^4} = \frac{1}{2^{32}}$. In our case the S-box and its input is not known. Therefore, we have to try all possible values of input and the two bytes key material of the S-box. Hence the probability is given by $\frac{(2^8)^3}{2^{32}} = \frac{1}{2^8}$.

Algorithm 2. DFA on Twofish

Input: $(L_0, L_1, L_2, L_3), (L'_0, L'_1, L'_2, L'_3)$
Output: 128-bit master key K

/*L_i and L'_i are the list of input-output differences corresponding to two different g-functions */

for $i = 0 \ldots 4$ **do**
    for *Each possible four differences of L_i* **do**
        Test Algorithm 1
        if (k_0, k_1, x) *found* **then**
            Save (k_0, k_1, x) in SK_i.
        end
    end
end

for $i = 0 \ldots 3$ **do**
    for *Each possible four differences of L'_i* **do**
        Test Algorithm 1.
        if (k_0, k_1, x') *found* **then**
            Save (k_0, k_1, x') in SK'_i.
        end
    end
end

for $i = 0 \ldots 3$ **do**
    for *Each elements of SK_i* **do**
        for *Each elements of SK'_i* **do**
            if (k_0, k_1) *of SK_i is equal to (k_0, k_1) of SK'_i* **then**
                Save (k_0, k_1, x, x').
            end
        end
    end
end
Get the value of X_0 and X_1 by combining the S-box inputs.
Get Y_0 and Y_1 from X_0 and X_1.
Get the corresponding (α, β) and (α', β').
Get K_4 and K_5 from $K_4 = X_0 \oplus C_0$ and $K_5 = X_1 \oplus C_1$.
Get the possible values of K_{38} and K_{39} by solving equation (5).
for *Each candidates of (K_{38}, K_{39})* **do**
    Get (A_2, B_2), and (A_{19}, B_{19}).
    Test equations (6) for (A_2, A_{19}) and (B_2, B_{19}).
    if *Both solutions found* **then**
        Order (W_e, W_o) and get K.
    end
end

return K

We have 2^{16} choices of the four input-output differences out of which the number of candidates giving the key is $\frac{2^{16}}{2^8} = 2^8$. Each of these candidates will give one hypotheses of the pair of S-box key bytes. This implies for a particular S-box, we will have on average 2^8 hypotheses of the pair of S-box key bytes. Similarly, we get 2^8 hypotheses of the same pair of key bytes from the second g function. The intersection of these two sets will uniquely determine the two key bytes and the S-box input. Finally, we have unique choice of the four S-box key and the two input words of the F function. From these values we uniquely determine the master key.

In-order to validate the analysis we have simulated the attack. A 3GHz Intel Core 2 Duo processor with 2GB RAM was used to perform the simulated attack. The code was written in C-programming language and compiled using gcc-4.4.3. The simulation was performed on 100 random keys. In each case forty random faults are induced in each of the S-boxes. The attack used total of 320 faulty ciphertexts and a fault-free ciphertexts. On an average the attack took 8 hours to reveal the secret key.

7   Conclusions

This is the first reported DFA on the AES finalist:Twofish. The proposed cipher, due to its integer addition and key-dependent S-boxes pose challenge to a differential analysis. The paper shows how a combination of approximation strategy and the observation that the key-dependent S-boxes make the differential properties stochastically inequivalent among the possible keys can reveal the key when the byte faults are induced in the cipher. The attack takes on average 320 faulty ciphertexts and a fault-free ciphertext to uniquely determine the master key with attack time complexity 2^{40}. The simulation result shows that the attack is indeed practical, taking around 8 hours on a standard platform.

References

1. Kocher, P.C., Jaffe, J., Jun, B.: Differential Power Analysis. In: Wiener, M. (ed.) CRYPTO 1999. LNCS, vol. 1666, pp. 388–397. Springer, Heidelberg (1999)
2. Boneh, D., DeMillo, R.A., Lipton, R.J.: On the Importance of Checking Cryptographic Protocols for Faults (Extended Abstract). In: Fumy, W. (ed.) EURO-CRYPT 1997. LNCS, vol. 1233, pp. 37–51. Springer, Heidelberg (1997)
3. Biham, E., Shamir, A.: Differential Fault Analysis of Secret Key Cryptosystems. In: Kaliski Jr., B.S. (ed.) CRYPTO 1997. LNCS, vol. 1294, pp. 513–525. Springer, Heidelberg (1997)
4. Skorobogatov, S.P., Anderson, R.J.: Optical Fault Induction Attacks. In: Kaliski Jr., B.S., Koç, Ç.K., Paar, C. (eds.) CHES 2002. LNCS, vol. 2523, pp. 2–12. Springer, Heidelberg (2003)
5. Giraud, C.: DFA on AES. In: Dobbertin, H., Rijmen, V., Sowa, A. (eds.) AES 2005. LNCS, vol. 3373, pp. 27–41. Springer, Heidelberg (2005)
6. Piret, G., Quisquater, J.-J.: A Differential Fault Attack Technique against SPN Structures, with Application to the AES and KHAZAD. In: Walter, C.D., Koç, Ç.K., Paar, C. (eds.) CHES 2003. LNCS, vol. 2779, pp. 77–88. Springer, Heidelberg (2003)
7. Moradi, A., Shalmani, M.T.M., Salmasizadeh, M.: A Generalized Method of Differential Fault Attack Against AES Cryptosystem. In: Goubin, L., Matsui, M. (eds.) CHES 2006. LNCS, vol. 4249, pp. 91–100. Springer, Heidelberg (2006)
8. Mukhopadhyay, D.: An Improved Fault Based Attack of the Advanced Encryption Standard. In: Preneel, B. (ed.) AFRICACRYPT 2009. LNCS, vol. 5580, pp. 421–434. Springer, Heidelberg (2009)

9. Tunstall, M., Mukhopadhyay, D., Ali, S.: Differential Fault Analysis of the Advanced Encryption Standard Using a Single Fault. In: Ardagna, C.A., Zhou, J. (eds.) WISTP 2011. LNCS, vol. 6633, pp. 224–233. Springer, Heidelberg (2011)

10. Ali, S.S., Mukhopadhyay, D.: Differential Fault Analysis of AES-128 Key Schedule Using a Single Multi-byte Fault. In: Prouff, E. (ed.) CARDIS 2011. LNCS, vol. 7079, pp. 50–64. Springer, Heidelberg (2011)

11. Ali, S., Mukhopadhyay, D.: A Differential Fault Analysis on AES Key Schedule Using Single Fault. In: Breveglieri, L., Guilley, S., Koren, I., Naccache, D., Takahashi, J. (eds.) FDTC, pp. 35–42. IEEE (2011)

12. Ali, S., Mukhopadhyay, D.: An Improved Differential Fault Analysis on AES-256. In: Nitaj, A., Pointcheval, D. (eds.) AFRICACRYPT 2011. LNCS, vol. 6737, pp. 332–347. Springer, Heidelberg (2011)

13. Hemme, L.: A Differential Fault Attack Against Early Rounds of (Triple-)DES. In: Joye, M., Quisquater, J.-J. (eds.) CHES 2004. LNCS, vol. 3156, pp. 254–267. Springer, Heidelberg (2004)

14. Chen, H., Wu, W., Feng, D.: Differential Fault Analysis on CLEFIA. In: Qing, S., Imai, H., Wang, G. (eds.) ICICS 2007. LNCS, vol. 4861, pp. 284–295. Springer, Heidelberg (2007)

15. Takahashi, J., Fukunaga, T.: Improved Differential Fault Analysis on CLEFIA. In: Breveglieri, L., Gueron, S., Koren, I., Naccache, D., Seifert, J.-P. (eds.) FDTC, pp. 25–34. IEEE Computer Society (2008)

16. Clavier, C., Gierlichs, B., Verbauwhede, I.: Fault Analysis Study of IDEA. In: Malkin, T. (ed.) CT-RSA 2008. LNCS, vol. 4964, pp. 274–287. Springer, Heidelberg (2008)

17. Trichina, E., Korkikyan, R.: Multi Fault Laser Attacks on Protected CRT-RSA. In: Breveglieri, et al. (eds.) [40], pp. 75–86

18. Coron, J.-S., Giraud, C., Morin, N., Piret, G., Vigilant, D.: Fault Attacks and Countermeasures on Vigilant's RSA-CRT Algorithm. In: Breveglieri, et al. (eds.) [40], pp. 89–96

19. Pellegrini, A., Bertacco, V., Austin, T.M.: Fault-based attack of RSA authentication. In: DATE, pp. 855–860. IEEE (2010)

20. Fukunaga, T., Takahashi, J.: Practical Fault Attack on a Cryptographic LSI with ISO/IEC 18033-3 Block Ciphers. In: Breveglieri, et al. (eds.) [41], pp. 84–92

21. Agoyan, M., Dutertre, J.-M., Naccache, D., Robisson, B., Tria, A.: When Clocks Fail: On Critical Paths and Clock Faults. In: Gollmann, D., Lanet, J.-L., Iguchi-Cartigny, J. (eds.) CARDIS 2010. LNCS, vol. 6035, pp. 182–193. Springer, Heidelberg (2010)

22. Canivet, G., Maistri, P., Leveugle, R., Clédière, J., Valette, F., Renaudin, M.: Glitch and Laser Fault Attacks onto a Secure AES Implementation on a SRAM-Based FPGA. J. Cryptology 24(2), 247–268 (2011)

23. Barenghi, A., Bertoni, G., Parrinello, E., Pelosi, G.: Low Voltage Fault Attacks on the RSA Cryptosystem. In: Breveglieri, et al. (eds.) [41], pp. 23–31

24. Barenghi, A., Hocquet, C., Bol, D., Standaert, F.-X., Regazzoni, F., Koren, I.: Exploring the Feasibility of Low Cost Fault Injection Attacks on Sub-threshold Devices through an Example of a 65nm AES Implementation. In: Juels, A., Paar, C. (eds.) RFIDSec 2011. LNCS, vol. 7055, pp. 48–60. Springer, Heidelberg (2012)

25. Agoyan, M., Dutertre, J.-M., Mirbaha, A.-P., Naccache, D., Ribotta, A.-L., Tria, A.: How to flip a bit? In: IOLTS, pp. 235–239. IEEE (2010)

26. Quisquater, J.-J., Samyde, D.: Eddy current for Magnetic Analysis with Active Sensor. Springer (2002)

27. Schneier, B., Kelsey, J., Whiting, D., Wagner, D., Hall, C.: Twofish: A 128-Bit Block Cipher, http://www.schneier.com/paper-twofish-paper.pdf
28. http://www.schneier.com/twofish-products.html
29. Ferguson, N.: Impossible Differentials in Twofish. Twofish Technical Report 5 (October 5, 1999), http://www.schneier.com/paper-twofish-impossible.pdf
30. Lucks, S.: The Saturation Attack - a Bait for Twofish. Cryptology ePrint Archive, Report 2000/046 (2000), http://eprint.iacr.org/
31. Murphy, S., Robshaw, M.J.B.: Differential Cryptanalysis, Key-dependent S-boxes, and Twofish (2000), http://csrc.nist.gov/encryption/aes/round2/comments/20000515-smurphy.pdf
32. Moriai, S., Yin, Y.L.: Cryptanalysis of Twofish (II) (2011)
33. Daemen, J., Rijmen, V.: The Design of Rijndael: AES - The Advanced Encryption Standard. Springer (2002)
34. Nyberg, K.: Generalized Feistel Networks. In: Kim, K., Matsumoto, T. (eds.) ASIACRYPT 1996. LNCS, vol. 1163, pp. 91–104. Springer, Heidelberg (1996)
35. Saha, D., Mukhopadhyay, D., RoyChowdhury, D.: A Diagonal Fault Attack on the Advanced Encryption Standard. Cryptology ePrint Archive, Report 2009/581 (2009), http://eprint.iacr.org/
36. Bhasin, S., Danger, J.-L., Guilley, S., Selmane, N.: Security Evaluation of Different AES Implementations Against Practical Setup Time Violation Attacks in FPGAs. In: Tehranipoor, M., Plusquellic, J. (eds.) HOST, pp. 15–21. IEEE Computer Society (2009)
37. Lipmaa, H., Moriai, S.: Efficient Algorithms for Computing Differential Properties of Addition. In: Matsui, M. (ed.) FSE 2001. LNCS, vol. 2355, pp. 336–350. Springer, Heidelberg (2002)
38. Lipmaa, H.: On Differential Properties of Pseudo-Hadamard Transform and Related Mappings (Extended Abstract). In: Menezes, A., Sarkar, P. (eds.) INDOCRYPT 2002. LNCS, vol. 2551, pp. 48–61. Springer, Heidelberg (2002)
39. Mukhopadhyay, D.: Design and Analysis of Cellular Automata Based Cryptographic Algorithms. IACR Ph.D database (2006), http://www.iacr.org/phds/?p=detail&entry=609
40. Breveglieri, L., Joye, M., Koren, I., Naccache, D., Verbauwhede, I. (eds.): 2010 Workshop on Fault Diagnosis and Tolerance in Cryptography, FDTC 2010, Santa Barbara, California, USA, August 21. IEEE Computer Society (2010)
41. Breveglieri, L., Gueron, S., Koren, I., Naccache, D., Seifert, J.-P. (eds.): Sixth International Workshop on Fault Diagnosis and Tolerance in Cryptography, FDTC 2009, Lausanne, Switzerland, September 6. IEEE Computer Society (2009)

Improved Differential Cache Attacks on SMS4

Phuong Ha Nguyen[1], Chester Rebeiro[2],
Debdeep Mukhopadhyay[2], and Huaxiong Wang[1]

[1] Division of Mathematical Sciences
School of Physical and Mathematical Sciences
Nanyang Technological University, Singapore
ng0007ha@e.ntu.sg, hxwang@ntu.edu.sg
[2] Department of Computer Science and Engineering
Indian Institute of Technology Kharagpur
Kharagpur, India
{chester,debdeep}@cse.iitkgp.ernet.in

Abstract. Block ciphers that have Feistel structures are prone to a class of cache attacks known as *differential cache attacks*, which monitor power or timing side-channels to reveal the secret key. Differential cache attacks were first demonstrated on the block cipher CLEFIA, which has a type-2 generalized Feistel structure. In this paper we improve the attack methodology by showing that a sophisticated method of choosing plaintexts can result in a considerable reduction in attack complexity. This coupled with other cryptanalytic techniques, when applied to the block cipher SMS4, requires just 2^{10} plaintexts to recover the SMS4 secret key from power traces for a 64 byte cache line. Further, the attack becomes more dangerous for large cache lines. For example, with a 128 byte cache line, only 52 power traces are required. Experimental validation of the complete attack has been done on an Intel Xeon microprocessor. Further we suggest an alteration to the SMS4 algorithm that can counter this attack.

Keywords: Block-cipher, SMS4, differential cache attack.

1   Introduction

Cache attacks are a class of side-channel attacks that target implementations of ciphers that use lookup tables. They were first prophesied by Kelsey et al. in [11] and then theoretically modeled by Page in [14]. In [20] and [21], the first cache attacks were successfully demonstrated on MISTY1, DES, and 3-DES. Since then there have been several variants of cache attacks that either developed new techniques or enhanced previous techniques.

Cache attacks can be classified into three depending on the method of acquiring side-channel information. These are *timing*, *access*, and *trace*. Attacks based on traces [2,5,9,10,14,16,25] make use of power measurements or electro-magnetic analysis to gain information about the memory accesses made by the cipher. These attack make use of the fact that a cache miss takes more power and time compared to a cache hit. Works such as [5] and [16] demonstrate that even with a

M. Kutyłowski and M. Yung (Eds.): Inscrypt 2012, LNCS 7763, pp. 29–45, 2013.

single power trace it is possible to extract significantly large amounts of information about the memory accesses. On the other hand, attacks that monitor timing of an encryption require several measurements [4,17,19,20,21,22]. They however can be mounted remotely [3,6,7] and applied in virtualization environments [23] as they do not require to be in close proximity to the device under attack.

For ciphers having a Feistel structure, a trace attack that utilized the differential properties of the s-box was proposed in [16] and used to recover the secret key of CLEFIA. The attack, which is known as *differential cache-trace* attack, was improved in [18] and also applied to CAMELLIA in [15]. In the present paper we attack the SMS4 block cipher using an enhanced differential cache attack. The SMS4 cipher [1] is used in the WAPI (WLAN Authentication and Privacy Infrastructure) standard to protect WLAN products in China. SMS4 has a Feistel structure but differs from CLEFIA and CAMELLIA in that it has a variant of type-1 generalized structure, compared to the type-2 structure in CLEFIA and the classical Feistel structure in CAMELLIA. In this paper we show that ciphers with a structure like SMS4 are prone to more powerful differential cache attacks, which exploit the structure properties. The attack on SMS4 presented in this paper, not only reduces the number of plaintexts required, but also the uncertainty of the key space that is to be searched by brute-force. On a standard 64 byte cache line machine, the number of power traces required is $2^{9.2}$ for an attack. This reduces the key space from 2^{128} to 2^{30}. On 128 byte cache line, $2^{5.7}$ power traces are capable of reducing the key space to 2^{31}. The contributions of the paper is as follows:

- We develop a sophisticated method of choosing plaintexts for SMS4 due to which the number of plaintexts required drastically reduce.
- The differential properties of the cipher is exploited to further improve the attack strength.
- Several cryptanalytic techniques are provided to minimize the uncertainty of the secret key.
- We show that the adversary can maximize the attack efficiency if the cache line is half the size of the table. The efficiency is increased by reusing plaintexts and exploiting information present in a cache miss. In such cases, the number of power traces required is as less as 52.
- We present an actual application of the attack on SMS4 which is time-driven. The attack is performed on an Intel Xeon server, and can be completed in less than 30 minutes. It shows that our algorithm is applicable to not only power traces but also timing.
- We propose a method to protect the master key of the SMS4.

The rest of the paper is organized as follows. Section 2 summarizes the idea of differential cache attacks. In section 3, the description of SMS4 block cipher is provided. Then in section 4 we describe the improved attack on SMS4. We detail the improved attack methodology and explain the cryptanalytic techniques developed. This section also has the analysis of the attack with different cache line sizes. Section 5 has the experimental evaluation of the attack using timing side-channels, while in section 6, a modification to SMS4 is presented to protect against the differential cache attack. The final section has the conclusion of the paper.

2   Differential Cache Attacks

In [16] the differential cache attack was introduced for ciphers with the Feistel structure. We follow the explanation in [16] in order to introduce the attack technique.

Consider a 2-round Feistel cipher as shown in Figure 1. There are 2-keys k_0 and k_1 each of n bits, and two inputs in_0 and in_1. The s-box has 2^l elements implemented by a lookup table. Assume that m elements of the table share a cache line, which means that the table occupies $2^l/m$ cache lines. Now, suppose in_1 is chosen such that the second s-box access collides with the first then,

$$\langle in_0 \oplus k_0 \rangle = \langle S[in_0 \oplus k_0] \oplus in_1 \oplus k_1 \rangle, \tag{1}$$

where $\langle \cdot \rangle$ denotes $(l - log_2 m)$ most significant bits. This results in the reduction of the uncertainty for k_0 and k_1 from $2l$ to $l + m$. Next, suppose in_0', in_1' is another pair satisfying Equation 1, then a difference equation can be derived as follows:

$$\langle in_0 \oplus in_1 \oplus in_0' \oplus in_1' \rangle = \langle S[in_0 \oplus k_0] \oplus S[in_0' \oplus k_0] \rangle \tag{2}$$

Based on the property of the s-box S, the key k_0 can be uniquely recovered by using Equation 2 with a certain number of pairs of (in_0, in_1). We denote this number of inputs required by N_r. The value of N_r strongly depends on s-box S and the size of the cache line. In this paper, we show how carefully chosen values for the inputs can be used to further reduce the uncertainty of the keys, thereby reducing the value of N_r.

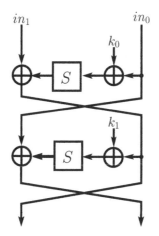

Fig. 1. Two Round Feistel Structure [16]

3   The SMS4 Block Cipher

SMS4 is a 128-bit block cipher released in 2006 [1]. There have been several published works, such as [12,13,24], which analyzed the security of SMS4. The cipher uses a 128 bit key and has 32-rounds. Each round comprises of a Feistel structure as shown in Figure 2(a). The inputs to round i $(0 \leq i \leq 31)$ are four 32 bit words X_i, X_{i+1}, X_{i+2}, X_{i+3}. Each round of SMS4 generates the word X_{i+4} as follows [24]:

$$
\begin{aligned}
X_{i+4} &= F(X_i, X_{i+1}, X_{i+2}, X_{i+3}) \\
&= X_i \oplus T(X_{i+1} \oplus X_{i+2} \oplus X_{i+3} \oplus RK_i),
\end{aligned}
\tag{3}
$$

where RK_i $(0 \leq i \leq 31)$ is a 32 bit round key and T is a function comprising of a layer of substitution followed by a diffusion. Four rounds of the cipher are shown in Figure 2(b). In a similar manner 32 rounds are present, and the ciphertext comprises of $(X_{31}|X_{32}|X_{33}|X_{34})$.

In each round, the 32-bit inputs (X_i) and round key RK_i are divided into 4 parts, each of 8 bits. These are respectively denoted $X_{i,0}, X_{i,1}, X_{i,2}, X_{i,3}$ and $RK_{i,0}, RK_{i,1}, RK_{i,2}, RK_{i,3}$. The round keys are generated from the secret key using a key expansion algorithm. Readers are directed to [8] for details about the key expansion.

Substitution is achieved by four similar 8×8 s-boxes denoted $S_3(\cdot)$, $S_2(\cdot)$, $S_1(\cdot)$, and $S_0(\cdot)$. The input to the s-box S_j, where $0 \leq j \leq 3$ is $(X_{i,j} \oplus X_{i+1,j} \oplus X_{i+2,j} \oplus X_{i+3,j} \oplus RK_{i,j})$.

Diffusion is provided by an L function defined as follows.

$$
\begin{aligned}
C &= L(B) \\
&= B \oplus (B <<< 2) \oplus (B <<< 10) \oplus (B <<< 18) \oplus (B <<< 24),
\end{aligned}
\tag{4}
$$

where $<<< i$ represents circular left rotation by i bits and B is the output of the substitution layer. That is $B = (S_3(\cdot)_{(7\ldots0)}|S_2(\cdot)_{(7\ldots0)}|S_1(\cdot)_{(7\ldots0)}|S_0(\cdot)_{(7\ldots0)})$. Similarly,

$$
\begin{aligned}
B <<< 2 &= (S_3(\cdot)_{(5\ldots0)}|S_2(\cdot)_{(7\ldots0)}|S_1(\cdot)_{(7\ldots0)}|S_0(\cdot)_{(7\ldots0)}|S_3(\cdot)_{(7,6)}) \\
B <<< 10 &= (S_2(\cdot)_{(5\ldots0)}|S_1(\cdot)_{(7\ldots0)}|S_0(\cdot)_{(7\ldots0)}|S_3(\cdot)_{(7\ldots0)}|S_2(\cdot)_{(7,6)}) \\
B <<< 18 &= (S_1(\cdot)_{(5\ldots0)}|S_0(\cdot)_{(7\ldots0)}|S_3(\cdot)_{(7\ldots0)}|S_2(\cdot)_{(7\ldots0)}|S_1(\cdot)_{(7,6)}) \\
B <<< 24 &= (S_0(\cdot)_{(7\ldots0)}|S_3(\cdot)_{(7\ldots0)}|S_2(\cdot)_{(7\ldots0)}|S_1(\cdot)_{(7\ldots0)})
\end{aligned}
\tag{5}
$$

4   The Improved Differential Cache Attack on SMS4

From the key schedule it can be easily deduced that the entire 128 bit SMS4 secret key can be uniquely recovered from four round keys RK_0, RK_1, RK_2, and RK_3 [8]. In this section we describe the methodology of our attack on SMS4. We assume that the cache line is of size m bytes, and the table used to implement the s-box is of 2^l bytes. The number of most significant bits revealed from each

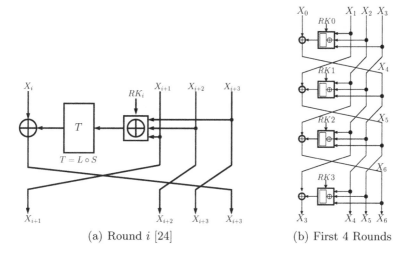

(a) Round i [24]   (b) First 4 Rounds

Fig. 2. Round Structure of SMS4

cache access is therefore $n = l - \log_2 m$. In the remainder of this section we show how these n bits can be used to reveal round keys RK_0, RK_1, RK_2, and RK_3, thus recovering the SMS4 secret key. The analysis is based on the assumption that no part of the table is present in cache at the start of the encryption and once data is loaded into cache it is not flushed out.

4.1   Step 1: Recovering RK_0

Let a plaintext (X_0, X_1, X_2, X_3) be chosen such that there are 7 cache hits out of the 8 table accesses in the first 2 rounds (Note that the first memory access can never be a cache hit by our assumption of a flushed cache at the start of encryption). The following equations can then be derived:

For Round 0:

$$\langle X_{1,0} \oplus X_{2,0} \oplus X_{3,0} \oplus RK_{0,0}\rangle = \langle X_{1,1} \oplus X_{2,1} \oplus X_{3,1} \oplus RK_{0,1}\rangle$$
$$= \langle X_{1,2} \oplus X_{2,2} \oplus X_{3,2} \oplus RK_{0,2}\rangle \qquad (6)$$
$$= \langle X_{1,3} \oplus X_{2,3} \oplus X_{3,3} \oplus RK_{0,3}\rangle$$

For Round 1:

$$\langle X_{1,0} \oplus X_{2,0} \oplus X_{3,0} \oplus RK_{0,0}\rangle$$
$$= \langle X_{0,0} \oplus X_{2,0} \oplus X_{3,0} \oplus RK_{1,0} \oplus T(RK_0 \oplus X_1 \oplus X_2 \oplus X_3)_0\rangle$$
$$= \langle X_{0,1} \oplus X_{2,1} \oplus X_{3,1} \oplus RK_{1,1} \oplus T(RK_0 \oplus X_1 \oplus X_2 \oplus X_3)_1\rangle \qquad (7)$$
$$= \langle X_{0,2} \oplus X_{2,2} \oplus X_{3,2} \oplus RK_{1,2} \oplus T(RK_0 \oplus X_1 \oplus X_2 \oplus X_3)_2\rangle$$
$$= \langle X_{0,3} \oplus X_{2,3} \oplus X_{3,3} \oplus RK_{1,3} \oplus T(RK_0 \oplus X_1 \oplus X_2 \oplus X_3)_3\rangle$$

Such a plaintext can be chosen adaptively as follows. For round 0, choose arbitrary values of X_0, X_2, X_3, $X_{1,0}$, $X_{1,2}$, and $X_{1,3}$. First vary $X_{1,1}$ until a cache hit is obtained in the second table access. Then vary $X_{1,2}$ until the second cache hit is obtained, and finally $X_{1,3}$ until the third cache hit is obtained. In a similar way 4 cache hits can be obtained in the second round by varying each byte of X_0 one after the other. Such an adaptive ordering of choosing plaintexts is required in order to prevent any ambiguities in the detection of collisions.

Let $P = (X_0, X_1, X_2, X_3)$ and $P' = (X_0', X_1', X_2', X_3')$ be two such plaintexts which satisfy Equations 6 and 7 and $P \neq P'$, then we have the following equations:

$$\langle RK_{0,1} \rangle = \langle X_{1,1} \oplus X_{2,1} \oplus X_{3,1} \oplus X_{1,0} \oplus X_{2,0} \oplus X_{3,0} \oplus RK_{0,0} \rangle$$
$$\langle RK_{0,2} \rangle = \langle X_{1,2} \oplus X_{2,2} \oplus X_{3,2} \oplus X_{1,0} \oplus X_{2,0} \oplus X_{3,0} \oplus RK_{0,0} \rangle \qquad (8)$$
$$\langle RK_{0,3} \rangle = \langle X_{1,3} \oplus X_{2,3} \oplus X_{3,3} \oplus X_{1,0} \oplus X_{2,0} \oplus X_{3,0} \oplus RK_{0,0} \rangle$$

$$\langle X_{1,0} \oplus X_{0,0} \oplus X_{1,0}' \oplus X_{0,0}' \rangle$$
$$= \langle T(RK_0 \oplus X_1 \oplus X_2 \oplus X_3)_0 \oplus T(RK_0 \oplus X_1' \oplus X_2' \oplus X_3')_0 \rangle$$
$$\langle X_{1,1} \oplus X_{0,1} \oplus X_{1,1}' \oplus X_{0,1}' \rangle$$
$$= \langle T(RK_0 \oplus X_1 \oplus X_2 \oplus X_3)_1 \oplus T(RK_0 \oplus X_1' \oplus X_2' \oplus X_3')_1 \rangle \qquad (9)$$
$$\langle X_{1,2} \oplus X_{0,2} \oplus X_{1,2}' \oplus X_{0,2}' \rangle$$
$$= \langle T(RK_0 \oplus X_1 \oplus X_2 \oplus X_3)_2 \oplus T(RK_0 \oplus X_1' \oplus X_2' \oplus X_3')_2 \rangle$$
$$\langle X_{1,3} \oplus X_{0,3} \oplus X_{1,3}' \oplus X_{0,3}' \rangle$$
$$= \langle T(RK_0 \oplus X_1 \oplus X_2 \oplus X_3)_3 \oplus T(RK_0 \oplus X_1' \oplus X_2' \oplus X_3')_3 \rangle$$

Using Equation 8, the uncertainty of key RK_0 reduces from 2^{32} to 2^{32-3n}. Equation 9 can be used to further filter the 2^{32-3n} candidates for RK_0. To determine uniquely the correct value for RK_0, we need to repeat the filtering for several pairs of plaintexts (P, P'). Let N_{r_0} denote the number of pairs of plaintexts that are required to uniquely determine the key. The value of N_{r_0} depends on the s-box, diffusion properties of the T function, and the cache line size (m). If m increases then N_{r_0} also increases, as the bits revealed from the cache hits reduce. In fact, N_{r_0} can be theoretically estimated. Since Equation 9 can be considered $4n$-bit filter and there are $(32 - 3n)$ unknown key bits, N_{r_0} is around $\lceil (32 - 3n)/4n \rceil$.

If the size of the table is 256 bytes, then the number of measurements required to uniquely determine RK_0 is $7\rho N_{r_0} 2^n$, where ρ is the number of measurements required to distinguish a cache hit from a miss. Note that this approach is different from the previous attacks [15,16,18], because it retrieves the entire 32 bits of the round key simultaneously, while the previous attacks target 8 bits at a time. Targeting 8 bits at a time would require several more plaintexts to uniquely determine the entire round key. Further, during the process of recovering RK_0, there are $4n$ bits of RK_1 that are also revealed (i.e $\langle RK_{1,0}\rangle, \langle RK_{1,1}\rangle, \langle RK_{1,2}\rangle, \langle RK_{1,3}\rangle$). This information was not utilized in the previous attacks [15,16,18]. On the other hand we use this information here to reduce the search space in the next step of the attack.

4.2 Step 2: Recovering RK_1

A straight forward application of the technique in [16] to obtain RK_1 requires choosing plaintexts such that there are 11 cache hits in the first 3 rounds (3 in the first, 4 in the second, and 4 in the third). We note that X_1, X_2, and X_3 contribute in the memory accesses in all 3 rounds, and (as seen in the earlier step to find RK_0), X_0 and X_1 are chosen based on X_2 and X_3. This *dependence* between the input words results in large number of plaintexts required. A naïve technique to obtain cache hits in the third round requires to check all 2^{32} candidates of X_2 thus resulting in $7\rho N_{r_1} 2^{32+n}$ measurements, where N_{r_1} is the number of pairs (P, P') needed to uniquely determine RK_1. Unless an alternate method of choosing plaintexts is developed, it cannot be directly applied to SMS4. Our approach focuses on the process of choosing X_0, X_1, X_2, and X_3. That is the choice of the value of X_i is not based on the choice of the value of X_j, $i, j \in \{0, 1, 2\}$.

The method requires keeping $X_2 = X_3$ and yet obtaining 11 cache hits in the first 3 rounds. By setting $X_2 = X_3$, the value $X_2 \oplus X_3$ is nullified in round 0 and round 1. This makes the procedure of choosing plaintexts that collide in Round 0, 1, 2 independent. Cache hits in round 0 can be obtained by using X_1, while X_0 can be used to obtain cache hits in round 1. For round 2, X_3 can be used. When 11 cache hits are obtained in the first three rounds, the following equations can be deduced.

For round 0:

$$\langle X_{1,0} \oplus RK_{0,0}\rangle = \langle X_{1,1} \oplus RK_{0,1}\rangle$$
$$= \langle X_{1,2} \oplus RK_{0,2}\rangle \qquad (10)$$
$$= \langle X_{1,3} \oplus RK_{0,3}\rangle$$

For Round 1:

$$\langle X_{1,0} \oplus RK_{0,0}\rangle = \langle X_{0,0} \oplus RK_{1,0} \oplus T(RK_0 \oplus X_1)_0\rangle$$
$$= \langle X_{0,1} \oplus RK_{1,1} \oplus T(RK_0 \oplus X_1)_1\rangle$$
$$= \langle X_{0,2} \oplus RK_{1,2} \oplus T(RK_0 \oplus X_1)_2\rangle \qquad (11)$$
$$= \langle X_{0,3} \oplus RK_{1,3} \oplus T(RK_0 \oplus X_1)_3\rangle$$

For round 2:

$$\langle X_{1,0} \oplus RK_{0,0}\rangle = \langle X_{3,0} \oplus X_{1,0} \oplus X_{0,0} \oplus T(RK_0 \oplus X_1)_0 \oplus RK_{2,0} \oplus T(RK_1 \oplus X_0 \oplus T(RK_0 \oplus X_1))_0\rangle$$
$$= \langle X_{3,1} \oplus X_{1,1} \oplus X_{0,1} \oplus T(RK_0 \oplus X_1)_1 \oplus RK_{2,1} \oplus T(RK_1 \oplus X_0 \oplus T(RK_0 \oplus X_1))_1\rangle$$
$$= \langle X_{3,2} \oplus X_{1,2} \oplus X_{0,2} \oplus T(RK_0 \oplus X_1)_2 \oplus RK_{2,2} \oplus T(RK_1 \oplus X_0 \oplus T(RK_0 \oplus X_1))_2\rangle$$
$$= \langle X_{3,3} \oplus X_{1,3} \oplus X_{0,3} \oplus T(RK_0 \oplus X_1)_3 \oplus RK_{2,3} \oplus T(RK_1 \oplus X_0 \oplus T(RK_0 \oplus X_1))_3\rangle$$

$$(12)$$

Note that Equations 10 and 11 are the same as that in 6 and 7 with the condition that $x_2 = x_3$. RK_1 can be recovered using Equations 11 and 12, and the previously determined value of RK_0 using a procedure similar to step 1 of the attack. Additionally $4n$ bits of RK_2 are also obtained. The number of additional measurements required to retrieve RK_1 is $3\rho N_{r_1} 2^n$ and N_{r_1} is theoretically estimated as $\lceil (32 - 4n)/4n \rceil$.

4.3   Step 3: Recovering RK_2

In order to recover RK_2, collisions are required in rounds 3 and 4. We propose two methods to determine RK_2. One which uses X_2 to obtain collisions in the 4th round and the other which uses X_3.

Using X_2:   Suppose the following restrictions are made on the choice of the input plaintext

$$X_0 = 0$$
$$X_1 = X_3 \oplus R$$
$$X_3 = T(RK_0 \oplus X_2 \oplus R) \oplus RK_0 \oplus RK_1 \oplus R,$$

where R is set to $\langle RK_2 \rangle$, which was found in the previous step of the attack. Then $X_4 = T(RK_0 \oplus X_2 \oplus R)$, $X_5 = X_1 \oplus X_4$, and the memory accesses in the third round are to the constant location $\langle 0 \rangle$ and independent of X_2. The plaintext input X_2 and X_3 can then be used to obtain cache hits in the 4th round thus resulting in the following equation

$$\langle RK2_i \oplus RK3_i \rangle = \langle X_{2,i} \oplus X_{3,i} \oplus T(\langle 0 \rangle)_i \rangle, \tag{13}$$

where $0 \leq i \leq 3$.

However when power traces are used, a cache hit thus obtained can be due to collisions in the 4th round or $RK0 \oplus X_2 \oplus R$ in the first and second rounds. Thus resulting in ambiguities about the collision. In previous works on differential cache attacks [15,16,18], such ambiguities were resolved by using probabilistic techniques. In the next part of the section we show that X_3 can be used to eliminate this ambiguity in a deterministic manner.

Using X_3:   We first set $X_2 = X_3$ as before. Next, we set $X_4 = X_5$. This is made possible using X_0 and X_1.

$$X_1 = RK_1 \oplus T(0).$$
$$X_0 = RK_1 \oplus T(RK_0 \oplus X_1). \tag{14}$$

Setting X_0 and X_1 as in Equation 14 makes both X_4 and X_5 equal to RK_1. Thus, making the accesses to the s-boxes in the third round dependent solely on X_3. The value of X_3 (and X_2, since the equality holds) is chosen such that the

access to the lookup table for the first s-box in Round 4 collides with the last
s-box access in Round 3 (Figure 2(b)), then,

$$\langle X_{3,3} \oplus RK_{2,3} \rangle = \langle X_{3,0} \oplus RK_{3,0} \oplus T(RK_2 \oplus X_3)_0 \rangle \qquad (15)$$

In order to choose plaintext so that the above equation holds, we use the inputs
$X_{3,1}$ and $X_{3,2}$, and exploit the s-box and diffusion properties of T.

Consider $\langle T(RK_2 \oplus X_3)_0 \rangle$. Using the diffusion properties given in Equations
4 and 5, it can be written as follows.

$$
\begin{aligned}
\langle T(RK_2 \oplus X_3)_0 \rangle = & S_0((RK_2 \oplus X_3)_0)_{(7 \cdots 7-n+1)} \\
& \oplus S_0((RK_2 \oplus X_3)_0)_{(5 \cdots 5-n+1)} \\
& \oplus S_2((RK_2 \oplus X_3)_2)_{(5 \cdots 5-n+1)} \\
& \oplus S_3((RK_2 \oplus X_3)_3)_{(5 \cdots 5-n+1)} \\
& \oplus S_1((RK_2 \oplus X_3)_1)_{(7 \cdots 7-n+1)},
\end{aligned}
\qquad (16)
$$

where n is the number of bits revealed from the cache attack. This depends on
the cache line size and the size of the table. We analyze for different values of n
in the range 1 to 5. From Equation 16, it can be seen that the required cache
collision in Equation 15 can be obtained by keeping $X_{3,0}$ and $X_{3,3}$ fixed and
varying $\langle T(RK_2 \oplus X_3)_0 \rangle$ using the inputs $X_{3,1}$ and $X_{3,2}$. Instead of trying all
256 values of $X_{3,1}$ or $X_{3,2}$, we use an analysis of SMS4 to minimize the search.
This depends on the properties of the s-box and the value of n and is summarized
in Table 1.

Table 1. Bits to be Manipulated in X_3 in order to obtain Equation 15

n	Bit to be Manipulated in X_3	Number of Trials
1	Byte 1, bit 0 to get a collision in $S_{1,7}$	2
	Byte 2, bit 0 to get a collision in $S_{2,5}$	
2	Byte 1, bits 0,1,2, and 4 to get a collision in $S_{1,(7,6)}$	16
	Byte 2, bits 0,1,2, and 3 to get a collision in $S_{2,(5,4)}$	
3	Byte 1, bits 0,1,2,3, and 4 to get a collision in $S_{1,(7,6,5)}$	32
	Byte 2, bits 0,1,2,3, and 4 to get a collision in $S_{2,(5,4,3)}$	
4	Byte 1, bits 0,1,2,3,4, and 5 to get a collision in $S_{1,(7,6,5,4)}$	64
	Byte 2, bits 0,1,2,3,4, and 6 to get a collision in $S_{2,(5,4,3,2)}$	
5	Byte 1, bits 0,1,2,3,4,5, and 6 to get a collision in $S_{1,(7,6,5,4,3)}$	128
	Byte 2, bits 0,1,2,3,4,5 and 6 to get a collision in $S_{2,(5,4,3,2,1)}$	

$S_{i,j}$ means the ith s-box, j^{th} bit $[(0 \leq i \leq 3)$ and $(0 \leq j \leq 7)]$

Let (P, P') be a pair of plaintexts satisfying Equation 15, then we have the
following equation:

$$\langle X_{3,3} \oplus X'_{3,3} \oplus X_{3,0} \oplus X'_{3,0} \rangle = \langle T(RK_2 \oplus X_3)_0 \oplus T(RK_2 \oplus X'_3)_0 \rangle \qquad (17)$$

We choose a certain N_{r_2} pairs of (P, P') large enough to uniquely determine the correct key RK_2. The number N_{r_2} depends on n and properties of the function $T(\cdot)$. If n is small then the filter is weak. For example, when $n = 1$ (i.e 128 byte cache line and 256 byte table), even with $N_{r_2} \geq 25$, the number of possible key candidates is around 74. If $n \geq 3$, then N_{r_2} is theoretically estimated as $\lceil (32 - 4n)/n \rceil$. The number of plaintexts needed for recovering RK_2 is $N_{r_2} 2^{n+2}$, where $2^{n+2}, n \geq 2$ is in Table 1 or $N_{r_2} 2$ in case n=1. In the next part of this section we present three methods for reducing the set of key candidates.

1. **Using Intersecting Sets:** This can be made more efficient by observing that each row in Table 1 depicts two ways of satisfying Equation 15. Either by varying the bits of $X_{3,1}$ or the bits of $X_{3,2}$. We first obtain the set of candidates keys ($S1$) by satisfying Equation 15 using $X_{3,1}$ and keeping $X_{3,2}$ fixed. Then we obtain another set $S2$, containing candidate keys obtained by keeping $X_{3,2}$ fixed and varying $X_{3,1}$. The correct key is always present in the intersection set $(S1 \cap S2)$. We found that for $n = 1$, $N_{r_2} = 44$ is sufficient to uniquely identify RK_2, i.e 22 collisions for each $X_{3,1}$ and $X_{3,2}$. If $n = 2$ then $N_{r_2} = 24$. Notably, this technique is used for $n = 1$ or $n = 2$ because the filter is weak.

   To clarify the method, the following example is shown. Let $n = 1$, $RK_2 = (RK_{2,3}, RK_{2,2}, RK_{2,1}, RK_{2,0}) = (1130101)_{16}$. If we manipulate only $X_{3,1}$ or $X_{3,2}$ to get the collision, the lower bound N_{r_2} computed from the experiment is 25. If however, we use both $X_{3,1}$ and $X_{3,2}$, N_{r_2} is around 44. Table 2 lists example key candidates obtained in set $S1$ and set $S2$. All the key candidates in $S1$ are different in the second byte, while in $S2$ the third byte varies. Hence, the correct key is uniquely recovered from the intersection of $S1$ and $S2$.

2. **Reusing Plaintexts:** The number of plaintexts is reduced by reusing the plaintexts generated for Equation 12, i.e plaintexts used for finding collisions for $X_{3,1}, X_{3,2}$. With the same argument above, the plaintexts for finding collision for $X_{3,1}$ and $X_{3,2}$ can be reused to find the collision in this step. Since $N_{r_0} = 10$ in case of m=128, the number N_{r_2} is reduced from 44 to 24. In case of that $n \geq 2$, then reduction is not much.

Table 2. Example for Determining RK_2

	$S1$	$S2$
0	$(\mathbf{1130101})_{16}$	$(1040101)_{16}$
1	$(1130601)_{16}$	$(1050101)_{16}$
2	$(1138801)_{16}$	$(1055101)_{16}$
$\vdots$	$\vdots$	$\vdots$
15	$(1132501)_{16}$	$(\mathbf{1130101})_{16}$
16	$(1132601)_{16}$	$(1180101)_{16}$
$\vdots$	$\vdots$	$\vdots$
62	$(1137e01)_{16}$	$(17c0101)_{16}$
63	$(1137f01)_{16}$	$(17d0101)_{16}$

3. **Using Cache Misses:** Although this method can be tailored for any value of n, it is most suited for $n = 1$, i.e 128 byte cache lines, because of the following lemma.

Lemma 1. *In case of 128-byte cache line, the cache miss and hit provide the same information for the attack due to the size of collision being 1 bit.*

According to the lemma, for a given plaintext, Equations 10, 11, and 12 can be constructed by observing the cache miss and cache hit. If a cache miss is observed, then adding one would give the required equation. By using this method, the number of plaintexts required to recover RK_0 and RK_1 reduces to 10. For the case of RK_2, the number of plaintexts reduces to 42 (with reusing). In all, the number of plaintexts to recover all three keys (RK_0, RK_1, and RK_2) is around 52.

In order to show how efficiently the techniques improve the number of pairs of (P, P') needed in case of 128-byte cache line or $n = 1$, we summarize the results above.

(a) Normal attack: $7N_{r_0}2 + 7N_{r_1}2 + N_{r_2}2 \approx 7 \times 10 \times 2 + 3 \times 10 \times 2 + 44 \times 2$
    $= 288$.
(b) Reusing Plaintexts, we can reuse 10 $X_{3,1}$ and 10 $X_{3,2}$ in Equation 12. Hence, we have: $\approx 7 \times 10 \times 2 + 3 \times 10 \times 2 + (22-10) \times 2 = 224$.
(c) Using Cache Misses and Reusing Plaintexts: $N_{r_0} + N_{r_2} = 10 + 44\text{-}2$
    $= 52$.

Where $N_{r_1} \approx N_{r_0}$ and the values of $N_{r_i}, 1 \leq i \leq 3$ are provided in Table 3.

4.4   Step 4: Recovering RK_3

During the process of find RK_2 we have also obtained n bits of RK_3. The remaining bits of RK_3 is found by brute force. For this we require one valid pair of plaintext and ciphertext (called *the golden pair*). Then, for every guessed value of RK_3 (there are 2^{32-n} guesses), we reverse the key scheduling to obtain a candidate key. The candidate key is correct if the ciphertext obtained by encrypting the given plaintext with the candidate key matches the golden ciphertext.

4.5   The Total Theoretical Number of Plaintexts Needed for Attack

If we have q plaintexts $(P_1, ... P_q)$, then the number of pairs (P, P') can be at least $q + 1 \approx q$ and at most C_2^q. In our case, we create q pairs from q given plaintexts. Denote N the total number of plaintexts need for attack, then

$$N = \rho(2^n(7N_{r_0} + 3N_{r_1}) + 2^{n+2}N_{r_2})$$
$$\approx \rho 2^n(10N_{r_0} + 4N_{r_2}), n \geq 2. \tag{18}$$

Where theoretical value and practical value of N_{r_0} and N_{r_2} are described in Table 3.

Table 3. Attack Complexity vs Cache Line Size

Number of Collision - $n = 8 - \log_2 m$	1 bit	2 bits	3 bits	4 bits	5 bits
theoretical N_{r_0}	$\lceil 7, 25 \rceil$	$\lceil 3, 25 \rceil$	2	2	2
practical N_{r_0}	10	4	2	2	2
theoretical N_{r_2}	x	x	$\lceil 6, 6 \rceil$	4	2
practical N_{r_2}	44	24	8	4	2
$\log_2$(Number of plaintexts needed)	5.7	9.2	8.8	9.3	10
$\log_2$(Candidate Keys)	31	30	29	28	27

4.6 Analysis

We analyze the attack algorithm by simulating the attack with various cache line sizes. The aim of the analysis was to estimate the number of pairs of plaintexts required for the attack (i.e. N_{r_0}, N_{r_1} and N_{r_2}), and also the number of candidate keys remaining at the end of the attack. Notably, if the power trace is used, then $\rho = 1$, and the number of plaintexts needed for the attack is presented in Table 3 as well. Table 3 presents the analysis assuming that the table occupies 256 bytes (i.e $l = 8$).

5   Experimental Evaluation

To practically mount the attack, the adversary requires to distinguish between a cache hit and a miss. There are two ways this can be done: either using power (or electro-magnetic) traces or by timing the encryption. A single power trace can reveal significant information about each memory access made by the cipher. For example in [16], all memory access patterns in a round were simultaneously revealed by monitoring a single power trace using an oscilloscope.

Attacks that use timing are not so straightforward. Here the cipher is a black box as compared to a gray box in power side-channels. The timing adversary only observes the time for encryption, from which individual memory access patterns must be deciphered. Several timing measurements are required in order to distinguish a single memory access. Although more difficult, the advantage of the timing side-channel is that it can be mounted remotely [6,3,7] and even in a virtualization environment [23]. In this section we present the general procedure for a timing attack and then its application to SMS4.

5.1   The Timing Attack Algorithm

From the cache-timing perspective, the cipher implementation can be considered as a series of r memory accesses to a lookup table stored in memory. The accesses to the table depend on the key material (k) and the initial or intermediate state of the cipher (d) and has the form $d \oplus k$. Note that the initial state is the plaintext input. To launch the cache-timing attack, one access to the table (say $d_i \oplus k_i$

where $0 \leq i < r-1$) is kept constant and another access (say $d_j \oplus k_j$, $i < j \leq r-1$) is traversed through every possible memory block that the table can occupy. For example if the table has 2^l elements and the size of the cache line is m, then the table occupies $2^l/m$ memory blocks. Traversing every block is possible by setting $\langle d_j \oplus k_j \rangle$ so that it takes all values from 0 to $\frac{2^l}{m} - 1$. For a constant $\langle d_i \oplus k_i \rangle$ and each value taken by $\langle d_j \oplus k_j \rangle$, the remaining memory accesses are made to random locations by varying the plaintext until a distribution of the timing can be built. We thus obtain $\frac{2^l}{m}$ distributions of which the distribution with the average time most different from the others resulted in the collision. For the collision the following relation is revealed $\langle d_i \oplus k_i \rangle = \langle d_j \oplus k_j \rangle$. The details of this procedure is presented in Algorithm 1

Algorithm 1. Algorithm to Find Collision

    Input: locations of i and j, where $0 \leq i < j \leq r$
1 **begin**
2   Choose values of plaintext such that $\langle d_i \oplus k_i \rangle$ is a constant
3   **foreach** $s \in \{0, 1, 2, \ldots, \frac{2^l}{m} - 1\}$ **do**
4   **for** *several number of times* **do**
5   Choose values of plaintext such that $\langle d_j \rangle = s$ and the remaining accesses are random
6   Trigger encryption and obtain the time required
7   **end**
8   **end**
9   **return** *The value of s with the most deviant average time*
10 **end**

The reason the algorithm works is that in the memory access $\langle d_j \oplus k_j \rangle$, there is exactly one memory block which collides with $\langle d_i \oplus k_i \rangle$ in every encryption. This results in a distribution which is visibly different compared to the other distributions.

5.2   Application to SMS4

We now apply Algorithm 1 to the various steps of the attack.

Determining RK0 and RK1: For $RK0$ Equation 6 needs to be first obtained. To obtain the first equality in Equation 6, we keep $\langle X_{1,0} \oplus X_{2,0} \oplus X_{3,0} \rangle$ constant (this is the d_i·in Algorithm 1) and then vary $\langle X_{1,1} \oplus X_{2,1} \oplus X_{3,1} \rangle$ from 0 to $\frac{2^l}{m} - 1$ (this is the d_j in the algorithm). All other plaintext bytes are varied randomly. One of the $\frac{2^l}{m} - 1$ timing distributions thus obtained will have an average timing which is considerably different from the other three. This distribution results in a collision and would yield the equation $\langle X_{1,0} \oplus X_{2,0} \oplus X_{3,0} \oplus RK_{0,0} \rangle = \langle X_{1,1} \oplus X_{2,1} \oplus X_{3,1} \oplus RK_{0,1} \rangle$, thus the first equality in Equation 6 is obtained. In a similar way, the other equalities in Equation 6 can be obtained by appropriately choosing d_j. It can be noted that Algorithm 1 can be easily modified to obtain all required equalities simultaneously.

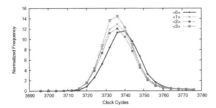
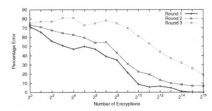

(a) Part of the Timing Distribution Obtained while determining the first Equality in Equation 6

(b) Error in Detecting a Collision vs Number of Encryptions

Fig. 3. Experimental Evaluation on an Intel Xeon Server (E5606)

To obtain the first equality of Equation 7, another requirement for $RK0$, we place $\langle d_i \rangle$ as $\langle X_{1,0} \oplus X_{2,0} \oplus X_{3,0} \rangle$ as before, and $\langle d_j \rangle$ as $\langle X_{0,0} \rangle$. In a similar manner the other equalities of Equation 7 can be obtained.

For $RK1$, Equations 10,11, and 12 needed to be determined. The former two equations can be determined as was done for $RK0$. To determine 12, $\langle d_i \rangle$ must be kept at $\langle X_{1,0} \rangle$ and $\langle d_j \rangle$ to $\langle X_{3,0} \rangle$. Further in order to identify the collision, the term $T(RK_1 \oplus X_0 \oplus T(RK_0 \oplus X_1))$ is to be kept constant by keeping X_0 and X_1 constant.

Determining RK2 : Two methods to determine RK2 have been presented in Section 4.3. One uses X_2 and the other X_3. While the X_3 method will work for power side-channels, it will fail in timing attacks. The reason being as follows. The required equation to be be satisfied is Equation 15. While left hand side of the equation can be kept as M_i, the right hand side cannot be used as M_j because $T(RK_2 \oplus X_3)_0$ cannot be computed. We can therefore apply only the X_2 method although ambiguities still arise due to the bytes in $RK2$. This requires Equation 13 to be fulfilled. d_i is 0 in this case and d_j is the right hand side of the equation.

5.3   Experimental Results

We use an Intel Xeon (E5606) as a target platform for the attack. The Xeon has a 32KB L1 data cache which is 8 way set associative. The unified L2 cache is 256KB and is also 8 way associative. There is also an L3 cache of 8MB which is 16 way set associative. The cache line size in all cases in 64 bytes.

The SMS4 implementation which was attacked was written in C and used a single table of 256 bytes to implement the s-box. Thus $2^l = 256$, $m = 64$, and the number of bits revealed by a cache collision is $n = log_2(2^l/m) = 2$. In order to distinguish a collision, several encryptions are required in order to build the timing distribution. Figure 3(a) shows the partial timing distributions obtained for the first equality in Equation 6. Since $n = 2$, there are 4 possible timing distributions, labeled $\langle 0 \rangle$, $\langle 1 \rangle$, $\langle 2 \rangle$, and $\langle 3 \rangle$. The figure clearly shows the distribution corresponding to $\langle 0 \rangle$ having a higher average compared to the other 3. Thus indicating a collision. The graph was built after monitoring 2^{22} encryptions.

The accuracy with which a collision is detected depends on the number of measurements monitored. Figure 3(b) shows the error percentage in detecting collisions for rounds 1, 2, and 3. It can be seen that as the number of measurements taken increases, the error in detecting a collision reduces.

6   Modified SMS4 to Protect against Differential Cache Attacks

There are several methods to counter cache attacks. Many of the counter measures would be able to prevent the differential cache attack as well. All countermeasures either try to randomize memory accesses or eliminate the dependence of the key on the memory accesses. Methods to do this include eliminating lookup tables, or constructing a table small enough to put in a single cache line. However, the encryption speed of the cipher is drastically affected without the cache, while implementing the cipher without tables or with a small table can result in large number of computations, thus hampering performance.

In this section we show a modification to the SMS4 algorithm that would prevent the attack. This is based on the following observations.

1. All the round keys are recovered independently.
2. It is not easy to recover many round keys.
3. The master key K is computed by using several consecutive round keys.
4. The master key K need to be protected and not the values of round keys.

Our aim is to protect the master key, that is, even if the adversaries recover some of the round keys, they still cannot recover K. It means that the recovered information, i.e, round keys, are made be not useful or not enough to recover the master key. Hence, even if the adversary collects signifcant information from the side channel, he cannot use this information for anything. This can be realized by using a simple trick: prevent the adversary from recovering the sub-keys, which are used to obtain the master key.

In the case of SMS4, the master key K is obtained by first recovering few round keys, and then reversing the key schedule. To protect the master key, we require the number of round keys generated from the key scheduling algorithm is increased. In the current key schedule algorithm of SMS4, 32 round keys are generated : RK_0 to RK_{31}. The key schedule algorithm can be modified to generate additional round keys RK_{32} to RK_{63}. Then, $RK_0 \oplus RK_{32}$, ..., $RK_3 \oplus RK_{35}$ are used as round keys instead of RK_0, ..., RK_{31}.

In this scenario, the adversary can apply the attack to recover the values $RK_0 \oplus RK_{32}$, ..., $RK_3 \oplus RK_{35}$ but the values of sub-keys $RK_0, \ldots, RK_3$ are still hidden. Therefore, the master key still be in secure. This simple modification only requires additional number of sub-keys to be generated. The structure of the cipher, its security, and the speed of encryption / decryption are not altered with this modification.

7   Conclusion

In this paper, the improved differential-cache attack is studied on SMS4. The improved attack exploits more information obtained from the cache leakage, and requires just around 600 plaintexts for a 64 byte cache line. A sophisticated method of choosing plaintexts coupled with several cryptanalytic techniques is applied to reduce the number of plaintexts needed, and there by the entropy of the key. An analysis of the attack complexity is made for various cache line sizes. The analysis shows that for a large cache line size, such as 128 bytes, as little as 52 plaintexts are sufficient. The paper also shows a modification to the SMS4 algorithm which can prevent this attack without any overhead in performance.

References

1. Specification of SMS4, Block Cipher for WLAN Products- SMS4 (in Chinese), http://www.oscca.gov.cn/UpFile/200621011642319790.pdf
2. Acıiçmez, O., Koç, Ç.K.: Trace-Driven Cache Attacks on AES (Short Paper). In: Ning, P., Qing, S., Li, N. (eds.) ICICS 2006. LNCS, vol. 4307, pp. 112–121. Springer, Heidelberg (2006)
3. Acıiçmez, O., Schindler, W., Koç, Ç.K.: Cache Based Remote Timing Attack on the AES. In: Abe, M. (ed.) CT-RSA 2007. LNCS, vol. 4377, pp. 271–286. Springer, Heidelberg (2006)
4. Bernstein, D.J.: Cache-timing Attacks on AES. Tech. rep. (2005)
5. Bertoni, G., Zaccaria, V., Breveglieri, L., Monchiero, M., Palermo, G.: AES Power Attack Based on Induced Cache Miss and Countermeasure. In: ITCC (1), pp. 586–591. IEEE Computer Society (2005)
6. Brumley, D., Boneh, D.: Remote Timing Attacks are Practical. Computer Networks 48(5), 701–716 (2005)
7. Crosby, S.A., Wallach, D.S., Riedi, R.H.: Opportunities and Limits of Remote Timing Attacks. ACM Trans. Inf. Syst. Secur. 12(3) (2009)
8. Diffie, W., Ledin, G.: SMS4 Encryption Algorithm for Wireless Networks (translated). Cryptology ePrint Archive, Report 2008/329 (2008), http://eprint.iacr.org/
9. Fournier, J.J.A., Tunstall, M.: Cache Based Power Analysis Attacks on AES. In: Batten, L.M., Safavi-Naini, R. (eds.) ACISP 2006. LNCS, vol. 4058, pp. 17–28. Springer, Heidelberg (2006)
10. Gallais, J.F., Kizhvatov, I., Tunstall, M.: Improved Trace-Driven Cache-Collision Attacks against Embedded AES Implementations. In: Chung, Y., Yung, M. (eds.) WISA 2010. LNCS, vol. 6513, pp. 243–257. Springer, Heidelberg (2011)
11. Kelsey, J., Schneier, B., Wagner, D., Hall, C.: Side Channel Cryptanalysis of Product Ciphers. J. Comput. Secur. 8(2,3), 141–158 (2000)
12. Li, R., Sun, B., Li, C., You, J.: Differential Fault Analysis on SMS4 using a single fault. Inf. Process. Lett. 111(4), 156–163 (2011)
13. Liu, F., Ji, W., Hu, L., Ding, J., Lv, S., Pyshkin, A., Weinmann, R.P.: Analysis of the SMS4 Block Cipher. In: Pieprzyk, J., Ghodosi, H., Dawson, E. (eds.) ACISP 2007. LNCS, vol. 4586, pp. 158–170. Springer, Heidelberg (2007)
14. Page, D.: Theoretical use of cache memory as a cryptanalytic side-channel. IACR Cryptology ePrint Archive 2002, 169 (2002)

15. Poddar, R., Datta, A., Rebeiro, C.: A Cache Trace Attack on CAMELLIA. In: Joye, M., Mukhopadhyay, D., Tunstall, M. (eds.) InfoSecHiComNet 2011. LNCS, vol. 7011, pp. 144–156. Springer, Heidelberg (2011)
16. Rebeiro, C., Mukhopadhyay, D.: Cryptanalysis of CLEFIA Using Differential Methods with Cache Trace Patterns. In: Kiayias, A. (ed.) CT-RSA 2011. LNCS, vol. 6558, pp. 89–103. Springer, Heidelberg (2011)
17. Rebeiro, C., Mukhopadhyay, D., Takahashi, J., Fukunaga, T.: Cache Timing Attacks on CLEFIA. In: Roy, B., Sendrier, N. (eds.) INDOCRYPT 2009. LNCS, vol. 5922, pp. 104–118. Springer, Heidelberg (2009)
18. Rebeiro, C., Poddar, R., Datta, A., Mukhopadhyay, D.: An Enhanced Differential Cache Attack on CLEFIA for Large Cache Lines. In: Bernstein, D.J., Chatterjee, S. (eds.) INDOCRYPT 2011. LNCS, vol. 7107, pp. 58–75. Springer, Heidelberg (2011)
19. Tiri, K., Acıiçmez, O., Neve, M., Andersen, F.: An analytical model for time-driven cache attacks. In: Biryukov, A. (ed.) FSE 2007. LNCS, vol. 4593, pp. 399–413. Springer, Heidelberg (2007)
20. Tsunoo, Y., Saito, T., Suzaki, T., Shigeri, M., Miyauchi, H.: Cryptanalysis of DES Implemented on Computers with Cache. In: Walter, C.D., Koç, Ç.K., Paar, C. (eds.) CHES 2003. LNCS, vol. 2779, pp. 62–76. Springer, Heidelberg (2003)
21. Tsunoo, Y., Tsujihara, E., Minematsu, K., Miyauchi, H.: Cryptanalysis of Block Ciphers Implemented on Computers with Cache. In: International Symposium on Information Theory and Its Applications, pp. 803–806 (2002)
22. Tsunoo, Y., Tsujihara, E., Shigeri, M., Kubo, H., Minematsu, K.: Improving Cache Attacks by Considering Cipher Structure. Int. J. Inf. Sec. 5(3), 166–176 (2006)
23. Weiß, M., Heinz, B., Stumpf, F.: A cache timing attack on AES in virtualization environments. In: Keromytis, A.D. (ed.) FC 2012. LNCS, vol. 7397, pp. 314–328. Springer, Heidelberg (2012)
24. Zhang, L., Zhang, W., Wu, W.: Cryptanalysis of Reduced-Round SMS4 Block Cipher. In: Mu, Y., Susilo, W., Seberry, J. (eds.) ACISP 2008. LNCS, vol. 5107, pp. 216–229. Springer, Heidelberg (2008)
25. Zhao, X., Zhang, F., Guo, S., Wang, T., Shi, Z., Liu, H., Ji, K.: MDASCA: An Enhanced Algebraic Side-Channel Attack for Error Tolerance and New Leakage Model Exploitation. In: Schindler, W., Huss, S.A. (eds.) COSADE 2012. LNCS, vol. 7275, pp. 231–248. Springer, Heidelberg (2012)

An Extension of Fault Sensitivity Analysis Based on Clockwise Collision

Yang Li, Kazuo Ohta, and Kazuo Sakiyama

Department of Informatics, The University of Electro-Communications
1-5-1 Chofugaoka, Chofu, Tokyo 182-8585, Japan
{liyang,kazuo.ohta,sakiyama}@uec.ac.jp

Abstract. This paper proposes an extension of fault sensitivity analysis based on *clockwise collision*. The original FSA attack uses the fault injections to exploit the sensitivity of calculations against the fault injections. While the clockwise collision fault sensitivity analysis (CC-FSA) uses the fault injections to detect the occurrence of the clockwise collision and to recover the secret key. Clockwise collision is a phenomenon for iterative hardware circuits, which leads to nearly impossible setup-time violations. Take an AES S-box as an instance, clockwise collision occurs when the S-box inputs for two consecutive clock cycles are identical in value. As a result, the combinational circuit in the second clock cycle has almost no signal toggle and a negligible critical path delay. This paper proposes and verifies the concept of CC-FSA using the clock-glitch-based fault injections and an unprotected AES implementation. We investigate the key recovery method for CC-FSA with a noisy data set and we consider CC-FSA can help the previous collision-based model-less FSA attack to identify the final 8-bit secret information without additional data and negligible computational overhead.

Keywords: side-channel analysis, fault analysis, fault sensitivity analysis, AES.

1 Introduction

In the recent decade, the security of cryptographic devices, e.g., smart cards, is practically threatened by the emergence of side-channel attacks. On the one hand, the secret information is leaking as the side channel leakage such as the power consumption [4], the electro-magnetic radiation [3,13] and so on. On the other hand, the fault-based attacks, which were first proposed in 1997 [2], recover the secret information based on intentionally injected computational faults. The well known fault analyses include the differential fault analysis (DFA) [1], the safe-error attacks [19] and the differential behavior analysis [15]

Recently, a new type of fault analysis named fault sensitivity analysis (FSA) was proposed in 2010 [6] and extended in 2011 [5,9]. In the FSA attack, the fault injection is considered with a new property named fault injection intensity, which describes the strength of the fault injection. The FSA attackers try to obtain

M. Kutyłowski and M. Yung (Eds.): Inscrypt 2012, LNCS 7763, pp. 46–59, 2013.

the critical fault injection intensity that corresponds to the threshold between the fault-free and the faulty operations. The critical fault injection intensity is related to the sensitive information of the critical path delay, which depends on the intermediate values used in the calculation. The secret key is possible to be recovered by analyzing the measured data of the fault sensitivity leakage.

This paper demonstrates a phenomenon named *clockwise collision* that leads to the negligible critical path delay and the nearly impossible setup-time violation, and proposes an extension of FSA named *clockwise collision fault sensitivity analysis (CC-FSA)*. The fault injection based on setup-time violation occurs when the period of a clock cycle is shorter than the critical path delay of the calculation. An example of setup-time violation based practical fault attack was shown by Selmane et al. [18]. For hardware circuits with an iterative architecture, the signal transitions in a combinational circuit are related to the calculation inputs in both the previous and the current clock cycles. The input in the previous clock cycle determines the initial calculation state of the combinational circuit, while the input in the current clock cycle determines the calculation result and the final state of the combinational circuit. The clockwise collision is the case that the input data of a combinational circuit are identical in value for two consecutive clock cycles. When a clockwise collision occurs, the combinational circuit is given to perform the same calculation using the same input data for two consecutive clock cycles. However, since the calculation is already performed in the first clock cycle, there is no calculation performed in the second clock cycle. Therefore there is no signal toggle in the second clock cycle for the combinational circuit, which causes a negligibly short critical path delay. Consequently, a setup-time violation is nearly impossible to be triggered for the second clock cycle when the clockwise collision occurs.

In the CC-FSA attack against AES, the attackers focus on the occurrence of the clockwise collision for AES S-boxes. The fault injections are used to detect the S-box calculations with the impossible setup-time violations. The detection of the clockwise collision leads to the leakage of the sensitive information of the intermediate values and the successful key recovery.

In this paper, we show a series of experiments for the verification of the attack concept, and test the strength of the proposed attack. Our experiments are based on the clock-glitch-based fault injections against an unprotected hardware AES implementation on the ASIC of SASEBO-R [14]. First, we perform some preliminary experiments to verify the two-round data dependency for the signal transitions of an AES S-box. Then, we verify the attack concept of CC-FSA that the setup-time violation is very difficult to be triggered for the AES S-box when the input data for two consecutive cycles collides in value, i.e., Hamming distance (HD) is 0. After the verification of the CC-FSA concept, we perform the attack experiment that uses only 1 fault injection to each plaintext. We find that no fault is injected to the clockwise colliding S-boxes, but there are also many noise data that the S-box calculation is still fault-free even no clockwise collision occurs. Then we propose the solutions to extract the secret key from the noisy data. Lastly, we consider that the CC-FSA attack can be combined with the collision-based model-less FSA attacks proposed in [5, 9]. Since the FSA attack in [5, 9] only recovers the key byte difference, the secret key space cannot be restricted to below 2^8. We note that the CC-FSA attack can be used to help identifying the last 8 secret key bits using no additional data and little computational overhead.

The rest of this paper is organized as follows. In Sect. 2, we briefly review the previous work. In Sects. 3 and 4, we explain the performed preliminary experiments and explain the concept of the clockwise collision. In Sect. 5, we show the attack experiments and the key recovery result. Section 6 discusses some extensions of the CC-FSA attack and Sect. 7 concludes the paper.

2   Previous Work

To perform a DFA attack, the attackers require pairs of fault-free and faulty ciphertexts and the information about the injected fault. When the fault injection method is based on the setup-time violation, the mostly used fault model against AES is the random byte fault model, in which some byte-wise faults are injected usually with unknown position and unknown faulty value. When the attack target is AES, the representative attack was proposed by Piret and Quisquater in 2003 [12].

Based on a guess of some partial key bits, some partial decryption calculation is performed for the pair of fault-free and faulty ciphertexts. The difference between the fault-free and faulty intermediate values is calculated and compared with the known information of the injected fault. When the calculated intermediate value difference cannot match the injected fault, the corresponding key guess is known to be invalid. Keeping on eliminating the invalid keys to restrict the key space, the secret key can be identified with enough pairs of fault-free and faulty ciphertexts. For the DFA attacks, the information of the injected fault, the exact value of the faulty ciphertexts and the detailed algorithm of the attack target are required [16].

2.1   Fault Sensitivity Analysis

Different from the DFA attack, the FSA attack tries to exploit the secret key without any detailed fault model and without using the value of the faulty outputs [6]. To achieve the mentioned freedom, the FSA attack introduces the concept of fault injection intensity to the fault-based attacks.

The fault injection intensity describes how much the current working environment is different from the normal working environment. As an example, the higher the frequency of a faulty clock-glitch, the stronger the fault injection intensity is. In the FSA attack, the faulty ciphertext is used to identify whether or not the faulty ciphertext occurs and to obtain the fault sensitivity (FS) leakage. The key recovery is based on the data-dependency of the FS leakage. When a fault-detection system is applied, the DFA attacks cannot work since the attackers cannot access the value of the faulty outputs. However, the abnormal behaviors after the fault injection can still be identified, and hence the FSA attack is still applicable.

Note that in the original FSA attack proposal in [6], the secret key is recovered with some FS leakage models. For example, it is found that the FS of pprm1 S-box [10] (1 stage Positive Polarity Reed-Muller) is proportional to the Hamming weight of the S-box input. Therefore, with the Hamming weight (HW) model used, the secret key byte for AES-pprm1 can be identified. For the attack details, we refer to [6]. Hereafter, the FSA attack that requires a hypothesis leakage model is referred as the *model FSA* attack. Generally, it is difficult to construct a leakage model that can describe the data-dependency of the FS leakage.

In 2011, the model FSA attack has been improved in two aspects [9]. First, the FSA attack is combined with the correlation-enhanced collision distinguisher [8]. The result of breaking all the AES cores on SASEBO-R including the ones with various types of side-channel countermeasures demonstrates the strength of this attack. We note another independent work of [5] has the similar contents to the first contribution of [9]. The second contribution of [9] is showing how to additionally use the faulty ciphertexts as another leakage to break masking AES countermeasures.

In both [5,9], the FS leakage model is not required by using a collision-based distinguisher. Instead of the secret key itself, the key byte difference is targeted in the collision-based distinguisher. With a guess of a key byte difference, the similarity of the data-dependency is compared for the FS leakage from two S-box instances. Without any leakage model, the key space for AES-128 can be restricted from 2^{128} to 2^8. After that, an exhaustive search based on a pair of plaintext-ciphertext or the attack on the second to last AES round are required to identify the final 8 secret bits. Hereafter, we refer this type of FSA attack as the *model-less FSA* attack. Later we explain the proposed CC-FSA attack can help the model-less FSA attack to identify the final 8 secret bits without using additional measurements and with a negligible computational cost.

2.2   Usage of Faulty Output in FSA

As mentioned in the Sect. 2.1, the largest characteristic of the FSA attack is no requirement of the faulty value in its key recovery. However, to perform the attacks shown in [5,6,9] smoothly, the attackers should be able to inject fault or to verify the calculation result in the accuracy of byte or bit. As shown in [9], the FS information useful for the key recovery are usually byte-wise or bit-wise. Actually, in most of the attacks shown in [5,6,9], the value of the faulty outputs are used to check the byte-wise or bit-wise correctness of the calculation result.

When the attack target is a 128-bit data path AES implementation as in [5,6] and this paper, it is difficult to inject a setup-time violation to a specific byte position. The value of the faulty output is useful to verify the correctness of a certain byte (bit) of the calculation result. However, no faulty value for any byte or bit is used in the key recovery analysis.

The experiment setup in the rest of this paper is similar to the one used in [5,6,9], so we also consider that the faulty value is known by the attackers in

order to have a smooth evaluation of the proposed attack. Note that in case that
the attackers can control the fault injection byte position, e.g., attacking an 8-bit
data path AES implementation, the value of the faulty output is not required
for both the existing FSA attacks and the proposed CC-FSA attack since the
byte-wise FS leakage can be measured based on observing the correctness of the
128-bit calculation results.

3   Preliminary Experiments

3.1   Target Hardware Structure

This paper focuses on the cryptographic ciphers with an iterative looping architecture such as AES [11], in which the whole calculation is composed of a
round function. Figure 1 shows a general and straightforward structure of an
iterative architecture hardware circuit. The clock signal *clk* synchronizes the iterative calculations. The period of each clock cycle determines the calculation
time for each round. At the beginning of each clock cycle, the calculation result
of the previous clock cycle *r_in* is kept in the register and becomes the input for
the combinational circuit *r_out*.

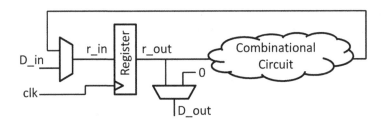

Fig. 1. Structure of an iterative architecture hardware circuit

The calculation in each clock cycle is a process of signal transitions from the
initial state to the final state. The input value and the logics in the combinational
circuit determine the final state for each clock cycle, which also becomes the
initial state for the next clock cycle. Thus, the signal transitions as well as the
side-channel leakage are related to the input data for two consecutive cycles,
i.e., both the current and the previous clock cycles. Even for the same circuit
processing on the same input data in the current cycle, the signal transitions
inside the combinational circuit can be totally different due to the difference of
the input data in the previous clock cycle.

3.2   2-Round Input Data Dependency

In this section, we experimentally verify the 2-round input data dependency for
the signal transitions of the combinational circuit. Our experiments are based on

a 128-bit AES-comp implementation in the ASIC on SASEBO-R, whose S-box is implemented based on the composite field arithmetic [17]. The target AES-comp implementation does not have any side-channel attack countermeasures and each AES round including the SubBytes (SB), the ShiftRows (SR), the MixColumns (MC) and the AddRoundKey (AK) takes one clock cycle to finish.

In this experiment, we use the faulty ciphertexts under various fault injection intensities to observe the signal transitions inside the combinational circuit. The setup-time violation is triggered by an illegal clock signal with a glitch in the final AES round, and the period of the glitch clock cycle can be freely controlled.

Hereafter, we use K, I, C and C' to denote the round key, the round input, the fault-free ciphertext and the faulty ciphertext, respectively. The superscript and the subscript are used to denote the byte position and the round number, respectively. The 16 bytes of the 128-bit AES state is numbered from 0 to 15 in the direction from the most significant byte to the least significant byte. For example, I_9^0 is the most significant byte of the 9th AES round input.

Focusing on the 0th byte, we have $C^0 = \text{SB}(I_{10}^0) \oplus K_{10}^0$ and $C'^0 = \text{SB}'(I_{10}^0) \oplus K_{10}^0$, where $\text{SB}(\cdot)$ and $\text{SB}'(\cdot)$ are the fault-free and faulty S-box calculations. Note that K_{10}^0 cannot be affected by the clock-glitch since it is calculated in the previous clock cycle. Therefore, we have the difference between C^0 and C'^0, i.e., ΔC, equals to the difference between $\text{SB}(I_{10}^0)$ and $\text{SB}'(I_{10}^0)$, i.e., $(\Delta \text{SB}(I_{10}^0))$. In our experiments, we use ΔC as an indicator to observe the signal transitions during the S-box calculation.

To verify the 2-round input data dependency, we choose three plaintexts P1, P2, and P3 in our experiments satisfying $I_{9_{P1}}^0 = I_{9_{P2}}^0 \neq I_{9_{P3}}^0$ and $I_{10_{P1}}^0 = I_{10_{P2}}^0 = I_{10_{P3}}^0$. We decrease the voltage of the power supply to the LSI core from 1.2V to 0.85 V for the easier fault injections. Then, we gradually increase the frequency of the glitch clock cycle from 88 to 164 MHz and we observe the change of C^0. For each step of the frequency change, we repeat the same AES calculation for 100 times. Based on the faulty ciphertexts, we calculate the error (bit-flip) rate for each bit of C^0 at each step of the clock-glitch frequency. The error rate curves for 8-bit of C_{P1}^0, C_{P2}^0 and C_{P3}^0 against various clock-glitch frequencies are shown in the top three rows in Fig. 2. From left to right, the 8 sub-figures in each row correspond to the most significant bit to the least significant bit [1].

As shown in Figs. 2(a) and 2(b), due to the fact that $I_{9_{P1}}^0 = I_{9_{P2}}^0$ and $I_{10_{P1}}^0 = I_{10_{P2}}^0$, the error rate curves for all the 8 bits are very similar to each other. On the other hand, for P3, since $I_{9_{P1}}^0 = I_{9_{P2}}^0 \neq I_{9_{P3}}^0$, the error rate curves of Fig. 2(c) are significantly different for those for P1 and P2, e.g., for the 2nd, 4th, and 5th MSB. This result verifies that the signal transitions inside the combinational circuit are related to the input data for two consecutive clock cycles. We can also observe the error rate curves for P1, P2 and P3 are all similar for the 8th MSB, and the 2nd MSB for P1 and P2 is not affected by any fault injection at all. Our future work includes more detailed analysis of these error rate curves to exploit the internal signal transitions.

---

[1] Note that the error rate becomes zero for the fault injection with high frequencies since the AES core ignores these clock-glitches.

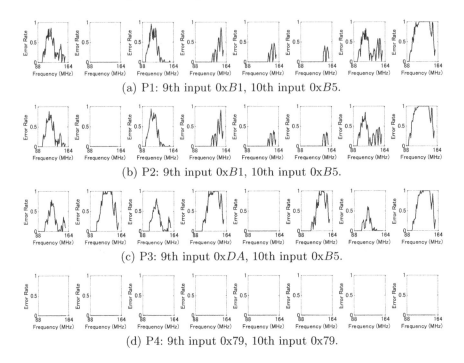

(a) P1: 9th input 0x$B1$, 10th input 0x$B5$.

(b) P2: 9th input 0x$B1$, 10th input 0x$B5$.

(c) P3: 9th input 0xDA, 10th input 0x$B5$.

(d) P4: 9th input 0x79, 10th input 0x79.

Fig. 2. Bit-wise error rate against the frequency of clock-glitch

4 Clockwise Collision

4.1 Clockwise Collision and Impossible Setup-Time Violation

The preliminary experiments verified the fact that the signal transitions inside the combinational circuit are related to the input data for two consecutive clock cycles. Therefore we consider a special case that the input data for two consecutive cycles collides in value for an independent combinational circuit, e.g., the AES S-box. We name this data collision the *clockwise collision* and we expect that it can lead to some special side-channel leakage such as a nearly impossible setup-time violation.

When the clockwise collision occurs, the combinational circuit is given the same input data for two consecutive clock cycles, so that there is almost no calculation performed in the second clock cycle since the initial state is already the desired calculation result. Therefore there is almost no signal toggle in the second clock cycle for the combinational circuit, which causes a negligibly short critical path delay. Consequently, a setup-time violation is nearly impossible to be triggered for the second cycle when the clockwise collision occurs.

Following the same experiment in Sect. 3, we verify the error rate for C^0 when the S-box input data for the 9th and 10th rounds collide in value, i.e., $I_9^0 = I_{10}^0$. We prepare a plaintext P4 so that $I_9^0 = I_{10}^0 = 0x79$, then we count the error rate and plot the error rate curves for 8-bit of C^0 in Fig. 2(d). As shown in Fig. 2(d), the setup-time violation cannot be triggered in our experiment for all the tested fault injection intensities. The tests of the other byte positions and using other plaintexts also verify the impossible setup time violation against the clockwise colliding S-boxes.

Although the last AES round has three round operations as SB, SR and MC, most of the critical path delay is caused by the SB operation. Due to the clockwise collision for the AES S-box, there is no toggle in the S-box circuit and the wires for registers have a stable fault-free value right after several XOR calculations for the AK operation. Unless the period of the clock-glitch is shorter than the timing of several XOR calculations, the setup-time violation cannot be triggered, which explains the all zero error curves in our experiments.

4.2   Clockwise Collision Fault Sensitivity Analysis

We explained that when the clockwise collision occurs, it is nearly impossible to trigger a setup-time violation. This impossible setup-time violation can be used to detect the clockwise collision and linked to a key recovery attack, which we call the *clockwise collision fault sensitivity analysis (CC-FSA)*.

In the CC-FSA attack, we assume that the attackers can detect the clockwise collision by performing fault injections with various fault injection intensities. Take AES as the attack target, we assume the attackers can inject the fault in the final AES round. In general, the clockwise collision between the 9th and 10th rounds for an S-box occurs with a probability of $1/256$. Since there are 16 S-boxes in total for the AES state, the attackers can expect one clockwise colliding S-box from the final AES round for encrypting 16 random plaintexts. After detecting the clockwise colliding S-box and knowing its position, the information of the sensitive intermediate values is obtained, i.e., $I_9^{\mathrm{SR}^{-1}(i)} = I_{10}^i$, where $i \in \{0, \cdots, 15\}$ and $\mathrm{SR}^{-1}(\cdot)$ denotes a map of byte position for an inverse SR operation.

In the following discussion, we explain the process of linking the information leakage of the intermediate values to the successful key recovery. In order to

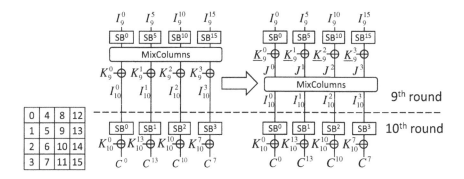

Fig. 3. AES state (left), 4 bytes in the final 2 AES rounds (right)

simplify the analysis, we change the sequence of MC and AK in the 9th AES round in the following analysis. Consequently, the added 9th round key K_9 becomes $\underline{K}_9 = \mathrm{MC}^{-1}(K_9)$ as shown in Fig. 3, where $\mathrm{MC}^{-1}(\cdot)$ denotes an inverse MC operation.

As shown in Fig. 3, taking $i = 0$ as an example that $I_9^0 = I_{10}^0$, we have

$$J^0 \oplus \underline{K}_9^0 = C^0 \oplus K_{10}^0, \tag{1}$$

where J^0 can be calculated using 4 ciphertext bytes and 4 final round key bytes as $K_{10}^0, K_{10}^{13}, K_{10}^{10}$ and K_{10}^7. From Eq. (1), we have

$$J^0 \oplus C^0 = \underline{K}_9^0 \oplus K_{10}^0. \tag{2}$$

As long as the 0th S-box calculation, i.e., SB^0 in the final AES round is a clockwise colliding S-box, $J^0 \oplus C^0$ is a fixed value of $\underline{K}_9^0 \oplus K_{10}^0$. For the ciphertexts with the clockwise collision of $I_9^0 = I_{10}^0$, the correctness of each key candidate of $\{K_{10}^0, K_{10}^{13}, K_{10}^{10}, K_{10}^7\}$ can be verified by calculating the value of J^0 and see whether or not the calculated $J^0 \oplus C^0$ always has the same value. Only for the correct key guess, the calculated $J^0 \oplus C^0$ is a fixed value. The similar conclusion also applies to the clockwise collision for other S-boxes. The same procedure can be repeated for all the byte positions, after that both K_9 and K_{10} can be correctly identified.

5   Experimental Verification of CC-FSA

5.1   Detection of Clockwise Collision S-Boxes

When considering the ideal fault injection results, the existence of the clockwise colliding S-boxes for the final AES round calculation can be distinguished using 1 fault injection for each plaintext. Under a strong fault injection, a faulty value from the unfinished S-box calculation is supposed to be stored into registers, while the fault-free result is stored for the clockwise colliding S-box.

Table 1. Number of Clockwise Collision S-boxes and Faulty Ciphertext Byte

Colliding/Faulty or not	Number of occurrences (percentage)
Clockwise collision, fault-free ciphertext byte	6341 (0.4%)
Clockwise collision, faulty ciphertext byte	**0 (0.0%)**
No Clockwise collision, faulty ciphertext byte	1483120 (92.7%)
No Clockwise collision, fault-free ciphertext byte	110539 (6.9%)

To verify the attack concept, we use ASIC AES-comp implementation on SASEBO-R to perform the following attack experiments. We use 100000 random plaintexts with each being encrypted twice. One is for the faulty-free output, and the other one is for the faulty output under a fault injection with a strong intensity. The fault-free and faulty ciphertexts are obtained with a normal clock signal of 24 MHz and a faulty clock signal with a glitch clock cycle of 148 MHz at the final AES round, respectively.

With the known key, we summarize the result about the clockwise colliding S-boxes and the faulty ciphertext bytes in Table 1. As show in the lines 1 and 2 in Table 1, all of the clockwise colliding S-boxes are not affected by the fault injections. In other words, for the S-box calculations that are affected by the fault injections, we can be sure that no clockwise collision occurs for them. However, on the other hand, for all the fault-free ciphertext bytes, not all of them are corresponding to the occurrence of the clockwise collision as shown in lines 1 and 4 of Table 1.

In our experiment setup, 1 fault injection for each plaintext can only offer a noisy data set. Actually as shown in Table 1, most of the fault-free ciphertext bytes do not correspond to the clockwise colliding S-boxes. It is expected that the repetition of the fault injections to these fault-free ciphertext bytes can reduce the number of false clockwise collisions. However, it requires more times of fault injections and it is difficult for the attackers to know when all the false clockwise collision can be eliminated. Therefore, we consider the key recovery of the CC-FSA attack is generally performed using the noisy data sets.

5.2 Key Recovery Using Noisy Data Set

In this section, we present two general solutions for the key recovery of the CC-FSA attack in the presence of noisy data. After comparing the expected computational complexities for two solutions, we pick up the one with less complexity and show the key recovery result based on the noisy data set shown in Table 1.

- Solution 1: Using the ciphertext bytes that are affected by the fault injections, the attackers can check whether $J^{\mathrm{SR}^{-1}(i)} \oplus C^i$ covers all the 256 values. For the correct key guess, the calculated $J^{\mathrm{SR}^{-1}(i)} \oplus C^i$ cannot have the value as $\underline{K}_9^{\mathrm{SR}^{-1}(i)} \oplus K_{10}^i$. While for a wrong key guess, the calculated $J^{\mathrm{SR}^{-1}(i)} \oplus C^i$ can be considered as a random value that can cover all the 256 possible values. The key guess can be eliminated from the key space when all 256 values occurs for $J^{\mathrm{SR}^{-1}(i)} \oplus C^i$.

  For a wrong key guess, the expected number of required ciphertexts that leads to the collection of all 256 byte values is about $\sum_{i=1}^{256} 256/i \approx 1567$. Hence, it is expected that after 1567 ciphertexts are used, one can eliminate about half of the wrong key candidates. Note that when 1567 ciphertexts are used in the key recovery, the computational complexity already become $2^{32} \cdot 1567 \approx 2^{42.6}$.

- Solution 2: Using the ciphertext bytes that are not affected by the fault injections, the attackers can check whether $J^{\mathrm{SR}^{-1}(i)} \oplus C^i$ has a frequently occurring value that occurs with a probability much larger than $1/256$. For a wrong key guess, the calculated $J^{\mathrm{SR}^{-1}(i)} \oplus C^i$ is uniformly distributed so that each value occurs with a probability of $1/256 \approx 0.4\%$. However when the key guess is correct, there is a frequently occurring value for $J^{\mathrm{SR}^{-1}(i)} \oplus C^i$ as $\underline{K}_9^{\mathrm{SR}^{-1}(i)} \oplus K_{10}^i$. For example for the data set shown in Table 1, the clockwise collision accounts for $6341/(110539 + 6341) \approx 5.4\%$ of the ciphertext bytes without fault injected. The recovery complexity of solution 1 is expected to be smaller than that of the solution 2. Assuming 1567 ciphertexts are used in the key recovery of solution 2, about $1567 \cdot 5.4\% \approx 85$ clockwise collisions occur, which means a certain value occurs for 85 times for $J^{\mathrm{SR}^{-1}(i)} \oplus C^i$. While for the wrong key guesses, the expect number of the occurrences for each value is about $1567/256 = 6.1$. Therefore, we can see the probability of a fail key identification is negligible for the solution 2 after using 1567 ciphertexts, while only half key candidates can be eliminated in solution 1.

Since solution 2 offers the key recovery with less complexity cost, we apply the solution 2 to the data shown in Table 1 and show the result. Considering N ciphertexts $C_i, i = 1, 2, \ldots, N$ whose 0th S-box of the final AES round is not affected by the fault injections are used in the key recovery, Alg. 1 shows the detailed procedures to recover $\{K_{10}^0, K_{10}^{13}, K_{10}^{10}, K_{10}^7\}$.

Algorithm 1. Key Recovery Using Solution 2

Input: N ciphertexts $C_i, i = 1, 2, \cdots, N$ that have no fault injected at the 0th S-box of the final AES round, SB^0
Output: 4 key-byte: $K_{10}^0, K_{10}^{13}, K_{10}^{10}, K_{10}^7$
for $K_g = 0$ to $2^{32} - 1$ **do**
   $\mathrm{Cnt}[256] = 0$;
   for $i = 1$ to N **do**
      Calculate J^0 using (C_i, K_g);
      $\mathrm{Cnt}[J^0 \oplus C_i^0]$++;
   end for
   $\mathrm{MaxCnt}[K_g]$=max(Cnt);
end for
Return argmax_{K_g} $\mathrm{MaxCnt}[K_g]$

In Alg. 1, $\max(\cdot)$ finds the maximum number of a vector and the K_g corresponding to the maximum of $MaxCnt$ is expected to be the correct key. In order to restrict the computational cost to a reasonable level, we used $N = 400$ in our key recovery test. That is to say, we use 400 ciphertexts whose 0th S-box are not affected by the fault injections. Note that we need about 6450 random plaintexts to collect all these 400 plaintexts in our experiment.

After the execution of Alg. 1, the correct 4 key-byte is identified with $MaxCnt$ being 25. Meanwhile, the maximum $MaxCnt$ for all the wrong key candidates is 18. Actually for $2^{31.9995}$ false key candidates, the value of $MaxCnt$ is fewer than 12. The complexity of the key recovery is about $400 \cdot 2^{32} = 2^{40.6}$ of 1-round AES decryption, which takes a few hours to finish using a PC.

The key recovery complexity for CC-FSA is relatively larger compared to the traditional side-channel analysis and the fault-based attacks such as DFA, the original FSA attacks. The reason is that the leakage used in CC-FSA is related to the intermediate values in the second to last AES round. However, the CC-FSA attack has its advantage over the DFA attacks and the original FSA attacks about the attackers' ability of the fault injection. Compared to the DFA attacks, the CC-FSA attack does not require the successful fault injections under a certain fault model. Compared to the original FSA attacks, the CC-FSA attack requires less detailed control of the fault injection intensity. For the original FSA attacks, the attackers require to distinguish the difference of fault sensitivities for different S-box inputs, while the CC-FSA attack only requires the fault injections with some strong fault injection intensities, even the fault injections with unstable fault injection intensities are enough for the CC-FSA attack.

6   Combine CC-FSA with Model-Less FSA

In this section, we discuss the possibility of combining the CC-FSA with the model-less FSA attack.

As mentioned in the Sect. 2.1, the key space can be only restricted to an 8-bit space for the model-less FSA attacks. In order to identify the key, it usually requires a plaintext-ciphertext pair for the exhaustive search or the attack against the second to last round. In other words, the secret key is difficult to be identified when the attackers cannot access any plaintext or more FS data from another AES round.

We note that the information leakage used in the CC-FSA attack is not discussed in the previous model-less FSA attacks although the data acquirement process is exactly the same. In the collision-based model-less FSA attacks, the fault sensitivity data are used to reveal the collision of input data for the S-box calculations in the final AES round. On the other hand, CC-FSA uses the fault sensitivity data to detect the collision of the S-box input data in two consecutive clock cycles. We consider the concept of CC-FSA can help the collision-based model-less FSA to identify the key from the 8-bit key space.

The procedure is rather simple. After the key space is restricted to $2^8 = 256$, the attacker already have a large amount of FS data, which is supposed to contain the clockwise colliding S-boxes as long as the FS data corresponding to more than 16 plaintexts. Each 128-bit key candidate can be used to calculate the related intermediate values using the ciphertexts, and to find the expected clockwise colliding S-boxes. After that, the correctness of the current key guess can be verified by checking the FS leakage for the expected clockwise colliding S-boxes. Only for the correct key candidate, the attackers can find that the faults are very difficult to be injected for these clockwise colliding S-boxes. Thus, CC-FSA can help the model-less FSA attack to identify the secret key without using additional measurements and with a computational cost of testing 2^8 key candidates.

7   Conclusion

This paper demonstrated an overlooked fault-based side-channel phenomenon named clockwise collision that leads to the nearly impossible setup-time violations. We considered this phenomenon can be used in the fault-based attacks and we proposed the clockwise collision fault sensitivity analysis. Based on the clock-glitch based fault injections, we show a successful key recovery using CC-FSA in which only 1 fault injection is performed for each plaintext. In our attack experiments, we proposed and verified the CC-FSA attack concept and its key recovery algorithm using the noisy data set. Finally, we consider CC-FSA is a low-cost solution to identify the final secret bits for the model-less FSA attacks. The future work is to consider the application of CC-FSA against the side-channel attack countermeasures.

Acknowledgments. This research was partially supported by Strategic International Cooperative Program (Joint Research Type), Japan Science and Technology Agency.

References

1. Biham, E., Shamir, A.: Differential Fault Analysis of Secret Key Cryptosystems. In: Kaliski Jr., B.S. (ed.) CRYPTO 1997. LNCS, vol. 1294, pp. 513–525. Springer, Heidelberg (1997)
2. Boneh, D., DeMillo, R.A., Lipton, R.J.: On the Importance of Checking Cryptographic Protocols for Faults (Extended Abstract). In: Fumy, W. (ed.) EUROCRYPT 1997. LNCS, vol. 1233, pp. 37–51. Springer, Heidelberg (1997)
3. Gandolfi, K., Mourtel, C., Olivier, F.: Electromagnetic Analysis: Concrete Results. In: Koç, Ç.K., Naccache, D., Paar, C. (eds.) CHES 2001. LNCS, vol. 2162, pp. 251–261. Springer, Heidelberg (2001)
4. Kocher, P.C., Jaffe, J., Jun, B.: Differential Power Analysis. In: Wiener, M. (ed.) CRYPTO 1999. LNCS, vol. 1666, pp. 388–397. Springer, Heidelberg (1999)
5. Li, Y., Ohta, K., Sakiyama, K.: New Fault-Based Side-Channel Attack Using Fault Sensitivity. IEEE Transactions on Information Forensics and Security 7(1), 88–97 (2012)
6. Li, Y., Sakiyama, K., Gomisawa, S., Fukunaga, T., Takahashi, J., Ohta, K.: Fault Sensitivity Analysis. In: Mangard, Standaert (eds.) [7], pp. 320–334
7. Mangard, S., Standaert, F.-X. (eds.): CHES 2010. LNCS, vol. 6225. Springer, Heidelberg (2010)
8. Moradi, A., Mischke, O., Eisenbarth, T.: Correlation-Enhanced Power Analysis Collision Attack. In: Mangard, Standaert (eds.) [7], pp. 125–139
9. Moradi, A., Mischke, O., Paar, C., Li, Y., Ohta, K., Sakiyama, K.: On the Power of Fault Sensitivity Analysis and Collision Side-Channel Attacks in a Combined Setting. In: Preneel, B., Takagi, T. (eds.) CHES 2011. LNCS, vol. 6917, pp. 292–311. Springer, Heidelberg (2011)
10. Morioka, S., Satoh, A.: An Optimized S-Box Circuit Architecture for Low Power AES Design. In: Kaliski Jr., B.S., Koç, Ç.K., Paar, C. (eds.) CHES 2002. LNCS, vol. 2523, pp. 172–186. Springer, Heidelberg (2003)

11. National Institute of Standards and Technology. Advanced Encryption Standard. NIST FIPS PUB 197 (2001)
12. Piret, G., Quisquater, J.-J.: A Differential Fault Attack Technique against SPN Structures, with Application to the AES and KHAZAD. In: Walter, C.D., Koç, Ç.K., Paar, C. (eds.) CHES 2003. LNCS, vol. 2779, pp. 77–88. Springer, Heidelberg (2003)
13. Quisquater, J.-J., Samyde, D.: ElectroMagnetic Analysis (EMA): Measures and Counter-Measures for Smart Cards. In: Attali, I., Jensen, T. (eds.) E-smart 2001. LNCS, vol. 2140, pp. 200–210. Springer, Heidelberg (2001)
14. Research Center for Information Security (RCIS). Side-channel attack standard evaluation board (SASEBO),
    `http://www.rcis.aist.go.jp/special/SASEBO/CryptoLSI-en.html`
15. Robisson, B., Manet, P.: Differential Behavioral Analysis. In: Paillier, P., Verbauwhede, I. (eds.) CHES 2007. LNCS, vol. 4727, pp. 413–426. Springer, Heidelberg (2007)
16. Sakiyama, K., Li, Y., Iwamoto, M., Ohta, K.: Information-Theoretic Approach to Optimal Differential Fault Analysis. IEEE Transactions on Information Forensics and Security 7(1), 109–120 (2012)
17. Satoh, A., Morioka, S., Takano, K., Munetoh, S.: A Compact Rijndael Hardware Architecture with S-Box Optimization. In: Boyd, C. (ed.) ASIACRYPT 2001. LNCS, vol. 2248, pp. 239–254. Springer, Heidelberg (2001)
18. Selmane, N., Guilley, S., Danger, J.-L.: Practical Setup Time Violation Attacks on AES. In: EDCC, pp. 91–96. IEEE Computer Society (2008)
19. Yen, S.-M., Joye, M.: Checking Before Output Not Be Enough Against Fault-Based Cryptanalysis. IEEE Trans. Computers 49(9), 967–970 (2000)

A Robust Fuzzy Extractor without ECCs

Jintao Yao, Kangshun Li, Mingwu Zhang, and Min Zhou

College of Informatics, South China Agricultural University,
Guangzhou 510642, China
justin_yjt@163.com

Abstract. Fuzzy extractors are important secure schemes that are used to extract reliably reproducible uniform randomness from noise and biased biometric data. It is well known that the error-correction codes (ECCs) only work best when the noise patterns likely to occur are completely random, and typical error-correction codes are unable to capitalize on the errors with low entropy. Consequently, a new robust fuzzy extractor without ECCs was proposed and constructed. Our fuzzy extractor adopts the error-correction method based on incoming $(1 - \theta)$-neighborhood and extracts more min-entropy under the condition of not-uniform noise patterns than those using standard error-correction codes. In addition, we also analyzed the proposed scheme's correctness and efficiency, and proved its security and robustness mainly. The result shows that the proposed fuzzy extractor has the better practical value.

Keywords: Biometric data, error correction code, robustness, fuzzy extractor, noise patterns.

1 Introduction

Remote authentication brings a formidable challenge to service providers and a frequent hassle to consumers. Identity theft is just one example of the difficulty in establishing online trust. Main reason of this problem happening is that digital authentication requires a strong secret. Generally, passwords have been an accepted form of authentication, but individuals rarely choose strong passwords[1]. As a result, passwords are typically subject to brute-force and dictionary attacks[2]. Stronger secrets, such as strong symmetric keys and the private key of a public-private key pair, can be stored on a device within the possession of a user. However, the device itself may be subject to attack and management of these secrets can become complex. Greater levels of security are achieved by longer human-generated passwords. It is well-known that biometric data provides a broad source of producing secret with high min-entropy, so biometric-based authentication is a potential candidate to replace password-based authentication by providing the complete authentication mechanism. Biometric-based authentication protocol requires that user first enrolls her biometrics into the authentication server, where the stored biometric is called reference template. Later, when user authenticates her to the server, a fresh biometric or presentation sample is captured and compared with the reference template. In addition

M. Kutyłowski and M. Yung (Eds.): Inscrypt 2012, LNCS 7763, pp. 60–68, 2013.

to authentication, biometrics has also been used as a source of human identification. The dual use of biometrics as a secret and identifier incorporate the concerns of both security and privacy. As a result, the protection of biometric information is of utmost importance[3].

All known biometric data has been combined with cryptography. Familiar method is to monolithically bind a cryptographic key with the biometric template of a user stored in the database(server) in such a way that the key cannot be revealed without a successful biometric authentication[4, 5]. However, biometrics remains unchanged for a long period, and storing biometric templates in plaintext on an authentication server increases the risk of exposure. Once the server is compromised, all biometrics in the credential database will be revealed and hard to recover. The other method is to directly produce and use secret string from biometric data instead of storing biometric templates[6–9]. Unfortunately, biometrics is inconsistent and most biometric data are noisy in the sense that the capturing devices and extraction algorithms introduce inevitable noises. Moreover, conventional cryptographic primitives do not tolerate even the slightest change in the data. In order to use biometric data in cryptographic schemes as above, an important general problem to be solved is to convert noisy non-uniform inputs (biometric data) into reliably reproducible, uniformly random strings. Fortunately, secure sketch and fuzzy extractor were proposed as a generic method to noise-tolerantly reconstruct or extract a secret R from noisy biometric data w by publishing a helper data P, which is stored on public device. Noise-tolerance means that if the input changes to some w' but remains sufficiently close in some appropriate metric space, the string R can be reproduced exactly. Here, R extracted from w can be used a key in a cryptographic application but unlike traditional keys. However, it is important to note that R remains uniformly random even given P. Because some redundancy is necessary to correct the noise and helper data necessarily decreases the entropy of w. But the problem can be addressed partially by carefully constructing P in such a way as to limit the amount of information an attacker can be obtain about w. Unfortunately, fuzzy extractor described above only against a passive attack in which an adversary observes P and tries to learn something about extractor R. However, if an adversary modifies P as it is sent to the user holding w', there are no guarantees about the reproduced R. Boyen et al proposed a stronger notion of robust fuzzy extractors[10], which provides strong guarantees against such an active attack. Specifically, the user holding w' can detect any tampering of P and output a special value "$\perp$" (fail). Robust fuzzy extractors are useful not only in the single-party setting, but also in interactive settings, where two parties are trying to derive a key from a shared (slightly different in the fuzzy case) secret w that either is non-uniform or about which some limited information is known to the adversary. Dodis et al gave a formal definition and construction of robust fuzzy extractor[11], which can extract R of length $2(m - n/2 + \log \delta)/3$, where the length of w is n, the entropy of w is m, and δ is the probability that the adversary violates robustness. Robust fuzzy extractor constructed by Cramer et al

extracts almost the entire entropy m reduced by an amount related to security and, in the fuzzy case, to error tolerance.

However, an additional challenge to fuzzy extractor is to address the fuzziness of two slightly different biometric readings. Generally, fuzzy extractors are obtained by adding error correcting information to P, to enable it to compensate for errors. When R is reproduced, fuzzy extractors use error-correcting codes(ECCs) to remove noise in biometric data. The specific constructions depend on the kinds of errors that can occur. It is well known that standard ECCs work best on (binary) strings under the condition that the likely to occurring noise patterns are completely random. However, when the biometric feature vector is mapped into a binary string, the noise patterns are not always nicely compatible with a representation in terms of binary strings. Of course, an ECC is capable of dealing with errors no matter what their probability distribution is, but the price is to increase the number of redundancy bits in the code is far higher than what an 'ideal' code would have. Therefore, typical ECCs are not able to capitalize on the low entropy of the errors, since they must be able to correct the 'worst case' errors, and consequently a large part of the entropy present in the source gets wasted. Skoric *et al* constructed a practical error correction method extracting more information than typical ECCs under the case of very non-uniform noise probabilities[12], but their scheme is only secure against passive attack. In this paper, we proposed a robust fuzzy extractor without ECCs. The extractor uses multiple almost universal hash functions ($AUHFs$) like in [12] on the same biometric data to generate public string and authentication key. The error-correcting procedure of our extractor is simple, and there are the better efficiency and security against both passive attack and active attack.

The paper proceeds as follows: In section 2, we give the basic notions such as fuzzy extractor, statistical distance, $AUHFs$ and incoming $(1-\theta)$-neighborhood. The detailed construction of our fuzzy extractor is described in Section 3. We provide the performance analysis and security proofs in Section 4. Finally, we make a conclusion in Section 5.

2   Preliminaries

Let U_l denote the uniform distribution on $\{0,1\}^l$. Let W, W' be two probability distributions over some metric space . Let l be the number of bits of the extracted from biometric data w. let the length of w be n and the entropy of w be m. Let i be random seed.

Definition 1. Statistical distance

$$SD\left(W,W'\right) = \max_{T \subseteq M}\left\{\Pr[W \in T] - \Pr[W' \in T]\right\}$$

$$= \frac{1}{2}\sum_{w \in M} |\Pr_W[w] - \Pr_{W'}[w]| \tag{1}$$

*Where, **Pr[]** is probability value. In particular, they are said to be ε-close if $SD(W,W') \leq \varepsilon$.*

Definition 2. Min-entropy

$$H_\infty(W) = -\log(\max_w \Pr[W = w]) \tag{2}$$

The min-entropy of a distribution tells us how many nearly uniform random bits can be extracted from it.

Definition 3. Average Min-entropy

$$\tilde{H}_\infty(W|E) = -\log(\underset{e \leftarrow E}{\boldsymbol{E}}(2^{-H_\infty(W|E)})) \tag{3}$$

Where, E is side information of W, and $\boldsymbol{E}()$ is mathematical expectation

Definition 4. (n, m, l, ε)-strong extractor
Let $Ext : \{0,1\}^n \rightarrow \{0,1\}^l$ be a polynomial time probabilistic function which uses r bits of randomness. We say that Ext is an efficient (n, m, l, ε)-strong extractor if for all min-entropy m distributions W on $\{0,1\}^n$, $SD((Ext(W; I), (U_l, I)) \leq \varepsilon$, where I is uniform on $\{0,1\}^r$.

Definition 5. (n, m, t, ε)-fuzzy extractor
An (n, m, t, ε)-fuzzy extractor is a pair of efficient randomized procedures ($\boldsymbol{Gen}()$, $\boldsymbol{Rep}()$) such that the following hold:

- *The generation procedure $\boldsymbol{Gen()}$, on input $w \in \boldsymbol{M}$, outputs an extracted string $R \in \{0,1\}^l$ and a helper string $P \in \{0,1\}^*$. The reproduction procedure $\boldsymbol{Rep}()$ takes an element $w' \in \boldsymbol{M}$ and a string $P \in \{0,1\}^*$ as inputs.*
- *$\boldsymbol{Correctness}$. If $dis(w, w') \leq t$ and $(R, P) \leftarrow \boldsymbol{Gen}(w)$, then $\boldsymbol{Rep}(w', P)) = R$.*
- *$\boldsymbol{Security}$. For any distribution W over $\boldsymbol{M}$ with min-entropy m, the string R is close to uniform even conditioned on the value of P. Formally, if $H_\infty(W) \geq m$ and $(R, P) \leftarrow \boldsymbol{Gen}(w)$, then we have $SD((R, P), U_l \times P) \leq \varepsilon$.*
- *$\boldsymbol{Efficiency}$. A fuzzy extractor is efficient if $\boldsymbol{Gen()}$ and $\boldsymbol{Rep()}$ run in expected polynomial time.*
- *Specially, the $\boldsymbol{robustness}$ is required to hold only if $\boldsymbol{Rep()}$ outputs " $\perp$ " when helper string P is modified.*

Definition 6. Incoming $(1 - \theta)$-neighborhood
Let $\theta \in (0, 1)$ be a fixed parameter. Let $W, W' \in \boldsymbol{M}$ be the enrolment measurement and the verification measurement. A set $\boldsymbol{B} \subset \boldsymbol{M}$ is called an incoming $(1 - \theta)$-neighborhood of w' if:

$$\sum_{w \in B} \Pr[W = w | W' = w'] \geq 1 - \theta \tag{4}$$

The set of all incoming $(1 - \theta)$-neighborhoods of w' is denoted as $\boldsymbol{B}_{1-\theta}^{in}(w')$.

Definition 7. η-almost universal hash functions
Let $\eta > 0$, let $\Re, \aleph$ and $\Im$ be finite sets. Let $\{\Phi_r\}_{r \in \Re}$ be a family of hash functions from $\aleph$ to $\Im$. The family is called $\{\Phi_r\}_{r \in \Re}$-almost universal hash functions ($\eta - AUHFs$) iff, for R drawn uniformly from $\Re$, it holds $\Pr[\Phi_r(w) = \Phi_r(w')] \leq \eta$.

3 Robust Fuzzy Extractor without ECCs

Before our scheme is described, we assume the case where the noise patterns in biometric data are not-uniform, but number of noise patterns that are likely to occur is limited.

– **Initial Setup**

Two legitimate parties (*Alice* and *Bob*) communicating by channel of communications beforehand agree on two almost universal families of hash functions $\{\Psi_t\}_{t\in T} : \mathbf{M} \to \{0,1\}^k$ and $\{\Gamma_c\}_{c\in C} : \mathbf{M} \to \{0,1\}^r$, which are $2^{-k}(1 + \delta_\Psi) - AUHF$ and $2^{-r}(1 + \delta_\Gamma) - AUHF$ respectively. In additions, a message authentication code with key manipulation security (KMS-MAC)[13] is also agreed on, and let the length of authentication code $\tilde{\sigma}$ generated by KMS-MAC be d. Abstractly, this authentication code is keyed by a random element of finite group, and remains secure even if the key is stored publicly. Specially, Common Reference String (CRS) includes random $\{t, c\}$, and $\{\Psi, \Gamma, MAC, k, r\}$ are public knowledge.

– **Gen**$(w; i)$

- *Alice* gets a enrollment biometric data $w \in \{0,1\}^n$ as input, and she parses w as two strings a and b of lengths $n-v$ and v, namely $a \in F_{2^{n-v}}$ and $b \in F_{2^v}$ (F is a finite field, and the construction is not sensitive to the choice of representation of field elements as bit strings and words as long as addition in the field corresponds to exclusive-or of bit strings). And then, *Alice* chooses a random $i \in F_{2^{n-v}}$, compute $\{s = \Psi_t(w), sk = \Gamma_c(w), \tilde{\sigma} = MAC_{sk}(s), ia \in F_{2^{n-v}}\}$, let $R = [ia]_{v+1}^{n-2v}$ be the extracted random key and let $\sigma = [ia]_1^v + b$ be the authentication code used to authenticate i. Finally, Alice sets $P = (i, s, \sigma, \tilde{\sigma})$.
- *Alice* sends P to *Bob*. Without loss of generality, because the channel may be unauthentic, the unbounded adversary *Eve* can modify P to $\mathbf{A}(P) = P' = (i', s', \sigma', \tilde{\sigma}')$.

– **Rep**$(w'; P')$

- Once *Bob* gets a authentication biometric data $w' \in \{0,1\}^n$ and helper data $P' = (i', s', \sigma', \tilde{\sigma}')$, he reads $\{t, c\}$ from CRS. Where, w is different from w and holds $dis(w, w') \leq t$.
- *Bob* chooses a neighborhood $B \in \mathbf{B}_{1-\theta}^{in}(w')$ and compiles a list $L = \{w_j \in B : \Psi_t(w_j) = s'\}$, where $j = 0, 1, 2, ...$ If $L = \phi$ is empty, **Rep**$(w'; P')$ aborts in failure.
- For all $w_j \in L$, *Bob* computes $sk_j = \Gamma_c(w_j)$, and checks if $\tilde{\sigma}' = MAC_{sk_j} - (s')$. In the event that a single match $w*$ occurs, w' is corrected to w accurately, and then is also considered to have succeeded. Otherwise, if there are no matches, or more than one, then **Rep**$(w'; P')$ aborts in failure.

- Again, *Bob* parses w as two strings a and b of lengths n-v and v, and checks if $\sigma' = [i'a]_1^v + b$. If the answer is positive, *Bob* accepts $R' = [i'a]_{v+1}^{n-2v}$ as the reproducible secret key. Otherwise, *Bob* gets " $\perp$ ", and **Rep**$(w'; P')$ aborts in failure.

4   Performance Analysis and Security Proofs

Lemma 1 (Leftover Hash Lemma, [11]). *For* $l, m, \varepsilon > 0$, *if* $\mathbf{H} = \{h_i : \{0,1\}^n \to \{0,1\}^l\}_{i \in I}$ *is a* $(2^{-l}(1+4\varepsilon^2) - 2^{-m}) - almost\ universal\ family,\ then\ \mathbf{H}$ *is a strong* $(m, \varepsilon) - average\text{-}case\ extractor\ (where\ the\ index\ of\ the\ hash\ function$ *is the seed to the extractor). In particular,* $\mathbf{H}$ *is a strong* $(m, \varepsilon) - average\text{-}case$ *extractor if* $\mathbf{H}$ *is universal and* $l \le m + 2 + 2 \log \varepsilon$.

Obviously, Lemma 1 indicates that *AUHFs* can be used as strong extractor to construct the fuzzy extractors.

Lemma 2 ([11]). *If* $SD((A, B), C \times D)) \le \alpha$, *then* $SD((A, B), C \times B)) \le 2\alpha$.

4.1   Correctness Analysis

First of all, **Gen**$(w; i)$ in the constructed robust fuzzy extractor uses $2^{-k}(1 + \delta_\Psi) - AUHF$ and $2^{-r}(1 + \delta_\Gamma) - AUHF$ respectively to extract the public help data P and random string R. At the same time, when *Bob* reconstructs random string using **Rep**$(w'; P)$, the enrollment biometric data $w \in \{0,1\}^n$ owned by *Alice* and authentication biometric data $w' \in \{0,1\}^n$ owned by *Bob* satisfy the inequality $dis(w, w') \le t$. Therefore Bob can get a reproducible secret key $R \leftarrow Rep(w', P)$ if the adversary *Eve* would not modify the public help data P. According to **Definition 4**, the constructed robust fuzzy extractor holds correctness.

4.2   Efficiency Analysis

First of all, the constructed fuzzy extractor uses two short almost universal hash functions to generate public string s and MAC key *sk*, which makes the constructed fuzzy extractor have the better efficiency than one constructed by Dodis *et al* in [11]. The reason is that computation of a short *AUHFs* can be done easily. In additions, the constructed fuzzy extractor uses the method of incoming $(1 - \theta)$-neighborhood to correct errors, and the hardware such as error correcting circuit for implementation is reduced, which makes the error-correcting procedure more simple. In a word, if incoming $(1 - \theta)$-neighborhood is not too large, the constructed fuzzy extractor is practical and efficient.

4.3   Security Proof against Passive Attack

Theorem 1. *Although the passive adversary have obtained public data* $P = (i, s, \sigma, \tilde{s})$, *the extracted* R *keeps the uniform distribution, that is,* $SD((R, P), U_{n-2v} \times P) \le \varepsilon$, *where* $\varepsilon = 2^{(n-v-m+k+r)/2}$.

Proof. First of all, we suppose $h_i(a, b) = (\sigma, R)$. For any $w \neq w'$, we have $(a, b) \neq (a', b')$ and compute $\Pr_i[h_i(a, b) = h_i(a', b')] = \Pr_i[[ia]_1^v - [ia']_1^v = b - b' \wedge [ia]_{v+1}^{n-v} = [ia']_{v+1}^{n-v}$. If $a = a'$ then $b \neq b'$, and thus this probability is 0; Otherwise, if $a \neq a'$, then this probability is at most 2^{v-n}. Therefore, we have $\Pr_i[h_i(a, b) = h_i(a', b')] = 2^{v-n}$. Consequently, we proved that $\{h_i(a, b)\}$ is $2^{v-n}(1 + \delta_{\mathbf{H}}) - AUHFs$. Because $\{s, \tilde{s}\}$ is public, min-entropy of input will be reduced $k + r$. In additions, R's security is directly related to (i, σ). Applying Lemma 1, we have $SD((R, P), U_{n-2v} \times U_{n-v} \times U_v \times U_k \times U_d) \leq 2^{(n-v-m+k+r)/2-1}$, and applying Lemma 2, we have $SD((R, P), U_{n-2v} \times P) \leq 2^{(n-v-m+k+r)/2}$.

4.4 Security Proof against Active Attack

Theorem 2. *Let biometric space be $\mathbf{M} = \{0, 1\}^n$, and setting $v = (n - l)/2$, our construction is a $(n, m, t, \varepsilon)-fuzzy$ extractor with robustness δ. For any $(n, m, \varepsilon, \delta) > 0$, satisfying $l = n - 2v \leq 2m - n + 2\max\{m + \log\delta, -k - r + 2\log\varepsilon\}$.*

Proof. We suppose that the active adversary, who can modify the public data, knows nothing about w, w'. Therefore, if the adversary wants to succeed in breaking the robustness of our fuzzy extractor, he has to exactly forge a $\{s', \tilde{\sigma}'\}$ so that there exists a point $\tilde{w}'$ in the neighborhood $B \in \mathbf{B}_{1-\theta}^{in}(w')$ of w' holding $\Psi_t(\tilde{w}') = s'$ and $\tilde{\sigma}' = MAC_{sk}(s')$. All known that the key of KMS- MAC can not be modified[14], so it is impossible for the adversary to exactly forge $\tilde{\sigma}'$. Therefore, the adversary must exactly forge s' so that he has a chance of success. However, although the adversary can find some $s \neq s'$ holding $\Psi_t(\tilde{w}') = s'$ for some $\tilde{w}'$ close to w', he has to guess since he has no knowledge of w'. So the adversary's probability of success is at most 2^{-m}, which completely depends on the min-entropy m of w'. Call(i, σ, i', σ') a transcript and denote it by π. Note that the number of possible transcript is at most $2^{|\sigma|} = v$. Let *win* be the event that the adversary succeeds. Now we can evaluate the probability that the adversary will succeed. We have:

$$\Pr[win]$$
$$\leq \sum_w \Pr[s', \tilde{\sigma}'] \sum_{a,b} \Pr_w[a||b] \sum_\pi [[ia]_1^v + b = \sigma \wedge A(i, \sigma) = (i', \sigma')$$
$$\wedge [i'a]_1^v + b = \sigma']$$
$$= 2^{-m} \sum_\pi A(i, \sigma) = (i', \sigma') \sum_{a,b} \Pr_w[a||b][[i'a]_1^v + b = \sigma'] \wedge [ia]_1^v + b = \sigma]$$
$$= 2^{-m} \sum_\pi \Pr_{a||b \leftarrow w}[[ia]_1^v - [i'a]_1^v = \sigma - \sigma' \wedge b = \sigma - [ia]_1^v]$$
$$\leq 2^{-m} \sum_\pi 2^{n-2v-m}$$
$$\leq 2^{n-v-2m}.$$

If we want to achieve robustness δ and an extracted R that is ε-close to uniform, we obtain the following constraints on v:

$$\begin{cases} l = |R| = n - 2v > 0 \\ 2^{n-v-2m} \leq \delta \\ 2^{(n-v-m+k+r)/2} \leq \varepsilon \end{cases}$$

$$\Rightarrow \begin{cases} v < n/2 \\ v \geq n - 2m - \log \delta \\ v \geq n - m + k + r - 2 \log \varepsilon \end{cases}$$

We would like to set v as small as possible to extract the largest possible R. Thus we set:

$$v = n - m - \max\{m + \log \delta, -k - r + 2 \log \varepsilon\}.$$

So, we can extract a random string of l bits.

$$\begin{aligned} l &= n - 2v \\ &\leq 2m - n + 2 \max\{m + \log \delta, -k - r + 2 \log \varepsilon\}. \end{aligned}$$

5 Conclusion

In this paper, we proposed a robust fuzzy extractor without ECCs that provides the correctness, efficiency, provable security and robustness. In the proposed fuzzy extractor, two almost universal hash functions are used to generate helper data and authentication key. Incoming $(1 - \theta)$−neighborhood is used to correct errors and error-correcting procedure is very simple, which makes the proposed fuzzy extractor practical. So the proposed fuzzy extractor can be used in biometric-based authentication and data secure requirement environments. The next work is how to construct an efficient robust fuzzy extractor based on block randomness source so for reducing the length of random seed, and improving the efficiency and practicality much more.

Acknowledgment. The authors grateful thank the anonymous reviewers for their valuable comments and suggestion that greatly helped us to improve the contents of this paper. This paper is supported in part by National Natural Science Foundation of China under grants No.70971043, No.61272404, Natural Science Foundation of Guangdong Province of China under Grant No.S2012010010383.

References

1. Klein, D.V.: Foiling the attacker-A survey of, and improvement to, password security. In: 2nd USENIX Workshop on Security (USENIX 1990), pp. 5–14. USENIX Association, Portland (1990)

2. Morris, R., Thompson, K.: Password security: A case history. Communications of the ACM 22(11), 594–597 (1979)
3. Huff, P.D.: Fuzzy Extractors Using an Improved Set Intersection Function. Technical Report, James Madison University, Computer Science, USA (2008)
4. Clancy, T.C., Kiyavash, N., Lin, D.J.: Secure smartcard-based fingerprint authentication. In: ACM SIGMM 2003 Multimedia, Biometrics Methods and Applications Workshop, pp. 45–52. ACM Press, New York (2003)
5. Uludag, U., Pankanti, S., Prabhakar, S., Jain, A.K.: Biometric Cryptosystems: Issues and Challenges. IEEE Transaction on Multimedia Security for Digital Rights Management 92(6), 948–960 (2004)
6. Juels, A., Sudan, M.: A fuzzy vault scheme. Designs, Codes and Cryptography 38(2), 237–257 (2006)
7. Juels, A., Wattenberg, M.: A fuzzy commitment scheme. In: 6th ACM Conference on Computer and Communication Security, pp. 28–36. ACM Press, New York (1999)
8. Boyen, X.: Reusable cryptographic fuzzy extractors. In: 11th ACM Conference on Computer and Communications Security, pp. 82–91. ACM Press, Washington (2004)
9. Dodis, Y., Ostrovsky, R., Reyzin, L., Smith, A.: Fuzzy extractors: How to generate strong keys from biometrics and other noisy data. SIAM Journal on Computing 38(1), 97–139 (2007)
10. Boyen, X., Dodis, Y., Katz, J., Ostrovsky, R., Smith, A.: Secure remote authentication using biometric data. In: Cramer, R. (ed.) EUROCRYPT 2005. LNCS, vol. 3494, pp. 147–163. Springer, Heidelberg (2005)
11. Dodis, Y., Katz, J., Reyzin, L., Smith, A.: Robust fuzzy extractors and authenticated key agreement from close secrets. In: Dwork, C. (ed.) CRYPTO 2006. LNCS, vol. 4117, pp. 232–250. Springer, Heidelberg (2006)
12. Skoric, B., Tuyls, P.: An efficient fuzzy extractor for limited noise. In: 30th Symposium on Information Theory on the Benelux, pp. 28–29. IEEE Press, New York (2009)
13. Cramer, R., Dodis, Y., Fehr, S., Padró, C., Wichs, D.: Detection of algebraic manipulation with applications to robust secret sharing and fuzzy extractors. In: Smart, N. (ed.) EUROCRYPT 2008. LNCS, vol. 4965, pp. 471–488. Springer, Heidelberg (2008)
14. Skoric, B., Obi, C., Verbitskiy, E., Schoenmakers, B.: Sharp lower bounds on the extractable randomness from non-uniform sources. Information and Computation 209(8), 1184–1196 (2011)

An Efficient Rational Secret Sharing Protocol Resisting against Malicious Adversaries over Synchronous Channels

Yang Yu and Zhanfei Zhou

State Key Laboratory of Information Security
Institute of Information Engineering, Chinese Academy of Sciences
Beijing 100093, P.R. China
{yyu,zhouzhanfei}@is.ac.cn

Abstract. Current works solve the problem of rational secret sharing from one or some, but not all, of the following aspects: achieving a more appealing equilibrium concept, avoiding strong communication models and resisting against adversaries. To address one issue above, they need to lower the satisfaction in other issues. In this paper we construct a t-out-of-n rational secret sharing protocol, which achieves an enhanced notion of *computational strict Nash equilibrium with respect to adversary structure* $\mathcal{A}$, runs over synchronous (non-simultaneous) broadcast channels and tolerates a malicious adversary who controls a minority of players. To the best of our knowledge, compared with current works tolerating adversaries, we are the first to yield positive results in all the three research aspects above. The feasibility of our protocol is based on the use of publicly verifiable secret sharing. Under the assumptions related to discrete logarithm and ElGamal cryptosystem, computational bounded players have an incentive not to deviate no matter how adversaries behave.

Keywords: Rational secret sharing, game theory, malicious adversary, computational strict Nash equilibrium, synchronous channel.

1 Introduction

1.1 Background

Secret sharing studies the problem that the dealer shares a secret among players such that an authorized subset of players can recover the secret but an unauthorized subset of players can get no information about the secret, it is fundamental in the area of secure multiparty computation (SMPC). Rational secret sharing (RSS), proposed by Halpern and Teague in 2004 [7], considers the problem of secret sharing in the game-theoretic model where all players are rational. Different from honest players and malicious players, rational players behave in their interests and try to get the maximum payoffs. It is assumed that they prefer to get the secret and prefer that the fewer players who get the secret

M. Kutyłowski and M. Yung (Eds.): Inscrypt 2012, LNCS 7763, pp. 69–89, 2013.

the better. Since the work of Halpern and Teague, many works have been devoted to rational secret sharing, such as [1,10,9,5,16], they focus on the following aspects.

Equilibrium Standard. The goal of rational secret sharing is to motivate all players to follow the protocol, hence, Halpern and Teague proposed the notion of *Nash equilibrium which survives the iterated deletion of weakly dominated strategies* as a security standard. But this notion is a weak guarantee, Kol and Naor [9] pointed out that a strategy that survives iterated deletion of weakly dominated strategies (iterated admissibility) may be undesirable, and suggested the notion of *strict Nash equilibrium* which requires that a player suffers losses if he deviates. However, the works [7,9] achieved the equilibrium notions they proposed by assuming the existence of simultaneous channels. After that Fuchsbauer et al. [5] achieved *a computational version of strict Nash equilibrium* in the synchronous model, but their scheme cannot resist against the attack of malicious adversaries.

Communication Channel. To design rational secret sharing protocols, the works [7,6,10] relied on the strong communication primitives of *simultaneous broadcast channels* to ensure the symmetry in the times that players get information. However, simultaneous communication is hard to be achieved, because it requires that all players move simultaneously and no player can observe other players' messages before he moves. Thus, several works [12,5,15] have been devoted to realizing rational secret sharing in the *synchronous* model, where the protocol runs in a series of rounds and only one player moves in each round. By delaying the signal indicating whether a given iteration is valid or not, the works [5,15] constructed efficient schemes over synchronous channels. By considering the mixture of rational players and honest players, Ong et al. [12] realized fairness over standard broadcast channels. However, these protocols may be problematic when some players are corrupted by malicious adversaries.

The Adversary Model. To guarantee the same security properties as in usual cryptographic model, some works [10,2,11] proposed to study rational secret sharing resisting against adversaries, there are two kinds. Abraham et al. [1] first considered rational players with unexpected utilities who do not respond to incentives the way we expect as adversaries. Then Altabari et al.[2] improved the protocol of [8] to resist against rational adversaries. Since malicious players in real-life executions behave arbitrarily and do not aim to get the secret, Lysyanskaya and Triandopoulos [10] proposed that it is appropriate to treat these players as malicious adversaries who behave irrationally and cannot be motivated. They realized multiparty computation for t-NCC functions in the mixed-behavior model consisting of adversaries and rational players, which can tolerate an adversary controlling at most $t - 2$ players, but the solution is not suitable for rational secret sharing. Different from previous works, [11] modeled rational secret sharing in the repeated game (the game is repeated several times and players get a payoff for each game), and introduced a *repeated rational secret sharing* protocol tolerating malicious players. However, it is undesirable that the protocols in [10,1,2] rely on simultaneous communication, moreover, another noticeable point of all protocols above is that they can only achieve a Nash equilibrium surviving iterated deletion, which is too weak.

Problem Statement. Achieving a stronger equilibrium concept than Nash equilibrium, avoiding simultaneous communication and resisting against adversaries are three separate development directions of rational secret sharing. Current schemes have been developed tolerating adversaries, but they are less satisfactory in other two aspects. There is no improvement to rational secret sharing from all the three aspects.

1.2   Our Contribution

In this paper we design a t-out-of-n ($t \leq \lceil \frac{n}{2} \rceil$) rational secret sharing protocol tolerating an irrational adversary controlling a minority of players based on a publicly verifiable secret sharing (PVSS) scheme. It runs over synchronous (non-simultaneous) broadcast channels and achieves *a computational strict Nash equilibrium with respect to adversary structure* $\mathcal{A}$. Our work has advantages over previous solutions in the adversary model, we get rid of the simultaneous communication, moreover, the equilibrium concept we achieve is much stronger than the notion of Nash equilibrium that current works achieved.

2   Definition

2.1   Secret Sharing

In Shamir's t-out-of-n threshold secret sharing protocol, to share a secret $s \in \mathbb{Z}_q$, the dealer chooses a polynomial $f(x)$ of degree $t-1$, such that the constant term is s, then he publishes n distinct points $x_1, \ldots, x_n$ in field $\mathbb{Z}_q^*$ and sends $f(x_i)$ to P_i as his share. At least t players can recover the secret by using Lagrange interpolation, but less than t players cannot get any information about the secret. If the dealer is honest, the shares received by each player should be consistent. Here we describe what it means to be consistent.

Definition 1. *Given* $S = \{s_1, \ldots, s_n\}$, $x_1, \ldots, x_n$ *are* n *fixed distinct points, if there exists a polynomial* $f(x)$ *of degree* $t-1$ ($t \leq n$)*, such that* $f(x_i) = s_i, \forall s_i \in S$*, then we say the that values in* $\{s_1, \ldots, s_n\}$ *are consistent, and that* $f(0)$ *is recovered from* S *consistently.*

2.2   Game Theoretic Model

We introduce a new game-theoretic model of *the mixed-behavior game with respect to adversary structure* for rational secret sharing where adversaries exist. Compared with the standard game model where all players are rational, our mixed-behavior game gives a description of the behaviors of adversaries.

Definition 2. *The mixed-behavior game Γ with respect to adversary structure $\mathcal{A}$ consists of*

- A finite set $P = \{P_i | i \in \{1, \ldots, n\}\}$ (the set of **players**), adversary structure $\mathcal{A} \subset 2^P$ satisfies that $\forall A \in \mathcal{A}$, if $A' \subseteq A$ then $A' \in \mathcal{A}$. For any adversary $A \in \mathcal{A}$ we denote rational player set $R = P \backslash A$.
- For each $P_i \in P$ a nonempty set AC_i (the set of **actions** available to P_i), and let $AC = AC_1 \times AC_2 \times \ldots \times AC_n$ be the set of action profiles.
- A set of sequences $H = \{(\boldsymbol{a}^k)_{k=0,\ldots,T} | \boldsymbol{a}^k \in AC, T \in \mathbb{N}\}$ that satisfies the following properties.

  - $\boldsymbol{a}^0 = \varnothing \in H$
  - If $(\boldsymbol{a}^k)_{k=0,\ldots,K} \in H$ and $L < K$ then $(\boldsymbol{a}^k)_{k=0,\ldots,L} \in H$
  - If an infinite sequence $(\boldsymbol{a}^k)_{k=0,\ldots}$ satisfies $(\boldsymbol{a}^k)_{k=0,\ldots,L} \in H$ for every positive integer L then $(\boldsymbol{a}^k)_{k=0,\ldots} \in H$

  Each member of H is a history. A history $(\boldsymbol{a}^k)_{k=0,\ldots,K} \in H$ is **terminal** if there is no $\boldsymbol{a}^{K+1}$ such that $(\boldsymbol{a}^k)_{k=0,\ldots,K+1} \in H$ or if it is infinite. The set of terminal histories is denoted Z.
- A function u_i (the **utility function** of player P_i) for each player $P_i \in P$, which assigns to each terminal history a real value, $u_i : Z \longrightarrow \mathbb{R}$. Let $\boldsymbol{u} = u_1 \times u_2 \times \ldots \times u_n$ be the utility profile.

We assume that in the game there exists a malicious adversary who takes no care of his outcome and behaves maliciously (does not behave according to what specified by the protocol). We do not limit his capability, he behaves arbitrarily and may deviate from the prescribed strategy even if doing so is not favorable to him. The adversary corrupts a subset of rational players before the game starts, gets all their information, takes full control of them and decides how to move in the following protocol. We use adversary structure $\mathcal{A}$ to model the subsets of players which are corrupted by the adversary, and treat all corrupted players as malicious throughout the protocol. Players do not know which subset of players has been corrupted and what the adversaries will do.

The game proceeds in a sequence of actions (AC). Players are perfectly informed of history H, which records the actions that have occurred, and then decide their plans of actions based on other players' behaviors. The action that P_i chooses in each step is determined by his strategy, it is a function from the non-terminal histories to his actions, $\sigma_i : H \backslash Z \longrightarrow AC_i$. S_i denotes the set of strategies of player P_i, let $S = S_1 \times \ldots \times S_n$ be the set of strategy profiles. A history after which no more choices have to be made is terminal, which corresponds to an outcome of the protocol. A utility function u_i is used to describe the preference of P_i over the outcomes, $u_i(h)$ refers to P_i's utility after the terminal history $h \in Z$. Since each terminal history is determined by a strategy profile, we define the *outcome* $O(\boldsymbol{\sigma})$ to be the terminal history that results when each player $P_i \in P$ follows the precepts of σ_i. That is, $O(\boldsymbol{\sigma})$ is the (possibly infinite) history $(a^0, \ldots, a^K) \in Z$ such that for $0 \leq k < K$, $\boldsymbol{\sigma}(a^0, \ldots, a^k) = a^{k+1}$. Now we can define the utility function on strategies, let $u_i(\boldsymbol{\sigma}) = u_i(O(\boldsymbol{\sigma}))$.

2.3   Utility Assumption

The adversaries are irrational, unlike rational players, they have no preference over the outcomes, so they cannot be motivated and may follow the strategy which seems bad. They behave arbitrarily, unpredictably or even maliciously, and they do not aim to learn the secret, so we do not have to consider their payoffs and we treat their utilities as empty ones. We assume that rational players do not take care of the outputs of adversaries, and the utility of a rational player depends on both his own output and other rational players' outputs. Following [7], we assume that players prefer to get the secret first, and then prefer the fewest number of other rational players who get the secret, which can be formalized as follows. In the rational secret sharing protocol, for a given adversary $A \in \mathcal{A}$, a strategy profile $\boldsymbol{\sigma}$, $out(\boldsymbol{\sigma}) = (o_1, \ldots, o_n)$ such that (1) $o_i = 1$ *iff* player $P_i \in R$ can get the secret when all players stick to $\boldsymbol{\sigma}$, and $o_i = 0$ otherwise, (2) $o_j = 0$ if $P_j \in A$. For $P_i \in R$ it holds that:

1. $u_i(\boldsymbol{\sigma}) = u_i(\boldsymbol{\tau})$ if $out(\boldsymbol{\sigma}) = out(\boldsymbol{\tau})$
2. $u_i(\boldsymbol{\sigma}) > u_i(\boldsymbol{\tau})$ if $out_i(\boldsymbol{\sigma}) = 1$ and $out_i(\boldsymbol{\tau}) = 0$
3. $u_i(\boldsymbol{\sigma}) > u_i(\boldsymbol{\tau})$ if $out_i(\boldsymbol{\sigma}) = out_i(\boldsymbol{\tau})$, $out_j(\boldsymbol{\sigma}) \leq out_j(\boldsymbol{\tau})$ for all $j \neq i$ and there exists a $P_k \in R$, $k \neq i$ such that $out_k(\boldsymbol{\sigma}) < out_k(\boldsymbol{\tau})$

U_i^+ denotes the utility of P_i when P_i learns the secret but other rational players do not, U_i denotes the utility of P_i when all rational players learn the secret, U_i^- denotes the utility of P_i when P_i himself learns no secret. It follows that $U_i^+ > U_i > U_i^-$. Furthermore, we assume that the secret is chosen from domain $\mathbb{Z}_q$, players can guess the secret with probability $1/q$. U_i^r denotes the utility that P_i gets when he tries to guess the secret, $U_i^r = \frac{1}{q}U_i^+ + (1 - \frac{1}{q})U_i^-$. We assume that $U_i^r < U_i$, or else players may gain without running the protocol. Moreover, we assume there is a non-negligible difference between U_i and U_i^r. That is, there exists a polynomial $p(\cdot)$ such that for all sufficiently large k's it holds that $U_i > U_i^r + \frac{1}{p(k)}$.

2.4   Definition of Game-Theoretic Equilibrium

Definition 3. *We say that a function ν is negligible if for every constant $c \geq 0$ there exists an integer k_c such that $v(k) < k^{-c}$ for all $k \geq k_c$.*

Following [5], we define what it means to follow the protocol in our model first. Since players have bounded computing power, their strategies can be seen as probabilistic polynomial-time interactive Turing machines. We measure equivalence of strategies according to their views. Given the prescribed strategy profile $\sigma = \sigma_1 \times \ldots \times \sigma_n$ of protocol Π, let $\sigma_{R\setminus i} = \times_{P_j \in R\setminus P_i} \sigma_j$ denote the strategy profile of rational players except P_i. We have the following definition.

Definition 4. *Given an adversary $A \in \mathcal{A}$, denote $P_{R\setminus i} = \{P_j | j \neq i, P_j \in R\}$. Let the adversary A follow the strategy profile $\tau_A \in S_A$, the rational players R follow the strategy profile σ_R. Define the random variable $\text{View}_{-i}^{\sigma_R, \tau_A}$ as follows:*

> *Let Trans denote the messages sent by P_i not including any message sent by P_i after he writes to his output tape. $\text{View}_{-i}^{\sigma_R, \tau_A}$ includes the information given by the dealer to P_{-i}, the random coins of P_{-i} and the (partial) transcript Trans.*

Fix a strategy ρ_i and an algorithm T. Define the random variable $\text{View}_{-i}^{T, \rho_i}$ as follows:

> *When the players interact, P_i follows ρ_i, $P_{R\setminus i}$ follow $\sigma_{R\setminus i}$, adversaries follow τ_A. Let Trans denote the messages sent by P_i. Algorithm T, given the entire view of P_i, output an arbitrary truncation Trans' of Trans (defining a cut-off point and deleting any messages sent after that point). $\text{View}_{-i}^{T, \rho_i}$ includes the information given by the dealer to P_{-i}, the random coins of P_{-i} and the (partial) transcript Trans'.*

Strategy ρ_i yields equivalent player with respect to Π, denoted $\rho_i \approx \Pi$, if $\forall A \in \mathcal{A}$, $\forall \tau_A \in S_A$ there exists a PPT algorithm T such that for all PPT distinguishers D:

$$|Prob[D(1^k, \text{View}_{-i}^{T, \rho_i}) = 1]| - |Prob[D(1^k, \text{View}_{-i}^{\sigma_R, \tau_A}) = 1]| \leq negl(k)$$

where $negl(k)$ is a negligible function.

From the definition above, a strategy which yields equivalent player with respect to Π should tolerate the deviations of a certain number of adversaries, but may differ from the prescribed strategy when the player can be sure that one rational player deviates, it may even deviate from σ after the player gets the output, and we call it *equivalent strategy* for short.

Intuitively, in the rational secret sharing protocol running over synchronous channels, the players who broadcast shares later have the privilege to identify the real secret. Once they learn the significant information, they are no longer afraid of being punished, and they would like to deviate from the protocol because of rationality. This deviation cannot be avoided, but it may cause a problem that not all the players can learn the secret in a protocol inducing a standard (strict) equilibrium in the synchronous model. The standard equilibrium can only guarantee that a rational player cannot prevent any player from learning the secret on condition that all other rational players follow the protocol. However, in the synchronous model the requirement that all remaining rational players follow cannot be satisfied, because they would like to deviate after they learn the secret. When a certain number of players deviate from the protocol, some players may not be able to learn the secret. Hence, the standard equilibrium is too weak for the synchronous model. To achieve fairness that all players can still get the secret in this situation, it should be required that even if some other rational players follow the equivalent strategies, deviating will not be better than following for any player, i.e. no one will be prevented from learning the secret.

In addition, since adversaries cannot be motivated to follow and their deviation may induce rational players to deviate, we enhance the standard notion of strict Nash equilibrium to tolerate adversaries. Considering computational limitations, we give the following definition of computational strict Nash equilibrium with respect to $\mathcal{A}$. It is appealing that rational players have an incentive not to deviate before outputting, and the fairness can be satisfied even if players deviate after getting the outputs. Let $Eqv_i(\boldsymbol{\sigma})$ be the union of σ_i and the set of the strategy ρ_i of P_i which yields equivalent with respect to Π, $Eqv_R(\boldsymbol{\sigma}) = \times_{P_i \in R} Eqv_i(\boldsymbol{\sigma})$.

Definition 5. *Let $\boldsymbol{\sigma}$ be the prescribed strategy profile of the protocol Π, Π induces a computational strict Nash equilibrium with respect to the adversary structure $\mathcal{A}$ if it satisfies:*

1. *For each $P_i \in R$ and each deviating strategy $\sigma_i' \in S_i$ $\sigma_i' \not\approx \Pi$, it is satisfied that: $\forall A \in \mathcal{A}$, $\forall \boldsymbol{\tau}_A \in S_A$ there is a $c > 0$ such that $u_i(\sigma_i, \boldsymbol{\sigma}_{R\backslash i}, \boldsymbol{\tau}_A) \geq u_i(\sigma_i', \boldsymbol{\sigma}_{R\backslash i}, \boldsymbol{\tau}_A) + \frac{1}{k^c}$ for infinitely many values k, that is, $u_i(\sigma_i, \boldsymbol{\sigma}_{R\backslash i}, \boldsymbol{\tau}_A) - u_i(\sigma_i', \boldsymbol{\sigma}_{R\backslash i}, \boldsymbol{\tau}_A)$ is non-negligible.*
2. *For each $P_i \in R$, $\forall \rho_i \approx \Pi$ $(\rho_i \neq \sigma_i)$, it holds that $u_i(\rho_i, \boldsymbol{\rho}_{R\backslash i}, \boldsymbol{\tau}_A) \leq u_i(\sigma_i, \boldsymbol{\rho}_{R\backslash i}, \boldsymbol{\tau}_A) + negl(k)$, $\forall \boldsymbol{\rho}_{R\backslash i} \in Eqv_{R\backslash i}(\boldsymbol{\sigma})$, $\forall A \in \mathcal{A}$, $\forall \boldsymbol{\tau}_A \in S_A$.*

The sufficiently strong notion of computational strict Nash equilibrium with respect to $\mathcal{A}$ requires that no matter how the adversaries behave, a player suffers losses if he deviates before getting the output, and that when other rational players follow the equivalent strategies, he cannot increase his payoff by a non-negligible amount if he deviates after getting the output. The last point models the fact that we cannot force P_i to send correct messages once he can be sure that the protocol is finished. However, this definition guarantees that even if rational players deviate after outputting, the fairness can still be satisfied with probability $1 - \epsilon$ (ϵ is negligible).

3 Publicly Verifiable Secret Sharing

Consider such a problem in secret sharing: in many applications the dealer and the shareholders do not trust each other, the dealer may distribute incorrect shares in the distribution phase and shareholders may reveal incorrect shares in the reconstruction phase. These problems are also apparent in our mixed-behavior model, moreover the adversary may accuse when receiving consistent shares in order to halt the protocol. The publicly verifiable secret sharing (PVSS) scheme provides an approach for all players to verify that a share is consistent with other shares without revealing any information about the secret. Hence, it cannot only detect forged messages but also prevent the adversary from declaring an accusation against an honest dealer. We will use it as a tool for detecting deviations in our rational secret sharing protocol.

Let p and q denote large primes such that q divides $p-1$, G_q is the unique subgroup of $\mathbb{Z}_p^*$ of order q, and g, h, G, H denote the independently chosen generators of G_q such that no one knows $\log_g h, \log_G H$. A publicly known element $x_i \in \mathbb{Z}_q^*$ is assigned to each P_i. A commonly used method for verifying the consistency of shares in PVSS works as follows, the dealer shares c through $f(x) = c + a_1 x + \ldots + a_{t-1} x^{t-1}$, publishes the commitments to the coefficients $g^c, g^{a_1}, \ldots, g^{a_{t-1}}$, and sends the share $f(x_i)$ to P_i, it satisfies that $g^{f(x_i)} = g^c \prod_{j=1}^{t-1} (g^{a_j})^{x_i^j}$. However, this approach is problematic when being used in our RSS protocol, because whether c equals zero or not can be revealed from g^c, from which players can recognize the valid iteration in advance (some protocols set c to be zero in the valid iteration). Pedersen's VSS scheme requires the committer to compute $g^c h^r$ as a commitment to c by using r, denoted $E(c, r) = g^c h^r$. It is not suitable for our protocol either, because players can learn g^c before revealing their shares just after r is calculated.

In order to guarantee the privacy of the iteration status before the secret is recovered, g^c should be private. For this reason, we propose a publicly verifiable secret sharing scheme in this section, which satisfies that the shares can be verified, and most importantly, no information about g^c is revealed during the protocol under the Decision Diffie-Hellman assumption. Our construction for PVSS is based on Pedersen's VSS scheme [13] and Stadler's PVSS scheme [14], but we make some necessary modifications to it so that it is applicable for our RSS protocol. We use a generalization of the Chaum and Pedersen protocol [4] as a subprotocol to prove the equality of the contents of two commitments, denoted $DLEV(g, h, G, H, l_1, l_2)$. (Generators $g, h, G, H \in G_q$ are public.) The prover publishes two commitments, i.e. $l_1 = g^c h^r$ and $l_2 = G^c H^r$, then he proves that l_1, l_2 are both commitments to c for r as follows:

1. The prover chooses w, w' randomly, and sends $a_1 = g^w h^{w'}$ and $a_2 = G^w H^{w'}$ to the verifier.
2. The verifier chooses b randomly and sends it to the prover.

3. The prover opens $u = w - c \cdot b \bmod q$ and $u' = w' - r \cdot b \bmod q$.
4. The verifier checks that $a_1 = (g^u h^{u'}) \cdot l_1^b$ and $a_2 = (G^u H^{u'}) \cdot l_2^b$.

Lemma 1. *Two commitments $l_1 = g^{c_1} h^{r_1}$ and $l_2 = G^{c_2} H^{r_2}$ are published by the prover, under the Discrete Logarithm assumption, if the verifier accepts the verification $DLEV(g, h, G, H, l_1, l_2)$, then it means that $c_1 = c_2$ and $r_1 = r_2$. We say that the contents of l_1 and l_2 are equal.*

Proof. We assume that the prover can find two two-tuples (c, r) and (c', r') such that $l_1 = g^c h^r$ and $l_2 = G^{c'} H^{r'}$ are accepted by the verifier. We can get that:

$$a_1 = g^w h^{w'} = g^u h^{u'} \cdot (g^c h^r)^b = g^{u+c \cdot b} \cdot h^{u'+r \cdot b}$$

satisfies $w = u + c \cdot b$, $w' = u' + r \cdot b$. Let $a_2 = G^w H^{w'}$, it also holds that:

$$a_2 = G^w H^{w'} = G^u H^{u'} \cdot (G^{c'} H^{r'})^b = G^w H^{w'} G^{(c'-c)b} H^{(r'-r)b}$$

and in particular $G^{(c'-c)b} H^{(r'-r)b} = 1$, then we can get that
$$\log_G H = \frac{c-c'}{r'-r} (mod\ q)$$

Therefore, if the prover can pass the verification when cheating, then computing discrete logarithm becomes feasible. □

Denote the initial protocol of Chaum and Pedersen [4] by $LEV(g, G, g^c, G^c)$, which is used to verify whether the discrete logarithm of g^c to the base g equals the discrete logarithm of G^c to the base G. It is similar to $DLEV(g, h, G, H, g^c h^r, G^c H^r)$ except $r = 0$ and is much more simple. We will use it for verification in our RSS protocol. We omit the description of it here which can be found in [4].

3.1 Verifiable Encryption

When the dealer distributes encrypted shares over a broadcast channel, he needs to make the encrypted shares publicly verifiable. We adopt the verifiable encryption scheme of [14]. It is a protocol for verifying that a pair (M, N) encrypts the discrete logarithm of a public element $V_i = G_i^{v_i}$, denoted $VES(v_i, G_i^{v_i})$. The details appear in Appendix A.

Under the Decision-Diffie-Hellman assumption, computing v_i from $G_i^{v_i}$ and (M, N) is hard. Moreover, the dealer can cheat successfully with negligible probability. We omit the proof here, which can be found in [14]. In fact, the negligible probability of a successful cheat has no bad influence on our rational secret sharing scheme, because P_i can verify the decrypted v_i by checking the commitment $G_i^{v_i}$, and then he opens his private key once it is forged, so that the malicious dealer is sure to be caught. Thus if the dealer can pass the verification we believe that the decryption is true.

3.2   PVSS Scheme

In this section, we give the construction of a t-out-of-n publicly verifiable secret sharing scheme. Under the Discrete Logarithm assumption, the dealer cannot succeed in sharing inconsistently. Given generators g, h of G_q which are chosen randomly so that no one knows $log_g h$, each P_i chooses $z_i \in_R \mathbb{Z}_q^*$ as his private key and publishes $G_i = g^{z_i}, H_i = h^{z_i}$ as his public keys.

Distribution of the shares

1. The dealer D wants to share a secret $c \in \mathbb{Z}_q$ among all players $P_1, \ldots, P_n$, and he chooses a $t-1$ degree polynomial $F(x)$ with coefficients in $\mathbb{Z}_q$:
$$F(x) = c + \alpha_1 x + \ldots + \alpha_{t-1} x^{t-1}$$
   D computes $c_i = F(x_i)$ for $i \in \{1, \ldots, n\}$ and publishes a commitment to c for a randomly chosen value $r \in \mathbb{Z}_q$: $E_0 = E(c, r) = g^c h^r$.
2. D chooses $\beta_1, \ldots, \beta_{t-1} \in \mathbb{Z}_q$ randomly and broadcasts commitments $E_i = E(\alpha_i, \beta_i) = g^{\alpha_i} h^{\beta_i}$ to each α_i for $i \in \{1, \ldots, t-1\}$. D can get another $t-1$ degree polynomial $R(x) = r + \beta_1 x + \ldots + \beta_{t-1} x^{t-1}$.
3. D computes $r_i = R(x_i)$ and sends (c_i, r_i) to player P_i for $i \in \{1, \ldots, n\}$ by applying the verifiable encryption scheme, D calculates and sends out cipher-texts, then each P_i recovers c_i and r_i from them.
4. D also publishes commitments $A_i = G_i^{c_i}, B_i = H_i^{r_i}$ for $i \in \{1, \ldots, n\}$.

Verification of the shares

1. The verification of $G_i^{c_i} H_i^{r_i}$
   D proves to all players that the contents of $g^{c_i} h^{r_i}$ and $A_i B_i = G_i^{c_i} H_i^{r_i}$ are equal through $DLEV(g, h, G_i, H_i, g^{c_i} h^{r_i}, A_i B_i)$ for $i \in \{1, \ldots, n\}$. In fact, players can compute $g^{c_i} h^{r_i}$ from the commitments:
$$g^{c_i} h^{r_i} = \prod_{j=0}^{t-1} E_j^{x_i^j}$$
2. The verification of c_i and r_i
   D runs the protocol $VES(c_i, G_i^{c_i})$ and $VES(r_i, H_i^{r_i})$, if he can pass the verification, then P_i receives a share consistent with others.

Reconstruction

   Each P_i broadcasts c_i and r_i, together with a proof that the shares published are the discrete logarithm of A_i to G_i and the discrete logarithm of B_i to H_i respectively. After all shares have been verified, players reconstruct c by using Lagrange interpolation, $c = \Sigma_{i=1}^t \gamma_i c_i$. ($\gamma_i$ is a Lagrange coefficient)

In the distribution phase, the dealer broadcasts the commitments to the coefficients $g^{\alpha_i} h^{\beta_i}$, from which the consistency of shares can be verified, and distributes the shares c_i and r_i by using the verifiable encryption scheme. In the verification phase, the dealer proves that the decrypted c_i, r_i are correct, and that the shares are distributed consistently through the polynomials that he commits to. Under the assumption of Decision Diffie-Hellman, no information about the secret is revealed from the commitments. Moreover, similar to [13], if the dealer passes the verification then the consistency of shares can be guaranteed. A proof of the following theorem appears in Appendix B.

Theorem 1. *Under the Decision Diffie-Hellman assumption, the PVSS scheme is secure: (1) If the dealer passes the verification, any subset of at least t players can reconstruct the same secret. (2) Any subset of less than t players cannot get any information about the secret.*

4 Rational Secret Sharing Protocol

In this section we give a t-out-of-n $(t \leq \lceil \frac{n}{2} \rceil)$ rational secret sharing protocol that is resilient to an adversary corrupting less than $t - 1$ players. We only need the existence of synchronous broadcast channels (but non-simultaneous), and assume all players to be computationally bounded. After the initialization, our protocol runs in a sequence of iterations, which is a frequently used technique for RSS, with the property that the secret s can be recovered in the valid iteration, and no information about s is revealed in the invalid iteration.

Our scheme depends on the masking of the secret in each iteration. Following the same high-level approach as in [3,15], players recover a "one-time" secret $s + c$ in each iteration, where c is negotiated by a part of players randomly and is unknown to them, and players can get s only when $c = 0$. To run the protocol over a synchronous channel, we require players to identify whether the current iteration is valid or not after reconstructing $s + c$. The key in this process is that no information about c except that whether c equals 0 or not should be revealed when players check c. Players do so by verifying whether $g^{c\kappa}$ equals 1 or not (κ is a non-zero value) so as to keep s private. If $g^{c\kappa} = 1$, players can be convinced that the reconstructed $s + c$ equals s, otherwise the given iteration is invalid and players cannot learn c from $g^{c\kappa}$.

Different from the previous protocol where there is no adversary, our goal is to motivate all rational players to follow even if adversaries try to induce them to deviate. To that end, we require the above PVSS scheme, through which players verify the correctness of shares and catch a minority of deviations, and we punish deviating players by disqualifying them. These methods guarantee that a player decreases his payoff by deviating independently of the behaviors of adversaries.

4.1   Construction

Let g,h be the independently chosen generators of G_q, hence no player knows the discrete logarithm of h to g. Each P_i chooses $z_i \in_R \mathbb{Z}_q^*$ as his private key and publishes $G_i = g^{z_i}$ and $H_i = h^{z_i}$ as his public keys.

Initialization. The dealer only needs to be active in the initial stage. To share $s \in \mathbb{Z}_q$, the dealer chooses a $t-1$ degree polynomial $f(x) = s+a_1 x+\ldots+a_{t-1}x^{t-1}$ with coefficients in $\mathbb{Z}_q$ randomly. The dealer calculates $s_i = f(x_i)$ and sends it to P_i as his share, and publishes a commitment to each s_i: $X_i = G_i^{s_i}$.

Each Iteration. Each iteration includes two phases: new shares generation phase and reconstruction phase. In the first phase players negotiate about a random value c and generate the shares of the "one-time" secret $s + c$ for this iteration. In the second phase the unknown value $s+c$ is reconstructed first. After verifying the validity of shares, players mask c and g^c by randomly choosing $\kappa_i \in \mathbb{Z}_q^*$ ($i \in \{1,\ldots,n\}$) and publishing $g^{c\kappa_1\ldots\kappa_n}$, which equals 1 in the valid iteration. We give the formal specification of the protocol in the l-th iteration as follows:

New shares generation

1. Players choose a subset of t players randomly together such that each P_i is chosen with probability $\frac{t}{n}$, w.l.o.g denoted $P' = \{P_1,\ldots,P_t\}$. Each $P_i \in P'$ chooses $\tilde{c}_i \in \mathbb{Z}_q$ randomly, such that $\tilde{c}_i$ equals 0 with probability δ_0 and equals each $d \in \mathbb{Z}_q^*$ with probability $\frac{1-\delta_0}{q-1}$, and then shares $\tilde{c}_i$ through the PVSS scheme described above.

   In the PVSS scheme, P_i commits to $\tilde{c}_i$ for a randomly chosen $\tilde{r}_i \in \mathbb{Z}_q$. Denote by $\tilde{C}_i(x) = \tilde{c}_i + \tilde{\alpha}_{i1}x + \ldots + \tilde{\alpha}_{i(t-1)}x^{t-1}$ the polynomial for sharing $\tilde{c}_i$. P_i chooses $\tilde{\beta}_{ij} \in \mathbb{Z}_q$ and gets a polynomial $\tilde{R}_i(x) = \tilde{r}_i + \tilde{\beta}_{i1}x + \ldots + \tilde{\beta}_{i(t-1)}x^{t-1}$. P_i sends $\tilde{c}_{ih} = \tilde{C}_i(x_h)$ and $\tilde{r}_{ih} = \tilde{R}_i(x_h)$ to P_h, and publishes the following commitments to the shares ($j \in \{1,\ldots,t-1\}, h \in \{1,\ldots,n\}$): $\tilde{E}_{i0} = E(\tilde{c}_i,\tilde{r}_i)$, $\tilde{E}_{ij} = E(\tilde{\alpha}_{ij},\tilde{\beta}_{ij})$, $G_h^{\tilde{c}_{ih}}$, $H_h^{\tilde{r}_{ih}}$.

   Disqualify P_i if he fails. Halt the protocol and output a random guess of the secret if there are at most $n - t + 1$ players stay.

2. Calculate the shares of $c = \sum_{k=1}^{t} \tilde{c}_k$ and $r = \sum_{k=1}^{t} \tilde{r}_k$ by adding corresponding shares as follows:
$$c_i = \sum_{k=1}^{t} \tilde{c}_{ki}, \quad r_i = \sum_{k=1}^{t} \tilde{r}_{ki}$$

3. Calculate the commitments to the shares of c and r as follows ($i \in \{1,\ldots,n\}, j \in \{0,\ldots,t-1\}$):
$$E_j = \prod_{k=1}^{t} \tilde{E}_{kj}, \quad Y_i = G_i^{c_i} = \prod_{k=1}^{t} G_i^{\tilde{c}_{ki}}$$

4. Each P_i calculates his share of $s + c$ by adding s_i and c_i.

Reconstruction

Stage 1: *reconstructing $s^{(l)} = s + c$*

Players take turns to broadcast their shares of $s + c$, and verify the authenticity of P_i's share by checking: $G_i^{s_i+c_i} = X_i Y_i$. It is required that:

(1) Disqualify P_i if his share cannot satisfy the equation above, or else we say that $s_i + c_i$ is credible.

(2) Halt the protocol if the credible shares broadcasted are inconsistent or at most $n - t + 1$ credible shares have been broadcasted, and then output a random guess of the secret.

(3) Reconstruct $s^{(l)}$ from these credible shares consistently if there are more than $n - t + 1$ credible shares which are consistent.

Stage 2: *checking c*

1. Each P_i chooses $\kappa_i \in_R \mathbb{Z}_q^*$ and publishes $K_i = g^{\kappa_i}$. Let $\kappa = \prod_{i=1}^n \kappa_i$.
2. Players compute $g^{c_i\kappa}$ for $i \in \{1, \ldots, n\}$ as follows. (Take $g^{c_i\kappa}$ as an example)

   (a) P_i calculates $g^{c_i\kappa_i}$ and publishes it, then P_i verifies its correctness through $LEV(G_i, K_i, G_i^{c_i}, g^{c_i\kappa_i})$, that is he verifies the discrete logarithm of $G_i^{c_i}$ to the base G_i is equivalent to the discrete logarithm of $g^{c_i\kappa_i}$ to the base g^{κ_i}.

   (b) Players take turns to calculate as follows, start from P_{i+1}, then $P_{i+2},\ldots,P_n,P_1,\ldots,P_{i-1}$. After P_{i-1} finishes, they can get $g^{c_i\kappa}$. We assume that it is P_j's turn now. P_j calculates and publishes $g^{c_i\kappa_i\cdots\kappa_j}$ after $g^{c_i\kappa_i\cdots\kappa_{j-1}}$ has been published by P_{j-1}, then P_j implements $LEV(g, g^{c_i\kappa_i\cdots\kappa_{j-1}}, K_j, g^{c_i\kappa_i\cdots\kappa_j})$.

   (c) We say $g^{c_i\kappa}$ is credible if it is calculated successfully. If someone fails when computing $g^{c_i\kappa}$, then players disqualify him and restart Stage 2 unless $g^{c\kappa}$ has been calculated, in which case players enter Step 3.

   (d) Halt the protocol and output $s^{(l)}$ if at most $n - t + 1$ players stay or the credible shares that have been calculated are inconsistent.

3. Reconstruct $g^{c\kappa}$ from credible shares (w.l.o.g from the first t shares) as follows: $g^{c\kappa} = \prod_{i=1}^t (g^{c_i\kappa})^{\gamma_i}$, γ_i is a Lagrange coefficient.
4. Output $s^{(l)}$ and terminate the protocol if $g^{c\kappa}$ equals 1, otherwise, proceed to the next iteration after disqualifying the deviating players.

Remark 1. *The fact that the parameter c is negotiated by t players instead of all players is due to malicious behavior of adversaries. An adverse P_i can make the probability of $c = 0$ very low by not choosing $\tilde{c}_i$ according to δ_0. However, when these t players are all rational players who follow the protocol, $c = \sum_{i=1}^t \tilde{c}_i$ equals 0 with the probability $p = \frac{1}{q} + \frac{(\delta_0 \cdot q - 1)^t}{q(q-1)^{t-1}}$ (c may equal zero when each $\tilde{c}_i$ equals zero or one of the $\tilde{c}_i$ equals the opposite of the sum of the others). According to our protocol, c is negotiated by t rational players with the probability at least $\binom{n-t+2}{t} / \binom{n}{t}$. Since the protocol terminates when $c = 0$, we can avoid very low probability of termination by setting δ_0 appropriately.*

Remark 2. *The use of $g^{c\kappa}$ for checking c is to ensure the privacy of c in the invalid iteration. Obviously, broadcasting the shares of c directly will not do. In addition, it is more secure to open $g^{c\kappa}$ than open g^c, even if players can learn $c\kappa$ from some special $g^{c\kappa}$, they cannot learn c from $c\kappa$ because of the unknown κ.*

4.2 Analysis

It is obvious that the deviations of adversaries will be caught if all rational players follow the protocol. Since the adversaries are at most $t - 2$, the correct shares revealed are more than t, so that an authorized subset of at least t honest players can recover the real secret from their shares at last. Now we first prove the privacy of the protocol, i.e. during the protocol an unauthorized subset cannot learn any information about the secret.

Theorem 2. *Under the Discrete Logarithm assumption, no information about s is revealed to any subset of less than t players before the reconstruction stage of the last iteration. Under the Decision Diffie-Hellman assumption, no information about c is revealed to any subset of less than t players before the second stage of the reconstruction phase.*

Proof. In the first phase, the commitments $G_i^{s_i}, G_i^{c_i}, H_i^{r_i}, g^{c_i} h^{r_i}$ are published. However, players cannot compute s_i, c_i from these commitments, or else computing discrete logarithm becomes feasible. Thus less than t players have no enough shares and cannot reconstruct s or c. In the first stage of reconstruction phase, $s + c$ can be reconstructed, but players can only learn the sum of unknown s_i and c_i, so s and c keeps private. When checking c in the invalid iteration, only $g^{c\kappa} \neq 1$ can be calculated, under the discrete logarithm assumption, no information about c except that c does not equal 0 is revealed, thus s cannot be calculated from $s + c$.

In the PVSS scheme, no information about g^{c_i} is revealed under the Decision Diffie-Hellman assumption, so even if $c = 0$ players cannot learn it. Moreover, c and g^c keep private when players reconstruct $s + c$. Thus players cannot learn c in advance. The result holds.   □

From the analysis above, it is obvious that no information about the secret is reveal in the invalid iteration because s is masked by using $s + c$, and no one can learn the iteration status in advance. Next we need to prove that the protocol leads to a computational strict Nash equilibrium. We first consider a problem that in our mixed-behavior model whether the rational secret sharing protocol can resist against $t - 1$ malicious players or not. As pointed out by [10], if the adversary can control $t-1$ players, he may send $t-1$ shares to $n-2t+2$ rational players, so that these rational players can recover the secret without running the protocol after verifying the validity of the shares by themselves. This situation is extremely undesirable, the remaining $t - 1$ players cannot recover the secret any longer because rational players would not like to participant in the protocol after learning the secret. To avoid this problem we allow the adversary to control at most $t - 2$ players. Now we give the proof of our result. (We assume that a given iteration is valid with probability β.)

Theorem 3. *The (t, n) RSS protocol Π runs in the mixed-behavior model where rational players and irrational adversaries coexist, $\mathcal{A}$ denotes the adversary structure which consists of subsets of less than $t-1$ players, Π induces a computational strict Nash equilibrium with respect to $\mathcal{A}$, if there exists a polynomial p such that for all sufficiently large k's it holds that $\frac{U_i - U_i^r}{U_i^+ - U_i^r} - \delta_0 > \frac{1}{p(k)}$.*

Proof. In RSS, it is unavoidable that cryptographic primitives may be broken before the last iteration with negligible probability, because RSS may execute in an exponential number of iterations. Thus, we consider the case that the cheating players share parameters inconsistently without being caught. Let $\varepsilon(k)$ be the negligible probability that rational P_i succeeds in doing so. Let $A \in \mathcal{A}$ be any adversary set of size at most $t - 2$, and $\varepsilon'(k)$ denotes the negligible probability that at least one of the adversaries succeeds in deviating. If adversaries share inconsistently then rational players cannot recover the secret no matter whether they follow, because they cannot distinguish incorrect shares. Otherwise, as long as all rational players follow the protocol, all deviations of $(\leq t - 2)$ adversaries are sure to be caught and the secret can be recovered. Thus, when all rational players follow, the utility that P_i gets is at least $U_i^r \varepsilon'(k) + U_i(1 - \varepsilon'(k))$.

σ denotes the prescribed strategy profile in the protocol Π. τ_A denotes an arbitrary strategy of a given adversary $A \in \mathcal{A}$. We assume that rational players except P_i stick to the prescribed protocol σ, P_i follows the deviating strategy $\sigma_i' \not\approx \Pi$, which denotes the strategy that P_i deviates from σ_i before outputting the real secret. We first prove that σ_i is strictly better than σ_i' no matter how adversaries behave. We need to consider the following three deviating cases: (1) P_i shares inconsistently through the PVSS scheme or keeps silent when players generate new shares. (2) P_i broadcasts a forged share of $s + c$ or keeps silent in the reconstruction stage. (3) P_i deviates when checking c.

We analyze the situation where P_i deviates in the first case. Caught_i denotes the fact that P_i is caught deviating. Valid denotes the fact that P_i deviates in the valid iteration. Before the reconstruction phase P_i will be caught once he keeps silent. We now analyze the situation where P_i tries to share inconsistently. If P_i succeeds in distributing inconsistent shares while adversaries do not, then the protocol will halt in the reconstruction stage. P_i will be the only player who learns the secret if the current iteration is valid with probability β, but he cannot learn the secret in the invalid iteration with probability $1 - \beta$. If P_i cannot succeed in deviating, then he will be disqualified, which happens with probability $1 - \varepsilon(k)$. The expected utility that P_i gets by deviating is

$$
\begin{aligned}
&u_i(\sigma_i', \sigma_{R \setminus i}, \tau_A) \\
&\leq U_i^r \cdot \mathsf{Prob}[\overline{\mathsf{Caught}_A}] + U_i^+ \cdot \mathsf{Prob}[\overline{\mathsf{Caught}_i} \wedge \mathsf{Caught}_A \wedge \mathsf{Valid}] \\
&\quad + U_i^r \cdot \mathsf{Prob}[\overline{\mathsf{Caught}_i} \wedge \mathsf{Caught}_A \wedge \mathsf{Invalid}] \\
&\quad + U_i^r \cdot (\mathsf{Prob}[\mathsf{Caught}_i \wedge \mathsf{Caught}_A \wedge \mathsf{Valid}] \\
&\quad + \mathsf{Prob}[\mathsf{Caught}_i \wedge \mathsf{Caught}_A \wedge \mathsf{Invalid}])
\end{aligned}
$$

$$= U_i^r \varepsilon'(k) + U_i^+ \varepsilon(k)(1 - \varepsilon'(k))\beta + U_i^r \varepsilon(k)(1 - \varepsilon'(k))(1 - \beta)$$
$$+ U_i^r [(1 - \varepsilon(k))(1 - \varepsilon'(k))\beta + (1 - \varepsilon(k))(1 - \varepsilon'(k))(1 - \beta)]$$
$$= U_i^r \varepsilon'(k) + U_i(1 - \varepsilon'(k)) + (U_i^r - U_i)(1 - \varepsilon'(k))$$
$$+ (U_i^+ - U_i^r)\varepsilon(k)(1 - \varepsilon'(k))\beta$$

where $(U_i^+ - U_i^r)\varepsilon(k)(1 - \varepsilon'(k))\beta = \eta(k)$ is negligible.

It follows that $\forall A \in \mathcal{A}$, $\forall \boldsymbol{\tau}_A \in S_A$,

$$u_i(\boldsymbol{\sigma}_R, \boldsymbol{\tau}_A) \geq u_i(\sigma_i', \boldsymbol{\sigma}_{R \setminus i}, \boldsymbol{\tau}_A) + (U_i - U_i^r)(1 - \varepsilon'(k)) - \eta(k)$$

We can notice that $(U_i - U_i^r)(1 - \varepsilon'(k))$ is positive and non-negligible, $\eta(k)$ is negligible, so that $(U_i - U_i^r)(1 - \varepsilon'(k)) - \eta(k)$ is positive and non-negligible. Thus, following the protocol is strictly better than deviating for P_i.

In the second case, (1) We assume that the shares are generated consistently, P_i forges his share or does not broadcast anything in stage 1, but he will be caught and be disqualified. Even if all $t - 2$ adversaries deviate when P_i deviates, there are at least t players who follow the protocol, so the deviation of P_i will not interface with other players' reconstruction of $s + c$. Thus, if $s + c$ happens to be the real secret, P_i will get utility U_i, if it is fake then P_i can only guess the secret and get utility U_i^r. Considering the probability that adversaries share inconsistently in the first phase, the expected utility of P_i with this deviation is at most $U_i^r \varepsilon'(k) + (1 - \varepsilon'(k))(\beta U_i + (1 - \beta)U_i^r)$, we have $\forall A \in \mathcal{A}$, $\forall \boldsymbol{\tau}_A \in S_A$,

$$u_i(\boldsymbol{\sigma}_R, \boldsymbol{\tau}_A) \geq u_i(\sigma_i', \boldsymbol{\sigma}_{R \setminus i}, \boldsymbol{\tau}_A) + (1 - \varepsilon'(k))(1 - \beta)(U_i - U_i^r)$$

(2) After $s + c$ has been recovered, P_i can deviate by quitting and outputting $s + c$. However, all players have gotten $s + c$, they can output the real secret in the valid iteration and the fake secret in the invalid iteration. In this case, P_i can get $U_i \beta + U_i^r(1 - \beta)$, we have $\forall A \in \mathcal{A}$, $\forall \boldsymbol{\tau}_A \in S_A$,

$$u_i(\boldsymbol{\sigma}_R, \boldsymbol{\tau}_A) \geq u_i(\sigma_i', \boldsymbol{\sigma}_{R \setminus i}, \boldsymbol{\tau}_A) + (1 - \varepsilon'(k) - \beta)(U_i - U_i^r)$$

P_i can also output $s + c - \tilde{c}_i$ when c is negotiated by P_i and other $t - 1$ players. If $c - \tilde{c}_i = 0$, then only P_i can learn the secret, and the maximum probability is δ_0 (when $t - 2$ of these $t - 1$ players are adversaries who always choose 0). Thus, the utility P_i can get is at most $U_i^+ \delta_0 + U_i^r(1 - \delta_0)$, we have $\forall A \in \mathcal{A}$, $\forall \boldsymbol{\tau}_A \in S_A$,

$$u_i(\boldsymbol{\sigma}_R, \boldsymbol{\tau}_A) \geq u_i(\sigma_i', \boldsymbol{\sigma}_{R \setminus i}, \boldsymbol{\tau}_A) + \varepsilon'(k)(U_i^r - U_i) + \frac{1}{p(k)}(U_i^+ - U_i^r)$$

Since $(1 - \varepsilon'(k))(1 - \beta)(U_i - U_i^r)$, $(1 - \varepsilon'(k) - \beta)(U_i - U_i^r)$, $\varepsilon'(k)(U_i^r - U_i) + \frac{1}{p(k)}(U_i^+ - U_i^r)$ are positive and non-negligible, following the protocol is strictly better than deviating.

In the third case, P_i deviates when checking c. There are two possible cases. The first one is that P_i computes $g^{c_j \kappa}$ ($j \in \{1, \ldots, n\}$) with a value different from what he commits to. The second one is that P_i keeps silent. In both cases, P_i will be caught and be disqualified, so we do not distinguish between them. If P_i deviates before t credible shares $g^{c_j \kappa}$ have been calculated, then players restart Stage 2 at once after disqualifying P_i. In this situation, even if $t - 2$ adversaries deviate, the protocol will halt and all players will have the same output value. Thus P_i gets U_i in the valid iteration, but can only get U_i^r in the invalid iteration, and his deviation results in the expected utility $U_i\beta + U_i^r(1-\beta)$. If P_i follows the protocol then $g^{c\kappa}$ can be calculated. If the current iteration is valid then all players learn the secret, or else they continue the protocol that may be interrupted when adversaries share inconsistently in the subsequent iterations with negligible probability. Thus P_i gets $U_i\beta + (1-\beta)(\varepsilon'(k)U_i^r + (1 - \varepsilon'(k))U_i)$ by following. We can get that $\forall A \in \mathcal{A}$, $\forall \boldsymbol{\tau}_A \in S_A$,

$$u_i(\boldsymbol{\sigma}_R, \boldsymbol{\tau}_A) \geq u_i(\sigma_i', \boldsymbol{\sigma}_{R\setminus i}, \boldsymbol{\tau}_A) + (1 - \varepsilon'(k))(1 - \beta)(U_i - U_i^r)$$

It follows that P_i suffers losses by deviating, since $(1 - \varepsilon'(k))(1 - \beta)(U_i - U_i^r)$ is positive and non-negligible.

As we analyzed above, P_i will decrease his payoff by a non-negligible amount if he deviates before learning the secret no matter how adversaries behave. Thus, the deviating strategy σ_i' is strictly worse than the prescribed strategy σ_i.

We next consider the scenario where all rational players follow the strategy profile $\boldsymbol{\rho}_R \in Eqv_R(\boldsymbol{\sigma})$, that is all rational players would deviate from the protocol after they can output the secret, and they would not deviate before they can output the secret when there are less than $t-1$ players deviate. We show that in this situation each P_i cannot gain by deviating after learning the secret. When checking c in the valid iteration, players calculate the share $g^{c_i\kappa}$ one by one, w.l.o.g. we assume that the shares are calculated in this order $g^{c_1\kappa}, ..., g^{c_n\kappa}$. If the first $t-1$ shares have been calculated and published, then P_{t-1} will be the first player who learns the iteration status after finishing the computation of $g^{c_t\kappa}$. If the current iteration is valid, then P_{t-1} may deviate by keeping silent or forging shares. However his lie is sure to be caught. If $t-2$ players (may be adversaries) have deviated, then the protocol halts and all players output $s^{(r)}$. If less than $t-2$ players have deviated, then players restart stage 2. Similarly, in the resumption of stage 2 the player who finishes the computation of the t'th share can learn the secret in advance and then would like to deviate. No matter what the adversaries do and no matter whether P_i deviates or not, at last the following two scenarios occur: (1) The protocol halts when the $(t-1)$'th deviating player occurs. In this situation all players can output the real secret, because the secret has been reconstructed during the first stage of reconstruction phase. (2) Less than $t-1$ players deviate, at least $n-t+1$ credible shares are calculated and $g^{c\kappa}$ is reconstructed. In both scenarios above, all players can learn the secret at last. If the current iteration is invalid, $\boldsymbol{\rho}$ is just $\boldsymbol{\sigma}$. In addition, P_i can get the secret s directly by breaking the cryptographic primitives with negligible probability. When some $t-2$ players keep silent, P_i can increase his utility from U_i to U_i^+ by quitting. However, since it happens with negligible probability, P_i can only increase his overall utility by a negligible amount by following ρ_i.

From the above analysis we can know that P_i cannot gain by deviating after learning the secret, even if all other rational players follow the equivalent strategies. For each rational player P_i, $\forall \boldsymbol{\rho}_R \in Eqv_R\boldsymbol{\sigma}$, it holds that:

$$u_i(\boldsymbol{\rho}_R, \boldsymbol{\tau}_A) \leq u_i(\sigma_i, \boldsymbol{\rho}_{R\setminus i}, \boldsymbol{\tau}_A) + negl(k), \quad \forall A \in \mathcal{A}, \forall \boldsymbol{\tau}_A \in S_A$$

The negligible term is derived from the broken of cryptographic primitives.

Therefore, we can conclude that the prescribed strategy of the protocol induces a computational strict Nash equilibrium with respect to adversary structure $\mathcal{A}$. □

4.3 Discussion

Equilibrium. Our scheme is the first to induce a computational strict Nash equilibrium with respect to adversary structure $\mathcal{A}$. This solution concept extends the notion of strict Nash equilibrium to resist against adversaries, it is much stronger than the notion of Nash equilibrium surviving iterated deletion of weakly dominated strategies, which previous protocols tolerating adversaries ([10,11,2]) can only achieve.

Communication Channel. Our RSS protocol only needs synchronous broadcast channels. However, previous works with respect to adversaries [10,2,1] required simultaneous communication.

Adversary Resilience. Our protocol motivates all rational players to follow the protocol independently of the attacks of adversaries. Compared with previous works, we do not limit the ability of adversaries, and our solution guarantees the same properties as in cryptography.

5   Conclusion

We show how to realize a t-out-of-n secret sharing protocol that is resilient to irrational adversaries over standard (synchronous) broadcast channels in this paper. We rely on the publicly verifiable secret sharing scheme to detect deviations, so that the reconstruction of the secret will not be interrupted even if a small number of players deviate. Moreover, the deviating players are punished by being disqualified. Compared with Nash equilibrium that current works with respect to adversaries can achieve, our protocol achieves an enhanced notion of computational strict Nash equilibrium with respect to adversary structure $\mathcal{A}$. In addition, we can tolerate less than one half of all players being corrupted by a malicious adversary without using simultaneous communication.

References

1. Abraham, I., Dolev, D., Gonen, R., Halpern, J.: Distributed computing meets game theory: robust mechanisms for rational secret sharing and multiparty computation. In: Proceedings of the Twenty-Fifth Annual ACM Symposium on Principles of Distributed Computing, PODC 2006,, pp. 53–62. ACM, New York (2006)
2. Altabari, N., Krohmer, A., Molter, H., Tarrach, T.: A rational secret sharing scheme robust against malicious players (2009)
3. Asharov, G., Lindell, Y.: Utility dependence in correct and fair rational secret sharing. In: Halevi, S. (ed.) CRYPTO 2009. LNCS, vol. 5677, pp. 559–576. Springer, Heidelberg (2009)

4. Chaum, D., Pedersen, T.P.: Wallet databases with observers. In: Brickell, E.F. (ed.) CRYPTO 1992. LNCS, vol. 740, pp. 89–105. Springer, Heidelberg (1993)
5. Fuchsbauer, G., Katz, J., Naccache, D.: Efficient rational secret sharing in standard communication networks. In: Micciancio, D. (ed.) TCC 2010. LNCS, vol. 5978, pp. 419–436. Springer, Heidelberg (2010)
6. Dov Gordon, S., Katz, J.: Rational secret sharing, revisited. In: De Prisco, R., Yung, M. (eds.) SCN 2006. LNCS, vol. 4116, pp. 229–241. Springer, Heidelberg (2006)
7. Halpern, J.Y., Teague, V.: Rational secret sharing and multiparty computation: extended abstract. In: Proceedings of the Thirty-Sixth Annual ACM Symposium on Theory of Computing, STOC 2004, pp. 623–632 (2004)
8. Kol, G., Naor, M.: Cryptography and game theory: Designing protocols for exchanging information. In: Canetti, R. (ed.) TCC 2008. LNCS, vol. 4948, pp. 320–339. Springer, Heidelberg (2008)
9. Kol, G., Naor, M.: Games for exchanging information. In: STOC, pp. 423–432 (2008)
10. Lysyanskaya, A., Triandopoulos, N.: Rationality and adversarial behavior in multiparty computation. In: Dwork, C. (ed.) CRYPTO 2006. LNCS, vol. 4117, pp. 180–197. Springer, Heidelberg (2006)
11. Maleka, S., Shareef, A., Pandu Rangan, C.: Rational secret sharing with repeated games. In: Chen, L., Mu, Y., Susilo, W. (eds.) ISPEC 2008. LNCS, vol. 4991, pp. 334–346. Springer, Heidelberg (2008)
12. Ong, S.J., Parkes, D.C., Rosen, A., Vadhan, S.: Fairness with an honest minority and a rational majority. In: Reingold, O. (ed.) TCC 2009. LNCS, vol. 5444, pp. 36–53. Springer, Heidelberg (2009)
13. Pedersen, T.P.: Non-interactive and information-theoretic secure verifiable secret sharing. In: Feigenbaum, J. (ed.) CRYPTO 1991. LNCS, vol. 576, pp. 129–140. Springer, Heidelberg (1992)
14. Stadler, M.: Publicly Verifiable Secret Sharing. In: Maurer, U. (ed.) EUROCRYPT 1996. LNCS, vol. 1070, pp. 190–199. Springer, Heidelberg (1996)
15. Zhang, Y., Tartary, C., Wang, H.: An efficient rational secret sharing scheme based on the Chinese remainder theorem. In: Parampalli, U., Hawkes, P. (eds.) ACISP 2011. LNCS, vol. 6812, pp. 259–275. Springer, Heidelberg (2011)
16. Zhang, Z., Liu, M.: Unconditionally secure rational secret sharing in standard communication networks. In: Rhee, K.-H., Nyang, D. (eds.) ICISC 2010. LNCS, vol. 6829, pp. 355–369. Springer, Heidelberg (2011)

Appendix A: Verifiable Encryption

It is a protocol for verifying that a pair (M, N) encrypts the discrete logarithm of a public element $V_i = G_i^{v_i}$, denoted $VES(v_i, G_i^{v_i})$.

Let q be a large prime so that $p' = (q-1)/2$ is also prime, G_i is a generator of G_q, f is a fixed element of order p' in $\mathbb{Z}_q^*$, P_i chooses $z_i' \in_R \mathbb{Z}_{p'}$ as his private key and publishes $y_i = f^{z_i'} (mod\ q)$ as his public key. To encrypt $v_i \in \mathbb{Z}_q^*$, the dealer D chooses $\varepsilon_i \in \mathbb{Z}_{p'}$ randomly and computes $(M, N) = (f^{\varepsilon_i}, v_i^{-1} \cdot y_i^{\varepsilon_i})$.

P_i can decrypt (M, N) by calculating

$$v_i = (f^{\varepsilon_i})^{z_i'} / (v_i^{-1} \cdot y_i^{\varepsilon_i})$$

Then the dealer proves to all players that the decryption of (M, N) is just the discrete logarithm of $V_i = G_i^{v_i}$ to G_i. Actually, if (M, N) equals $(f^{\varepsilon_i}, v_i^{-1} \cdot y_i^{\varepsilon_i})$, then it holds that

$$V_i^N = (G_i^{v_i})^{v_i^{-1} \cdot y_i^{\varepsilon_i}} = G_i^{y_i^{\varepsilon_i}}$$

So the dealer needs to prove that the double discrete logarithm of V_i^N to the base G_i, y_i equals the discrete logarithm of M to the base f. They repeat the following scheme T times:

1. The dealer randomly chooses $w \in \mathbb{Z}_{p'}$, publishes $t_f = f^w$ and $t_{G_i} = G_i^{y_i^w}$.
2. The verifiers send $b \in_R \{0, 1\}$ to the dealer.
3. The dealer responses with $r = w - b \cdot \varepsilon_i$.
4. The verifiers check
   (a) $t_f = f^r \cdot M^b = f^w$.
   (b) $t_{G_i} = G_i^{y_i^r}$ when $b = 0$
   (c) $t_{G_i} = (V_i^N)^{y_i^r}$ when $b = 1$

Appendix B: Proof of Theorem 1

We recall the Diffie-Hellman assumption and the Decision Diffie-Hellman assumption briefly. The Diffie-Hellman assumption states that given g^α, g^β it is infeasible to compute $g^{\alpha\beta}$. The Decision Diffie-Hellman assumption states that given g^α, g^β, it is infeasible to determine whether a given g^γ equals $g^{\alpha\beta}$ or not.

Firstly we consider the privacy of shares. In the distribution phase the dealer publishes commitments to each c_i for r_i, according to [13] the commitment $E(c_i, r_i)$ protects the privacy of c_i, r_i unconditionally. The dealer also publishes the commitments $G_i^{c_i}$ and $H_i^{r_i}$, c_i and r_i keep private under the Discrete Logarithm assumption. Furthermore, it follows from the soundness of Stadler's verifiable encryption scheme that no information about c_i and r_i is revealed from the encrypted values under the assumption of Discrete logarithm and Decision Diffie-Hellman. We can get that, assume that computing discrete logarithm is hard and breaking ElGamal cryptosystem is hard, players cannot compute other players' shares, so that less than t players cannot compute c. This can be expressed by the following theorem. Let $shares_B$ denote all shares received by players in B from the dealer during the protocol.

Lemma 2. *In the (t, n) public verifiable secret sharing scheme, for any player subset B of size less than t, it holds that*

$$Pr[players\ in\ B\ learn\ c|shares_B] = Pr[players\ in\ B\ learn\ c]$$

Proof. We consider the subset of size $t - 1$ first, let $B = \{P_1, \ldots, P_{t-1}\}$. Note that $shares_B = (c_1, r_1, \ldots, c_{t-1}, r_{t-1})$.

For every $c \in \mathbb{Z}_q$, there exists a polynomial f of degree at most $t - 1$ satisfies

$$f(0) = c$$
$$f(x_b) = c_b \quad for \quad b = \{1, \ldots, t - 1\}$$

It follows that players cannot recover the secret from $t-1$ shares. Furthermore, the subset of size $< t-1$ has fewer shares, so c also keeps private. $\qquad\square$

In our protocol, $G_i^{c_i}$ and $H_i^{r_i}$ can be seen as the encryption of g^{c_i} and h^{r_i} respectively. As we pointed out early that it may be dangerous for our rational secret sharing protocol if players can break the encryption and get g^{c_i}. In fact, breaking the encryption is equivalent to the Diffie-Hellman problem.

Lemma 3. *Under the Diffie-Hellman assumption, it is infeasible to break the encryption of shares: $G_i^{c_i}$ and $H_i^{r_i}$.*

Proof. Given $G_i^{c_i} = g^{z_i \cdot c_i}$, $G_i = g^{z_i}$, breaking the encryption means computing g^{c_i} from $g^{z_i \cdot c_i}$ and g^{z_i}, which is equivalent to computing g^{β} from $g^{\alpha\beta}$ and g^{α}. If we can solve this problem, then given g^{α} and g^{β}, we can compute $g^{\beta^{-1}}$ from g^1 and g^{β}, so that we can compute $g^{\alpha \cdot \beta}$ from g^{α} and $g^{\beta^{-1}}$. This means that Diffie-Hellman problem can be settled. $\qquad\square$

Our rational secret sharing protocol requires that g^c cannot be revealed before the reconstruction stage. The commitment $g^{c_i} h^{r_i}$ reveals no information of c_i and r_i, moreover, the above result shows that players except P_i cannot compute g^{c_i}, but it cannot guarantee that no information about g^{c_i} is revealed. We prove the following result which holds under the Decision Diffie-Hellman assumption.

Lemma 4. *Under the Decision Diffie-Hellman assumption, less than t players cannot get any information about g^c or h^r.*

Proof. Here, we prove that no information about g^c is revealed, the proof of h^r is similar. We start from subset of $t-1$ players, w.l.o.g. denoted $P_1, \ldots, P_{t-1}$, they can learn $g^{c_1}, \ldots, g^{c_{t-1}}$. If they can get some information about g^c then they can get partial information about g^{c_j} $(j > t-1)$ from its encryption $G_j^{c_j} = g^{z_j \cdot c_j}$. Writing $G_j^{c_j} = g^{z_j \cdot c_j} = g^{\alpha \cdot \beta}$, $G_j = g^{\alpha}$, we suppose that a player can determine whether the decrypted share g^{β} is equal to a given g^{δ} or not. In this situation, given g^{α}, g^{β}, g^{θ}, if the player can output whether $g^{\theta/\alpha}$ equals g^{β} with inputs g^{θ}, g^{α}, then we can determine whether g^{θ} equals $g^{\alpha \cdot \beta}$ or not. This is a contradiction with the Decision Diffie-Hellman assumption. $\qquad\square$

Next we need to prove the consistency of shares in the PVSS scheme.

Lemma 5. *Under the Discrete Logarithm assumption, if all players accept their shares in the publicly verifiable secret sharing scheme, then their shares are consistent.*

Proof. According to [13], the dealer can succeed in distributing inconsistent shares unless he can settle Discrete Logarithm problem, so that the shares being committed are consistent. Moreover, following from Lemma 1, the discrete logarithm of $G_i^{c_i}$ equals the content c_i of $g^{c_i} h^{r_i}$. Thus, all players can make sure that the shares distributed are consistent. $\qquad\square$

It follows from the Lemmas above that the commitments and encryptions do not reveal any information about the secret, and the shares held by players are consistent with the secret. We can get the result.

Visual Cryptography
for Natural Images and Visual Voting

Teng Guo[1,2], Feng Liu[1], and ChuanKun Wu[1]

[1] State Key Laboratory of Information Security, Institute of Information Engineering,
Chinese Academy of Sciences, Beijing 100093, China
[2] University of Chinese Academy of Sciences, Beijing 100190, China
{guoteng,liufeng,ckwu}@iie.ac.cn

Abstract. Visual cryptography is a type of secret sharing which encodes
a secret image into several shadow images in such a way that the stacking
of certain images printed on transparencies will reveal the secret. The decryption is done directly by the human visual system without any extra
calculations. Most of previous researches essentially handle only binary
images, as the underling encoding matrices are all Boolean matrices. For
gray-level image, we need to halftone it into binary image before encoding. Although binary image can be used to simulate gray-level image, its
visual quality is deteriorated, especially for fine images. The first part
of this paper presents a method to provide much more gray-levels than
previous schemes, given the same pixel expansion, and thus establishes
the visual cryptography scheme suitable for natural images. The second
part of this paper presents a visual voting scheme that need no counting
process and guarantees anonymity.

Keywords: Visual cryptography, Secret sharing, Gray pixel, Visual
voting.

1 Introduction

Visual cryptography is a type of secret sharing in which the secret can be decoded
directly by the human visual system without any extra calculations. Most previous
works on visual cryptography basically deal with binary images, as the underling
encoding matrices are all Boolean matrices. For natural images such as color images or gray-level images, we generally need to preprocess them before encoding.
As colors can be decomposed into three independent channels RGB with some intensities, essentially we only need to process gray-level images. Binary image can
be used to simulate gray-level image, although the visual quality is deteriorated,
especially for fine images. Nakajima and Yamaguchi noticed this drawback and
proposed a scheme to provide more gray-levels [13]. For 2 out of 2 visual cryptography scheme ((2,2)-VCS) with pixel expansion m, they provide approximately $\frac{m}{2}$
gray-levels. This paper describes a method to provide much more gray-levels than
previous researches, given the same pixel expansion. For (2,2)-VCS with pixel expansion 4, Naor and Shamir's scheme provides 2 gray-levels, and Nakajima and

M. Kutyłowski and M. Yung (Eds.): Inscrypt 2012, LNCS 7763, pp. 90–101, 2013.

Yamaguchi's scheme provides 3 gray-levels, while the proposed scheme provides 11 gray-levels. We cannot determine the exact number of gray-levels that the proposed scheme provides for arbitrary pixel expansion m, on the other hand, we show that this number is lower bounded by $\frac{m(m+1)}{2} + 1$ and upper bounded by $\frac{m(m+1)(m+2)}{6} + 1$. It is easy to see that as m increase, the proposed scheme provide much more gray-levels than previous schemes. The rich gray-levels in the decoded image will allow us to obtain pleasing visual qualities and thus establish the visual cryptography scheme suitable for natural images. The method that we adopt is by allowing gray pixels on shadow images. The stacking of two gray pixels is first introduced in [5], but they only use it trivially, for black (of gray-level degree 0) and white (of gray-level degree 255) pixels. Previous papers on color VCS [7,11] all rely on some underling Boolean basis matrices. The proper fractional matrices that we propose are supposed to substitute those underling Boolean basis matrices to provide much more gray-levels. To the best of our knowledge, this is the first attempt to non-trivially use the stacking of two gray pixels that are not of gray-level degrees 0 or 255 in the basis matrix level. This work develops a framework for the study of gray pixel VCS (GVCS) in the basis matrix level and gives an efficient solution for (2,2)-GVCS, while leaves many interesting open problems to further studies, see Section 4 for some details.

In the second part of the paper, we propose a visual voting scheme that suits for situations where there are two candidates and odd number of voters in total and no one abstains from voting. The voting result can be seen by simply stacking all submitted shadow images without needing to count the number of votes. Besides, the proposed scheme guarantees anonymity that after the election, each voter's vote is only known to himself and others have no idea about it.

This paper is organized as follows. Gray pixel VCS is discussed in Section 2. A visual voting scheme is presented in Section 3. The paper is concluded in Section 4.

2   Visual Cryptography for Natural Images

Visual cryptography dealing with natural images generally has the following steps: 1, natural images are decomposed into three independent channels that can be seen as three gray-level images; 2, the gray-level images are transformed to binary images by some halftone technique; 3, binary images are encoded by conventional VCS; 4, three independent channels are merged into one shadow image printed on a transparency; 5, each transparency is distributed to its supposed owner. Many image processing techniques are combined with VCS to improve its visual quality [18,17,10,8], but the shadows and the decoded images are still limited to the stacking result of binary images. To step over this limitation and provide more gray-levels, we introduce gray pixels on shadows.

This section contains four parts: firstly we give some background knowledge of the stacking of two gray pixels; secondly we develop a framework for analyzing GVCSs; thirdly we propose an efficient solution for (2,2)-GVCS; at last, the above solution is used to encode color images.

2.1   The Model of Stacking Two Gray Pixels

Light transmittance rate (LRT) can be used to represent gray-levels. Suppose we have a unit of light transmitting through a gray transparency with LRT $\frac{1}{2}$, then we get a half unit of light. In computer representation, we use numbers 0 to 255 to represent 256 gray-levels, where 0 represents pure black and 255 represents pure white. If we set a unite of light as gray-level 255, then after transmitting through a gray transparency with LRT $\frac{1}{2}$, we get a light of gray-level $\frac{255}{2} \approx 128$. If we have a unit of light transmitting through a gray transparency with LRT $\frac{1}{5}$, then we get a fifth unit of light, and in computer representation, we get a light of gray-level $\frac{255}{5} = 51$. The LRT of the stacking result of two gray transparencies with LRTs $\alpha_1, \alpha_2 \in [0,1]$ can be expressed (approximately) as $\alpha_1 \times \alpha_2$, see [5]. A pixel of LRT 0 is pure black and a pixel of LRT 1 is pure white. According to the above stacking rule, we know that $0 \times 0 = 0$ and $0 \times 1 = 0$ and $1 \times 0 = 0$ and $1 \times 1 = 1$. Only the stacking of two white pixels will results in a white pixel, which is the same as the stacking rule of Naor and Shamir, see [14]. Hence the stacking rule in [5] can be seen as a generalization of that in [14], from the binary case to the gray-level case. Although Cimato. et al. proposed the stacking rule of two gray pixels in [5], they did not adopt the stacking of two gray pixels in their proposed basis matrices. To the best of our knowledge, this is the first attempt to non-trivially use the stacking of two gray pixels that are not of gray-levels 0 or 255 in the basis matrix level.

2.2   The Model of Gray Pixel Visual Cryptography

We first set up our notations. Let X be a subset of participants $\{1, 2, \cdots, n\}$ and let $|X|$ be the cardinality of X. Suppose S is an $n \times m$ proper fractional matrix, in which each item is a fraction and lies between 0 and 1. Let $S[X]$ denote the matrix S constrained to rows in X, then $S[X]$ is a $|X| \times m$ matrix. We denote by $H(S[X])$ the sum of the multiplication results of rows of $S[X]$.

In a gray pixel visual cryptography scheme (GVCS) with n participants, we share one pixel at a time. Suppose the pixel's gray-levels are divided into t non-overlapping parts, which can be taken as an affine transform. If the pixel's gray-level is in part i, then we randomly permutate the columns of S_i and distribute the j-th $(0 \leq j \leq n)$ row to share j, in which each proper fraction denotes a pixel's LRT. Formally, (k, n)-GVCS is defined as follows:

Definition 1 ((k, n)-GVCS). *The $n \times m$ proper fractional matrices $(S_1, \ldots, S_t)$ constitute a (k, n)-GVCS if the following conditions hold:*

1. *(Contrast) For any participant set X with $|X| \geq k$, we denote $l_X = H(S_0[X])$, and denote $h_X = H(S_1[X])$. It holds that $0 \leq l_X < h_X \leq m$.*
2. *(Security) For any participant set Y with $|Y| \leq k - 1$, $(S_1, \ldots, S_t)$ are all equal up to a column permutation.*

Remark: If $t = 2$ and (S_1, S_2) are both Boolean matrices, then our definition of (k, n)-GVCS coincides with the commonly accepted definition of (k, n)-VCS [14,1].

GVCS is best understood by an example. The following four basis matrices define a (2,2)-GVCS with 4 gray levels.

$$S_1 = \begin{bmatrix} 0\frac{1}{2}1 \\ 1\frac{1}{2}0 \end{bmatrix} \text{ and } S_2 = \begin{bmatrix} 0\frac{1}{2}1 \\ \frac{1}{2}10 \end{bmatrix} \text{ and } S_3 = \begin{bmatrix} 0\frac{1}{2}1 \\ \frac{1}{2}01 \end{bmatrix} \text{ and } S_4 = \begin{bmatrix} 0\frac{1}{2}1 \\ 0\frac{1}{2}1 \end{bmatrix}$$

The total LRTs of the stacking results of rows of S_i ($1 \le i \le 4$) are $\frac{1}{4}$, $\frac{1}{2}$, 1 and $\frac{5}{4}$ respectively.

2.3   Efficient Solutions for (2,2)-GVCS

Now we consider (2,2)-GVCS with arbitrary pixel expansion, say $m + 1$, the pixels' LRTs in a block are set to be $T = \{0, \frac{1}{m}, \ldots, \frac{m-1}{m}, 1\}$. The basis matrices can be expressed as $S = \binom{T}{perm(T)}$, where $perm(T)$ denotes some permutation of T. The decoded LRT of S is $H(S) = \sum_{i=0}^{m} \frac{i}{m} \times perm(i)$ where $perm(i)$ denotes the i-th element of $perm(T)$. We would like to pick up a sequence of basis matrices $S_1, S_2, \ldots, S_n$ that is strictly increasing w.r.t. decoded LRTs. Since the length of the sequence is equal to the number of decoded LRTs, it is expected to be as large as possible. A naive approach to find such a sequence is by listing all possible permutations and their decoded gray-levels, and then by picking up a matrix for all possible decoded LRTs. But as $m + 1$ becomes large, the number of all possible permutations $(m + 1)!$ becomes enormous and this method will become inefficient w.r.t. both time and space. Besides, the following Theorem states that there cannot be too many number of decoded LRTs. From another perspective, many different permutations correspond to the same decoded LRT.

Theorem 1. *Considering $S = \binom{T}{perm(T)}$, where $T = \{0, \frac{1}{m}, \ldots, \frac{m-1}{m}, 1\}$ and $perm(T)$ denotes all possible permutations of T, the number of all possible decoded LRTs of S is at most $\frac{m(m+1)(m+2)}{6} + 1$.*

Proof: The case of largest decoded LRT is:

$$S_n = \begin{bmatrix} 0 & \frac{1}{m} & \frac{2}{m} & \cdots & \frac{m-1}{m} & 1 \\ 0 & \frac{1}{m} & \frac{2}{m} & \cdots & \frac{m-1}{m} & 1 \end{bmatrix}$$

$$\text{where } H(S_n) = \sum_{i=0}^{m} \frac{i^2}{m^2} = \frac{m(m+1)(2m+1)}{6m^2}$$

The case of smallest decoded LRT is:

$$S_1 = \begin{bmatrix} 0 & \frac{1}{m} & \frac{2}{m} & \cdots & \frac{m-1}{m} & 1 \\ 1 & \frac{m-1}{m} & \frac{m-2}{m} & \cdots & \frac{1}{m} & 0 \end{bmatrix}$$

$$\text{where } H(S_1) = \sum_{i=0}^{m} \frac{i(m-i)}{m^2} = \frac{m(m+1)(m-1)}{6m^2}$$

As the decoded LRT of S is $H(S) = \sum_{i=0}^{m} \frac{i}{m} \times perm(i)$ where $perm(i)$ denotes the i-th element of $perm(T)$, if we take m^2 as the denominator of $H(S)$, then the numerator of $H(S)$ must be an integer between $\frac{m(m+1)(m-1)}{6}$ and $\frac{m(m+1)(2m+1)}{6}$. Thus the number of all possible $H(S)$ is at most $\frac{m(m+1)(2m+1)}{6} - \frac{m(m+1)(m-1)}{6} + 1 = \frac{m(m+1)(m+2)}{6} + 1$. $\qquad\square$

In the following, we try to give a lower bound on the number of decoded LRTs. The method is by picking up a sequence of permutations of $\{0, 1, \ldots, m\}$ that will result in a larger sum $\sum_{i=0}^{m} i \times perm(i)$ and is as long as possible. From sorting theory, we know that bubble sorting from the reverse sequence $(m, m-1, \ldots, 1, 0)$ to the positive sequence $(0, 1, \ldots, m-1, m)$ will result in such a sequence of permutations. Bubble sort works by repeatedly stepping through the list to be sorted, comparing each pair of adjacent items and swapping them if they are in the wrong order [9]. The pass through the list is repeated until no swaps are needed, which indicates that the list is sorted.

As the decoded gray-level can be easily calculated from the decoded LRT and vise versa, sometimes we abuse their names and do not distinguish between them. The following lemma associates the number of decoded gray-levels with the number of swap steps in bubble sort.

Lemma 1. *Each swap step in bubble sort increase the sum* $\sum_{i=0}^{m} i \times perm(i)$ *where $perm(i)$ denotes the i-th element of the being sorted sequence.*

Proof: Suppose the sequence before the swap step is $t_0, t_1, \ldots, t_i, t_{i+1}, \ldots, t_m$ and the sequence after the swap is $t_0, t_1, \ldots, t_{i+1}, t_i, \ldots, t_m$. From the swap condition, we know that $t_{i+1} < t_i$ holds, which leads to $i \times t_i + (i+1) \times t_{i+1} < i \times t_{i+1} + (i+1) \times t_i$. Hence $\sum_{j=0}^{m} j \times t_j < \sum_{j=0}^{i-1} j \times t_j + i \times t_{i+1} + (i+1) \times t_i + \sum_{j=i+2}^{m} j \times t_j$ holds. $\qquad\square$

The following lemma gives the number of swap steps in bubble sorting from the reverse sequence to the positive sequence.

Lemma 2. *The number of swap steps in bubble sorting from the reverse sequence $(m, m-1, \ldots, 1, 0)$ to the positive sequence $(0, 1, \ldots, m-1, m)$ is $\frac{m(m+1)}{2}$.*

Proof: The inversion table $b_0, b_1, \ldots, b_m$ of the reverse sequence is $m, m-1, m-2, \ldots, 1, 0$, where b_j is the number of elements to the left of j that are greater than j. In each swap step of bubble sort, we adjust a pair of adjacent numbers which reduce one number in the inversion table by 1. Hence in total, we need $\sum_{i=0}^{m} i = \frac{m(m+1)}{2}$ swap steps from the reverse sequence to the positive sequence. $\qquad\square$

From Lemma 1 and Lemma 2, we can get $\frac{m(m+1)}{2}+1$ basis matrices by running bubble sort algorithm, which are strictly increasing w.r.t. decoded gray-levels. Combining with Theorem 1, we have the following theorem:

Theorem 2. *Considering* $S = \binom{T}{perm(T)}$, *where* $T = \{0, \frac{1}{m}, \ldots, \frac{m-1}{m}, 1\}$ *and* $perm(T)$ *denotes all possible permutations of* T, *the number of all possible decoded gray-levels of* S *must be an integer in the interval from* $\frac{m(m+1)}{2}+1$ *to* $\frac{m(m+1)(m+2)}{6}+1$.

Before using a GVCS with t gray-levels to encode images, an affine transform is needed to map all possible gray-levels in the secret image into numbers $1, \ldots, t$. Then basis matrix S_i is used to encode pixels of gray-levels mapped to number i. A typical technique is by dividing all possible gray-levels in the secret image into t equal parts. For example, for (2,2)-GVCS with 11 gray-levels, all possible gray-levels in the secret image, say $0 - 255$ can be divided into 11 almost equal parts: gray-levels $23 \times (i-1)$ to $23 \times i - 1$ are encoded by S_i, where $i = 1, 2, \ldots, 11$.

To give more intuitive ideas about (2,2)-GVCS, we give the following example to illustrate the difference between the proposed scheme and previous schemes.

Example 1. The following eleven basis matrices define a (2,2)-GVCS with 11 gray-levels.

$$S_1 = \begin{bmatrix} 0 & \frac{1}{3} & \frac{2}{3} & 1 \\ 1 & \frac{2}{3} & \frac{1}{3} & 0 \end{bmatrix} \text{ and } S_2 = \begin{bmatrix} 0 & \frac{1}{3} & \frac{2}{3} & 1 \\ 1 & \frac{1}{3} & \frac{2}{3} & 0 \end{bmatrix} \text{ and } S_3 = \begin{bmatrix} 0 & \frac{1}{3} & \frac{2}{3} & 1 \\ \frac{2}{3} & 1 & 0 & \frac{1}{3} \end{bmatrix} \text{ and } S_4 = \begin{bmatrix} 0 & \frac{1}{3} & \frac{2}{3} & 1 \\ \frac{2}{3} & \frac{1}{3} & 1 & 0 \end{bmatrix}$$

$$S_5 = \begin{bmatrix} 0 & \frac{1}{3} & \frac{2}{3} & 1 \\ 1 & \frac{2}{3} & \frac{1}{3} & 0 \end{bmatrix} \text{ and } S_6 = \begin{bmatrix} 0 & \frac{1}{3} & \frac{2}{3} & 1 \\ \frac{2}{3} & 0 & 1 & \frac{1}{3} \end{bmatrix} \text{ and } S_7 = \begin{bmatrix} 0 & \frac{1}{3} & \frac{2}{3} & 1 \\ \frac{2}{3} & \frac{1}{3} & 0 & 1 \end{bmatrix} \text{ and } S_8 = \begin{bmatrix} 0 & \frac{1}{3} & \frac{2}{3} & 1 \\ 0 & \frac{2}{3} & 1 & \frac{1}{3} \end{bmatrix}$$

$$S_9 = \begin{bmatrix} 0 & \frac{1}{3} & \frac{2}{3} & 1 \\ \frac{1}{3} & 0 & 1 & \frac{2}{3} \end{bmatrix} \text{ and } S_{10} = \begin{bmatrix} 0 & \frac{1}{3} & \frac{2}{3} & 1 \\ 0 & \frac{2}{3} & \frac{1}{3} & 1 \end{bmatrix} \text{ and } S_{11} = \begin{bmatrix} 0 & \frac{1}{3} & \frac{2}{3} & 1 \\ 0 & \frac{1}{3} & \frac{2}{3} & 1 \end{bmatrix}$$

The total LRTs of the stacking results of S_i ($1 \le i \le 11$) are $\frac{4}{9}, \frac{5}{9}, \frac{6}{9}, \frac{7}{9}, \frac{8}{9}, \frac{9}{9}, \frac{10}{9}, \frac{11}{9}, \frac{12}{9}, \frac{13}{9}$ and $\frac{14}{9}$ respectively.

NaorShamir's scheme with pixel expansion 4 is constituted by the following matrices:

$$S_0^{NS} = \begin{bmatrix} 0011 \\ 0011 \end{bmatrix} \text{ and } S_1^{NS} = \begin{bmatrix} 0011 \\ 1100 \end{bmatrix}$$

NakajimaYamaguchi's scheme with pixel expansion 4 is constituted by the following matrices:

$$S_1^{NY} = \begin{bmatrix} 0011 \\ 0011 \end{bmatrix} \text{ and } S_2^{NY} = \begin{bmatrix} 0011 \\ 0101 \end{bmatrix} \text{ and } S_3^{NY} = \begin{bmatrix} 0011 \\ 1100 \end{bmatrix}$$

In summary, we have Table 1, from which we can see that our method significantly increase the number of decoded gray-levels compared to previous method. In Table 1, PE represents the pixel expansion and $N_{PE=m}$ represents the number of decoded gray-levels with pixel expansion m.

Table 1. The number of decoded gray-levels for different schemes and different pixel expansions

Schemes	$N_{PE=3}$	$N_{PE=4}$	$N_{PE=m+1}$
NaorShamir [14]	2	2	2
NakajimaYamaguchi [13]	2	3	$\approx \frac{m+1}{2} + 1$
This paper	4	11	$\geq \frac{m(m+1)}{2} + 1$

3   Visual Voting

In this section, we propose a visual voting scheme that suits for situations where there are two candidates and odd number of voters in total and no one abstains from voting. The voting result can be seen by simply stacking all submitted shadow images without needing to count the number of votes. Besides, the proposed scheme guarantees anonymity that after the election, each voter's vote is only known to himself and others should have no idea about it.

Now we turn to the technical part. In overall, the proposed visual voting scheme is based on visual cryptography. Suppose the voting scheme contains $2n+1$ voters and two candidates, then a visual voting scheme can be realized by an $(n+1, 2n+1)$-VCS. Let the pixel expansion of the given $(n+1, 2n+1)$-VCS be m. The vote is just a shadow image with pixel expansion $2m$. Suppose all votes are denoted as $V_1^A, V_2^A, \ldots, V_{2n+1}^A$ and $V_1^B, V_2^B, \ldots, V_{2n+1}^B$, where V_i^A and V_i^B are handed to voter i and the voter i will submit vote V_i^A if he supports candidate A and will submit vote V_i^B if he supports candidate B. All votes are noise-like shadow images and cannot be distinguished, which guarantees voters' anonymity. On the other hand, we must allow voter i to distinguish between V_i^A and V_i^B, so that he can submit his vote properly according to his mind. We can achieve this aim by first distributing the voting image for A and then distributing the voting image for B. During the voting process, all voters must make a choice between the two candidates and submit their votes and and no one can abstain from voting. After collecting all parties' submitted votes, we need to align them carefully to get the voting result. We can combine the proposed voting scheme with some shift tolerant techniques [12,16] to make it more convenient to get the voting result. After the voting result is declared, the remaining votes should be collected and destroyed. As transparencies and printers are easy to obtain and the voting images can be generated in advance, the proposed scheme is convenient to use.

Informally, the voting images are generated as follows: we first write the two candidates' names on two images with equal size, say images A and B. As A and B are just binary textual images, we can use the extensively studied binary VCS [14,1,4,6,2,3,15] as building block. Let the pixel expansion of the given $(n+1, 2n+1)$-VCS be m, having basis matrices M_0 and M_1 for encoding white and black pixels respectively. From the $2m$ positions in a block, we first randomly choose m of them as region 1, and the remaining m positions are denoted as region 2. For the j-th block of the voting images V_i^A ($i = 1, 2, \ldots, 2n+1$), region

1 is encoded with M_0 (resp. M_1) if the j-th pixel of image A is white (resp. black), and region 2 is filled with white pixels. For the j-th block of the voting images V_i^B $(i = 1, 2, \ldots, 2n + 1)$, region 1 is filled with white pixels and region 2 is encoded with M_0 (resp. M_1) if the j-th pixel of image B is white (resp. black). Repeat the above process until all blocks on voting images have been filled. To get an intuitive idea of the above process, one can see Fig.1.

Formally, the voting images' generation process can be stated as follows.

Construction 1. *Suppose images A and B both have q pixels, in which each pixel corresponds to a block of $2m$ pixels on the voting image.*

Input: *two secret images, say A and B.*
Output: *$2n + 1$ voting images $V_1^A, V_2^A, \ldots, V_{2n+1}^A$ for A and $2n + 1$ voting images $V_1^B, V_2^B, \ldots, V_{2n+1}^B$ for B.*
Step 0.   *Generate $4n + 2$ blank images, each having $2qm$ pixels. The images are denoted as $V_1^A, V_2^A, \ldots, V_{2n+1}^A$ and $V_1^B, V_2^B, \ldots, V_{2n+1}^B$.*
Step 1.   *For $j = 0$ to $q - 1$ do the following:*
Step 2. *Randomly choose m numbers from $\{1, 2, \ldots, 2m\}$ as set R1, and the remaining m numbers constitute set R2.*
Step 3.   *If $A[j]$ and $B[j]$ are both white pixels*
Step 4.   *For the j-th block of the voting images V_i^A $(i = 1, 2, \ldots, 2n + 1)$, we encode positions R1 with permuted M_0 and fill positions R2 with white pixels. For the j-th block of the voting images V_i^B $(i = 1, 2, \ldots, 2n + 1)$, we encode positions R2 with permuted M_0 and fill positions R1 with white pixels.*
Step 5.   *Else if $A[j]$ is a white pixel and $B[j]$ is a black pixel*
Step 6.   *For the j-th block of the voting images V_i^A $(i = 1, 2, \ldots, 2n + 1)$, we encode positions R1 with permuted M_0 and fill positions R2 with white pixels. For the j-th block of the voting images V_i^B $(i = 1, 2, \ldots, 2n + 1)$, we encode positions R2 with permuted M_1 and fill positions R1 with white pixels.*
Step 7.   *Else if $A[j]$ is a black pixel and $B[j]$ is a white pixel*
Step 8.   *For the j-th block of the voting images V_i^A $(i = 1, 2, \ldots, 2n + 1)$, we encode positions R1 with permuted M_1 and fill positions R2 with white pixels. For the j-th block of the voting images V_i^B $(i = 1, 2, \ldots, 2n + 1)$, we encode positions R2 with permuted M_0 and fill positions R1 with white pixels.*
Step 9.   *Else if $A[j]$ and $B[j]$ are both black pixels*
Step 10.   *For the j-th block of the voting images V_i^A $(i = 1, 2, \ldots, 2n + 1)$, we encode positions R1 with permuted M_1 and fill positions R2 with white pixels. For the j-th block of the voting images V_i^B $(i = 1, 2, \ldots, 2n + 1)$, we encode positions R2 with permuted M_1 and fill positions R1 with white pixels.*
Step 11.   *End if*

To give an intuitive idea of the proposed voting scheme, we give the following example.

Example 2. The voting scheme contains two candidates, say *Alice* and *Bob*, and three voters, say $P1$, $P2$ and $P3$. We first write each candidate's name on an image. Image A contains *Alice*'s name and image B contains *Bob*'s name. We use the (2,3)-VCS for binary images as a building block. The (2,3)-VCS is defined by the following two Boolean basis matrices, where $M0$ is used to encode a white pixel and $M1$ is used to encode a black pixel.

$$M0 = \begin{bmatrix} 100 \\ 100 \\ 100 \end{bmatrix}, M1 = \begin{bmatrix} 100 \\ 010 \\ 001 \end{bmatrix}.$$

The encoding process of the i-th pixel of images A and B can be seen in Fig. 1.

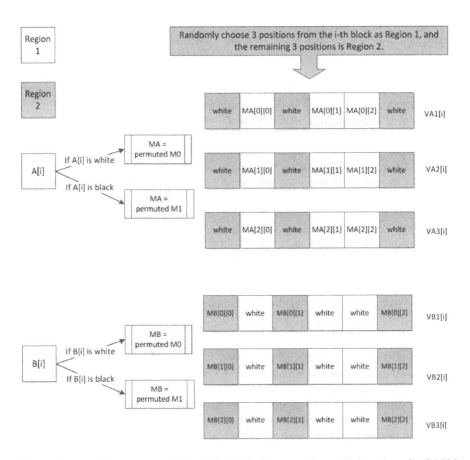

Fig. 1. The encoding process of the i-th pixel of images A and B based on (2,3)-VCS

After all pixels of images A and B have been encoded, we get the voting images: $VA1, VA2, VA3, VB1, VB2$ and $VB3$, in which $VA1$, $VA2$ and $VA3$ (resp. $VB1$, $VB2$ and $VB3$) are the votes for candidate A (resp. B). We first distribute the voting images for A and then distribute the voting images for B, enabling each party himself can distinguish between his vote for A and his vote for B. Then the parties submit their votes for their supporting candidate according to their mind. The election result can be seen by stacking the submitted votes. After the declaration of the election result, the remaining votes hold by parties are taken back and all votes are destroyed.

Theorem 3. *Given an* $(n+1, 2n+1)$*-VCS with pixel expansion* m*, Construction 1 implements a visual voting scheme with pixel expansion* $2m$*.*

Proof: Each block on voting images is divided into two non-overlapping regions of equal size m. One region is for the encoded pixels of image A and the other region is for the encoded pixels of image B. As there are exactly $2n+1$ submitted voting images, from the pigeonhole principle, it is easy to know that there are at least $n+1$ voting images for some candidate, and the other candidate must have less than or equal to n voting images. Assume without loss of generality that candidate A has at least $n+1$ voting images and candidate B has less than or equal to n voting images. From the contrast condition of $(n+1, 2n+1)$-VCS, we know that regions that have encoded pixels of image A can reveal the name of candidate A. From the security condition of $(n+1, 2n+1)$-VCS, we know that regions that have encoded pixels of image B are even and provide no trace of the name of candidate B. In overall, we can see the name of candidate A. Furthermore, from the security condition of $(n+1, 2n+1)$-VCS, we know that for any $1 \leq i \leq 2n+1$, the i-th row of M_0 and the i-th row of M_1 have the same number of black pixels, which are uniformly distributed in every block of voting images hold by voter i that guarantees anonymous of voters. □

Although the proposed visual voting scheme is only suitable for situations, where there are two candidates and odd number of voters in total, and no one abstains from voting, it has the following special advantages:

1. Each voting image is noise-like, which guarantees anonymous of voters.
2. The election result can be seen by stacking the votes, without any counting process.

4   Conclusion

This paper contains two parts: 1, we provide an efficient solution for (2,2)-GVCS with much more gray-levels than previous (2,2)-VCSs. 2, we propose a visual voting scheme that suits for situations where there are two candidates and odd number of voters in total and no one abstains from voting. The proposed visual voting scheme has the "stacking to see" property and guarantees anonymous of voters.

Our work suggests several interesting directions for future research. First, the number of gray-levels for the proposed (2,2)-GVCS with pixel expansion m is proved to be between $\frac{m(m+1)}{2}+1$ and $\frac{m(m+1)(m+2)}{6}+1$ in this paper. One further study is how to close this gap or determine the exact number of gray-levels for the proposed (2,2)-GVCS with pixel expansion m. Second, as we only provide efficient solutions for (2,2)-GVCS, another further study is how to extend the idea to more general access structures, like (k, k) or (k, n) access structure. Third, proposing new visual voting schemes that relax any constrain of the proposed visual voting scheme is a nice work.

Acknowledgements. This work was supported by NSFC grant No. 60903210, the "Strategic Priority Research Program" of the Chinese Academy of Sciences No. XDA06010701 and the IIE Cryptography Research Project No. Y2Z0011102.

References

1. Ateniese, G., Blundo, C., De Santis, A., Stinson, D.R.: Visual cryptography for general access structures. Information and Computation 129, 86–106 (1996)
2. Blundo, C., De Bonis, A., De Santis, A.: Improved schemes for visual cryptography. Designs, Codes and Cryptography 24, 255–278 (2001)
3. Blundo, C., Cimato, S., De Santis, A.: Visual cryptography schemes with optimal pixel expansion. Theoretical Computer Science 369, 169–182 (2006)
4. Blundo, C., De Santis, A., Stinson, D.R.: On the contrast in visual cryptography schemes. Journal of Cryptology 12(4), 261–289 (1999)
5. Cimato, S., De Prisco, R., De Santis, A.: Colored visual cryptography without color darkening. Theoretical Computer Science 374, 261–276 (2007)
6. Hofmeister, T., Krause, M., Simon, H.U.: Contrast-optimal k out of n secret sharing schemes in visual cryptography. Theoretical Computer Science 240(2), 471–485 (2000)
7. Hou, Y.C.: Visual cryptography for color images. Pattern Recognition 1773, 1–11 (2003)
8. Kang, I.K., Arce, G.R., Lee, H.K.: Color extended visual cryptography using error diffusion. IEEE Transactions on Image Processing 20(1), 132–145 (2011)
9. Knuth, D.E.: The Art of Computer Programming. Sorting and Searching, vol. 3. Addison-Wesley (1998)
10. Liu, F., Wu, C.K.: Embedded extended visual cryptography schemes. IEEE Transactions on Information Forensics & Security 6(2), 307–322 (2011)
11. Liu, F., Wu, C.K., Lin, X.J.: Colour visual cryptography schemes. IET Information Security 2, 151–165 (2008)
12. Liu, F., Wu, C.K., Lin, X.J.: The alignment problem of visual cryptography schemes. Designs, Codes and Cryptography 50, 215–227 (2009)
13. Nakajima, M., Yamaguchi, Y.: Extended visual cryptography for natural images. In: WSCG Conference 2002, pp. 303–412 (2002)
14. Naor, M., Shamir, A.: Visual cryptography. In: De Santis, A. (ed.) EUROCRYPT 1994. LNCS, vol. 950, pp. 1–12. Springer, Heidelberg (1995)
15. Shyu, S.J., Chen, M.C.: Optimum pixel expansions for threshold visual secret sharing schemes. IEEE Transactions on Information Forensics and Security 6(3), 960–969 (2011)

16. Wang, D.S., Dong, L., Li, X.B.: Towards shift tolerant visual secret sharing schemes. IEEE Transactions on Information Forensics and Security 6(2), 323–337 (2011)
17. Wang, Z.M., Arce, G.R., Di Crescenzo, G.: Halftone visual cryptography via error diffusion. IEEE Transactions on Information Forensics and Security 4(3), 383–396 (2009)
18. Zhou, Z., Arce, G.R., Di Crescenzo, G.: Halftone visual cryptography. IEEE Transactions on Image Processing 15(8), 2441–2453 (2006)

RCCA Security
for KEM+DEM Style Hybrid Encryptions

Yuan Chen and Qingkuan Dong

State Key Laboratory of Integrated Service Networks (ISN),
Xidian University, Xi'an 710071, P.R. China
yuanchen@xidian.edu.cn, qkdong@mail.xidian.edu.cn

Abstract. RCCA security is a weaker notion than CCA security, and has been proven to be sufficient for several cryptographic tasks. This paper adapts RCCA security to the most popular hybrid paradigms, KEM+DEM and Tag-KEM/DEM.

It is open to construct an RCCA-secure scheme more efficient than CCA-secure ones. In the setting of Tag-KEM, we solve this by presenting a natural RCCA-secure RSA-based Tag-KEM scheme, named as RSA-TKEM, which is more efficient than all existing methods for constructing a CCA-secure RSA-based Tag-KEM scheme.

Unfortunately, combining our RSA-TKEM with passive secure one-time pad following Tag-KEM/DEM paradigm yields an RCCA-insecure hybrid encryption. This shows passive security of DEM is not sufficient now, and Tag-KEM/DEM looses its advantage over KEM+DEM. In spite of this and for completeness, we show RCCA secure DEMs are still sufficient to achieve RCCA-secure hybrid encryptions by following Tag-KEM/DEM.

In addition, we show RCCA-secure KEM is sufficient for achieving CCA-secure hybrid encryptions. This is done by introducing a new hybrid paradigm, named as KEM/Tag-DEM, where the ciphertext of KEM is used as a tag for Tag-DEM scheme rather than reversely in Tag-KEM/DEM, so that the security of KEM can be weakened to RCCA one. Tag-DEMs can be constructed as efficiently as DEMs, so RCCA-secure KEMs more efficient than CCA-secure ones become more appealing.

1 Introduction

The notion of Replayable CCA (RCCA) security for Public-Key Encryption (PKE) is introduced in [10]. It is a weakened variant of CCA security where the decryption oracle answers 'test' whenever it is asked to decrypt any ciphertext that decrypts to either of the questioned messages m_0 or m_1, even if this ciphertext is different from the challenge ciphertext. Accordingly, even if the adversary can tweak the challenge ciphertext without affecting the embedded plaintext (such a feature is called benign-malleability in [20]), sending it to the decryption oracle does not help the adversary determine which of the questioned messages is hidden.

M. Kutyłowski and M. Yung (Eds.): Inscrypt 2012, LNCS 7763, pp. 102–121, 2013.

RCCA-security is proven to be sufficient for several cryptographic tasks in [10] and is believed to be sufficient for all the uses of CCA-secure encryptions in [5,20]. It also makes it possible to consider secure rerandomizable encryptions [13,17]. We can hope that a weaker definition might give rise to more efficient constructions but this has so far not been the case. There is no known instance of RCCA-secure public-key encryption that is more efficient than known CCA-secure ones as so far.

For hybrid encryptions, RCCA security was first considered in [10]. [10] shows the natural combination of an RCCA-secure PKE and an RCCA-secure Symmetric-Key Encryption (SKE) is RCCA-secure as a PKE, which is consistent with the well known CCA case. Furthermore, an RCCA-secure PKE can be made CCA-secure if combined with a CCA-secure SKE in such a way that the ciphertext of the PKE is also input to the SKE encryption. This shows the sufficiency of RCCA security of PKE for achieving CCA-secure hybrid encryptions. The two hybrid schemes named as HE1 and HE2 are shown in Table 1.

However, the work in [10] only relates to limited hybrid frameworks consisting of PKE and SKE. There are more efficient and general paradigms to realize hybrid encryptions, such as KEM+DEM [11] and Tag-KEM/DEM [3].

Table 1. RCCA-security related hybrid encryptions of PKE and SKE in [10]

	PKE	SKE	Security
HE1	Input K Output $\psi =$ $PKE.Enc_{pk}(K)$	Input M Output $\chi=$ $SKE.Enc_K(M)$	IND-RCCA+IND-RCCA $\Rightarrow$ IND-RCCA
HE2	Input K Output $\psi=$ $PKE.Enc_{pk}(K)$	Input (M, ψ) Output $\chi=$ $SKE.Enc_K(\psi\|M)$	IND-RCCA+IND-CCA $\Rightarrow$ IND-CCA

KEM uses asymmetric techniques to encrypt a symmetric key, while DEM uses a symmetric cipher to encrypt the message using the key from the KEM. KEM can be built more efficiently than PKE, and DEM can be a one-time SKE, these make KEM+DEM paradigm more efficient.

For some security reasons and to capture wider variety, Masayuki Abe, et al introduced Tag-KEM/DEM framework ([3], [2], [4]). A Tag-KEM scheme takes also a *tag* as its input. The novelty of Tag-KEM/DEM lies in using the ciphertext of DEM part as the tag input to Tag-KEM. This binding way of ciphertexts makes it possible to yield CCA-secure hybrid encryptions by a DEM scheme secure simply against a passive attacker (we shortened this security for DEM as one-time security). This weakening may be the most prominent advantage of Tag-KEM/DEM.

This paper adapts RCCA security to those more general hybrid paradigms and consider whether or not similar desired properties hold as for hybrid encryptions of PKE and SKE.

1.1 Our Contributions

We first consider RCCA security for KEM+DEM paradigm. Adapting the notion of RCCA security to KEM is also done in [3] for a different purpose. It is believed in [20] that if KEM and DEM are benign malleable, then so is the hybrid encryption. We substitutes more general RCCA-security for benign malleability. That is, IND-RCCA+IND-RCCA⇒IND-RCCA. This consists with the CCA situation, as desired.

We also adapt RCCA security to Tag-KEM/DEM, but find some different status. Firstly, a natural and efficient RCCA-secure Tag-KEM construction is possible. We present such an RSA-based one in Section 3, named as RSA-TKEM. The security is proved in the random oracle model [8]. RSA-TKEM is almost as efficient as the well known RSA-KEM in [20] with only one more hash and an XOR operation. Particularly, the scheme has no ciphertext redundancy, thus no validity check of ciphertext or tag part. This is different from all existing CCA-secure schemes as much as we know of and makes the scheme more efficient. We give a short comparison with those most efficient CCA-secure RSA-based Tag-KEMs in Table 2, where f denotes the RSA permutation, MAC is a message authentication code, H is a hash function, the final ciphertext is ψ, and $|\cdot|$ denotes the length. It can be seen from the table that our RSA-TKEM has least ciphertext expansion.

Table 2. A comparison with existing efficient CCA-secure RSA-based Tag-KEMs

Schemes	In [1]	In [3] Section 4.2	In [3] Section 5.3	RSA-TKEM
Description of encapsulation	$x = r\|H(r,\tau)$ $\psi = f(x)$	$\sigma = MAC(\tau)$ $\psi = f(r)\|\sigma$	$\sigma = H(r\|\tau)$ $\psi = f(r)\|\sigma$	$s = f(r)$ $\psi = f(r) \oplus H(\tau)$
Ciphertext length	$|r| + |H(r,\tau)|$	$|r| + |MAC(\tau)|$	$|r| + |H(r,\tau)|$	$|r|$
Security	IND-CCA	IND-CCA	IND-CCA	IND-RCCA

For Tag-KEM/DEM, one may hope IND-RCCA+One-time security⇒IND-RCCA. Unfortunately, this is not the case. Combining the above RSA-TKEM and passive secure one-time pad yields a counterexample. An adversary when receives the challenge ciphertext (ψ^*, χ^*) can randomly choose a χ', compute $H(\chi')$ and $H(\chi^*)$, then query $(\psi = \psi^* \oplus H(\chi^*) \oplus H(\chi'), \chi')$ to its decryption oracle. Let the answer be m', with all but negligible probability, $m' \neq$ 'test'. The adversary can then obtain the K underlying (ψ^*, χ^*) by computing $K = \chi' \oplus m'$.

In fact, passive security for DEM is not sufficient now. Note that if in an RCCA-secure Tag-KEM, an adversary can only tweak (ψ^*, τ^*) to (ψ, τ) with $\tau = \tau^*$ and without affecting the encapsulated key, then passive security for DEM is sufficient. However, this is not the case, generally. Furthermore, we can prove RCCA security for DEM will be sufficient generally. The proof is given in Section 4.2. But this time Tag-KEM/DEM looses its advantage over KEM+DEM. It is interesting to notice that a little weakening of security requirement of Tag-KEM results in a total insecurity. This somewhat explains the gap between KEM+DEM and Tag-KEM/DEM paradigms.

Finally, we prove RCCA-security for KEM is sufficient for hybrid encryption as desired. To do this, we generalize HE2 in Table 1 to a new hybrid paradigm named as KEM/Tag-DEM. KEM/Tag-DEM uses a similar idea behind Tag-KEM/DEM, but rather than use the ciphertext of DEM as a tag for Tag-KEM, we use the ciphertext of KEM as a tag for Tag-DEM. Since in Tag-KEM/DEM the binding way of ciphertexts makes it possible for the CCA-security of Tag-KEM to provide integrity to the tag, the ciphertext of DEM there, so can it in our paradigm for the CCA security of Tag-DEM to compensate the malleability of KEM. This makes it possible to achieve CCA-security by RCCA-secure KEM and CCA-secure Tag-DEM. The formal treatment and possible constructions are shown in Section 5.

The CCA-security of KEM/Tag-DEM and the RCCA one of KEM+DEM actually show that RCCA-secure KEM is sufficient for constructing hybrid encryption, just as we desired: for RCCA-security, follow KEM+DEM; for CCA-security, follow KEM/Tag-DEM. We summarize all three hybrid paradigms related security results in Table 3.

Table 3. The three hybrid paradigms and their security

Hybrid paradigm	Security results
KEM+DEM	IND-CCA + IND-CCA $\Rightarrow$ IND-CCA([11])
	IND-RCCA + IND-RCCA $\Rightarrow$ IND-RCCA (by Th2)
Tag-KEM/DEM	IND-CCA + One-time security $\Rightarrow$ IND-CCA([3])
	IND-RCCA + One-time security $\nRightarrow$ IND-RCCA (counterexample)
	IND-RCCA + IND-RCCA $\Rightarrow$ IND-RCCA (by Th3)
KEM/Tag-DEM	IND-RCCA + IND-CCA $\Rightarrow$ IND-CCA (by Th4)

Importance of KEM/Tag-DEM. Compared to Tag-KEM/DEM, one may think KEM/Tag-DEM achieves less improvement. However, CCA-secure DEMs and Tag-DEMs can be easily and efficiently built, while CCA-secure KEMs and Tag-KEMs cost much, weakening the security requirement of KEM to RCCA-security may be beneficial. In most KEMs, the valid ciphertext of a encapsulated key is uniquely determined, this makes it difficult to build efficient and natural RCCA-secure KEM, especially when rerandomizable one is taken into consideration [13]. Nevertheless, as illustrated in [10], a CCA-secure KEM may only achieve RCCA-security in practical protocols when allowing for arbitrary padding to ciphertexts (in order to align the length) or more than one representation of ciphertexts. That time, KEM/Tag-DEM will achieve advantages over KEM+DEM paradigm.

KEM/Tag-DEM shows the diversity of hybrid encryptions and has additional practical values. In practice there are always associated data to DEM [18], thus including the ciphertext of KEM brings no significant difference in efficiency, and may "offload" as much cryptographic work from the slower KEM part onto the faster DEM part. In addition, in Tag-KEM/DEM, a receiver generally need the entire ciphertext to derive the encapsulated key, which makes it extremely unsuitable for streaming processing, while KEM/Tag-DEM suffers no such problem.

1.2 Further Discussions and Related Works

From the above, to achieve RCCA-secure hybrid encryptions, we need RCCA-secure DEMs. In [10], it has been pointed out that RCCA-secure SKE can be given by the "encrypt-then-authenticate" paradigm using a regular secure MAC (but not a strong one, which means given pairs of messages and their mac values, it is not possible to find another valid mac value for any messages), which means given pairs of messages and their mac values, it is not possible to find a valid mac value for any other messages, but may be possible to find a different valid mac value for someone of these messages. RCCA-secure DEM can be given in the same way. Thus, a regular secure but not strong MAC may helps in obtaining an RCCA-secure hybrid encryptions more efficient than CCA-secure ones. However, most MAC schemes are deterministic and the verification is done by re-computation, finding a different valid mac value for the same message is impossible. A randomized or multi-valued MAC is needed. [15] gives some examples, but just conceptual.

In [3], Abe et al. also showed how to obtain a CCA-secure hybrid encryption from an RCCA-secure KEM by making it to be a CCA-secure Tag-KEM. Their method can be explained by our new paradigm in another way. And since in Tag-DEM it is no need to provide privacy but integrity of tag τ, then using the same techniques in constructing deterministic authenticated-encryption in [19] gives more efficient schemes.

There are some other weaker security notions for KEM except RCCA-security, such as CCCA-security in [14] and LCCA-security in [3]. These security notions whose strength depend on the chosen predict are not strictly weaker than CCA-security. Since in RCCA security, a special 'test' is returned when a replay is detected, no direct relation exists between these notions.

2 Preliminaries

2.1 CCA and RCCA Security Notions for PKE

A public-key encryption scheme consists of three algorithms. Probabilistic PKE.Gen that on input the security parameter k, generates public and private-keys (pk, sk), pk defines the message space $\mathcal{M}$. Probabilistic PKE.Enc encrypts a message $m \in \mathcal{M}$ into a ciphertext c. PKE.Dec decrypts c, outputs either $m \in \mathcal{M}$ or a special symbol $\perp \notin \mathcal{M}$. An obvious soundness condition applies.

We say a PKE is IND-CCA secure if for every probablistic polynomial-time oracle machine $\mathcal{A}_E$ plays the following game, its advantage $Adv^{\mathsf{cca}}_{\mathsf{pke}, \mathcal{A}_E}(k) = |Pr[\tilde{b} = b] - \frac{1}{2}|$ is negligible in k.

[GAME.PKE]
Step 1. $(pk, sk) \leftarrow \mathsf{PKE.Gen}(1^k)$
Step 2. $(m_0, m_1, v) \leftarrow \mathcal{A}_E^{\mathcal{O}}(pk)$
Step 3. $b \leftarrow \{0, 1\}$, $c \leftarrow \mathsf{PKE.Enc}_{pk}(m_b)$.
Step 4. $\tilde{b} \leftarrow \mathcal{A}_E^{\mathcal{O}}(v, c)$

By $\mathcal{O}$, we denote $\mathsf{PKE.Dec}_{sk}(\cdot)$. In Step 4, $\mathcal{A}_E$ is restricted not to ask c to $\mathcal{O}$.

IND-RCCA security is defined all the same except that the decryption oracle returns 'test' for any ciphertext decrypts to m_0 or m_1 in step 4. Let [RGAME.PKE] denote the game and $Adv^{\mathsf{rcca}}_{\mathsf{pke},\mathcal{A}_E}(k)$ the advantage.

2.2   KEM+DEM and Related Security Notions

A key encapsulation mechanism (KEM) consists of three algorithms. Probabilistic $\mathsf{KEM.Gen}$ that on input 1^k outputs a public/private key pair (pk, sk), pk defines the key space $\mathcal{K}_K$. Probabilistic encapsulation algorithm $\mathsf{KEM.Enc}$ that on input 1^k and a public key pk, outputs a pair (dk, ψ), where $dk \in \mathcal{K}_K$ is a key and ψ is its ciphertext. Decapsulation algorithm $\mathsf{KEM.Dec}$, on input sk and ψ, outputs either a key $dk \in \mathcal{K}_K$ or the special symbol $\perp$. An obvious soundness condition applies.

IND-CCA security for KEM is defined by the following game.

[GAME.KEM]
Step 1. $(pk, sk) \leftarrow \mathsf{KEM.Gen}(1^k)$
Step 2. $v \leftarrow \mathcal{A}_K^{\mathcal{O}}(pk)$
Step 3. $(dk_1, \psi) \leftarrow \mathsf{KEM.Enc}_{pk}()$, $dk_0 \leftarrow \mathcal{K}_K$, $\delta \leftarrow \{0,1\}$.
Step 4. $\tilde{\delta} \leftarrow \mathcal{A}_K^{\mathcal{O}}(v, \psi, dk_\delta)$
$\mathcal{O}$ denotes $\mathsf{KEM.Dec}_{sk}(\cdot)$. In Step 4, $\mathcal{A}_K$ is restricted not to ask ψ to $\mathcal{O}$.

For IND-RCCA security, all is the same except that the decryption oracle returns 'test' for any ciphertext decrypts to dk_0 or dk_1 in step 4, as done in [3].

A data encapsulation mechanism (DEM) is a one-time symmetric-key encryption, consists of two algorithms. Deterministic $\mathsf{DEM.Enc}$ that takes as input 1^k, a key dk and a message m, outputs a ciphertext χ. Deterministic $\mathsf{DEM.Dec}$ that takes as input a dk and a ciphertext χ, outputs a message m or the special symbol $\perp$. An obvious soundness condition applies.

The one-time security (or passive security) and IND-CCA security of DEM is defined respectively by the following game when $\mathcal{O}$ is null and $\mathsf{DEM.Dec}_{dk}(\cdot)$. In Step 3, $\mathcal{A}_D$ is restricted not to ask χ to $\mathcal{O}$.

[GAME.DEM]
Step 1. $(m_0, m_1, v) \leftarrow \mathcal{A}_D^{\mathcal{O}}(1^k)$
Step 2. $dk \leftarrow \mathcal{K}_D$, $b \leftarrow \{0,1\}$, $\chi \leftarrow \mathsf{DEM.Enc}_{dk}(m_b)$.
Step 3. $\tilde{b} \leftarrow \mathcal{A}_D^{\mathcal{O}}(v, \chi)$

For IND-RCCA security, all is the same except that the decryption oracle returns 'test' for any ciphertext decrypts to m_0 or m_1 in step 3.

KEM+DEM hybrid paradigm works as follows, and [11] shows that if KEM and DEM are IND-CCA secure then the following HPKE is IND-CCA secure (as a public-key encryption).

Function: HPKE.Enc$_{pk}(m)$
$(dk, \psi) \leftarrow$ KEM.Enc$_{pk}()$
$\chi \leftarrow$ DEM.Enc$_{dk}(m)$
Output $c = (\psi, \chi)$

Function: HPKE.Dec$_{sk}(c)$
$(\psi, \chi) \leftarrow c$
$dk \leftarrow$ KEM.Dec$_{sk}(\psi)$
$m \leftarrow$ DEM.Dec$_{dk}(\chi)$
Output m

2.3 Tag-KEM/DEM Hybrid Framework and Related Security Notions

A Tag-KEM scheme consists of the following algorithms. Probabilistic TKEM.Gen generates public/private-key pair (pk, sk), pk defines spaces for tags and encapsulated keys denoted by $\mathcal{T}$ and $\mathcal{K}_K$. Probabilistic TKEM.Key outputs one-time key $dk \in \mathcal{K}_D$ and internal state information ω, $\mathcal{K}_D$ is the key-space of DEM. Probabilistic TKEM.Enc encapsulates dk (embedded in ω) into ψ along with τ. TKEM.Dec recovers dk from ψ and τ. An obvious soundness condition applies.

Let $\mathcal{O}$ be the decapsulation oracle TKEM.Dec$_{sk}(\cdot, \cdot)$, the IND-CCA security of a Tag-KEM is defined by the following game:

[GAME.TKEM]
Step 1. $(pk, sk) \leftarrow$ TKEM.Gen(1^k)
Step 2. $v_1 \leftarrow \mathcal{A}_T^{\mathcal{O}}(pk)$
Step 3. $(\omega, dk_1) \leftarrow$ TKEM.Key(pk), $dk_0 \leftarrow \mathcal{K}_D$, $\delta \leftarrow \{0, 1\}$.
Step 4. $(\tau, v_2) \leftarrow \mathcal{A}_T^{\mathcal{O}}(v_1, dk_\delta)$
Step 5. $\psi \leftarrow$ TKEM.Enc(ω, τ)
Step 6. $\tilde{\delta} \leftarrow \mathcal{A}_T^{\mathcal{O}}(v_2, \psi)$

In Step 6, A_T is restricted not to ask (ψ, τ) to decryption oracle $\mathcal{O}$. IND-RCCA security for Tag-KEM can be derived in the same way as for KEM.

The novel generic construction of Tag-KEM/DEM which uses the ciphertext output by the DEM as the tag is as follows, and [3] shows that if Tag-KEM is CCA secure and DEM is passive secure then the hybrid HPKE scheme is CCA secure.

Function: HPKE.Enc$_{pk}(m)$
$(\omega, dk) \leftarrow$ TKEM.Key(pk)
$\chi \leftarrow$ DEM.Enc$_{dk}(m)$
$\psi \leftarrow$ TKEM.Enc$_{pk}(\omega, \chi)$
Output $c = (\psi, \chi)$

Function: HPKE.Dec$_{sk}(c)$
$(\psi, \chi) \leftarrow c$
$dk \leftarrow$ TKEM.Dec$_{sk}(\psi, \chi)$
$m \leftarrow$ DEM.Dec$_{dk}(\chi)$
Output m

3   The Proposed RCCA-Secure Scheme: RSA-TKEM

Our RSA-TKEM is very simple and has a tight reduction, just like RSA-KEM in [20]. The description is as follows (for simplicity, we assume all elements are expressed as binary strings):

- Gen(1^λ): The same as RSA and also output a hash function H maps a bit string of arbitrary length to appropriate one (allowing the XOR). Let $((n, e), (n, d))$

denotes the public-private key pair (pk, sk). The pk also defines the output key length l.

- Key(pk): Generate a random number $r \in \{0, 1, ..., n - 1\}$, then compute $K = G(r)$, where G is a KDF function (see [11]), it maps elements of $\mathbb{Z}_n$ to bit strings of length l. Output $(K, \omega = r)$.
- Enc$_{pk}(\omega, \tau)$: Compute $s = r^e \mod n$ and $y = s \oplus H(\tau)$. Output y.
- Dec$_{sk}(y, \tau)$: Compute $s = y \oplus H(\tau)$, $r = s^d \mod n$ and $K = G(r)$. Output K.

Note that in the scheme a hash of tag is XORed to s to yield the ciphertext rather than concatenated inside or outside the encryption operation of the underlying one-way function, so that there is no validity check operation in the decryption. In fact, a ciphertext-tag pair with different τ (except for collision) but same y will result in a different decryption, which ensures the security[1].

3.1   Security

The security of RSA-TKEM can be analyzed in the random oracle model when G is modeled as a random oracle. The formal theorem states as follows:

Theorem 1. *RSA-TKEM is IND-RCCA secure assuming the hardness of RSA problem. Particularly,*

$$Adv^{rcca}_{tkem, \mathcal{A}} \leq \varepsilon_{rsa, \mathcal{B}} + q_D \cdot \varepsilon_{ch} + \frac{q_D}{nBound}. \tag{1}$$

where

- ε_{ch} *is the advantage of finding a collision of H;*
- q_D *is a bound on the number of decryption oracle queries made by $\mathcal{A}$;*
- $nBound$ *is an lower bound on n;*
- $\mathcal{B}$ *is an algorithm for solving a random instance of the RSA problem, $\varepsilon_{rsa, \mathcal{B}}$ is the success probability. $\mathcal{B}$ runs in time roughly the same as that of $\mathcal{A}$; more precisely, the running time is that of $\mathcal{A}$, plus the time to perform q_G exponentiations modulo n, where q_G is a bound on the number of random oracle queries made by $\mathcal{A}$, and the time to perform q_D hash and XOR operations, Where q_D is a bound on the number of decryption oracle queries.*

PROOF. The proof is quite similar to that of RSA-KEM in [20], and follows the common game-modifying method. On the way of modifying the game, we use the following lemma.

Lemma 1. *(Shoup's Lemma [11]) Let P, Q, and F be events defined on some probability space, such that $\Pr[P \wedge \neg F] = \Pr[Q \wedge \neg F]$, then $|\Pr[P] - \Pr[Q]| \leq \Pr[F]$.*

---

[1] RSA-TKEM achieves publicly-detectable RCCA security [10]. Although weaker private-detectable or rerandomizable [13,17] ones are more desired, the scheme is sufficient for our purpose.

Let G_0 be the original attack game RGAME.TKEM played by adversary $\mathcal{A}$, and let S_0 be the event that $\mathcal{A}$ correctly guesses the hidden bit b in game G_0, and S_i be the same event in the following games. Let (y^*, τ^*) denote the target ciphertext-tag pair, and let $r^* = (y^* \oplus H(\tau^*))^{1/e} \in \mathbb{Z}_n$.

We next define a game G_1 that is the same as game G_0, except that if a ciphertext-tag pair (y, τ) with $y \oplus H(\tau) = y^* \oplus H(\tau^*) = s^*$ was submitted to the decryption oracle prior to the invocation of the encryption oracle, then the game is halted. Let F_1 be the event that game G_1 is halted as above. Since $y \oplus H(\tau)$ has the same length as n, and a smarter $\mathcal{A}$ can always choose (y, τ) satisfying $y \oplus H(\tau)$ in $\mathbb{Z}_n$, so $\Pr[F_1] \leq q_D/n \leq q_D/nBound$, and since games G_0 and G_1 proceed identically until F_1 occurs, it follows by Lemma 1 that $|\Pr[S_0] - \Pr[S_1]| \leq q_D/nBound$.

We then define a game G_2 that is the same as G_1, except that if a ciphertext (y^*, τ) with $H(\tau) = H(\tau^*)$ was queried by the adversary $\mathcal{A}$ after the invocation of the encryption oracle, we halt the game. Let F_2 be the event that game G_2 is halted as above. Since τ^* is chosen by $\mathcal{A}$ itself, if $\mathcal{A}$ can find a collision (τ_1, τ_2) for H then it can use one of them as τ^*. So, $\Pr[F_2] \leq \varepsilon_{ch}$, and since games G_1 and G_2 proceed identically until F_2 occurs, it follows that $|\Pr[S_1] - \Pr[S_2]| \leq \varepsilon_{ch}$.

Finally, we define a game G_3 that is the same as G_2, except that if (1)the target ciphertext is generated by an independent and randomly choosen s^*, and $y^* = s^* \oplus H(\tau^*)$ and (2) the adversary ever queries G at r^*, then we halt the game.

It is clear by construction that $\Pr[S_3] = 1/2$, since the key $G(r^*)$ is independent of everything else that is accessible to the adversary in game G_3, either directly or indirectly. Indeed, only the encryption oracle evaluates G at r^* in this game.

Let F_3 be the event that game G_3 is halted as above. It is clear that both games G_2 and G_3 proceed identically until F_3 occurs, and so we have $|\Pr[S_2] - \Pr[S_3]| \leq \Pr[F_3]$.

We claim that $\Pr[F_3] \leq \varepsilon_{rsa,\mathcal{B}}$ for an RSA inversion adversary $\mathcal{B}$ whose runtime is bounded as described in the theorem. $\mathcal{B}$ takes as input a random RSA modulus n, an RSA exponent e, and a random element $s^* \in \mathbf{Z}_n$. It creates a public key using n and e, and then lets adversary $\mathcal{A}$ run in game G_3. When $\mathcal{A}$ chooses a tag τ^* and then invokes the encryption oracle, $\mathcal{B}$ responds to $\mathcal{A}$ with $s^* \oplus H(\tau^*)$, where s^* is the above-mentioned input to $\mathcal{B}$.

$\mathcal{B}$ simulates the random oracle G as well as the decryption oracle by maintaining two lists: G&D-list and D-list. The lists are initially empty and have entries of the form (r, g, s) and (s, g) respectively, where $s = r^e$.

$\mathcal{B}$ answers $\mathcal{A}$'s random oracle queries to G and decryption oracle queries as follows:

Simulation for G queries
If $r \in$ G&D-list then return the corresponding g
Else compute $s = r^e$
    If $s \in$ D-list then return the corresponding g, add (r, g, s) in G&D-list
    Else choose a random $g \in \mathcal{K}_D$, add (r, g, s) in G&D-list, return g.

Simulation for Decryption queries
Compute $s = y \oplus H(\tau)$
If $s = s^*$ then return 'test'
Else
 If $s \in$ G&D-list or $s \in$ D-list then return the corresponding g
 Else choose a random $g \in \mathcal{K}_D$, add (s, g) in D-list, return g.

$\mathcal{B}$ perfectly simulates the view of $\mathcal{A}$, and that $\mathcal{B}$ outputs a solution to the given instance of the RSA problem with probability equal to $\Pr[F_3]$.

 Collecting the probabilities, (1) follows immediately, that proves the theorem.   □

4 Considering RCCA Security for the Hybrid Paradigms

In this section we discuss the security results for achieving RCCA secure hybrid encryptions from the well known paradigm, KEM+DEM and Tag-KEM/DEM.

4.1 Obtaining RCCA-Security for KEM+DEM

For KEM+DEM paradigm, similar result holds when considering both CCA security and RCCA one (benign malleability). That is, if KEM and DEM are benignly malleable then KEM+DEM paradigm is also benignly malleable [20]. The proof is quite the same as that for HE1 in [10], we omit it here.

Theorem 2. *If both KEM and DEM are IND-RCCA secure then the Hybrid PKE scheme following KEM+DEM paradigm is IND-RCCA secure (as a public-key encryption scheme).*

4.2 Obtaining RCCA-Security for Tag-KEM/DEM

However, when we consider RCCA security for Tag-KEM/DEM, things will be different. Although RCCA-secure Tag-KEMs seem simple to be constructed, they cannot be used to obtain RCCA-secure hybrid encryptions when combined with just passive secure DEMs. Take the proposed RSA-TKEM as the RCCA-secure Tag-KEM and one-time pad as the passive secure DEM, this is easily to be seen. For the hybrid encryption to be RCCA-secure, CCA security, or rigorously, RCCA security for DEM should be asked again.

Theorem 3. *If both Tag-KEM and DEM are IND-RCCA secure then the hybrid scheme in Section 2.3 is IND-RCCA secure(as a PKE). In particular, for every $\mathcal{H}$, there exist $\mathcal{A}_T$ and $\mathcal{A}_D$ with*

$$Adv^{rcca}_{pke,\mathcal{H}}(k) \leq 2Adv^{rcca}_{tkem,\mathcal{A}_T}(k) + Adv^{rcca}_{dem,\mathcal{A}_D}(k) + \frac{q_D}{|\mathcal{K}_K|}. \tag{2}$$

where q_D is a bound on the number of decryption oracle queries made by an IND-RCCA attacker against HPKE, and l is the length of the key used in DEM.

The proof for Theorem 3 can be shown in a similar way as done for CCA secure Tag-KEM and passive secure DEM in [3], except that the adversary $\mathcal{A}_D$ against DEM must use its own decryption oracle to answer a query (ψ, χ) from the adversary $\mathcal{H}$ against HPKE when $\mathsf{TKEM.Dec}_{sk}(\psi, \chi) = \mathsf{TKEM.Dec}_{sk}(\psi^*, \chi^*)$. That is why CCA security for DEM is needed here.

PROOF. Let $\mathcal{H}$ be an adversary playing RGAME.PKE. We modify the game by using a random key dk^+ in place of the legitimate one generated by TKEM.Key in both the encryption and decryption oracle. Call this game RGAME.PKE'. Let T and T' be events that $\tilde{b} = b$ in RGAME.PKE and RGAME.PKE', respectively. Then we claim that $|\Pr[T] - \Pr[T']| \leq 2Adv^{rcca}_{\mathsf{tkem}}(k) + \frac{q_D}{|\mathcal{K}_K|}$, which is shown by constructing $\mathcal{A}_T$ that attacks the underlying TKEM scheme by using $\mathcal{H}$.

First $\mathcal{A}_T$ is given public-key pk and passes it to $\mathcal{H}$. Given m_0 and m_1 from $\mathcal{H}$, $\mathcal{A}_T$ requests the encryption oracle of RGAME.TKEM to obtain (dk_δ, ψ^*). $\mathcal{A}_T$ then selects $b \in \{0, 1\}$ and computes $\chi^* = \mathsf{DEM.Enc}_{dk_\delta}(m_b)$, and sends (ψ^*, χ^*) to $\mathcal{H}$.

$\mathcal{A}_T$ answers $\mathcal{H}$'s decryption query (ψ, χ) as follows:

- If $(\psi, \chi) \neq (\psi^*, \chi^*)$, then $\mathcal{A}_T$ just forwards (ψ, χ) to its own decryption oracle $\mathsf{TKEM.Dec}_{sk}(\cdot)$.
    - If $\bot$ is returned, then $\mathcal{A}_T$ returns $\bot$ to $\mathcal{H}$.
    - If 'test' is returned and $\chi \neq \chi^*$, then $\mathcal{A}_T$ uses dk_δ to decrypt χ.
        - If m_0 or m_1 is obtained, then $\mathcal{A}_T$ returns 'test' to $\mathcal{H}$.
        - Else $\mathcal{A}_T$ returns the result to $\mathcal{H}$.
    - If 'test' is returned and $\chi = \chi^*$, then $\mathcal{A}_T$ returns 'test' to $\mathcal{H}$.
    - If dk is returned, then $\mathcal{A}_T$ uses dk to decrypt χ.
        - If m_0 or m_1 is obtained, then $\mathcal{A}_T$ returns 'test' to $\mathcal{H}$.
        - Else $\mathcal{A}_T$ returns the result to $\mathcal{H}$.

The simulation is perfect unless ψ decrypts to dk_0 and thus 'test' is returned by $\mathsf{TKEM.Dec}_{sk}(\cdot)$ in RGAME.PKE. However, the probability of this event is $\frac{1}{|\mathcal{K}_K|}$ for each such query since in that case dk_0 is random and independent from the view of $\mathcal{H}$.

When $\mathcal{H}$ finally outputs $\tilde{b}$, if $\tilde{b} = b$ then $\mathcal{A}_T$ outputs $\tilde{\delta} = 1$, meaning dk_δ is the real key. Otherwise, $\mathcal{A}_T$ outputs $\tilde{\delta} = 0$. Accordingly, $|\Pr[\tilde{b} = b|\delta = 1] - \Pr[T]| \leq \frac{q_D}{|\mathcal{K}_K|}$, and $\Pr[\tilde{b} = b|\delta = 0] = \Pr[T']$. Therefore,

$$Adv^{rcca}_{\mathsf{tkem}, \mathcal{A}_T}(k) = |\Pr[\tilde{\delta} = \delta] - \frac{1}{2}|$$
$$= \frac{1}{2}|\Pr[\tilde{\delta} = 1|\delta = 1] - \Pr[\tilde{\delta} = 1|\delta = 0]|$$
$$= \frac{1}{2}|\Pr[\tilde{b} = b|\delta = 1] - \Pr[\tilde{b} = b|\delta = 0]|$$
$$\geq \frac{1}{2}|\Pr[T] - \Pr[T'] - \frac{q_D}{|\mathcal{K}_K|}|.$$

Hence, we have $|\Pr[T] - \Pr[T']| \leq 2Adv^{rcca}_{\mathsf{tkem}, \mathcal{A}_T}(k) + \frac{q_D}{|\mathcal{K}_K|}$.

Lastly, we show that $\mathcal{H}$ playing RGAME.PKE$'$ essentially conducts an IND-RCCA attack to DEM, i.e. we claim $|\Pr[T'] - \frac{1}{2}| \leq Adv^{rcca}_{\mathsf{dem}}(k)$. This is shown by constructing an RCCA attacker $\mathcal{A}_D$ to DEM. $\mathcal{A}_D$ first generate (pk, sk) by using PKE.Gen and gives pk to $\mathcal{H}$. When (m_0, m_1) has been chosen by $\mathcal{H}$, $\mathcal{A}_D$ forwards them to encryption oracle of RGAME.DEM and receives ciphertext χ^*. It then generates (dk^*, ψ^*) by using χ^* as a tag and following TKEM.Key and TKEM.Enc, and sends (ψ^*, χ^*) to $\mathcal{H}$. Note that the key dk^+ chosen by encryption oracle of RGAME.DEM and the one embedded in ψ^* are independent and randomly chosen. $\mathcal{A}_D$ answers $\mathcal{H}$'s decryption query (ψ, χ) as follows:

- If $(\psi, \chi) \neq (\psi^*, \chi^*)$, then $\mathcal{A}_D$ uses sk to decrypt (ψ, χ).
    - If the result is $\bot$, then $\mathcal{A}_D$ returns $\bot$ to $\mathcal{H}$.
    - If the result is dk^* and $\chi = \chi^*$ then $\mathcal{A}_D$ returns 'test' to $\mathcal{H}$.
    - If the result is dk^* and $\chi \neq \chi^*$ then $\mathcal{A}_D$ forwards χ to its own decryption oracle DEM.Dec$_{dk^+}(\cdot)$, and returns the result to $\mathcal{H}$.
    - If the result is $dk \neq dk^*$ then $\mathcal{A}_D$ uses dk to decrypt χ.
        - If m_0 or m_1 is obtained, then $\mathcal{A}_D$ returns 'test' to $\mathcal{H}$.
        - Else $\mathcal{A}_D$ returns the result to $\mathcal{H}$.

When $\mathcal{H}$ outputs $\tilde{b}$, $\mathcal{A}_D$ outputs $\tilde{b}$, too. $\mathcal{A}_D$ perfectly simulates RGAME.PKE$'$, and whenever $\mathcal{H}$ wins, so does $\mathcal{A}_D$. Hence $|\Pr[T'] - \frac{1}{2}| = Adv^{rcca}_{\mathsf{dem}, \mathcal{A}_D}(k)$.

In summary, we have:

$$|(\Pr[T] - \frac{1}{2}) - (\Pr[T'] - \frac{1}{2})| \leq 2Adv^{rcca}_{\mathsf{tkem}, \mathcal{A}_T}(k) + \frac{q_D}{|\mathcal{K}_K|}$$

$$Adv^{rcca}_{\mathsf{pke}, \mathcal{H}}(k) \leq 2Adv^{rcca}_{\mathsf{tkem}, \mathcal{A}_T}(k) + Adv^{rcca}_{\mathsf{dem}, \mathcal{A}_D}(k) + \frac{q_D}{|\mathcal{K}_K|}. \quad \square$$

5 KEM/Tag-DEM: From RCCA Security to CCA One

Consider the method in [10] that makes an RCCA-secure PKE to be CCA-secure one, we generalize it to be based on an RCCA-secure KEM scheme.

By using the ciphertext of KEM as a tag of DEM, we will let the security of DEM provide non-malleability for KEM.

5.1 Tag-DEM and the Hybrid Paradigm

A Tag-DEM is a one-time symmetric-key encryption scheme with a tag as an additional input. It consists of two algorithm. Deterministic TDEM.Enc takes an input 1^k, a key dk, a message m and a tag $\tau \in \mathcal{T}$, and outputs a ciphertext χ, $\mathcal{T}$ is the tag space. Deterministic TDEM.Dec takes as input 1^k, a key dk, a ciphertext χ and a tag τ, and outputs a message m or the special symbol $\bot$. An obvious soundness condition applies.

We define IND-CCA security for Tag-DEMs by the following game. $\mathcal{O}$ denotes TDEM.$\text{Dec}_{dk}(\cdot, \cdot)$. In Step 3, $\mathcal{A}_D$ is restricted not to ask (χ, τ) to $\mathcal{O}$.

[GAME.TDEM]
Step 1. $(m_0, m_1, \tau, v) \leftarrow \mathcal{A}_D(1^k)$
Step 2. $dk \leftarrow \mathcal{K}_D$, $b \leftarrow \{0, 1\}$, $\chi \leftarrow$ TDEM.$\text{Enc}_{dk}(m_b, \tau)$.
Step 3. $\tilde{b} \leftarrow \mathcal{A}_D^{\mathcal{O}}(v, \chi)$

Note that Tag-DEMs are deterministic symmetric-key encryptions with tag, and we only ask one-time CCA-security but not authenticity, this makes them weaker than authenticated encryptions with associated data [18], even a deterministic one.

Our KEM/Tag-DEM works as follows:

Function: HPKE.$\text{Enc}_{pk}(m)$
$(dk, \psi) \leftarrow$ KEM.$\text{Enc}_{pk}()$
$\chi \leftarrow$ TDEM.$\text{Enc}_{dk}(m, \psi)$
Output $c = (\psi, \chi)$

Function: HPKE.$\text{Dec}_{sk}(c)$
$(\psi, \chi) \leftarrow c$
$dk \leftarrow$ KEM.$\text{Dec}_{sk}(\psi)$
$m \leftarrow$ TDEM.$\text{Dec}_{dk}(\chi, \psi)$
Output m

Theorem 4. *If KEM is IND-RCCA secure and TDEM is IND-CCA secure then the Hybrid PKE scheme above is IND-CCA secure(as a public-key encryption scheme). In particular, for every $\mathcal{H}$, there exist $\mathcal{A}_K$ and $\mathcal{A}_D$ with*

$$Adv_{pke,\mathcal{H}}^{cca} \leq 2Adv_{kem,\mathcal{A}_K}^{rcca} + Adv_{tdem,\mathcal{A}_D}^{cca} + \frac{q_D}{|\mathcal{K}_K|}. \tag{3}$$

PROOF. Let $\mathcal{H}$ be an adversary playing GAME.PKE. We modify the game by using a random key dk^+ in place of the legitimate one generated by KEM.Enc in both the encryption and decryption oracle. Call this game GAME.PKE′. Let T and T' be events that $\tilde{b} = b$ in GAME.PKE and GAME.PKE′, respectively. Then we claim that $|\Pr[T] - \Pr[T']| \leq 2Adv_{kem,\mathcal{A}_K}^{rcca}(k)$, which is shown by constructing $\mathcal{A}_K$ that attacks the underlying KEM scheme by using $\mathcal{H}$.

First $\mathcal{A}_K$ is given pk and passes it to $\mathcal{H}$. Given m_0 and m_1 from $\mathcal{H}$, $\mathcal{A}_K$ requests the encryption oracle of RGAME.KEM to obtain (dk_δ, ψ^*). $\mathcal{A}_K$ then selects $b \in \{0, 1\}$ and computes $\chi^* = $ DEM.$\text{Enc}_{dk_\delta}(m_b, \psi^*)$, and sends (ψ^*, χ^*) to $\mathcal{H}$.

$\mathcal{A}_K$ answers $\mathcal{H}$'s decryption query (ψ, χ) as follows:

- If $\psi = \psi^*$ and so that $\chi \neq \chi^*$, then $\mathcal{A}_K$ uses dk_δ to decrypt (χ, ψ).
- If $\psi \neq \psi^*$, then $\mathcal{A}_K$ just forwards ψ to its own decryption oracle KEM.$\text{Dec}_{sk}(\cdot)$.
    - If $\perp$ is returned, then $\mathcal{A}_K$ returns $\perp$ to $\mathcal{H}$.
    - If 'test' is returned, then $\mathcal{A}_K$ uses dk_δ to decrypt (χ, ψ) by applying TDEM.$\text{Dec}_{dk_\delta}(\cdot, \cdot)$, returns the result to $\mathcal{H}$.
    - If dk is returned, then $\mathcal{A}_K$ uses this dk to decrypt (χ, ψ) by applying TDEM.$\text{Dec}_{dk}(\cdot, \cdot)$, and returns the result to $\mathcal{H}$.

When $\mathcal{H}$ finally outputs $\tilde{b}$, if $\tilde{b} = b$ then $\mathcal{A}_K$ outputs $\tilde{\delta} = 1$, meaning dk_δ is the real key. Otherwise, $\mathcal{A}_K$ outputs $\tilde{\delta} = 0$. Accordingly, $|\Pr[\tilde{b} = b|\delta = 1] - \Pr[T]| \leq \frac{q_D}{|\mathcal{K}_K|}$, and $\Pr[\tilde{b} = b|\delta = 0] = \Pr[T']$. Therefore, similar as in the proof of Theorem 3, we have $|\Pr[T] - \Pr[T']| \leq 2Adv_{\mathsf{kem}, \mathcal{A}_K}^{rcca}(k) + \frac{q_D}{|\mathcal{K}_K|}$.

Lastly, we show that $\mathcal{H}$ playing GAME.PKE$'$ essentially conducts an IND-CCA attack to TDEM, i.e. we claim $|\Pr[T'] - \frac{1}{2}| \leq Adv_{\mathsf{tdem}, \mathcal{A}_D}^{cca}(k)$. This is shown by constructing a CCA attacker $\mathcal{A}_D$ to DEM. $\mathcal{A}_D$ first generate (pk, sk) by using PKE.Gen and gives pk to $\mathcal{H}$. When (m_0, m_1) has been chosen by $\mathcal{H}$, $\mathcal{A}_D$ first generates (dk^*, ψ^*) by following KEM.Enc, then forwards (m_0, m_1, ψ^*) to encryption oracle of GAME.TDEM. When $\mathcal{A}_D$ receives ciphertext χ^*, it sends (ψ^*, χ^*) to $\mathcal{H}$. Note that the key chosen by encryption oracle of GAME.TDEM dk^+ and the one embedded in ψ^* are independent and randomly chosen. $\mathcal{A}_D$ answers $\mathcal{H}$'s decryption query (ψ, χ) as follows:

- If $\psi = \psi^*$ and so that $\chi \neq \chi^*$, then $\mathcal{A}_D$ forwards (χ, ψ) to its own decryption oracle DEM.Dec$_{dk^+}(\cdot, \cdot)$, and returns the result to $\mathcal{H}$.
- If $\psi \neq \psi^*$, then $\mathcal{A}_D$ uses sk to decrypt ψ.
  - If the result is $\perp$, then $\mathcal{A}_D$ returns $\perp$ to $\mathcal{H}$.
  - If the result is dk^*, then $\mathcal{A}_D$ forwards (χ, ψ) to its own decryption oracle DEM.Dec$_{dk^+}(\cdot, \cdot)$, and returns the result to $\mathcal{H}$.
  - If the result is $dk \neq dk^*$, then $\mathcal{A}_D$ uses this dk to decrypt χ.

When $\mathcal{H}$ outputs $\tilde{b}$, $\mathcal{A}_D$ outputs $\tilde{b}$, too. $\mathcal{A}_D$ perfectly simulates GAME.PKE$'$, and whenever $\mathcal{H}$ wins, so does $\mathcal{A}_D$. Hence $|\Pr[T'] - \frac{1}{2}| = Adv_{\mathsf{tdem}, \mathcal{A}_D}^{cca}(k)$.

In summary, we have (3) immediately. $\square$

We can illustrate the security result in anther view. In Tag-KEM/DEM paradigm, the ciphertext of DEM is used as the tag input to the encryption of Tag-KEM, this can weaken the security requirement for DEM. By the same reason, in our KEM/Tag-DEM paradigm, the use of ciphertext of KEM as the tag of DEM should weaken the security requirement of KEM. Now we proved the security is weakened to be IND-RCCA security. Whether it can be further weakened remains open.

5.2   Two Direct Constructions of CCA Secure Tag-DEM Schemes

In this section we present some methods for constructing IND-CCA secure Tag-DEM schemes from One-time secure DEMs. The first one is based on the double-encryption structure used to make RCCA-secure PKE CCA-secure in [10]:

Function: TDEM.Enc(dk, mk, m, τ)	**Function:** TDEM.Dec(dk, mk, χ, τ)
$c_1 \leftarrow$ DEM.Enc$_{dk}(m\|\tau)$	parse χ as $c_1\|c_2$
$c_2 \leftarrow$ MAC.Sign$_{mk}(c_1)$	If MAC.Ver$_{mk}(c_2, c_1) = 1$ then
Output $\chi = (c_1\|c_2)$	$m\|\bar{\tau} \leftarrow$ DEM.Dec(dk, c_1)
	Else output $\perp$ EndIf
	If $\bar{\tau} = \tau$ then output m Else output $\perp$

Theorem 5. *If DEM is One-time secure and MAC is one-time secure, then the above TDEM is IND-CCA secure. In particular, for every $\mathcal{A}_D$, there exists $\mathcal{B}$ with*

$$Adv^{cca}_{tdem,\mathcal{A}_D} \leq Adv^{ot}_{dem,\mathcal{B}} + q_D \cdot Adv^{forge}_{mac}. \qquad (4)$$

where q_D is a bound on the number of decryption oracle queries made by $\mathcal{A}_D$.

PROOF. Let $\mathcal{A}_D$ be an adversary playing GAME.TDEM, we construct a passive adversary $\mathcal{B}$ against DEM by using $\mathcal{A}_D$ as follows:

$\mathcal{B}$ forwards 1^k to $\mathcal{A}_D$. Given (m_0, m_1, τ^*) from $\mathcal{A}_D$, $\mathcal{B}$ computes $x_0 = m_0 \| \tau^*$ and $x_1 = m_1 \| \tau^*$, and requests (x_0, x_1) to the encryption oracle of GAME.DEM to obtain c^*. Then $\mathcal{B}$ let $c_1^* = c^*$, and randomly chooses mk from $\mathcal{K}_M$, computes $c_2^* = MAC.Sign_{mk}(c_1^*)$, sends $\chi^* = (c_1^*, c_2^*)$ to $\mathcal{A}_D$. For all decryption queries $(\chi = (c_1, c_2), \tau)$ from $\mathcal{A}_D$, $\mathcal{B}$ just returns $\perp$. Finally, when $\mathcal{A}_D$ outputs $\tilde{b}$, $\mathcal{B}$ outputs $\tilde{b}$, too.

For each decryption query, the simulation is correct unless $MAC.Ver(c_2, c_1) = 1$. Let Forge denote this event, we have $\Pr[\text{Forge}] \leq q_D \cdot Adv^{forge}_{mac}$, and (4) follows immediately. $\qquad \square$

The second method avoids double encryption and just makes the tag τ as an input part of MAC:

Function: TDEM.Enc(dk, mk, m, τ)	**Function:** TDEM.Dec(dk, mk, χ, τ)
$c_1 \leftarrow$ DEM.Enc$_{dk}(m)$	parse χ as $c_1 \| c_2$
$c_2 \leftarrow$ MAC.Sign$_{mk}(c_1 \| \tau)$	If MAC.Ver$_{mk}(c_2, c_1 \| \tau) = 1$ then
Output $\chi = (c_1 \| c_2)$	$m \leftarrow$ DEM.Dec(dk, c_1)
	Else output $\perp$ EndIf
	Output m.

Combined with an RCCA secure KEM, the above scheme coincides with the one in [3] to construct a CCA secure hybrid encryption from an RCCA secure KEM.

Theorem 6. *If DEM is One-time secure and MAC is one-time secure, then the above TDEM is IND-CCA secure. In particular, for every $\mathcal{A}_D$, there exists $\mathcal{B}$ with*

$$Adv^{cca}_{tdem,\mathcal{A}_D} \leq Adv^{ot}_{dem,\mathcal{B}} + q_D \cdot Adv^{forge}_{mac}. \qquad (5)$$

where q_D is a bound on the number of decryption oracle queries made by $\mathcal{A}_D$.

PROOF. Let $\mathcal{A}_D$ be an adversary playing GAME.TDEM, we construct a passive adversary $\mathcal{B}$ against DEM by using $\mathcal{A}_D$ as follows:

$\mathcal{B}$ forwards 1^k to $\mathcal{A}_D$. Given (m_0, m_1, τ^*) from $\mathcal{A}_D$, $\mathcal{B}$ lets $x_0 = m_0$, $x_1 = m_1$, and requests (x_0, x_1) to the encryption oracle of GAME.DEM to obtain c^*. Then $\mathcal{B}$ lets $c_1^* = c^*$, and randomly chooses mk from $\mathcal{K}_M$, computes $c_2^* = MAC.Sign_{mk}(c_1^* \| \tau^*)$, sends $\chi^* = (c_1^*, c_2^*)$ to $\mathcal{A}_D$.

For all decryption queries $(\chi = (c_1, c_2), \tau)$ from $\mathcal{A}_D$, $\mathcal{B}$ just returns $\perp$. Finally, when $\mathcal{A}_D$ outputs $\tilde{b}$, $\mathcal{B}$ outputs $\tilde{b}$, too.

The simulation is correct unless $\mathsf{MAC.Ver}(c_2, c_1 \| \tau) = 1$. Let Forge denote this event, we have $\Pr[\mathsf{Forge}] \leq q_D \cdot Adv_{\mathsf{mac}}^{\mathsf{forge}}$, and equation (5) follows immediately. $\qquad\square$

Additionally, Tag-DEMs can be built more efficiently from conventional IV-based encryption schemes as in deterministic authenticated encryptions [19]. Taking the tag τ as a header, in the encryption it is no need to require the privacy of τ. But there must be a way to bind the tag τ to the encrypted message and provide authenticity for both of them. For example, the SIV construction in [19] provides a method for constructing Tag-DEM with shorter ciphertext. Details can be found in Appendix.

Acknowledgment. This work is supported by the National Natural Science Foundations of China (No. 60970120) and the Fundamental Research Funds for the Central Universities (Nos. K50510010024 and K50511010009.).

References

1. Abe, M., Cui, Y., Imai, H., Kurosawa, K.: Tag-KEM from Set Partial Domain One-Way Permutations. In: Batten, L., Safavi-Naini, R. (eds.) ACISP 2006. LNCS, vol. 4058, pp. 360–370. Springer, Heidelberg (2006)
2. Abe, M., Gennaro, R., Kurosawa, K.: Tag-KEM/DEM: A new framework for hybrid encryption. Cryptology ePrint Archive: Report 2005/027 (2005)
3. Abe, M., Gennaro, R., Kurosawa, K., Shoup, V.: Tag-KEM/DEM: A new framework for hybrid encryption and a new analysis of Kurosawa-Desmedt KEM. In: Cramer, R. (ed.) EUROCRYPT 2005. LNCS, vol. 3494, pp. 128–146. Springer, Heidelberg (2005)
4. Abe, M., Gennaro, R., Kurosawa, K., Shoup, V.: Tag-KEM/DEM: A new framework for hybrid encryption. J. Cryptology 21(1), 97–130 (2008)
5. An, J.H., Dodis, Y., Rabin, T.: On the security of joint signature and encryption. In: Knudsen, L.R. (ed.) EUROCRYPT 2002. LNCS, vol. 2332, pp. 83–107. Springer, Heidelberg (2002)
6. Bellare, M., Desai, A., Pointcheval, D., Rogaway, P.: Relations among notions of security for public-key encryption schemes. In: Krawczyk, H. (ed.) CRYPTO 1998. LNCS, vol. 1462, pp. 26–45. Springer, Heidelberg (1998)
7. Bellare, M., Desai, A., Jokipii, E., Rogaway, P.: A concrete security treatment of symmetric encryption: analysis of the DES modes of operation. In: Proceedings of the 38th Symposium on Foundations of Computer Science, pp. 394–403. IEEE Press (1997)
8. Bellare, M., Rogaway, P.: Random oracles are practicala paradigm for designing efficient protocols. In: Proceedings of the First Annual Conference on Computer and Communications Security, pp. 62–73. ACM, New York (1993)
9. Bellare, M., Namprempre, C.: Authenticated encryption: Relations among notions and analysis of the generic composition paradigm. In: Okamoto, T. (ed.) ASIACRYPT 2000. LNCS, vol. 1976, pp. 531–545. Springer, Heidelberg (2000)

10. Canetti, R., Krawczyk, H., Nielsen, J.: Relaxing chosen-ciphertext security. In: Boneh, D. (ed.) CRYPTO 2003. LNCS, vol. 2729, pp. 565–582. Springer, Heidelberg (2003)
11. Cramer, R., Shoup, V.: Design and analysis of practical public-key encryption schemes secure against adaptive chosen ciphertext attack. Manuscript (December 17, 2001); SIAM Journal of Computing 33(1), 167–226 (2003)
12. Dent, A.W.: A designer's guide to KEMs. In: Paterson, K.G. (ed.) Cryptography and Coding 2003. LNCS, vol. 2898, pp. 133–151. Springer, Heidelberg (2003)
13. Groth, J.: Rerandomizable and replayable adaptive chosen ciphertext attack secure cryptosystems. In: Naor, M. (ed.) TCC 2004. LNCS, vol. 2951, pp. 152–170. Springer, Heidelberg (2004)
14. Hofheinz, D., Kiltz, E.: Secure Hybrid Encryption from Weakened Key Encapsulation. In: Menezes, A. (ed.) CRYPTO 2007. LNCS, vol. 4622, pp. 553–571. Springer, Heidelberg (2007)
15. Krawczyk, H.: The order of encryption and authentication for protecting communications (or: How secure is SSL?). In: Kilian, J. (ed.) CRYPTO 2001. LNCS, vol. 2139, pp. 310–331. Springer, Heidelberg (2001)
16. Kurosawa, K., Desmedt, Y.: A new paradigm of hybrid encryption scheme. In: Franklin, M. (ed.) CRYPTO 2004. LNCS, vol. 3152, pp. 426–442. Springer, Heidelberg (2004)
17. Prabhakaran, M.M., Rosulek, M.: Rerandomizable RCCA Encryption. In: Menezes, A. (ed.) CRYPTO 2007. LNCS, vol. 4622, pp. 517–534. Springer, Heidelberg (2007)
18. Rogaway, P.: Authenticated-Encryption with Associated-Data. In: Proceedings of the 9th Annual Conference on Computer and Communications Security (CCS-9), pp. 98–107. ACM, New York (2002)
19. Rogaway, P., Shrimpton, T.: Deterministic Authenticated-Encryption: A Provable-Security Treatment of the Key-Wrap Problem. Full version of: A Provable-Security Treatment of the Key-Wrap Problem. In: Vaudenay, S. (ed.) EUROCRYPT 2006. LNCS, vol. 4004, pp. 373–390. Springer, Heidelberg (2006)
20. Shoup, V.: ISO 18033-2: An emerging standard for public-key encryption, committee draft (2004), http://shoup.net/iso/

A   Message Authentication Code

MAC is a pair of algorithms (MAC.Sign, MAC.Ver). A key space $\mathcal{K}_M$ is defined by security parameter k. MAC.Sign takes a key $mk \in \mathcal{K}_M$ and a message $m \in {0,1}^*$ as inputs, and outputs a string σ. We say (σ, m) is valid with regard to mk if $\sigma = \text{MAC.Sign}_{mk}(m)$. MAC.Ver takes a triple (mk, σ, m) as input and outputs 1 if (σ, m) is valid with respect to mk, or outputs 0, otherwise.

We define a one-time chosen message attacking game, GAME.MAC. An adversary chooses an arbitrary message m and is given m's MAC σ created with mk randomly chosen from $\mathcal{K}_M$, it outputs (σ', m') which is different from (σ, m). The adversary wins if (σ', m') is valid with respect to the same mk. We say MAC is secure against one-time chosen message attack, or shorten as one-time secure, if any PPT adversary wins GAME.MAC with at most negligible probability in k, say $Adv_{\text{mac}}^{\text{forge}}(k)$.

B   The SIV Construction of Tag-DEM

B.1   Conventional IV-Based Encryption Scheme

Encryption modes like CBC and CTR are the so called conventional IV-based encryption schemes. Such a scheme is a tuple $\Pi = (\mathsf{K},\mathsf{E},\mathsf{D})$, where K is a probabilistic algorithm, which on input 1^k outputs a key $K \in \mathcal{K}$, $\mathcal{K}$ be the *key space*. E is a deterministic encryption algorithm that takes as input an IV from IV space $\mathcal{IV}$, a key dk and a message m, and outputs a ciphertext $C = \mathsf{E}_{dk}^{\mathcal{IV}}(m)$. D is a deterministic decryption algorithm that takes as input an IV, a key dk and a ciphertext C, and outputs a message m or the special symbol $\perp$. Obvious soundness condition applies.

Fix $\mathcal{IV} = \{0,1\}^n$. For simplicity, we assume Π is length-preserving. Let $\mathsf{E}_{dk}^{\$}$ be the probabilistic algorithm defined from E, which on input dk and m, randomly chooses IV from $\mathcal{IV}$, then computes C as $\mathsf{E}_{dk}^{\mathcal{IV}}(m)$.

For consistency, we only require find-then-guess security against passive attacker, and demand a random IV. This makes the security notion rather weak, but sufficient for our purposes. Let $\mathcal{A}_E$ be a polynomial-time oracle machine that plays the following game.

[GAME.Π]
Step 1. $(m_0, m_1, v) \leftarrow \mathcal{A}_E(1^k)$
Step 2. $dk \leftarrow \mathcal{K}$, $b \leftarrow \{0,1\}$, $(C, IV) \leftarrow \mathsf{E}_{dk}^{\$}(m_b)$.
Step 3. $\tilde{b} \leftarrow \mathcal{A}_E(v, C, IV)$
We define

$$Adv_{\Pi, \mathcal{A}_E}^{\mathsf{ot}}(k) = |Pr[\tilde{b} = b] - \frac{1}{2}|$$

and

$$Adv_{\Pi}^{\mathsf{ot}}(k) = max_{\mathcal{A}_E}(Adv_{\Pi, \mathcal{A}_E}^{\mathsf{ot}}(k)).$$

We say that Π is one-time secure if $Adv_{\Pi}^{\mathsf{ot}}(k)$ is negligible in k.

B.2   Arbitrary-Input PRFs

A pseudorandom function(PRF) is a map $F : \mathcal{K} \times \mathcal{X} \to \{0,1\}^n$ for some $n \geq 1$, $\mathcal{K}$ and $\mathcal{X}$ are fixed nonempty sets. F is pseudorandom if its input-output behavior is indistinguishable from that of a random function of the same domain and range.

We write $F_K(X)$ for $F(K, X)$. Let $Func(\mathcal{X}, \mathcal{Y})$ be the set of all functions from $\mathcal{X}$ to $\mathcal{Y}$ and let $Func(\mathcal{X}, n) = Func(\mathcal{X}, \{0,1\}^n)$. Regarding a function in $Func(\mathcal{X}, n)$ as the key, which associates a random string in $\{0,1\}^n$ to each $X \in \mathcal{X}$. The pseudorandomness of F is defined by the following game:

[GAME.PRF]
Step 1. $\rho \to Func(\mathcal{X}, n)$, $\mathcal{O}_0 \leftarrow \rho$, $K \leftarrow \mathcal{K}$, $\mathcal{O}_1 \leftarrow F_K$
Step 2. $\tilde{d} \leftarrow \mathcal{B}^{\mathcal{O}_d}$.
We define $Adv_{F, \mathcal{B}}^{\mathsf{prf}} = |Pr[\tilde{d} = 1|d = 1] - Pr[\tilde{d} = 1|d = 0]|.$

B.3 The Construction

The security notion used in [19] for DAE is stronger than our CCA one for Tag-DEM. For the consistency, we still use the CCA security defined in this paper.

Function: TDEM.Enc$(dk1, dk2, m, \tau)$	**Function:** TDEM.Dec$(dk1, dk2, \chi, \tau)$
$IV \leftarrow F_{dk1}(m, \tau)$	parse χ as $IV\|C$
$C \leftarrow E^{IV}_{dk2}(m)$	$m \leftarrow D^{IV}_{dk2}(C)$
Output $\chi = IV\|C$	$IV' \leftarrow F_{dk1}(m, \tau)$
	If $IV = IV'$ then output m
	Else output $\perp$

Theorem 7. *If $\Pi = (E, D)$ is a One-time secure IV-based encryption scheme with Iv-length n and F is a PRF, then the above TDEM is IND-CCA secure. In particular,*

$$Adv^{cca}_{tdem, \mathcal{A}_D} \leq Adv^{ot}_{\Pi, \mathcal{A}_E} + Adv^{prf}_{F, \mathcal{B}} + q_D/2^n. \tag{6}$$

where q_D is a bound on the number of decryption oracle queries made by an IND-CCA attacker against TDEM.

PROOF.   Let G_0 be the original attack game GAME.TDEM played by adversary $\mathcal{A}_D$, and let S_0 be the event that $\mathcal{A}$ correctly guesses the hidden bit b in game G_0. Let (ψ^*, τ^*) denote the target ciphertext-tag pair, and $IV^* = F_{dk1}(m_b, \tau^*)$, $C^* = E^{IV^*}_{dk2}(m_b)$ be the underlying IV and C. Thus, $\psi^* = IV^*\|C^*$.

We next define a game G_1 that is the same as game G_0, except that F_{dk1} is replaced by a random function $\rho \in Func(\mathcal{X}, n)$ in both the encryption and decryption oracle, where $\mathcal{X} = \mathcal{T} \times \{0, 1\}^*$, $\mathcal{T}$ is the tag space. And ρ is hidden from the view of $\mathcal{A}_D$. Let S_1 be the event in game G_1 corresponding to the event S_0.

We claim that there is a adversary $\mathcal{B}$ against the pseudorandomness of F_K, such that

$$|\Pr[S_1] - \Pr[S_0]| = Adv^{prf}_{F, \mathcal{B}}$$

$\mathcal{B}$ runs $\mathcal{A}_D$, forwards 1^k to $\mathcal{A}_D$. Given (m_0, m_1, τ^*) from $\mathcal{A}_D$, $\mathcal{B}$ chooses randomly $dk2$ and $b \leftarrow \{0, 1\}$, and asks (τ^*, m_b) to its $F_{dk1}(\cdot)$ or $\rho(\cdot)$ oracle, when obtains IV^*, it computes $C^* = E^{IV^*}_{dk2}(m_b)$, then returns $\psi^* = IV^*\|C^*$ to $\mathcal{A}_D$. For all decryption queries (χ, τ) from $\mathcal{A}_D$, $\mathcal{B}$ parses χ as $IV\|C$, since $\mathcal{B}$ knows $dk2$, it decrypts C and computes $m = D^{IV}_{dk2}(C)$, asks (m, τ) to its own oracle, check whether or not the returned IV' is equal to IV, if yes then return m else return $\perp$.

$\mathcal{B}$ perfectly simulates the oracles of $\mathcal{A}_D$. If $\mathcal{A}_D$ outputs $\tilde{b} = b$, then $\mathcal{B}$ outputs $\tilde{d} = 1$, else outputs $\tilde{d} = 0$.

Finally, we define a game G_2 that is the same as G_1, except that $\perp$ is returned for all decryption queries. Let S_2 be the event in the game G_2 corresponding to the event S_0.

Let F_2 be the event that a valid ciphertext $\psi = IV\|C$ has been asked by $\mathcal{A}_D$, then it follows by Lemma 1 that $|\Pr[S_2] - \Pr[S_1]| \leq \Pr[F_2]$. A ciphertext is valid only when $\rho(\tau, m) = IV$, where $m = \mathsf{D}_{dk2}^{IV}(C)$. Since ρ is a random function, this happens only with probability of $\frac{1}{2^n}$. Thus, $|\Pr[S_1] - \Pr[S_2]| \leq \Pr[F_2] \leq \frac{q_D}{2^n}$.

Furthermore, we claim that there is an adversary $\mathcal{A}_E$ under the sense of one-time security against Π, such that $|\Pr[S_2] - \frac{1}{2}| = Adv_{\Pi, \mathcal{A}_E}^{\mathsf{ot}}$.

$\mathcal{A}_E$ runs $\mathcal{A}_D$, forwards 1^k to $\mathcal{A}_D$. Given (m_0, m_1, τ^*) from $\mathcal{A}_D$, $\mathcal{A}_E$ asks (m_0, m_1) to its own encryption oracle $E_{dk}^\$(\cdot)$, when obtains the target ciphertext (C^*, IV^*), it forwards $IV^* \| C^*$ to $\mathcal{A}_D$. For all decryption queries (χ, τ) from $\mathcal{A}_D$, $\mathcal{A}_E$ returns $\bot$.

Since all ciphertexts decrypt to $\bot$, ρ loses its role in decryption, and a randomly chosen IV properly substitutes an IV computed by the random ρ. $\mathcal{A}_E$ perfectly simulates the oracles of $\mathcal{A}_D$. When $\mathcal{A}_D$ outputs $\tilde{b}$, $\mathcal{A}_E$ outputs $\tilde{d} = \tilde{b}$.

Collecting the probabilities, (6) will follow immediately, that proves the theorem. $\qquad\square$

Embedded Surface Attack on Multivariate Public Key Cryptosystems from Diophantine Equations

Jintai Ding[1,2], Ai Ren[2], and Chengdong Tao[3]

[1] Chongqing University
[2] University of Cincinnati
[3] South China University of Technology
{jintai.ding,chengdongtao2010}@gmail.com, renai@mail.uc.edu

Abstract. Let $X = (x_1, .., x_n)$ and $Y = (y_1, ..., y_m)$ be a pair of corresponding plaintext and ciphertext for a cryptosystem. We define an embedded surface of this cryptosystem as any polynomial equation:

$$E(X, Y) = E(x_1, .., x_n, y_1, ..., y_m) = 0,$$

which is satisfied by all such pairs. In this paper, we present a new attack on the multivariate public key cryptosystems from Diophantine equations developed by Gao and Heindl by using the embedded surfaces associated to this family of multivariate cryptosystems.

1 Introduction

The security of cryptosystems such as RSA, ECC, and Diffie-Hellman key exchange scheme, depends on assumptions about the hardness of certain number theoretic problems, such as the Integer Prime Factorization Problem or the Discrete Logarithm Problem. However, in 1994 Peter Shor [12] showed that quantum computers could break all public key cryptosystems that are based on these hard number theoretic problems. In recent years, significant efforts have been devoted to the search for alternative public key cryptosystems, which would remain secure in an era of quantum computers. Multivariate public key cryptosystems (MPKC) are one of the main families of cryptosystems that have the potential to resist quantum computer attacks.

The public key of a MPKC is a system of multivariate polynomials, mostly quadratic, over a finite field. This construction is based on the fact that solving a random multivariate polynomial system over a finite field is an NP-complete problem. In general, MPKCs have the following structure. Let k be a finite field with q elements. A public key is a map

$$\bar{F} : k^n \to k^m$$

constructed as:

$$\bar{F} = L_1 \circ F \circ L_2,$$

M. Kutyłowski and M. Yung (Eds.): Inscrypt 2012, LNCS 7763, pp. 122–136, 2013.

where L_1 and L_2 are are two random invertible affine transformations over k^m and k^n respectively. The central map $F : k^n \rightarrow k^m$ is a nonlinear multivariate polynomial map that has the property of being easily invertible computation-wise. The key of building a good MPKC is to find a good polynomial system F that makes the cryptosystem secure.

There are many attempts in building MPKC for encryption. For MPKCs, the encryption schemes standing in general are much slower than the signature schemes. Therefore, there is still a need to find good constructions for MPKCs for encryption.

In 2009, a new construction was built using a very different idea from before, namely one uses a special function solution to certain special Diophantine equation [8][7]. Even though, this construction also uses a triangular construction, Oil-Vinegar construction[11], the key component comes from certain special solutions of the Diophantine equation:

$$AB = CD + EF + GH + IJ + KL,$$

which is inspired by the construction in MFE[13], a generalization of HFE[10].

For this new family, the authors [7] propose three concrete cases for practical applications. They have very strong security claims, which is at the level of 2^{113} or higher. Also the decryption process is very efficient. By now, no one could yet find any weakness in the system.

1.1   The Contributions of This Paper

Let $X = (x_1, .., x_n)$ and $Y = (y_1, ..., y_m)$ be a pair of corresponding plaintext and ciphertext for any cryptosystem. We define an embedded surface of this cryptosystem as any polynomial equation:

$$E(X, Y) = E(x_1, .., x_n, y_1, ..., y_m) = 0,$$

which is satisfied by all such pairs. This name comes from the fact that this equation defines an algebraic surface in the space k^{m+n}, where all the plaintext and ciphertext pairs for this cryptosystems belong, or we can embed all the such pairs in such a surface.

In the case of MPKCs, the public key equation itself: $y_i = \bar{f}_i(x_1, ..., x_n)$, gives an embedded surface in k^{m+n}. In terms of attack on cryptosystems, one general approach should try to find the embedded surfaces that could help us to attack the systems. We call such an embedded surface a non-trivial embedded surface.

The first non-trivial embedded surface is used as the linerization equation by Patarin to defeat the Matsumomto-Imai MPKCs[10]:

$$\sum a_{i,j} x_i y_j + \sum b_i y_i + \sum c_i x_i + e = 0.$$

If we know the value of a ciphertext, this equation will give us a linear equation satisfied by the plaintext, which is very useful in attacking the system. This is also the idea used to build algebraic attack on AES.

Later, another embedded surface, a high order linerization equation is used in breaking the MFE MPKCs[3].

A natural question is:

can more general embedded surfaces other than linearization type of equations be useful to attack cryptosystems?

What we did in this paper is to give a positive answer to this question by using it to attack the new MPKCs from Diophantine equations.

What we observe is that, in the new MPKCs using the Diophantine equations, the decryption process actually implies that we can use the embedded surfaces to get what is done in the decryption process. Namely special embedded surfaces will help us to decrypt the message efficiently. In this case, the corresponding embedded surfaces will be in the form:

$$\sum A_{i,j,s,t} y_i y_j y_s y_t + \sum B_{i,j,s} y_i y_j y_s + \sum C_{i,j} y_i y_j +$$
$$\sum D_j y_j + \sum A'_{i,j,s,t} y_i y_j x_s^2 x_t^2 + \sum B'_{i,s,t} y_i x_s^2 x_t^2 + \sum C'_{i,j,s} y_i y_j x_s^2 +$$
$$\sum D'_{i,s} y_i x_s^2 + \sum E'_{s,t} x_s^2 x_t^2 + \sum H'_s x_s^2 + E = 0. \tag{1}$$

The embedded surfaces will produce equations in the form:

$$\sum A''_{s,t} x_s^2 x_t^2 + \sum B''_s x_s^2 + C'' = 0, \tag{2}$$

once the values of the ciphertext y_i are given. This enables us to derive new quadratic equations due to the fact that the field is of characteristic 2. This allows us to break the system efficiently. We could break the three systems proposed at the complexity of 2^{52}, 2^{61} and 2^{52} over the corresponding fields respectively.

This paper is organized as follows. In Section 2, we introduce the new MPKCs from Diophantine equations. In Section 3, we will present the cryptanalysis of the new MPKCs by using embedded surfaces. We conclude in Section 4.

2   Multivariate Public Key Cryptosystems from Diophantine Equations

In this section, we will present the MPKCs from Diophantine equations, and we will follow the notations in[7].

Let k be a finite field with q elements, and let $\mathcal{F}$ be an extension of k with degree d. In an MFE type ("medium field") construction, we fix a basis $\alpha_1, ..., \alpha_d$ of $\mathcal{F}$ over k, which identifies $\mathcal{F}$ with k^d via the natural map p : $\mathcal{F} \to k^d$:

$$p(a_1 \alpha_1 + ... + a_d \alpha_d) = (a_1, ..., a_d). \tag{3}$$

Then we view a polynomial $f \in \mathcal{F}[X_1, ..., X_n]$ component-wise over k by writing

$$X_i = x_{i1} \alpha_1 + ... + x_{id} \alpha_d,$$

and then

$$f = f_1 \alpha_1 + ... + f_d \alpha_d,$$

with $f_i \in k[x_{11}, ..., x_{nd}]$.

Throughout this paper, we assume that the finite field $\mathcal{F}$ has characteristic two. If the field is $GF(2)$, the embedded surfaces of (1) and (2) should be modified slightly, since there are not square terms.

2.1   The Origin of the Diophantine Equations

In the MFE MPKC, the key idea comes the fact that

$$det(M_1 M_2) = det(M_1) \times det(M_2),$$

for two 2×2 matrices:

$$M_1 = \begin{pmatrix} X_1 & X_2 \\ X_3 & X_4 \end{pmatrix}, \quad M_2 = \begin{pmatrix} X_5 & X_6 \\ X_7 & X_8 \end{pmatrix}.$$

This gives a quadratic polynomial solution to the the Diophantine equation over a polynomial ring $\mathcal{F}[X_1, ..., X_8]$:

$$AB = CD + EF,$$

namely

$$(X_1 X_4 + X_2 X_3)(X_5 X_8 + X_6 X_7) = (X_1 X_5 + X_2 X_7)(X_3 X_6 + X_4 X_8) + $$
$$(X_1 X_6 + X_2 X_8)(X_3 X_5 + X_4 X_7).$$

To build new type of MPKCs, Gao and Heindl were able to find solutions to the following new Diophantine equation:

$$AB = CD + EF + GH + IJ + KL,$$

over the ring $\mathcal{F}[X_1, ..., X_8, Y_1, ..., Y_8]$. In the context of their work, they rewrite this equation as

$$\psi_1 \psi_2 = f_1 f_2 + ... + f_9 f_{10}, \tag{4}$$

where each polynomial is quadratic and

- $\psi_1 \in \mathcal{F}[X_1, ..., X_8], \psi_2 \in \mathcal{F}[Y_1, ..., Y_n]$;
- $f_i \in \mathcal{F}[X_1, ..., X_8, Y_1, ..., Y_8]$, for $0 < i < 9$, are oil-vinegar polynomials;
- $f_i \in \mathcal{F}[X_1, ..., X_8, Y_1, ..., Y_8]$, $i = 9, 10$.

An oil-vinegar polynomial is a quadratic polynomial, where we divide the variables into two sets: the oil variables and the vinegar variables, and an oil-vinegar polynomial has not any quadratic terms with only oil variables:

$$\sum a_{ij} x_i x_j' + \sum b_{ij} x_i' x_j' + \sum c_j x_i + \sum d_j x_j' + e = 0,$$

where x_i are oil variables and x_j' are the vinegar variables.

The design starts with the polynomial ring

$$R = \mathcal{F}[x_1, x_2, x_3, x_4, y_1, y_2, y_3, y_4, z_1, z_2, z_3, z_4, w_1, w_2, w_3, w_4].$$

Let

$$p_{xy}^{ij} = x_i y_j + x_j y_i,$$

for $1 = i < j = 4$;

$$p^{ij}(x, y, z, w) = p_{xz}^{ij} + p_{yz}^{ij} + p_{yw}^{ij},$$

for $1 = i < j = 4$.

In algebraic geometry terms, the p_{xy}^{ij} are simply Plück coordinates, which are known to satisfy the quadratic relations:

$$\begin{aligned}
0 = {}& (p_{xy}^{12} + p_{zw}^{12})p^{34}(x, y, z, w) + (p_{xy}^{13} + p_{zw}^{13})p^{24}(x, y, z, w) + \\
& (p_{xy}^{14} + p_{zw}^{14})p^{23}(x, y, z, w) + (p_{xy}^{23} + p_{zw}^{23})p^{14}(x, y, z, w) + \\
& (p_{xy}^{24} + p_{zw}^{24})p^{13}(x, y, z, w) + (p_{xy}^{34} + p_{zw}^{34})p^{12}(x, y, z, w).
\end{aligned} \tag{5}$$

2.2 The Central Map

Let ρ be a ring homomorphism from R to $\mathcal{F}[X_1, ..., X_8, Y_1, ..., Y_8]$ induced by the map:

$$(x_1, x_2, x_3, x_4, y_1, y_2, y_3, y_4, z_1, z_2, z_3, z_4, w_1, w_2, w_3, w_4) \rightarrow$$
$$(X_1, X_3, Y_1 + Y_5, Y_3 + Y_7, X_4, X_2, Y_5, Y_7, X_5, X_7, Y_4 + Y_8, Y_2 + Y_6, X_8, X_6, Y_8, Y_6).$$

Let

$$\begin{aligned}
\psi_1 &= \rho(p_{xy}^{12} + p_{zw}^{12}) = X_1 X_2 + X_3 X_4 + X_5 X_6 + X_7 X_8 \\
\psi_2 &= \rho(p^{34}(x, y, z, w)) = Y_1 Y_2 + Y_3 Y_4 + Y_5 Y_6 + Y_7 Y_8 \\
f_1 &= \rho(p_{xy}^{13} + p_{zw}^{13}) = X_4 Y_1 + X_8 Y_4 + (X_1 + X_4) Y_5 + X_5 Y_8 \\
f_2 &= \rho(p^{24}(x, y, z, w)) = (X_2 + X_3) Y_2 + X_7 Y_3 + X_2 Y_6 + X_6 Y_7 \\
f_3 &= \rho(p_{xy}^{14} + p_{zw}^{14}) = X_8 Y_2 + X_4 Y_3 + X_5 Y_6 + (X_1 + X_4) Y_7 \\
f_4 &= \rho(p^{23}(x, y, z, w)) = X_7 Y_1 + (X_2 + X_3) Y_4 + X_6 Y_5 + X_2 Y_8 \\
f_5 &= \rho(p_{xy}^{23} + p_{zw}^{23}) = X_2 Y_1 + X_6 Y_4 + (X_2 + X_3) Y_5 + X_7 Y_8 \\
f_6 &= \rho(p^{14}(x, y, z, w)) = (X_1 + X_4) Y_2 + X_5 Y_3 + X_4 Y_6 + X_8 Y_7 \\
f_7 &= \rho(p_{xy}^{24} + p_{zw}^{24}) = X_6 Y_2 + X_2 Y_3 + X_7 Y_6 + (X_2 + X_3) Y_7 \\
f_8 &= \rho(p^{13}(x, y, z, w)) = X_5 Y_1 + (X_1 + X_4) Y_4 + X_8 Y_5 + X_4 Y_8 \\
f_9 &= \rho(p_{xy}^{34} + p_{zw}^{34}) = Y_1 Y_7 + Y_2 Y_8 + Y_3 Y_5 + Y_4 Y_6 \\
f_{10} &= \rho(p^{12}(x, y, z, w)) = X_1 X_7 + X_2(X_5 + X_8) + X_3 X_5 + X_4(X_6 + X_7)
\end{aligned}$$

Note that $f_1, ..., f_8$ are Oil-vinegar polynomials, where we can take either $X = (X_1, ..., X_8)$ or $Y = (Y_1, ..., Y_8)$ be the vinegar variables. This implies that, if either X or Y is known, we can use the polynomial equations coming from knowing the value of these polynomials to find the value of the other one by plugging in the values of variables given.

In terms of the original notation, we rename each ψ_j and f_j above as $\psi_{1,j}$ and $f_{1,j}$ respectively, and define $\psi_{i,1} = \psi_{1,1}$, and $f_{i,j} = f_{1,j}$, for i = 2, 3, 4, j = 1, 3, 5, 7, 9.

Again, in terms of the original notation, interchanging z with w in (5), we define

$$
\begin{aligned}
\psi_{2,2} &= \rho(p^{34}(x, y, w, z)), \\
f_{2,2} &= \rho(p^{24}(x, y, w, z)), \\
f_{2,4} &= \rho(p^{23}(x, y, w, z)), \\
f_{2,6} &= \rho(p^{14}(x, y, w, z)), \\
f_{2,8} &= \rho(p^{13}(x, y, w, z)), \\
f_{2,10} &= \rho(p^{12}(x, y, w, z)).
\end{aligned}
\tag{6}
$$

Similarly, by interchanging x with y in (5), we define $\psi_{3,2}$ and $f_{3,j}$, for j = 2, 4, 6, 8, 10; by interchanging x with y, and z with w in (5), we define $\psi_{4,2}$ and $f_{4,j}$, for j = 2, 4, 6, 8, 10. Then we have four identities:

$$
\psi_{i,1}\psi_{i,2} = f_{i,1}f_{i,2} + \ldots f_{i,9}f_{i,10},
\tag{7}
$$

for $0 < i < 5$.

The central map:

$$
(Z_1, ..., Z_{74}) = F(X_1, ..., X_{24}, Y_1, ..., Y_{32}),
$$

is defined as

$$
\begin{aligned}
Z_1 &= X_1 + \psi_{1,1}(X_1, ..., X_8) + \phi_1(X_1) \\
Z_2 &= X_2 + \psi_{1,2}(Y_1, ..., Y_8) + \phi_2(X_1, X_2) \\
Z_3 &= X_3 + \psi_{2,2}(Y_9, ..., Y_{16}) + \phi_3(X_1, X_2, X_3) \\
Z_4 &= X_4 + \psi_{3,2}(Y_{17}, ..., Y_{24}) + \phi_4(X_1, X_2, X_3, X_4) \\
Z_5 &= X_5 + \psi_{2,1}(X_9, ..., X_{16}) + \phi_5(X_1, X_2, X_3, X_4, X_5) \\
Z_6 &= X_6 + \psi_{3,1}(X_{17}, ..., X_{24}) + \phi_6(X_1, X_2, X_3, X_4, X_5, X_6) \\
Z_7 &= X_7 + \psi_{4,2}(Y_{25}, ..., Y_{32}) + \phi_7(X_1, X_2, X_3, X_4, X_5, X_6, X_7) \\
Z_{7+i} &= f_{1,i}(X_1, ..., X_8, Y_1, ..., Y_8) \quad i = 1, .., 10 \\
Z_{17+i} &= f_{2,i}(X_1, ..., X_8, Y_9, ..., Y_{16}) \quad i = 1, .., 10 \\
Z_{27+i} &= f_{2,i}(Y_1, ..., Y_8, Y_9, ..., Y_{16}) \quad i = 1, .., 8 \\
Z_{36} &= f_{2,10}(Y_1, ..., Y_8, Y_9, ..., Y_{16}) \\
Z_{36+i} &= f_{3,i}(X_1, ..., X_8, Y_{17}, ..., Y_{24}) \quad i = 1, .., 10 \\
Z_{46+i} &= f_{2,i}(X_9, ..., X_{16}, Y_9, ..., Y_{16}) \quad i = 1, .., 8 \\
Z_{55} &= f_{2,10}(X_9, ..., X_{16}, Y_9, ..., Y_{16}) \\
Z_{55+i} &= f_{3,i}(X_{17}, ..., X_{24}, Y_{17}, ..., Y_{24}) \quad i = 1, .., 8 \\
Z_{64} &= f_{3,10}(X_{17}, ..., X_{24}, Y_{17}, ..., Y_{24}) \\
Z_{64+i} &= f_{4,i}(X_9, ..., X_{16}, Y_{25}, ..., Y_{32}) \quad i = 1, .., 10
\end{aligned}
$$

Here ϕ_i are randomly chosen quadratic functions.

Note that $f_{2,9}(Y_1, ..., Y_8, Y_9, ..., Y_{16})$ is not explicitly in the central map due to the redundancy that

$$f_{2,9}(Y_1, ..., Y_8, Y_9, ..., Y_{16}) = f_{2,9}(X_1, ..., X_8, Y_9, ..., Y_{16}) = Z_{26}. \qquad (8)$$

Similar situation is also true for:

$f_{2,9}(X_9, ..., X_{16}, Y_9, ..., Y_{16})$ and $f_{3,9}(X_{17}, ..., X_{24}, Y_{17}, ..., Y_{24})$.

There are 7 oil-vinegar polynomial systems inside the central map:

1. $Z_8, ..., Z_{15}$, where $Y_1, ..., Y_8$ are viewed as oil variable and $X_1, ..., X_8$ are viewed as vinegar variables;
2. $Z_{18}, ..., Z_{25}$, where $Y_9, ..., Y_{16}$ are viewed as oil variable and $X_1, ..., X_8$ are viewed as vinegar variables;
3. $Z_{28}, ..., Z_{35}$, where $Y_1, ..., Y_8$ can be viewed either as oil or vinegar variables and $Y_9, ..., Y_{16}$ are viewed as the opposite variables;
4. $Z_{37}, ..., Z_{44}$, where $Y_{17}, ..., Y_{24}$ are viewed as oil variable and $X1, ..., X8$ are viewed as vinegar variables;
5. $Z_{47}, ..., Z_{54}$, where $X_9, ..., X_{16}$ are viewed as oil variable and $Y_9, ..., Y_{16}$ are viewed as vinegar variables;
6. $Z_{56}, ..., Z_{63}$, where $X_{17}, ..., X_{24}$ are viewed as oil variable and $Y_{17}, ..., Y_{24}$ are viewed as vinegar variables;
7. $Z_{65}, ..., Z_{72}$, where $Y_{25}, ..., Y_{32}$ are viewed as oil variable and $X_9, ..., X_{16}$ are viewed as vinegar variables.

The public key is constructed as a map from $k^{56 \times d}$ to $k^{74 \times d}$:

$$Y = (y_1, ..., y_{74 \times d}) = \bar{F}(x_1, ..., x_{56 \times d}) = L_1 \circ \Phi \circ F \circ \Phi' \circ L_2(x_1, ..., x_{56 \times d}),$$

where Φ' is the map from k^{56d} to $\mathcal{F}^{56}$ induced from the map P in (5), and Φ is the map from $\mathcal{F}^{74}$ to k^{74d} induced from P^{-1}.

2.3   The Decryption Process

The decryption process requires to invert the maps and the key is how to invert the central map.

The key step is first to unmask the triangular system $(Z_1, ..., Z_7)$, and to derive the value of $X_1, .., X_7$ and then X_8. The rest is just to solve the oil-vinegar systems. We start by focusing on the first three equations of the central map system.

We will first write some of the Diophantine equations satisfied by components of the central map. Let

$$g_1 = Z_8 Z_9 + Z_{10} Z_{11} + Z_{12} Z_{13} + Z_{14} Z_{15} + Z_{16} Z_{17}$$
$$= \psi_{1,1}(X_1...X_8)\psi_{1,2}(Y_1...Y_8),$$
$$g_2 = Z_{18} Z_{19} + Z_{20} Z_{21} + Z_{22} Z_{23} + Z_{24} Z_{25} + Z_{26} Z_{27}$$
$$= \psi_{2,1}(X_1...X_8)\psi_{2,2}(Y_9...Y_{16}), \qquad (9)$$
$$g_3 = Z_{28} Z_{29} + Z_{30} Z_{31} + Z_{32} Z_{33} + Z_{34} Z_{35} + Z_{26} Z_{36}$$
$$= \psi_{2,1}(Y_1...Y_8)\psi_{2,2}(Y_9...Y_{16}).$$

Note that Z_{26} appears in both g_2 and g_3 because of (7), (8).

Since

$$\psi_{2,1}(X_1, ..., X_8) = \psi_{1,1}(X_1, ..., X_8), \quad \psi_{2,1}(Y_1, ..., Y_8) = \psi_{1,2}(Y_1, ..., Y_8),$$

we have

$$h_1 = (g_1 g_2 g_3^{-1})^{1/2} = \psi_{1,1}(X_1, ..., X_8) \tag{10}$$
$$h_2 = g_1 h_1^{-1} = \psi_{1,2}(Y_1, ..., Y_8) \tag{11}$$
$$h_3 = g_2 h_1^{-1} = \psi_{2,2}(Y_9, ..., Y_{16}). \tag{12}$$

This allows us to compute the value of $\psi_{1,1}(X_1, ..., X_8)$, $\psi_{1,2}(Y_1, ..., Y_8)$ and $\psi_{2,2}(Y_9, ..., Y_{16})$.

Since we also have the Diophantine equations:

$$g_4 = Z_{37}Z_{38} + Z_{39}Z_{40} + Z_{41}Z_{42} + Z_{43}Z_{44} + Z_{45}Z_{46}$$
$$= \psi_{3,1}(X_1, .., X_8)\psi_{3,2}(Y_{17}, .., Y_{24}), \tag{13}$$
$$g_5 = Z_{47}Z_{48} + Z_{49}Z_{50} + Z_{51}Z_{52} + Z_{53}Z_{54} + Z_{26}Z_{55}$$
$$= \psi_{2,1}(X_9, .., X_{16})\psi_{2,2}(Y_9, .., Y_{16}), \tag{14}$$
$$g_6 = Z_{56}Z_{57} + Z_{58}Z_{59} + Z_{60}Z_{61} + Z_{62}Z_{63} + Z_{45}Z_{64}$$
$$= \psi_{3,1}(X_{17}, .., X_{24})\psi_{3,2}(Y_{17}, .., Y_{24}), \tag{15}$$
$$g_7 = Z_{65}Z_{66} + Z_{67}Z_{68} + Z_{69}Z_{70} + Z_{71}Z_{72} + Z_{73}Z_{74}$$
$$= \psi_{4,1}(X_9, .., X_{16})\psi_{4,2}(Y_{25}, .., Y_{32}). \tag{16}$$

Then, since

$$\psi_{3,1}(X_1, ..., X_8) = \psi_{1,1}(X_1, ..., X_8),$$

and

$$\psi_{4,1}(X_9, ..., X_{16}) = \psi_{2,1}(X_9, ..., X_{16}),$$

we have

$$h_4 = g_4 h_1^{-1} = \psi_{3,2}(Y_{17}, ..., Y_{24}), \tag{17}$$
$$h_5 = g_5 h_3^{-1} = \psi_{2,1}(X_9, ..., X_{16}), \tag{18}$$
$$h_6 = g_6 h_4^{-1} = \psi_{3,1}(X_{17}, ..., X_{24}), \tag{19}$$
$$h_7 = g_7 h_5^{-1} = \psi_{4,2}(Y_{25}, ..., Y_{32}). \tag{20}$$

Using the value of $h_1, ..., h_7$, we can restore the triangular structure of $Z_1, ..., Z_7$, and recover the values of $X_1, ..., X_7$.

Then we recover X_8 by using the value of $h_1 = \psi_{1,1}(X_1, ..., X_8)$, as long as X_7 is nonzero, or we can use Z_{17} to recover X_8 as long as X_2 is not zero.

One finishes the inversion of the central map by using the 1,2,4,5,6,7 oil-vinegar systems described in the section above to derive the remaining variables $X_9, ..., X_{24}$ and $Y_1, ..., Y_{32}$.

Note that the decryption process succeeds with a high probability but not 1, and our attack only deals with ciphertexts, whose decryption can be performed successfully as above.

2.4   Practical Parameters and Security Claims

The authors [7] suggested the following practical parameters:

1. $q = 2^{16}$, d=1, the number of variables 56, the number of public key polynomials 74, and the security level claim is 2^{113};
2. $q = 2^{16}$, d=2, the number of variables $56 \times 2 = 112$, the number of public
   key polynomials $74 \times 2 = 148$, and the security level claim is 2^{221};
3. $q = 2^{32}$, d=1, the number of variables 56, the number of public key polynomials 74, and the security level claim is 2^{114}.

3   Embedded Surface Attack

We will present the attack using the embedded surfaces.

3.1   Embedded Surface Attack

We will now concentrate our attack using the first suggested parameter. Namely
we have: $q = 2^{16}$, d=1, $\mathcal{F} = k = GF(2^{16})$, the number of variables is 56, the
number of public key polynomials is 74, and the security level claim is 2^{113}.

It is very clear that the key decryption process is in the relations (9), without
which the decryption will not be possible. Let us first rewrite these relations
explicitly as:

$$g_1 = h_1 \times h_2, \tag{21}$$

$$g_2 = h_1 \times h_3, \tag{22}$$

$$g_3 = h_2 \times h_3. \tag{23}$$

However, from these relations, we can derive the following very interesting relations:

$$g_1 g_2 = g_3 \times h_1^2,$$
$$g_2 g_3 = g_1 \times h_3^2, \tag{24}$$
$$g_1 g_3 = g_2 \times h_2^2.$$

Let us look at the first relation explicitly as:

$$(Z_8 Z_9 + Z_{10} Z_{11} + Z_{12} Z_{13} + Z_{14} Z_{15} + Z_{16} Z_{17}) \times$$
$$(Z_{18} Z_{19} + Z_{20} Z_{21} + Z_{22} Z_{23} + Z_{24} Z_{25} + Z_{26} Z_{27}) =$$
$$(Z_{28} Z_{29} + Z_{30} Z_{31} + Z_{32} Z_{33} + Z_{34} Z_{35} + Z_{26} Z_{36}) \times (\psi_{1,1}(X_1, ..., X_8))^2. \tag{25}$$

which can be further written in the form:

$$\sum a_{i,j,s,t} Z_i Z_j Z_s Z_t = \sum a'_{i,j,s,t} Z_i Z_j X_s^2 X_t^2. \tag{26}$$

or

$$\sum a_{i,j,s,t} Z_i Z_j Z_s Z_t - \sum a'_{i,j,s,t} Z_i Z_j X_s^2 X_t^2 = 0. \tag{27}$$

Here we would like to point out that this relation is true due to the fact that $\mathcal{F} = k$ is of characteristics 2, where

$$(a+b)^2 = a^2 + b^2.$$

This means that if

$$g_1 \times g_2 \times g_3 \neq 0,$$

an assumption required for decryption, again, due to the fact that $\mathcal{F} = k$ is of characteristics 2, if we have all relations in the form of (26), given the values of Z_i, we should be able to derive the values of

$$h_1^2 = (\psi_{1,1}(X_1, ..., X_8))^2,$$
$$h_2^2 = (\psi_{1,2}(Y_1, ..., Y_8))^2,$$
$$h_3^2 = (\psi_{2,2}(Y_9, ..., Y_{16}))^2,$$

and therefore the value of $h_1 = \psi_{1,1}(X_1, ..., X_8)$, $h_2 = \psi_{1,2}(Y_1, ..., Y_8)$ and $h_3 = \psi_{2,2}(Y_9, ..., Y_{16})$, by taking squareroot in k, a field of characteristic 2.

The above implies that, for the public key cryptosystem, for a pair of ciphertext and plaintext $(x_1, .., x_{56})$ and $(y_1, ..., y_{74})$, there are relations in the form:

$$\sum a_{i,j,s,t} y_i y_j y_s y_t + \sum b_{i,j,s} y_i y_j y_s + \sum c_{i,j} y_i y_j + \sum d_j y_j +$$
$$\sum a'_{i,j,s,t} y_i y_j x_s^2 x_t^2 + \sum b'_{i,s,t} y_i x_s^2 x_t^2 + \sum c'_{i,j,s} y_i y_j x_s^2 + \sum d'_{i,s} y_i x_s^2 +$$
$$\sum e'_{s,t} x_s^2 x_t^2 + \sum h'_s x_s^2 + e = 0, \tag{28}$$

which comes from (27). This new form is due to the affine transformations L_1 and L_2.

This can give us a none-trivial embedded surface, since if we are given the value of all y_i, we can derive polynomial equations in the form of

$$\sum a''_{s,t} x_s^2 x_t^2 + \sum b''_s x_s^2 + c'' = 0, \tag{29}$$

which gives us the value of polynomials corresponding to h_1 and h_2 and h_3, and they are not components in in the central map. This is true, as long as the corresponding value of $g_1 \times g_2 \times g_3$ is not zero, an assumption required for decryption.

The means that, if we get all the embedded surfaces as a linear space in the form of (28), we will actually be able to derive the corresponding value of h_1 and h_2 and h_3 for any valid (decryption possible)ciphertext $(y'_1, ..., y'_{74})$. If we amend those equations to the original system, in the context of original polynomial system derived from the known ciphertext, we will be able to derive the values corresponding to X_1, X_2, X_3.

Now, let us look at again the relations that are used to derive $h_3, .., h_7$ in the decryption process, which we will rewrite as:

$$h_4 h_1 = \psi_{3,2}(Y_{17}, ..., Y_{24})h_1 = g_4 =$$
$$Z_{37}Z_{38} + Z_{39}Z_{40} + Z_{41}Z_{42} + Z_{43}Z_{44} + Z_{45}Z_{46}, \tag{30}$$
$$h_5 h_3 = \psi_{2,1}(X_9, ..., X_{16})h_1 = g_5 =$$
$$Z_{47}Z_{48} + Z_{49}Z_{50} + Z_{51}Z_{52} + Z_{53}Z_{54} + Z_{26}Z_{55}. \tag{31}$$

and

$$h_6 h_4 = \psi_{3,1}(X_{17}, ..., X_{24})h_1 = g_6 =$$
$$Z_{56}Z_{57} + Z_{58}Z_{59} + Z_{60}Z_{61} + Z_{62}Z_{63} + Z_{45}Z_{64}, \tag{32}$$
$$h_7 h_5 = \psi_{4,2}(Y_{25}, ..., Y_{32})h_5 = g_7 =$$
$$Z_{65}Z_{66} + Z_{67}Z_{68} + Z_{69}Z_{70} + Z_{71}Z_{72} + Z_{73}Z_{74}. \tag{33}$$

This means, in the central map system, if we amend the h_1 and h_2 and h_3 to the map, and if we apply either Groebner basis algorithm like F_4 or F_5 of Faugere or the mutant XL family of algorithms [9],[2], in the first computation round when the algorithm reaches degree 4, we will derive the values of h_4 and h_5 as mutants, and in the next computation round, which is still at degree 4, we will derive h_6 and h_7 as mutants. This implies that we can derive the values of $X_4, .., X_7$ and therefore the value of X_8 as in the decryption process. Since the rest are just Oil-Vinegar type of systems, this further implies that we can solve the system at degree 4 using polynomial solving algorithms once the values h_1, h_2, h_3 are derived using the embedded surfaces in the form (28).

The above enables us to make a complete algorithm to attack the system.

1. **Step 1. Find all the embedded surfaces**

   Randomly pick

   $$\binom{74+4}{4} + \binom{56+2}{2} \times \binom{74+2}{2} = 1426425 + 4711050 = 6137475$$

   ciphertext and plaitext pairs derived from the public key, and substitute them into the equation in the form of (28), where the coefficients of the system are treated as variables. This will give us a set of linear equations with 6137475 variables over $GF(2^{16})$ and the same number of equations.

   Find the solutions for this set of linear equations. The solution space should be of dimension:

   $$(76 \times 75)/2 \times 76 + 76 \times 76 + 76 + 3 = 222455,$$

   where 222455 of them come from equations derived from the trivial relations from terms like $Z_i Z_j Z_k^2$, $Z_j^2 Z_i$ and Z_i^2, and only 3 of them is what we really need, namely the ones coming from (24).

2. **Step 2. Derive new equations from the embedded surfaces**

With the 222455 embedded surfaces, once given any valid ciphertext, we substitute it into the embedded surfaces, we will derive $74 + 3 = 77$ linearly independent degree 4 equations in the form:

$$\sum A_{s,t} x_s^2 x_t^2 \sum B_s x_s^2 + C = 0.$$

Then, we take the square root of these equations due to the fact that it is over a field of characteristic 2, namely

$$\sum A_{s,t}^{1/2} x_s x_t \sum B_s^{1/2} x_s + C^{1/2} = 0,$$

since

$$(\sum A_{s,t}^{1/2} x_s x_t \sum B_s^{1/2} x_s + C^{1/2})^2 = \sum A_{s,t} x_s^2 x_t^2 \sum B_s x_s^2 + C,$$

and comuting the square root over a field of of characteristic 2 is easy to do. This gives us a set of 77 linearly independent quadratic equations. All the public equations derived from the public key and the known ciphertext are already included in the span of this set of equations.

3. **Step 3. Reduce three variables**

Perform Gaussian elimination on this set of equations to look for an equation in the form of

$$\sum a_i x_i^2 + \sum b_i x_i + c = 0,$$

where

$$a_i = b_i^2 \times \alpha,$$

for a fixed constant α. Solving this quadratic equation will give us a linear in the form

$$\sum a_i x_i + b = 0.$$

This corresponds to deriving the value of X_1, which comes from Z_1 by eliminating $\psi_{1,1}(X_1, ..., X_8)$ due to the known value of $h_1 = \psi_{1,1}(X_1, \ldots, X_8)$. We will then substitute this linear equation into the system, and perform Gaussian elimination, which gives us again an equation in the form of

$$\sum a_i x_i^2 + \sum b_i x_i + c = 0,$$

where again

$$a_i = b_i^2 \times \alpha',$$

for a some fixed constant α'. Solving this quadratic equation will give us a linear equation in the form $\sum a_i x_i + b = 0$.

This corresponds to deriving the value of X_2, which comes from Z_2 and the known value of h_2.

We will repeat the process to derive a new linear equation, which corresponds to deriving the value of X_3 coming from Z_3 and the known value of h_3.

4. **Step 4. Solve the system**

> We will feed the new system including the 3 new linear equations into a Groebner solver like F_4 or the mutant XL algorithm. We will solve the systems at degree 4. This will give us the value of the whole plaintext.

In principle, we can merge Step 3 and Step 4 by using directly the algebraic solver like F_4 or the mutant XL algorithm, which will yield the same results.

3.2 The Complexity of the Attack

From the attacking steps, it is clear that the complexity of the attacks concentrates on **Step 1** and **Step 4**.

In Step 1, the key part is to solve a system of linear equations with $N = 6137475$ variables and the same number of equations. If we use usual Gaussian elimination, the complexity will be roughly

$$2N^3/3 = 154126724635276031250 \approx 2^{68},$$

over the field $GF(2^{16})$. Assume that we use the best optimized linear solver, we should have the complexity $N^{2.3} \approx 2^{52}$ theoretically.

In Step 4, we will need to solve a linear system roughly with $\binom{53+4}{4} = 395010$ variables and the same number of equations. Clearly this system is much smaller than the system above, whose complexity is much smaller.

Therefore, we conclude that if we use the optimized Gaussian elimination, the complexity will be roughly 2^{52} theoretically, and the complexity will be 2^{68} with usual Gaussian elimination. This complexity is based on operations over $GF(2^{16})$. The original security claim for the system is 2^{113} with the assumption of using the optimized Gaussian elimination.

3.3 The Complexity for Attacking the Other Two Systems

For the case, where $q = 2^{32}$ and $d=1$, the attack complexity will be precisely the same except that everything will be on a field over $GF(2^{32})$. The original security assumption is 2^{114} with the assumption of using the optimized Gaussian elimination.

As for the case, where $q = 2^{16}$, $d=2$, it is clear the complexity will be determined by solving a set of linear equations with the number of variables and equations as

$$N = \binom{2*74+4}{4} + \binom{2*56+2}{2} * \binom{2*74+2}{2} = 93352225.$$

If we use normal Gaussian elimination, the complexity will be roughly

$$2N^3/3 \approx 2^{79},$$

over the field $GF(2^{16})$. Assume that we use the best optimized linear solver, we should have the complexity $N^{2.3} \approx 2^{61}$ theoretically. The original security claim is 2^{221} with assumption of using the optimized Gaussian elimination.

Due to the memory constraints in our own equipments, we could not perform the experiments to attack the system in practice. But we did perform some small scale toy experiments, where we set some of the variables in the central map to be 0, to confirm that our attack works indeed.

3.4 Direct Algebraic Attack

One may ask what if we use F_4 or the mutant XL directly against the new MPKCs? One can see easily, our embedded surface actually implies that the degree of regularity of the systems [1] is actually 8, since each y_i is of degree 2 and our surface is actually of degree 4 in y_i. This means that the direct algebraic solver would be much less efficient since our method finishes at degree 4.

4 Conclusion

We present a new attack on the new MPKCs from Diophantine equations developed by Gao and Hendl. This attack uses embedded surfaces associated with the new MPKCs. We show that this new attack can break the system efficiently. We believe such an approach is a very useful approach, which can be applied on other types of systems including symmetric systems.

We would like to point out that our attack relies very much on the fact that the field is of characteristic 2. We believe it deserves further attention to seek possibilities to rebuild the system using fields of odd characteristics, whose security could be very different as pointed out in[4].

Acknowledgments. The work was partially supported by **Charles Phelps Taft Foundation** and the NSF of China under the grant #60973131 and the National Natural Science Foundation of China under grant No. U1135004 and 61170080.

References

1. Bardet, M., Faugère, J.-C., Salvy, B.: On the complexity of Gröbner basis computation of semi-regular overdetermined algebraic equations. In: International Conference on Polynomial System Solving - ICPSS, pp. 71–75 (November 2004)
2. Ding, J., Buchmann, J., Mohamed, M., Mohamed, W., Weinmann, R.-P.: Mutant xL. In: First International Conference on Symbolic Computation and Cryptography, SCC 2008 (2008)
3. Ding, J., Hu, L., Nie, X., Li, J., Wagner, J.: High order linearization equation (HOLE) attack on multivariate public key cryptosystems. In: Okamoto, T., Wang, X. (eds.) PKC 2007. LNCS, vol. 4450, pp. 233–248. Springer, Heidelberg (2007a)

4. Ding, J., Schmidt, D., Werner, F.: Algebraic attack on HFE revisited. In: Wu, T.-C., Lei, C.-L., Rijmen, V., Lee, D.-T. (eds.) ISC 2008. LNCS, vol. 5222, pp. 215–227. Springer, Heidelberg (2008)
5. Dubois, V., Gama, N.: The degree of regularity of HFE systems. In: Abe, M. (ed.) ASIACRYPT 2010. LNCS, vol. 6477, pp. 557–576. Springer, Heidelberg (2010)
6. Garey, M.R., Johnson, D.S.: Computers and intractability, A Guide to the theory of NP-completeness. W.H. Freeman, San Francisco (1979)
7. Gao, S., Heindl, R.: Multivariate public key cryptosystems from diophantine equations. Designs, Codes and Cryptography, 1–18 (November 2, 2011), doi:10.1007/s10623-011-9582-1
8. Heindl, R.A.: New directions in multivariate public key cryptography, Ph.D. Thesis, Clemson University. Mathematical Science - 2009 (2009)
9. Mohamed, M.S.E., Cabarcas, D., Ding, J., Buchmann, J., Bulygin, S.: MXL$_3$: An Efficient Algorithm for Computing Gröbner Bases of Zero-Dimensional Ideals. In: Lee, D., Hong, S. (eds.) ICISC 2009. LNCS, vol. 5984, pp. 87–100. Springer, Heidelberg (2010)
10. Patarin, J.: Cryptanalysis of the Matsumoto and Imai Public Key Scheme of Eurocrypt '88. In: Coppersmith, D. (ed.) CRYPTO 1995. LNCS, vol. 963, pp. 248–261. Springer, Heidelberg (1995)
11. Patarin, J.: The oil and vinegar signature scheme. Presented at the Dagstuhl Workshop on Cryptography (1997)
12. Shor, P.: Polynomial-time algorithms for prime factorization and discrete logarithms on a quantum computer. SIAM Rev. 41(2), 303–332 (1999)
13. Wang, L.-C., Yang, B.-Y., Hu, Y.-H., Lai, F.: A "Medium-field" multivariate public-key encryption scheme. In: Pointcheval, D. (ed.) CT-RSA 2006. LNCS, vol. 3860, pp. 132–149. Springer, Heidelberg (2006)

Verifiable Structured Encryption

Moesfa Soeheila Mohamad and Geong Sen Poh

Cryptography Lab, MIMOS Berhad
Technology Park Malaysia, 57000 Kuala Lumpur, Malaysia
{soeheila.mohamad,gspoh}@mimos.my

Abstract. Structured encryption schemes generalise symmetric searchable encryption (SSE) schemes by allowing encrypted search on arbitrarily structured data, instead of keyword-based search only. Both structured encryption and SSE schemes mainly consider security against passive adversaries, until recently where SSE schemes secure against active adversaries were proposed. This means in addition of querying encrypted data, the adversaries can modify encrypted data in the storage. SSE schemes secure against such adversaries are termed *verifiable SSE*. In this paper, we examine verifiable SSE and propose an extension for structured encryption under the active adversary setting. We first define verifiable structured encryption and its security under the notion of reliability similar to verifiable SSE, but with difference on how a tag for verifiability is defined. This is mainly due to the notions of semi-private data that does not exist in a verifiable SSE scheme. We then present constructions secure under this model and prove security of the constructions.

Keywords: verifiable symmetric searchable encryption, structured encryption.

1 Introduction

Symmetric searchable encryption (SSE) was introduced to address privacy concern on storing sensitive data into and retrieving sensitive data from a storage. A possible application scenario today is remote cloud storage. Such a storage facility is normally provided by a cloud storage provider. A user who stores data in this cloud storage may not necessarily trust the provider and hence the user may encrypt the data before storing them. However, if a user wishes to retrieve one specific file from the encrypted data, either the provider must be allowed to decrypt and retrieve the required data, or the encrypted data must be sent to the user. The provider will learn the data if the provider is allowed to decrypt, while sending the encrypted data back to the user for him to retrieve one specific file is inefficient. SSE schemes provide a way to search for the file and retrieve the file from the encrypted data without first decrypting the data. The underlying assumption is that the encrypted data consists of text documents and search can be performed based on keywords. Structured encryption, proposed by Chase and Kamara [5], extends the search capability from keywords to also include search

M. Kutyłowski and M. Yung (Eds.): Inscrypt 2012, LNCS 7763, pp. 137–156, 2013.

for arbitrarily structured data. The main reason for this is that new data may be stored in complex structure, such as web graphs or social networks, and keyword based search may not be able to retrieve all relevant data.

For both SSE and structured encryption, security is defined against passive adversaries. This means providing privacy (or confidentiality) as a whole for the data structure and stored data as well as the search tokens. Storage provider is honest-but-curious in the sense that he might try to guess the keywords or the encrypted data, but not modify them. Recently Kurosawa and Ohtaki [11] propose verifiable SSE schemes, in which the security is defined against active adversaries. It models the case where, for example, a malicious storage provider forging encrypted data or deleting some of this data. If such a storage provider is allowed, it is possible to create fake encrypted data entries in existing structured encryption schemes. This motivates us to consider the extension of such a security model to structured encryption since structured encryption provides broader and more flexible symmetric searchable encryption, in which a verifiable construct allows detection of modified data by a malicious storage provider.

Our Results. In the following we summarize our results.

- We introduce and define verifiable structured encryption against active adversaries. In particular, we extend the notion of *reliability* of verifiable SSE schemes by Kurosawa and Ohtaki [11] to structured encryption proposed by Chase and Kamara [5]. The main challenge in this extension lies in the different properties of structured encryption compared to a SSE scheme, where the output of the encryption function includes an encrypted data structure containing semi-private data in addition to the encrypted files. The semi-private data is considered public information and can be used to "link" to other encrypted data structure. Therefore, reliability must be preserved for both the data and the semi-private data. We address this by computing an authentication tag that binds together the index pointers to data in the data structure, and the semi-private data that is indexed under the same pointers. By doing this when an adversary manipulate the semi-private data, he will also need to generate an authentication tag for a pointer to data related to this semi-private data. Similarly if the adversary forge an encrypted data, he will need to generate an authentication tag for all relevant data that matches the semi-private data and index pointer for a submitted search token.
- We propose two instances of verifiable structured encryption scheme. These instances are the verifiable extension for the label and labeled graph schemes proposed by Chase and Kamara [5]. The verifiable label scheme gives a basic primitive for structured encryption, and the verifiable labeled graph scheme uses the verifiable label scheme to construct searchable encryption for graph-based data structure.

2   Related Work

Works on oblivious RAMs first examined by Goldreich and Ostrovsky [9], with a recent proposal in [12], can be used to construct searchable encryption schemes.

However, these schemes are inefficient in practice. In order to construct efficient and practical scheme, Song, Wagner and Perrig [13] introduced SSE schemes that contain symmetric encryption functions designed specifically for encryptions and searches of words in a document. The schemes can be built under sequential scanning or index tables. Sequential scanning is inefficient as the server sequentially scan through all documents to retrieve relevant documents based on the keywords. The index tables, on the other hand, leak information during updates, as was stated by Goh in [8].

Due to this, Goh proposed secure indexes based on Bloom filters but searchable encryption is just one of the applications that may utilise secure indexes. Furthermore the underlying security model against chosen keyword attacks does not require the underlying keyword tokens (or trapdoors) to be semantically secure. Hence Chang and Mitzenmacher [4] suggested stronger security model to address information leakage in Goh's secure indexes. However, Curtmola *et al.* in [6] pointed out that the security definition by Chang and Mitzenmacher can be easily met, even with SSE scheme that is insecure. Improved security notions on SSE schemes were thus proposed, with introduction of non-adaptive and adaptive chosen-keyword attacks. All these schemes consider passive adversary only. So recently Kurosawa and Ohtaki, in [11], proposed an adversarial model that take into account both passive and active adversaries, whereby an adversary may modify the data in storage and the data produced during search on the server. Kurosawa and Ohtaki then proceed to present a scheme termed as *verifiable SSE scheme* secure against these active adversaries. In another development based on the study of existing SSE schemes, a generalisation of SSE termed as *structured encryption* was proposed by Chase and Kamara [5]. Their proposal extends SSE on keyword-based data to arbitrarily-structured data, while the security model follows that of SSE before Kurosawa and Ohtaki, that is it only considers passive adversary.

There are also proposals of searchable encryption schemes based on public key cryptography. The first such scheme, known as *Public Key Encryption with keyword Search* (PEKS), was introduced by Boneh, Di Crescenzo, Ostrovsky and Persiano [2]. This PEKS scheme was further refined in [1]. Similar schemes known as Private Information Retrieval (PIR) were also proposed, such as in [3]. Unlike PEKS schemes that leak access patterns, PIR schemes provide full concealment of encrypted search. Recently a primitive known as fully homomorphic encryption [7] has become one of the main techniques to provide public-key based searchable encryption due to its capability to execute arbitrary operations on encrypted data. Our focus is on SSE and hence we will not examine further schemes based on public key settings.

3   Preliminaries

Following the notion of Chase and Kamara [5], we use $x \leftarrow \mathcal{A}$ to denote an algorithm $\mathcal{A}$ with an output x. Given n a positive integer, we denote $\{0,1\}^n$ as the set of binary string with length n, while the set of integers $\{1, \ldots, n\}$ is denoted as $[n]$. The empty set is $\emptyset$. We further use $|S|$ to refer to the cardinality of a set S, and given a string s, we use $|s|$ to refer to its bit length. For $\mathbf{v}$ a sequence of n elements, we denote v_i as its ith element. We also assume the existence of a static look up table $\mathcal{T}$ that support query operations. The look up table stores a pair of value (a, b), in such a way that when b is given, a can be retrieved efficiently. This means b serves as a search key. In particular, we will construct two look up tables. The first look up table is called a labeling, L, in which it stores pairs of (i, w) for $i \in [n]$ the indexes to messages containing keyword w. In this case given a keyword w as input to L, we have $L(w) = \{i \in [n] : (i, w) \in L\}$. We further denote $\max(L)$ as the size of the largest set $L(w)$. The second look up table is a dictionary, T, which contains pairs of encrypted data and encrypted keywords generated by the verifiable structured encryption scheme (as will be described in Sections 5 and 6).

3.1 Required Cryptographic Building Blocks

We require a CPA-secure symmetric encryption scheme $\Pi = (\mathsf{Gen}, \mathsf{Enc}, \mathsf{Dec})$, where Gen is a probabilistic key generation algorithm, Enc a probabilistic encryption algorithm and Dec a deterministic decryption algorithm. We also require pseudo-random functions (PRF) and pseudo-random permutations (PRP). Definitions for these building blocks can be found in [10].

3.2 Structured Encryption Schemes

In this section we describe structured encryption schemes proposed by Chase and Kamara [5]. A structured encryption scheme uses permutation and has properties known as associativity and chainability.

Induced Permutation. A structured encryption scheme uses PRP to permute the original locations (or indexes) of messages in a message sequence $\mathbf{m} = (m_1, \cdots, m_n)$ during the encryption process. By using the permutation, given an index to a ciphertext in the ciphertext sequence $\mathbf{c} = (c_1, \cdots, c_n)$, it is infeasible to deduce the original locations of the items in $\mathbf{m}$. This permutation is termed induced permutation [5]. We denote by π the induced permutation and for all $i \in [n]$, $m_i := \mathsf{Dec}(K, c_{\pi(i)})$. The inverse is π^{-1}.

Associativity. In this setting, a message input to a structured encryption scheme may contain a message sequence $\mathbf{m}$ and an associated data sequence $\mathbf{v}$. More specifically, a structured encryption scheme is said to be *associative* if the input message is defined as $\mathbf{M} = (\mathbf{m}, \mathbf{v}) = ((m_1, v_1), \ldots, (m_n, v_n))$, where m_i is a message to be encrypted and v_i a semi-private data. A semi-private data is data that can be revealed as public information given a matching query. In other words, the query operation in addition of returning the query results also returns semi-private data v_i related to the data items.

Chainability. It means simpler structures can be "chained" to form a more complex structure using the associativity property. A possible chaining is to assign tokens on queries or encrypted message items of a simple structure as the semi-private data.

Definition of Structured Encryption Schemes [5]. An *associative structured encryption scheme* is a tuple of five polynomial-time algorithms $\Sigma = ($Gen, Enc, Token, Query, Dec$)$, such that Gen is a probabilistic algorithm that generates a key K with input 1^k; Enc is a probabilistic algorithm that takes as input K, a data structure L and a sequence of private and semi-private data $\mathbf{M}$ and outputs an encrypted data structure γ and a sequence of ciphertexts $\mathbf{c}$; Token is a (possibly probabilistic) algorithm that takes as input K and a query q and outputs a search token τ; Query is a deterministic algorithm that takes as input an encrypted data structure γ and a search token τ and outputs a set of pointers $J \subseteq [n]$ and a sequence of semi-private data $\mathbf{v}_I = (v_i)_{i \in I}$, where $I = \pi^{-1}[J]$; Dec is a deterministic algorithm that takes as input K and a ciphertext c_j and outputs a message m_i. Detailed and exact definition of the scheme can be found in [5].

$(\mathcal{L}_1, \mathcal{L}_2)$-Security. In a structured encryption scheme (as well as SSE schemes), leakage on access and query patterns are allowed. Chase and Kamara [5] generalise definition of such leakages through two stateful leakage functions, $\mathcal{L}_1$ and $\mathcal{L}_2$. In brief, the $\mathcal{L}_1$ leakage function captures the leakage of size and length of the data items, that is, the information leaked by the encrypted data $(\gamma, \mathbf{c})$. On the other hand, $\mathcal{L}_2$ captures the leakage from the query and intersection patterns by the token τ and query q. The actual form of leakage depends on the definition of $(\mathcal{L}_1, \mathcal{L}_2)$ in a concrete scheme.

4   Verifiable Structured Encryption Schemes

In this section we define verifiable structured encryption schemes. Our security notions follow the *privacy* and *reliability* of Kurosawa and Ohtaki [11]. The notion of privacy is then adopted to the $(\mathcal{L}_1, \mathcal{L}_2)$-security against adaptive chosen keyword attack of Chase and Kamara [5].

The idea of search result reliability was introduced by Kurosawa and Ohtaki in [11] by extending SSE defined by Curtmola *et al.* in [6]. Reliability means the search result can be verified to contain exactly the documents containing the input keyword; no more, no less. Consequently the tags must be created for every document index in relation to every keyword. In other words, every document declares whether it contains a keyword, for all keywords. In more details, the scheme in [11] defines the look-up table L to have the size $2 \times N \cdot 2^\ell$ where N is the number of documents and 2^ℓ is the number of keywords. A permutation based on a PRP, $\pi_k(\cdot, \cdot)$, was also defined. For a document index i and a keyword w, the location $\mathrm{addr}_{w,i} = \pi_k(w, i)$ in L holds either $(i, \mathrm{tag}_{w,i} = \mathrm{MAC}(\mathrm{addr}_{w,i}, c_i))$ if document i contains w or $(\mathrm{dummy}, \mathrm{tag}_{w,i} = \mathrm{MAC}(\mathrm{addr}_{w,i}, \mathrm{dummy}))$ otherwise.

Consequently, by unforgeability of MAC, an adversary can neither add any ciphertext to a search result nor omit any ciphertext to a search result. Furthermore, the user can also detect if a ciphertext is replaced with a different one because each ciphertext is put with its index in the MAC.

For structured encryption defined by Chase and Kamara in [5], the dictionary, T, is the corresponding data to the look-up table L above. The dictionary contains one entry for each keyword and the size of the entry depends on the number of documents containing the keyword. Also, due to the associative nature of the scheme, each message is allowed to have semi-private data. So, every message index is paired with the message semi-private data. In short, a dictionary entry for keyword w is $\langle(\pi(i), v_i)\rangle_{i \in L(w)} \oplus F_{K_1}(w)$ where i is a message (or document) index, $\pi(i)$ the induced permutation on i, $F_{K_1}(w)$ is a PRF and $L(w)$ is the set of indices of documents which contains w. Furthermore, privacy is achieved by having the input to Query being a token calculated from the keyword, which means the keyword is not revealed to the storage service provider. The token is the search key (or location) in the dictionary.

Taking the same approach as Kurosawa and Ohtaki, we extend structured SSE to be verifiable by calculating tags for every element in a dictionary entry. The tags must link together the search key, the messages permuted index, the messages ciphertext and the messages semi-private data. Besides that, each dictionary entry will contain all index and data pairs, with an indicator of which index is in $L(w)$ and which index is not (following the dummy instance of Kurosawa and Ohtaki [11]). Another approach is to calculate the tag on the unmasked dictionary entry, and not individual elements. This approach would take away the flexibility provided by the original schemes where the user is sent only the indexes, and can choose which ciphertexts to download. By taking the first approach the verification algorithm may be made to verify individual results instead of verifying the whole search result.

4.1   Definition

A verifiable structured encryption scheme has similar characteristics of a structured encryption scheme. That is, induced permutation is used and the scheme is associative and chainable. Its differences from the definition of the usual structured encryption scheme lie in the inclusion of a Verify function and the authentication token Tags.

Definition 1. *A* verifiable structured encryption scheme *is a tuple of six polynomial-time algorithms* $\Sigma_v = $ (Gen, Enc, Token, Query, Verify, Dec) *where:*

- $K \leftarrow$ Gen(1^k) *is a probabilistic algorithm that generates a key K with input 1^k, where k is the security parameter;*
- $(\gamma, \mathbf{c}) \leftarrow$ Enc($K, L, \mathbf{M}$) *is a probabilistic algorithm that takes as input K, a data structure L and a sequence of private and semi-private data $\mathbf{M}$ and outputs an encrypted data structure γ and a sequence of ciphertexts $\mathbf{c}$;*
- $\tau \leftarrow$ Token(K, q) *is a (possibly probabilistic) algorithm that takes as input K and a query q and outputs a token τ;*
- $(J, \mathbf{v}_I, \text{Tags}) :=$ Query(γ, τ) *is a deterministic algorithm that takes as input an encrypted data structure γ and a token τ, and outputs a set of pointers $J \subseteq [n]$, a sequence of semi-private data $\mathbf{v}_I = (v_i)_{i \in I}$, where $I = \pi^{-1}[J]$, and a sequence of authentication tokens Tags;*

- accept/reject := Verify($K, \tau, J, \mathbf{c}_J, \mathbf{v}_I$, Tags) *is a deterministic algorithm that takes as input K, a search token τ, a sequence of pointers, a sequence of ciphertext, a sequence of semi-private data returned from the search and a sequence of authentication tokens* Tags, *and outputs* accept *if the inputs are authentic or* reject *otherwise.*
- m_j := Dec(K, c_j) *is a deterministic algorithm that takes as input K and a ciphertext $\mathbf{c}$ and outputs a message m_j.*

We say that Σ_v is correct if for all $k \in \mathbb{N}$, for all $K \leftarrow$ Gen(1^k), for all $(\gamma, \mathbf{c}) \leftarrow$ Enc($K, L, \mathbf{M}$), there is an induced permutation π such that for all queries q, for all $\tau \leftarrow$ Token(K, q) and for $(J, \mathbf{v}_I, \text{Tags}) :=$ Query(γ, τ) where:

- *for $j \in J$, m_i := Dec(K, c_j) for all $j \in [n]$ and $i = \pi^{-1}[j]$, and*
- Verify($K, \tau, J, \mathbf{c}_J, \mathbf{v}_I$, Tags) = accept.

4.2   Security Model

Consider an adversary who resides or has access to the storage. So, the adversary can obtain the ciphertexts and, the access and query patterns. Following definitions of structured encryption scheme (Section 3.2) and the verifiable version (Definition 1), we may observe the adversary has the encrypted data $(\gamma, \mathbf{c})$, the search token τ, the query results $(J, \mathbf{v}_I)$ and the authentication tokens Tags. Furthermore, the adversary is able to build a pattern of query results whenever queries are repeated. Following the notion in [5], the adversary can ascertain how frequent an identical query is made by defining a query pattern QP(q_t). In this case given $\mathbf{q}$ a non-empty sequence of queries, QP(q_t) is a binary vector of length t with a value 1 at location i whenever $q_t = q_i$, and a value 0 otherwise. The adversary is also able to obtain information on the access patterns whenever the same items are queried. Intersection pattern IP(q_t) can be defined on access patterns, where IP(q_t) is a sequence of length t with $f[I]$ at location t, where f is a fixed random permutation over $[n]$ and $I :=$ Query(δ, q_t). However, the *exact* items are not revealed since every item in the message sequence $\mathbf{m}$ is permuted using the induced permutation π. The above information accessible by the adversary is captured under the *privacy* notion. In addition the adversary can modify the encrypted data $(\gamma, \mathbf{c})$, search token τ and query results $(J, \mathbf{v}_I)$. This is captured under the *reliability* notion.

4.3   Privacy

This security notion, as defined by Kurosawa and Ohtaki [11] strengthened the definition of privacy from [6]. We adopt the notion to the definition of $(\mathcal{L}_1, \mathcal{L}_2)$-security by Chase and Kamara in [5]. The description of the **Real** and **Ideal** privacy games as defined in [5] is included in Appendix A. In these games, the adversary outputs 0 if it concludes it is playing **Real** and 1 for **Ideal**. Denote the adversary's output as **Real**$_{\Sigma_v} = b$ and **Ideal**$_{\Sigma_v} = b$ where $b \in \{0, 1\}$ and Σ_v is the verifiable structured encryption scheme.

The games are the more general form of the **Real** and **Sim** games as defined by Kurosawa and Ohtaki, with respect to the information gained by the adversary from encrypted data and search. Specifically for the definition of Kurosawa and Ohtaki, we have $\mathcal{L}_1(L, \mathbf{M})=(|m_1|, |m_2|, \ldots, |m_n|, \ell)$ and $\mathcal{L}_2(L,q) = L(q)$, where L is a labeling as stated in Section 3 and ℓ the maximum bit length of a message m_i. In the following we formalise the notion of privacy:

Definition 2. *A verifiable structured encryption scheme Σ_v is $(\mathcal{L}_1,\mathcal{L}_2)$-secure with adaptive chosen query attacks if there exists a probabilistic polynomial time (PPT) simulator* **S** *such that for all PPT adversaries* **A***, we have*

$$|Pr\left[\mathbf{Real}_{\Sigma_v} = 1\right]| - |Pr\left[\mathbf{Ideal}_{\Sigma_v} = 1\right]|$$

is negligible.

4.4   Reliability

The notion of reliability [11] defines security against active adversary. Here, we adapt the definition of reliability to the original structured encryption schemes for security against active adversary, instead of passive adversary only. The main difference between the definition in Kurosawa and Ohtaki's SSE scheme [11] and the definition in Chase and Kamara's structured encryption schemes is the existence of semi-private data and search results which do not include the ciphertexts in the structured encryption scheme.

Definition 3. *Let $(L, \mathbf{M}, \mathbf{W})$ be data created by the users, where* **W** *the set of all possible keywords (which include the query q), and $(\gamma,\mathbf{c})$ be the encrypted data. Suppose for a search token τ, we have $(J, \mathbf{v}_I, \mathtt{Tags}) \leftarrow \mathtt{Query}(\gamma, \tau)$. A result $(J^*, \mathbf{v}_I^*, \mathtt{Tags}^*)$ is invalid if $(J^*, \mathbf{v}_I^*) \neq (J, \mathbf{v}_I)$.*

A verifiable structured encryption scheme is said to achieve reliability *if for any $(L, \mathbf{M}, \mathbf{W})$ and after any sequence of queries $q_1, q_2, \ldots, q_t$, given a challenge $w \in \mathbf{W}$, an adversary* **A** *produces $(J^*, \mathbf{v}_I^*, \mathtt{Tags}^*)$ with $(J^*, \mathbf{v}_I^*)$ invalid for token τ_w, but $\mathtt{Verify}(K, \tau_w, J^*, \mathbf{c}_{J^*}, \mathbf{v}_J^*, \mathtt{Tags}^*) = \mathtt{Accept}$ with negligible probability.*

5   Verifiable Labels

In this section we describe our first instance of verifiable structured encryption scheme, vLabel, which is a verifiable version of the Label scheme proposed in [5, §5.2]. The scheme is similar to the Label scheme in [5], except that there is an additional `Verify` algorithm and generation of authentication tokens `Tags` by the `Search` algorithm. In this scheme, messages are searched by keywords. The verifiable label scheme can have semi-private data and is chainable. Verifiability of the scheme is achieved by demonstrating that it satisfies reliability.

5.1   Adding Reliability

Figure 1 illustrates the verifiable Label scheme. In order to achieve reliability, we have modified the structure of the dictionary T in the original Label scheme to enable verification of search result and stored data. Specifically, as shown in the Enc algorithm in Figure 1, for each keyword w, besides recording the index of messages containing w, the entry in T must also record the messages which do not contain w. The two types of record are distinguished by the value of the semi-private data of the message. For messages containing w, it would have its semi-private data in the entry. The other message indexes would only have dummy as semi-private data. This is seen in the encryption algorithm line 6 in Figure 1.

In the case where the scheme does not need to be associative, which means the semi-private data is not used, the encryption steps can be easily modified. For example we insert empty for the semi-private data if the message contains w. So Step 6 will change to,

- for each $i \in L(w)$, compute $\text{tag}_{w,\pi(i)} = \text{MAC}_{K_4}(\kappa_w, \pi(i), c_{\pi(i)}, \text{empty})$,
- for each $i \notin L(w)$, compute $\text{tag}_{w,\pi(i)} = \text{MAC}_{K_4}(\kappa_w, \pi(i), \text{dummy}, \text{dummy})$.

This way, Step 4 in the Search algorithm remains correct. In addition, the Verify algorithm at Step 2 becomes

$$t_j = \begin{cases} \text{MAC}_{K_4}(\tau, j, c_j, \text{empty}) & \text{if } j \in J, \\ \text{MAC}_{K_4}(\tau, j, \text{dummy}, \text{dummy}) & \text{if } j \notin J. \end{cases}$$

Every entry in the dictionary T is based on one keyword. With the construction as above, for each entry all message index is included. For reliability, one tag Tag is computed for each message index. The tag is calculated on the dictionary search key, permuted message index, ciphertext of the message and the semi-private data of the message. As a result any alterations in the encrypted messages or semi-private data, or their locations in the sequences will cause verification to fail. Also, the Verify algorithm would check by comparing the tags returned by the Search algorithm whether the indices returned are exactly the messages containing the searched keyword. If any index is omitted, the tags would not match because the semi-private data input is different. Similarly if a new index is inserted. Hence, reliability is achieved.

Table 1. An index database for query keyword w

Index	Keywords	query answers
1	w_1	w_2, w_3, w_4
2	w_2	w_3
$\vdots$	$\vdots$	$\vdots$
4	w_4	$\ldots$

Briefly, by using a hypothetical example, the scheme works as follow. Given the query and answers, an index database can be prepared as shown in Table 1. Then labeling on keyword w_1, $L(w_1)$, for example, will return message indexes $\{2,3,4\}$. We may execute the vLabel scheme for $L(w_1) = \{2,3,4\}$ in Table 1. The scheme first runs $\mathtt{Gen}(1^k)$ to generate K_1 and K_2 for PRFs, and K_4 for a message authentication code (MAC), where MAC is also a PRF such that MAC : $\{0,1\}^k \times \{0,1\}^* \to \{0,1\}^h$, in which h can be of 160 bits. It also uses a CPA-secure symmetric encryption scheme Π to generate a secret key K_3. Following from this, the encryption algorithm $\mathtt{Enc}$ is computed using the labeling L, input message $\mathbf{M} = (\mathbf{m}, \mathbf{v})$ for $\mathbf{m} = (m_1, m_2, m_3, m_4)$ and $\mathbf{v} = (v_1, v_2, v_3, v_4)$ assuming $n = 4$. We further assume the induced permutation as $\pi = (2, 1, 4, 3)$. Then the message sequence $\mathbf{m}$ is permuted using π, resulting in $\mathbf{m}^* = (m_2, m_1, m_4, m_3)$. Next each messages in $\mathbf{m}^*$ is padded so that all of them have the same length and these messages are encrypted using the symmetric encryption scheme Π, resulting in a ciphertext sequence $\mathbf{c} = (c_1, c_2, c_3, c_4)$. After that, following Step 6 in Figure 1, authentication tokens $\mathtt{tag}$ are computed using K_4 based on a MAC algorithm. The encrypted structure $\gamma = (a, b)$ is:

$$\big\langle (2, \mathtt{dummy}, \mathtt{tag}_{w_1,2}), (1, v_2, \mathtt{tag}_{w_1,1}), (4, v_3, \mathtt{tag}_{w_1,4}), (3, v_4, \mathtt{tag}_{w_1,3}) \big\rangle \oplus F_{K_1}(w_1),$$
$$H_{K_2}(w_1)$$

where $F : \{0,1\}^k \times \mathbf{W} \to \{0,1\}^{\max(L)\cdot(\log n + \omega)}$ and $H : \{0,1\}^k \times \mathbf{W} \to \{0,1\}^k$ are two PRFs and $|v_i| \le \omega$. In order to query $(\gamma, \mathbf{c})$ using keyword w_1, we first run $\mathtt{Token}$ to return $\tau := (F_{K_1}(w_1), H_{K_2}(w_1))$. Then $\mathtt{Search}$ uses $b = H_{K_2}(w_1)$ in τ as a search key to retrieve a from γ and exclusive-ors a with $F_{K_1}(w_1)$, resulting in the output $J = (1, 4, 3)$, $\mathbf{v}_I = (v_2, v_3, v_4)$ and $\mathtt{Tags} = (\mathtt{tag}_{w_1,2}, \mathtt{tag}_{w_1,1}, \mathtt{tag}_{w_1,4}, \mathtt{tag}_{w_1,3})$. The first entry in a with permuted index 2 and the semi-private data $\mathtt{dummy}$ is discarded, except for the tag $\mathtt{tag}_{w_1,2}$. Using $J = (1, 4, 3)$ as pointers, $\mathbf{c} = (c_1, c_3, c_4)$ can be retrieved. Verification will be successful if $\mathrm{MAC}_{K_4}(\kappa_w, 1, c_1, v_2)$ matches $\mathtt{tag}_{w_1,2}$, $\mathrm{MAC}_{K_4}(\kappa_w, 2, \mathtt{dummy}, \mathtt{dummy})$ matches $\mathtt{tag}_{w_1,1}$, $\mathrm{MAC}_{K_4}(\kappa_w, 4, c_4, v_3)$ matches $\mathtt{tag}_{w_1,4}$, and $\mathrm{MAC}_{K4}(\kappa_w, 3, c_3, v_4)$ matches $\mathtt{tag}_{w_1,3}$. Finally, the $\mathtt{Dec}_{K_3}$ algorithm decrypts c_1 to m_2, c_4 to m_3, and c_3 to m_4 as the messages containing keyword w_1.

Security Analysis. The scheme vLabel is defined from Label of the original structured encryption scheme, which achieves $(\mathcal{L}_1, \mathcal{L}_2)$-security under adaptive chosen keyword attack with $\mathcal{L}_1 = (|L|, \max(L), n, \ell)$ and $\mathcal{L}_2 = (|I|, \mathrm{QP}(w), \mathrm{IP}(w))$. We expect there is no additional leak from the ciphertexts and search due to the $\mathtt{Tags}$ assuming a secure MAC. If reliability (using the $\mathtt{Tags}$) is not in place, for example, the adversary may create new message m_i^A and v_i^A, and use the received search token τ to create new entry to the encrypted data structure γ, causing fake result to be returned to the user.

Proposition 1. *Suppose F and H are PRFs, Π is indistinguishable under CPA and $MAC(\cdot)$ is unforgeable under CPA and is pseudo-random, then the scheme vLabel achieves $(\mathcal{L}_1, \mathcal{L}_2)$-security under adaptive chosen keyword attack where $\mathcal{L}_1 = (|L|, \max(L), n, \ell)$ and $\mathcal{L}_2 = (|I|, QP(w), IP(w))$.*

vLabel $=$ (Gen, Enc, Token, Search, Verify, Dec)

$K \leftarrow$ Gen(1^k):

1. Generate three random binary sequences of length k, K_1, K_2 and K_4.
2. Generate $K_3 \leftarrow \Pi.$Gen(1^k).
3. Output $K := (K_1, K_2, K_3, K_4)$.

$(\gamma, \mathbf{c}) \leftarrow$ Enc(K, L, $\mathbf{M}$):

1. Parse $\mathbf{M}$ as $\mathbf{m}$ and the corresponding $\mathbf{v}$.
2. Choose a random permutation $\pi : [n] \to [n]$.
3. Pad every element of $\mathbf{m}$ so that they all have the same length, obtain $\mathbf{m}^*$.
4. Permute the elements in $\mathbf{m}^*$ using π.
5. For $1 \le j \le n$ compute $c_j \leftarrow \Pi.$Enc(K_3, m_j^*).
6. For each $w \in \mathbf{W}$ such that $L(w) \ne \emptyset$, compute $\kappa_w = H_{K_2}(w)$, and
   – for each $i \in L(w)$, compute $\mathbf{tag}_{w,\pi(i)} = $ MAC$_{K_4}(\kappa_w, \pi(i), c_{\pi(i)}, v_i)$
   – for each $i \notin L(w)$, compute $\mathbf{tag}_{w,\pi(i)} = $ MAC$_{K_4}(\kappa_w, \pi(i),$ dummy, dummy$)$
   – store in the dictionary T, associated to search key κ_w, the entry

$$\langle (j, x_j, \mathbf{tag}_{w,j})_{j=1,2,\ldots,n} \rangle \oplus F_{K_1}(w)$$

with

$$x_j = \begin{cases} v_{\pi^{-1}(j)} & \text{if } \pi^{-1}(j) \in L(w), \\ \text{dummy} & \text{if } \pi^{-1}(j) \notin L(w). \end{cases}$$

7. Output $\gamma := T$ and $\mathbf{c} = (c_1, \ldots, c_n)$.

$\tau :=$ Token(K, w):

1. Output $\tau := (F_{K_1}(w), H_{K_2}(w))$

$(J, \mathbf{v_I}, \mathbf{Tags}) :=$ Search(γ, τ):

1. Parse τ as (α, β).
2. Compute $\mathbf{s} := \gamma(\beta) \oplus \alpha$, where $\gamma(\beta)$ the entry stored in γ with search key β.
3. If β is not in γ then return $J = \emptyset$, $\mathbf{v}_I = \perp$, and $\mathbf{Tags} = \perp$.
4. Otherwise every element in $\mathbf{s}$ has the form $(j, v, \mathbf{tag})$. For $j = 1, 2, \ldots, n$, if $\mathbf{s}(j)$ has $v \ne$ dummy, then include j in J and v in $\mathbf{v}_I$.
5. Set $\mathbf{Tags} = \langle \mathbf{tag}_j \mid j = 1, 2, \ldots, n \rangle$.
6. Output J, $\mathbf{v}_I$, and $\mathbf{Tags}$.

$\{$Accept or Reject$\} :=$ Verify(K, τ, J, $\mathbf{c}_J$, $\mathbf{v}_I$, $\mathbf{Tags}$)

1. Let $\kappa_w = H_{K_2}(w)$, where κ_w is extracted from τ.
2. For $j = 1, 2, \ldots, n$, compute

$$t_j = \begin{cases} \text{MAC}_{K_4}(\kappa_w, j, c_j, v_i) & \text{if } j \in J, \\ \text{MAC}_{K_4}(\kappa_w, j, \text{dummy}, \text{dummy}) & \text{if } j \notin J. \end{cases}$$

3. For every $j \in J$, compare t_j to $\mathbf{tag}_j$ in $\mathbf{Tags}$.
4. Output Accept if all comparison returns true. Otherwise output Reject.

$m_j :=$ Dec(K, c_j): Output $g_j := \Pi.$Dec(K_3, c_j). $m_{\pi^{-1}(j)} :=$ Dec(K, c_j): output $m_{\pi^{-1}(j)} := \Pi.$Dec(K_3, c_j).

Fig. 1. The vLabel scheme

Proof. Given F and H are PRFs and Π is indistinguishable under CPA, we have a $(\mathcal{L}_1,\mathcal{L}_2)$-secure Label scheme under adaptive chosen keyword attack as stated in [5, Theorem 5.2]. That is to say there exists a simulator such that for any adversary **A**, we have

$$|Pr\,[\mathbf{Real}_{Label} = 1]| - |Pr\,[\mathbf{Ideal}_{Label} = 1]| \leqslant \epsilon_1.$$

In our scheme, reliability is added to this Label scheme by inserting `tag` in the elements of dictionary T, which are $\mathrm{MAC}_{K_4}(\cdot)$ of κ_w, j, v_i and c_j. By assumption $\mathrm{MAC}_{K_4}(\cdot)$ is indistinguishable from any random function, which means the probability that an adversary is able to decide correctly whether a given function is MAC or a random function is negligible, say ϵ_2.

Define game $G_0(0)$ as the $\mathbf{Real}_{vLabel}$ game and $G_0(1)$ as the $\mathbf{Ideal}_{vLabel}$ game. Further, define game G_1 as game G_0 with the function $\mathrm{MAC}_{K_4}(\cdot)$ replaced with a random function $R(\cdot)$.

Then, the $(\mathcal{L}_1,\mathcal{L}_2)$-security of vLabel which is defined by

$$|Pr\,[\mathbf{Real}_{vLabel} = 1]| - |Pr\,[\mathbf{Ideal}_{vLabel} = 1]|$$

can be written as

$$
\begin{aligned}
|Pr\,[\mathbf{Real}_{vLabel} &= 1]| - |Pr\,[\mathbf{Ideal}_{vLabel} = 1]| \\
&= |Pr\,[G_0(0) = 1] - Pr\,[G_0(1) = 1]| \\
&\leqslant |Pr\,[G_0(0) = 1] - Pr\,[G_1(0) = 1]| \quad\quad (1) \\
&+ |Pr\,[G_1(0) = 1] - Pr\,[G_1(1) = 1]| \quad\quad (2) \\
&+ |Pr\,[G_1(1) = 1] - Pr\,[G_0(1) = 1]|. \quad\quad (3)
\end{aligned}
$$

Notice that term (2) is in effect

$$|Pr\,[\mathbf{Real}_{Label} = 1]| - |Pr\,[\mathbf{Ideal}_{Label} = 1]|$$

which is negligible. By the definitions of the games, terms (1) and (3) reduces to the distance between $\mathrm{MAC}_{K_4}(\cdot)$ and $R(\cdot)$. Hence we have,

$$|Pr\,[\mathbf{Real}_{vLabel} = 1]| - |Pr\,[\mathbf{Ideal}_{vLabel} = 1]| \leqslant \epsilon_1 + 2\epsilon_2$$

which implies vLabel achieves $(\mathcal{L}_1,\mathcal{L}_2)$-security. $\square$

Proposition 2. *The scheme vLabel achieves reliability under chosen-keyword attack.*

Proof. Suppose there exists an adversary **A** who breaks reliability of vLabel. Then, for some $(\mathbf{M}, \mathbf{W})$ and after some query sequence $q_1, q_2, \ldots, q_t$, **A** can produce $(J^*, \mathbf{v}_J^*, \mathtt{Tags}^*)$ for a new query token τ such that $(J^*, \mathbf{v}_J^*)$ is invalid while $\mathtt{Verify}(K, \tau, J^*, \mathbf{v}_J^*, \mathbf{c}_J^*, \mathtt{Tags}^*) = \mathtt{accept}$.

Let the correct result from the server be $(J, \mathbf{v}_I, \texttt{Tags})$ and

$$\tau = (\alpha, \kappa_w)$$
$$J = (j_1, j_2, \ldots, j_s)$$
$$J^* = (j_1^*, j_2^*, \ldots, j_u^*)$$
$$\mathbf{v}_I = (v_1, v_2, \ldots, v_s)$$
$$\mathbf{v}_I^* = (v_1^*, v_2^*, \ldots, v_u^*)$$
$$\texttt{Tags}^* = (\texttt{tag}_1^*, \texttt{tag}_2^*, \ldots, \texttt{tag}_n^*).$$

Since $(J^*, \mathbf{v}_I^*) \neq (J, \mathbf{v}_I)$ while $|J| = |\mathbf{v}_I|$ and $|J^*| = |\mathbf{v}_I^*|$, there are three cases.

Case 1: $s = u$. Then there must be that for some $1 \leqslant i \leqslant u$, $(j_i^*, v_{j_i}^*) \notin (J, \mathbf{v}_I)$. Since $\texttt{Verify}(K, \tau, J^*, c_{J^*}, \mathbf{v}_J^*, \texttt{Tags}^*) = \texttt{Accept}$, it must be that for all such i, $\text{MAC}_{K_4}(\kappa_w, j_i^*, c_{j_i}^*, v_i^*) = \texttt{tag}_{j_i^*}^*$. Therefore $\mathbf{B}$ can submit $((\kappa_w, j_i^*, c_{j_i}^*, v_i^*), \texttt{tag}_{j_i^*}^*)$ as a forgery of MAC.

Case 2: $s < u$. In this case, there must be at least $u - s$ indices which are in J^* but not in J. By similar argument as in **Case 1**, $\mathbf{B}$ can submit as a forgery $((\kappa_w, j_i^*, c_{j_i}^*, v_i^*), \texttt{tag}_{j_i^*}^*)$ where j_i^* is one of indices which are in J^* but not in J.

Case 3: $s > u$. Then there must be at least $s - u$ indices in J which is not in J^*. So, $\mathbf{B}$ can choose one such index, say j_i^*, and submit $((\kappa_w, j_i^*, c_{j_i}^*, v_i^*), \texttt{tag}_{j_i^*}^*)$ as a forgery. This is a valid forgery by the same argument as in **Case 1**.

Hence, in all cases adversary $\mathbf{B}$ is able to submit a forgery of MAC. By the assumption that the MAC is secure against forgery, we conclude that there cannot be any adversary $\mathbf{A}$ who can break reliability of vLabel. □

6   Verifiable Labeled Graphs

In addition to the Label scheme, Chase and Kamara also proposed a labeled graph scheme known as LabGraph in [5, §6]. It combines a Label scheme and Graph schemes to allow for graph-based searches. The data are graphs with nodes labeled with keywords. The data is searched by keyword and subgraphs around the node labeled by the keyword are returned as the results. The main applications, for example, are web graphs and social networks. Such a scheme demonstrates capability of structured encryption to query complex data structure without losing the "links" between these structures, therefore providing more related results than just label or keyword searches. A verifiable version would be a natural extension for the original scheme, using our vLabel scheme. Nevertheless, we will need to first construct verifiable variant of the originally proposed Graph schemes, which we call vGraph, and then uses the vGraph together with the previousy proposed vLabel scheme to construct a verifiable LabGraph scheme in [5]. The resulting scheme is termed vLabGraph.

6.1   vGraph

A Graph scheme is defined in [5, §6] as a specific case of a Label scheme. In particular, it is a Label scheme with the data being graphs and the labeling being relations between a node and all other nodes connected to it. In these schemes, nodes are represented by integers. Specific Graph schemes called Graph$^+$ and Graph$^-$ were proposed. In the Graph$^+$ scheme, the labeling is the relation of a node A to nodes that A points to. While in the Graph$^-$ scheme, the labeling is the relation of all nodes pointing to a node A. For example, let G be the graph in Figure 2. Under the Graph$^+$ scheme, the labeling L^+ will be $\{(1,2),(2,4),(3,2),(3,4),(5,3)\}$. The same G under scheme Graph$^-$ will have labeling $L^-=\{(2,1),(2,3),(3,5),(4,2),(4,3)\}$.

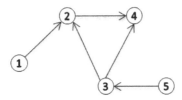

Fig. 2. Example data for Graph$^+$ and Graph$^-$

Figure 3 and Figure 4 describe our verfiable variants of Graph$^+$ and Graph$^-$ schemes which achieves reliability, termed as vGraph$^+$ and vGraph$^-$. We note that it is straightforward to transform the original Graph$^+$ and Graph$^-$ into vGraph$^+$ and vGraph$^-$ respectively. In both cases what is needed is to replace calls to Label by calls to vLabel. Also, we remark that since vGraph$^+$ and vGraph$^-$ do not have additional process besides calling vLabel, they inherit the security properties of vLabel directly. In other words, vGraph$^+$ and vGraph$^-$ achieves $(\mathcal{L}_1,\mathcal{L}_2)$-security under adaptive chosen keyword attack and reliability under chosen keyword attack.

Furthermore, since the inclusion of **tag** in the dictionary items does not affect $\mathcal{L}_1$ and $\mathcal{L}_2$ in vGraph$^+$ and vGraph$^-$, these schemes are chainable like vLabel. With this we are able to compose vLabGraph using vLabel, vGraph$^+$ and vGraph$^-$.

6.2   vLabGraph

We define the verifiable LabGraph scheme vLabGraph, which is composed from vLabel, vGraph$^+$ and vGraph$^-$. As in [5], the input data **m** is a sequence of messages whose links are captured in a directed graph G. The nodes of G holds the message indexes. First, the message relations within the graph structure is captured and encrypted using schemes vGraph$^+$ and vGraph$^-$. Then, search tokens under vGraph$^+$ and vGraph$^-$ for each node or message index are set as the semi-private data v_i of every message m_i. Next, the keywords are extracted from the messages and the labeling L is generated, relating each m_i to the keywords it contains. Finally, the data $\mathbf{M} = (\mathbf{m}, \mathbf{v})$ and L are input to the vLabel scheme for encryption. The collection of encrypted graph structures and encrypted documents are taken as the encrypted data under vLabGraph. Figure 5 provides description of the scheme.

---

vGraph$^+$ = (Gen, Enc, Token, Search, Verify, Dec)

$K \leftarrow$ Gen(1^k): Output $K \leftarrow$ vLabel.Gen(1^k).

$(\gamma, \mathbf{c}) \leftarrow$ Enc(K, G, $\mathbf{M}$):

1. Parse $\mathbf{M}$ as $\mathbf{m}$ and $\mathbf{v}$.
2. Construct labeling L that associates each m_i *with the set of nodes that node i points to in G.*
3. Output $(\gamma, \mathbf{c}) \leftarrow$ vLabel.Enc(K, L, $\mathbf{M}$).

$\tau \leftarrow$ Token(K, w): Output $\tau \leftarrow$ vLabel.Token(K, i).

$(J, \mathbf{v}_I, \textsf{Tags}) :=$ OutNeigh(γ, τ): Output $(J, \mathbf{v}_I, \textsf{Tags}) :=$ vLabel.Search(γ, τ).

{Accept or Reject} := Verify(K, τ, J, $\mathbf{c}_J$, $\mathbf{v}_I$, Tags): Output Accept or Reject by running vLabel.Verify(K, τ, J, $\mathbf{c}_J$, $\mathbf{v}_I$, Tags).

$m_{\pi^{-1}(j)} :=$ Dec(K, c_j): Output $m_{\pi^{-1}(j)} :=$ vLabel.Dec(K, c_j).

Fig. 3. The vGraph$^+$ scheme

---

vGraph$^-$ = (Gen, Enc, Token, Search, Verify, Dec)

$K \leftarrow$ Gen(1^k): Output $K \leftarrow$ vLabel.Gen(1^k).

$(\gamma, \mathbf{c}) \leftarrow$ Enc(K, G, $\mathbf{M}$):

1. Parse $\mathbf{M}$ as $\mathbf{m}$ and $\mathbf{v}$.
2. Construct labeling L that associates each m_i *with the set of nodes that point to node i in G.*
3. Output $(\gamma, \mathbf{c}) \leftarrow$ vLabel.Enc(K, L, $\mathbf{M}$).

$\tau \leftarrow$ Token(K, w): Output $\tau \leftarrow$ vLabel.Token(K, i).

$(J, \mathbf{v}_I, \textsf{Tags}) :=$ InNeigh(γ, τ): Output $(J, \mathbf{v}_I, \textsf{Tags}) \leftarrow$ vLabel.Search(γ, τ).

{Accept or Reject} := Verify(K, τ, J, $\mathbf{c}_J$, $\mathbf{v}_I$, Tags): Output Accept or Reject by running vLabel.Verify(K, τ, J, $\mathbf{c}_J$, $\mathbf{v}_I$, Tags).

$m_{\pi^{-1}(j)} :=$ Dec(K, c_j): Output $m_{\pi^{-1}(j)} :=$ vLabel.Dec(K, c_j).

Fig. 4. The vGraph$^-$ scheme

---

vLabGraph = (Gen, Enc, Token, Search, Verify, Dec)

$K \leftarrow$ **Gen**(1^k):

1. Generate $K^L \leftarrow$ vLabel.Gen(1^k)
2. Generate $K^+ \leftarrow$ vGraph$^+$.Gen(1^k).
3. Generate $K^- \leftarrow$ vGraph$^-$.Gen(1^k).
4. Set $K := (K^L, K^+, K^-)$.

$(\gamma, \mathbf{c}) \leftarrow$ **Enc**$(K, G, \mathbf{m})$:

1. Compute $(\gamma^+, \mathbf{c}^+) \leftarrow$ vGraph$^+$.Enc$(K^+, G, \mathbf{m})$
2. Compute $(\gamma^-, \mathbf{c}^-) \leftarrow$ vGraph$^-$.Enc$(K^-, G, \mathbf{m})$
3. For $1 \leq i \leq n$,
   - compute $\tau_i^+ \leftarrow$ vGraph$^+$.Token(K^+, i)
   - compute $\tau_i^- \leftarrow$ vGraph$^-$.Token(K^-, i)
4. Let L be the labeling generated from all the keywords in $\mathbf{m}$ and set $v_i = (\tau_i^+, \tau_i^-)$ to form $\mathbf{v} = (v_i)_i$
5. Compute $(\gamma^L, \mathbf{c}^L) \leftarrow$ vLabel.Enc$(K^L, L, \mathbf{M} = (\mathbf{m}, \mathbf{v}))$
6. Output $\gamma = (\gamma^L, \gamma^+, \gamma^-)$ and $\mathbf{c} = (\mathbf{c}^L, \mathbf{c}^+, \mathbf{c}^-)$

$\tau :=$ **Token**(K, w):

1. Output $\tau :=$ vLabel.Token(K^L, w)

$(J, \mathbf{v}_I, \mathsf{Tags}) :=$ **Subgraph**(γ, τ):

1. Compute $(J^L, \mathbf{v}_I, \mathsf{Tags}^L) \leftarrow$ vLabel.Search(γ, τ).
2. For all $j \in J^L$, parse $v_j = (\tau_j^+, \tau_j^-)$ and
   - Compute $(J_j^+, \mathsf{Tags}_j^+) \leftarrow$ vGraph$^+$.OutNeigh(γ^+, τ_j^+).
   - Compute $(J_j^-, \mathsf{Tags}_j^-) \leftarrow$ vGraph$^-$.InNeigh(γ^-, τ_j^-).
3. Set $J^+ = (J_j^+)_{j \in J^L}$ and $J^- = (J_j^-)_{j \in J^L}$.
4. Set $\mathsf{Tags}^+ = (\mathsf{tag}_j^+)_{j \in J^L}$ and $\mathsf{Tags}^- = (\mathsf{tag}_j^-)_{j \in J^L}$.
5. Output $J = (J^L, J^+, J^-)$, $\mathbf{v}_I^L$ and $\mathsf{Tags} = (\mathsf{Tags}^L, \mathsf{Tags}^+, \mathsf{Tags}^-)$.

$\{$Accept or Reject$\} :=$ **Verify**$(K, \tau, J, \mathbf{c}_J, \mathbf{v}_I^L, \mathsf{Tags})$

1. Compute $Z :=$ vLabel.Verify$(K^L, \tau, J^L, \mathbf{c}^L, \mathbf{v}^L, \mathsf{Tags}^L)$
2. For every $j \in J^L$, compute $Y_j :=$ vGraph$^+$.Verify$(K^+, \tau_j^+, J_j^+, \mathbf{c}_j^+, \mathbf{v}_j^+, \mathsf{Tags}_j^+)$
3. For every $j \in J^L$, compute $X_j :=$ vGraph$^-$.Verify$(K^-, \tau_j^-, J_j^-, \mathbf{c}_j^-, \mathbf{v}_j^-, \mathsf{Tags}_j^-)$
4. If $Z =$ Accept and for all $j \in J^L$, $Y_j =$ Accept and $X_j =$ Accept, then output Accept. Otherwise output Reject.

$m_{\pi^{-1}(j)} :=$ **Dec**(K, c_j): Output $m_{\pi^{-1}(j)} := \Pi$.Dec(K^L, c_j).

Fig. 5. The vLabGraph scheme

Security Analysis. Since vLabel, vGraph$^+$ and vGraph$^-$ are chainable, the composition vLabGraph is correct and does not leak more information. Our proposition follows.

Proposition 3. *Given that vLabel, vGraph$^+$ and vGraph$^-$ schemes are chainable and achieve ($\mathcal{L}_1^l$,$\mathcal{L}_2^l$)-security, ($\mathcal{L}_1^+$,$\mathcal{L}_2^+$)-security and ($\mathcal{L}_1^-$,$\mathcal{L}_2^-$)-security respectively under adaptive chosen keyword attack. Then the scheme vLabGraph also achieves ($\mathcal{L}_1$,$\mathcal{L}_2$)-security under adaptive chosen keyword attack with*

$$\mathcal{L}_1(G, L, \mathbf{m}) = (\mathcal{L}_1^l(L, \mathbf{m}), \mathcal{L}_1^+(G, \mathbf{m}), \mathcal{L}_1^-(G, \mathbf{m}))$$
$$\mathcal{L}_2(G, L, w) = (\mathcal{L}_2^l(L, w), (\mathcal{L}_2^+(G, i))_{i \in R(w)}, (\mathcal{L}_2^-(G, i))_{i \in R(w)})$$

where $R(w)$ is the set of nodes in G which contains w.

Proof. First we define the following games.

- **G_0** The privacy game for vLabGraph. Specifically, $G_0(0)$ is **Real**$_{vLabGraph}$ and $G_0(1)$ is **Ideal**$_{vLabGraph}$.
- **G_1** The game G_0 with the scheme vLabel in vLabGraph replaced by Label.
- **G_2** The game G_1 with the scheme vGraph$^+$ in vLabGraph replaced by Graph$^+$.
- **G_3** The game G_2 with the scheme vGraph$^-$ in vLabGraph replaced by Graph$^-$.

Now, using triangle inequality we have that

$$|Pr\,[G_0(0) = 1] - Pr\,[G_0(1) = 1]|$$
$$\leqslant |Pr\,[G_0(0) = 1] - Pr\,[G_1(0) = 1]| \tag{4}$$
$$+ |Pr\,[G_1(0) = 1] - Pr\,[G_2(0) = 1]| \tag{5}$$
$$+ |Pr\,[G_2(0) = 1] - Pr\,[G_3(0) = 1]| \tag{6}$$
$$+ |Pr\,[G_3(0) = 1] - Pr\,[G_3(1) = 1]| \tag{7}$$
$$+ |Pr\,[G_3(1) = 1] - Pr\,[G_2(1) = 1]| \tag{8}$$
$$+ |Pr\,[G_2(1) = 1] - Pr\,[G_1(1) = 1]| \tag{9}$$
$$+ |Pr\,[G_1(1) = 1] - Pr\,[G_0(1) = 1]| . \tag{10}$$

First, consider term (4) which is the difference of distributions between $G_0(0)=$**Real**$_{vLabGraph}$ and $G_1(0)$, where vLabel is replaced with Label. The difference between Label and vLabel is the generation of tags for verification produced by MAC of the vLabel scheme. In effect, the difference in the distribution is the difference of MAC and any PRF. By the assumption that vLabel achieves ($\mathcal{L}_1^l$,$\mathcal{L}_2^l$)-security, by Proposition 1 MAC is indistinguishable from PRF under chosen plaintext attack. Say, the adversary **A** can distinguish MAC from a random function with a negligible probability, ϵ_1. where ϵ_1 is negligible and R is any PRF. Hence

$$|Pr\,[G_0(0) = 1] - Pr\,[G_1(0) = 1]| \leqslant \epsilon_1.$$

The same argument holds for terms (5), (6), (8), (9) and (10).

Next, consider term (7). In game G_3, all verifiable schemes in vLabGraph is replaced by the original schemes. In effect, the resulting scheme is LabGraph. Since LabGraph achieves $(\mathcal{L}_1,\mathcal{L}_2)$-security [5, Theorem 6.2],

$$|Pr[G_3(0) = 1]| - |Pr[G_3(1)]| = |Pr[\textbf{Real}_{LabGraph} = 1]| - |Pr[\textbf{Ideal}_{LabGraph} = 1]|$$

which is negligible, say with value ϵ_2.

As a result,

$$|Pr[G_0(0) = 1] - Pr[G_0(1) = 1]| \leqslant 6\epsilon_1 + \epsilon_2$$

which is negligible. Therefore, vLabGraph achieves $(\mathcal{L}_1,\mathcal{L}_2)$-security under keyword chosen attack.   □

Proposition 4. *The vLabGraph scheme achieves reliability under chosen keyword attack.*

Proof. Assume there exists an adversary $\mathbf{A}$ who breaks reliability of vLabGraph. So, for a fixed $(\mathbf{M}, \mathbf{W})$ and after a few queries $w_1, w_2, \ldots, w_q$, $\mathbf{A}$ can produce $(J^*, \mathbf{v}_I^*, \textbf{Tags}^*)$ with $(J^*, \mathbf{v}_I^*)$ invalid but $\texttt{Verify}(K, \tau, J^*, \mathbf{v}_I^*, \mathbf{c}_{J^*}, \textbf{Tags}^*) = \texttt{Accept}$ with non-negligible probability. Since $J^* = (\tilde{J}^L, \tilde{J}^+, \tilde{J}^-)$, $\mathbf{v}_I^* = \tilde{\mathbf{v}}_I^L$ and $\textbf{Tags}^* = (\widetilde{\textbf{Tags}}^L, \widetilde{\textbf{Tags}}^+, \widetilde{\textbf{Tags}}^-)$, the assumption implies that at least one of the following holds:

- $(\tilde{J}^L, \tilde{\mathbf{v}}_I^L) \neq (J^L, \mathbf{v}_I^L)$ but

$$\texttt{vLabel.Verify}(K^L, \tau^L, \tilde{J}^L, \mathbf{c}_{\tilde{j}L}, \tilde{\mathbf{v}}_I^L, \widetilde{\textbf{Tags}}^L) = \texttt{Accept}$$

  where $(J^L, \mathbf{v}_I^L) = \texttt{vLabel.Search}(\tau)$.
- $\tilde{J}^+ \neq J^+$ but for every $x \in J^L$

$$\texttt{vGraph}^+.\texttt{Verify}(K^+, \tau_x^+, \tilde{J}_x^+, \mathbf{c}_{\tilde{j}_x^+}, \tilde{\mathbf{v}}_x^+, \widetilde{\textbf{Tags}}_x^+) = \texttt{Accept}$$

  where $J^+ = \texttt{vGraph}^+.\texttt{OutNeigh}(\tau_x)$.
- $\tilde{J}^- \neq J^-$ but for every $x \in J^L$

$$\texttt{vGraph}^-.\texttt{Verify}(K^-, \tau_x^-, \tilde{J}_x^-, \mathbf{c}_{\tilde{j}_x^-}, \tilde{\mathbf{v}}_x^-, \widetilde{\textbf{Tags}}_x^-) = \texttt{Accept}$$

  where $J^- = \texttt{vGraph}^-.\texttt{InNeigh}(\tau_x)$.

Consequently, $\mathbf{A}$ is able to break reliability of vLabel, vGraph$^+$ or vGraph$^-$, or any combination of them. Since it is assumed that vLabel, vGraph$^+$ and vGraph$^-$ achieve reliability, an adversary such as $\mathbf{A}$ cannot exist.   □

7   Conclusions

In this paper we proposed verifiable structured encryption schemes. We extended structured encryption schemes proposed in [5] to also achieve reliability in addition to privacy, by utilising the active adversary model defined in [11]. Reliability is accomplished by associating authentication tags to every item in the encrypted look up table of the structured encryption schemes. Furthermore, we adopt the definition of privacy under the $(\mathcal{L}_1,\mathcal{L}_2)$-security as defined in [5] but made stronger definition with condition set in [11]. We proved that the new schemes achieve $(\mathcal{L}_1,\mathcal{L}_2)$-security under adaptive chosen keyword attack and reliability under chosen keyword attack. We further provides verifiable variants of the Label and LabGraph schemes from [5].

References

1. Abdalla, M., Bellare, M., Catalano, D., Kiltz, E., Kohno, T., Lange, T., Malone-Lee, J., Neven, G., Paillier, P., Shi, H.: Searchable Encryption Revisited: Consistency Properties, Relation to Anonymous IBE, and Extensions. Journal of Cryptology 21, 350–391 (2008)
2. Boneh, D., Di Crescenzo, G., Ostrovsky, R., Persiano, G.: Public Key Encryption with Keyword Search. In: Cachin, C., Camenisch, J. (eds.) EUROCRYPT 2004. LNCS, vol. 3027, pp. 506–522. Springer, Heidelberg (2004)
3. Boneh, D., Kushilevitz, E., Ostrovsky, R., Skeith III, W.E.: Public Key Encryption That Allows PIR Queries. In: Menezes, A. (ed.) CRYPTO 2007. LNCS, vol. 4622, pp. 50–67. Springer, Heidelberg (2007)
4. Chang, Y.-C., Mitzenmacher, M.: Privacy Preserving Keyword Searches on Remote Encrypted Data. In: Ioannidis, J., Keromytis, A.D., Yung, M. (eds.) ACNS 2005. LNCS, vol. 3531, pp. 442–455. Springer, Heidelberg (2005)
5. Chase, M., Kamara, S.: Structured Encryption and Controlled Disclosure. In: Abe, M. (ed.) ASIACRYPT 2010. LNCS, vol. 6477, pp. 577–594. Springer, Heidelberg (2010)
6. Curtmola, R., Garay, J.A., Kamara, S., Ostrovsky, R.: Searchable Symmetric Encryption: Improved Definitions and Efficient Constructions. In: Juels, A., Wright, R.N., De Capitani di Vimercati, S. (eds.) ACM Conference on Computer and Communications Security, CCS 2006, pp. 79–88. ACM (2006)
7. Gentry, C.: A Fully Homomorphic Encryption Scheme. PhD thesis, Stanford University (2009)
8. Goh, E.-J.: Secure indexes. Cryptology ePrint Archive, Report 2003/216 (2003), http://eprint.iacr.org/2003/216/
9. Goldreich, O., Ostrovsky, R.: Software Protection and Simulation on Oblivious RAMs. Journal of the ACM 43(3), 431–473 (1996)
10. Katz, J., Lindell, Y.: Introduction to Modern Cryptography. Chapman & Hall/CRC (2007)
11. Kurosawa, K., Ohtaki, Y.: UC-Secure Searchable Symmetric Encryption. In: Keromytis, A.D. (ed.) FC 2012. LNCS, vol. 7397, pp. 285–298. Springer, Heidelberg (2012)
12. Shi, E., Hubert Chan, T.-H., Stefanov, E., Li, M.: Oblivious RAM with $o((\log N)^3)$ worst-case cost. In: Lee, D.H., Wang, X. (eds.) ASIACRYPT 2011. LNCS, vol. 7073, pp. 197–214. Springer, Heidelberg (2011)

13. Song, D.X., Wagner, D., Perrig, A.: Practical Techniques for Searches on Encrypted Data. In: SP 2000: Proceedings of the 2000 IEEE Symposium on Security and Privacy, p. 44. IEEE Computer Society (2000)

A The Games for Privacy

Description of the games in [5] for the definition of adversary under $(\mathcal{L}_1, \mathcal{L}_2)$-security.

The game **Real**(k) is as follows.

1. The adversary **A** generates data $(L, \mathbf{M})$ where $\mathbf{M} = (\mathbf{m}, \mathbf{v})$ and submit to the challenger.
2. The challenger runs $\mathtt{Gen}(1^k)$ to get the key K, and then encrypts the data $\mathtt{enc}(K, L, \mathbf{M})$ to output $(\gamma, \mathbf{c})$ which is given to **A**.
3. **A** chooses a query q_0 and submit to the challenger.
4. The challenger returns the token $\tau_0 = \mathtt{Token}(K, q_0)$.
5. For $t = 1, 2 \ldots, p(k)$ where $p(\cdot)$ is a polynomial,
   - Based on previous queries, **A** chooses query q_t.
   - The challenger returns the corresponding token $\tau_t = \mathtt{Token}(K, q_t)$.
6. **A** outputs a bit b.

The game **Ideal**(k)

1. The adversary **A** generates data $(L, \mathbf{M})$ where $\mathbf{M} = (\mathbf{m}, \mathbf{v})$ and gives to the challenger.
2. The challenger gives $\mathcal{L}_1(L, \mathbf{M})$ to the simulator **S**.
3. **S** generates and send $(\tilde{\gamma}, \tilde{\mathbf{c}})$ to **A**.
4. **A** submits a query q_0 to the challenger.
5. The challenger gives **S** $(\mathcal{L}_2(L, q_0), \mathbf{v}_{I_0})$.
6. **S** returns to **A** a token $\tilde{\tau}_0$.
7. For $t = 1, 2, \ldots, p(k)$ where $p(\cdot)$ is a polynomial,
   - Based on previous queries, **A** chooses query q_t.
   - **S** is given $(\mathcal{L}_2(L, q_t), \mathbf{v}_{I_t})$.
   - **S** returns a token $\tilde{\tau}_t$ to **A**.
8. **A** outputs a bit b.

Nested Merkle's Puzzles against Sampling Attacks⋆
(Extended Abstract)

Shlomi Dolev[1], Nova Fandina[1], and Ximing Li[2,1,⋆⋆]

[1] Department of Computer Science, Ben Gurion University of Negev
{dolev,fandina}@cs.bgu.ac.il
[2] Modern Education Technology Center, South China Agricultutral Unversity
ximing@post.bgu.ac.il

Abstract. We propose a new private key establishment protocol which is based on the Merkle's puzzles scheme. This protocol is designed to provide the honest parties the ability to securely and continuously communicate over an unprotected channel. To achieve the continuous security over unbounded communication sessions we propose to use a *nested* Merkle's puzzles approach where the honest parties repeatedly establish new keys and use previous keys to encrypt the puzzles of the current key establishment incarnation. We provide an implementation of the idea in the random oracle model and analyze its security. In addition, we implement the protocol in the standard cryptographic model, basing its security on the lattice shortest vector problem. The iterative nested scheme we propose enlarges the probability that the set of randomly chosen puzzles will contain hard puzzles, comparing with the probability that a single randomly chosen set consists of hard puzzles. Our nested Merkle puzzles scheme copes with δ-*sampling attack* where the adversary chooses to solve δ puzzles in each iteration of the key establishment protocol, decrypting the actual current communication when the adversary is lucky to choose the same puzzles the receiver chooses. We analyze the security of our schemes in the presence of such an attack.

1 Introduction

In his pioneering work [18] Merkle proposed a protocol for secret key agreement over insecure channels. The protocol enables the honest parties to agree on the key without any secret sharing prior to the time they wish to communicate securely. The protocol is based on *puzzles*. Puzzle is defined to be a cryptogram which is meant to be broken. When puzzle is broken (or solved) the information that was "en-puzzled" is revealed.

Suppose Alice and Bob want to establish a secret key while communicating only over public insecure channel. For this, Alice creates n puzzles. Each puzzle encapsulates two

---

⋆ Partially supported by Deutsche Telekom, Rita Altura Trust Chair in Computer Sciences, Lynne and William Frankel Center for Computer Sciences, Israel Science Foundation (grant number 428/11), Cabarnit Cyber Security MAGNET Consortium, Grant from the Institute for Future Defense Technologies Research named for the Medvedi of the Technion, and Israeli Internet Association, Grant from Guangdong Province Science Technology Plan (No. 2011B090400325).
⋆⋆ Corresponding author.

randomly chosen strings: id the "index" of the puzzle (which is possibly a function of part of the solution string) and key (possibly a function of another part of the solution string) serving as a key for the future secure communication. Alice sends all puzzles to Bob. Bob randomly chooses one puzzle to solve, spending the required amount of time for solving the chosen puzzle. After Bob has solved the puzzle, Bob has the id and the key that were en-puzzled by Alice. Bob sends id back to Alice. Now Alice and Bob can use key as their common secret key.

The security of this scheme is based on the disability of the adversary to know which puzzle Bob has chosen. Therefore, to find out the key the adversary Eve has to solve all (or at least a big portion of) the puzzles. Suppose it takes $O(n)$ time to solve one puzzle, then to agree on the key Alice and Bob will spend $O(n)$ time, while Eve will spend $O(n^2)$ time. Thus, the protocol has a polynomial level of security.

There is a wide line of research which investigates cryptography based on the Merkle's puzzles scheme [18,13,5,21,4]. We consider a scenario of long communication session and examine the question whether the original Merkle's puzzles protocol is secure enough to be used repeatedly during long interaction. Suppose Alice and Bob have agreed on a secret key, how long can they communicate securely using this key? After $O(n^2)$ time Eve will reveal the key. An intuitive proactive solution is to run the key agreement protocol again, after some time, to establish a fresh key for securing the next period, called round, of the communication session. For example, after using the previous key for $O(n)$ time. Unfortunately, this approach is insecure when coping with the attack described next. Consider an adversary which records all the information exchanged. Assume the adversary Eve is performing the following attack. In each round of the key agreement protocol Eve randomly chooses only one puzzle (or some constant number, δ, of the puzzles) to solve. If Eve is lucky, Eve will choose the same puzzle as Bob, and thus will be able to decrypt and listen to the communication in the current round of the session with the decrypted key! If Eve is unlucky, Eve will not be able to find out the key in the current portion of the session. Repeating, iteratively the key agreement protocol, there will be a round (one from every $O(n)$ rounds) in which Eve will guess the right puzzle with high probability. We call this attack the *sampling attack.*

To demonstrate the drawback of iterative repetition of the Merkle's scheme, we consider the following scenario. Assume Alice and Bob are two brokers that coordinate their actions every hour. First they establish a key using Merkle's puzzles scheme and then securely decide whether to buy or sell stock. Eve would like to decrypt their communication and decide whether to buy or sell stock accordingly. So, in case Eve is not lucky in choosing the puzzles to solve in a certain hour, Eve does not participate in the stock-exchange in that hour. In case Eve is lucky to choose the right puzzles to solve and decrypt the communication between Alice and Bob (essentially by performing the sampling attack) Eve buys or sells according to their plans in the specific hour.

In this paper we propose a key exchange protocol which is resistant to the sampling attack in terms of decreasing the probability of success of the adversary to find out a non-obsolete session key. The idea is to use the key agreement protocol repeatedly, but to keep every round be dependent on the previous ones. We use the secret keys established in the previous rounds to encrypt the puzzles in the next round. In this way Eve cannot start to solve puzzles without solving the puzzles from the previous rounds (assuming random oracle model or under assumption of the hardness of the random lattice shortest vector problem).

Moreover, in case puzzles are proven to be hard on average, we ensure that for a given computation time, the probability of Eve to solve all puzzles (that are needed to be solved in order to solve the current puzzle) is dramatically smaller than the probability to solve the single last puzzle. The single last puzzle has a non-negligible probability to be easy since, roughly speaking, the puzzle hardness is proven for the distribution of the randomly chosen puzzles rather than on the hardness of the easiest puzzle instance.

Related Work. In his original protocol Merkle proposed to implement puzzles as an encryption scheme. Since then various implementations were proposed, in the random oracle model as well as in standard cryptographic model. Security of the protocols, implemented in both models, were analyzed. Impagliazzo and Rudich [13] showed that there is no key exchange protocol in the oracle model in which the gap between the time spent by honest parties and the adversary is super polynomial. In addition, their result implied that there is no key exchange protocol based on a one-way function which is super polynomial secure and is of the standard black-box type.

Thus, the authors of [13] negatively answered the open question Merkle stated in his paper on whether it is possible to build a similar key agreement protocol that will have security gap bigger than polynomial. Barak and Ghidary [4] improved the result of [13] and proved that every key exchange protocol in the random oracle model in which the honest parties make at most n queries to the oracle can be broken by an adversary that performs $O(n^2)$ queries to the oracle. Namely, the Merkle's puzzles protocol is optimal in the random oracle model. In addition, from this paper it follows that any implementation (in any model) of the Merkle's puzzle protocol will allow only $O(n^2)$ security gap between the adversary and the honest parties. Nearly the same result is found in [5,21] but in different form. In [7,6] the authors propose to consider the Merkle's puzzles protocol in the quantum domain. The authors propose a model in which the honest parties (standard Turing machines) wish to establish a secret key in the presence of a quantum adversary.

Bounded Storage Model (BSM). The adversary with bounded storage was introduced by Cachin and Maurer [8]. The adversary can use unlimited computational power to compute any probabilistic function of some huge amount of public data, however the adversary can store information with less volume than the public data volume. The authors proved that the proposed private-key system and secret key agreement protocol are information-theoretically secure, under the assumption that the function's output size does not exceed the number of available storage bits. The BSM model was investigated in the scope of several application fields [19,10]. In contrast to the BSM adversary, in our proposed scheme, the adversary Eve is assumed to be able to store all the bits communicated by Alice and Bob. However Eve is unable to compute all the functions on the information before the communication becomes obsolete, due to computational power restrictions.

Bounded Time Model (BTM). The BTM adversary is present only during some period of time. Namely, the adversary is not exposed to all the communication between Alice and Bob. Alice and Bob cannot know when the adversary is present or not. For RFID privacy, Juels presented in [14] what he calls a minimalist model for tag privacy and security. The assumption in this model is that the adversary is able to perform a bounded number of queries in a man-in-the-middle attack. Dolev, Kopeetsky and Shamir proposed in [11] an information secure scheme which is based on the assumption that the information exchanged during at least $k > 1$ of every n successive communication sessions is not exposed to an adversary. Unlike the BTM adversary, in our proposed scheme, the adversary Eve continuously listens to the communication all the time.

Bounded computation model (BCM). This is the assumption on which modern cryptography is based. The assumption is that the adversary is computationally bounded. Usually, probabilistic polynomial time (PPT) bounded adversaries are under consideration. Time-release crypto is used in this model in order to establish secure communication. The goal of timed-release crypto, introduced in [17,20], is to encrypt a message in such a way that it will be readable at some specified time in the future (even without additional help from the sender) but not before then.

A natural approach for building a timed-release crypto scheme is the use of the time-lock puzzles, puzzles that take a pre-specified amount of time to solve (which is typically significantly longer than the time to generate the puzzle). One usage of time-lock-puzzles is in the scope of denial-of-service resistant authentication schemes [2]. Several possible implementations of these puzzles are suggested in [2]. Common implementations are based on the hardness of some (one way) computational problem (e.g., RSA).

Mohammad Mahmoody et al. in [16] proved the impossibility (assuming the random oracle model) to construct time-lock puzzle that require more parallel time to be solved than the total work required to generate the puzzle. They proved that every key-agreement protocol in the random-oracle model can be broken by a parallel attack with polynomially many queries to the random-oracle. Authors also give a construction of a time-lock puzzle with a linear gap in parallel time. Mahmoody et al. discussed in [15] another type of puzzles that are generated randomly without knowing the solution prior their generation. In the proposed schemes of this paper we consider a standard PPT Turing machine adversary.

Our Contribution. In this paper, we propose a scheme to improve the security and flexibility of the key exchange protocols which are based on the Merkle's puzzles scheme. We use the original Merkle's puzzles protocol as a brick to build a multiple round scheme which provides an infinite series of secret shared keys. Secret keys established in the previous rounds are used to protect the puzzles used in the present round. The concept of δ-*sampling attack* is proposed, which means an eavesdropping attacker that spends short time to solve only δ puzzles in each round of the protocol.

We propose two implementations of the nested protocol. The first implementation assumes an access of all the participants to the random oracle. This model is a pure theoretical model. A scheme which is proven to be secure in the random oracle model is not necessarily secure in the standard cryptographic model [9]. Thus, to obtain a provably secure nested Merkle's puzzles protocol in the standard model, we cannot just replace the oracle with some standard cryptographic primitive (e.g., one way function, hash function). Therefore, we provide an implementation of the Merkle's puzzles scheme (both for one round and for the nested rounds versions) based on specific assumption in the standard model. In more detail, we base our implementation on the hardness of a shortest vector problem in a random lattice [1,12].

Outline of the Paper. Following some preliminaries in Section 2, we review some known implementations of the Merkle's puzzles protocol and discuss their drawbacks in Section 3 . In Section 4 we suggest nested implementations of the Merkle's puzzles protocol (assuming the random oracle model). Then, in Section 5 we propose implementations of the original and nested Merkle's scheme in the standard cryptographic model. We analyze the performance and security of the implementations (in both models) in the presence of the δ-sampling attack. In Section 6, we discuss some possible improvements of the nested Merkle's protocol. Proofs are omitted from this extended abstract.

2 Settings

In this section the settings used throughout this paper are formally defined. We start with the standard definition of the key agreement protocol and its security. All the participants of the protocol are standard probabilistic polynomial time Turing machines. The key agreement protocol between two parties Alice and Bob is defined by instructions in the form of pseudo codes. In the beginning, each of the honest parties chooses random bits (independently) and executes the instructions. At the end of the protocol, Alice and Bob output two keys k_A and k_B in $\{0,1\}^n$ respectively. The protocol is correct if $k_A = k_B$ with probability negligibly below 1.

Definition 1. $d, \epsilon()$ *security of the key agreement protocol* Let Π be a key agreement protocol that involves two honest parties, Alice and Bob. Let n denote the security parameter. Let d be some constant, and $\epsilon()$ be some function with negligible values. We say that Π is ($d, \epsilon()$)-secure in the presence of the eavesdropping adversary Eve if the following holds.

 For any constant $d' < d$ any $O(n^{d'})$ time bounded Eve discovers Alice's and Bob's shared secret bit (on a random transcript of the protocol) with the probability bounded by $1/2 + \epsilon(n)$.

The protocol has quadratic security if it is $(d, \epsilon())$-secure for $d = 2$. We consider key agreement protocols which consist of rounds. In every round the honest parties send to each other puzzle information which requires computational effort to solve. After each round is finished a new secret key is established. We define a *usage parameter t* of the multiple round key agreement protocol. Intuitively, t is the time for legal usage (for encryption of the communication) of the new established secret key. For this type of protocols, we define and investigate the concept of δ-sampling attack. A sampling attack is an attack in which the adversary listens to the communication link all the time (and thus does not lose information) but in every round of the protocol does not spend too much time to perform computations. Instead the adversary randomly chooses a few puzzles to process (solve) in each round, and hopes this information will suffice to reveal the current key. If in some round Eve is lucky to choose the "right" puzzles, Eve will reveal the current session key exactly on the same time the honest parties have agreed on the key. If Eve is not lucky in some specific round, Eve will continue trying her fortune in the next round, while she is able to keep working (simultaneously) on the rest of the information which were not chosen at first. The goal of the adversary is to guess the subset of puzzles sent in a round, in order to get the secret key exactly at the time the honest parties establish it or during (or close enough after) the communication curried out by Alice and Bob using this secret key. We call such a key a *current* or a *non-obsolete* key. Intuitively, the protocol is safe against such an attacker, if the adversary's probability to discover the current session key used by the honest parties is very small and decreases with the continuation of the communication session.

Definition 2. *Usage parameter of the multiple round key agreement protocol*

Let t be some function. We say that the multiple round key agreement protocol has a usage parameter $t()$ if each secret key k that is established by the honest parties (in every round) is used by them as a session key during t units of time after the establishment of k.

- *The* life time *of the new established secret key is defined as the t units of time from its establishing.*
- *During its life time the secret key is called a* current *or a* non-obsolete *secret key.*

Definition 3. δ *- sampling adversary*

Let Π be a multiple round key agreement protocol between Alice and Bob. Let n be a security parameter. Assume a key agreement protocol consists of rounds of communication between Alice and Bob. Assume further that in each round n puzzles are exchanged between them. Let Eve be an eavesdropping adversary and $1 \leq \delta \leq n$. We say that Eve is performing δ-sampling attack if the following conditions hold:

- *Eve is present during the whole communication between Alice and Bob.*
- *In every round of the protocol, Eve chooses randomly δ puzzles being exchanged between Alice and Bob in the present round and stores all the rest in her memory (possibly for a later processing). Eve performs computational processing on the puzzles Eve has chosen.*

Note, the definition does not restrict Eve to continue to work on all the puzzles Eve has seen so far. Thus, in order to define the security of the protocol in the presence of such an adversary, we have to take into consideration the computational power of all the participants. We consider the setting in which all the parties have roughly the same power.

Definition 4. *(Weak) Security in the presence of the δ-sampling adversary*

Let Π be a multiple round key agreement protocol with a usage parameter t between Alice and Bob, in which puzzles are being exchanged between the participants in every round. Let Eve be an adversary that performs the δ-sampling attack. Denote $\epsilon()$ to be some function with negligible values, and $p()$ some function with values from $[0, 1]$, n is the security parameter. Assume that after each round of the protocol Alice and Bob output a secret key they have agreed on. Protocol Π is secure with a security level $p()$ in the presence of the δ-sampling adversary Eve if the following holds. For every round i of the protocol, the probability that Eve will discover the non-obsolete secret key which is established during this round, is bounded by $p(n, i) + \epsilon(n)$. The probability *is taken over a randomly chosen transcript of the whole execution of the protocol until the present round, and the randomness of Eve. $p()$ is denoted as the* security level *of the protocol.*

Note that in the above definition the power of the adversary is not directly mentioned as a parameter for the security, since the running time of a successful attacker can be derived from the parameter t and the time which is required to execute one round of the protocol. Moreover, the parameter δ of the adversary is encapsulated in the function $p()$.

3 Merkle's Puzzles Scheme

Merkle showed in [18] that it is possible to select a secret key over open communication channels without prior established secret. The method forces any adversary to spend square of the amount of the work required by the two communicants to agree on the key.

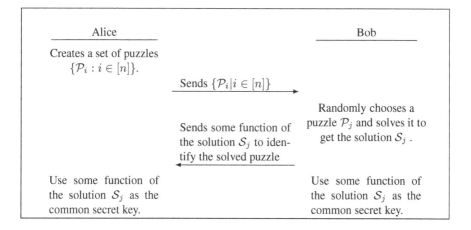

Fig. 1. Original Merkle's Puzzles Scheme

Fig. 1 schematically describes the Merkle's puzzles technique. To use this scheme, one has to choose a way to implement puzzles. In this section, we concentrate our attention on implementations in the random oracle model. Random oracle methodology was proposed as a middle ground between a formal proof of security and no proof at all. This approach suggests to analyze the security of protocols in an idealized world, in which a random oracle exists. In this model all parties have an access to the oracle that provides a truly random function. The performance of the scheme is measured in terms of the queries to the oracle. The main question, however, is whether a protocol proven to be secure in the random oracle model is secure in practice. Much research has been done to answer this question. In [9], the authors showed that it is not always secure to instantiate an oracle with one way function. In particular, [9] shows specific schemes, which are secure in the random oracle model, but totally insecure in *any* instantiation.

Thus, the proof of security of the protocol in the random oracle model gives some hope for its security in the standard model, in which the oracle can be replaced with a standard cryptographic primitives, but still requires a security proof for specific situation. Therefore, we first concentrate our attention on the implementation in the random oracle model. We provide a detailed description of the protocols, and analyze their security according to Definition 4. Then, we propose implementations in a more realistic world, namely, in the standard model.

3.1 Asymmetric Merkle's Puzzles

In this version of the protocol, puzzles are implemented as answers to queries to the random oracle. All the parties have an access to the same random oracle. In order to be able to use the protocol securely for obtaining more than one key (for example, by invoking the protocol several times), the protocol simulates an access to a *set* of random oracles. In more detail, one oracle can be viewed as a set of different oracles, by using the first part of its input string as an index of an oracle. TAG is a constant bit string of length a. Fig. 2 describes a possible implementation.

Let n be a security parameter and k some big enough constant, $k >> \log n$. Alice and Bob publicly agree on a constant string TAG of length a. An access to the oracle $\mathcal{O}$ is given. Assume $\mathcal{O} : \{0,1\}^{k+\log n} \to \{0,1\}^{2\log n+a}$.

1. Alice chooses a random set $\{(index_i, key_i, ID_i, M_i)|i \in [n], index_i \in \{0,1\}^k, key_i, ID_i, M_i \in \{0,1\}^{\log n}$. Alice computes the set $\{\mathcal{P}_i = \mathcal{O}_{index_i}(key_i) \oplus (ID_i, M_i, TAG)\}$ and sends $\{(index_i, \mathcal{P}_i)\}$ to Bob.
2. Bob randomly chooses a puzzle $(index_j, \mathcal{P}_j)$ and solves it by exhaustive search on the domain of the oracle $\mathcal{O}_{index_j}$. On getting the right key (Bob verifies it according to the TAG string) Bob finds the pair (ID_j, M_j). Then he sends ID_j back to Alice.
3. Alice and Bob use the solution M_j as the common secret key.

Fig. 2. Asymmetric Merkle's Puzzles in the Random Oracle Model

Solving the puzzle is a synonym to finding the pre-image of the specific random oracle. $\mathcal{O}_{index_i}$ denotes the oracle obtained from $\mathcal{O}$ by substitution the first k bits of its input string with $index_i$ bits. The honest party knows that it has found the right value by XORing the answer of the oracle with the puzzle and looking for the string TAG. Under assumptions of characteristics of the random oracle primitive, one's best method to solve the puzzle is to perform an exhaustive search on the pre-image domain. The security of the above protocol comes from the adversary's difficulty to detect the exact puzzle that Bob has selected. It will reveal partial information of the solution of the puzzle Bob has solved when Bob sends the ID back to Alice, but it does not leak information about the rest of the solution (namely, the shared secret key). This is due to the usage of the random oracle.

The time spent by honest parties in order to agree on the secret key in this implementation is as follows. Alice creates n puzzles. Assuming it takes a constant time to create one puzzle, Alice spends $O(n)$ time on the task. To solve one puzzle, Bob will spend $O(n)$ time. After Bob finishes his work, he sends the ID of the puzzle he has solved back to Alice. Thus, to agree on a secret key, the honest participants will spend together $O(n)$ time. For the adversary the best strategy to find out the key (in the worst case) is to solve all the puzzles Alice has sent. Therefore, by investing $O(n^2)$ time Eve will find the secret.

3.2   Symmetric Merkle's Puzzles

The protocol in Fig. 3 describes a symmetric version of the Merkle puzzles protocol, implemented in the random oracle model. The parties are given an access to an oracle $\mathcal{O}$. Alice and Bob each randomly choose n values, query the oracle on them and send the results to each other. They use an intersection set of the selected values as their common secret source.

Let n be a security parameter. An access to the random oracle $\mathcal{O}$ is given. $\mathcal{O}$: $\{0,1\}^{2\log n} \rightarrow \{0,1\}^{2\log n}$.

1. Alice chooses a random set $A = \{(M_i) : M_i \in \{0,1\}^{2\log n}, i \in [n]\}$, then queries $\{a_i = \mathcal{O}(M_i)\}$ and sends $\{a_i\}$ to Bob. At the same time, Bob chooses a random set $B = \{(M_j) : M_j \in \{0,1\}^{2\log n}, j \in [n]\}$, then computes $\{b_j = \mathcal{O}(M_j)\}$ and sends $\{b_j\}$ to Alice.
2. Alice and Bob find a common set $C = \{C_i : i \in l[n]\}$ such that $\mathcal{O}(C) = \{c_i : i \in l[n]\} = \{a_i : i \in [n]\} \cap \{b_j : j \in [n]\}$. If there are no common values, Alice and Bob return to the first step.
3. Alice and Bob output $\oplus_{i=1}^{l[n]} C_i$ as their common secret key.

Fig. 3. Symmetric Merkle's Puzzles in the Random Oracle Model

By the Birthday Paradox the intersection set is not empty with high probability, and thus Alice and Bob will agree on a key with high probability. If Alice and Bob have not gotten the same key, they will find this out while continuing communicating. Then, they can execute the protocol again to get a new key. The security of the protocol comes from the adversary's difficulty in finding all the pre-images of the intersection set. In this implementation, the best strategy of the adversary Eve is to query the oracle in a brute force manner in order to find the secret with the probability 1. The (expected) time required by the honest parties to establish a secret key is $O(n)$. The time required by the adversary to find a secret key is $O(n^2)$ in the worst case.

Theorem 1. *In the asymmetric scenario, the proposed Merkle's puzzle based key agreement protocol has quadratic security.*

The formal proof of the security of the Merkle's puzzle scheme in the random oracle model can be found in [4] and [5].

3.3 Starting Delay and Security Loss in Long Communications

One of the drawbacks of the original protocol (in both scenarios) is that it has fixed performance and security. Once the parameters of the protocol are fixed the security is also fixed. Thus, to achieve higher level of security the two parties need to send more information to each other before starting the actual communication. In the asymmetric case Alice has to send more puzzles to Bob in order to decrease the probability of Eve to succeed in guessing the right puzzle. In the symmetric version of the protocol, Alice and Bob have to query the oracle on a bigger domain, to force the adversary to spend more time on finding the secret key. Therefore, if two parties wish to agree on the secret key in order to use it as a communication key, the higher security level they need the more information they need to send *before* the actual communication. The protocol we propose in the sequel does not possess this characteristic.

Another drawback (which we have discussed in the introduction) of the original protocol is its performance when using it repeatedly, in rounds, to get different key for each round. Suppose a sequential execution of the Merkle's puzzles scheme. For the sake of easiness of discussion, consider asymmetric implementation. Namely, the multiple rounds key agreement protocol is obtained by the execution of the asymmetric Merkle's puzzle scheme in every round. In each round it takes $O(n)$ time for the honest parties to establish a fresh secret key. Let t be a usage parameter of this protocol. Then, the sampling attacker has $k_1 n + t$ time in order to find out a non-obsolete key in every round, for some constant k_1. Denote c the number of puzzles the adversary suffice to solve during the time $k_1 n + t$. The probability to find out a *non-obsolete* key in every round is $\frac{c}{n}$. Namely, according to Definition 4 the security level of such a protocol in the presence of the sampling adversary is the same in every round. Similar observation can be made assuming implementation of each round by symmetric Merkle's puzzle scheme. In contrast, the security level of the nested Merkle's puzzles protocol, that we propose, is growing with time. The probability that hard instances are chosen as puzzles that must be solved grows with time as well.

4 Nested Merkle's Puzzles

In order to deal with the above mentioned issues we propose a protocol which employs the following idea. Use the secret keys established in the previous round to protect the puzzles in the present round. Thus, the honest parties can run the protocol infinitely, while using the keys from the previous rounds as the session keys. With this method, parties do not need to wait in order to start to communicate securely. In addition, the security level (according to Definition 4) in such a scenario is growing with time.

4.1 Asymmetric Nested Merkle's Puzzles

The asymmetric scenario of the Merkle's puzzles key agreement protocol is given in Fig. 4. The beginning of the protocol is similar to the one round Merkle's puzzle

Let n be a security parameter, k be some big enough constant, $k \gg \log n$ and $m > 1, \alpha > 1$ are constants. Let $t(n)$ be a usage parameter. Alice and Bob publicly agree on the constant string TAG of length a. An access to the following oracles are given:

1. $\mathcal{O} : \{0,1\}^{k+\log n} \to \{0,1\}^{a+(m+1)\log n}$. By substituting the first k bits of the input of the oracle with the $index$ bits oracle $\mathcal{O}_{index}$ is obtained.
2. $\mathcal{O}_{Gen} : \{0,1\}^* \to \{0,1\}^{n \times (a+(m+1)\log n)}$

For each $i > 0$ define z_i to be the secret key which is established by Alice and Bob after the execution of round i. Define $\mathcal{Z}_i^\alpha = z_1 \| z_2 \| \dots \| z_{i-1}, if\ i \leq \alpha$, and $\mathcal{Z}_i^\alpha = z_{i-\alpha} \| z_{i-\alpha+1} \dots \| z_{i-1}, if\ i > \alpha$.

1. At the first round:
   (a) Alice chooses a random set $\{(index_i, key_i, ID_i, M_i) | i \in [n], index_i \in \{0,1\}^k, key_i, ID_i \in \{0,1\}^{\log n}, M_i \in \{0,1\}^{m \log n}$. Alice computes the set $\{\mathcal{P}_i = \mathcal{O}_{index_i}(key_i) \oplus (ID_i, M_i, TAG)\}$ and sends $\{(index_i, \mathcal{P}_i)\}$ to Bob.
   (b) Bob randomly chooses a puzzle $(index_j, \mathcal{P}_j)$ and solves it by exhaustive search on the domain of the oracle $\mathcal{O}_{index_j}$. On getting the right key (Bob verifies it according to the TAG string) Bob finds the pair (ID_j, M_j). Then he sends ID_j back to Alice.
   (c) Alice and Bob use the solution M_j as the common secret key, set $z_1 = M_j$.
2. At the ith round:
   (a) Alice generates n puzzles as described in the first round. Alice encrypts all of them and sends to Bob. The encryption of the puzzles is as follows: $\mathcal{O}_{Gen}(\mathcal{Z}_{i-1}^\alpha) \oplus (\mathcal{P}_1, \mathcal{P}_2 \dots \mathcal{P}_n)$.
   (b) When Bob receives encrypted puzzles, he uses the sequence of the secret keys established so far in order to decrypt. After the decryption, Bob does the same as in the first round. Namely, Bob randomly chooses one puzzle then solves it by exhaustive search on the pre-image domain of the appropriate oracle. On getting the solution of the puzzle (ID_j, M_j), Bob sends ID_j back to Alice.
   (c) On receiving Bob's message ID_j, Alice and Bob agree on a common key M_j and set $z_i = M_j$.
3. When the execution of the round i is finished, Alice and Bob can use the new established secret key z_i as the private key for secure communication during $t(n)$ time.

Fig. 4. Nested Merkle's Puzzles Protocol in Asymmetric Scenario Π_{NMP-A}

scheme. In order to protect the puzzles in the next round, parties are given an access to the oracle $\mathcal{O}_{Gen}$ which provides a one time pad string. In the i's round of the protocol the input to the oracle $\mathcal{O}_{Gen}$ is a concatenation of the secret keys which were established in the previous rounds. We call the input to $\mathcal{O}_{Gen}$ a seed. In every round of the protocol the seed is changed by a function on the most recently established secret keys. In that way we keep the next round be depended on the secret history of the previous rounds.

Eve may try to do a brute force search on the seed used in the current round to generate the one time pad string. This approach is not efficient for the adversary, as the length of the seeds in every round is set to $m \log n$, where m is chosen to be greater than 1. Therefore, brute force searching will take much more time.

4.2 Symmetric Nested Merkle's Puzzles

The symmetric variant of the Nested Merkle's puzzles appears in Fig. 5. All the parties are given an access to the oracles $\mathcal{O}_{index}$. In every round Alice and Bob agree on one of these oracles and start to work with it (a similar way to the original one round Merkle's puzzles scheme). However, the oracles $\{\mathcal{O}_{index}\}$ have, in some sense, a big domain. Therefore, in order to restrict the size of the working set, in every round Alice and Bob agree on a subset of the domain of the chosen oracle, thus, an access to the random oracle $\{\mathcal{O}_{Set}\}$ is provided. The input to the oracle is *set-index* string, and the output consists of the subset of the domain elements of the oracles $\{\mathcal{O}_{index}\}$. In every round of the protocol Alice randomly chooses the index of the oracle to be used and the set to work on. Alice encrypts her choice with the one time pad generated by an oracle $\mathcal{O}_H$ and sends to Bob. Now Alice and Bob can proceed to the next step. They act as in the one round Merkle's symmetric scheme. The only difference is the communication of the values of their choices to each other is encrypted by the one time pad generated by the oracle $\mathcal{O}_{Gen}$. The seeds to the oracles $\mathcal{O}_H$ and $\mathcal{O}_{Gen}$ are the secret history of Alice and Bob so far, exactly as in the asymmetric scenario.

4.3 Analysis of the Nested Scheme

First we note, that the usage parameter has to be smaller than n^2 (the time needed for Eve to find the secret key in the first round), in order to keep every round secure. In addition, the usage parameter has to be at least as the time required to the parties to establish a new key. In the analysis of the security we assume that the usage parameter $t()$ is chosen according to the above observations.

The parameter k defined in both schemes, represents the number of oracles which can be used through the protocol by the participants. The protocol uses different oracles in every round in order to protect the rounds against adversary that tabulates the queries of the oracle. Hence, the number of the different oracles has to be big enough. For example $k = 30$ defines 2^{30} different oracles, the number of the particles in the observable universe (suffices for the long enough communication).

Theorem 2. *The multiple round protocol in Fig. 4 (Fig. 5) is secure with the security level $p(n, i) = \left(\frac{\delta}{n}\right)^i$ $(p(n, i) = \left(\frac{\delta}{n^2}\right)^i)$ in the presence of the sampling adversary.*

Proof is omitted from this extended abstract.

5   Nested Merkle's Puzzles in the Standard Model

The implementations we suggest share some techniques with the secure unidirectional communication schemes that are based on magnifying computing gap [12]. Our scope is fullduplex (rather than unidirectional) communication that enables us to obtain new

Let n be a security parameter, k be some big enough constant, $k >> \log n$ and $m > 1, \alpha > 1$ are constants. An access to the following oracles are given:

1. An oracle $\mathcal{O} : \{0,1\}^{k+m\log n} \to \{0,1\}^{m\log n}$. By substituting the first k bits of the input of the oracle with the $index$ bits oracle $\mathcal{O}_{index} : \{0,1\}^{m\log n} \to \{0,1\}^{m\log n}$ is obtained.
2. Three oracles: $\mathcal{O}_{Set} : \{0,1\}^k \to \{0,1\}^{(n^2)m\log n}$; $\mathcal{O}_H : \{0,1\}^* \to \{0,1\}^{2k}$; $\mathcal{O}_{Gen} : \{0,1\}^* \to \{0,1\}^{mn\log n)}$.

For each $i > 0$ define z_i to be the secret key which is established by Alice and Bob after the execution of the round i. Define $\mathcal{Z}_i^{\alpha} = z_1||z_2||\dots||z_{i-1}, if \ i \leq \alpha$, and $\mathcal{Z}_i^{\alpha} = z_{i-\alpha}||z_{i-\alpha+1}\dots||z_{i-1}, if \ i > \alpha$.

1. At the first round:
   (a) Alice selects a random string $index \in \{0,1\}^k$ and a random string $set_{index} \in \{0,1\}^k$. Alice sends $(index, set_{index})$ (in clear text) to Bob.
   (b) Alice and Bob run the one-round Merkle's puzzles protocol, with the oracle $\mathcal{O}_{index}$ and the queries domain obtained by $\mathcal{O}_{Set}(set_{index})$. Namely, Alice and Bob choose their n values from the set of n^2 values resulted by $\mathcal{O}_{Set}(set_{index})$. After the execution Alice and Bob agree on the secret M_j ($M_j \in \{0,1\}^{m\log n}$), and set $z_1 = M_j$.
2. At the ith round:
   (a) Alice randomly selects a fresh $index$ and a fresh set_{index}. Alice sends the encryption of the chosen strings to Bob: $\mathcal{O}_H(\mathcal{Z}_i^{\alpha}) \oplus (index||set_{index})$.
   (b) As in the first round, Alice and Bob run the one-round Merkle's puzzles protocol with the oracle $\mathcal{O}_{index}$ and the queries domain $\mathcal{O}_{Set}(set_{index})$. But now, they send each other the encrypted values. Encryption is obtained by XORing the values with the one time pad string $\mathcal{O}_{Gen}(\mathcal{Z}_i^{\alpha})$.
   (c) Alice and Bob use $\mathcal{O}_{Gen}(\mathcal{Z}_i^{\alpha})$ to decrypt the information and proceed further according to the one-round Merkle's puzzles protocol.
3. At any point of the protocol, Alice and Bob can use the common secret key z_i as a session key for secure communication.

Fig. 5. Nested Merkle's Puzzles Protocol in Symmetric Scenario

schemes that cope with computationally stronger adversaries with relation to the adversaries considered in [12] (in [12] the adversaries are assumed to be slightly weaker than at least one of the honest parties).

Lattice problems have been studied for a long time. Various results have been proved. From the cryptographic point of view, the most important result was proven by Ajtai [1]. Roughly speaking, Ajtai showed that randomly generated instances of the lattice shortest vector problem are hard with high probability. In more detail, Ajtai provided a randomized construction procedure for (hard on average) instances of lattice called *random lattice problem*. Ajtai proved that if there is a probabilistic polynomial time algorithm solving a shortest vector problem in a random lattice, then there is an efficient probabilistic algorithm solving (with very high probability) some known worst-case lattice problems in *every* lattice in Z^n, which are believed to be hard. In this section we provide a detailed description of the implementations of the nested Merkle's puzzles schemes, basing them on the random lattice problem and its average case hardness, which was formally proven by Ajtai. In the next definition and thereafter we denote variables that represent vectors using a bold font.

Definition 5. Random Lattice Shortest Vector Problem

For a given integer n, choose c_1, c_2 such that $m = c_1 n \log n$ and $q = n^{c_2}$ are integers, and the following holds: $c_2 \geq 7$, and $n \log q < m < \frac{q}{2n^4}$ and $m < n^2$. $m - 1$ vectors $\mathbf{v}_1, \mathbf{v}_2, \ldots, \mathbf{v}_{m-1}$ are chosen randomly from the set Z_q^n. Then, $m - 1$ values $\delta_1, \delta_2, \ldots \delta_{m-1}$ are chosen randomly from the set $\{0, 1\}$ and the following vector computed $\mathbf{v}_m = -\sum_{i=1}^{m-1} \delta_i v_i \mod q$. The resulted set of m vectors $(\mathbf{v}_1, \mathbf{v}_2, \ldots \mathbf{v}_m)$ defines a random variable γ. A set $\Lambda(\gamma, q)$ is defined to be the set of all vectors $\mathbf{h}$ in Z_q^m for which $\sum h_i v_i \equiv 0 \mod q$. The length of the vector $\mathbf{h}$ is the usual Euclidean norm (l_2). The random problem defined as follows: given the value of (γ, q) as an input, find a vector in $\Lambda(\gamma, q)$ of length less than n.

Note, that the vector $(\delta_1, \delta_2, \ldots \delta_{m-1}, 1) \in \Lambda(\gamma, q)$ and its length is less than $\sqrt{m} < n$.

5.1 One Round Merkle's Puzzles

We start describing the implementation of one round of the protocol. Asymmetric and symmetric cases are considered. We provide an analysis of the performance and security of the implementations. For the best of our knowledge, this is the first implementation of the Mekle's Puzzles protocol based on a concrete computationally hard on average problem.

Asymmetric Merkle's Puzzles. First we consider the asymmetric scenario. Each puzzle is implemented by an instance of the random lattice problem. Namely, the set of vectors obtained by the value of the random variable λ defines the puzzle. We say that the participant of the protocol randomly generates a puzzle with the parameters (n, m, q), if the participant generates the value of the random variable in the way described in Definition 5. To solve the puzzle means to find a vector in the $\Lambda(\gamma, q)$ whose length is less than n. As we have noted before, one of the possible solutions is the vector of coordinates $(\delta_1, \delta_2, \ldots \delta_{m-1}, 1)$ which is generated during the construction. (Note, that it is enough to consider as a solution only $(\delta_1, \delta_2, \ldots \delta_{m-1})$. However, it is not necessary that each puzzle has only one solution. We address this point in our constructions. The protocol consisting of one round is described in Fig. 6.

The idea is to implement a puzzle as a quadruplet of the instances of the random lattice problem. Alice randomly creates n quadruplets of puzzles, along with their solutions. Then Alice sends all these puzzles, as clear (not encrypted) text to Bob. Bob randomly chooses one quadruplet from the puzzles, and tries to solve it, by applying a brute force search. If he finds more than one solution, he will choose the first according to the lexicographical order. When he finds the solutions to all the puzzles of his choice, he has to inform Alice about the quadruplet he has chosen. For that, Bob Xors solutions of the first two puzzles and sends the result back to Alice. Alice tests all the solutions for the puzzles she has. In that way, Alice knows about the puzzle Bob has chosen, and they establish a secret key.

The security parameter is n. Alice and Bob publicly agree on the parameters (m, q) (as required by the definition of the random lattice problem).

1. Alice randomly generates n quadruplets of puzzles, $\langle \mathcal{P}_{index1}, \mathcal{P}_{index2}, \mathcal{P}_{secret1}, \mathcal{P}_{secret2} \rangle$. Totally $4n$ different puzzles. Alice sends all the puzzles to Bob, in clear text.
2. Bob randomly chooses one of the quadruplets and, by brute force, finds the solutions $\mathbf{s}_1, \mathbf{s}_2, \mathbf{s}_3, \mathbf{s}_4$ for all the four puzzles.
3. Bob computes $\mathbf{s}_1 \oplus \mathbf{s}_2$ and sends back to Alice.
4. Upon receiving the notification from Bob, Alice verifies which pair of the puzzles from the quadruplets fits the message. If Alice can not find the matching between the solutions she has and the notification message, she restarts the protocol.
5. Alice and Bob output $key = (\mathbf{s}_3, \mathbf{s}_4)$ as their common secret key.

Fig. 6. One Round in the Standard Model (Asymmetric Scenario)

Let n, t be the security parameters. Alice and Bob publicly generate a puzzle with the parameters (n, m, q) (as required by the random lattice problem). Define the randomly chosen vectors by $\mathbf{r}_1, \dots \mathbf{r}_{m-1}$.

1. Alice randomly chooses t vectors $\{\mathbf{a}_1, \mathbf{a}_2 \dots, \mathbf{a}_t\}$ from $\{0, 1\}^{m-1}$. For each vector $\mathbf{a}_i = \{\delta_1^{a_i}, \delta_2^{a_i}, \dots, \delta_n^{a_i}\}$, Alice computes $\mathbf{v}_i^a = \sum \delta_j^{a_i} \mathbf{r}_j$.
2. Bob generates t vectors $\{\mathbf{b}_1, \dots \mathbf{b}_t\}$ and computes the set of values $\{\mathbf{v}_i^b\}$, in the same way as Alice.
3. Alice and Bob send all the computed t vectors to each other.
4. By the Birthday Paradox, with high probability, Alice and Bob will find an intersection set of vectors $\{\mathbf{v}_i : i \in l[n]\}$. If there are no common values, Alice and Bob return to the first step.
5. For every common vector $\mathbf{v}_i$, Alice and Bob know the corresponding solution vector $\mathbf{c}_i = \{\delta_j^{c_i} : j \in l[n]\}$. They output $key = XOR_{j=1}^{j=l[n]} \mathbf{c}_j$ as their common secret key.

Fig. 7. One Round in the Standard Model (Symmetric Scenario)

Symmetric Merkle's Puzzles. In this scenario we implement a puzzle in the same way as in the asymmetric case. Detailed description of the symmetric implementation appears in Fig. 7.

Alice and Bob publicly generate a puzzle R, with the parameters (n, m, q). Denote the random vectors obtained by this generation as $\mathbf{r}_1, \dots, \mathbf{r}_{m-1}$. The parameters n, m and q are chosen as required by the definition of the random lattice problem. Alice and Bob randomly choose coordinates of the linear combination of the vectors. The number of such coordinates should be sufficient for the Birthday Paradox to be applied. Namely, Alice and Bob randomly choose number of vectors $\mathbf{a}_1, \dots, \mathbf{a}_{m-1}$ and $\mathbf{b}_1, \dots, \mathbf{b}_{m-1}$. Each vector is from the set $\{0, 1\}^n$. Then, they compute the following values, for each vector, Alice computes $\mathbf{v}_i^a = \sum \delta_j^{a_i} \mathbf{r}_j$. Bob does the same, computing the values $\mathbf{v}_i^b$ (δ of his choice). Then, Alice and Bob send each other the values they obtained, a_i, b_i. Thus, by the Birthday Paradox, with very high probability the intersection set is not empty. Alice and Bob set their secret to be an appropriate sum.

The number of the samples Alice and Bob each have to perform has to be sufficient in order for the Birthday Paradox to be applied. Alice and Bob choose vectors from the $\{0,1\}^{m-1}$. The size of this set is $O(2^m)$. Recall that $m = O(n \log n)$, hence the size of the set is $O(n^n)$. Therefore, Alice and Bob have to choose $O(\sqrt{n^n})$ vectors each. Thus, when running the scheme, we care to set up the protocol with the proper value of n, which will enable an efficient performance. In other words, we will choose a small value of n.

Implementation Details and Security. The security of the above implementations relays on the hardness of the random instances of the lattice shortest vector problem and on the security of the OTP scheme. Assuming the random lattice shortest vector problem is hard on average, it will be hard for Eve to solve the puzzles from the intersection set. Namely, Eve cannot solve the puzzles very fast, by cryptanalysis. Thus, the delay in time needed to solve the puzzle by Eve will keep the above implementation secure (with the quadratic security gap). Even if SVP turns out to be easy to solve in the future, it does not affect the security of our protocol, as long as protocol participants and Eve use the same techniques to solve the puzzles. Namely, the main ingredient needed for the protocol to be secure is the proof of equivalent work of Eve and the protocol participants.

In the asymmetric scenario, Bob sends back the XOR of the solutions of the pair of the chosen puzzle, alternatively hash of one solution or hash of the XORed solutions. The XOR of the solutions is used to disable Eve using the solution of one puzzle to check which of the puzzles the solution belongs to. The degree in which Eve may correlate puzzles and the solutions depends on many parameters. Here, we consider a model in which the adversary can only verify for each pair of a puzzle and a solution whether the solution is the solution of the puzzle or not. Therefore XORing (two randomly selected) solutions of two puzzles blocks the ability of Eve to check whether the XORed solutions belong to certain puzzles or not. The use of hash function may serve as a way to encapsulate the above security issue in the security of the hash function.

5.2   Nested Implementation

We provide a very high level idea of the nested implementation of the protocol. Detailed discussions on implementation is omitted from this extended abstract. We describe the procedure for the asymmetric case, though the symmetric case nested protocol can be constructed in a similar fashion.

The first round is implemented as described in Section 5.1. In every next (dependent) round, Alice and Bob use keys obtained from the previous rounds to protect all the communication in the current round. In more detail, Alice and Bob use previous keys as seed to the pseudo random generator to produce pseudo random bit string. (For example, we can use generators which are based on the lattice problems [3]). Then bit string is used as one time pad to protect all the information in the current round.

In order to start work on the current round, Eve has to find out the matrix of the current round. Note, that when encoding the matrix, Alice does not use any TAG within it. Since Bob knows the key, the honest parties do not need to use TAGs to identify the right encryptions. Therefore, the adversary cannot find out the right matrix in every session, even by performing an exhaustive search on the key. Hence, in order to reveal the new secret key, Eve has to know the secret keys from the previous rounds.

6   Discussions

The asymmetric nested protocol we have proposed possesses the following property: the honest parties have to wait for each other. Bob must wait while Alice sends puzzles, and Alice must wait while Bob exhaustively searches the solutions of the puzzles. We can improve the security of the system by efficient use of "free" time. Namely, the participants will accelerate the rate of the sending of the puzzles.

The main observation is that, in principle, Alice does not need wait for the acknowledgment from Bob about the ID of the puzzle he has chosen. Alice can just send puzzles to Bob all the time, without getting a respond from Bob. At the beginning, Alice will send the puzzles to Bob in the clear text. At the first time Alice receives the information from Bob, Alice will set the common secret key and use it to encrypt the following puzzles she communicates to Bob. At any point of time, until Alice receives new information from Bob, Alice keeps sending puzzles encrypted by the most recently established secret key. Upon receiving fresh information from Bob, Alice updates the secret key. The strategy of Bob changes from selecting one puzzle in every round of the nested protocol, to selecting one puzzle at any time he wants. Bob just selects a puzzle at some point of time he likes and tries to solve it. When he finishes he sends ID back to Alice.

Namely, there is no clear boundary between different rounds in the improved protocol, all the rounds mixed together. The security of such an implementation increases, because the number of puzzles sent during some period of time is bigger than in the original nested protocol. We call this improved protocol *fast* nested Merkle's Puzzles protocol.

Acknowledgment. The authors would like to thank Niv Gilboa for valuable discussions. They also thank Mohammad Mahmoody for comments on an early draft. Thanks to anonymous Referees for their very careful reviews of the paper that include many important points and will improve significantly the clarity of this paper.

References

1. Ajtai, M.: Generating hard instances of lattice problems. Electronic Colloquium on Computational Complexity (ECCC) 3(7) (1996)
2. Aura, T., Nikander, P., Leiwo, J.: DOS-resistant authentication with client puzzles. In: Christianson, B., Crispo, B., Malcolm, J.A., Roe, M. (eds.) Security Protocols 2000. LNCS, vol. 2133, pp. 170–177. Springer, Heidelberg (2001)

3. Banerjee, A., Peikert, C., Rosen, A.: Pseudorandom functions and lattices. In: Pointcheval, D., Johansson, T. (eds.) EUROCRYPT 2012. LNCS, vol. 7237, pp. 719–737. Springer, Heidelberg (2012)

4. Barak, B., Mahmoody-Ghidary, M.: Merkle puzzles are optimal — an $o(n^2)$-query attack on any key exchange from a random oracle. In: Halevi, S. (ed.) CRYPTO 2009. LNCS, vol. 5677, pp. 374–390. Springer, Heidelberg (2009)

5. Biham, E., Goren, Y.J., Ishai, Y.: Basing weak public-key cryptography on strong one-way functions. In: Canetti, R. (ed.) TCC 2008. LNCS, vol. 4948, pp. 55–72. Springer, Heidelberg (2008)

6. Brassard, G., Høyer, P., Kalach, K., Kaplan, M., Laplante, S., Salvail, L.: Merkle puzzles in a quantum world. In: Rogaway, P. (ed.) CRYPTO 2011. LNCS, vol. 6841, pp. 391–410. Springer, Heidelberg (2011)

7. Brassard, G., Salvail, L.: Quantum merkle puzzles. In: ICQNM, pp. 76–79. IEEE Computer Society (2008)

8. Cachin, C., Maurer, U.M.: Unconditional security against memory-bounded adversaries. In: Kaliski Jr., B.S. (ed.) CRYPTO 1997. LNCS, vol. 1294, pp. 292–306. Springer, Heidelberg (1997)

9. Canetti, R., Goldreich, O., Halevi, S.: The random oracle methodology, revisited. J. ACM 51(4), 557–594 (2004)

10. Dolev, S., Gilboa, N., Kopeetsky, M., Persiano, G., Spirakis, P.G.: Information security for sensors by overwhelming random sequences and permutations. In: Al-Shaer, E., Keromytis, A.D., Shmatikov, V. (eds.) ACM CCS, pp. 669–671 (2010)

11. Dolev, S., Kopeetsky, M., Shamir, A.: RFID authentication efficient proactive information security within computational security. Theory Comput. Syst. 48(1), 132–149 (2011)

12. Dolev, S., Korach, E., Uzan, G.: MAGNIFYING COMPUTING GAPS establishing encrypted communication over unidirectional channels (Extended abstract). In: Masuzawa, T., Tixeuil, S. (eds.) SSS 2007. LNCS, vol. 4838, pp. 253–265. Springer, Heidelberg (2007)

13. Impagliazzo, R., Rudich, S.: Limits on the provable consequences of one-way permutations. In: Johnson, D.S. (ed.) STOC, pp. 44–61 (1989)

14. Juels, A.: Minimalist cryptography for low-cost RFID tags (Extended abstract). In: Blundo, C., Cimato, S. (eds.) SCN 2004. LNCS, vol. 3352, pp. 149–164. Springer, Heidelberg (2005)

15. Mahmoody, M., Moran, T., Vadhan, S.: Non-interactive time-stamping and proofs of work in the random oracle model. Cryptology ePrint Archive, Report 2011/553 (2011), http://eprint.iacr.org/

16. Mahmoody, M., Moran, T., Vadhan, S.: Time-lock puzzles in the random oracle model. In: Rogaway, P. (ed.) CRYPTO 2011. LNCS, vol. 6841, pp. 39–50. Springer, Heidelberg (2011)

17. Mao, W.: Timed-release cryptography. Cryptology ePrint Archive, Report 2001/014 (2001), http://eprint.iacr.org/

18. Merkle, R.C.: Secure communications over insecure channels. Commun. ACM 21(4), 294–299 (1978)

19. Moran, T., Shaltiel, R., Ta-Shma, A.: Non-interactive time stamping in the bounded-storage model. J. Cryptology 22(2), 189–226 (2009)

20. Rivest, R.L., Shamir, A., Wagner, D.A.: Time-lock puzzles and timed-release crypto. Technical report, Cambridge, MA, USA (1996)

21. Sotakova, M.: Breaking one-round key-agreement protocols in the random oracle model. Cryptology ePrint Archive, Report 2008/053 (2008), http://eprint.iacr.org/

Optimizing Guessing Strategies for Algebraic Cryptanalysis with Applications to EPCBC

Michael Walter[1,*], Stanislav Bulygin[2,3,**], and Johannes Buchmann[2,3]

[1] University of California, San Diego,
Department of Computer Science and Engineering,
9500 Gilman Drive, Mail Code 0404, La Jolla, CA 92093-5004, USA
miwalter@eng.ucsd.edu
[2] Technische Universität Darmstadt, Department of Computer Science
Hochschulstraße 10, 64289 Darmstadt, Germany
buchmann@cdc.informatik.tu-darmstadt.de
[3] Center for Advanced Security Research Darmstadt - CASED
Mornewegstraße 32, 64293 Darmstadt, Germany
Stanislav.Bulygin@cased.de

Abstract. In this paper we demonstrate how to use Mixed Integer Linear Programming to optimize guessing strategies for algebraic cryptanalysis with applications to the block cipher EPCBC. Using our optimized guessing strategy we are able to attack 5 rounds of EPCBC-96 and 8 rounds of EPCBC-48 faster than brute force using one and two known plaintexts resp. Finally, we are able to identify a class of weak keys for which the attack is faster than brute force for up to 7 rounds of EPCBC-96. Alongside results on EPCBC we believe that the proposed technique of optimized guessing is a useful tool in a more general context of algebraic cryptanalysis.

Keywords: Algebraic Cryptanalysis, Lightweight Cryptography, Guessing Strategies, Mixed Integer Linear Programming.

1 Introduction

Recent years have seen a drastic increase in the importance of embedded systems. More and more objects in the world around us are being equipped with some circuitry, giving rise to a seemingly endless potential of intelligent and convenient solutions to today's problems. As a consequence, small and cheap hardware, like RFID tags or printed integrated circuits, is being developed. However, for many applications these low resource devices need to be able to provide security properties, like privacy and authenticity. This is achieved by employing cryptographic algorithms. Many "classical" algorithms have not been designed to be implemented on small devices and are thus not suitable for this purpose. For this reason, the relatively young field of lightweight cryptography tries to cater to

---

* Supported in part by NSF grant CNS-1117936.
** Supported by the grant DFG BU630/22-1.

M. Kutyłowski and M. Yung (Eds.): Inscrypt 2012, LNCS 7763, pp. 175–197, 2013.

that need by designing cryptographic primitives that can be implemented with a small hardware footprint, while still preserving security.

The main challenge in lightweight cryptography – to reduce the hardware footprint as far as possible while maintaining acceptable performance and security levels – requires careful analysis of every new cryptosystem that is being proposed. While the proposals tend to get smaller and smaller in terms of hardware footprint, one needs to make sure that these primitives still meet the claimed security properties. It seems plausible that algebraic cryptanalysis could be a powerful approach to the analysis of lightweight primitives, since the restrictions on the hardware footprint also pose restrictions on the algebraic complexity of these primitives. The crucial step in algebraic cryptanalysis is solving an algebraic system describing the primitive in question. There are several techniques available to tackle this problem. So far one of the most efficient methods has been the SAT solving, due to the vast amounts of research during the past decades regarding solving the satisfiability problem in propositional logic. It has been employed in the analysis of several primitives [1, 5, 8, 9, 19]. We will follow this methodology and also employ SAT solving.

In this work we will analyze a recently proposed lightweight primitive, the block cipher EPCBC [22], which follows the design principles of the PRESENT [2] block cipher. We will focus on attacks with a low data complexity. We are aware of the success of statistical attacks on PRESENT (e.g. [6]) and that they are probably applicable to EPCBC with similar success due to the similarity to PRESENT. However, these attacks require a large amount of known (or chosen) plain-/ciphertext pairs. This might not always be a realistic scenario. The authors of [22] describe a possible application of their cipher that involves a library using RFID tags to manage their books and someone borrowing a book on cancer treatment, which is obviously very private information. There should be no illegitimate way to read out the Electronic Production Code (EPC) used to identify the book. While in this case it may be possible to walk into the library and obtain a large amount of plain-/ciphertext pairs to mount a statistical attack, there are several scenarios where this is not true. For example, it is plausible that a hospital manages their medical devices using RFID tags. In this case it is doubtful that it is easy to obtain enough plain-/ciphertext pairs to mount a statistical attack. In contrast, a successful attack with low data complexity would enable an adversary to gain knowledge of who is walking out of the hospital, for example with a catheter. So in this context, algebraic attacks with low data complexity, although generally breaking fewer rounds, should be considered as a complement to cryptanalysis tools, rather than a competitor to statistical attacks. Moreover, studying attacks with low data complexity is important to rule out the temptation to use less rounds in a scenario, where gathering large amount of data is (practically) impossible. An interesting approach for low data complexity attacks on AES is described in [16].

Our contribution goes beyond the analysis of a specific block cipher. We introduce a novel technique to optimize guessing strategies in algebraic cryptanalysis using Mixed Integer Linear Programming (MILP). Guessing strategies play an important role in algebraic cryptanalysis to estimate the complexity of theoretical attacks or demonstrate certain weaknesses [1, 10, 17]. At first sight it is not clear how a guessing strategy should be selected, as there is no established approach yet. We address this problem by introducing a clear criterion based on information propagation for guessing strategies and introduce a new technique to select a guessing strategy that optimizes this criterion. We show how this new technique can be applied to EPCBC and how it can even be used to identify classes of weak keys. While we demonstrate the technique using a specific block cipher, this approach is applicable, and should be considered, in a more general context.

MILP has been used as a tool for cryptanalysis for some time now, either as a solving technique [4] or as a tool of finding useful differential properties [14]. In this work we use MILP to facilitate algebraic cryptanalysis.

The next section gives a brief overview of the primitive under consideration and Section 3 outlines our results of an algebraic attack applied to EPCBC without guessing. We introduce the concept of guessing strategies in Section 4, where we also demonstrate how to optimize guessing strategies for EPCBC and give our results for both versions of EPCBC. Finally, we summarize our results in Section 5 and outline some future work.

2   Description of EPCBC

EPCBC is a lightweight block cipher proposed by Yap et al. in 2011 [22]. The design of this cipher is mainly driven by two objectives. Firstly, being a lightweight cipher, EPCBC is supposed to provide a maximum of security with a very low hardware footprint. Secondly, the cipher is designed for a specific purpose, namely to provide secure encryption for Electronic Product Codes (EPC). EPCs are codes with a bit length of 96 in their smallest variant. The authors of [22] observed that so far there are no lightweight block ciphers with a suitable block size for EPCs. To remedy this they propose two ciphers, one with block size $b = 48$ and one with block size $b = 96$. Both variants have a key length of 96 bits. We will denote them by EPCBC-48 and EPCBC-96, respectively.

The cipher is heavily inspired by PRESENT. Accordingly, the key schedule and the encryption algorithm exhibit very strong structural similarities to the encryption algorithm of PRESENT. This has the advantage that some security proofs for PRESENT directly carry over to EPCBC.

2.1   Key Schedule

Both versions of EPCBC run in 32 rounds with a final key addition at the end resulting in 33 subkeys. The key schedules are outlined in Algorithm 1 and 2, largely following the terminology of [22]. Note, that for EPCBC-48 the key schedule is built of 8 separate 4-round PRESENT-like and very similar permutations, which have a block size of 48 and related initial values, and only differ in the constant addition. This will be useful during our attack, where we will denote each of these permutations as a *block*. The following are the layers of the key schedule algorithm:

Table 1. EPCBC S-Box (hex)

input	0 1 2 3 4 5 6 7 8 9 A B C D E F
output	C 5 6 B 9 0 A D 3 E F 8 4 7 1 2

Algorithm 1. EPCBC-48 key schedule

(LKeystate, RKeystate) = 96-bit key
Subkey[0] ← LKeystate
for $i = 0 \to 7$ do
   temp ← LKeystate ⊕ RKeystate
   for $j = 0 \to 3$ do
      RKeystate ← sBoxLayer(RKeystate)
      RKeystate ← pLayer(RKeystate)
      RKeystate ← RKeystate ⊕ $(4i + j)$
      Subkey[$4i + j + 1$] ← RKeystate
   end for
   LKeystate ← RKeystate
   RKeystate ← temp
end for

Algorithm 2. EPCBC-96 key schedule

Keystate = 96-bit key
Subkey[0] ← Keystate
for $i = 0 \to r - 1$ do
   Keystate ← sBoxLayer(Keystate)
   Keystate ← pLayer(Keystate)
   Keystate ← Keystate ⊕ i
   Subkey[$i + 1$] ← Keystate
end for

---

sBoxLayer. The substitution layer of EPCBC and PRESENT are identical up to the number of S-Boxes. For completeness, the definition of the 4-bit S-Box is given in Table 1.

pLayer. The permutation layer also strongly resembles the one of PRESENT. Bit j is moved to position $P(j)$ with

$$P(j) = \begin{cases} j \cdot \frac{b}{4} \mod b - 1 & \text{if } 0 \leq j \leq b - 2 \\ b - 1 & \text{if } j = b - 1 \end{cases} ,$$

2.2 Encryption

The encryption process is mainly borrowed from PRESENT and is described by Algorithm 3 for both versions of EPCBC. The STATE is initialized with the plaintext and subsequently the round function is applied r times to it. Finally, the last subkey is added, after which STATE contains the ciphertext. For both versions of EPCBC r is 32. The functions sBoxLayer and pLayer are identical to the ones of the key schedule described in the previous section. One round of EPCBC-48 is depicted in Figure 1, where s_i is the i-th state, k_i the i-th subkey and s_{i+1} the next state. Note, that the encryption process and the key schedule exhibit a strong structural symmetry, which allows for significant information flow, as we will see below.

Algorithm 3. EPCBC Encryption

---
for $i = 0 \rightarrow r - 1$ **do**
    STATE $\leftarrow$ STATE $\oplus$ Subkey[i]
    STATE $\leftarrow$ sBoxLayer(STATE)
    STATE $\leftarrow$ pLayer(STATE)
end for
STATE $\leftarrow$ STATE $\oplus$ Subkey[r]

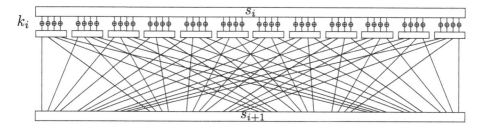

Fig. 1. One round of EPCBC-48

3 Algebraic Attack without Guessing

Since EPCBC is a recently proposed block cipher, the analytic effort targeting this cipher is very limited so far. As far as we know, the only cryptanalysis to date is the preliminary analysis in the proposal itself [22]. The authors comment on algebraic cryptanalysis but use a more or less rule-of-thumb estimation to argue that EPCBC is secure against algebraic attacks. This estimation is partially justified, since it is mainly based on results due to analysis of PRESENT, but a more thorough examination is necessary to ensure that the cipher meets the claimed security properties. The authors of [22] estimate the number of variables in the polynomial system corresponding to the encryption and key schedule of EPCBC-48 to be at least 6240 and the number of equations to 16380 (12480 and 32760 for EPCBC-96). This might be a valid estimation if restricting the degree of the equations to 2, which can make sense for certain solving algorithms. However, when employing SAT solving, this may not be true. Our algebraic representation consists of 4656 variables and 4608 equations for EPCBC-48, and 6240 and 6144 for EPCBC-96. In both cases, a quarter of the equations has degree two and the rest degree three, because the degree of the equations is determined by the representation of the S-Box operation (cf. Equations (1) to (4)).

For the algebraic attack we generated the polynomials in the Boolean polynomial ring relating the inputs and outputs to each other, with additional variables for each intermediate state in the key schedule and encryption. The crucial part of the equation generation is the way the S-Box operation is represented as it is the only non-linear operation. As pointed out by the authors of [22], the S-Box operation can be represented by 21 equations of degree two. Using these equations and Gröbner basis techniques, we generated four explicit equations describing for each output variable y_i its dependence on the input variables x_i, i.e. $y_i = f_i(x_0, x_1, x_2, x_3)$:

$$y_0 = x_0 + x_1 \cdot x_2 + x_2 + x_3 \tag{1}$$

$$y_1 = x_0 \cdot x_1 \cdot x_2 + x_0 \cdot x_1 \cdot x_3 + x_0 \cdot x_2 \cdot x_3 + x_1 \cdot x_3 + x_1 + x_2 \cdot x_3 + x_3 \tag{2}$$

$$y_2 = x_0 \cdot x_1 \cdot x_3 + x_0 \cdot x_1 + x_0 \cdot x_2 \cdot x_3 + x_0 \cdot x_3 + x_1 \cdot x_3 + x_2 + x_3 + 1 \tag{3}$$

$$y_3 = x_0 \cdot x_1 \cdot x_2 + x_0 \cdot x_1 \cdot x_3 + x_0 \cdot x_2 \cdot x_3 + x_0 + x_1 \cdot x_2 + x_1 + x_3 + 1 \tag{4}$$

We generated the polynomial system for EPCBC-48 and EPCBC-96, respectively, with successively increasing round numbers r starting with $r = 1$ using the open source mathematics software system SAGE [20]. In theory, substituting the values of the known plain-/ciphertext pairs into the system and solving the system recovers the key. To solve the system we converted it into an instance of the satisfiability problem using the PolyBoRi CNF converter[1] and applied the SAT solver CryptoMiniSat [18] to it. We implemented and evaluated the algebraic attack (without guessing) on round reduced versions of EPCBC-b for $b \in \{48, 96\}$ in the known plaintext scenario. If not stated otherwise, throughout this paper our attacks use the minimal number of known plain-/ciphertext pairs to uniquely determine the key, i.e. one known pair for EPCBC-96 and two for EPCBC-48. We evaluated the approach for each version and r using the following experiment 100 times. First, we chose a key and plaintext(s) at random and computed the corresponding ciphertext(s). Then, we set the variables corresponding to the plain-/ciphertext pairs in the polynomial system accordingly and attempted to solve the system. The average solving times and standard deviations are listed in Table 2 for $1 \le r \le 3$. The attack was practically infeasible for larger r with our resources, which consisted of a test server with processors of type *Quad-Core AMD Opteron(tm) Processor 8356* operating at a frequency of 2.3 GHz and using a 64-bit Linux kernel in version 2.6.32. Only one core was used for the experiments.

---

[1] https://bitbucket.org/malb/algebraic_attacks/src/ce81112bbce4/
polybori-cnf-converter.py

Table 2. Standard algebraic known plaintext attack on EPCBC-48 (left) and EPCBC-96 (right)

r	1	2	3	r	1	2	3
avg in s	0.0077	0.27	458.3	avg in s	0.017	0.28	556.7
stdev in s	0.004	0.013	866.4	stdev in s	0.005	0.014	2282.7

4   Guessing Strategies

Despite the problems caused by the lack of efficiency of algebraic cryptanalysis, results for many primitives can often still be obtained by employing *guessing strategies*. For this, a certain number of variables of the polynomial system is fixed to either correct values or a guess and thus yielding a practically solvable system. To explore the implications of results obtained by following a guessing strategy, consider a block cipher with a key of length b. We denote the *expected* time required to find a solution of the corresponding polynomial system as t_{true}^b. To denote the *expected* time required to prove that such a system does not have a solution, we use t_{false}^b. Finally, we will denote the time needed to encrypt a plaintext by t_{eval}. Typically, results from guessing strategies involve one of the two scenarios. In the first scenario we assume part of the key is revealed to the adversary by some oracle. For a good cryptographic primitive there should be no way to recover the rest of the key faster than by brute-forcing the remaining key bits. This means, if we can show that for a block cipher and a set of k revealed secret bits

$$t_{true}^{b-k} < 2^{b-k-1} \cdot t_{eval} \tag{5}$$

holds, we have demonstrated a weakness in the primitive. Practical examples of this scenario are side-channel attacks, where additional information is available to the adversary due to the exploitation of physical properties of an implementation [12,15].

   In the second scenario guessing is used to estimate the complexity of an algebraic attack without assuming any knowledge of the secret. Any algorithm that recovers the key faster than the brute-force attack is considered to be an attack, even if it is practically infeasible, in which case it is of theoretical nature. So, assume that we can show by sufficiently sampling t_{false}^{b-k} and t_{true}^{b-k}, that

$$2^{k-1} \cdot t_{false}^{b-k} + t_{true}^{b-k} < 2^{b-1} \cdot t_{eval} \tag{6}$$

$$t_{false}^{b-k} + \frac{t_{true}^{b-k}}{2^{k-1}} < 2^{b-k} \cdot t_{eval} \tag{7}$$

holds for a given primitive. Note that the left hand side of (6) is the *expected* time needed to find a solution to the polynomial system by repeatedly guessing k out of the b secret bits and solving the reduced system. Indeed, we expect to run through half of the possible guesses ($2^{k-1} \cdot t_{false}^{b-k}$) before we hit the correct guess (t^{b-k}_{true}). It follows that in this case we have found a theoretical attack for the given primitive employing algebraic techniques, even though we might not be able to estimate t^b_{true}. For sufficiently large k the inequality can be simplified further, since the term involving t^{b-k}_{true} is negligible, yielding an upper bound for t^{b-k}_{false} only.

Note that in the second scenario the attacker is free to choose the variables for which he will guess values. Not surprisingly, it may happen that Equation (7) holds for one choice of k variables, but does not for another. So in the former case we have a successful attack, whereas in the latter we do not. Therefore, the question arises which variables to guess. In this work we call a set of variables, where the guessing will take place, a *guessing strategy*. While employing guessing strategies is a standard approach in algebraic analysis, there is no established method in selecting a strategy. We want to remedy this by defining a clear criterion for the quality of a guessing strategy and showing how to optimize this criterion in a systematic way.

4.1 Information Propagation

EPCBC is an iterative block cipher. This means that the next state in the encryption and the key schedule is computed from the previous state via a round function. A round function is almost the same for all rounds of a cipher (up to maybe adding some round-dependent constants and the like). It follows that some information about a state can be deduced when information about the previous state is known. In algebraic cryptanalysis the states usually correspond to certain variables in the polynomial system, so information about some variables can propagate to other variables. For example, consider Figure 2 which depicts one round of the key schedule in EPCBC-48 (neglecting the constant addition). The figure shows a set of S-Boxes at the top and at the bottom, and in between the permutation layer is illustrated. The old state is the input of the S-Boxes at the top and the new state is the input of the S-Boxes at the bottom. If we know the input of one of the S-Boxes at the top, we obviously also know the output of this specific S-Box and thus four of the bits of the new state. On the other hand, if we had known four bits at random positions at four *different* S-Boxes of the input state, we could not have deduced the values of any bits of the new state. This is obvious when considering Equations (1) to (4): no matter which x-variable is known, we cannot deduce the value of any y-variables. In contrast, if the values of x_1, x_2, and x_3 are all known to be 0, then we know for sure that $y_1 = 0$. It follows, that revealing the values of different bits yields different information gain, which can even depend on the values of the variables. The same holds for guesses: guessing bits at the input of the round may impose values for bits in the new state and thus decrease the number of unknowns in the system. Since the difference between actually known bits, i.e. bits revealed to the adversary, and guessed bits is irrelevant for information propagation, we will use these terms in this work interchangeably in the context of information propagation.

The difference in the number of inferable bits is even magnified when considering more rounds and a larger number of known or guessed bits. So, guessing

k variables of a polynomial system can reduce the number of variables in the system by far more than only k variables. We show in this work that solvers can benefit from this propagated information – the more information inferable from the guesses the shorter the solving times. Although we do not claim that the amount of propagated information is the only factor that influences the solving times for different guessing strategies, our experiments suggest that it is definitely an important one. Consequentially, our goal is to find guessing strategies that maximize the information gain in order to optimize solving times for the reduced polynomial systems.

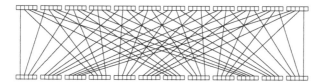

Fig. 2. One round of the key schedule of EPCBC-48

4.2   Optimizing Information Flow Using MILP

We introduce two MILP models that compute guessing strategies in order to maximize the information flow for EPCBC-96. We will address EPCBC-48 in the next subsection. For an introduction to MILP, see for example [7] or any other book on Mathematical Programming. Recall that for a given $c \in \mathbb{R}^n$, $A \in \mathbb{R}^{m \times n}$, $b \in \mathbb{R}^m$, and $p \in \{0, \cdots, n\}$ an MILP is defined as:

$$\max_x \{c^T x | Ax \leq b, \, x \in \mathbb{Z}^p \times \mathbb{R}^{n-p}\} \tag{8}$$

Note that for the purpose of information flow maximization we can neglect the constant addition of the key schedule, since the constants are publicly known. Furthermore, we can circumvent the key addition as well, due to the strong symmetry of the key schedule and the encryption process. When guessing bits only in the first state of the key schedule, i.e. in the master key, all of these bits correspond to known bits in the plaintext and the knowledge is thus propagated through the first key addition layer of the encryption process. As this is true for all guessed key bits, every propagated bit in the key schedule corresponds to a known bit in the encryption process. So, if bits are only guessed in the input of the key schedule, the information flow in the key schedule and encryption process are identical. It follows that we only have to model the key schedule without the constant addition, i.e. a network of interleaved substitution and permutation layers, and maximize the information flow.

Simple Propagation Model. First we introduce a simple model in the sense that we assume that the output bits of a certain S-Box can only be learned if all of its input bits are known. For this, let us assume a network consisting of r

rounds of the EPCBC-96 key schedule (without constant addition). The state width is denoted by b. For the model we introduce a Boolean decision variable $x_{i,j}$ for every bit of the state in each round with the semantics that $x_{i,j} = 1$ iff the j-th bit is known after round i. Accordingly, the model will contain b variables for each round that is modeled and b additional variables for the initial state. The objective function is now straight-forward:

$$\max \sum_{i=0}^{r} \sum_{j=0}^{b-1} x_{i,j} \quad . \tag{9}$$

Similarly, we can easily limit the number of bits we want to guess to an arbitrary integer k:

$$\sum_{j=0}^{b-1} x_{0,j} \leq k. \tag{10}$$

Finally, we have to translate the semantics of the decision variables into our model. For this consider an arbitrary S-Box in round i and let x_{i,j_0}, x_{i,j_1}, x_{i,j_2}, x_{i,j_3} be the variables corresponding to the input bits of this S-Box. Note, that the variables corresponding to the output bits of the S-Box are $x_{i+1,P(j_0)}$, $x_{i+1,P(j_1)}$, $x_{i+1,P(j_2)}$, $x_{i+1,P(j_3)}$. This is illustrated in Figure 3. To model the propagation of information through this S-Box, we include the following set of constraints:

$$x_{i+1,P(j_t)} \leq x_{i,j_s} \quad \text{for all } t, s \in \{0, \cdots, 3\}. \tag{11}$$

This set of constraints ensures that an output bit of the S-Box is only known, i.e. $x_{i+1,P(j_t)} = 1$, if all the input bits are known. This is ensured by the fact that we maximize the sum of known/learned bits. Including this set of constraints for every S-Box in every round models the information flow for the whole network. This will result in $16 \cdot 24 = 384$ constraints for each round that is modeled.

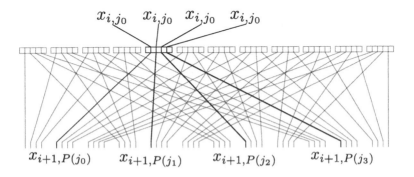

Fig. 3. Decision variables for one S-Box

We solved this MILP using a MILP solver[2] for $r = 4$ rounds and $k = 64$ guesses. A drawback of our method is that the model is increasingly hard to solve for more rounds. However, our result showed that information propagation does not extend beyond round three, so the solutions is optimal for all rounds larger than three. One result is depicted in Appendix A. It consists of guessing the leftmost 64 bits of the master key. There are two more optimal solutions: one is guessing the rightmost 64 bits, and the other one is guessing the leftmost 32 and the rightmost 32 bits. By guessing according to one of these strategies we are able to infer at least $z = 160$ additional bits. Accounting for the bits propagated in the encryption, this sums up to reducing the polynomial system by at least 384 variables. The estimations of t_{true}^{32} and t_{false}^{32} resulting from averaging the results of 100 runs each using the strategy in Appendix A can be found in Table 3. To estimate a lower bound for t_{eval} we accounted one processor cycle for each substitution and each constant or key addition layer during the encryption of a plaintext and the key schedule and assumed the same processor speed as our experiments were run with (cf. Section 3). The results show that the algebraic attack using our guessing strategy (or having the corresponding bits revealed) is significantly faster than the brute-force attack up to $r = 5$. Specifically, we were able to achieve a speed-up factor of nearly 90 for the 5-round version of EPCBC-96 for t_{false}^{32}.

Table 3. Comparison of t_{true}^{32} (left) and t_{false}^{32} (right) for EPCBC-96 with the brute-force attack

r	4	5	6	r	4	5	6
$2^{31} \cdot t_{eval}$ in s	14.9	18.7	22.4	$2^{32} \cdot t_{eval}$ in s	29.9	37.3	44.8
avg in s	0.12	0.39	1687.5	avg in s	0.062	0.42	4324.7
stdev in s	0.006	0.023	2941.1	stdev in s	0.040	0.038	5614.7

We compared our strategy with 10 random strategies. For each of these strategies we selected 16 out of the 24 S-Boxes of the first substitution layer of the key schedule randomly and selected their input bits as a guessing strategy. Running the same experiment with them as we did for our optimized strategy showed that 8 of the 10 strategies yield attacks that are slower than the brute-force attack. For 2 of the strategies the attack is also faster than brute-force, but the speed-up factor is less than 3.

Remark 1. It seems intuitive to apply a meet-in-the-middle attack, where bits in the first and in the last subkey are guessed and the propagated information "overlaps" in the middle. This can serve to quickly reject a large portion of incorrect guesses if the overlapping information does not match. However, using MILP techniques we were able to show that for $r = 6$ it is not possible to achieve overlapping information with less than $k = 100$ guessed bits. Furthermore, we

---

[2] IBM ILOG CPLEX V12.1 under the academic license.

were able to show that at least $k = 80$ guessed bits are needed to achieve this for $r = 5$. With $k = 80$ and $r = 5$ a maximum of 6 overlapping bits is possible, which means that the number of guesses can be reduced from 2^{80} to 2^{74}. We carried out experiments and applied the same bounds we used throughout this paper. The results strongly suggest that a meet-in-the-middle attack does not work in this context.

S-Box Adjusted Propagation Model. For many S-Boxes some information about the output can still be inferred even if the input is only partially known. For example, if the second, third, and fourth bits of the input of the S-Box used in EPCBC are known or assumed to have the value 0, then the second and third bit of the output must have the values 0 and 1, respectively (cf. Equations (1) to (4)). We will denote such relations as *masks*. The bits correspond directly to variables in the algebraic system, which represent their values and thus the terms *bit* and *algebraic variable* can be used interchangeably in certain context. In contrast, recall that the values of the decision variables of the MILP only represent knowledge of the values of the corresponding bits, not the values of the bits themselves. To clarify this distinction we will use the terms *algebraic variable* and *decision variable* in the following.

Again, consider an arbitrary S-Box in round i with the input bits corresponding to the decision variables x_{i,j_0}, x_{i,j_1}, x_{i,j_2}, x_{i,j_3} and output bits to the decision variables $x_{i+1,P(j_0)}$, $x_{i+1,P(j_1)}$, $x_{i+1,P(j_2)}$, $x_{i+1,P(j_3)}$. The concatenation of the values these variables take on can be seen as 8-dimensional binary vectors and the constraints in (11) describe a 0/1-polytope in 8-dimensional space that contains all points that represent a valid information flow through an S-Box. For example, this polytope contains the points $(1,1,1,1,1,1,1,1)$ and $(1,0,1,0,0,0,0,0)$, which represent the information flow with fully known input propagated to the output and partial input that is not propagated, respectively. The polytope does not contain the point $(0,1,1,1,0,1,1,0)$, as would be desired for the example of the EPCBC S-Box mask above. To remedy this we can construct the polytope using its vertex representation, i.e. we construct the polytope as the convex hull of the set of points that all describe a valid information flow. Subsequently, the vertex representation can be converted into a set of equations and inequalities describing the same polytope using the Double Description Method[3] [13]. Including this set of constraints into the MILP instead of the constraints in (11) for every S-Box yields an MILP that models the information flow for a specific S-Box and specific values.

We are aware that this method neglects the fact that only certain values for partially known inputs of an S-Box actually yield information about certain output bits. This can result in an invalid information propagation being computed if several partial inputs are used in subsequent rounds. A conceivable example using aforementioned EPCBC S-Box relation is depicted in Figure 4. Here the partial input is used to infer that the second and third output bit of an S-Box are

---

[3] Fukuda's `cddlib` (`http://www.ifor.math.ethz.ch/~fukuda/cdd_home/`) accessed through the SAGE interface.

0 and 1. Furthermore, the third output bit is part of partially known input of an S-Box in the subsequent round itself, but assumed to be 0 in order to allow for further information to be gained. This yields a conflict and thus the information propagation is invalid. This is due to the MILP model using Boolean decision variables and only distinguishing known and unknown bits, but not their values. We will explain how we dealt with conflicts when discussing the solution.

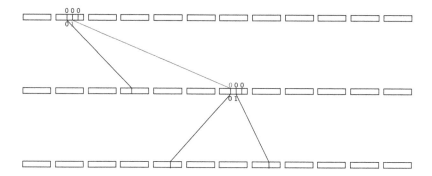

Fig. 4. Example of conflict in EPCBC network

The set of vertices (comprising values of decision variables) corresponding to masks (comprising values of algebraic variables) for the EPCBC S-Box, which can be found by brute-force, is listed in Appendix B. To this set we added the vertex representing full information flow $(1, 1, 1, 1, 1, 1, 1, 1)$ and the vertices for partially known inputs that do not yield a mask, i.e. where the information is lost. Applying the Double Description Method to the resulting set yielded 181 inequalities. As they need to be included for each S-Box, this results in 4344 constraints for each round that is modeled. The number of decision variables is still the same as for the simple model. We solved the MILP for $r = 5$ and the result is depicted in Appendix C.[4] The information flow is invalid as it contains several conflicts as explained above. However, close inspection of the result reveals, that there is a set of crucial S-Boxes that allows for significant information propagation, if the mask conditions are satisfied for the algebraic variables corresponding to these S-Box inputs. In the illustration in Appendix C these are the S-Boxes with the numbers, which represent the values the algebraic variables need to have for the respective S-Box to yield the depicted information flow. A "+" means that either value works. For the key schedule to take advantage of this S-Box adjusted information flow, there are 55 algebraic variables at the output of round 2 that need to have a specific value each. We will denote the corresponding bits by *active* bits. A key will be denoted as *weak*, if the key schedule applied to it results in inner states, i.e. subkeys, meeting these requirements. There must be 2^{41} weak keys since two rounds of the key schedule yield a 96-bit permutation.

---

[4] For readability the lines representing known bits in the permutation layer of round two and three are drawn in light gray. This has no special meaning.

Known Plaintext Attack on Weak Keys. We simulated the attack on EPCBC-96 with $r = 6$ rounds and a random known plain-/ciphertext pair for each of the 2^9 guesses. Specifically, we fixed the bits in the third round of the key schedule to the required values (the values in Appendix C), enumerated all possible values for the bits with the "+", and for each of them obtained the values for our guess by inverting the two rounds of the key schedule for this set of bits only. In the simple model we had the luxury of achieving the same information flow in the key schedule and the encryption, as the flow was independent of the values of the variables. The information flow now under consideration is dependent of the values of the variables and since the weakness of the keys only ensures the correct values for the key schedule, the information flow does not hold for the encryption. There is still information being propagated, but it is unlikely to be as much as during the key schedule. However, relying on the high information flow during the key schedule, we were able to reduce the number variables of the system by 440 on average. The result is shown in Table 4 and shows speed-up factors of $2^{3.6}$ and $2^{4.2}$ compared to the brute-force attacks. The attack was practically infeasible for $r = 7$.

Table 4. Comparison of t_{true}^{32} (left) and t_{false}^{32} (right) for weak keys and random plaintext to brute-force attack for EPCBC-96

r	6	r	6
$2^{31} \cdot t_{eval}$ in s	22.4	$2^{32} \cdot t_{eval}$ in s	44.8
avg in s	1.85	avg in s	2.42
stdev in s	2.93	stdev in s	3.11

Chosen Plaintext Attack on Weak Keys. The attack can be sped up by also maximizing the information flow for the encryption process. Due to the symmetry of the key schedule and the encryption process, we need the algebraic variables corresponding to partial inputs of the same set of S-Boxes to have the same values as the ones in the key schedule. Due to the key addition layer, these active bits are required to be 0 during the encryption. Given a key, such a plaintext can be constructed easily by fixing the 55 active bits to 0, choosing arbitrary values for the remaining bits and applying two rounds of decryption to this constructed state. Note that the choice of the plaintext is dependent on the choice of the guess. This is not a problem in case the correct values of the key bits are known, since an attacker can simply choose the plaintext as just explained. However, in case the key bits are not known and need to be guessed, this would mean the adversary would have to choose a new plaintext for each guess. This obviously results in a very high data complexity, which we are trying to avoid. For this reason, we propose to choose a plaintext for one of the guesses and reuse the same plaintext for each following guess. The hope here, which is confirmed by our experiments, is that due to the structural similarity of all the weak keys the chosen plaintext is still relatively weak for all of them.

Now it is possible to construct a chosen plaintext attack under the assumption that the key is weak. After selecting the first guess, we can choose a plaintext as outlined above and run our attack. We applied the attack to EPCBC-96 for $r \in \{6, 7\}$ with 100 randomly chosen weak keys each, guessing correctly and randomly (but also weak). The polynomial system was reduced by 497 variables on average in case the key bits are known, and by 470 variables in case they are guessed. The results are listed in Table 5. Again, our estimation of t_{true}^{32} is on the left and the one of t_{false}^{32} is on the right. The estimations show that when given a set of 64 weak key bits, for $r = 6$ recovering the remaining 32 bits in a chosen plaintext scenario is more efficient using the algebraic attack than using a brute-force attack (in which we accounted for the weak key assumption), exhibiting a speed-up factor of more than 2^5. Also, recovering the key under the assumption that it is weak by enumerating the 2^9 sets of weak key bits and solving the reduced system is more efficient than brute-forcing all 2^{41} weak keys by a factor of more than $2^{6.5}$.

Table 5. Comparison of t_{true}^{32} (left) and t_{false}^{32} (right) for weak keys and chosen plaintext to brute-force attack for EPCBC-96

r	6	7	r	6	7
$2^{31} \cdot t_{eval}$ in s	22.4	26.1	$2^{32} \cdot t_{eval}$ in s	44.8	52.3
avg in s	0.5	71.0	avg in s	0.47	7968.8
stdev in s	0.037	86.4	stdev in s	0.039	15194.2

The results also show that this attack is not faster than the brute-force for $r = 7$. However, we experimented with using more plaintexts. The results for the case that the correct values of the key bits are known are shown in Figure 5. The horizontal line in the figure represents the upper bound imposed by the brute-force attack. The results show that the attack on 7 rounds is faster than brute-force with a speed-up factor of up to 2.7 if using more than one plaintext. In the case where the key bits are guessed the attack was also drastically sped up by using multiple plaintexts, but not enough to yield an attack faster than the brute-force attack. For this reason we neglect the results here.

In this attack we only considered one optimal solution returned by the MILP solver to the information flow maximization problem. Preliminary tests showed that there are multiple optimal solutions, which might lead to further classes of weak keys. Some of these might even make attacks on more rounds of EPCBC-96 possible. To explore more sets of weak keys some automation of the attack is necessary, especially in the handling of conflicts. In this work we did this manually – how to do this algorithmically remains open for future work.

Finally, we want to remark on the drastic difference of observed average hardness of the polynomial system when guessing 64 bits of general keys in contrast to the weak keys just discussed. In Table 3 (left) for $r = 6$ the average solving time is reported to be $1687.5s$ with a standard deviation of $2941.1s$. Obviously,

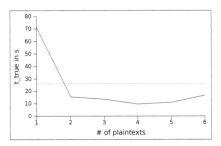

Fig. 5. Comparison of t_{true}^{32} for weak keys of EPCBC-96 with $r = 7$ and several numbers of known plaintexts to brute-force attack

different instances that were tested exhibit a large inhomogeneity regarding their hardness. Very low corresponding average solving time and standard deviation for weak keys in Table 5 for $r = 6$ suggest that the hardness of the instances is at least related to the amount of propagated information. As a consequence, apart from identifying a class of weak keys, this section serves as support for the claim made in Section 4.1: the more information can be inferred by guessing a set of bits, the easier the problem is to solve.

4.3   EPCBC-48

We also employed guessing strategies to obtain results for EPCBC-48 for $r > 3$. While the approach outlined above for EPCBC-96 is also applicable to EPCBC-48 with minor modifications, the difference in the key schedule of EPCBC-48 (cf. Algorithm 1) allows for another approach. Observe that a 4-block permutation is carried out on RKeystate to obtain the next four subkeys. While RKeystate is initialized with the right part of the key, after each block of the key schedule RKeystate is updated using temp. The first value temp takes on is the sum of the left part and the right part of the key. In consequence, if the left and right parts of the key are known to have a certain difference, the second block of the key schedule is initialized with this known *difference vector* and we can easily compute the subkeys number 5 to 8. Attacking 8 rounds of EPCBC-48 under the assumption that the difference vector of the key is known should not be harder than attacking 4 rounds under the same assumption. Thus, we can either assume an oracle to reveal the 48-bit difference vector to the adversary or guess the difference vector.

Naturally, a brute-force adversary can also take advantage of this property. If an adversary obtains a plain-/ciphertext pair encrypted under a key of which he knows the difference vector, he only has to brute-force at most 2^{48} different keys. Note, that even when attacking EPCBC-48 with $4 < r \leq 8$ the adversary only has to encrypt 4 rounds for each potential key, since he can precompute the last subkeys and thus compute the inner state of the encryption at the end of round 4 using the ciphertext. To sum up, assuming the knowledge of the difference vector, the expected time to recover the key for $r \leq 8$ is: $2^{47} \cdot \min\{r, 4\} \cdot t_r$, where t_r denotes the runtime of one round of the cipher. Again, we accounted one processor cycle for each substitution and each addition layer and assumed the same processor speed as for our experiments. With these assumptions a brute-force attack recovering the remaining 48 bits when the difference vector is revealed takes almost 17 days for $4 \leq r \leq 8$, providing the upper bound for t_{true}^{48}. The upper bound for t_{false}^{48} is twice as large.

We tested this approach assuming knowledge of the correct difference vector and then guessing the difference vector randomly. The results are listed in Table 6. As expected, the hardness of the problem does not increase with increasing r for $4 \leq r \leq 8$ and the 8-round version of EPCBC-48 exhibits weaknesses here. With our estimations of t_{true}^{48} (Table 6, left) we achieve a speed-up factor of more than 2^{12} in case the correct difference vector is known and more than 2^{10} (Table 6, right) in case it is guessed randomly, compared to the brute-force adversary. We did also test a different approach where we applied the optimization techniques above, but guessing the difference vector outperformed any optimized strategy we obtained. However, the complexity of the algebraic attack increases steeply for $r = 9$. This is not surprising, since the internal state of the encryptions cannot be computed because the last subkey is not known (or guessed), even though four intermediate subkeys are still known.

Table 6. Algebraic known plaintext attack on EPCBC-48 with known (left) and guessed (right) difference vector

r	4	5	6	7	8
avg in s	175.0	156.4	283.0	164.7	142.1
stdev in s	291.3	247.3	605.1	250.0	250.5

r	4	5	6	7	8
avg in s	1133.9	817.8	826.9	1296.3	1236.7
stdev in s	1630.4	1051.8	1318.8	2699.9	1850.7

This approach suggests a generalization to guessing the initial value of the last block of the key schedule for arbitrary r. Due to this structural weakness of the key schedule, we can reduce breaking the r-round cipher faster than a brute-force attack on the 96-bit key to breaking the $(r - 4)$-round cipher faster than a brute-force attack on 48 bits of the key.

5   Conclusion

In this work we introduced a novel technique to improve guessing strategies in the algebraic cryptanalysis of PRESENT-like primitives using Mixed Integer Linear Programming on the example of EPCBC. In addition to introducing a systematic approach to optimizing guessing strategies, we also showed how to use these techniques to identify classes of weak keys. We analyzed both versions of EPCBC using algebraic methods with the following results:

- We found practical attacks for EPCBC-48 and EPCBC-96 with up to 3 out of the 32 rounds.
- We presented a theoretical attack on EPCBC-48 with up to 8 rounds.
- We presented a theoretical attack on EPCBC-96 with up to 5 rounds.
- We identified a class of 2^{41} weak keys for EPCBC-96 with up to 7 rounds.

Our attacks mainly exploit two structural weaknesses of the cipher. In both versions of the cipher the encryption process and the key schedule exhibit a strong symmetry. This allows for a lot of information propagation. Furthermore, the way the 96-bit key is processed in EPCBC-48 to produce the subkeys allows for a very efficient guessing strategy, where whole blocks of successive subkeys can be computed from known or guessed bits. Even though our attacks do not yet threaten the full cipher, we recommend avoiding such weaknesses in the design of block ciphers. Especially in light of side-channel attacks these weaknesses can prove to be fatal to the security of a cipher.

One might argue that at least for the simple model the use of MILP is an overkill since an exhaustive search of all guessing strategies that guess at 4-bit blocks corresponding to S-Boxes in the first round could have achieved the same result. However, this is only true in this particular case, since the choice of 4-bit blocks is relatively obvious. In contrast, the MILP approach is very flexible. For example, using exhaustive search it would not have been that easy to rule out meet-in-the-middle attacks (cf. Remark 1). Furthermore, an exhaustive search fails when considering primitives for which it does not make sense to restrict the guessing to the first round. For example, the permutation of SPONGENT [3] does not involve a key addition layer, but rather a constant addition layer. It follows that guessing does not need to be restricted to the first round when attacking SPONGENT algebraically.

The techniques introduced in this work are not limited to the application to EPCBC or SPONGENT. In fact, they are not even limited to PRESENT-like primitives. The method of optimizing guessing strategies can be employed in the algebraic analysis of any primitive, where information about known variables may propagate through the algebraic system. Depending on the nature of the targeted primitive this only requires modifications to the MILP model. It would be interesting to apply our techniques to other primitives, for example LBLOCK [21] or SPONGENT.

Our analysis of weak keys could be improved by extending the MILP approach to take into account the values of the known bits, not only whether they are known or unknown. This could avoid conflicts as they were observed in Section 4.2 and thus aid the automation of the process of identifying weak keys. This, in turn, bears the potential of recovering more classes of weak keys of EPCBC-96, which we believe have a relatively high information flow and are therefore linked to solutions of the corresponding MILP model.

Moreover, our technique suffers from the complexity of the MILP model. We were only able to solve the model for up to certain round numbers. In some cases and for small k this does not compromise optimality since information does not extend any further but for larger k or other primitives this might not hold anymore. Our analysis could profit from advances in MILP in general and improvements of the model itself.

Finally, there is room for improvement when choosing the guessing parameter k – the number of variables to guess. While our decisions regarding this parameter were mainly driven by considerations about the practicality of our experiments, other decisions might yield a better overall complexity of the attack by improving the trade-off between available information and number of values to guess.

References

1. Bard, G.V., Courtois, N.T., Nakahara Jr., J., Sepehrdad, P., Zhang, B.: Algebraic, AIDA/Cube and Side Channel Analysis of KATAN Family of Block Ciphers. In: Gong, G., Gupta, K.C. (eds.) INDOCRYPT 2010. LNCS, vol. 6498, pp. 176–196. Springer, Heidelberg (2010)

2. Bogdanov, A., Knudsen, L.R., Leander, G., Paar, C., Poschmann, A., Robshaw, M., Seurin, Y., Vikkelsoe, C.: PRESENT: An Ultra-Lightweight Block Cipher. In: Paillier, P., Verbauwhede, I. (eds.) CHES 2007. LNCS, vol. 4727, pp. 450–466. Springer, Heidelberg (2007)

3. Bogdanov, A., Knežević, M., Leander, G., Toz, D., Varıcı, K., Verbauwhede, I.: SPONGENT: A Lightweight Hash Function. In: Preneel, B., Takagi, T. (eds.) CHES 2011. LNCS, vol. 6917, pp. 312–325. Springer, Heidelberg (2011)

4. Borghoff, J., Knudsen, L.R., Stolpe, M.: Bivium as a mixed-integer linear programming problem. In: Parker, M.G. (ed.) Cryptography and Coding 2009. LNCS, vol. 5921, pp. 133–152. Springer, Heidelberg (2009)

5. Bulygin, S., Buchmann, J.: Algebraic Cryptanalysis of the Round-Reduced and Side Channel Analysis of the Full PRINTCipher-48. In: Lin, et al. (eds.) [11], pp. 54–75

6. Collard, B., Standaert, F.-X.: A Statistical Saturation Attack against the Block Cipher PRESENT. In: Fischlin, M. (ed.) CT-RSA 2009. LNCS, vol. 5473, pp. 195–210. Springer, Heidelberg (2009)

7. Conejo, A.J., Castillo, E., Minguez, R., Garcia-Bertrand, R.: Decomposition techniques in mathematical programming. Engineering and science applications. Springer, Berlin (2006)

8. Courtois, N.T., Bard, G.V.: Algebraic Cryptanalysis of the Data Encryption Standard. In: Galbraith, S.D. (ed.) Cryptography and Coding 2007. LNCS, vol. 4887, pp. 152–169. Springer, Heidelberg (2007)

9. Courtois, N.T., Bard, G.V., Wagner, D.: Algebraic and Slide Attacks on KeeLoq. In: Nyberg, K. (ed.) FSE 2008. LNCS, vol. 5086, pp. 97–115. Springer, Heidelberg (2008)

10. Debraize, B., Goubin, L.: Guess-and-determine algebraic attack on the self-shrinking generator. In: Nyberg, K. (ed.) FSE 2008. LNCS, vol. 5086, pp. 235–252. Springer, Heidelberg (2008)

11. Lin, D., Tsudik, G., Wang, X. (eds.): CANS 2011. LNCS, vol. 7092. Springer, Heidelberg (2011)

12. Mohamed, M.S.E., Bulygin, S., Zohner, M., Heuser, A., Walter, M., Buchmann, J.: Improved algebraic side-channel attack on AES. In: IEEE HOST 2012, pp. 146–151 (2012)

13. Motzkin, T.S., Raiffa, H., Thompson, G.L., Thrall, R.M.: The Double Description Method. In: Kuhn, H.W., Tucker, A.W. (eds.) Contributions to the Theory of Games II. Princeton University Press (1953)

14. Mouha, N., Wang, Q., Gu, D., Preneel, B.: Differential and linear cryptanalysis using mixed-integer linear programming. In: Wu, C.-K., Yung, M., Lin, D. (eds.) Inscrypt 2011. LNCS, vol. 7537, pp. 57–76. Springer, Heidelberg (2012)

15. Oren, Y., Renauld, M., Standaert, F.-X., Wool, A.: Algebraic side-channel attacks beyond the hamming weight leakage model. In: Prouff, E., Schaumont, P. (eds.) CHES 2012. LNCS, vol. 7428, pp. 140–154. Springer, Heidelberg (2012)

16. Rogaway, P. (ed.): CRYPTO 2011. LNCS, vol. 6841. Springer, Heidelberg (2011)

17. Simonetti, I., Faugère, J.-C., Perret, L.: Algebraic Attack Against Trivium. In: First International Conference on Symbolic Computation and Cryptography, SCC 2008, Beijing, China. LMIB, pp. 95–102 (April 2008)

18. Soos, M.: Cryptominisat 2.5.0. In: SAT Race Competitive Event Booklet (July 2010)

19. Soos, M.: Grain of Salt – an Automated Way to Test Stream Ciphers through SAT Solvers. In: Tools 2010: Proceedings of the Workshop on Tools for Cryptanalysis 2010, pp. 1–2 (2010)

20. Stein, W.A., et al.: Sage Mathematics Software (Version 4.7.2). The Sage Development Team (2011), http://www.sagemath.org

21. Wu, W., Zhang, L.: LBlock: A lightweight block cipher. In: Lopez, J., Tsudik, G. (eds.) ACNS 2011. LNCS, vol. 6715, pp. 327–344. Springer, Heidelberg (2011)

22. Yap, H., Khoo, K., Poschmann, A., Henricksen, M.: EPCBC - A Block Cipher Suitable for Electronic Product Code Encryption. In: Lin, et al. (eds.) [11], pp. 76–97

A   Solution of the Simple Propagation Model for EPCBC-96

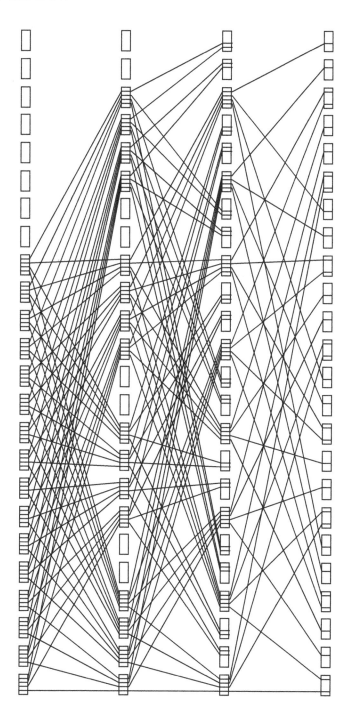

B   Information Flow in EPCBC S-Box

mask		vertex
*000	→	*01* $(0, 1, 1, 1, 0, 1, 1, 0)$
*001	→	*1** $(0, 1, 1, 1, 0, 1, 0, 0)$
*010	→	*00* $(0, 1, 1, 1, 0, 1, 1, 0)$
*011	→	**10 $(0, 1, 1, 1, 0, 0, 1, 1)$
*100	→	*1** $(0, 1, 1, 1, 0, 1, 0, 0)$
*101	→	***1 $(0, 1, 1, 1, 0, 0, 0, 1)$
*110	→	***1 $(0, 1, 1, 1, 0, 0, 0, 1)$
*111	→	**00 $(0, 1, 1, 1, 0, 0, 1, 1)$
0*00	→	0*1* $(1, 0, 1, 1, 1, 0, 1, 0)$
0*01	→	11** $(1, 0, 1, 1, 1, 1, 0, 0)$
0*10	→	**01 $(1, 0, 1, 1, 0, 0, 1, 1)$
0*11	→	*0*0 $(1, 0, 1, 1, 0, 1, 0, 1)$
1*00	→	1*** $(1, 0, 1, 1, 1, 0, 0, 0)$
1*01	→	0**1 $(1, 0, 1, 1, 1, 0, 0, 1)$
1*10	→	*0** $(1, 0, 1, 1, 0, 1, 0, 0)$
1*11	→	*1*0 $(1, 0, 1, 1, 0, 1, 0, 1)$

mask		vertex
00*0	→	*0*1 $(1, 1, 0, 1, 0, 1, 0, 1)$
00*1	→	***0 $(1, 1, 0, 1, 0, 0, 0, 1)$
01*0	→	01** $(1, 1, 0, 1, 1, 1, 0, 0)$
01*1	→	1*** $(1, 1, 0, 1, 1, 0, 0, 0)$
10*0	→	*0*0 $(1, 1, 0, 1, 0, 1, 0, 1)$
10*1	→	*11* $(1, 1, 0, 1, 0, 1, 1, 0)$
11*0	→	1**1 $(1, 1, 0, 1, 1, 0, 0, 1)$
11*1	→	0*0* $(1, 1, 0, 1, 1, 0, 1, 0)$
001*	→	*0** $(1, 1, 1, 0, 0, 1, 0, 0)$
010*	→	*11* $(1, 1, 1, 0, 0, 1, 1, 0)$
011*	→	**0* $(1, 1, 1, 0, 0, 0, 1, 0)$
100*	→	**1* $(1, 1, 1, 0, 0, 0, 1, 0)$
101*	→	***0 $(1, 1, 1, 0, 0, 0, 0, 1)$
110*	→	**01 $(1, 1, 1, 0, 0, 0, 1, 1)$
**11	→	***0 $(0, 0, 1, 1, 0, 0, 0, 1)$
*0*0	→	*0** $(0, 1, 0, 1, 0, 1, 0, 0)$

C   Solution of the S-Box Adjusted Model for EPCBC-96

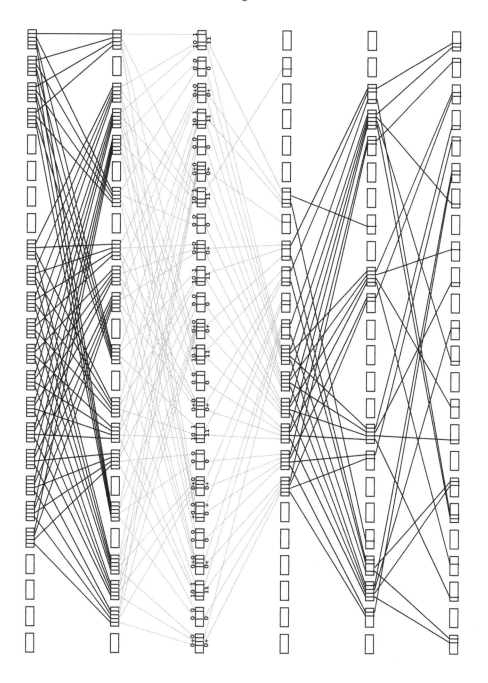

A General Model for MAC Generation
Using Direct Injection

Harry Bartlett[1,2], Mufeed AlMashrafi[1,2], Leonie Simpson[1,2], Ed Dawson[1,2],
and Kenneth Koon-Ho Wong[1]

[1] Institute for Future Environments
[2] Science and Engineering Faculty,
Queensland University of Technology
GPO Box 2434, Brisbane Qld 4001, Australia
{h.bartlett,lr.simpson,e.dawson,kk.wong}@qut.edu.au,
almashrafi@student.qut.edu.au

Abstract. This paper presents a model for generating a MAC tag by
injecting the input message directly into the internal state of a nonlinear
filter generator. This model generalises a similar model for unkeyed hash
functions proposed by Nakano *et al*. We develop a matrix representation
for the accumulation phase of our model and use it to analyse the security of the model against man-in-the-middle forgery attacks based on
collisions in the final register contents. The results of this analysis show
that some conclusions of Nakano *et al* regarding the security of their
model are incorrect. We also use our results to comment on several recent MAC proposals which can be considered as instances of our model
and specify choices of options within the model which should prevent
the type of forgery discussed here. In particular, suitable initialisation
of the register and active use of a secure nonlinear filter will prevent an
attacker from finding a collision in the final register contents which could
result in a forged MAC.

Keywords: MAC, Hash functions, Stream ciphers, Forgery attacks, SSS,
SOBER128, NLSv2.

1 Introduction

In the context of cryptography, Message Authentication Codes (MACs) are used
to provide assurance of message integrity. MACs share some properties with hash
functions and are often calculated similarly.

In this paper, we extend a model proposed by Nakano *et al* [7] for unkeyed
hash functions to a model for MAC generation. We develop a matrix description
of this model and use this to provide a security analysis of our model against
man-in-the-middle forgery attacks based on MAC collisions.

The structure of our paper is as follows. In Section 2, we discuss the properties
of MAC functions, describe our model for generating MACs using stream ciphers
and discuss how this model relates to Nakano *et al*'s model for unkeyed hash

M. Kutyłowski and M. Yung (Eds.): Inscrypt 2012, LNCS 7763, pp. 198–215, 2013.

functions. In Section 3, we develop the matrix representation for this model, and in Section 4, we present a security analysis based on this matrix representation – including a revision to Nakano *et al*'s analysis of their model. In Section 5, we briefly discuss current MAC proposals which are described by our model, including the implications of our security analysis for these proposals, before presenting a summary and conclusions from our work in Section 6.

2   Description of MAC Model

Message Authentication Codes ("MACs" or "MAC tags") are widely used to provide assurance of message integrity for either plaintext or ciphertext messages. These applications are referred to as authentication and authenticated encryption respectively. In the context of authenticated encryption, a MAC tag can be generated from either the plaintext or the ciphertext. To encompass both of these possibilities, we use the term "message" to refer to whichever of the plaintext and ciphertext is being used as the input to the MAC generation process.

To be classified as secure, a MAC algorithm is required to satisfy the following properties [6]:

1. ease of computation
2. compression to a fixed bit-length
3. *computation resistance*: given zero or more text-MAC pairs $(x_i, \text{MAC}(x_i)$, it is computationally infeasible to compute a text-MAC pair $(x, \text{MAC}(x)$ for any new input $x \neq x_i$ (including possibly for the case where $\text{MAC}(x) = \text{MAC}(x_i)$ for some i).

For parties not knowing the secret key of the MAC, property 3 above implies the classical hash function requirements of *preimage resistance, second-preimage resistance* and *collision resistance*.

MAC generation is performed in three phases. In the first phase, the message is prepared by padding with any value which is predefined in the specification of the cipher. This process is performed either to avoid any insertion forgery attacks or to match the length of the message with the size of each stage in the internal state, or both. Also in this phase, the internal state of the integrity component of the cipher is initialised using a keystream sequence which is generated using a secret key and optional public IV. In the second phase, the message is accumulated into the state of the integrity component using the accumulation function. The accumulation function can update this state in either of two ways: the state can be updated directly with the message contents or it can be updated indirectly by using the message bits to control the accumulation of unknown keystream bits into the state. After the whole message has been processed, the final phase occurs: the contents of the internal state are processed using a finalisation function to form a MAC tag for the input message.

In another paper [1], we have presented and analysed a general model for the full process of generating a MAC tag using indirect injection. In the current paper, we consider the case where the input message is accumulated directly into the internal state of the stream cipher and propose a general model for the second phase of MAC generation in this case. This model does not explicitly include the other two MAC generation phases and is an extension of a hash function model proposed by Nakano *et al* [7].

2.1   Our Model

We consider the case of injecting a message directly into the state of the keystream generator for a stream cipher. For simplicity, we use a nonlinear filter generator which consists of one linear feedback shift register (LFSR) and a nonlinear filter function, as the state is contained in a single register. We assume the components of this nonlinear filter generator are selected for their security properties. That is, the feedback polynomial of the LFSR is a primitive polynomial and the filter function is nonlinear, balanced and with high correlation immunity. This provides resistance to various types of attacks on stream ciphers. During the message accumulation phase, the LFSR is updated according to its feedback function (denoted by y_t) and we also allow the output of the nonlinear filter (denoted by z_t) to be accumulated into the internal state of the LFSR simultaneously with the input message (denoted by m_t), as shown in Figure 1.

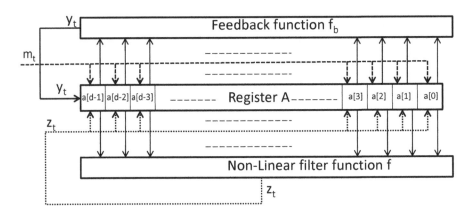

Fig. 1. General model for MAC generation using the input message directly

In general, we assume that the LFSR is a word-based register, which we denote as Register A. (Note: in terms of our model, a binary LSFR is a special case of a word-based register in which the word length is 1 bit and the addition operation is equivalent to binary XOR.) There are three possible inputs to each stage in A: the first is either the feedback word y_t for stage $a[d-1]$ or the content of stage $a[i+1]$ for stage $a[i]$ with $0 \le i \le d-2$; the second and third inputs are the input message word m_t and the nonlinear filter output word z_t. These three inputs can be fed into the register stages in one of two ways: either by combining

m_t and/or z_t with either y_t or $a[i+1]$ using the register's addition operation, or by replacing the content of the relevant stage with the chosen combination of m_t and z_t. Our model incorporates both these alternatives, as discussed in Section 3 below.

2.2 How This Generalise Nakano *et al*'s model

Nakano *et al* [7] considered the situation of using a binary LFSR with an associated nonlinear filter to generate an unkeyed hash function for a given message, a process they describe as injecting the message into the internal state of the hash function. They then provided a security analysis for two configurations of injecting the message and filter output directly into the LFSR, namely (1) XORing them into the last stage of the register and (2) XORing them together into several regularly spaced stages of the register. Since they are considering unkeyed hash functions, they assume that the attacker knows the plaintext and the corresponding hash value and look at ways of manipulating a message in order to find collisions between the hash functions of distinct messages.

Our proposal generalises this model in two ways: both by generalising the register from a binary register to a word-based register and by extending the context from generating unkeyed hash functions to the formation of MACs for either authentication only or authenticated encryption applications. This widened context requires the use of a key and IV, as described above, whereas Nakano *et al* use no key and assume that the LFSR is initialised with zeroes. They also assume that the (plaintext) message is known, but we note that this will not usually be the case in authenticated encryption applications.

The generalisation to word-based registers is a straightforward extension which recognises the growing use of such registers in recent stream cipher proposals. The word based LFSR can be more efficient in software especially when the finite field that underlies the LFSR operations is suited to a processor. The best choices for such a field are the Galois fields $GF(2^w)$, where w is the size of item in the entire processor used by the application. All the elements and the coefficients of the recurrence relation in this field will then utilise one unit of storage in this processor.

3   Matrix Representation

As we are dealing in general with a word-based register, we note that the addition operation used in evaluating the register feedback may be either modular addition or bitwise XOR, according to the cipher specification. In the following derivation, the matrix operations used to describe the register update process in our model are assumed to incorporate this same addition operation, which we denote using $\oplus$. To maintain consistency between the numbering of the register stages and matrix elements, we index the rows and columns of our matrices from zero.

We first note that the autonomous operation of the LFSR can be described in terms of a matrix equation [5,8] as follows. Referring to Figure 1 we suppose the LFSR A has d stages, which we denote as $a[0], a[1], \ldots, a[d-1]$ and that the feedback function f_b of A is described by the equation $f_b = c_0 a[0] \oplus c_1 a[1] \oplus \cdots \oplus c_{d-1} a[d-1]$. If we represent the contents of register A at time t by the vector $A_t = (a_t[0]\ a_t[1]\ \cdots\ a_t[d-1])^T$ then the contents of register A at time $t+1$ can be represented by the equation $A_{t+1} = CA_t$ where

$$
C = \begin{pmatrix}
0 & 1 & 0 & \cdots & \cdots & 0 & 0 \\
0 & 0 & 1 & \cdots & \cdots & 0 & 0 \\
\vdots & \ddots & \ddots & \ddots & \ddots & \ddots & \vdots \\
\vdots & \ddots & \ddots & \ddots & \ddots & \ddots & \vdots \\
0 & \cdots & \cdots & 0 & 0 & 1 & 0 \\
0 & \cdots & \cdots & \cdots & 0 & 0 & 1 \\
c_0 & c_1 & \cdots & \cdots & \cdots & c_{d-2} & c_{d-1}
\end{pmatrix}
$$

is the usual companion matrix of the register A.

We now extend this equation to incorporate the injection of the message and the filter output into the register, by writing:

$$
A_{t+1} = CA_t \oplus m_t \sigma_m \oplus z_t \sigma_z \tag{1}
$$

where σ_m and σ_z are vectors of zeroes and ones indicating which stages of the register the message word and the output filter word, respectively, are injected into. More specifically,

$$
\sigma_{m,i} = \begin{cases} 0, & m_t \text{ is not injected into stage } i, \\ 1, & m_t \text{ is injected into stage } i \end{cases}
$$

and similarly

$$
\sigma_{z,i} = \begin{cases} 0, & z_t \text{ is not injected into stage } i, \\ 1, & z_t \text{ is injected into stage } i. \end{cases}
$$

If the injection method is replacement rather than combination (by addition) with the updated register contents, then we adapt C by replacing the one in the relevant row by a zero. Thus C takes the form:

$$
C = \begin{pmatrix}
0 & 1 & 0 & \cdots & \cdots & \cdots & \cdots & 0 \\
\vdots & \ddots & \ddots & \ddots & \ddots & \ddots & \ddots & \vdots \\
0 & \cdots & 0 & 1 & 0 & \cdots & \cdots & 0 \\
0 & \cdots & \cdots & 0 & 0 & 0 & \cdots & 0 \\
0 & \cdots & \cdots & \cdots & 0 & 1 & 0 & \cdots & 0 \\
\vdots & \ddots & \ddots & \ddots & \ddots & \ddots & \ddots & \vdots \\
0 & \cdots & \cdots & \cdots & \cdots & 0 & 0 & 1 \\
c_0 & c_1 & \cdots & \cdots & \cdots & \cdots & c_{d-2} & c_{d-1}
\end{pmatrix} \quad \leftarrow (\text{row } i)
$$

where row i corresponds to the register stage whose contents are being replaced. If the value of the input message and/or filter output replaces the contents of more than one stage of register A, then all the rows corresponding to these stages in matrix C are set to zero in the same manner as for stage i in the equation above.

Note that our model actually allows for a mixture of the above alternatives as well, that is, for the situation where m_t and/or z_t are injected into some stages using addition and others using replacement. The non-zero entries in σ_m and σ_z indicate which stages m_t and z_t respectively are injected into, while the zero rows in C indicate the stages for which this injection is done by replacement. (For all other indicated stages, the injection will be by combination (addition) with the updated contents of that stage.)

Now let l be the length of the input message in words. We take Equation 1 and iterate it l times to obtain the corresponding equation for the complete accumulation phase. For simplicity, we assume initially that the filter output is not injected into the LFSR, that is, that σ_z is an all-zero vector. Successively iterating Equation 1 gives us

$$A_1 = CA_0 \oplus \sigma_m m_0$$
$$A_2 = C(CA_0 \oplus \sigma_m m_0) \oplus \sigma_m m_1 = C^2 A_0 \oplus C\sigma_m m_0 \oplus \sigma_m m_1$$
$$\vdots$$
$$A_l = C^l A_0 \oplus C^{l-1}\sigma_m m_0 \oplus C^{l-2}\sigma_m m_1 \oplus \cdots \oplus C\sigma_m m_{l-2} \oplus \sigma_m m_{l-1}$$
$$= C^l A_0 \oplus K_m M_{l-1}$$

where $K_m = (C^{l-1}\sigma_m \ C^{l-2}\sigma_m \ \cdots \ C\sigma_m \ \sigma_m)$ and $M_{l-1} = (m_0 \ m_1 \ \cdots \ m_{l-2} \ m_{l-1})^T$.

Returning to the general case, where σ_z is non-zero, a similar analysis yields the final equation for the register contents A_l at the end of the accumulation phase

$$A_l = C^l A_0 \oplus K_m M_{l-1} \oplus K_z Z_{l-1} \tag{2}$$

where $K_z = (C^{l-1}\sigma_z \ C^{l-2}\sigma_z \ \cdots \ C\sigma_z \ \sigma_z)$, $Z_{l-1} = (z_0 \ z_1 \ \cdots \ z_{l-2} \ z_{l-1})^T$ and K_m and M_{l-1} are as defined above.

4   Security Analysis

Under the direct injection model for MAC generation, the message accumulation phase plays a critical role in the security of the MAC generation process. Any collision which occurs in this phase for any two distinct messages using the same keystream sequence will result in the same MAC tag being generated for both messages regardless of the process performed in the other two phases of MAC generation (preparation and finalisation). In this section, we therefore analyse the security of the message accumulation process for direct message injection with respect to forgery attacks based on collisions. More particularly, we consider a man-in-the-middle style forgery attack, as follows.

Suppose that for a message M, a MAC tag $\text{MAC}_{K,IV}(M)$ is generated using key K and a known IV. The sender intends to transmit the message-MAC tag pair to a particular receiver. Assume a man-in-the-middle attacker intercepts the message-MAC tag pair, and tries to modify M and possibly also $\mathrm{MAC}_{K,IV}(M)$ to calculate a valid MAC tag $\mathrm{MAC}_{K,IV}(M')$ for a modified message M'. The attacker then sends the new pair $(M', \mathrm{MAC}_{K,IV}(M'))$ to the intended recipient. If it is possible to alter M to M' and provide a valid $\mathrm{MAC}_{K,IV}(M')$ without any knowledge of the keystream sequences used to generate $\mathrm{MAC}_{K,IV}(M)$, the forgery attack is then successful.

In the following section, we analyse the general case for collisions in our model, using the matrix formulation derived above. In doing so, we consider for completeness the case where the message and the initial contents of the register are known. We note, however, that a MAC cannot be secure under these conditions, since any attacker can replicate the initial state of the register and obtain the corresponding final state for any message by simply accumulating that message in the normal way. In the context of authenticated encryption, this includes the case where the accumulated message is the ciphertext, but not the case where the accumulated message is the plaintext (which should be unknown to the attacker). Following this analysis, we apply our results to give a revised analysis of Nakano *et al*'s model for hash functions.

4.1   Analysis of Collisions in the General Model

Recall from Section 2.1 that we allow two methods for inserting the message and nonlinear filter output words into the LFSR of our model, namely combination (by addition) with the updated register contents or replacement of those contents. We consider first the situations where the inserted words are combined with the updated contents. It is also convenient to divide the analysis into cases according to whether the nonlinear filter is used in the accumulation process.

(1) Insertion Using Addition Only

Case 1: If nonlinear filter is not used
In this case Equation 2 reduces to $A_t = C^t A_0 \oplus K_m M_{t-1}$. Since the nonlinear filter output is not used, all the operations in the accumulation process are linear. Provided the message is longer than d words, it is then possible to manipulate the message to force a collision for two distinct messages without knowing the contents of the original message or the initial contents of the register. This capability follows directly from the matrix formulation of K_m according to the following theorem:

Theorem 1. *Assume that $\sigma_m \neq 0$ and consider the set $U = \{u_i = C^i \sigma_m | i \geq 0\}$.*
(a) If C is a companion matrix of full rank (that is, if $c_0 \neq 0$), then there is a positive number $n \leq d$ such that any n consecutive columns $C^{i+n-1} \sigma_m, \ldots,$ $C^{i+1} \sigma_m, C^i \sigma_m$ in K_m form a basis for $span\{U\}$.
(b) If C is the companion matrix for a LFSR with a primitive feedback polynomial of degree d, then any d consecutive columns in K_m form a basis for $span\{U\}$.

Proof. We first show that $\sigma_m, C\sigma_m, \ldots, C^{n-1}\sigma_m$ form a basis for span$\{U\}$. Since C is non-singular, it follows that this also applies to $C^i\sigma_m, C^{i+1}\sigma_m, \ldots,$ $C^{i+n-1}\sigma_m$ for any $i \geq 0$.

Let n be the largest integer for which the vectors $\sigma_m, C\sigma_m, \ldots, C^{n-1}\sigma_m$ are linearly independent. (Since $\sigma_m \neq \mathbf{0}$, $n > 0$.) Then we must have $C^n\sigma_m = a_0\sigma_m \oplus a_1 C\sigma_m \oplus \ldots \oplus a_{n-1}C^{n-1}\sigma_m$ for some $a_0, a_1, \ldots, a_{n-1}$. But then $C^{n+1}\sigma_m = a_0 C\sigma_m \oplus a_1 C^2\sigma_m \oplus \ldots \oplus a_{n-2}C^{n-1}\sigma_m \oplus a_{n-1}C^n\sigma_m$ can obviously be expressed in this form as well and it follows by induction that the same is true for $C^j\sigma_m$ for any $j \geq n$. Thus $\sigma_m, C\sigma_m, \ldots, C^{n-1}\sigma_m$ form a basis for span$\{U\}$.

Now consider $|U|$ and recall that each stage of a word-based register contains a word of size w bits. If the LFSR has a primitive feedback polynomial of degree d, then U must cycle through all $2^{wd} - 1$ non-zero vectors in $\{0, 1, \ldots, 2^w - 1\}^d$, which implies that any basis for span$\{U\}$ in this case must contain d vectors. But this case gives the maximum possible value for $|U|$, so for a general LFSR we must have $n \leq d$.   □

Based on this theorem, we may write, for example, $C^{l-1}\sigma_m = a_1 C^{l-2}\sigma_m + \ldots + a_d C^{l-d-1}\sigma_m$ with $a_1, a_2, \ldots, a_d$ not all zero. If we now consider the process of multiplying these columns of K_m by the first $d + 1$ words of M_{l-1} (as part of the MAC accumulation process), we see that any non-zero change in m_0 can be cancelled out by making suitable changes in the words m_1 to m_d. Hence a collision will occur and as a result of that an attacker can send a forged MAC tag utilising this type of collision attack. In fact, by a similar argument, it is clear that up to $l - d$ words of the message can be manipulated at will in this way, with the resulting changes in A_l being cancelled out by suitable changes in the remaining d words of the message.

Note that the above result applies whether the initialisation of register A is known or unknown, since all the operations are linear.

If the model under this assumption is used for authentication only, then the message is the plaintext which is known to the attacker. It follows that the attacker will also know the plaintext of the forged message. (In fact, as noted above, he has freedom to choose up to $l - d$ words of this forged message.) If the model is used for authenticated encryption, the plaintext will not normally be known, but an attacker can still forge a MAC tag by manipulating the ciphertext. (If the input message to the MAC accumulation process is ciphertext, the above analysis applies directly; if the input message is plaintext, the result follows provided that the plaintext has been encrypted using a binary additive stream cipher with a keystream that is independent of the message and the MAC generation process.)

Case 2: If nonlinear filter is used

As noted previously, the following analysis assumes that the nonlinear filter used in the accumulation process is secure from attack. If we include this nonlinear filter in the accumulation process for the input message, then there are three further cases for message and filter output injection into the internal states.

Case 2a: Message and initial state known, $\sigma_m = \sigma_z$. Then $K_m = K_z$ and we can still manipulate the input message. Since we are accumulating $(m_t \oplus z_t)$ and z_t can be determined at each step, we see that m_t can be adjusted as required to achieve the same result as before and hence force the collision to occur.

Case 2b: Message and initial state known, $\sigma_m \neq \sigma_z$. Then $K_m \neq K_z$ and so it may not be possible to adjust for the effects of z_t. In principle any change in z_t at a single time point can be counteracted by a suitable combination of manipulated message words $m_{t+1}, \ldots, m_{t+d}$, but these changes may then result in changes to later words of Z, and there is no guarantee that all of these can be adjusted for. It may be possible to manipulate the register contents to obtain a collision for some special cases of message and initial register contents, but these cases would be extremely rare. Note, however (as remarked previously) that this case is nonetheless insecure because message and initialisation are both known.

Case 2c: Either message or initial state unknown. In this case, the unknown inputs to the nonlinear filter function and the assumed security of this function guarantee that z_t cannot be determined with better than brute force probability, so (even where $\sigma_m = \sigma_z$) it is not possible to determine how to manipulate m_t to get the desired result. Thus, the accumulation process will be secure in this case. This result underscores the need in authentication applications for the register to be initialised with key-dependent (unknown) values.

(2) Insertion with Replacement

As before, we consider two cases according to whether the filter output is used.

Case 1: If nonlinear filter is not used
If the filter output is not used, we can apply a similar analysis to the one given above, to show that a collision can be forced during the accumulation process. The first part of the previous proof still applies, to show that $\sigma_m, C\sigma_m, \ldots, C^{n-1}\sigma_m$ form a basis for span$\{U\}$, so a forgery can still be obtained for any message of length $l > d$. However, the matrix C no longer has full rank, so the result cannot be extended to any n consecutive columns of K_m.

In practice, this is not a serious restriction, since the columns $\sigma_m, C\sigma_m, \ldots, C^{n-1}\sigma_m$ in K_m are those which multiply the final n words $m_l - n, \ldots, m_l - 1$ of the message. Thus, the first $l - n$ words of the message can be modified at will in the forgery and the resulting changes in A_l can then be cancelled out by suitable changes in the remaining n words of the message.

In fact, by considering the form of K_m for this insertion alternative a little more closely, we can see that if the message words are inserted into stage i of the register, then only $n - i - 1$ of the final n words need to be used for this purpose. (More specifically, these are the words $m_{l-n}, \ldots, m_{l-i-2}$, and the final $i + 1$ words are not used.)

To demonstrate this claim, consider the vector $C\sigma_m$, calculated as follows

$$
\begin{pmatrix}
0 & 1 & 0 & \cdots & & & & & & 0 \\
\vdots & \ddots & \ddots & \ddots & \ddots & \ddots & \ddots & \ddots & & \vdots \\
0 & \cdots & 0 & 1 & 0 & \cdots & & & & 0 \\
0 & \cdots & \cdots & 0 & 0 & 0 & \cdots & & & 0 \\
0 & \cdots & \cdots & & 0 & 1 & 0 & \cdots & & 0 \\
\vdots & \ddots & \ddots & \ddots & \ddots & \ddots & \ddots & \ddots & & \vdots \\
0 & \cdots & & & & & 0 & 0 & & 1 \\
c_0 & c_1 & \cdots & & & & & & c_{d-2} & c_{d-1}
\end{pmatrix}
\begin{pmatrix}
\sigma_{m,0} \\
\sigma_{m,1} \\
\vdots \\
\\
\sigma_{m,d-2} \\
\sigma_{m,d-1}
\end{pmatrix}
=
\begin{pmatrix}
\sigma_{m,1} \\
\sigma_{m,2} \\
\vdots \\
\sigma_{m,i} \\
0 \\
\sigma_{m,i+2} \\
\vdots \\
\sigma_{m,d-1} \\
c^T \sigma_m
\end{pmatrix}
$$

where the zero occurs in row i of $C\sigma_m$ and we have used c^T to denote the final row of matrix C and $c^T \sigma_m$ to denote its product with the column vector σ_m. Successive multiplications by C will continue to move the elements of the vector (including any zeroes) further up the column, inserting a new element in the final position and also inserting an extra zero at row i at each iteration. Thus the final form of K_m will be:

$$
K_m =
\begin{pmatrix}
0 & \cdots & 0 & \sigma_{m,i} & \cdots & \cdots & \sigma_{m,1} & \sigma_{m,0} \\
\vdots & \ddots & 0 & 0 & \ddots & \ddots & \sigma_{m,2} & \sigma_{m,1} \\
\vdots & & \ddots & \vdots & \vdots & \ddots & \vdots & \vdots \\
\vdots & & \ddots & \vdots & \vdots & \ddots & \sigma_{m,i} & \sigma_{m,i-1} \\
0 & \cdots & 0 & 0 & \cdots & \cdots & 0 & \sigma_{m,i} \\
c^T C^{l-d+i+1}\sigma_m & \cdots & \cdots & \cdots & \cdots & \cdots & \sigma_{m,i+2} & \sigma_{m,i+1} \\
\vdots & & \ddots & \ddots & \ddots & \ddots & \ddots & \vdots \\
\vdots & & \ddots & \ddots & \ddots & \ddots & \ddots & \vdots \\
c^T C^{l-3}\sigma_m & \cdots & \cdots & \cdots & c^T \sigma_m & \sigma_{m,d-1} & \sigma_{m,d-2} \\
c^T C^{l-2}\sigma_m & \cdots & \cdots & \cdots & c^T C\sigma_m & c^T \sigma_m & \sigma_{m,d-1}
\end{pmatrix}
$$

It is clear from this result that the final contents of stages $a[0]$ to $a[i]$ of the LFSR are affected only by the final $i + 1$ words (m_{l-i-1} to m_{l-1}) of the message. Since a change made to any earlier word cannot affect the final content of these stages, these words are not needed to adjust for any such changes. It is also clear that the remaining stages can all be manipulated by using only the words $m_{l-n}, \dots, m_{l-i-2}$ (which are multiplied by the remaining $n - i - 1$ vectors in the basis for U).

Note: If the message is inserted by replacement into $k > 1$ stages, say $i_1 < i_2 < \cdots < i_k$, then a similar argument shows that the final $i^* + 1$ words are not used, where $i^* = \max(i_1, i_j - i_{j-1} - 1$ for $j > 1)$ and we only need to use the $n - i_k - 1$ message words $m_{l-n-i^*+i_k}, \dots, m_{l-i^*-2}$ to cancel out the changes introduced by any earlier words. Since the index $l-n-i^*+i_k > l-n$, this actually increases the number of words that can be freely modified in the forgery.

Case 2: If nonlinear filter is used

If the filter output is used, then the arguments from Case 2 of alternative (1) apply as given previously and lead to a similar conclusion. That is, collisions can again be forced if both the input message and initialisation are known and the input message and the filter output are injected into the same stages, but not if either the input message or initialisation is unknown.

A summary of the conclusions from these analyses is presented in Table 1.

Table 1. Summary of the analysis for MAC generation using direct message injection

Cases	Nonlinear filter	Message/Register initialisation	Other condition	Forced collisions?	Overall Outcome
1	not used	any	—	Yes	not secure (collisions)
2a	used	both known	$\sigma_m = \sigma_z$	Yes	not secure (collisions)
2b	used	both known	$\sigma_m \neq \sigma_z$	Unlikely	not secure – other
2c	used	either unknown	—	No	secure

4.2   Applying Our Results to Nakano *et al*'s Model

As mentioned previously, Nakano *et al* [7] analysed two configurations for injecting the message and filter output directly into the binary register of a nonlinear filter generator to generate a hash value, namely (1) XORing them into the last stage of the register and (2) XORing them together into several regularly spaced stages of the register. For the first configuration, they concluded that the full register can be manipulated using the input message and hence that it is easy to force a collision. For the second configuration, they injected the message into r stages at intervals of d/r and claimed that the probability of obtaining a collision in this case will be $2^{-d(1-1/r)/2}$.

Since both configurations are described by Case 2a in Table 1, we conclude that an attacker can easily obtain a collision in both cases. Thus our analysis confirms their conclusion for the first configuration but contradicts their conclusion for the second configuration. As long as the filter output is injected into the same stages as the message (and provided the register initialisation is known), it is always possible to use the message bit m_t to adjust for the known value of the filter output bit z_t as well as for the changes made to earlier message bits. The only constraint in obtaining a guaranteed collision using this process is that the length of the input message must be greater than d bits.

5   Current Proposals Described by Our Model

In this section, we examine three stream ciphers with authentication mechanisms which can be considered as instances of the general model presented in Section 2.1. All three ciphers are word based, with word sizes of either 16 or 32 bits. These algorithms are SSS [3], NLSv2 [4] and SOBER-128 [2]. In this section, we do not consider the provision of confidentiality but investigate the integrity assurance component only. In particular, the following subsections describe the accumulation process for the input message for each cipher; we also provide comments on the security of this process in each case, based on our analysis above.

5.1   SSS

The SSS stream cipher [3] uses a word size of 16 bits, so operations are performed over $GF(2^{16})$. The accumulation register A has 17 stages and uses the feedback function $f_b = a[15] \oplus a[4] \oplus \delta a[0]$, where δ is a non-trivial element of $GF(2^{16})$ chosen by the cipher designers and $\oplus$ is the bitwise XOR operation. This cipher does not use a nonlinear filter and the input message word is accumulated directly into the final stage $a[16]$ of the register by combining it (using bitwise XOR) with the feedback word, as shown in Figure 2. Note also that the input message is the plaintext message, which is unknown to an attacker, and that the register is initialised using keystream.

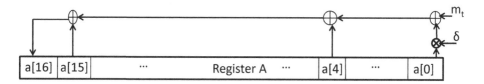

Fig. 2. Message accumulation mechanism in SSS

For these specifications, $\sigma_z = \mathbf{0}$ in our model, $\sigma_m = (0\,0 \cdots 0\,1)^T$ and the final row of the companion matrix is $c^T = (\delta\,0\,0\,0\,1\,0 \cdots 0\,1\,0)$; further the matrix K_m can be constructed as:

$$
K_m =
\begin{pmatrix}
\cdots & 0 & 1 & 0 & 1\,0\,0\,0\,0\,0\,0\,0\,0\,0\,0\,0\,0\,0\,0\,0 \\
\cdots & 1 & 0 & 1 & 0\,1\,0 \cdots \cdots \cdots \cdots \cdot 0 \\
\cdots & 0 & 1 & 0 & 1\,0\,1\,0 \cdots \cdots \cdots \cdots 0 \\
\cdots & 1 & 0 & 1 & 0\,1\,0\,1\,0 \cdots \cdots \cdots 0 \\
\cdots & 0 & 1 & 0 & 1\,0\,1\,0\,1\,0 \cdots \cdots \cdot 0 \\
\cdots & 1 & 0 & 1 & 0\,1\,0\,1\,0\,1\,0 \cdots \cdots 0 \\
\cdots & 0 & 1 & 0 & 1\,0\,1\,0\,1\,0\,1\,0 \cdots \cdots 0 \\
\cdots & 1 & 0 & 1 & 0\,1\,0\,1\,0\,1\,0\,1\,0 \cdots \cdot 0 \\
\cdots & 0 & 1 & 0 & 1\,0\,1\,0\,1\,0\,1\,0\,1\,0 \cdots \cdot 0 \\
\cdots & 1 & 0 & 1 & 0\,1\,0\,1\,0\,1\,0\,1\,0\,1\,0 \cdots 0 \\
\cdots & 1 & 1 & 0 & 1\,0\,1\,0\,1\,0\,1\,0\,1\,0\,1\,0 \cdots 0 \\
\cdots & 1 & 1 & 1 & 0\,1\,0\,1\,0\,1\,0\,1\,0\,1\,0\,1\,0 \cdots 0 \\
\cdots & 0 & 1 & 1 & 1\,0\,1\,0\,1\,0\,1\,0\,1\,0\,1\,0 \cdots 0 \\
\cdots & 1 & 0 & 1 & 1\,1\,0\,1\,0\,1\,0\,1\,0\,1\,0\,1\,0 \cdot 0 \\
\cdots & 1+\delta & 1 & 0 & 1\,1\,1\,0\,1\,0\,1\,0\,1\,0\,1\,0\,1\,0\,0 \\
\cdots & 1 & 1+\delta & 1 & 0\,1\,1\,1\,0\,1\,0\,1\,0\,1\,0\,1\,0\,1\,0 \\
\cdots & 2+2\delta & 1 & 1+\delta & 1\,0\,1\,1\,1\,0\,1\,0\,1\,0\,1\,0\,1\,0\,1
\end{pmatrix}
$$

Based on the description above, SSS is considered to be Case 1 in Table 1; as discussed in Section 4.1, the MAC accumulation process in this cipher is therefore not secure against forgery attacks based on collisions.

However, for SSS the input message words are also used to generate keystream words by a self synchronous process. This process is beyond the scope of our analysis, which focuses on the MAC accumulation process only. Because the keystream is generated using a self synchronous mechanism, manipulating the input message words results in different output keystream words and so the resulting ciphertext will be changed unpredictably. So the fact that SSS uses a self synchronous stream cipher instead of using a nonlinear filter in the accumulation process will prevent this type of collisions. Even if the register A of the accumulation process uses a known initialisation such as zero values, this additional mechanism prevents the attacker from generating a MAC that corresponds with the received message.

5.2   NLSv2

NLSv2 [4] uses a word size of 32 bits, so operations are performed over $GF(2^{32})$. The accumulation register A has eight stages and uses the feedback function $f_b = a[5] \oplus \delta a[0]$, where δ is here a non-trivial element of $GF(2^{32})$ chosen by the cipher designers and $\oplus$ is again the bitwise XOR operation. This cipher also does not use a nonlinear filter and the input message word is again accumulated directly into the final stage (here $a[8]$) of the register by combining it with the feedback word, as shown in Figure 3. Note that the input message is again the plaintext message, which is unknown to an attacker, and that register A is initialised with keystream.

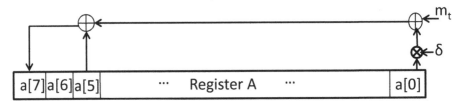

Fig. 3. Message accumulation mechanism in NLSv2

For these specifications, we again have $\sigma_z = \mathbf{0}$ and $\sigma_m = (0\,0\cdots 0\,1)^T$, but here the final row of the companion matrix is $c^T = (\delta\,0\,0\,0\,0\,1\,0\,0)$ and the matrix K_m is:

$$K_m = \begin{pmatrix}
\cdots & \delta & 0 & 1 & 0 & 0 & 1 & 0 & 0 & 1 & 0 & 0 & 0 & 0 & 0 & 0 \\
\cdots & 1 & \delta & 0 & 1 & 0 & 0 & 1 & 0 & 0 & 1 & 0 & 0 & 0 & 0 & 0 \\
\cdots & 0 & 1 & \delta & 0 & 1 & 0 & 0 & 1 & 0 & 0 & 1 & 0 & 0 & 0 & 0 \\
\cdots & 2\delta & 0 & 1 & \delta & 0 & 1 & 0 & 0 & 1 & 0 & 0 & 1 & 0 & 0 & 0 \\
\cdots & 1 & 2\delta & 0 & 1 & \delta & 0 & 1 & 0 & 0 & 1 & 0 & 0 & 1 & 0 & 0 \\
\cdots & 0 & 1 & 2\delta & 0 & 1 & \delta & 0 & 1 & 0 & 0 & 1 & 0 & 0 & 1 & 0 \\
\cdots & 3\delta & 0 & 1 & 2\delta & 0 & 1 & \delta & 0 & 1 & 0 & 0 & 1 & 0 & 0 & 1 & 0 \\
\cdots & 1 & 3\delta & 0 & 1 & 2\delta & 0 & 1 & \delta & 0 & 1 & 0 & 0 & 1 & 0 & 0 & 1
\end{pmatrix}$$

Based on the description above, NLSv2 is also considered to be Case 1 in Table 1, and again the MAC accumulation process in this cipher is therefore not secure against forgery attacks based on collisions.

However, the input message word in NLSv2 is also accumulated at the same time into a different register. This accumulation process is not linear as a nonlinear function is used when the input message is accumulated into this other register. In this case, manipulating the input message words will affect the nonlinear register in an unpredictable manner. Introducing any differences in the input message word to force a collision in the linear register will result in different contents in the nonlinear register. So when the attacker tries to modify another message word to cancel the difference that was introduced in the linear register by the previously modified message word, this word will also introduce another different word in the second register and so the attacker cannot control that collision in this way. So the fact that NLSv2 uses both a linear and a nonlinear register for message accumulation prevents simultaneous collisions in the two registers. Even if the initialisation of A is known, the attacker cannot manipulate the input message to obtain collisions in both registers at the same time.

5.3 SOBER-128

SOBER-128 [2] has a word size of 32 bits, so operations are performed over $GF(2^{32})$. The register A has 17 stages, with a feedback function of $f_b = a[15] \oplus a[4] \oplus \delta a[0]$ where δ is again a non-trivial element of $GF(2^{32})$ chosen by the cipher designers and $\oplus$ is the bitwise XOR operation. In this cipher, a nonlinear filter is used, and the output from this filter is inserted into the register by using it to replace the previous contents of stage $a[4]$, as shown in Figure 4. The input message is accumulated into the register via the nonlinear filter as follows: the input message word is combined with the previous contents of stage $a[4]$ by addition modulo 2^{32}, and the output of this operation then forms an input word to the nonlinear filter. Note also that the input message is again the plaintext message, which is unknown to an attacker, and that register A is again initialised with keystream.

For SOBER-128, the filter output z_t depends directly on the message word m_t and m_t is not injected separately into the register, so σ_m is effectively all zeroes. As noted above, the filter output z_t replaces the old contents of stage $a[4]$, so

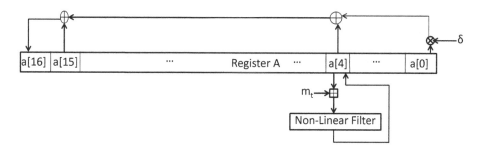

Fig. 4. Message accumulation mechanism in SOBER-128

σ_z in this case will be given by $(0\,0\,0\,0\,1\,0\cdots0\,0)^T$. If we denote the nonlinear filter function in Figure 4 as f, then we have $z_t = f(m_t + a_t[4])$ where $+$ is an addition modulo 2^{32}. For these specifications, C is a modified companion matrix with a final row of $c^T = (\delta\,0\,0\,0\,1\,0\cdots0\,1\,0)$ and a row of zeroes corresponding to stage $a[4]$ of the register, namely

$$C = \begin{pmatrix}
0\,1\,0\,0\,0\,0\,0\,0\,0\,0\,0\,0\,0\,0\,0\,0\,0\,0 \\
0\,0\,1\,0\,\cdot\,\cdot\,\cdot\,\cdot\,\cdot\,\cdot\,\cdot\,\cdot\,\cdot\,\cdot\,\cdot\,0 \\
0\,0\,0\,1\,0\,\cdot\,\cdot\,\cdot\,\cdot\,\cdot\,\cdot\,\cdot\,\cdot\,\cdot\,0 \\
0\,0\,0\,0\,1\,0\,\cdot\,\cdot\,\cdot\,\cdot\,\cdot\,\cdot\,\cdot\,0 \\
0\,0\,0\,0\,0\,0\,0\,0\,0\,0\,0\,0\,0\,0\,0\,0\,0\,0 \\
0\,\cdot\,\cdot\,\cdot\,0\,1\,0\,\cdot\,\cdot\,\cdot\,\cdot\,\cdot\,\cdot\,0 \\
0\,\cdot\,\cdot\,\cdot\,\cdot\,0\,1\,0\,\cdot\,\cdot\,\cdot\,\cdot\,\cdot\,0 \\
0\,\cdot\,\cdot\,\cdot\,\cdot\,\cdot\,0\,1\,0\,\cdot\,\cdot\,\cdot\,\cdot\,0 \\
0\,\cdot\,\cdot\,\cdot\,\cdot\,\cdot\,\cdot\,0\,1\,0\,\cdot\,\cdot\,\cdot\,0 \\
0\,\cdot\,\cdot\,\cdot\,\cdot\,\cdot\,\cdot\,\cdot\,0\,1\,0\,\cdot\,\cdot\,0 \\
0\,\cdot\,\cdot\,\cdot\,\cdot\,\cdot\,\cdot\,\cdot\,\cdot\,0\,1\,0\,\cdot\,0 \\
0\,\cdot\,\cdot\,\cdot\,\cdot\,\cdot\,\cdot\,\cdot\,\cdot\,\cdot\,0\,1\,0\,\cdot\,0 \\
0\,\cdot\,\cdot\,\cdot\,\cdot\,\cdot\,\cdot\,\cdot\,\cdot\,\cdot\,\cdot\,0\,1\,0\,0 \\
0\,\cdot\,\cdot\,\cdot\,\cdot\,\cdot\,\cdot\,\cdot\,\cdot\,\cdot\,\cdot\,0\,1\,0\,0 \\
0\,\cdot\,\cdot\,\cdot\,\cdot\,\cdot\,\cdot\,\cdot\,\cdot\,\cdot\,\cdot\,\cdot\,0\,1\,0 \\
0\,0\,0\,0\,0\,0\,0\,0\,0\,0\,0\,0\,0\,0\,0\,0\,0\,1 \\
\delta\,0\,0\,0\,1\,0\,0\,0\,0\,0\,0\,0\,0\,0\,0\,1\,0
\end{pmatrix}$$

It is also interesting to construct the matrix K_z in this case; we have:

$$K_z = \begin{pmatrix}
\cdots & 0 & 0 & 0 & 0 & 0 & 0 & 0 & 0 & 0 & 0 & 0 & 0 & 0 & 0 & 1 & 0 & 0 & 0 & 0 \\
\cdots & 0 & \cdot & \cdot & \cdot & \cdot & \cdot & \cdot & \cdot & \cdot & \cdot & \cdot & \cdot & \cdot & \cdot & \cdot & 0 & 1 & 0 & 0 & 0 \\
\cdots & 0 & \cdot & & & & & & & & & & & & \cdot & 0 & 0 & 1 & 0 & 0 \\
\cdots & 0 & \cdot & & & & & & & & & & & \cdot & \cdot & 0 & 0 & 0 & 1 & 0 \\
\cdots & 0 & 0 & 0 & 0 & 0 & 0 & 0 & 0 & 0 & 0 & 0 & 0 & 0 & 0 & 0 & 0 & 0 & 0 & 1 \\
\cdots & \delta^+ & 0 & \delta^+ & 0 & 1 & 0 & 1 & 0 & \cdot & \cdot & \cdot & \cdot & \cdot & \cdot & \cdot & \cdot & \cdot & \cdot & 0 \\
\cdots & 0 & \delta^+ & 0 & \delta^+ & 0 & 1 & 0 & 1 & 0 & \cdot & \cdot & \cdot & \cdot & \cdot & \cdot & \cdot & \cdot & 0 \\
\cdots & \delta^+ & 0 & \delta^+ & 0 & \delta^+ & 0 & 1 & 0 & 1 & 0 & \cdot & \cdot & \cdot & \cdot & \cdot & \cdot & 0 \\
\cdots & 0 & \delta^+ & 0 & \delta^+ & 0 & \delta^+ & 0 & 1 & 0 & 1 & 0 & \cdot & \cdot & \cdot & \cdot & 0 \\
\cdots & \delta^+ & 0 & \delta^+ & 0 & \delta^+ & 0 & \delta^+ & 0 & 1 & 0 & 1 & 0 & \cdot & \cdot & \cdot & 0 \\
\cdots & 0 & \delta^+ & 0 & \delta^+ & 0 & \delta^+ & 0 & \delta^+ & 0 & 1 & 0 & 1 & 0 & \cdot & \cdot & 0 \\
\cdots & \delta^+ & 0 & \delta^+ & 0 & \delta^+ & 0 & \delta^+ & 0 & \delta^+ & 0 & 1 & 0 & 1 & 0 & \cdot & \cdot & 0 \\
\cdots & 0 & \delta^+ & 0 & \delta^+ & 0 & \delta^+ & 0 & \delta^+ & 0 & \delta^+ & 0 & 1 & 0 & 1 & 0 & \cdot & 0 \\
\cdots & \delta^+ & 0 & \delta^+ & 0 & \delta^+ & 0 & \delta^+ & 0 & \delta^+ & 0 & \delta^+ & 0 & 1 & 0 & 1 & 0 & \cdot & 0 \\
\cdots & 0 & \delta^+ & 0 & \delta^+ & 0 & \delta^+ & 0 & \delta^+ & 0 & \delta^+ & 0 & \delta^+ & 0 & 1 & 0 & 1 & 0 & \cdot & 0 \\
\cdots & \delta^+ & 0 & \delta^+ & 0 & \delta^+ & 0 & \delta^+ & 0 & \delta^+ & 0 & \delta^+ & 0 & 1 & 0 & 1 & 0 & 0 \\
\cdots & 0 & \delta^+ & 0 & \delta^+ & 0 & \delta^+ & 0 & \delta^+ & 0 & \delta^+ & 0 & \delta^+ & 0 & 1 & 0 & 1 & 0
\end{pmatrix}$$

where we have used δ^+ to denote $1+\delta$ for brevity. In this case, the columns $C^{16}\sigma_z$ and $C^{15}\sigma_z$ can be seen to provide a basis for all "previous" columns ($C^{16+j}\sigma_z$ for $j > 0$). If this were a K_m matrix and the initialisation was known, then only the words m_{l-16} and m_{l-17} would need to be modified in order to compensate for any changes in the previous words of the message.

Returning to the specifics of this cipher, we note from the description above that the accumulation process of the input message words involves using a non-linear filter in the accumulation register, that the register A is initialised with keystream words and that the input message words that are accumulated into the register are the plaintext words, which are assumed to be unknown to the attacker. Based on these features, SOBER-128 is considered to be case 2c in Table 1; as discussed in Section 4.1 above, the MAC accumulation process for this cipher should therefore be secure against forgery attacks based on collision in this case.

We note that there is nonetheless a reported forgery attack on SOBER-128 [9] which uses the same method of introducing differences in the input message words and cancelling out this difference after a certain number of clocks. We also note, however, that this attack is not due to the weakness of the accumulation process itself but rather to the weakness of the nonlinear filter that is used in the accumulation process. We assumed in setting up our model that a secure nonlinear filter is used in the filter generator, and it is clear from this example that the security of the accumulation process for this direct injection model relies (among other things) on the strength of this nonlinear filter.

6   Summary and Conclusions

This paper considers the process of generating MAC tags by injecting the input message and optionally the nonlinear filter output directly into the internal state of a nonlinear filter keystream generator comprising a LFSR and a nonlinear filter function. It describes a general model for the accumulation phase of this process and provides a security analysis of this model. The model we describe extends a model of Nakano *et al* for generating unkeyed hash values, generalising it to the case of word-based registers and extending the context from generating unkeyed hash functions to generating MACs (requiring the use of a key and IV). In this model, the message being accumulated could be either plaintext or ciphertext and the plaintext will not necessarily be known to the attacker.

In our model, we consider two alternative methods for injecting the message and the filter output into the internal state (LFSR) of the generator. The first method is to combine the input message and/or the filter output with the updated content of the relevant stages using the register's addition operation (XOR for binary registers). The second method is to replace the previous content of the relevant stages with the new combination of the input message and the filter output. The model also allows the possibility that the first alternative might be used in some stages of the register and the second alternative in other stages;

the security analysis for this situation would be similar to those reported here for the two separate alternatives.

Having described our model, we develop a matrix representation for the accumulation phase of MAC generation. Using this matrix representation, we provide a security analysis of the general model and describe conditions under which a collision can be forced which would enable a man-in-the-middle forgery to be successful. Specifically we show that suitable initialisation of the register and active use of the nonlinear filter prevent an attacker from finding a collision in the final register contents which would result in a forged MAC.

We use the results of this analysis to revisit Nakano *et al*'s analysis of their model. In particular, our analysis enables us to show, contrary to their conclusions, that collisions can always be forced in the entire register under their second configuration (injecting the message and filter output together into multiple stages of the register). We also applied the results of our security analysis to three existing authentication proposals which use direct injection in the accumulation phase of MAC generation. We found in two cases (SSS and NLSv2) that the accumulation mechanism used is not secure by itself. However in both cases, additional features of the authentication mechanism were used to overcome this weakness. For example, use of a self synchronous construction prevents an attacker from forging a valid MAC in the SSS stream cipher. In the third case (SOBER-128) the accumulation mechanism should be secure, except for the weakness of the nonlinear filter that was used.

Based on our analyses, we recommend the following procedures to prevent collision attacks when using this model in the accumulation phase of MAC generation:

- Use a secure nonlinear filter in the accumulation process and ensure that its output is injected into at least one stage of the register.
- Initialise the internal state of the LFSR with key-dependent secret values.
- When injecting the message and filter output into any stage of the LFSR, combine them with the updated contents of the stage using the register's addition operation rather than replacing the updated contents.
- For added security, inject the message and the filter output into different sets of LFSR stages.

The concept of generating MAC tags by injecting the message directly into the internal state of a cipher's integrity component can obviously be applied to other structures apart from the nonlinear filter generator considered in this paper. We considered this simple structure in order to demonstrate our approach for developing and analysing models of the MAC generation process in this case. Although it would be more complex, the same approach can be used to construct a similar model for other such structures.

Acknowledgement. Mufeed AlMashrafi was supported by a PhD scholarship from the Government of Oman.

References

1. AlMashrafi, M., Bartlett, H., Simpson, L., Dawson, E., Wong, K.K.-H.: Analysis of indirect message injection for MAC generation using stream ciphers. In: Susilo, W., Mu, Y., Seberry, J. (eds.) ACISP 2012. LNCS, vol. 7372, pp. 138–151. Springer, Heidelberg (2012)
2. Hawkes, P., Paddon, M., Rose, G.G.: Primitive specification for SOBER-128. IACR ePrint Archive, 473:476 (2003), http://eprint.iacr.org/2003/81
3. Hawkes, P., Paddon, M., Rose, G.G., de Vries, M.W.: Primitive Specification for SSS
4. Hawkes, P., Paddon, M., Rose, G.G., de Vries, M.W.: Primitive Specification for NLSv2. eSTREAM, ECRYPT Stream Cipher Project, Report 2006/036 (2006), http://www.ecrypt.eu.org/stream
5. Lidl, R., Niederreiter, H.: Finite fields. Encyclopedia of Mathematics and its Applications, vol. 20. Cambridge University Press (1997)
6. Menezes, A.J., van Oorschot, P.C., Vanstone, S.A.: Handbook of Applied Cryptography. CRC Press (1997)
7. Nakano, Y., Cid, C., Fukushima, K., Kiyomoto, S.: Analysis of Message Injection in Stream Cipher-Based Hash Functions. In: Lopez, J., Tsudik, G. (eds.) ACNS 2011. LNCS, vol. 6715, pp. 498–513. Springer, Heidelberg (2011)
8. Wardlaw, W.P.: A matrix model for the linear feedback shift register. Dtic Document, Naval Research Lab, Washington, DC (1989)
9. Watanabe, D., Furuya, S.: A MAC forgery attack on SOBER-128. In: Roy, B., Meier, W. (eds.) FSE 2004. LNCS, vol. 3017, pp. 472–482. Springer, Heidelberg (2004)

Collision Attacks on Variant of OCB Mode and Its Series

Zhelei Sun, Peng Wang, and Liting Zhang

State Key Laboratory of Information Security
Institute of Information Engineering of Chinese Academy of Sciences
{zhlsun,wp}@is.ac.cn, zhangliting@is.iscas.ac.cn

Abstract. Three versions of OCB appeared in the literature: OCB1, OCB2 and OCB3. Ferguson pointed out that OCB1 could not resist against collision attacks, which was improved by Mathiassen. Zhang, Xing and Yang made the first attempt to improve OCB1 against this prevailing attack in blockcipher modes of operation, and proposed a new authenticated encryption mode OCB-ZXY, using offset dependent plaintext block transformation (ODPBT) technique. Our research shows that: 1) OCB-ZXY still cannot resist against collision attacks. 2) OCB2 and OCB3 also suffer from collision attacks, even more severely than OCB1. 3) Even if OCB2 and OCB3 adopt the ODPBT technique, collision attacks still exist.

Keywords: OCB, collision attack, authenticated encryption.

1 Introduction

During the past few years, considerable effort has been made to construct authenticated encryption (AE) schemes, which provide both privacy and authenticity protections, such as IAPM [7], OCB [14], CCM [15], EAX [2], CWC [8] and GCM [12]. Briefly, privacy means that it is impossible for adversaries to obtain any information of plaintext from the known ciphertext; authenticity means that it is impossible for adversaries to make a forgery which cannot be caught by the authentication mechanism.

OCB [14](Offset Codebook), designed by Rogaway, Bellare, Black and Krovetz, is an AE scheme based on blockcipher, in which every block of message only needs to be processed once in order to achieve both privacy and authenticity. This kind of one-pass AE scheme is more efficient than the two-pass constructions [13], such as CCM [15], EAX [2], CWC [8] and GCM [12].

Three versions of OCB appeared in the literature: OCB1 [14], OCB2 [13] and OCB3 [9]. OCB1 is the original one; OCB2 is refined from OCB1 using the concept of tweakable blockcipher [10]; OCB3 [13], the final version, has the best software performance among OCB series. Before encryption, OCB series partition the message M into blocks $M_1 \cdots M_m$, where all but the last block are full, then each block except the last one is encrypted using a blockcipher invocation to get the ciphertext block $C_i = E_K(M_i \oplus \Delta_i) \oplus \Delta_i$, $i = 1, \cdots, m-1$,

M. Kutyłowski and M. Yung (Eds.): Inscrypt 2012, LNCS 7763, pp. 216–224, 2013.

where the offset Δ_i is a value relevant to the nonce and the key of the scheme and can be updated from the previous known offset easily. From the view of tweakable blockcipher, the function of offset is to make encryptions of the blocks independent from each other under the same blockcipher key. The core of authentication mechanism is the generation of the tag, which need not process the message blocks once again, only encrypt the Checksum, which is mainly the exclusive-or (XOR) of message blocks.

Shortly after the publication of OCB1, Ferguson pointed out that [3] OCB1 could not resist against collision attack, which is prevailing in blockcipher modes of operation, such as CBC encryption mode [1] and CBC-MAC authentication mode [6]. Later on, this attack was improved by Mathiassen [11]. Typically, collision attacks wait for the moment that the inputs to the blockcipher collide during the process of the mode, and then break the security of the mode thoroughly. The collision of inputs can be seen as a birthday problem, so the complexity of collision attacks is usually $O(2^{n/2})$, where n is the block length of the underlying blockcipher. After the collision detection, both Ferguson's and Mathiassen's attacks modify the ciphertext blocks in some way, with Checksum unchanged, so the modified ciphertext can pass the authentication mechanism successfully.

Although the collision attack generally does not violate the security proofs of modes, it is a severe problem particularly for 64-bit blockcipher mode. It is valuable to design modes which have security beyond birthday bound, such as CHM [4] and CIP [5] AE modes proposed by Iwata. In 2010, Zhang, Xing and Yang made the first attempt to improve OCB1 against collision attacks [16], proposing a new AE mode, which we name OCB-ZXY. OCB-ZXY adds offset dependent plaintext block transformation (ODPBT) before the Checksum calculation, trying to prevent attackers from modifying the ciphertext without being caught by the authentication mechanism.

Our contributions. Our research shows that: 1) OCB-ZXY still cannot resist against collision attacks while using offset dependent plaintext block transformation(ODPBT), which changes the way to calculate the Checksum. We observe that ODPBT has two fixed points 0^n and 1^n, and it is a linear function for any offsets. We use these two properties to show that once a collision is detected we still can make a successful forgery. Our attack only needs one more query to the encryption algorithm compared with the previous attacks given by Ferguson and Mathiassen. 2) OCB2 and OCB3 also suffer from collision attack, even more severely than OCB1. Once collision is detected, we can obtain all the values of offsets in OCB2, and related values of offsets in OCB3. The forgery can directly make use of the methods in [3,11]. 3) Even if OCB2 and OCB3 adopt the ODPBT technique, collision attacks still exist.

2   OCB Series and OCB-ZXY

We begin with some basic definitions and notations.

A *blockcipher* is a function $E : \mathcal{K} \times \{0,1\}^n \to \{0,1\}^n$, where $E_K(\cdot) = E(K, \cdot)$ is a permutation for all $K \in \mathcal{K}$, $\mathcal{K}$ is a *key space*. In OCB Series and OCB-ZXY AE modes, the block length of underlying blockcipher is 128, i.e., $n = 128$.

An authenticated encryption (with associated-data) scheme is a three-tuple $\pi = (\mathcal{K}, \mathcal{E}, \mathcal{D})$. $\mathcal{K}$ is the *key space* which coincides with the key space of the underlying blockcipher in OCBs. The *encryption algorithm* $\mathcal{E}$ takes in a key $K \in \mathcal{K}$, a nonce N, a message M, and associated data A, then returns a ciphertext C and a tag Tag. The *decryption algorithm* $\mathcal{D}$ takes in a key $K \in \mathcal{K}$, a nonce N, a ciphertext C, a tag Tag and associated data A, then returns a plaintext M or a distinguished value $\perp$. In the following descriptions of OCBs, we only give the encryption algorithms.

Let $GF(2^n)$ be the *finite field* with 2^n points. We denote *multiplication* in $GF(2^n)$ as $\cdot$. Without confusion, we often denote the point in $GF(2^n)$ as a string or a integer number interchangeably. For example, the string $0^{126}10 \in \{0,1\}^{128}$ in $GF(2^{128})$ is equivalent to the integer 2. *Gray code* is an ordering $\gamma_0, \gamma_1, \cdots, \gamma_{2^n-1}$ of $\{0,1\}^n$ such that successive points differ (in the Hamming sense) by just one bit. $ntz(i)$ is the number of trailing 0-bits in the binary representation of i, for example, $ntz(3) = 0$ and $ntz(4) = 2$. str2num is a function which turns a string to a integer number. $X^{\lll n}$ is a bit-rotation of X to the left of n positions.

2.1   OCB1, OCB2 and OCB3

We divide the encryption algorithms of OCB series into three stages: Initialization, Ciphertext Generation and Tag Generation.

1) *Initialization*: The initialization stage completes two tasks, partition of the message M into blocks $M_1 \cdots M_m$, where all but the last block are full, and calculation of the initial offset Δ_0.

- In OCB1: $\Delta_0 = E_K(N \oplus L)$, where $L = E_K(0^{128})$.
- In OCB2: $\Delta_0 = E_K(N)$.
- In OCB3: $\Delta_0 = H_L(N)$, where H is a universal hash function.

2) *Ciphertext Generation*: During this stage, the plaintext blocks are encrypted to get ciphertext blocks along with offsets updated.

$$C_i \leftarrow E_K(M_i \oplus \Delta_i) \oplus \Delta_i, \ i = 1, \cdots, m - 1.$$

The offset Δ_i can be easily updated from previous Δ_{i-1}.

- In OCB1, $\Delta_i = \Delta_0 \oplus \gamma_i \cdot L = \Delta_{i-1} \oplus 2^{ntz(i)} \cdot L$, where γ_i is the ith element of the Gray code, $L = E_K(0^n)$ and $\Delta_0 = E_K(N \oplus L)$.
- In OCB2, $\Delta_i = 2^i \cdot \Delta_0 = 2 \cdot \Delta_{i-1}$.
- In OCB3, $\Delta_i = \Delta_0 \oplus 4 \cdot \gamma_i \cdot L = \Delta_{i-1} \oplus 2^{2+ntz(i)} \cdot L$.

3) *Tag Generation*: In this stage, Checksum is calculated, and then encrypted into Tag:

$$\text{Checksum} \leftarrow M_1 \oplus \cdots \oplus M_{m-1} \oplus g_K(M_m),$$
$$\text{Tag} \leftarrow E_K(\text{Chesksum} \oplus \Delta_*) \oplus h_K(A).$$

where g is a function dealing with the last plaintext block, Δ_* is a new offset value, and h is a function dealing with associated data(A), which does not exist in OCB1. Here we will not give all the details of g and h in OCBs, but stress that when we modify the ciphertext blocks in some way, the corresponding Checksum is unchanged, then the resulting ciphertext with the previous tag can pass the authentication mechanism, or in other words we constitute a successful forgery. The encryption algorithm of OCB1 is given in Fig. 2.

2.2   Previous Attacks on OCB1

Ferguson points out that [3] OCB1 does not resist against collision attack, which is improved by Mathiassen [11]. Both Ferguson's and Mathiassen's attacks proceed in two steps. The first step detects a collision of inputs to the blockcipher by querying about $2^{n/2}$ blocks. The second step modifies the ciphertext without modifying the authentication tag. The difference is that Ferguson's attack modifies four blocks of the ciphertext, while Mathiassen's attack only modifies two blocks. Although the collision attack does not violate the provable security result of OCB1 [14], it is a severe problem particularly for 64-bit blockcipher mode. We review that in OCB1 the offset

$$\Delta_i = \Delta_0 \oplus \gamma_i \cdot L.$$

First step: Ferguson observed that [3]

$$\left.\begin{array}{r} X_i = X_j \\ \Rightarrow Y_i = Y_j \end{array}\right\} \Rightarrow M_i \oplus C_i = M_j \oplus C_j.$$

$X_i = M_i \oplus \Delta_i$ and $X_j = M_j \oplus \Delta_j$ are two inputs of blockcipher, which is just the collision we need, $Y_i = C_i \oplus \Delta_i$ and $Y_j = C_j \oplus \Delta_j$ are two corresponding outputs of blockcipher. The key fact $M_i \oplus C_i = M_j \oplus C_j$, can be regarded as a way to detect collisions with a probability of $1/2$ [3]. Once the detection is successful, we get the value of L [3],

$$X_i = X_j \Rightarrow M_i \oplus M_j = \Delta_i \oplus \Delta_j = L \cdot (\gamma_i \oplus \gamma_j) \Rightarrow L = (M_i \oplus M_j) \cdot (\gamma_i \oplus \gamma_j)^{-1}.$$

which is used in the forgery [3,11]. It is also the first step of our attack on OCB-ZXY.

Second step: In Mathiassen's attack [11], two ciphertext blocks C_p and C_q are modified into $C'_p = C_q \oplus (\gamma_p \oplus \gamma_q) \cdot L$ and $C'_q = C_p \oplus (\gamma_p \oplus \gamma_q) \cdot L$ respectively, which results in a successful forgery. We try to use L to make a forgery like [11], which is the exact one that the author of [16] wants to avoid, changing the existing ciphertext without being caught by the authentication mechanism.

2.3   OCB-ZXY

Zhang, Xing and Yang made the first attempt to improve OCB1 against collision attacks, and proposed a new authenticated encryption mode OCB-ZXY [16], using offset dependent plaintext block transformations (ODPBT) before the Checksum calculation. We describe ODPBT in Fig.1. For the plaintext block M_i and the corresponding offset Δ_i, ODPBT updates Δ_i into $\Delta_i \oplus i$, partitions M_i and Δ_i into 32-bit small blocks, and makes left bit-rotations of the plaintext blocks using the last five bits of the offset blocks.

We describe the encryption algorithms of OCB-ZXY and OCB1 in Fig.2, which illustrates the differences between OCB-ZXY and OCB1.

During the processing, the main differences between OCB-ZXY and OCB1 are $h()$ and ODPBT. The rest remains the same with OCB1. Function $h()$ is a collision resistance hash function intent to compress an arbitrary length header with the origin nonce into a fixed length nonce. Zhang, Xing and Yang tried to use ODPBT before calculating Checksum to defeat the collision attack. They even estimated that after collision detection the success probability of Mathiassen's forgery is 2^{-20} [16] if $n = 128$. Unfortunately, it is not the case, and collision attacks still exist.

```
ODPBT (M_i, Δ_i):
    Δ_i ← Δ_i ⊕ i
    S_{i,j} ← str2num (a_{j×32+4}a_{j×32+3}a_{j×32+2}a_{j×32+1}a_{j×32})
    (where j = 0, 1, ··· l − 1, l = n/32, Δ_i = a_{n−1} ··· a_1 a_0)
    M_i ← M_{i,l−1}^{≪S_{i,l−1}} || ··· || M_{i,1}^{≪S_{i,1}} || M_{i,0}^{≪S_{i,0}}
    (where M_i = M_{i,l−1} || ··· || M_{i,1} || M_{i,0})
    return M_i
```

Fig. 1. ODPBT (offset dependent plaintext block transformation)

```
00:    N ← h(H‖N)
01:    Partition M into M_1 ··· M_m
02:    L ← E_K(0^n)
03:    Δ_0 ← E_K(N ⊕ L)
04:    Checksum ← 0^n
05:    for i = 1 to m do
06:        Δ_i ← γ_i · L ⊕ Δ_0
07:    for i = 1 to m − 1 do
08:        C_i ← E_K(M_i ⊕ Δ_i) ⊕ Δ_i
09:        M_i ← ODPBT(M_i, Δ_i)
10:        Checksum ← Checksum ⊕M_i
11:    X_m ← len(M_m) ⊕ L · 2^{−1} ⊕ Δ_m
12:    Y_m ← E_K(X_m)
13:    C_m ← Y_m ⊕ M_m
14:    Checksum ← Checksum ⊕C_m0^* ⊕ Y_m
15:    Tag = E_K(Checksum ⊕Δ_m)
```

Fig. 2. Encryption algorithms of OCB-ZXY and OCB1. OCB1 is obtained by canceling the boxed statements (Line 00 and 09).

3   Collision Attack on OCB-ZXY

In this section we describe a collision attack on OCB-ZXY. It turns out that once a collision is detected we still can make a successful forgery.

We observe that ODPBT has the following two properties.

Property 1. For any offsets, ODPBT does not change the value of 0^n or 1^n:

$$\text{ODPBT}(0^n, \Delta_i) = 0^n, \text{ODPBT}(1^n, \Delta_i) = 1^n.$$

Property 2. For any offsets, ODPBT is a linear function:

$$\text{ODPBT}(X, \Delta_i) \oplus \text{ODPBT}(Y, \Delta_i) = \text{ODPBT}(X \oplus Y, \Delta_i).$$

Our attack has three steps.

1) *Collision detection*: This step is the same as the step one in previous attack of OCB1. Query a plaintext about $2^{n/2}$ blocks and wait for a collision. Once a collision is detected, we can obtain the value L, which can be used for calculating the XOR of any two offsets $\Delta_i \oplus \Delta_j = (\gamma_i \oplus \gamma_j) \cdot L$.

2) *Special plaintext query*: Query a random plaintext $M_1, M_2, \ldots, M_m$ with the restriction that $M_p \oplus M_q = \Delta_p \oplus \Delta_q \oplus 1^n$.

3) *Ciphertext modification*: Modify the ciphertext blocks C_p and C_q into

$$C'_p = C_q \oplus \Delta_p \oplus \Delta_q,$$

and

$$C'_q = C_p \oplus \Delta_p \oplus \Delta_q.$$

We can prove that the resulting ciphertext and tag constitute a successful forgery.

We denote the input and the output of blockcipher of ith block encryption as X_i and Y_i, and the corresponding value after ciphertext modification as X'_i and Y'_i.

$$Y'_p = C'_p \oplus \Delta_p = C_q \oplus \Delta_p \oplus \Delta_q \oplus \Delta_p = Y_q,$$

$$Y'_q = C'_q \oplus \Delta_q = C_p \oplus \Delta_p \oplus \Delta_q \oplus \Delta_q = Y_p.$$

The modification of the ciphertext makes the two outputs of blockcipher interchanged, therefore $X'_p = X_q$, $X'_q = X_p$. The new plaintext blocks are

$$M'_p = X'_p \oplus \Delta_p = X_q \oplus \Delta_p = M_q \oplus \Delta_q \oplus \Delta_p,$$

$$M'_q = X'_q \oplus \Delta_q = X_p \oplus \Delta_q = M_p \oplus \Delta_p \oplus \Delta_q.$$

It is needed that the changes of the ciphertext won't affect the Checksum. The original Checksum without considering the rest plaintext blocks is,

$$\text{ODPBT}(M_p, \Delta_p) \oplus \text{ODPBT}(M_q, \Delta_q). \tag{1}$$

After the ciphertext modification, the new Checksum without considering the rest plaintext blocks is,

$$\text{ODPBT}(M'_p, \Delta_p) \oplus \text{ODPBT}(M'_q, \Delta_q) \qquad (2)$$

$$= \text{ODPBT}(M_q \oplus \Delta_p \oplus \Delta_q, \Delta_p) \oplus \text{ODPBT}(M_p \oplus \Delta_p \oplus \Delta_q, \Delta_q).$$

By property 2, (1)=(2) if and only if

$$\text{ODPBT}(M_p \oplus M_q \oplus \Delta_p \oplus \Delta_q, \Delta_p) = \text{ODPBT}(M_p \oplus M_q \oplus \Delta_p \oplus \Delta_q, \Delta_q).$$

But in the second step the plaintext has the restriction that $M_p \oplus M_q = \Delta_p \oplus \Delta_q \oplus 1^n$, or $M_p \oplus M_q \oplus \Delta_p \oplus \Delta_q = 1^n$. By property 1, (1)=(2) holds. So after the modification, the Checksum and Tag remain unchanged. In the process, we make two queries, one for collision detection with a length about $2^{n/2}$ blocks, the other is a restricted message for forgery, so the complexity of attack is $O(2^{n/2})$. Since the bound of privacy and authenticity are both $O(\sigma^2/2^n)$(where σ means the aggregate length of the blocks queried by the adversary), which equals to the bound of birthday, when $\sigma \approx 2^{n/2}$, it will be very possible for an adversary to make a successful attack with a probability of 1.

4   Collision Attacks on OCB2 and OCB3

Collision attack on OCB2: In OCB2, the offset

$$\Delta_i = 2^i \cdot \Delta_0,$$

if we detect collision $X_i = X_j$, i.e. $M_i \oplus \Delta_i = M_j \oplus \Delta_j$, then

$$\Delta_0 = (M_i \oplus M_j) \cdot (2^i \oplus 2^j)^{-1}.$$

Therefore we know all the offsets. This is different from OCB1, OCB-ZXY and OCB3, of which we only know the related value of offsets $\Delta_i \oplus \Delta_j$.

When we modify the ciphertext, we can directly make use of the methods in [3,11]. For example we can set $C'_p = C_q \oplus \Delta_p \oplus \Delta_q$ and $C'_q = C_p \oplus \Delta_p \oplus \Delta_q$ without the restriction of M_p and M_q, which will successfully goes through the authentication mechanism. Besides, because we know all the offsets, we can even change arbitrary ciphertext block resulting in any special value of the corresponding output of the blockcipher.

Collision attack on OCB3: In OCB3, the offset

$$\Delta_i = \Delta_0 \oplus 4 \cdot \gamma_i \cdot L,$$

if we detect collision $X_i = X_j$, i.e. $M_i \oplus \Delta_i = M_j \oplus \Delta_j$, then

$$L = (M_i \oplus M_j) \cdot (4 \cdot \gamma_i \oplus 4 \cdot \gamma_j)^{-1}.$$

Therefore we know all the related value of offsets $\Delta_i \oplus \Delta_j$.

When we modify the ciphertext, we can also directly make use of the methods in [3,11]. So the existing attacks based on collision detection almost directly apply to both OCB2 and OCB3. From the point of view, they are no more secure than OCB1.

What about OCB2(3) + ODPBT? From the above analysis, we see that even if ODPBT technique is added to OCB2 and OCB3, they still can not resist against collision attack. We can apply the collision attack on OCB-ZXY to these new schemes.

5   Conclusion

In this paper, we focus on collision attack on a variant of OCB modes and its series, OCB-ZXY, OCB2 and OCB3. Although OCB-ZXY adopts the ODPBT technique, we can still modify a special ciphertext without caught by the authentication mechanism. OCB2 and OCB3 also suffer from the collision attack, even if they adopt the ODPBT technique, our attacks apply to them. What's more, all of our work don't violate the security proofs of OCBs. All these authenticated encryption schemes can not resist again collision attacks. Once a collision is detected we can make a successful forgery.

Acknowledgment. This research is supported by the National Natural Science Foundation Of China (No. 60903219, 61272477, 61202422) and the Strategic Priority Research Program of Chinese Academy of Sciences under Grant XDA06010702.

References

1. Bellare, M., Desai, A., Jokipii, E., Rogaway, P.: A concrete security treatment of symmetric encryption. In: FOCS, pp. 394–403. IEEE Computer Society (1997)
2. Bellare, M., Rogaway, P., Wagner, D.: The EAX mode of operation. In: Roy, B., Meier, W. (eds.) FSE 2004. LNCS, vol. 3017, pp. 389–407. Springer, Heidelberg (2004)
3. Ferguson, N.: Collision attacks on OCB. Comments to NIST (2002),
   http://csrc.nist.gov/groups/ST/toolkit/BCM/documents/comments/General_Comments/papers/Ferguson.pdf
4. Iwata, T.: New blockcipher modes of operation with beyond the birthday bound security. In: Robshaw, M.J.B. (ed.) FSE 2006. LNCS, vol. 4047, pp. 310–327. Springer, Heidelberg (2006)
5. Iwata, T.: Authenticated encryption mode for beyond the birthday bound security. In: Vaudenay, S. (ed.) AFRICACRYPT 2008. LNCS, vol. 5023, pp. 125–142. Springer, Heidelberg (2008)
6. Jia, K., Wang, X., Yuan, Z., Xu, G.: Distinguishing and second-preimage attacks on CBC-like MACs. In: Garay, J.A., Miyaji, A., Otsuka, A. (eds.) CANS 2009. LNCS, vol. 5888, pp. 349–361. Springer, Heidelberg (2009)
7. Jutla, C.S.: Encryption modes with almost free message integrity. In: Pfitzmann, B. (ed.) EUROCRYPT 2001. LNCS, vol. 2045, pp. 529–544. Springer, Heidelberg (2001)

8. Kohno, T., Viega, J., Whiting, D.: CWC: A high-performance conventional authenticated encryption mode. In: Roy, B., Meier, W. (eds.) FSE 2004. LNCS, vol. 3017, pp. 408–426. Springer, Heidelberg (2004)

9. Krovetz, T., Rogaway, P.: The software performance of authenticated-encryption modes. In: Joux, A. (ed.) FSE 2011. LNCS, vol. 6733, pp. 306–327. Springer, Heidelberg (2011)

10. Liskov, M., Rivest, R.L., Wagner, D.: Tweakable block ciphers. In: Yung, M. (ed.) CRYPTO 2002. LNCS, vol. 2442, pp. 31–46. Springer, Heidelberg (2002)

11. Mathiassen, J.E.: Improved collision attack on OCB (2005), http://www.ii.uib.no/publikasjoner/texrap/pdf/2005-306.pdf

12. McGrew, D.A., Viega, J.: The galois/counter mode of operation (GCM) (2004), http://csrc.nist.gov/groups/ST/toolkit/BCM/

13. Rogaway, P.: Efficient instantiations of tweakable blockciphers and refinements to modes OCB and PMAC. In: Lee, P.J. (ed.) ASIACRYPT 2004. LNCS, vol. 3329, pp. 16–31. Springer, Heidelberg (2004)

14. Rogaway, P., Bellare, M., Black, J., Krovetz, T.: OCB: a block-cipher mode of operation for efficient authenticated encryption. In: Reiter, M.K., Samarati, P. (eds.) ACM Conference on Computer and Communications Security, pp. 196–205. ACM (2001)

15. Whiting, D., Housley, R., Ferguson, N.: Counter with CBC-MAC (CCM) (2002), http://csrc.nist.gov/groups/ST/toolkit/BCM/

16. Zhang, S., Xing, G., Yang, Y.: An efficient scheme of authenticated encryption with associated data. In: Proc. Chinese Control and Decision Conf. (CCDC), pp. 4217–4221 (2010)

The Security and Performance of "GCM" when Short Multiplications Are Used Instead

Kazumaro Aoki and Kan Yasuda

NTT Secure Platform Laboratories

Abstract. We study the security and performance of an *altered* Galois/Counter Mode (GCM) of operation. Recent studies (e.g. Krovetz and Rogaway FSE 2011) show that GCM performs rather poorly in modern software implementation because of polynomial hashing in the large field $\mathrm{GF}(2^n)$ (n denotes the block size of the underlying cipher). This paper investigates whether we can use polynomial hashing in the ring $\mathrm{GF}(2^{n/2}) \times \mathrm{GF}(2^{n/2})$ instead. Such a change would normally compromise the level of security down to $\Theta(2^{n/4})$. Nonetheless, our security proofs show that we can avoid such degradation by masking *and then encrypting* the hash result, guided by the tentative suggestion made by Ferguson in 2005. We also provide experimental data showing that the modified GCM runs at 1.777 cycles per byte on an Intel Sandy Bridge processor. This makes about 31% reduction from 2.59 cycles per byte of Gueron's GCM implementation presented at Indocrypt 2011.

Keywords: GCM, polynomial hash, nonce, authenticated encryption.

1 Introduction

This work is about the block-cipher mode GCM (Galois/Counter Mode) [21] which is designed for nonce-based authenticated encryption. GCM is widely standardized by ANSI [2], IEEE [7,8], ISO/IEC [16] and NIST [24]. GCM is employed by various cryptographic protocols including IPsec [9,10], SSH [12] and TLS/SSL [11]. Regrettably, GCM is not one of the fastest modes in the category (e.g. [19]). In this work we show that, by introducing fairly minor modifications to GCM, we are able to bring significant gains in performance while retaining $\Theta(2^{n/2})$ security (n is the block size of the underlying block cipher).

Background and Motivation: GCM Well-Designed but Often Slow. Let us first carry out a careful review of GCM, focusing on its operational aspects. We then find out that the software performance of GCM is its primary disadvantage, even though GCM has other remarkable properties. The performance issue about the otherwise sound GCM motivates us to change slightly the architecture of GCM for greater efficiency.

See Fig. 1 for a graphic description of the GCM encipherment algorithm using a 128-bit block cipher $E_K(\cdot)$. Here IV is a nonce, A associated data, P a plaintext, C the ciphertext and T the authentication tag. The symbol $\odot$ denotes

M. Kutyłowski and M. Yung (Eds.): Inscrypt 2012, LNCS 7763, pp. 225–245, 2013.
© Springer-Verlag Berlin Heidelberg 2013

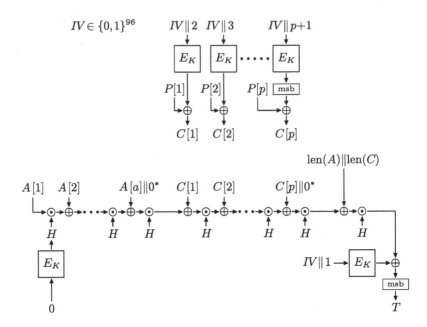

Fig. 1. The Original GCM Specified in SP800-38D When $\text{len}(IV) = 96$

a multiplication in the binary field $\text{GF}(2^{128})$. As Fig. 1 describes, GCM is a "two-pass" mode of operation—for each message block, one needs to carry out one invocation to the block cipher plus one multiplication in the field $\text{GF}(2^{128})$[1]. Hence GCM generally runs slower than a "one-pass" scheme such as OCB [26], the overhead being mainly the 128-bit multiplications.

Despite the fact that GCM is a two-pass construction, GCM has been standardized by a number of organizations and adopted by quite a few security protocols, as mentioned above. The reasons behind the choice of GCM could be:

- **No Block-Cipher Inverse.** The decipherment process of GCM does not require the inverse E^{-1}. This is due to the fact that GCM utilizes the CTR (Counter) mode for encryption and polynomial hashing for authentication. The absence of cipher inverse brings a benefit of smaller code size and enables us to prove security based on a weaker assumption about the cipher (e.g. PRP rather than Strong PRP; see Sect. 4 for the definition of PRP).
- **Authentication-Only Usage.** The authentication part of GCM can be used naturally as an independent *nonce-based* MAC (Message Authentication Code) algorithm as in GMAC [10]. GMAC innately processes A-only data when P is the empty string ε (see [25] for issues about associated data).

---

[1] The cost for one multiplication in $\text{GF}(2^{128})$ is comparable with one block cipher encryption on software environments, and a fast hardware implementation of one multiplication in $\text{GF}(2^{128})$ requires similar gate counts of one block cipher encryption. Thus, we regard that GCM is two-pass instead of one-pass.

- **Online Processing.** GCM is "online"—a plaintext P can be processed as soon as it is (partially) received and needs to be read only once for both encryption and authentication. Specifically, in GCM, once $P[i]$ is read, it can be immediately discarded after an xor or overwritten with the xor.
- **Parallelizability.** GCM is parallelizable both in its encryption (CTR) and in its authentication (polynomial hashing). Moreover, the design of GCM combines the CTR mode and the polynomial hash without causing major stalls, from which we would expect GCM to achieve high throughput for sufficiently large data.

To our knowledge there exist no research results that have cogently argued against GCM's advantages described in the first three items. As to the fourth item, on the other hand, the high performance of GCM has become questionable since the recent observations made by Krovetz and Rogaway [19]. They demonstrated rather poor performance of GCM on modern CPUs, GCM running much slower than one would expect from a two-pass construction. The performance overhead of GCM comes mainly from the long multiplications "$\odot$" in $GF(2^{128})$. This is the case also for the latest Intel processors that are equipped with dedicated instructions [14] of short, 64-bit carry-less multiplications.

Therefore, we would like to make small modifications to the GCM architecture in order to increase its efficiency, while maintaining the attractive features described above. Naturally we shall change the type of multiplication in polynomial hashing, so that the change would improve its performance, in particular the software performance on the current Intel processors.

Our Contributions. Given the performance issue of GCM, we devise a novel, altered version of GCM. The basic idea is to use multiplications in the smaller field $GF(2^{n/2})$, or more precisely, in the ring $GF(2^{n/2}) \times GF(2^{n/2})$. In this way we fully utilize Intel's instruction set of 64-bit carry-less multiplications when $n = 128$. We prove the security of the modified GCM, while giving experimental results to show that the new scheme is indeed faster. We believe this is the first example of an authenticated-encryption scheme that utilizes half-size polynomial hashing and attains $\Theta(2^{n/2})$ security[2].

- **GCM/2$^+$ Construction: Ferguson [5] Revisited.** Simply altering the type of multiplication would cause degradation in security down to $\Theta(2^{n/4})$. In order to retain $\Theta(2^{n/2})$ security (which is the bound of the original GCM), we introduce a subtle structural change to the authentication part—we *encrypt* the authentication tag, following up the suggestive hint from Ferguson [5]. We name the new mode GCM/2$^+$ to represent the two changes introduced. See Fig. 2 for a pictorial representation of GCM/2$^+$. The symbol $\otimes$ denotes a multiplication in the ring $GF(2^{n/2}) \times GF(2^{n/2})$. Note that GCM/2$^+$ is able to omit the final multiplication owing to the extra block-cipher call. We also point out that, although only $len(A)$ is input to the left

---

[2] In Document 1 of [1], multiplications in $GF(2^{n/2})$ are used for integrity. However, the tag length is only $(n/4)$-bit.

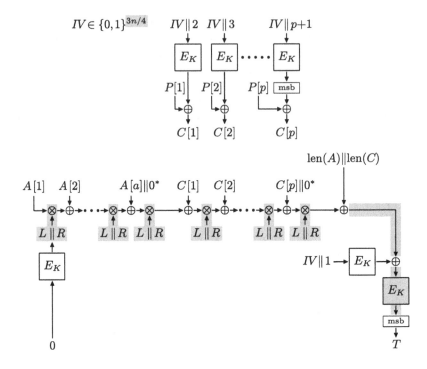

Fig. 2. GCM/2$^+$: The Changes from GCM Are Grayed

Table 1. Comparison of Security Bounds

GCM/2$^+$ Security (This work)[*]	GCM Security [21][**]
$\dfrac{17\sigma^2}{2^n} + \dfrac{2\ell q_\perp}{2^{n/2}} + \dfrac{q_\perp}{2^t}$	$\dfrac{0.5(\sigma' + 2q)^2}{2^n} + \dfrac{4q(\sigma' + 2q)}{2^n} + \dfrac{\ell q}{2^t}$

---

[*] σ is the total length of queries, ℓ the maximum length of each query, $q_\perp$ the maximum number of forgery attempts and t the tag length.

[**] σ' denotes the total length of plaintext queries and q the maximum number of queries.

half and only len(C) to the right half, xoring len(A)$\|$ len(C) suffices to make the scheme secure.

- **Proofs of Security: New Type of $\Theta(2^{n/2})$ Bound.** Our analysis shows that the new mode achieves security of a $\Theta(2^{n/2})$ bound in a fashion distinctly different from the original GCM. See Table 1. To prove the new bound, we rely on the game-playing techniques [3]. Our proofs, in particular the authenticity proof, become more complicated than those of GCM.
- **Proofs of Speed on Intel Processors.** We provide data for software implementation of GCM/2$^+$. Our experimental results demonstrate that

Table 2. Our Experimental Results and Comparison with Previous Figures

| Mode | Performance (cycles per byte) | | Data length | Source |
	Sandy Bridge	Westmere		
GCM/2$^+$	1.777	2.355	16KB	This work
	1.784	2.364	8KB	//
	1.804	2.381	4KB	//
	1.926	2.477	1KB	//
GCM	2.59	—	16KB	[6]
	2.67	3.90	4KB	//
	2.898	3.452	8KB	OpenSSL 1.0.1c
	—	3.505	16KB	[20]
	—	3.597	4KB	//
	—	3.85	1KB	[14]
CTR	0.658	1.158	4KB	This work
	0.83	1.30	1KB	[6]
	0.916	1.332 (1.26***)	8KB	OpenSSL 1.0.1c
	—	1.222	4KB	[20]
	—	1.316	1KB	//

*** This number can be found in the comments of `openssl-1.0.1c/crypto/aes/asm/aesni-x86_64.pl`; other OpenSSL figures are our measurements.

GCM/2$^+$ does indeed give improved performance over GCM on the modern Intel CPUs. Our implementation of GCM/2$^+$ runs at 1.777 cycles per byte on an Intel Sandy Bridge CPU, the figure making about 31% reduction from Gueron's implementation of GCM [6]. To compare our results with figures available for GCM, we also conduct experiments with a former-generation Westmere processor.[3] See Table 2 for the summary of our experimental results and for the comparison with previous figures in the literature. Note that GCM/2$^+$ is a proof of concept to use a multiplication in $GF(2^{n/2}) \times GF(2^{n/2})$ for a polynomial hash. We do not provide numerical input and output examples of our implementation.

Our techniques are independent from SGCM [28] and from MGCM [22]. Our half-size multiplication can be possibly combined with the techniques of SGCM or of MGCM to obtain desired performance of the authentication part; see Sect. 7 where we shall discuss more about the combination with SGCM.

Intuition behind Our Construction: Why Secure? Let us explain why GCM/2$^+$ is secure. We give reasons for the $\Theta(2^{n/2})$ security that is achieved despite using short multiplications. We focus on the collision of hash values. Note that by taking the advantage of associated data A (and setting P to be the

---

[3] Our implementation is optimized for Sandy Bridge; we run the same source code on Westmere just by selecting a different compiler option (`-msse4` instead of `-mavx`).

null string ε), an adversary can fully control the input to the polynomial hash. By fixing, say, the right half of the input (corresponding to the hash function in variable R), an adversary can cause a collision after about $2^{n/4}$ queries.

However, such a collision would not directly affect the security of the *authenticated-encryption* mode GCM/2^+ owing to the presence of a nonce IV. Such a collision has no impact on the encipherment oracle, because every time the encipherment algorithm is invoked, a fresh n-bit random mask $E_K(IV\|1)$ is xored onto the entire ($n/2 + n/2 = n$ bits) hash result, making colliding hash values insignificant.

One might think that a problem arises when a collision occurs between the encipherment and decipherment oracles with the same IV. However, recall that an adversary is *nonce-respecting* and is allowed to make only one query to the encipherment oracle for each IV, which means that the probability of such a collision across the oracles increases only *linearly* with the number of queries (forgery attempts) to the decipherment oracle. As a result, the security of GCM/2^+ remains at $\Theta(2^{n/2})$.

Intuition Behind Our Results: Why Faster? Let us explain why GCM/2^+ is faster. We give a theoretical justification of the performance improvement. Let $\textbf{time}(\text{CTR})$ denote the time consumed by the CTR mode and $\textbf{time}(\text{Hash}^\odot)$ that by the polynomial hashing of GCM. Then roughly the time consumed by GCM can be written as the sum $\textbf{time}(\text{CTR}) + \textbf{time}(\text{Hash}^\odot)$.

The bulk of $\textbf{time}(\text{Hash}^\odot)$ comes from the multiplications in the "long" field $\text{GF}(2^{128})$. Recall that one multiplication $\odot$ in $\text{GF}(2^{128})$ would cost three 64-bit multiplications (even) if the Karatsuba method [17] is used, which is the case of OpenSSL 1.0.1c (and probably the case of most other "fast" implementations). On the other hand, one multiplication $\otimes$ in the ring $\text{GF}(2^{64}) \times \text{GF}(2^{64})$ would cost only two 64-bit multiplications. Therefore, the time consumed by GCM/2^+ is expected to be roughly $\textbf{time}(\text{CTR}) + 2/3 \cdot \textbf{time}(\text{Hash}^\odot)$, and the difference $1/3 \cdot \textbf{time}(\text{Hash}^\odot)$ significantly contributes to boosting software performance.

Organization of the Paper. We define the GCM/2^+ mode of operation in Sect. 2. We give its design rationale in Sect. 3, explaining the changes from the original GCM. We define security notions in Sect. 4. Security proofs are given in Sect. 5. Our software implementation results are presented in Sect. 6. In Sect. 7 we end the paper with making remarks on the hardware performance analysis, on the weak keys of the polynomial hash used in GCM/2^+ and on a slightly different method of implementation.

2   GCM/2^+ Specification

In this section we define the new mode GCM/2^+ and explain basic symbols and notation that we use in the paper. Algorithms 1 and 2 define the encipherment and decipherment processes of the GCM/2^+ mode, respectively. The algorithms call an n-bit block cipher $E_K : \{0,1\}^n \to \{0,1\}^n$, where n is divisible by 4.

Algorithm 1. The $\text{GCM}/2^+$ Encipherment $\mathcal{E}_{E_K}(IV, A, P)$

Input: a nonce $IV \in \{0,1\}^{3n/4}$, associated data $A \in \{0,1\}^*$,
      a plaintext $P \in \{0,1\}^*$, a key $K \in \{0,1\}^k$
Output: a ciphertext $C \in \{0,1\}^*$, a tag $T \in \{0,1\}^t$

1 $C \leftarrow \text{CTR}_{E_K}(IV, P); \; L\|R \xleftarrow{n/2} E_K(0); \; V \leftarrow \text{Hash2}^{\otimes}_{L\|R}(A, C)$
2 $J \leftarrow E_K(IV\| \langle 1 \rangle_{n/4}); \; T \leftarrow \text{msb}_t(E_K(V \oplus J)); \textbf{ return } C\|T$

Algorithm 2. The $\text{GCM}/2^+$ Decipherment $\mathcal{D}_{E_K}(IV, A, C, T)$

Input: a nonce $IV \in \{0,1\}^{3n/4}$, associated data $A \in \{0,1\}^*$,
      a ciphertext $C \in \{0,1\}^*$, a tag $T \in \{0,1\}^t$, a key $K \in \{0,1\}^k$
Output: a plaintext $P \in \{0,1\}^*$ or a reject symbol $\perp$

1 $L\|R \xleftarrow{n/2} E_K(0); \; V \leftarrow \text{Hash2}^{\otimes}_{L\|R}(A, C)$
2 $J \leftarrow E_K(IV\| \langle 1 \rangle_{n/4}); \; T_* \leftarrow \text{msb}_t(E_K(V \oplus J))$
3 **if** $T = T_*$ **then return** $P \leftarrow \text{CTR}_{E_K}(IV, C)$ `/* valid integrity */`
4 **else return** $\perp$ `/* invalid */`

The subroutines are defined in Algorithms 3, 4 and 5. Please refer back to Fig. 2 for an illustration of the encipherment algorithm $\mathcal{E}$.

Our primary interest is the case when E is AES [23], which means $n = 128$ and $n/2 = 64$. In this case we choose an irreducible polynomial $f(u) := u^{64} \oplus u^4 \oplus u^3 \oplus u \oplus 1 \in \text{GF}(2)[u]$ to represent the finite field $\text{GF}(2^{64})$. A binary string $X = X_{63}X_{62}\cdots X_0$ is regarded as a polynomial $X_{63} \cdot u^{63} \oplus X_{62} \cdot u^{62} \oplus \cdots \oplus X_0$ interchangeably. Throughout the paper we use u as a variable of polynomials.

- **Encipherment $\mathcal{E}$ and Decipherment $\mathcal{D}$.** See Algorithms 1 and 2. The operation $L\|R \xleftarrow{n/2} E_K(0)$ means that the encryption of $0 = 0^n \in \{0,1\}^n$ is assigned to the variables L and R, with L being the leftmost $n/2$ bits and R the remaining $n/2$ bits. Given a non-negative integer i, we write $\langle i \rangle_m$ for denoting the m-bit representation of the integer i using a natural conversion.

Algorithm 3. The $\text{CTR}_{E_K}(IV, X)$ Subroutine

Input: a nonce $IV \in \{0,1\}^{3n/4}$, data $X \in \{0,1\}^*$, a key $K \in \{0,1\}^k$
Output: (un)masked data $Y \in \{0,1\}^*$ `/* used for en/decipherment */`

1 **if** $X = \varepsilon$ **then** $Y \leftarrow \varepsilon$ `/* X empty string */`
2 **else**   `/* non-empty */`
3     $X[1]\|X[2]\|\cdots\|X[x] \xleftarrow{n} X$
4   **for** $i = 1$ **to** x **do** $Y[i] \leftarrow \text{msb}_{\text{len}(X[i])}(E_K(IV\| \langle i+1 \rangle_{n/4})) \oplus X[i]$
5     $Y \leftarrow Y[1]\|Y[2]\|\cdots\|Y[x]$
6 **end**
7 **return** Y

Algorithm 4. The $\text{Hash2}^{\otimes}_{L\|R}(A, C)$ Subroutine

---

Input: associated data $A \in \{0,1\}^*$, a ciphertext $C \in \{0,1\}^*$,
      a key $L\|R \in \{0,1\}^{n/2} \times \{0,1\}^{n/2}$
Output: a hash value $V \in \{0,1\}^n$

1 $\bar{A} \leftarrow A\|0^*$; $\bar{C} \leftarrow C\|0^*$; $X \leftarrow \langle \text{len}(A)\rangle_{n/2}$; $Y \leftarrow \langle \text{len}(C)\rangle_{n/2}$
2 **return** $V \leftarrow \text{Hash1}^{\otimes}_{L\|R}(\bar{A}\|\bar{C}\|X\|Y)$

Algorithm 5. The $\text{Hash1}^{\otimes}_{L\|R}(X)$ Subroutine

---

Input: a bit string $X \in \{0,1\}^{n+}$,   /* $|X|$ a positive multiple of n */
      a key $L\|R \in \{0,1\}^{n/2} \times \{0,1\}^{n/2}$
Output: a hash value $V \in \{0,1\}^n$

1 $X[1]\|X[2]\| \cdots \|X[x] \xleftarrow{n} X$; $V \leftarrow 0$
2 **for** $i = 1$ **to** x **do** $V \leftarrow ((L\|R) \otimes V) \oplus X[i]$ /* short multiplication */
3 **return** V

The leftmost bit is the most significant bit. The function $\text{msb}_i(X)$ outputs the leftmost (significant) i bits of the string X. The tag length t is a positive integer less than or equal to n. Unless otherwise stated, within a statement operations are performed from right to left. So the statement **return** $X \leftarrow Y$ is a shorthand for $X \leftarrow Y$; **return** X.

- **CTR Subroutine.** See Algorithm 3. Given a non-empty string X, the notation $X[1]\|X[2]\| \cdots \|X[x] \xleftarrow{n} X$ represents the partitioning operation into n-bit strings; we have $X[1]\|X[2]\| \ldots \|X[x] = X$, where $|X[i]| = n$ for $1 \leq i \leq x - 1$ and $1 \leq |X[x]| \leq n$. The function $\text{len}(X)$ returns the bit length of a string $X \in \{0,1\}^*$. The returned value is a non-negative integer.
- **Hash Functions Hash2$^{\otimes}$ and Hash1$^{\otimes}$.** See Algorithms 4 and 5. Given a string X, the notation $X\|0^*$ means padding a minimum number of zero bits so that the bit length of the resulting string becomes divisible by n. No bit is padded if X is the null string ε. We write $\{0,1\}^{n+}$ for meaning the set of strings whose bit length is a positive multiple of n. The symbol $\otimes$ represents the short multiplication used in our polynomial hash. To be precise, given two strings $X, Y \in \{0,1\}^n$, let $X_1\|X_2 \xleftarrow{n/2} X$ and $Y_1\|Y_2 \xleftarrow{n/2} Y$. We then define the product $X \otimes Y \in \{0,1\}^n$ as $(X_1 \cdot Y_1)\|(X_2 \cdot Y_2)$, where $X_1 \cdot Y_1$ and $X_2 \cdot Y_2$ are multiplications in the smaller field $\text{GF}(2^{n/2})$. Note that we write $X \odot Y$ for denoting the standard multiplication in $\text{GF}(2^n)$ which is not the same as $X \otimes Y$.

3   Design Rationale

In this section we explain how we have reached the new design; we elaborate on the differences between GCM/2$^+$ and the original GCM. The changes are:

- **Fixed *IV* Length.** The original GCM accepts *IV* of any length, but recently it has been pointed out by Iwata et al. [15] that the security proof of the case $IV \neq 96$ was buggy (and its "repair" is not trivial). Therefore, for the sake of simplicity we fix the nonce length to $3n/4$ bits, which corresponds to 96 when $n = 128$. Actually, GCM treats 96 as $n - 32$ [21,24], not $3n/4$. However, we consider 2^{32} blocks to be too short for the future case of $n > 128$ and hence adopt $3n/4$ instead.
- **Half-Size Multiplication.** GCM/2$^+$ utilizes the Cartesian product $\otimes$ of two $n/2$-bit multiplications. One may think that we might be able to go further; e.g. product of four $n/4$-bit multiplications, etc.. Unfortunately we were unable to do so. The half size $n/2$ seems the smallest to keep $\Theta(2^{n/2})$ security in this style of construction.
- **No Final Multiplication.** The multiplication at the end of hashing, after xoring $len(A)\| len(C)$, is removed for better efficiency. This omission is made possible because of the extra block-cipher call described below.
- **Encrypted Tag.** This is an essential change. We quote from Ferguson [5, §7] who, after having presented an attack on GCM for short authentication tags (the attack does not invalidate the security proof of GCM), pointed out a possible modification to enhance GCM's security:[4]

    > *CWC (a competing mode) solves this very same problem by encrypting the hash result with the block cipher before xorring it with a block of the key stream [2]. As far as we can see this construction would resolve the GCM short-tag authentication weakness.*
    >
    > *We must point out that we have not done any cryptanalysis or security proofs for this modified version of GCM. We strongly urge people not to use this version until cryptanalytical review and security proofs have been completed.*

    We follow this direction, except that we encrypt the hash result *after* xoring it with a block of the key stream (*xor-then-encrypt*). With the order reversed (*encrypt-then-xor*) we were unable to prove a desired level of security.

The half-size multiplications must be used in combination with the extra encryption. Without it GCM/2$^+$ would not be as secure as we expect in this work.

4   Security Definitions

We basically follow the security notions defined by McGrew and Viega in their work of GCM [21]. We give an adversary $\mathcal{A}$ (an oracle machine) access to the encipherment oracle $\mathcal{E}(\cdot, \cdot, \cdot)$ and, possibly, to the decipherment oracle $\mathcal{D}(\cdot, \cdot, \cdot, \cdot)$. The $\mathcal{E}$-oracle takes (IV, A, P) as its input and returns $C\|T$. The $\mathcal{D}$-oracle takes (IV, A, C, T) as its input and returns either P or $\perp$. The queries to the two oracles can be interleaved. We also comply with the notion of *nonce-respecting* given by McGrew and Viega [21]—we demand that an adversary $\mathcal{A}$ never repeats the

---

[4] The citation [2] in the quote corresponds to the reference [18] in this work.

same IV in its queries to the same oracle. However, an $\mathcal{E}$-query and a $\mathcal{D}$-query can share the same IV.

Let $\mathcal{A}^{\mathcal{O}(\cdot),\cdots}$ be the value returned by $\mathcal{A}$ after its interaction with oracles $\mathcal{O}(\cdots),\cdots$. We would like to measure the distinguishing advantage

$$\Pr[\mathcal{A}^{\mathcal{E}(\cdot,\cdot,\cdot),\mathcal{D}(\cdot,\cdot,\cdot,\cdot)} = 1] - \Pr[\mathcal{A}^{\$(\cdot,\cdot,\cdot),\perp(\cdot,\cdot,\cdot,\cdot)} = 1], \tag{1}$$

where $\$(\cdot,\cdot,\cdot)$ is a random oracle that returns a random string of $|P| + t$ bits upon an input (IV, A, P) and $\perp(\cdot,\cdot,\cdot,\cdot)$ is a reject oracle that always returns $\perp$ upon any input (IV, A, C, T). The probabilities are taken over the random coins used by the oracles and also over internal coins of $\mathcal{A}$, if any. Note that (1) can be divided into $\Pr[\mathcal{A}^{\mathcal{E}(\cdot,\cdot,\cdot),\perp(\cdot,\cdot,\cdot,\cdot)} = 1] - \Pr[\mathcal{A}^{\$(\cdot,\cdot,\cdot),\perp(\cdot,\cdot,\cdot,\cdot)} = 1]$ and $\Pr[\mathcal{A}^{\mathcal{E}(\cdot,\cdot,\cdot),\mathcal{D}(\cdot,\cdot,\cdot,\cdot)} = 1] - \Pr[\mathcal{A}^{\mathcal{E}(\cdot,\cdot,\cdot),\perp(\cdot,\cdot,\cdot,\cdot)} = 1]$, corresponding to privacy and authenticity defined below [27]. For the sake of presentation we take this "security = privacy + authenticity" approach.

PRP Assumption. The security of $\mathrm{GCM}/2^+$ and that of GCM are based on the exactly same assumption about the underlying cipher. We assume that our underlying block cipher E is a secure Pseudo-Random Permutation (PRP) in the sense of [21]. This is the only assumption we need for proving the security of $\mathrm{GCM}/2^+$. Under this assumption we can safely replace E_K with a truly random permutation $\pi : \{0,1\}^n \to \{0,1\}^n$. It then remains to prove the security of "$\mathrm{GCM}/2^+[\pi]$" consisting of the algorithms $\mathcal{E}_\pi(IV, A, P)$ and $\mathcal{D}_\pi(IV, A, C, T)$.

Privacy Definition. We define the privacy advantage as

$$\mathrm{Adv}^{\mathrm{priv}}_{\mathrm{GCM}/2^+[\pi]}(\mathcal{A}) := \Pr_\pi[\mathcal{A}^{\mathcal{E}_\pi(\cdot,\cdot,\cdot)} = 1] - \Pr_\$[\mathcal{A}^{\$(\cdot,\cdot,\cdot)} = 1].$$

Note that the reject oracle is removed, as it is redundant.

Authenticity Definition. We define the authenticity advantage as

$$\mathrm{Adv}^{\mathrm{auth}}_{\mathrm{GCM}/2^+[\pi]}(\mathcal{A}) := \Pr_\pi[\mathcal{A}^{\mathcal{E}_\pi(\cdot,\cdot,\cdot),\mathcal{D}_\pi(\cdot,\cdot,\cdot,\cdot)} \text{ forges}],$$

where "forges" means that the oracle $\mathcal{D}_\pi(\cdot,\cdot,\cdot,\cdot)$ returns some $P \neq \perp$. We forbid $\mathcal{A}$ from making a *trivial winning* query, a query (IV, A, C, T) to the decipherment oracle $\mathcal{D}_\pi$ such that the value (C, T) is obtained through some previous query to the encipherment oracle $\mathcal{E}_\pi(IV, A, P)$. Without loss of generality we also assume that $\mathcal{A}$ does not make a *trivial losing* query, a query (IV, A, C, T') to the decipherment oracle with $T' \neq T$ after receiving $(C, T) \leftarrow \mathcal{E}_\pi(IV, A, P)$.

5   Security Proofs of $\mathrm{GCM}/2^+$

This section is devoted to proving the $\Theta(2^{n/2})$ security of $\mathrm{GCM}/2^+$. We first prove privacy and then authenticity.

Algorithm 6. Privacy Game

---

1 **Initialization:**

2   for *each* $X \in \{0,1\}^n$ do $\varphi(X) \leftarrow \{\}$ /* φ everywhere undefined */

3     $X \leftarrow 0; L \| R \xleftarrow{n/2} \varphi(X) \xleftarrow{\$} \{0,1\}^n;$ **bad** $\leftarrow 0$

4 **end**

5 **Run:** $\mathcal{A}^{\mathcal{E}(\cdot,\cdot,\cdot)}$

Privacy Proof of GCM/2$^+$. In the case of the original GCM with len(IV) = 96, the security proof for privacy can be fairly direct and clear, once the underlying block cipher E_K is replaced with a random function φ. A proof can be based on the observation that all of $C[1], C[2], \ldots, C[p], T$ are values xored with outputs of the random function $\varphi(\cdot)$ with fresh input values. The freshness is guaranteed by the fact that IV is a nonce.

Unfortunately, in the case of GCM/2$^+$, we need a bit more work even after replacing the block cipher E_K with a random function φ. The difference comes from the encrypted tag—the value T might not be "random" if its preimage is "old" due to a collision with some previous input to the function $\varphi(\cdot)$. The proof of the following theorem is based on the evaluation of such collision probabilities:

Theorem 1 (Privacy of GCM/2$^+$). *For any adversary $\mathcal{A}$ making queries to its encipherment oracle, the total length of queries being at most σ blocks, we have*

$$\mathrm{Adv}^{\mathrm{priv}}_{\mathrm{GCM}/2^+[\pi]}(\mathcal{A}) \leq \frac{7\sigma^2}{2^n},$$

where the length of a query (IV, A, P) is the length, in blocks, of the string $IV \| A \| P$.

Proof. We first replace the random permutation π with a random function $\varphi : \{0,1\}^n \to \{0,1\}^n$. By the PRP-PRF switching lemma [3], we get $\mathrm{Pr}_\pi\big[\mathcal{A}^{\mathcal{E}_\pi(\cdot,\cdot,\cdot)} = 1\big] - \mathrm{Pr}_\varphi\big[\mathcal{A}^{\mathcal{E}_\varphi(\cdot,\cdot,\cdot)} = 1\big] \leq 0.5(1 + \sigma + q)(\sigma + q)/2^n$, where q denotes the maximum number of queries made by $\mathcal{A}$. So now we are to evaluate the quantity

$$\mathrm{Pr}_\varphi\big[\mathcal{A}^{\mathcal{E}_\varphi(\cdot,\cdot,\cdot)} = 1\big] - \mathrm{Pr}_\$\big[\mathcal{A}^{\$(\cdot,\cdot,\cdot)} = 1\big]. \tag{2}$$

The rest of the privacy proof is based on game-playing techniques. See Algorithm 6 which rewrites the privacy definition in a game style. In the code, a random function φ is lazily sampled, where the symbol $\{\}$ means "undefined." Also, when two or more operations are written in a sequence within a statement, we perform them from right to left (e.g. $A \leftarrow B \leftarrow C$ is equivalent to $B \leftarrow C; A \leftarrow B$).

See Algorithm 7 which describes the encipherment oracle $\mathcal{E}_\varphi$. It can be directly and easily verified that the code without the boxed statements corresponds to

---

Algorithm 7. Simulation of $\mathcal{E}$-Oracle

---

1 **Upon** α-*th query* $\left(IV^{(\alpha)}, A^{(\alpha)}, P^{(\alpha)} \right)$ *to* $\mathcal{E}$-*oracle* **do:**

2   **if** $P^{(\alpha)} = \varepsilon$ **then** $C^{(\alpha)} \leftarrow \varepsilon$ /* begin CTR mode */

3   **else**

4         $P^{(\alpha)}[1] \| P^{(\alpha)}[2] \| \cdots \| P^{(\alpha)}[p] \stackrel{n}{\leftarrow} P^{(\alpha)}$

5   **for** $i = 1$ **to** p **do**

6             $X \leftarrow IV^{(\alpha)} \| \langle i+1 \rangle_{n/4}$; **if** $\varphi(X) \neq \{\}$ **then** $\mathbf{bad} \leftarrow 1$ $\boxed{\varphi(X) \leftarrow \{\}}$

7   **if** $\varphi(X) = \{\}$ **then** $\varphi(X) \stackrel{\$}{\leftarrow} \{0,1\}^n$

8             $C^{(\alpha)}[i] \leftarrow \mathrm{msb}_{\mathrm{len}\,(P^{(\alpha)}[i])}\!\left(\varphi(X) \right) \oplus P^{(\alpha)}[i]$

9   **end**

10         $C^{(\alpha)} \leftarrow C^{(\alpha)}[1] \| C^{(\alpha)}[2] \| \cdots \| C^{(\alpha)}[p]$

11   **end**   /* end CTR mode */

12     $V^{(\alpha)} \leftarrow \mathrm{Hash2}^{\otimes}_{L\|R}\!\left(A^{(\alpha)}, C^{(\alpha)} \right)$; $X \leftarrow IV^{(\alpha)} \| \langle 1 \rangle_{n/4}$

13   **if** $IV^{(\alpha)}$ *is new and* $\varphi(X) \neq \{\}$ **then** $\mathbf{bad} \leftarrow 1$ $\boxed{\varphi(X) \leftarrow \{\}}$

14   /* ''new'' condition for authenticity proof; same below */

15   **if** $\varphi(X) = \{\}$ **then** $\varphi(X) \stackrel{\$}{\leftarrow} \{0,1\}^n$

16     $J^{(\alpha)} \leftarrow \varphi(X)$; $X \leftarrow V^{(\alpha)} \oplus J^{(\alpha)}$

17   **if** $\left(IV^{(\alpha)}, A^{(\alpha)}, C^{(\alpha)} \right)$ *is new and* $\varphi(X) \neq \{\}$ **then** $\mathbf{bad} \leftarrow 1$ $\boxed{\varphi(X) \leftarrow \{\}}$

18   **if** $\varphi(X) = \{\}$ **then** $\varphi(X) \stackrel{\$}{\leftarrow} \{0,1\}^n$

19     $T^{(\alpha)} \leftarrow \mathrm{msb}_t\!\left(\varphi(X) \right)$; **return** $C^{(\alpha)} \| T^{(\alpha)}$

20 **end**

---

the $\mathcal{E}_\varphi(\cdot, \cdot, \cdot)$ oracle, whereas the code with the boxed statements to the $\$(\cdot, \cdot, \cdot)$ oracle. With abuse of notation we write $\mathcal{E}^{\$}_\varphi(\cdot, \cdot, \cdot)$ for the oracle simulation described in Algorithm 7 including the boxed statements. We can then write, by the fundamental lemma of game-playing [3], that

$$(2) = \Pr\!\left[\mathcal{A}^{\mathcal{E}_\varphi(\cdot,\cdot,\cdot)} = 1 \right] - \Pr\!\left[\mathcal{A}^{\mathcal{E}^{\$}_\varphi(\cdot,\cdot,\cdot)} = 1 \right] \leq \Pr\!\left[\mathcal{A}^{\mathcal{E}^{\$}_\varphi(\cdot,\cdot,\cdot)} \text{ sets } \mathbf{bad} \right].$$

Now we see that the set $\mathrm{Dom}\,\varphi$, the "domain" (the set of defined input points) of the function φ, consists of the following values:

- $X = 0$ at line 3 in Algorithm 6,
- $X = IV \| \langle i \rangle_{n/4}$ with $i \in \{1, 2, \ldots\}$, at lines 6 and 13 in Algorithm 7, and
- $X = V \oplus J$ at line 17 in Algorithm 7.

Let us first evaluate the probability that $\mathbf{bad}$ gets set at line 6 or 13. Since $IV^{(\alpha)}$ is a nonce and i is non-zero, we see that the value $X = IV^{(\alpha)} \| \langle i \rangle_{n/4}$ collides only with some previously defined $V^{(\beta)} \oplus J^{(\beta)}$ ($\beta < \alpha$). The adversary learns nothing about the values $V^{(\beta)} \oplus J^{(\beta)}$ except that they might have or might not have collided with 0 or with some previous $IV^{(\beta)} \| \langle j \rangle_{n/4}$. Therefore, the overall probability that **bad** gets set at line 6 or 13 is at most

$$\sum_{\alpha=1}^{q} \sum_{i=1}^{\ell^{(\alpha)}} \frac{\#\{V^{(\beta)} \oplus J^{(\beta)}\}_{\beta < \alpha}}{2^n - \#\operatorname{Dom} \varphi} \le \sum_{\alpha=1}^{q} \frac{\ell^{(\alpha)} \cdot (\alpha - 1)}{2^n - 2^{n-1}} \le \frac{2\sigma q - 2\sigma}{2^n}, \qquad (3)$$

where $\#$ means the cardinality of the set and $\ell^{(\alpha)}$ the length (in blocks) of the α-th query. Of course we have $\ell^{(1)} + \ell^{(2)} + \cdots + \ell^{(q)} \le \sigma$. Note that the initial denominator in (3) is not 2^n, because we shall need this strict evaluation later in the authenticity proof (the same applies below).

Next we evaluate the probability that **bad** gets set at line 17. Observe that in $\mathcal{E}_\varphi^\$ (\cdot, \cdot, \cdot)$ the value $J^{(\alpha)}$ gets always sampled at the preceding line. So the overall probability that **bad** gets set at line 17 is at most

$$\sum_{\alpha=1}^{q} \frac{\#\{0\} + \#\{IV^{(\beta)} \| \langle j \rangle_{n/4}\}_{\beta < \alpha, j \le \ell^{(\beta)}} + \#\{V^{(\beta)} \oplus J^{(\beta)}\}_{\beta < \alpha}}{2^n - \#\operatorname{Dom} \varphi}$$

$$\le \sum_{\alpha=1}^{q} \frac{1 + \left(\ell^{(1)} + \ell^{(2)} + \cdots + \ell^{(\alpha-1)}\right) + (\alpha - 1)}{2^n - 2^{n-1}} \le \frac{2\sigma q - 2\sigma + q(q+1)}{2^n}, \qquad (4)$$

from which we obtain $\operatorname{Adv}_{\operatorname{GCM}/2^+[\pi]}^{\operatorname{priv}}(\mathcal{A}) \le (\text{PRP-PRF}) + (3) + (4) \le 7\sigma^2/2^n$ using the fact $\sigma \ge q$. $\qquad \square$

Authenticity Proof of GCM/2+. In the case of the original GCM with $\operatorname{len}(IV) = 96$, the authenticity proof can be done as in the very standard argument of a Carter-Wegman MAC [31], reducing the security to the almost xor universality of polynomial hashing using an n-bit random variable. Unfortunately, this type of reduction would not work for GCM/2+; it would only yield a $\Theta(2^{n/4})$ bound.

To overcome this difficulty, we again utilize game-playing techniques. Our authenticity proof builds upon the privacy proof. The following theorem guarantees a rather unusual form of $\Theta(2^{n/2})$ security.

Theorem 2 (Authenticity of GCM/2+). *For any adversary $\mathcal{A}$ making queries to its encipherment and decipherment oracles, each query being at most ℓ blocks and the total length of queries being at most σ blocks, we have*

$$\operatorname{Adv}_{\operatorname{GCM}/2^+[\pi]}^{\operatorname{auth}}(\mathcal{A}) \le \frac{10\sigma^2}{2^n} + \frac{2\ell q_\perp}{2^{n/2}} + \frac{q_\perp}{2^t},$$

where $q_\perp$ denotes the maximum number of queries (forgery attempts) to the decipherment oracle.

Before we start to make a proof of Theorem 2, we need to show the following property of the hash function $\operatorname{Hash2}_{L \| R}^\otimes$:

Lemma 1. *Given two inputs $(A, C) \ne (A', C')$, the equality $\operatorname{Hash2}_{L \| R}^\otimes(A, C) = \operatorname{Hash2}_{L \| R}^\otimes(A', C')$ implies at least one of the following:*

Algorithm 8. Authenticity Game

---

1 **Initialization:**
2 | for *each* $X \in \{0,1\}^n$ **do** $\varphi(X) \leftarrow \{\}$ /* φ everywhere undefined */
3 | $X \leftarrow 0$; $L \| R \xleftarrow{n/2} \varphi(X) \xleftarrow{\$} \{0,1\}^n$; **bad** $\leftarrow$ **win** $\leftarrow 0$
4 **end**
5 **Run:** $\mathcal{A}^{\mathcal{E}(\cdot,\cdot,\cdot),\mathcal{D}(\cdot,\cdot,\cdot,\cdot)}$

- *A non-trivial polynomial equation in* $\mathrm{GF}(2^{n/2})[L]$,
- *Such an equation in* $\mathrm{GF}(2^{n/2})[R]$, *or*
- *An inconsistent equation of the form* (*some non-zero constant*) $= 0$.

Proof. The equality yields two equations in $\mathrm{GF}(2^{n/2})$, treating L and R as unknowns. If $\mathrm{len}(A) \neq \mathrm{len}(A')$ then we have either an equation in L or an inconsistent equation. Similarly, if $\mathrm{len}(C) \neq \mathrm{len}(C')$ then we have an equation in R or an inconsistent equation. On the other hand, if $\mathrm{len}(A) = \mathrm{len}(A')$ and $\mathrm{len}(C) = \mathrm{len}(C')$, then we must have some index i such that $A[i] \neq A'[i]$ or $C[i] \neq C'[i]$, which implies an equation in L or an equation in R.   □

Proof (of Theorem 2)
As in the privacy proof we first replace the random permutation π with a random function $\varphi : \{0,1\}^n \to \{0,1\}^n$. By the PRP-PRF switching lemma, we obtain the inequality $\Pr_\pi[\mathcal{A}^{\mathcal{E}_\pi(\cdot,\cdot,\cdot),\mathcal{D}_\pi(\cdot,\cdot,\cdot,\cdot)} \text{ forges}] \leq 0.5(\sigma + q + 1)(\sigma + q)/2^n + \Pr_\varphi[\mathcal{A}^{\mathcal{E}_\varphi(\cdot,\cdot,\cdot),\mathcal{D}_\varphi(\cdot,\cdot,\cdot,\cdot)} \text{ forges}]$.

See Algorithm 8 for the authenticity game and Algorithm 9 for the simulation of $\mathcal{D}$-oracle. We abort the game as soon as the adversary succeeds in forgery. The events at lines 4 and 9 do not necessarily imply a forgery, but for the sake of security proof we become rather generous to the adversary. Then we have $\Pr_\varphi[\mathcal{A}^{\mathcal{E}_\varphi(\cdot,\cdot,\cdot),\mathcal{D}_\varphi(\cdot,\cdot,\cdot,\cdot)} \text{ forges}] \leq \Pr[\mathcal{A}^{\mathcal{E}_\varphi(\cdot,\cdot,\cdot),\mathcal{D}_\varphi(\cdot,\cdot,\cdot,\cdot)} \text{ sets } \textbf{win}]$.

We can now modify $\mathcal{E}$-oracle in the exactly same way as before. We introduce **bad** flags and the succeeding boxed statements as in Algorithm 6. Again with abuse of notation let us write $\mathcal{E}_\varphi^\$(\cdot,\cdot,\cdot)$ to indicate the $\mathcal{E}$-oracle described in Algorithm 6 including the execution of boxed statements. Then, by the fundamental lemma of game playing, we obtain $\Pr[\mathcal{A}^{\mathcal{E}_\varphi(\cdot,\cdot,\cdot),\mathcal{D}_\varphi(\cdot,\cdot,\cdot,\cdot)} \text{ sets } \textbf{win}] \leq \Pr[\mathcal{A}^{\mathcal{E}_\varphi^\$(\cdot,\cdot,\cdot),\mathcal{D}_\varphi(\cdot,\cdot,\cdot,\cdot)} \text{ sets } \textbf{bad}] + \Pr[\mathcal{A}^{\mathcal{E}_\varphi^\$(\cdot,\cdot,\cdot),\mathcal{D}_\varphi(\cdot,\cdot,\cdot,\cdot)} \text{ sets } \textbf{win}]$. The rest of the proof is devoted to evaluating the probabilities that **bad** and **win** get set in the game $\mathcal{A}^{\mathcal{E}_\varphi^\$(\cdot,\cdot,\cdot),\mathcal{D}_\varphi(\cdot,\cdot,\cdot,\cdot)}$. We divide our analysis into the following cases:

1. **Pr[bad] at Line 6 or 13.** Identical to (3) in the privacy proof. Note that the strict evaluation of the denominator becomes necessary here.
2. **Pr[bad] at Line 17.** Consider the α-th query to the $\mathcal{E}_\varphi^\$(\cdot,\cdot,\cdot)$ oracle.
   (a) $J^{(\alpha)}$ **Gets Sampled.** Identical to (4) in the privacy proof.
   (b) $J^{(\alpha)}$ **Does Not Get Sampled.** This case means that $IV^{(\alpha)}$ is old, having been already used in some previous β-th ($\beta < \alpha$) query to $\mathcal{D}$-oracle, so that $IV^{(\alpha)} = IV^{(\beta)}$. Then $IV^{(\beta)}$ was new when the β-th query

---

Algorithm 9. Simulation of $\mathcal{D}$-Oracle

---

1 **Upon** α-*th query* $\left(IV^{(\alpha)}, A^{(\alpha)}, C^{(\alpha)}, T^{(\alpha)}\right)$ *to* $\mathcal{D}$-*oracle* **do**
        `/* α a serial number of queries to the oracles ` $\mathcal{E}$ ` and ` $\mathcal{D}$ ` */`
2     $V^{(\alpha)} \leftarrow \mathrm{Hash2}^{\otimes}_{L\|R}\left(A^{(\alpha)}, C^{(\alpha)}\right);\ X \leftarrow IV^{(\alpha)} \| \langle 1 \rangle_{n/4}$
3   **if** $IV^{(\alpha)}$ *is new and* $\varphi(X) \neq \{\}$ **then**
4 | **win** $\leftarrow 1$; **Abort**   `/* let adversary win */`
5   **end**
6   **if** $\varphi(X) = \{\}$ **then** $\varphi(X) \xleftarrow{\$} \{0,1\}^n$
7     $J^{(\alpha)} \leftarrow \varphi(X);\ X \leftarrow V^{(\alpha)} \oplus J^{(\alpha)}$
8   **if** $\varphi(X) \neq \{\}$ **then**
9 | **win** $\leftarrow 1$; **Abort**   `/* let adversary win */`
10   **else** $\varphi(X) \xleftarrow{\$} \{0,1\}^n$
11     $T^{(\alpha)}_* \leftarrow \mathrm{msb}_t\left(\varphi(X)\right)$
12   **if** $T^{(\alpha)} = T^{(\alpha)}_*$ **then**   `/* successful forgery */`
13 | **win** $\leftarrow 1$; **Abort**   `/* CTR mode removed */`
14   **else return** $\perp$
15 **end**

---

was made to $\mathcal{D}$-oracle. Since the adversary has not won the game at the α-th query to $\mathcal{E}$-oracle, the value $J^{(\beta)}$ must have been sampled at the β-th query.

  i. $\boldsymbol{V^{(\alpha)} \oplus J^{(\alpha)} \neq V^{(\beta)} \oplus J^{(\beta)}}$. This implies that the value $V^{(\alpha)} \oplus J^{(\alpha)}$ collides with some already-defined domain point whose value has nothing to do with the random value $J^{(\alpha)} = J^{(\beta)}$. Hence, the probability of this event can be bounded in the same way as (4). Here we rely on the strict evaluation of the denominator in (4).

  ii. $\boldsymbol{V^{(\alpha)} \oplus J^{(\alpha)} = V^{(\beta)} \oplus J^{(\beta)}}$. The equality implies $V^{(\alpha)} = V^{(\beta)}$. Since $\left(IV^{(\alpha)}, A^{(\alpha)}, C^{(\alpha)}\right)$ is new and $IV^{(\alpha)} = IV^{(\beta)}$, we must have $\left(A^{(\alpha)}, C^{(\alpha)}\right) \neq \left(A^{(\beta)}, C^{(\beta)}\right)$. We can then use Lemma 1. The probability of this event is at most $\ell / \left(2^{n/2} - \ell q_\perp\right)$, as the equation in L (or in R) has a degree at most ℓ.

3. **Pr[win] at Line 4.** Included in case 1.
4. **Pr[win] at Line 9.** Consider the α-th query to the $\mathcal{D}(\cdot, \cdot, \cdot, \cdot)$ oracle.

  (a) $\boldsymbol{J^{(\alpha)}}$ **Gets Sampled.** Included in case 2a.

  (b) $\boldsymbol{J^{(\alpha)}}$ **Does Not Get Sampled.** This case means that $IV^{(\alpha)}$ is old, having been already used in some previous β-th ($\beta < \alpha$) query to the oracle $\mathcal{E}^{\$}_\varphi(\cdot, \cdot, \cdot)$, so that $IV^{(\alpha)} = IV^{(\beta)}$. Then $IV^{(\beta)}$ was new when the β-th query was made, so the value $J^{(\beta)}$ must have been sampled at the β-th query.

    i. $\boldsymbol{V^{(\alpha)} \oplus J^{(\alpha)} \neq V^{(\beta)} \oplus J^{(\beta)}}$. Similar to case 2(b)i.

    ii. $\boldsymbol{V^{(\alpha)} \oplus J^{(\alpha)} = V^{(\beta)} \oplus J^{(\beta)}}$. Since we exclude trivial winning and losing queries, we must have $\left(A^{(\alpha)}, C^{(\alpha)}\right) \neq \left(A^{(\beta)}, C^{(\beta)}\right)$. The rest is similar to case 2(b)ii.

5. **Pr[win] at Line 13.** Since the adversary has not won the game, the point $V^{(\alpha)} \oplus J^{(\alpha)}$ was undefined, and the value $\varphi(V^{(\alpha)} \oplus J^{(\alpha)})$ has just been sampled at the preceding line. So the probability that $T = T^{(\alpha)}$ holds is at most $1/2^t$.

Using the fact $\sigma \geq q$, we can sum up the probabilities as

$$\mathrm{Adv}^{\mathrm{auth}}_{\mathrm{GCM}/2^+[\pi]}(\mathcal{A}) \leq (\mathrm{PRP\text{-}PRF}) + (3) + (4) + (4) + \sum_{\alpha=1}^{q_\perp} \frac{\ell}{2^{n/2} - \ell q_\perp} + \sum_{\alpha=1}^{q_\perp} \frac{1}{2^t}$$

$$\leq \frac{10\sigma^2}{2^n} + \frac{2\ell q_\perp}{2^{n/2}} + \frac{q_\perp}{2^t},$$

as desired. $\square$

6   Software Implementation of GCM/2$^+$-AES-128

We explain our benchmark trials. We describe the configuration of our experiments and also the methods that we use for boosting our implementation.

Configuration for Benchmark. Detailed information concerning our experiments are as follows:

- **CPU.** Westmere, which is a shrunk version of the Nehalem core, is the first generation CPU that is equipped with the new AES instruction set (AES-NI). The current Sandy Bridge is the second generation. Westmere and Sandy Bridge are also equipped with the carry-less multiplication instruction set, CLMUL. Our Westmere and Sandy Bridge CPUs are Intel E5-606 (2.13GHz) and Xeon E3-1225 (3.10GHz), respectively. These CPUs are not equipped with the Hyper-Threading Technology. We turn off both the Turbo Boost Technology and the Enhanced Intel SpeedStep Technology.
- **OS.** We run FreeBSD/amd64 9.1-RELEASE on the Sandy Bridge processor as an operating system.
- **Language.** Our implementation is written in the C language with intrinsic functions such as _mm_clmulepi64_si128. Our source code is optimized for Sandy Bridge but can be also executed on Westmere. We use ports/lang/gcc46 (gcc 4.6.4 20121123) as our compiler with the options "-O3 -funroll-loops -maes -mpclmul -mavx" for Sandy Bridge. For Westmere we change the last option to "-msse4."
- **Data.** We implement GCM/2$^+$ only for the case of null associated data (i.e. $A = \varepsilon$). The functions in our implementation require (1) a pointer to the ciphertext, (2) a pointer to the plaintext, (3) key-dependent constants and (4) the length, in bytes, of the plaintext. The pointers to data are assumed to be aligned along the 4KB boundary, and the length of the plaintext is assumed to be a multiple of 8 blocks (128 bytes).

- **Measurement.** We measure the clock cycles by the standard sequence of `cpuid`, `rdtsc`, `/* call the function to be measured */`, `rdtscp`. We include the overhead of function calls into the clock cycles but exclude the overhead of the timing-measurement code from the obtained cycles. We choose the minimum number of clock cycles from 2^{16} trials. We do this for making the clock cycles stable, avoiding machine interrupts, cache misses, branch mispredictions and other lags.
- **OpenSSL.** We also pick numbers generated by OpenSSL 1.0.1c, which is built on `ports/security/openssl` in our configuration. We use the speed measurement code in the command line interface of OpenSSL as "`openssl speed -evp aes-128-{ctr,gcm}`" and convert the numbers to the unit of cycles per byte. The command "`openssl speed`" averages the performance in three seconds. Thus the figures in Table 2 are measured by different methodologies, and we should be careful with the numbers when comparing small decimals.

Boosting the Software Performance. Our implementation is faster than theoretically expected. As we have discussed in Sect. 1, GCM/2^+ is expected to run in $\mathbf{time}(\text{CTR}) + 2/3 \cdot \mathbf{time}(\text{Hash}^{\odot})$. Let us focus on the Sandy Bridge numbers in Table 2. For OpenSSL 1.0.1c, $\mathbf{time}(\text{CTR})$ and $\mathbf{time}(\text{Hash}^{\odot})$ are 0.916 and 1.982 ($= 2.898 - 0.916$) cycles per byte, respectively. Then GCM/2^+ is expected to run at about 2.237 ($= 0.916 + 2/3 \cdot 1.982$) cycles per byte. However, our implementation runs at 1.777 cycles per byte, which is much faster. In the following we explain what methods are used in our implementation for increasing the speed. Several methods are already discussed in the Intel white paper [14].

- **AES-NI Pipeline Optimization.** We unroll the innermost loop eight times, because the latency and the throughput of the AES-round instruction are 8 and 1 clock cycles, respectively, on a Sandy Bridge. The latency and the throughput of PCLMULQDQ are 14 and 8 clock cycles, respectively, on a Sandy Bridge, which mean that eight times should be sufficient.
- **Counter-Mode Caching.** We employ the counter-mode caching, which can be found in, for example, [4, §3.4]. We also reduce the critical path using the technique described in [20, Fig.4]. In our source code we do not do function stitching [13], as we expect our compiler to do an adequate job, since the CTR mode part in our mode is well optimized and there is very small room to speed the implementation up.
- **Polynomial Hashing.** We precompute $(L\|R)^{\otimes j}$ for $j = 1, 2, \ldots, 8$ and perform the multiplications in $\bigoplus_{j=0}^{7} C[8i + j + 1] \otimes (L\|R)^{\otimes(7-j)}$ in parallel. We then apply "lazy reduction."
  1. **Polynomial Multiplication in GF(2)[u].** On a Sandy Bridge or Westmere CPU, this step can be realized via the CLMUL instruction. PCLMULQDQ multiplies a 64-bit by a 64-bit and produces a 128-bit result. Hence, the polynomial multiplication in GF(2)[u] (for that in GF(2^{64})) is implemented in a straightforward way.

Algorithm 10. Reduction $B^H \cdot u^{64} \oplus B^L \bmod f(u)$ Using Table Lookup

---

1 $X_0 \leftarrow B^H \oplus (B^H)^{\ll 1}$
2 $X_1 \leftarrow X_0 \oplus X_0^{\ll 3}$
3 $X_2 \leftarrow X_1 \oplus \mathrm{err}\big((B^H)^{\gg 60}\big)$
4 **return** $X_2 \oplus B^L$

---

2. **Reduction Modulo $f(u)$.** This step requires several shifts and xors.
   We optimize the computation of this step.
   (a) **Initial Reduction.** Recall that we use the reduction polynomial
       $f(u) = u^{64} \oplus u^4 \oplus u^3 \oplus u \oplus 1$. Let $B^H(u) \cdot u^{64} \oplus B^L(u)$ be a multiplication
       result, where $\deg B^H$, $\deg B^L < 64$. Applying $u^{64} \equiv u^4 \oplus u^3 \oplus u \oplus$
       $1 \bmod f(u)$, we get $B^H(u) \cdot u^{64} \oplus B^L(u) \equiv (u^4 \oplus u^3 \oplus u \oplus 1) \cdot B^H(u) \oplus$
       $B^L(u) \bmod f(u)$. Unfortunately, $\deg\big((u^4 \oplus u^3 \oplus u \oplus 1) \cdot B^H(u)\big)$ may
       still exceed 63, in which case we need further reduction.
   (b) **Remaining in XMM Registers.** Dealing with the excess part is
       one of the most costly operations. We can do this either in general-
       purpose registers or in XMM. We do this on the latter, because only
       XMM registers can be used with CLMUL and AES instruction sets.
       Note that remaining in XMM registers will impose limitations on the
       usage of shift instructions.
   (c) **Further Reduction Using Table Lookup.** Observe that $B^H(u) \cdot$
       $u^{64} \bmod f(u)$ can be written as $B^H \oplus (B^H)^{\ll 1} \oplus (B^H)^{\ll 3} \oplus (B^H)^{\ll 4} \oplus$
       $\mathrm{err}(B^H_{63} \| B^H_{62} \| B^H_{61} \| B^H_{60})$, where $X^{\ll i}$ is the i-bit left shift of X ($=$
       $X \cdot u^i \bmod u^{64}$) and err is the function for "error" terms. The first
       terms $B^H \oplus (B^H)^{\ll 1} \oplus (B^H)^{\ll 3} \oplus (B^H)^{\ll 4} = (B^H \oplus (B^H)^{\ll 1}) \oplus (B^H \oplus$
       $(B^H)^{\ll 1})^{\ll 3}$ can be efficiently computed. The problem is to compute
       $\mathrm{err}(B^H_{63} \| B^H_{62} \| B^H_{61} \| B^H_{60})$. Notice that B^H_{63} must be always 0, since B^H
       was the upper-half of a multiplication result. We can then precom-
       pute a table for $\mathrm{err}(0 \| B^H_{62} \| B^H_{61} \| B^H_{60})$ in advance without knowing the
       plaintext or the key. Such a precomputed table consists of only 2^3
       elements. Even if we implement two reductions in parallel for 128-bit
       data, the size of the table is only 2^6. Algorithm 10 describes this re-
       duction method, where $X^{\gg i}$ is the i-bit right shift of X. Note that
       $(B^H)^{\ll 1}$ can be realized via addition to itself ($B^H + B^H \in \mathbb{Z}/2^{64}\mathbb{Z}$).
       Also note that we can run SIMD operations for handling two 64-bit
       words in an XMM register.

7   Remarks

We briefly comment on the hardware performance of GCM/2$^+$. We also comment
on the weak keys of the polynomial hash in the ring $\mathrm{GF}\big(2^{n/2}\big) \times \mathrm{GF}\big(2^{n/2}\big)$. Given
the recent study by Saarinen [28], we mention another version of GCM/2$^+$ using
a Sophie-Germain prime number. Finally, we devise another reduction method
modulo $f(u)$.

Hardware Consideration. Sato et al. [30] showed that the hardware implementation of GCM can yield "very high" throughput, supporting the theoretical analysis of pipelined GCM-AES-128 by McGrew and Viega [21, §3.1]. Let us analyze how the changes for GCM/2^+ would affect its hardware performance.

The multiplication in $\mathrm{GF}(2^{n/2}) \times \mathrm{GF}(2^{n/2})$ can be realized in hardware as efficiently as, if not more efficiently than, the multiplication in $\mathrm{GF}(2^n)$. The omission of the final multiplication in GCM/2^+ may also contribute to performance improvement. On the other hand, the extra block-cipher encryption (to produce the authentication tag) in GCM/2^+ causes a pipeline stall, as McGrew and Viega pointed out for CWC and for OCB [21].

Weak Keys in $\mathrm{GF}(2^{n/2}) \times \mathrm{GF}(2^{n/2})$. We explain the class of "weak" keys (in the sense of [29]) of the polynomial hash in $\mathrm{GF}(2^{n/2}) \times \mathrm{GF}(2^{n/2})$. The bottom line is that the scale is roughly comparable to the weak keys of the usual polynomial hash in the binary field $\mathrm{GF}(2^{n/2})$.

Suppose we have $L = 0$. Then the hash key $L\|R$ is a weak key in $\mathrm{GF}(2^{n/2}) \times \mathrm{GF}(2^{n/2})$ irrespective of the value R. So there are $2^{n/2}$-many weak keys of this type. Moreover, considering the cycling attack [29], we know more weak keys, since some non-zero L can also be weak. Nonetheless, this observation does not violate our security proofs, as the total number of keys is 2^n. To be more precise, we can compute the expected cycle length of a key in our polynomial hash to be $2^{63.8}$, whereas that in the usual polynomial hash in $\mathrm{GF}(2^{64})$ is $2^{63.3}$ and that in $\mathrm{GF}(2^{128})$ is $2^{127.3}$. However, a long message should not be used for GCM/2^+, and a message of 2^{64} blocks generates a trivial forgery attack, but such a long message violates the security proof for authenticity.

When $n = 128$ we could use, for example, a Sophie-Germain prime number $p = 2^{64} + 3103$ and hash in the ring $\mathbb{Z}/p\mathbb{Z} \times \mathbb{Z}/p\mathbb{Z}$, following [28]. The use of $p = 2^{64} + 3103$ would diminish the majority of weak keys, possibly at the cost of small terms related to "3103." Note that this would not improve our authenticity bound, because generic attacks (without exploiting the weak keys) would break GCM/2^+ at the complexity of the bound.

Algorithm 11. Constant-Time Reduction $B^\mathrm{H} \cdot u^{64} \oplus B^\mathrm{L} \bmod f(u)$

---

1 $X_0 \leftarrow (B^\mathrm{H})^{\gg 60}$

2 $X_1 \leftarrow B^\mathrm{H} \oplus X_0$

3 $X_2 \leftarrow B^\mathrm{H} \oplus X_1^{\ll 1} \oplus (B^\mathrm{H})^{\gg 61} \oplus (X_0 \& 1)$

4 $X_3 \leftarrow B^\mathrm{L} \oplus X_2 \oplus X_2^{\ll 3}$

5 **return** X_3

Constant-Time Reduction Method. This method is slower but does not require a precomputed table. Notice that $\mathrm{err}(0\|B_{62}^\mathrm{H}\|B_{61}^\mathrm{H}\|B_{60}^\mathrm{H})$ can be written as $B_{62}^\mathrm{H} \cdot u^6 \oplus B_{61}^\mathrm{H} \cdot u^5 \oplus (B_{60}^\mathrm{H} \oplus B_{62}^\mathrm{H}) \cdot u^4 \oplus (B_{60}^\mathrm{H} \oplus B_{61}^\mathrm{H} \oplus B_{62}^\mathrm{H}) \cdot u^3 \oplus B_{61}^\mathrm{H} \cdot u^2 \oplus (B_{60}^\mathrm{H} \oplus B_{62}^\mathrm{H}) \cdot u \oplus (B_{60}^\mathrm{H} \oplus B_{61}^\mathrm{H}) = D \cdot u^3 \oplus D$, where $D = B_{62}^\mathrm{H} \cdot u^3 \oplus B_{61}^\mathrm{H} \cdot u^2 \oplus (B_{60}^\mathrm{H} \oplus B_{62}^\mathrm{H}) \cdot u \oplus (B_{60}^\mathrm{H} \oplus B_{61}^\mathrm{H})$. Thus, the reduction $B^\mathrm{H} \cdot u^{64} \oplus B^\mathrm{L} \bmod f(u)$ can be computed as in Algorithm 11.

Acknowledgements. We thank the anonymous reviewers for their constructive comments.

References

1. 3GPP: Specification of the 3GPP Confidentiality and Integrity Algorithms UEA2 & UIA2 (2009), http://www.gsma.com/technicalprojects/fraud-security/security-algorithms/
2. ANSI: Fibre Channel Security Protocols (FC-SP) rev 1.74. INCITS working draft proposed (2006)
3. Bellare, M., Rogaway, P.: The security of triple encryption and a framework for code-based game-playing proofs. In: Vaudenay, S. (ed.) EUROCRYPT 2006. LNCS, vol. 4004, pp. 409–426. Springer, Heidelberg (2006)
4. Bernstein, D.J., Schwabe, P.: New AES software speed records. In: Chowdhury, D.R., Rijmen, V., Das, A. (eds.) INDOCRYPT 2008. LNCS, vol. 5365, pp. 322–336. Springer, Heidelberg (2008)
5. Ferguson, N.: Authentication weaknesses in GCM. Comments Submitted to NIST Modes of Operation (2005)
6. Gueron, S.: Software optimizations for cryptographic primitives on general purpose x86_64 platforms. In: Bernstein, D.J., Chatterjee, S. (eds.) INDOCRYPT 2011. LNCS, vol. 7107, pp. 399–400. Springer, Heidelberg (2011)
7. IEEE MAC Security Task Group: 802.1ae—Media Access Control (MAC) security draft 5.1. IEEE Standards Association (2006)
8. IEEE Security in Storage Working Group: P1619.1 Authenticated encryption. IEEE Standards Association (2007)
9. IETF: The use of Galois/Counter Mode (GCM) in IPsec Encapsulating Security Payload (ESP). RFC 4106 (2005)
10. IETF: The use of Galois Message Authentication Code (GMAC). RFC 4543 (2006)
11. IETF: AES Galois Counter Mode (GCM) cipher suites for TLS. RFC 5288 (2008)
12. IETF: AES Galois Counter Mode for the Secure Shell Transport Layer Protocol. RFC 5647 (2009)
13. Intel Corporation: Fast Cryptographic Computation on Intel Architecture Processors Via Function Stitching (2010)
14. Intel Corporation: Intel Carry-Less Multiplication Instruction and its Usage for Computing the GCM Mode — Rev 2 (2010)
15. Iwata, T., Ohashi, K., Minematsu, K.: Breaking and repairing GCM security proofs. In: Safavi-Naini, R., Canetti, R. (eds.) CRYPTO 2012. LNCS, vol. 7417, pp. 31–49. Springer, Heidelberg (2012)
16. JTC 1: Information Technology—Security Techniques—Authenticated Encryption. ISO/IEC 19772 (2009)
17. Karatsuba, A.A., Ofman, Y.P.: Multiplication of many-digital numbers by automatic computers. Proceedings of the USSR Academy of Sciences 145, 293–294 (1962)
18. Kohno, T., Viega, J., Whiting, D.: CWC: A high-performance conventional authenticated encryption mode. Cryptology ePrint Archive: Report 2003/106 (2003)
19. Krovetz, T., Rogaway, P.: The software performance of authenticated-encryption modes. In: Joux, A. (ed.) FSE 2011. LNCS, vol. 6733, pp. 306–327. Springer, Heidelberg (2011)

20. Manley, R., Gregg, D.: A program generator for Intel AES-NI instructions. In: Gong, G., Gupta, K.C. (eds.) INDOCRYPT 2010. LNCS, vol. 6498, pp. 311–327. Springer, Heidelberg (2010)

21. McGrew, D.A., Viega, J.: The security and performance of the Galois/Counter Mode (GCM) of operation. In: Canteaut, A., Viswanathan, K. (eds.) INDOCRYPT 2004. LNCS, vol. 3348, pp. 343–355. Springer, Heidelberg (2004)

22. Meloni, N., Nègre, C., Hasan, M.A.: High performance GHASH and impacts of a class of unconventional bases. J. Cryptographic Engineering 1(3), 201–218 (2011)

23. NIST: Advanced Encryption Standard (AES). FIPS Publication 197 (2001)

24. NIST: Recommendation for block cipher modes of operation: Galois/Counter Mode (GCM) for confidentiality and authentication. Special Publication 800-38D (2007)

25. Rogaway, P.: Authenticated-encryption with associated-data. In: ACM CCS 2002, pp. 98–107. ACM Press (2002)

26. Rogaway, P., Bellare, M., Black, J., Krovetz, T.: OCB: A block-cipher mode of operation for efficient authenticated encryption. In: Reiter, M.K., Samarati, P. (eds.) ACM CCS 2001, pp. 196–205. ACM (2001)

27. Rogaway, P., Shrimpton, T.: A provable-security treatment of the key-wrap problem. In: Vaudenay, S. (ed.) EUROCRYPT 2006. LNCS, vol. 4004, pp. 373–390. Springer, Heidelberg (2006)

28. Saarinen, M.-J.O.: SGCM: The Sophie Germain counter mode. Cryptology ePrint Archive: Report 2011/326 (2011)

29. Saarinen, M.-J.O.: Cycling attacks on GCM, GHASH and other polynomial MACs and hashes. In: Canteaut, A. (ed.) FSE 2012. LNCS, vol. 7549, pp. 216–225. Springer, Heidelberg (2012)

30. Satoh, A., Sugawara, T., Aoki, T.: High-speed pipelined hardware architecture for Galois counter mode. In: Garay, J.A., Lenstra, A.K., Mambo, M., Peralta, R. (eds.) ISC 2007. LNCS, vol. 4779, pp. 118–129. Springer, Heidelberg (2007)

31. Wegman, M.N., Carter, L.: New hash functions and their use in authentication and set equality. J. Comput. Syst. Sci. 22(3), 265–279 (1981)

Estimating Resistance
against Multidimensional Linear Attacks:
An Application on DEAN

Risto M. Hakala, Atle Kivelä, and Kaisa Nyberg

Department of Information and Computer Science,
Aalto University,
P.O. Box 15400, FI-00076 Aalto, Finland
{risto.m.hakala,atle.kivela,kaisa.nyberg}@aalto.fi

Abstract. In this paper, we investigate an algorithm which can be used to compute improved estimates of squared correlations of linear approximations over key-alternating block ciphers. The algorithm was previously used by Cho [5] to compute estimates of expected squared correlations and capacities of multidimensional linear approximations of PRESENT. The goal of this paper is to investigate the applicability and usefulness of this algorithm for a nonbinary AES-like symmetric key-alternating block cipher DEAN designed by Baignères et al. [2] who estimated that the best LLR-based distinguisher will require the full code book of about 2^{60} known plaintext blocks to succeed over four rounds of DEAN. We give evidence that there is an LLR-based multidimensional linear distinguisher with estimated data complexity 2^{50} over six rounds of DEAN. Turning this to a (partial) key-recovery attack over the full eight-round DEAN is likely to succeed.

Keywords: distinguishing attack, linear cryptanalysis, symmetric-key cipher, SPN network, cipher on general group.

1 Introduction

Linear cryptanalysis is one of the most important cryptanalytic methods for symmetric key ciphers. Estimates of data complexities of linear attacks against iterated block ciphers are based on estimates of squared correlations of linear approximations involved in the attack. The estimate used by Matsui [13] is obtained by computing an upper bound to the squares of all averaged trail correlations using the Piling-up lemma. Given the maximum round correlations, this estimate is easy to compute just by multiplication of the maximum correlations from each round and still widely used when making statements about ciphers' resistance against linear cryptanalysis. Subsequently, Nyberg [15] proposed to compute instead the squared correlations first and then take the average over the keys. This so called linear hull estimate leads to more accurate predictions about ciphers' strength against linear cryptanalysis, in particular, for ciphers where linear approximations with nonzero correlations over one round are numerous but the

M. Kutyłowski and M. Yung (Eds.): Inscrypt 2012, LNCS 7763, pp. 246–262, 2013.

correlations are small in absolute value. The SPN block cipher PRESENT [4] is a good example of this phenomenon as demonstrated by Nakahara et al. [14, see Fig. 2] and later by Cho [5].

Computation of the linear hull estimate of squared correlation is in general a difficult problem. In theory, one can apply the idea of correlation matrices proposed by Daemen et al. [7], but instead, use matrices of squared correlations. An application of this approach was shown for DES in Theorem 2 of [15]. Unfortunately, it is not practical to compute on full (squared) correlation matrices, since the number of rows and columns is equal to the elements in the round data space. Therefore, different heuristics must be used to reduce the sizes of the matrices. In the case of PRESENT, accurate reductions can be achieved by restricting to matrices with nonzero values assigned only on elements that correspond to (squared) correlation of linear approximations with single-bit input and output masks. In his multidimensional linear attack on PRESENT, Cho [5] devised an iterative algorithm to compute products of matrices of squared correlations with nonzero values occurring only for single-bit masks of only nine out of sixteen S-boxes at each round. More complete and accurate estimates of squared correlations of single-bit approximations were obtained for PRESENT by Leander [9]. Since the absolute values of all nonzero correlations of single-bit trails are equal, it suffices to count the number of all such single-bit linear approximations. This method of Leander is equivalent to using matrices of squared correlations of all single-bit round approximations.

The goal of this paper is to apply the idea of squared correlation matrices to a very different cipher than PRESENT and investigate what kind of heuristics can be used to reduce the size of the correlation matrices and computational workload while still achieving useful estimates of the data complexity of linear attacks. We chose the cipher DEAN, which is an AES-like nonbinary cipher proposed by Baignères et al. [2]. In spite of significant differences, DEAN shares with PRESENT the property that the absolute values of correlations of one-round linear approximations are small and there is a large number of approximations with nonzero correlation, but an essential difference is due to the correlations taking on largely varying values. According to preliminary estimates using the Piling-up lemma, the designers claim that eight rounds should be sufficient for DEAN to resist linear attacks. No specific key schedule was designed for DEAN. In this paper, we give evidence that there is an LLR-based linear distinguisher with estimated data complexity 2^{50} over six rounds of DEAN. Turning this to a (partial) key-recovery attack over the full eight rounds of DEAN is very likely to succeed, whatever the key schedule might be.

The contributions of the paper can be summed up as follows:

- We use the general approach of computing iteratively products of squared correlation matrices, and we apply it for computing average squared correlations and capacities of distributions related to multidimensional linear cryptanalysis.
- Since also non-Boolean functions and operations has been used on the diffusion and key-addition layer in symmetric ciphers, e.g., in SAFER [11,12] and

DEAN [2], we extend this approach so that it can be applied in the general setting when non-Boolean approximations are used.

– We suggest heuristics for the block cipher DEAN to make the computation of squared absolute correlations feasible while still obtain relevant information.
– The smallest multidimensional approximations over DEAN have either too large memory requirement or too large data complexity to allow testing in practice. Therefore we design a reduced version of DEAN and test the algorithm on it.
– We show that in case of DEAN, the data complexity estimate based on the squared average correlations and computed using the Piling-up lemma does not give relevant security guarantees against advanced linear attacks that make use of the linear hull effect and multidimensional extensions of linear attacks.

We will start in Sect. 2 by presenting the generalized notions of nonlinearity defined using a Fourier transform on arbitrary finite groups. Then in Sect. 3 linear cryptanalysis will be described in the setting of a general group. Then we present the algorithm for computing the expected capacity in Sect. 4. The LLR and χ^2 statistics of distinguishing distributions and their data complexities are discussed in Sect. 5. After a brief description of DEAN in Sect. 6, its linear approximations are investigated in Sect. 7. Our results for DEAN are given in Sect. 8 and in Sect. 9 we present some experimental results derived using a modified DEAN. We conclude the paper in Sect. 10.

2   Preliminaries

2.1   Basic Definitions

Let A be a finite Abelian group written additively. A character χ of A is a homomorphism from A into the multiplicative group of complex numbers of absolute value one. A trivial character τ is defined as $\tau(x) = 1$ for all $x \in A$. For every character χ of A, there is a conjugate character $\overline{\chi}$ defined by $\overline{\chi}(x) = \overline{\chi(x)}$ for all $x \in A$, where the bar denotes complex conjugation. It follows that $\overline{\chi}(x) = \chi(-x)$ for all $x \in A$.

Let q be a positive integer. We use $\mathbb{Z}_q$ to denote the ring of integers modulo q. For a real number z, we denote $e(z) = \exp(2\pi i z)$ and $e_q(z) = e(z/q)$. The functions χ_a, $a = 0, \ldots, q-1$, defined by

$$\chi_a(x) = e_q(ax) \quad \text{for all } x \in \mathbb{Z}_q,$$

form the set of characters of the additive group $\mathbb{Z}_q$, see [10]. More generally, given, in addition, a positive integer n, the functions

$$\chi_a = \prod_{i=1}^{n} \chi_{a_i},$$

where $a = (a_1, \ldots, a_n) \in \mathbb{Z}_q^n$ and each χ_{a_i}, $i = 1, \ldots, n$, is a character of $\mathbb{Z}_q$, form the group of characters on the additive group $\mathbb{Z}_q^n$. For $q = 2$, we get the characters

$$\chi_a(x) = (-1)^{a_1 x_1 + \cdots + a_n x_n}, \quad x = (x_1, \ldots, x_n) \in \mathbb{Z}_2^n, \, a = (a_1, \ldots, a_n) \in \mathbb{Z}_2^n,$$

which are used in linear cryptanalysis of binary ciphers.

2.2   Fourier Transform and Correlation

Nonlinearity of functions over finite Abelian groups is usually measured using their Fourier transform. To recall the definitions of these notions, we follow the conventions used in [2,8]. Let A be a finite Abelian group and ϕ be a complex-valued function on A and χ a character on A. The Fourier transform of ϕ with respect to χ is defined as

$$\hat{\phi}(\chi) = \sum_{\eta \in A} \phi(\eta) \overline{\chi}(\eta).$$

Now let f be a function from a finite Abelian group A to another finite Abelian group B, and let χ and ψ be characters on A and B, respectively. The Fourier transform of f with respect to χ and ψ is defined as

$$\hat{f}(\psi, \chi) = \sum_{\eta \in A} (\psi \circ f)(\eta) \overline{\chi}(\eta),$$

where $(\psi \circ f)(\eta)$ denotes the composition $\psi(f(\eta))$.

Let $\hat{f}(\psi, \chi)$ be a Fourier transform defined as above. The pair (ψ, χ) is called the linear approximation of f, where χ the input character and ψ the output character. The complex number

$$\frac{1}{|A|} \hat{f}(\psi, \chi)$$

is called the correlation (or bias) of the linear approximation (ψ, χ) and denoted by $c(\psi \circ f, \chi)$. If χ is the trivial character τ, we will simply use $c_f(\psi)$ to denote the correlation $c(\psi \circ f, \tau)$.

Let us denote by $p_f(\eta)$ the probability $\Pr(f(x) = \eta)$ taken over the uniform distribution of x over A. The sequence $\{p_f(\eta) \, | \, \eta \in B\}$ is called the distribution of f and is denoted by p_f. It follows that

$$c_f(\psi) = \frac{1}{|A|} \sum_{x \in A} (\psi \circ f)(x) = \sum_{\eta \in B} p_f(\eta)\psi(\eta) = \widehat{p_f}(\overline{\psi}).$$

Parseval's theorem then yields the identity

$$\sum_{\psi} |c_f(\psi)|^2 = |B| \sum_{\eta \in B} p_f(\eta)^2. \tag{1}$$

2.3 Capacity

Let p be a probability distribution with support B. Nonuniformity of p is measured using the capacity $C(p)$ defined as

$$C(p) = |B| \sum_{\eta \in B} \left(p(\eta) - \frac{1}{|B|} \right)^2.$$

Let $f \colon A \to B$ be a function with probability distribution p_f. In our analysis we are interested in the nonuniformity of p_f. The following theorem describes how the capacity of p_f, also called the capacity of f and denoted by $C(f)$, can be computed if the correlations $c_f(\psi)$ are known for all nontrivial characters ψ of B. The corresponding theorem for Boolean functions is given in [1].

Theorem 1. *Let f be defined as before. Then*

$$C(f) = \sum_{\psi \neq \tau} |c_f(\psi)|^2. \tag{2}$$

Proof. We get from the definition of $C(f)$ that

$$C(f) = |B| \sum_{\eta \in B} \left(p_f(\eta)^2 - 2p_f(\eta)\frac{1}{|B|} + \frac{1}{|B|^2} \right) = |B| \sum_{\eta \in B} p_f(\eta)^2 - 1.$$

The theorem follows from (1), when we observe that $c_f(\psi) = 1$ for the trivial character $\psi = \tau$.   □

3   Linear Approximation of a Block Cipher

Let A be a finite Abelian group written additively. The encryption function $\mathcal{E}_K$ of an R-round iterated key-alternating block cipher on A is specified by a sequence of round functions $g_1, \ldots, g_R$ on A and a key $K = (K_1, \ldots, K_R) \in A^R$ such that the encryption $\mathcal{E}_K(x)$ of plaintext $x \in A$ is computed as

$$x_0 = x,$$
$$x_r = g_r(x_{r-1} + K_r) \quad \text{for } r = 1, \ldots, R,$$
$$\mathcal{E}_K(x) = x_R.$$

We denote by G_{K_r} the round function such that $G_{K_r}(x) = g_r(x + K_r)$. Given a linear approximation (χ_r, χ_{r-1}) of G_{K_r}, its correlation is equal to

$$c(\chi_r \circ G_{K_r}, \chi_{r-1}) = \frac{1}{|A|} \sum_{x \in A} \chi_r(g_r(x + K_r))\overline{\chi}_{r-1}(x) = \chi_{r-1}(K_r)c(\chi_r \circ g_r, \chi_{r-1}).$$

Let $K \in A^R$ and let (ψ, χ) be a linear approximation of $\mathcal{E}_K$. As it is the composition of the round functions, its correlation can be given using the following formula

$$c(\psi \circ \mathcal{E}_K, \chi) = \sum_{\chi_1, \ldots, \chi_{R-1}} \prod_{r=1}^{R} \chi_{r-1}(K_r)c(\chi_r \circ g_r, \chi_{r-1}),$$

where $\chi_0 = \chi$ and $\chi_R = \psi$. The proof of this result is a straightforward gener-alization of the same result in the binary case, see [6] or [16].

As frequently observed for modern block ciphers the correlation may vary a lot with the key. Therefore, to measure the strength of a linear approximation, the expected squared absolute value of the correlation is frequently used. The proof of the following theorem is also a generalization of the proof in binary case, see [15]. An alternative proof using the Markov property is given in [2].

Theorem 2. *Let* $g_1, \ldots, g_R$ *be the round functions of an* R-*round key-alternat-ing iterated block cipher* $\mathcal{E}_K$ *on a finite Abelian group* A *with the key* $K = (K_1, \ldots, K_R)$. *If* K *is drawn from the uniform distribution on* A^R, *then*

$$\mathrm{E}_K(|c(\psi \circ \mathcal{E}_K, \chi)|^2) = \sum_{\chi_1, \ldots, \chi_{R-1}} \prod_{r=1}^{R} |c(\chi_r \circ g_r, \chi_{r-1})|^2,$$

where $\chi_0 = \chi$ *and* $\chi_R = \psi$.

4   Computing Expected Capacity

As before, let $\mathcal{E}_K$ be an iterated key-alternating block cipher on a finite Abelian group A. Since the size of the whole distribution of values $\{(x, \mathcal{E}_K(x)) \mid x \in A\}$ is intractable, as computing its capacity would require to compute the sum of the squared absolute correlations for all characters of $A \times A$, a cryptanalyst must restrict attention to a subgroup of characters. In the applications to be considered in this paper, such character subgroups are formed by characters on subgroups of $A \times A$.

Let B be a subgroup of $A \times A$. The characters of such subgroup are simply restrictions of the characters of the entire group. We denote by f_K a mapping from A to B, which is a composition of the block cipher mapping $x \mapsto (x, \mathcal{E}_K(x))$ and a homomorphic projection σ from $A \times A$ to B. By Theorem 1 the capacity of f_K can be computed as

$$C(f_K) = \sum_{\psi \neq \tau} |c_{f_K}(\psi)|^2,$$

where the summation is taken over all nontrivial characters ψ of B.

Let us now assume that $B = A' \times B'$, where A' and B' are subgroups of A. Then characters of $A' \times B'$ are of the form $\psi = \chi' \times \psi'$ and $c_{f_K}(\psi) = c(\psi' \circ \mathcal{E}_K, \chi')$. To obtain the expected value C of the capacity of $C(f_K)$ we can take the expected value of the squared absolute correlation $|c(\psi' \circ \mathcal{E}_K, \chi')|^2$ of the linear approximation (ψ', χ') of the iterated block cipher and then sum over all nontrivial characters χ' and ψ'. Then we get under the assumption that the keys K are uniformly distributed in A^R, the following expression:

$$C = \mathrm{E}_K(C(f_K)) = \sum_{\chi_0, \ldots, \chi_R} \prod_{r=1}^{R} |c(\chi_r \circ g_r, \chi_{r-1})|^2,$$

where the summation is taken over all nontrivial characters $\chi_0 = \chi'$ of A' and $\chi_R = \psi'$ of B'.

It was observed by Cho [5] that this expression can be computed for a binary cipher PRESENT using an iterative procedure from round to round. For a general key-alternating iterative block cipher we can now formulate the iterative algorithm as follows:

$$\Gamma_0(\chi_0) = 1 \quad \text{for all } \chi_0 \text{ of } A',$$

$$\Gamma_r(\chi_r) = \sum_{\chi_{r-1} \neq \tau} |c(\chi_r \circ g_r, \chi_{r-1})|^2 \Gamma_{r-1}(\chi_{r-1}) \quad \text{for } r = 1, \dots, R,$$

$$C = \sum_{\chi_R \neq \tau} \Gamma_R(\chi_R).$$

If B is not the form $A' \times B'$ as assumed above, the same algorithm can be used to compute the (reduced) linear hull effect $E_K(|c_{f_K}(\psi)|^2)$, for each character ψ of B, and then sum them up over ψ.

Many correlations of linear approximations over intermediate rounds will trivially vanish, but still the number of characters with nonzero correlation is usually too large. This means that in practice only a lower bound of the capacity can be determined using this algorithm. How to select the sets of intermediate masks must be determined for each cipher separately, and requires different heuristic strategies to be used.

In the cryptanalysis of PRESENT in [5] the strategy was to restrict to single-bit linear approximations over S-boxes. Such approximations will also on the next round involve only one S-box. In the evaluations of the capacities of distributions constructed for the DEAN cipher later in this paper, the goal is the same, i.e., to minimize the number of S-boxes that are simultaneously active in one iteration round of the algorithm.

5   Data Complexity of Distinguishing Distributions

Linear distinguishing attack is an implementation of a statistical hypothesis test that operates on the following principles: A set of samples is collected and a linear transformation is applied to them. A statistical hypothesis test is used to decide whether the given set of samples is drawn from a uniform distribution or from the cipher.

The distribution is collected in the following way. As before, our focus is on a block cipher defined using the encryption function $\mathcal{E}_K \colon A \to A$. Suppose that we have N data pairs (x_t, y_t), $t = 1, \dots, N$, belonging to $A \times A$ and let σ denote a homomorphic projection from $A \times A$ to B, where B is a subgroup of $A \times A$. For all $\eta \in B$, we compute

$$q(\eta) = N^{-1}|\{1 \leq t \leq N \mid \sigma(x_t, y_t) = \eta\}|.$$

The sequence $q = \{q(\eta) \mid \eta \in B\}$, forms the distribution that is studied in the hypothesis test. We say that the distribution originates from the cipher if $y_t = \mathcal{E}_K(x_t)$ for some unknown key K and for $t = 1, \dots, N$.

The decision can be done using different test statistics. They depend on the attack model which is chosen based on the information obtained from the cipher in theoretical analysis. In this paper we consider two attack models. In the first model, it is assumed that the data obtained from the cipher is drawn according to one unknown distribution from a family of distributions p_i, $i = 1, \ldots, \ell$. Then to test whether a given distribution q is drawn from the cipher or from the uniform distribution p_0, the attacker will compute the LLR statistic

$$\mathrm{LLR}(q \mid p_i) = \sum_{\eta \in B} q(\eta) \log \frac{p_0(\eta)}{p_i(\eta)}$$

for $i = 1, \ldots, \ell$. If the minimum of the values $\mathrm{LLR}(q \mid p_i)$ is negative, the hypothesis that q originates from the cipher is accepted. According to Theorem 8 of [3], the success probability of this attack is significant as soon as the sample size is larger than the inverse of the minimum of the Chernoff information between p_0 and p_i. Further, by the result of [3], it is known that if p_i is close to uniform, this Chernoff information can be estimated by $\frac{1}{8 \ln 2} C(p_i)$. In linear cryptanalysis, the distributions p_i are typically permutations of each other and hence have the same capacity equal to the average capacity taken over the keys. Then we estimate that the success probability of this LLR distinguisher is significant at least for about half of the keys as soon as the sample size exceeds eight times the inverse of the average capacity.

For modern ciphers designed to have differentially uniform and highly nonlinear components and efficient diffusion layer, it tends to be infeasible to determine small sets of data distributions such that for each key the data obtained from the cipher would follow one of these distributions. Also the correlations and capacities of small distributions may vary significantly with the keys, but as the size of the distribution grows, and more linear approximations are involved, the capacities typically vary less with the keys [5]. Then one can use a test statistic that is directly related to the capacity. A distinguisher can be based on the test statistic T calculated from the data as follows:

$$T = MN \sum_{\eta \in B} \left(q(\eta) - \frac{1}{M} \right)^2,$$

where $q = \{q(\eta)\}$ is the sample distribution, M is the size of the support of the distribution, that is, $M = |B|$, and N is the number of available data pairs. If the distribution $\{q(\eta)\}$ originates from the cipher, then the expected value of T/N, for all sufficiently large N, can be estimated by the expected capacity of the cipher distribution. On the other hand, if the distribution $\{q(\eta)\}$ originates from a random M-valued source which takes on each value η equally likely, then T follows χ^2 distribution with $M-1$ degrees of freedom. In this case the expected value of T/N is $(M-1)/N$ for all N.

Vaudenay [17] showed that for close-to-uniform distribution p with support of cardinality M, the data requirement of the χ^2 distinguisher T can be given as

$$N_{\chi^2} = \frac{\lambda \sqrt{M}}{C(p)},$$

where λ is a small constant. It is straightforward to derive the estimate

$$\lambda \approx (\sqrt{2} + 2)\Phi^{-1}(P_S),$$

where P_S is the required success probability. For $P_S = 0.95$ we have $\lambda \approx 8$.

For a fixed size of the distributions, the data complexities of LLR-based optimal distinguisher and the χ^2 distinguisher were previously shown to be equal up to a constant [1]. As shown above, this constant is proportional to the square root of the size of the support of the distribution, and therefore must be taken into account when the distinguisher uses large distributions.

6   DEAN

DEAN18 [2] is a toy cipher that encrypts blocks of 18 decimal digits. Since this is the only cipher from the DEAN family considered in this paper, we will call it DEAN. Its general structure, depicted in Fig. 1, closely resembles AES. A block is represented as a 3×3 array of elements from the additive group $\mathbb{Z}_{10} \times \mathbb{Z}_{10}$. The cipher has R rounds, each of which consists of the following operations:

- *AddRoundKeys*, which performs digit-wise addition of round key to input (modulo 10);
- *SubBytes*, which applies fixed bijective substitution box to each two-digit element of array;
- *ShiftRows*, which shifts each row of the block to the left over an offset equal to the row number (starting from 0);
- *MixColumns*, which multiplies each column of the input by the matrix

$$M = \begin{pmatrix} \alpha & 1 & 1 \\ 1 & \alpha & 1 \\ 1 & 1 & \alpha \end{pmatrix},$$

where the multiplication of an element $(a, b) \in \mathbb{Z}_{10}^2$ by α is defined by $\alpha \cdot (a, b) = (a + b, -a)$ (and $1 \cdot (a, b) = (a, b)$). The matrix M is an MDS matrix with branch number four, which means that for a nonzero input vector, at least four out of the six components of the input and output of the matrix multiplication are nonzero.

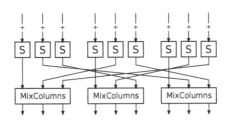

Fig. 1. One round of DEAN

7   Linear Approximations over DEAN

When applying the method described in Sect. 4 for DEAN, we set $A = (\mathbb{Z}_{10}^2)^9$. The characters in this group are given in terms of masks $\mathbf{a}$ such that

$$\chi_{\mathbf{a}}(x) = \prod_{i=1}^{9} e_{10}(a_{i1}x_{i1})e_{10}(a_{i2}x_{i2}), \quad \text{where}$$

$$x = (x_1, \ldots, x_9), \quad x_i = (x_{i1}, x_{i2}) \in \mathbb{Z}_{10}^2,$$

$$\mathbf{a} = (a_1, \ldots, a_9), \quad a_i = (a_{i1}, a_{i2}) \in \mathbb{Z}_{10}^2.$$

The elements a_i in a mask $\mathbf{a}$ are referred to as component masks. Given masks $\mathbf{a}$ and $\mathbf{b}$, we use $c(\mathbf{a}, \mathbf{b})$ to denote the correlation $c(\chi_{\mathbf{a}} \circ f, \chi_{\mathbf{b}})$, where f is the round function of DEAN.

When computing capacities of distributions for DEAN, we are facing the task of identifying sufficiently many linear trails with sufficiently large correlations. The smaller the number of active S-boxes on cipher rounds the larger the correlation. By (2) large correlations also contribute to the nonuniformity of the distribution. Moreover, with small number of S-boxes also the computation of the expected capacity of the plaintext-ciphertext pairs is feasible.

To define the suitable trails on DEAN we use the notion of *selection pattern*.

Definition 1. *A selection pattern* $\mathbf{p} = [p_1 \ldots p_9]$ *for DEAN is a string, where* $p_i \in \{0, *\}$ *for* $i = 1, \ldots, 9$. *Succession of a selection pattern* $\mathbf{p_1}$ *on a round of the cipher by a pattern* $\mathbf{p_2}$ *on the next round is denoted by* $\mathbf{p_1} \longrightarrow \mathbf{p_2}$. *Given a pattern* $\mathbf{p} = [p_1 \ldots p_9]$ *and a mask* $\mathbf{a} = (a_1, \ldots, a_9)$, *we write* $\mathbf{a} \in \mathbf{p}$ *if and only if* $a_i \neq 0$ *implies that* $p_i = *$ *for* $i = 1, \ldots, 9$.

Hence, a single pattern succession can be used to define a set of linear trails over DEAN. An example of a pattern succession over three rounds of DEAN is given in Appendix A. In a pattern succession, the first pattern and the last pattern are called the input pattern and the output pattern, respectively.

The MDS matrix used on the diffusion round sets a lower bound to the number of active S-boxes: on two subsequent rounds the minimum number of active S-boxes is four. If an upper bound is set to the Hamming weight for successions over three or more rounds, then four is the least such an upper bound. This can also be achieved as shown in Appendix A.

When calculating the number of all nonzero component masks in $\mathbb{Z}_{10}^2$ involved in these linear approximations over three rounds with a fixed input mask, it suffices to determine the number of active MixColumn transformations. When one of the four nonzero component masks at the input and the output of the MixColumn is given, the remaining three are uniquely determined. Each such initial component mask can be freely selected. There are six active MixColumn transformations in the example, so the total number of nonzero component masks involved in this trail is 99^6.

Algorithm 1 describes how to compute a lower bound for the average capacity of the distribution of pairs of input and output data segments of R-round DEAN. Note that the first round is obtained for free due to Parseval's theorem.

Algorithm 1. Computes an estimate for the average capacity for DEAN

Input: Definition of suitable trails using selection patterns $\mathbf{p}_r$, $r = 1, \ldots, R$.
Output: Lower bound for the sum of averages squared correlations of all linear
      trails using masks corresponding to the selection patterns.
Memory: Arrays $\Gamma_{\text{thisRnd}}[\cdot]$ and $\Gamma_{\text{prevRnd}}[\cdot]$ storing squared correlations for
      every independent mask combination on two successive rounds.

foreach $\mathbf{a} \in \mathbf{p}_1$ **do**
    $\lfloor$ $\Gamma_{\text{thisRnd}}(\mathbf{a}) \leftarrow 1$;
for $r \leftarrow 2$ **to** R **do**
    prevRnd $\leftarrow$ thisRnd;
    foreach $\mathbf{a} \in \mathbf{p}_r$ **do**
        foreach $\mathbf{b} \in \mathbf{p}_{r-1}$ **do**
            $\lfloor$ $\Gamma_{\text{thisRnd}}[\mathbf{a}] \leftarrow \Gamma_{\text{thisRnd}}[\mathbf{a}] + \Gamma_{\text{prevRnd}}[\mathbf{b}] \cdot |c(\mathbf{a}, \mathbf{b})|^2$;

return $\sum_{\mathbf{a} \in \mathbf{p}_R} \Gamma_{\text{thisRnd}}[\mathbf{a}]$

---

8 Capacity Estimates for DEAN

Using Algorithm 1, we studied two different types of linear approximations of
DEAN for different number of rounds. The purpose was to find effective linear
distinguishers for DEAN with sample distributions of different sizes. The results
are presented in Table 1, where (i) and (ii) denote the two approximation types, R
denotes the number of rounds in DEAN, and C denotes the capacity estimate for
the approximation. The estimated data requirements for the LLR distinguisher
and the χ^2 distinguisher are denoted by N_{LLR} and N_{χ^2} in the table. They were
computed as described in Sect. 5 with exponents rounded to the nearest integer.

Type (i) and type (ii) approximations were specified by defining fixed input
and output patterns for the approximation. In type (i) approximations, both the
input pattern and the output pattern have four nonzero components with fixed
positions. In type (ii) approximations, there are two fixed nonzero components in
both patterns. The sample distribution size M is hence $10^{16} \approx 2^{53.2}$ for type (i)
and $10^8 \approx 2^{26.6}$ for type (ii). These numbers also define the memory requirements
for the distinguishers.

Table 1. Complexities of type (i) and type (ii) distinguishers for DEAN

	(i)			(ii)		
R	C	N_{LLR}	N_{χ^2}	C	N_{LLR}	N_{χ^2}
3	2^{-12}	2^{15}	2^{42}	2^{-33}	2^{36}	2^{49}
4	2^{-23}	2^{26}	2^{53}	2^{-38}	2^{41}	2^{54}
5	2^{-35}	2^{38}	2^{65}	2^{-43}	2^{46}	2^{59}
6	2^{-47}	2^{50}	2^{77}	2^{-75}	2^{78}	2^{91}
7	2^{-58}	2^{61}	2^{88}	2^{-80}	2^{83}	2^{96}

Using the aforementioned specifications, we determined a set of R-round pattern successions for both types of approximations. To limit the time it takes to compute C, we limited the number of active MixColumns transformations in two subsequent rounds of each succession. We used four as a limit for type (i) and five as a limit for type (ii). Then we chose the input pattern and the output pattern for each approximation such that there would be as many pattern successions as possible. For type (i), we chose $[*0**0*000]$ to be the input pattern and the output pattern regardless of the number of rounds in DEAN. Taking into account the properties of the MDS matrix, we can deduce that the number of pattern successions is 3^{R-2} for type (i). The input and output patterns for type (ii) are presented in Table 2. For it, the number of successions is 3^{R-3} for $R = 3, 4, 5$ and $2 \cdot 3^{R-4}$ for $R = 6, 7$.

Table 2. The input and output patterns for type (ii) approximations

R	Pattern successions
3	$[*0000*000] \longrightarrow \cdots \longrightarrow [*0000000*]$
4	$[*0000*000] \longrightarrow \cdots \longrightarrow [*0*000000]$
5	$[*0*000000] \longrightarrow \cdots \longrightarrow [*0*000000]$
6	$[*0000*000] \longrightarrow \cdots \longrightarrow [*0000000*]$
7	$[*0000*000] \longrightarrow \cdots \longrightarrow [*0*000000]$

In our experiments, the correlations for individual linear trails were very evenly distributed for most masks. Hence, including the correlations of more trails and masks gives significantly larger estimates for the capacities than without them. Moreover, due to the diffusion properties of the MixColumn transformation, changing the positions of the nonzero component masks in the input or the output of the transformation does not have a significant effect on the results. Thus, there are many input and output patterns that give essentially the same results as the ones presented for type (i) and type (ii) approximations.

Due to the efficient diffusion round, it is not possible to restrict the number of active components and achieve small distributions for all numbers of rounds. For $R = 4$ it is possible to find distinguishers with only one S-box active on the first round and one on the last round. It turns out that any of the S-boxes can be selected for the first round and the last round. Moreover, before the last summation over the output characters, one can see that the values produced for all output characters are about equal, each being about 2^{-53}. Hence restricting to one coordinate in the output (which has the group size 10) and the two coordinates in the input, will produce a distribution with cardinality $M = 10^3$ and expected capacity $2^{-49.7}$. The data requirement for the LLR distinguisher of this distribution would be $2^{52.7}$ and for the χ^2 distinguisher $2^{59.6}$.

Baignères et al. [2] estimated that about 2^{61} samples are required to distinguish a four-round DEAN from a random permutation using the LLR distinguisher. According to the more accurate estimates given in this paper, the data requirement for a LLR distinguisher over four rounds is bounded from above by 2^{26} or by 2^{41} depending on the size of the distribution. We also presented evidence that a four-round DEAN can be distinguished from a random permutation using χ^2 with 2^{53} samples using multidimensional linear approximations of type (i). For the best attack given in Table 1, the data complexity does not reach the full code book until seven rounds. It means that eight rounds as suggested by the designers of DEAN is not sufficient.

9   Practical Experiments

We implemented the algorithm for computing capacities of cipher distributions and tested it in practice. As shown in the previous section, only type (ii) distinguishers have practical memory requirements, but unfortunately, the smallest estimated data requirement for the χ^2 distinguisher of type (ii) is still too large for running practical experiments. Therefore, we designed a smaller version of the DEAN algorithm with the same S-box and MDS matrix, but with a reduced block size of 10^{12}. The resulting three-round block cipher, which we call Vice DEAN, is depicted in Fig. 2. As with full DEAN, diffusion is added after the S-boxes by permuting the elements in the block. For the first round, the structure of the permutation is insignificant and an identity mapping can be used. The round keys are added before the S-boxes as in full DEAN, but they have been omitted from the figure for clarity.

We computed estimates of the capacity of the distribution consisting of two components in the input and two components in the output. The size of the distribution is $M = 10^8$. We first ran the algorithm over the pattern succession depicted in Fig. 2 and obtained an estimate $2^{-19.9}$. We then replaced the pattern [*0*000] before the last MixColumns layer by [**0000] and obtained the same estimate. These two selection patterns use the minimum number of active S-boxes, and are fast to compute. By summing up the estimates obtained using these separate sets of trails gives us the estimate $2^{-18.9}$ of the capacity. Finally, we ran the algorithm counting over all possible trails, i.e., using the selection pattern [***000] before the last MixColumns layer, and obtained the complete value $2^{-13.3} \approx 10^{-4}$ of the capacity. This example demonstrates that restricting to selection patterns with minimal number of S-boxes gives only very rough lower bounds to the capacities, and consequently, all estimates of data complexities given in Table 1 are much larger than the true values.

If the statistical model of the χ^2 distinguisher presented in Sect. 5 is correct, we can deduce that for distribution of size $M = 10^8$ and capacity 10^4 the distinguisher has high success probability for about $8 \cdot 10^8$ data. We ran the following practical experiment to test the correctness of this estimate. Two sets of samples were generated, one from 20 different initializations from a random number generator, and a second set of 20 different samples of randomly generated plaintext and ciphertext pairs of Vice DEAN. The experiment is illustrated in Fig. 3. The two sets are fully separated already as the sample sizes exceeds $8 \cdot 10^8$ as predicted.

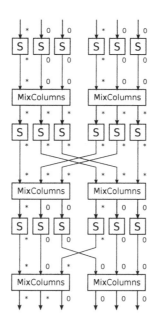

Fig. 2. The Vice DEAN algorithm and a pattern succession

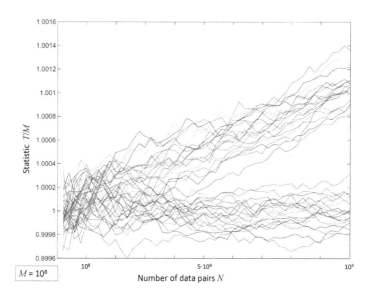

Fig. 3. Results from the experiment on Vice DEAN

10   Conclusions

In this paper, we investigated how to compute estimates of expected squared correlations and capacities of linear approximations over key-alternating block ciphers. Previously, Cho [5] had presented an iterative algorithm customized to PRESENT for estimating these quantities. Based on the same approach, we proposed a general purpose algorithm for computing capacities of distributions related to multidimensional linear cryptanalysis. Previous methods of counting trails with about equal correlations used for the PRESENT cipher do not work in general case, where the trails are numerous and their values vary a lot. Using the method investigated in this paper, it is possible, also for ciphers other than PRESENT, to obtain better estimates of resistance against linear cryptanalysis compared to the traditional method, which is based on the upper bound to the bias of the best single linear approximation trail.

We used the algorithm to estimate expected capacities of multidimensional linear approximations of the nonbinary SPN network DEAN [2]. All this analysis is done without the need to specify a key schedule. The underlying theoretical assumption of this method is that the round keys are statistically independent and uniformly distributed. If DEAN is equipped with a reasonable key schedule such that it does not violate the assumption significantly, then the results given in Table 1 indicate that at least five rounds are needed before the data complexity of the χ^2 distinguisher exceeds the full code book bound 2^{60}. If moreover, resistance against the LLR distinguisher is wanted, then more rounds are needed, since the full code book bound is not broken until seven rounds with the LLR distinguisher. In [2], it was estimated that the data complexity of the best LLR distinguisher would exceed the code book bound already with four rounds of DEAN.

Acknowledgements. We wish to thank the anonymous reviewers for their helpful comments. The research work of the first author has been supported by Helsinki Doctoral Programme in Computer Science - Advanced Computing and Intelligent Systems, Academy of Finland (project #122736), Nokia Foundation, and KAUTE Foundation.

References

1. Baignères, T., Junod, P., Vaudenay, S.: How far can we go beyond linear cryptanalysis? In: Lee, P.J. (ed.) ASIACRYPT 2004. LNCS, vol. 3329, pp. 432–450. Springer, Heidelberg (2004)
2. Baignères, T., Stern, J., Vaudenay, S.: Linear cryptanalysis of non binary ciphers. In: Adams, C., Miri, A., Wiener, M. (eds.) SAC 2007. LNCS, vol. 4876, pp. 184–211. Springer, Heidelberg (2007)
3. Baignères, T., Vaudenay, S.: The complexity of distinguishing distributions (invited talk). In: Safavi-Naini, R. (ed.) ICITS 2008. LNCS, vol. 5155, pp. 210–222. Springer, Heidelberg (2008)

4. Bogdanov, A., Knudsen, L.R., Leander, G., Paar, C., Poschmann, A., Robshaw, M.J.B., Seurin, Y., Vikkelsoe, C.: PRESENT: An ultra-lightweight block cipher. In: Paillier, P., Verbauwhede, I. (eds.) CHES 2007. LNCS, vol. 4727, pp. 450–466. Springer, Heidelberg (2007)
5. Cho, J.Y.: Linear cryptanalysis of reduced-round PRESENT. In: Pieprzyk, J. (ed.) CT-RSA 2010. LNCS, vol. 5985, pp. 302–317. Springer, Heidelberg (2010)
6. Daemen, J., Rijmen, V.: The Design of Rijndael – AES, the Advanced Encryption Standard. Springer (2002)
7. Daemen, J., Govaerts, R., Vandewalle, J.: Correlation matrices. In: Preneel, B. (ed.) FSE 1994. LNCS, vol. 1008, pp. 275–285. Springer, Heidelberg (1995)
8. Drakakis, K., Gow, R., McGuire, G.: APN permutations on $\mathbb{Z}_n$ and Costas arrays. Discrete Applied Mathematics 157(15), 3320–3326 (2009)
9. Leander, G.: On linear hulls, statistical saturation attacks, PRESENT and a cryptanalysis of PUFFIN. In: Paterson, K.G. (ed.) EUROCRYPT 2011. LNCS, vol. 6632, pp. 303–322. Springer, Heidelberg (2011)
10. Lidl, R., Niederreiter, H.: Finite fields, 2nd edn. Encyclopedia of mathematics and its applications, vol. 20. Cambridge University Press (1997)
11. Massey, J.L.: SAFER K-64: A byte-oriented block-ciphering algorithm. In: Anderson, R. (ed.) FSE 1993. LNCS, vol. 809, pp. 1–17. Springer, Heidelberg (1994)
12. Massey, J.L.: SAFER K-64: One year later. In: Preneel, B. (ed.) FSE 1994. LNCS, vol. 1008, pp. 212–241. Springer, Heidelberg (1995)
13. Matsui, M.: Linear cryptanalysis method for DES cipher. In: Helleseth, T. (ed.) EUROCRYPT 1993. LNCS, vol. 765, pp. 386–397. Springer, Heidelberg (1994)
14. Nakahara Jr., J., Sepehrdad, P., Zhang, B., Wang, M.: Linear (hull) and algebraic cryptanalysis of the block cipher PRESENT. In: Garay, J.A., Miyaji, A., Otsuka, A. (eds.) CANS 2009. LNCS, vol. 5888, pp. 58–75. Springer, Heidelberg (2009)
15. Nyberg, K.: Linear approximation of block ciphers. In: De Santis, A. (ed.) EUROCRYPT 1994. LNCS, vol. 950, pp. 439–444. Springer, Heidelberg (1995)
16. Nyberg, K.: Correlation theorems in cryptanalysis. Discrete Applied Mathematics 111(1-2), 177–188 (2001)
17. Vaudenay, S.: An experiment on DES statistical cryptanalysis. In: Gong, L., Stern, J. (eds.) CCS 1996, pp. 139–147. ACM Press (1996)

A   An Example of a Linear Approximation over DEAN

The pattern succession

$$[*0***0000] \longrightarrow [0***0*000] \longrightarrow [000**00**] \longrightarrow [*0***0000]$$

is depicted in Fig. 4. Each selection pattern in this pattern succession has the Hamming weight four which is the least upper bound for the Hamming weights in successions over three or more rounds. In type (i) approximations presented in Sect. 8, the input and output patterns also have four nonzero components.

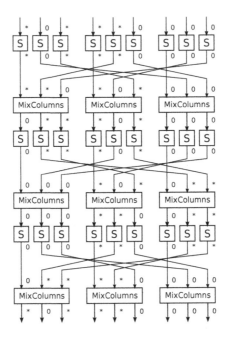

Fig. 4. An example of a pattern succession over three rounds of DEAN

Fast Evaluation of T-Functions
via Time-Memory Trade-Offs

Tao Shi[1], Vladimir Anashin[2], and Dongdai Lin[3,*]

[1] Institute of Software, Chinese Academy of Sciences,
University of Chinese Academy of Sciences
shitao@is.iscas.ac.cn
[2] Faculty of Computational Mathematics and Cybernetics,
Lomonosov Moscow State University
vladimir.anashin@u-picardie.fr
[3] The State Key Laboratory of Information Security, Institute of Information
Engineering, Chinese Academy of Sciences
ddlin@iie.ac.cn

Abstract. We present two low time-cost methods to evaluate arbitrary
T-function on k-bit words; both methods use only fast computer instructions (integer addition and/or bitwise logical instructions) and calls to
memory. The methods can be applied in a design of T-function-based
stream ciphers for fast encryption software in heavy-traffic networks.

1 Introduction

For years linear feedback shift registers (LFSRs) over a 2-element field $\mathbb{F}_2$ have
been one of the most important building blocks in keystream generators of stream
ciphers. LFSRs can easily be designed to produce binary sequences of the longest
period (that is, of length $2^k - 1$ for a k-cell LFSR over $\mathbb{F}_2$); LFSRs are fast and
easy to implement in hardware. However, sequences produced by LFSRs have
linear dependencies that may make it easy for the cryptanalysts to construct
attacks on the whole cipher. To make output sequences of LFSRs more secure
these linear dependencies must be destroyed by a properly chosen filter; this is
the filter that carries the major cryptographical load making the whole cipher
secure.

During these years, T-functions were found to be useful tools to design fast
cryptographic primitives and ciphers based on usage on both arithmetic (addition, multiplication) and logical operations, see [30, 11, 12, 14, 13, 15, 18, 17, 16,
21, 26, 10, 27, 28, 23]. Loosely speaking, a T-function is a map of k-bit words

---

* The research of the first and the third authors are partially supported by 973 Program 2011CB302400, NSFC 60970152, the Strategic Priority Research Program of
the Chinese Academy of Sciences under Grant XDA06010701; the second author is
partially supported by Chinese Academy of Sciences visiting professorship for senior
international scientists grant 2009G2-11 and Russian Foundation for Basic Research
grant 12-01-00680-a.

M. Kutyłowski and M. Yung (Eds.): Inscrypt 2012, LNCS 7763, pp. 263–275, 2013.

into k-bit words such that each i-th bit of image depends only on low-order bits $0, ..., i$ of the pre-image. Various methods are known to construct transitive T-functions (the ones that produce sequences of the longest possible period, 2^k), see [3, 4, 6, 9, 5, 2, 1, 21, 22, 14, 13, 15, 17, 11]. Transitive T-functions have been considered as a candidate to replace LFSRs in keystream generators of stream ciphers, see e.g. [10, 30, 12, 16, 26, 27] since sequences produced by T-function-based keystream generators are proved to have a number of good cryptographic properties, e.g., high linear and 2-adic complexity, uniform distribution of sub-words, etc., see [3, 20, 1, 31]. Furthermore, the filter in these generators can also be T-function based, see [3, Subsection 10.3.1]. Therefore, being implemented in a software, the performance of the corresponding T-function based stream cipher is completely determined by how fast the evaluation of a T-function is: Given a T-function f and an k-bit word x, the computation of the k-bit word $f(x)$ must be as fast as possible to provide high overall performance of the software.

In practice, a T-function is implemented in software as a *straight line program*, i.e., as composition of basic computer instructions that include numerical ones (e.g., integer addition and multiplication of integers represented by base-2 expansions), bitwise logical ones (e.g., $\vee$, a bitwise logical 'or'; $\wedge$, a bitwise logical 'and', etc.) The run-time complexities of all these instructions are quite different. Bitwise logical instructions (as well as integer addition) are the fastest ones, whereas integer multiplication are significantly slower: For instance, the run-time complexity of integer multiplication of two k-bit words is of order $k^{\log_2 3}$ with the use of Karatsuba's algorithm of fast multiplication, of order $k^{\log 5/\log 3}$ with the use of Toom-3 algorithm, and of order $k \log k \log \log k$ with the use of Schönhage-Strassen algorithm. It is worth noticing that the latter algorithm (as well as recent Fürer's algorithm which has even asymptotically better run-time bit complexity) are effective only for very large k, larger than $2^{2^{15}}$. Note also that whenever a univariate T-function is used in a stream cipher as a state update function, to obtain a sufficiently long period one must use longer machine words (e.g. 128-bit words on 64-bit machines) thus also slowing down the performance in the case when multiplications are used in composition of the T-function. These considerations force one to conclude that it might be reasonable to avoid (or to restrict) usage of integer multiplications in a composition of a T-functions to achieve better performance and to completely avoid such operations as raising to powers, inversion, etc. However, this significantly reduces the class of T-functions. Moreover, using only integer additions and bitwise logical operations in a composition of a T-function may result in sharp irregularities in distribution of the corresponding key stream, see [3, Sections 11.1–11.2]. Thus, it would be highly desirable to develop a method with a small run-time complexity to evaluate *arbitrary* T-function.

The main goal of the paper is to present two methods of this sort. To evaluate a T-function on k-bit words, either of the methods demands not more than k calls to memory, not more than k bitwise and's $\wedge$ and not more than k integer additions modulo 2^k, or, respectively xor's $\oplus$ (=bitwise additions modulo 2).

The second one of these methods (the one that uses xor's) is suitable for parallel computing and can be used in design T-function-based stream ciphers that operate with very long words.

In the real world, the structure of stream cipher today is getting more and more complex, the design of primitives should be more and more flexible. The method we develope here is suitable for various cipher designs, and provides more flexibility in the stream cipher design: one can almost 'randomly' choose a series of data(corresponding to the expansion coefficients of the T-function). For example, for counter dependent PRNG like the one used in stream cipher ABC, the T-function for states updating is changing permanently, and our method can be used to fast generating of new state updating functions.

In our constructions we use techniques of non-Archimedean dynamics (see monograph [3] on the theme); that is, we expand T-functions onto the whole space $\mathbb{Z}_2$ of 2-adic integers or, respectively on the space $\mathbb{F}_2[[X]]$ of formal power series over a two-element field $\mathbb{F}_2$ and study corresponding dynamical systems on these spaces: We use representation of a T-function via van der Put series over $\mathbb{Z}_2$ or over $\mathbb{F}_2[[X]]$.

The paper is organized as follows:

- Section 2 concerns basics of the non-Archimedean theory for T-functions;
- Section 3 describes the two mentioned methods;
- we conclude in Section 4.

2 Non-archimedean Theory of T-Functions: Brief Survey

In this Section, we introduce basics of what can be called a non-Archimedean approach to T-functions. For the full theory see monograph [3] or expository paper [1]. We start with a definition of a T-function and show that T-functions can be treated as continuous functions defined on and valued in the space $\mathbb{Z}_2$ of 2-adic integers or, respectively, in the space $\mathbb{F}_2[[X]]$ of formal power series over a field $\mathbb{F}_2 = \{0, 1\}$. Then we introduce basics of 2-adic arithmetic and of 2-adic Calculus that we will need to state our main results. There are many comprehensive monographs on p-adic numbers and p-adic analysis that contain all necessary definitions and proofs, see e.g. [19, 25, 29] or introductory chapters in [3]; so further in the section we introduce 2-adic numbers in a somewhat informal manner.

It is worth noticing here that the theory of T-functions (which actually are functions that satisfy a Lipschitz condition with a constant 1 w.r.t. 2-adic metric) was developed by mathematicians during decades prior to first publication of Klimov and Shamir on T-functions [14] in 2003, and in a much more general setting, for arbitrary prime p, and not only for $p = 2$. Moreover, various criteria of invertibility and single cycle property of T-functions were obtained within p-adic ergodic theory (see e.g. [9, 4]) nearly a decade prior to the first publication of Klimov and Shamir on T-functions [14].

2.1   T-Functions

In general an univariate T-function f is a mapping

$$(\chi_0; \chi_1; \chi_2; \ldots) \overset{f}{\mapsto} (\psi_0(\chi_0); \psi_1(\chi_0, \chi_1); \psi_2(\chi_0, \chi_1, \chi_2); \ldots), \qquad (1)$$

where $\chi_j \in \{0,1\}$, and each $\psi_j(\chi_0, \ldots, \chi_j)$ is a Boolean function in Boolean variables $\chi_0, \ldots, \chi_j$. T-functions may be viewed as mappings from non-negative integers to non-negative integers: e.g., a univariate T-function f sends a number with the base-2 expansion $\chi_0 + \chi_1 \cdot 2 + \chi_2 \cdot 2^2 + \cdots$ to the number with the base-2 expansion $\psi_0(\chi_0) + \psi_1(\chi_0, \chi_1) \cdot 2 + \psi_2(\chi_0, \chi_1, \chi_2) \cdot 2^2 + \cdots$ Further in the paper we refer to these Boolean functions $\psi_0, \psi_1, \psi_2, \ldots$ as *coordinate functions* of a T-function f. If we restrict T-functions to the set of all numbers whose base-2 expansions are no longer than k, then we refer to these restrictions as *T-functions on k-bit words*. We may associate the set of all k-bit words to the set $\{0, 1, \ldots, 2^k - 1\}$ of all residues modulo 2^k; the latter set constitutes the residue ring $\mathbb{Z}/2^k\mathbb{Z}$ w.r.t. modulo 2^k operations of addition and multiplication. Naturally we can get the T-function on k-bit words by the map $mod\ 2^k$ (the reduction modulo 2^k, i.e.,taking the first k digits in the representation of f). Accordingly, an n-variate T-function is a mapping

$$\left(\alpha_0^\downarrow, \alpha_1^\downarrow, \alpha_2^\downarrow, \ldots\right) \mapsto \left(\Phi_0^\downarrow\left(\alpha_0^\downarrow\right), \Phi_1^\downarrow\left(\alpha_0^\downarrow, \alpha_1^\downarrow\right), \Phi_2^\downarrow\left(\alpha_0^\downarrow, \alpha_1^\downarrow, \alpha_2^\downarrow\right), \ldots\right), \qquad (2)$$

where $\alpha_i^\downarrow \in \mathbb{F}_2^n$ is a Boolean columnar n-dimensional vector over a 2-element field $\mathbb{F}_2 = \{0,1\}$, and $\Phi_i^\downarrow \colon (\mathbb{F}_2^n)^{i+1} \to \mathbb{F}_2^m$ maps $(i+1)$ Boolean columnar n-dimensional vectors $\alpha_0^\downarrow, \ldots, \alpha_i^\downarrow$ to m-dimensional columnar Boolean vector $\Phi_i^\downarrow\left(\alpha_0^\downarrow, \ldots, \alpha_i^\downarrow\right)$. The determinative property of T-functions (which might be used to state equivalent definition of a T-function) is *compatibility* with all congruences modulo powers of 2: Given a (univariate) T-function f, if $a \equiv b \pmod{2^s}$ then $f(a) \equiv f(b) \pmod{2^s}$. Vice versa, every compatible map is a T-function. Important examples of T-functions are basic machine instructions: integer arithmetic operations (addition, multiplication,...); bitwise logical operations ($\vee$, $\oplus$, $\wedge$, $\neg$); some their compositions (masking, shifts towards high order bits, and mod 2^i, the reduction modulo 2^i). A composition of T-functions is a T-function (for instance, *any polynomial with integer coefficients is a T-function*).

2.2   The Rings $\mathbb{Z}_2$ and $\mathbb{F}_2[[X]]$

As it follows directly from the definition, any T-function {can be} well-defined on the set $\mathbb{Z}_2$ of all infinite binary sequences $\ldots \delta_2(x)\delta_1(x)\delta_0(x) = x$, where $\delta_j(x) \in \{0,1\}$, $j = 0, 1, 2, \ldots$. Arithmetic operations (addition and multiplication) with these sequences could be defined via standard "school-textbook" algorithms of addition and multiplication of natural numbers represented by base-2 expansions. Each term of a sequence that corresponds to the sum (respectively, to the product) of two given sequences could be calculated by these algorithms within a finite number of steps. Thus, $\mathbb{Z}_2$ is a commutative ring with respect to the so defined addition and multiplication. The ring $\mathbb{Z}_2$ is called the ring of 2-*adic integers*. The ring $\mathbb{Z}_2$ contains a subring $\mathbb{Z}$ of all rational integers. Moreover, the ring $\mathbb{Z}_2$ contains all rational numbers that can be represented by irreducible fractions with odd denominators. For instance, $\ldots 01010101 \times \ldots 00011 = \ldots 111$, i.e., $\ldots 01010101 = -1/3$ since $\ldots 00011 = 3$ and $\ldots 111 = -1$. Sequences with only finite number of 1-s correspond to non-negative rational integers in their base-2 expansions, sequences with only finite number of 0-s correspond to negative rational integers, while eventually periodic sequences (that is, sequences that become periodic starting with a certain place) correspond to rational numbers represented by irreducible fractions with odd denominators: For instance, $3 = \ldots 00011$, $-3 = \ldots 11101$, $1/3 = \ldots 10101011$, $-1/3 = \ldots 1010101$. So the j-th term $\delta_j(u)$ of the corresponding sequence $u \in \mathbb{Z}_2$ is merely the j-th digit of the base-2 expansion of u whenever u is a non-negative rational integer, $u \in \mathbb{N}_0 = \{0, 1, 2, \ldots\}$.

What is important, the ring $\mathbb{Z}_2$ is a metric space with respect to the metric (distance) $d_2(u, v)$ defined by the following rule: $d_2(u, v) = \|u - v\|_2 = 1/2^n$, where n is the smallest non-negative rational integer such that $\delta_n(u) \neq \delta_n(v)$, and $d_2(u, v) = 0$ if no such n exists (i.e., if $u = v$). For instance, $d_2(3, 1/3) = 1/8$. The function $d_2(u, 0) = \|u\|_2$ is the *2-adic absolute value* of u, and $\mathrm{ord}_2 u = -\log_2 \|u_2\|_2$ is the 2-adic valuation of u. Note that if $u \in \mathbb{N}_0$, the valuation $\mathrm{ord}_2 u$ is merely the exponent of the highest power of 2 that divides u (thus, loosely speaking, $\mathrm{ord}_2 0 = \infty$, so $\|0\|_2 = 0$). This means, in particular, that

$$\|a - b\|_2 \leq 1/2^k \text{ if and only if } a \equiv b \pmod{2^k}$$

for $a, b \in \mathbb{Z}$.

Now we can represent every 2-adic integer $x = \ldots \delta_2(x)\delta_1(x)\delta_0(x)$ (where $\delta_i(x) \in \{0, 1\}$, $i = 0, 1, 2, \ldots$) as the series $x = \sum_{i=0}^{\infty} \delta_i(x) \cdot 2^i$; (where $\delta_i(x) \in \{0, 1\}$, $i = 0, 1, 2, \ldots$). The series are called *canonic 2-adic expansion* of the 2-adic integer x; the series converges to x with respect to the 2-adic metric.

Infinite binary strings can also be treated as elements of another ring, the ring $\mathbb{F}_2[[X]]$ of formal power series (in variable X) over a field $\mathbb{F}_2 = \{0, 1\}$: to every (left-infinite) binary string $\ldots \delta_2(x)\delta_1(x)\delta_0(x) = x$, where $\delta_j(x) \in \{0, 1\}$, $j = 0, 1, 2, \ldots$ we put into the correspondence the formal power series $\sum_{i=0}^{\infty} \delta_i(x)X^i$. We stress that *addition in the ring* $\mathbb{F}_2[[X]]$ *corresponds to the operation* $\oplus$, *the bitwise addition modulo 2; that is, to the computer instruction 'xor'*.

Metric (and absolute value) on the ring $\mathbb{F}_2[[X]]$ are defined exactly in the same way as on the ring $\mathbb{Z}_2$; thus, metric spaces $\mathbb{F}_2[[X]]$ and $\mathbb{Z}_2$ are *isometric* to each other (however, $\mathbb{F}_2[[X]]$ and $\mathbb{Z}_2$ are *non-isomorphic* rings). Note that in the ring of power series the counter-part of the operation $\mathrm{mod} 2^i \colon \mathbb{Z}_2 \to \mathbb{Z}/2^i\mathbb{Z}$, the reduction modulo 2^i of a 2-adic integer, is the operation $\mathrm{mod}\, X^i$ which puts into the correspondence to the series $\sum_{i=0}^{\infty} \delta_i(x)X^i$ a *polynomial* $(\sum_{i=0}^{\infty} \delta_i(x)X^i)$ mod $X^i = \sum_{i=0}^{i-1} \delta_i(x)X^i$ *over a field* $\mathbb{F}_2$.

2.3   Van der Put Series of T-Functions

Once the metric is defined, one defines notions of convergent sequences, limits, continuous functions on the metric space, and convergent series if the space is a commutative ring. We will need a special sort of convergent series to represent T-functions, the *van der Put series*. We remind definition and some properties of van der Put series following [25, 29].

Given a continuous function $g\colon \mathbb{Z}_2 \to \mathbb{Z}_2$, there exists a unique sequence $B(0), B(1), B(2), \ldots$ of 2-adic integers such that

$$g(x) = \sum_{m=0}^{\infty} B(m)\chi(m, x) \tag{3}$$

for all $x \in \mathbb{Z}_2$, where

$$\chi(m, x) = \begin{cases} 1, \text{ if } \|x - m\|_2 \leq 2^{-n} \\ 0, \text{ otherwise} \end{cases}$$

and $n = 1$ if $m = 0$; n is uniquely defined by the inequality $2^{n-1} \leq m \leq 2^n - 1$ otherwise. The right side series in (3) is called the *van der Put series* of the function g. Note that the sequence $B(0), B(1), \ldots, B(m), \ldots$ of van der Put coefficients of the function f tend 2-adically to 0 as $m \to \infty$, and the series converges uniformly on $\mathbb{Z}_2$.

The number n in the definition of $\chi(m, x)$ has a very natural meaning; it is just the number of digits in a base-2 expansion of $m \in \mathbb{N}_0$: Given $m \in \mathbb{N}_0$ denote via $\lfloor \log_2 m \rfloor$ the largest rational integer that is either less than, or equal to, $\log_2 m$; then

$$\lfloor \log_2 m \rfloor = (\text{the number of digits in a base-2 expansion for } m) - 1;$$

henceforth $n = \lfloor \log_2 m \rfloor + 1$ for all $m \in \mathbb{N}_0$ (we put $\lfloor \log_2 0 \rfloor = 0$).

Accordingly, any continuous function $g\colon \mathbb{F}_2[[X]] \to \mathbb{F}_2[[X]]$ has a unique representation via van der Put series of form similar to that of (3):

$$g(x) = \sum_{\alpha \in \mathbb{F}_2[X]} B_\alpha \chi(\alpha, x) \tag{4}$$

where $B_\alpha \in \mathbb{F}_2[[X]]$, and $\mathbb{F}_2[X]$ is the ring of all polynomials in variable X over $\mathbb{F}_2$, and

$$\chi(\alpha, x) = \begin{cases} 1, \text{ if } \|x - \alpha\|_2 \leq 2^{-\deg \alpha - 1} \\ 0, \text{ otherwise} \end{cases}$$

(we assume that $\deg 0 = 0$). Again, we stress that summation in (4) is in $\mathbb{F}_2[[X]]$; that is, the summation is $\oplus$, a bitwise addition modulo 2 (and also $x - \alpha = x \oplus \alpha$). Note that the order of summation in (4) is not important: The peculiarity of the non-Archimedean metric is that the series converges independently on the order of terms.

And of course, it is worth noticing that van der Put coefficients for the same continuous function g are different depending on whether we consider the map

g as a transformation of the ring $\mathbb{Z}_2$ or of the ring $\mathbb{F}_2[[X]]$ (if the both are considered as a space of infinite binary strings).

What is most important within the scope of the paper is that all T-functions are *continuous* functions of 2-adic variables since *all T-functions satisfy Lipschitz condition with a constant 1 with respect to the 2-adic metric*, and vice versa.

Indeed, it is obvious that the function $f \colon \mathbb{Z}_2 \to \mathbb{Z}_2$ satisfies the condition $\|f(u) - f(v)\|_2 \le \|u - v\|_2$ for all $u, v \in \mathbb{Z}_2$ if and only if f is compatible, since the inequality $\|a - b\|_2 \le 1/2^k$ is just equivalent to the congruence $a \equiv b$ (mod 2^k). A similar property holds for n-variate T-functions (we just consider the product metric $\| \ \|_2$ on the n-Cartesian power $\mathbb{Z}_2^n$). So we conclude:

T-functions = compatible functions = 1-Lipschitz functions.

This implies in particular that given a T-function $f \colon \mathbb{Z}_2 \to \mathbb{Z}_2$ and $k \in \mathbb{N} = \{1, 2, 3, \ldots\}$, the map f mod $2^k \colon z \mapsto f(z)$ mod 2^k is a well-defined transformation of the residue ring $\mathbb{Z}/2^k\mathbb{Z} = \{0, 1, \ldots, 2^k - 1\}$; actually the reduced map f mod 2^k is a T-function on k-bit words.

The following functions satisfy Lipschitz condition with a constant 1 and thus are T-functions, and so also be used in compositions of cryptographic primitives:

- subtraction $(u, v) \mapsto u - v$;
- exponentiation $(u, v) \mapsto (1 + 2u)^v$; and in particular raising to negative powers, $u \mapsto (1 + 2u)^{-n}$;
- division $(u, v) \mapsto \frac{u}{1+2v}$.

As metric spaces $\mathbb{Z}_2$ and $\mathbb{F}_2[[X]]$ are isometric to each other, *one may express arbitrary T-function both via van der Put series over $\mathbb{Z}_2$ and via van der Put series over $\mathbb{F}_2[[X]]$*.

Theorem 1 (Anashin-Khrennikov-Yurova, [8]). *The map $f \colon \mathbb{Z}_2 \to \mathbb{Z}_2$ is a T-function if and only it can be represented as*

$$f(x) = \sum_{m=0}^{\infty} b(m) 2^{\lfloor \log_2 m \rfloor} \chi(m, x), \tag{5}$$

where $b(m) \in \mathbb{Z}_2$ for $m = 0, 1, 2, \ldots$

Theorem 2 (D. Lin, T. Shi and Z. Yang, [24]). *A continuous function $f \colon \mathbb{F}_2[[X]] \to \mathbb{F}_2[[X]]$ is a T-function if and only if it can be expressed as*

$$f(x) = \sum_{\alpha \in \mathbb{F}_2[X]} b_\alpha X^{\deg \alpha} \chi(\alpha, x) \tag{6}$$

for suitable $b_\alpha \in \mathbb{F}_2[[X]]$, $\alpha \in \mathbb{F}_2[X]$.

2.4   Invertibility and Single Cycle Property

Given $k \in \mathbb{N}$, a T-function $f \colon \mathbb{Z}_2 \to \mathbb{Z}_2$ is said to be *bijective modulo 2^k* iff it is invertible on k-bit words; that is, iff the reduced map f mod $2^k \colon \mathbb{Z}/2^k\mathbb{Z} \to \mathbb{Z}/2^k\mathbb{Z}$ is a permutation on the residue ring $\mathbb{Z}/2^k\mathbb{Z}$. Similarly, a T-function $f \colon \mathbb{Z}_2 \to \mathbb{Z}_2$ is said to be *transitive modulo 2^k* iff it is a single cycle on k-bit words; that is, iff the reduced map f mod 2^k: $\mathbb{Z}/2^k\mathbb{Z} \to \mathbb{Z}/2^k\mathbb{Z}$ is a permutation on the residue ring $\mathbb{Z}/2^k\mathbb{Z}$ with the only cycle (hence, with the cycle of length 2^k).

Definition 1. *We say that a T-function f: $\mathbb{Z}_2 \to \mathbb{Z}_2$ is bijective if and only if f is bijective modulo 2^n for all $n \in \mathbb{N}$; we say that f is transitive if and only if f is transitive modulo 2^n for all $n \in \mathbb{N}$.*

Actually the above definition is a theorem that is proved in the p-adic ergodic theory, see [3] for details. *The bijectivity and/or transitivity properties of T-functions can be expressed in terms of van der Put series:*

Theorem 3 (Anashin-Khrennikov-Yurova, [8]). *The map f: $\mathbb{Z}_2 \to \mathbb{Z}_2$ is a bijective T-function if and only if coefficients $b(m)$ of its van der Put series (5) satisfy the following conditions:*

1. $b(0) + b(1) \equiv 1 \pmod 2$,
2. $\|b(m)\|_2 = 1$, if $m \geq 2$.

The map f: $\mathbb{Z}_2 \to \mathbb{Z}_2$ is a transitive T-function if and only if coefficients $b(m)$ of its van der Put series (5) satisfy the following conditions:

1. $b(0) \equiv 1 \pmod 2$;
2. $b(0) + b(1) \equiv 3 \pmod 4$;
3. $b(2) + b(3) \equiv 2 \pmod 4$;
4. $\|b(m)\|_2 = 1$, if $m \geq 2$;
5. $\sum_{m=2^{n-1}}^{2^n-1} b(m) \equiv 0 \pmod 4$, if $n \geq 3$.

Theorem 4 (D. Lin, T. Shi and Z. Yang, [24]). *Let a T-function f: $\mathbb{F}_2[[X]] \to \mathbb{F}_2[[X]]$ be represented via van der Put series (6). The T-function f is bijective if and only if the following conditions hold simultaneously:*

1. $b_0 + b_1 \equiv 1 \pmod X$, and
2. $\|b_\alpha\|_2 = 1$ if $\deg \alpha \geq 1$.

The T-function f is transitive if and only if the following conditions hold simultaneously:

1. $b_0 \equiv 1 \pmod X$;
2. $b_0 + b_1 \equiv X + 1 \pmod {X^2}$;
3. $b_X + b_{1+X} \equiv X \pmod {X^2}$;
4. $\|b_\alpha\|_2 = 1$, if $\deg \alpha \geq 1$;
5. $\sum_{\alpha=X^{n-1}}^{X^{n-1}+\cdots+X+1} b_\alpha \equiv X \pmod {X^2}$, if $n \geq 3$.

3   Methods

In this section, we use van der Put series to expand T-functions, the representation can be used to evaluate a T-function via a knapsack-like algorithm. It is faster to evaluate a T-function compared to representation via other known expansions,i.e., Mahler series or via coordinate functions. From what has been said in Subsection 2.3 it follows that given arbitrary T-function f on k-bit words, $f\colon \mathbb{F}_2^k \to \mathbb{F}_2^k$, it may be represented in either of two forms,

$$f(x) = \sum_{m=0}^{2^k-1} b(m) 2^{\lfloor \log_2 m \rfloor} \chi(m, x), \tag{7}$$

$$f(x) = \bigoplus_{\alpha=0}^{1+X+\cdots+X^{k-1}} b(\alpha) X^{\deg \alpha} \chi(\alpha, x), \tag{8}$$

where $\sum$ stands for summation modulo 2^k of k-bit words considered as base-2 expansions of integers from $\{0, 1, \ldots, 2^k - 1\}$ (that is, for a summation with carry) , whereas $\bigoplus$ stands for a bitwise summation modulo 2 (that is, without carry).

Note that although in the first case the k-bit words are considered as base-2 expansions of integers, and as polynomials over $\mathbb{F}_2$ of degree $< k$ in the second case, actually in both cases we deal with k-bit words. That is, there is a natural one-to-one correspondence between integers m from $\{0, 1, \ldots, 2^k - 1\}$, polynomials α (over $\mathbb{F}_2$) from $\{0, 1, X, \ldots, \}$ and k-bit words from $\mathbb{F}_2^k$: If we successively enumerate bits in words by $0, 1, 2, \ldots$ from right to left, then to every k-bit word $w \in \mathbb{F}_2^k$ we put into the correspondence the number $m_w \in \{0, 1, \ldots, 2^k - 1\}$ whose base-2 expansion is w and a polynomial α_w whose coefficients agree with w (e.g., $\alpha_{0\ldots0} = 0$, $\alpha_{0\ldots01} = 1$, $\alpha_{0\ldots010} = X$, $\alpha_{1\ldots1} = X^{k-1} + \cdots + X + 1$, etc.).

Accordingly, the coefficients $b(m) 2^{\lfloor \log_2 m \rfloor}$ and $b(\alpha) X^{\deg \alpha}$ are also just k-bit words that have not less than $\lfloor \log_2 m \rfloor$ (respectively, not less than $\deg \alpha$) zeros in rightmost positions. Now, if we arrange the coefficients into a $2^k \times k$ table T_f whose entries are numbered with k-bit words from $0\cdots00$ to $1\cdots11$, the evaluation of $f(x)$ is just a summation (by $+$, or, respectively, by $\bigoplus$) of entries of the table T_f such that the values of characteristic functions $\chi(m, x)$ (or, respectively, $\chi(\alpha, x)$) are 1. Now, given a k-bit word $x \in \mathbb{F}_2^k$, all m (or, respectively, all α) such that $\chi(m, x) = 1$ (respectively, $\chi(\alpha, x) = 1$) can be found as follows.

Let w_ℓ, $\ell = 1, 2, \ldots, k$, be a k-bit word with 0 at all positions except of the rightmost positions $0, 1, \ldots, \ell - 1$ where there is 1; that is, w is a base-2 expansion of integer $2^\ell - 1$ (or, respectively, w_ℓ corresponds to the polynomial $X^{\ell-1} + \cdots + X + 1$). The following proposition holds:

Proposition 1. *Given a k-bit word $x \in \mathbb{F}_2^k$, under the natural one-to-one correspondence between integers m from $\{0, 1, \ldots, 2^k - 1\}$, polynomials α over $\mathbb{F}_2$ of degree $< k$ and k-bit words,*

$$\{m \colon \chi(m, x) = 1\} = \{\alpha \colon \chi(\alpha, x) = 1\} = \{x \wedge w_\ell \colon \ell = 1, 2, \ldots, k\}.$$

Proof. Indeed, from definitions of the 2-adic absolute value $\| \ \|_2$ and of characteristic functions $\chi(m, x)$, $\chi(\alpha, x)$ (see Subsections 2.2 and 2.3), we have that

- $\chi(m, x) = 1$ if and only if $m \equiv x \pmod{2^{1 + \lfloor \log_2 m \rfloor}}$;
- $\chi(\alpha, x) = 1$ if and only if $\alpha \equiv x \pmod{X^{1 + \deg \alpha}}$.

Now we note that $x \bmod 2^{1+\lfloor \log_2 m \rfloor} = x \wedge w_{1+\lfloor \log_2 m \rfloor}$, $x \bmod X^{1+\deg \alpha} = x \wedge w_{1+\deg \alpha}$, and the assertion follows. □

Now, given the table $T_f = [B(w): w \in \mathbb{F}_2^k]$, every k-bit word $f(x)$ can be calculated via either of procedures $\mathbf{P}(x, f, \boxplus)$, where $\boxplus \in \{+, \oplus\}$:

```
    if  x ∧ w₁ < 1  then  S := B(0···00)
                    else  S := B(0···01);
    f(x) := S;
    i := 1;
C:  if  i = k  then STOP
              else
                    i := i + 1;
                    if  x ∧ wᵢ < 2^{i-1}  then  f(x) := f(x)
                                          else  f(x) := f(x) ⊞ B(x ∧ wᵢ);
              repeat C.
```

It can be easily seen that to compute $f(x)$, either of procedures $\mathbf{P}(x, f, \boxplus)$, $\boxplus \in \{+, \oplus\}$, uses not more than k memory calls $B(w)$, not more than k compare instruction $</\not<$ for integers, not more than k bitwise and's $\wedge$, and not more than $k-1$ integer additions $+$ modulo 2^k (i.e., with carry) or, respectively, bitwise additions $\oplus$ modulo 2 (i.e., without carry) of k-bit words. Note that if necessary, the compare instruction $x \wedge w_i < 2^{i-1}$ can be replaced by the instruction whether $x \wedge 2^{i-1}$ is 0 or not: just note that 2^{i-1} corresponds to the word with 1 at the $(i-1)$-th position with 0 at the rest positions.

We also note that the procedure $\mathbf{P}(x, \oplus)$ are more appropriate to the long words computing case, since there are no carries to leftmost bits during summation.

Finally, from Theorems 3 and 4 it follows how one should arrange the table T_f to provide the corresponding T-function f be bijective (=invertible) or transitive (=with a single cycle property). For instance, to ensure the T-function is invertible, only one of the entries $B(0 \cdots 00)$ and $B(0 \cdots 01)$ must have 1 at the rightmost position, and, for the rest entries, if ℓ is leftmost position in the k-bit word $\chi_{k-1} \cdots \chi_0$ such that $\chi_\ell = 1$, then the entry $B(\chi_{k-1} \cdots \chi_0)$ must have 1 at the ℓ-th position as well (recall that bits at rightmost positions $0, 1, \ldots, \ell - 1$ must be 0 due to Theorems 1 and 2).

Respectively, to ensure the T-function f has a single cycle property one should arrange the table T_f in a similar manner, in accordance with conditions 1-5 of Theorems 3 and 4 accordingly. We note that conditions 1-4 being re-stated in terms of words are the same for both procedures $\mathbf{P}(x, f, +)$ and $\mathbf{P}(x, f, \oplus)$; there is a slight difference only in condition 5.

It is worth noticing here that in practical cases to ensure the T-function is invertible or has a single cycle property, the table T_f may contain *significantly less than 2^k entries*: Indeed, to ensure these properties we actually need only to have few bits of the entries fixed in due positions to satisfy conditions of

Theorems 3 and/or 4. Therefore, some of the entries (may be, most of the entries) of the table T_f may be calculated on-the-fly by certain fast procedures rather then stored in memory. Time-memory interplay of this sort can be used to achieve optimal time-memory consumption for the procedure. We illustrate the latter interplay by an example of a procedure $\mathbf{P}_{m,d}(x)$ that evaluates invertible T-function on k-bit words; the procedure needs memory of $2^m \times k$ memory arranged in a table of 2^m k-bit words, m is fixed, $1 < m < k$.

Take and fix some $(k-m)$-bit word d that has 1 in the rightmost position; that is, d is a base-2 expansion of a positive odd integer which we denote via the same symbol d. Given $k > i > m$, the integer $2^i d \bmod 2^k$ corresponds to the k-bit word $u_i(d)$ that has 0 in all rightmost positions $0, 1, \ldots, i-1$ and 1 at the i-th position (actually it is the word d shifted to i positions left). Set $B(0\cdots 00)$ and $B(0\cdots 01)$ so that only one of them has 1 in the rightmost position. Then the procedure $\mathbf{P}_{m,d}(x)$ is as follows:

```
    if  x ∧ w₁< 1 then  S := B(0···00)
                 else  S := B(0···01);
    f(x) := S;
    i := 1;
C:  if  i = k then STOP
              else
                  i := i + 1;
                  if  i < m then
                              if  x ∧ wᵢ < 2^{i-1} then  f(x) := f(x)
                              else  f(x) := f(x) ⊞ B(x ∧ wᵢ);
                          else
                              if  x ∧ wᵢ < 2^{i-1} then  f(x) := f(x)
                              else  f(x) := f(x) ⊞ uᵢ(d);
                  repeat C.
```

Of course, the above procedure $\mathbf{P}_{m,d}(x)$ is a toy example only; however, it illustrates the very idea of time-memory trade-offs in development of T-function-based primitives to achieve better performance and usage of memory.

4   Conclusion

In the paper, we have presented two methods of fast computation of values of arbitrary T-function on k-bit words. Either of the methods uses not more than k calls to memory, not more than k bitwise and's $\wedge$ and not more than k integer additions modulo 2^k, or, respectively, xor's $\oplus$ (=bitwise additions modulo 2). The second of these methods (the one that uses xor's) is suitable for large scale data computing and can be used in design T-function-based stream ciphers that operate with very long words. Both methods use a specially organised array of k-bit words.

References

[1] Anashin, V.: Non-Archimedean theory of T-functions. In: Proc. Advanced Study Institute Boolean Functions in Cryptology and Information Security. NATO Sci. Peace Secur. Ser. D Inf. Commun. Secur., vol. 18, pp. 33–57. IOS Press, Amsterdam (2008)

[2] Anashin, V.: Non-Archimedean ergodic theory and pseudorandom generators. The Computer Journal 53(4), 370–392 (2010), doi:10.1093/comjnl/bxm101

[3] Anashin, V., Khrennikov, A.: Applied Algebraic Dynamics. de Gruyter Expositions in Mathematics, vol. 49. Walter de Gruyter GmbH & Co., Berlin (2009)

[4] Anashin, V.S.: Uniformly distributed sequences of p-adic integers. Mathematical Notes 55(2), 109–133 (1994)

[5] Anashin, V.S.: Uniformly distributed sequences in computer algebra, or how to constuct program generators of random numbers. J. Math. Sci. 89(4), 1355–1390 (1998)

[6] Anashin, V.S.: Uniformly distributed sequences of p-adic integers, II. Discrete Math. Appl. 12(6), 527–590 (2002)

[7] Anashin, V.S., Khrennikov, A.Y., Yurova, E.I.: Characterization of ergodicity of p-adic dynamical systems. Doklady Mathematics 83(3), 1–3 (2011)

[8] Anashin, V.S., Khrennikov, A.Y., Yurova, E.I.: T-functions revisited: New criteria for bijectivity/transitivity. Designs, Codes and Cryptography (2012), doi:10.1007/s10623-012-9741-z

[9] Anashin, V.: Uniformly distributed sequences over p-adic integers. In: Shparlinsky, I., van der Poorten, A.J., Zimmer, H.G. (eds.) Proceedings of the Int'l Conference on Number Theoretic and Algebraic Methods in Computer Science, Moscow, June-July, 1993, pp. 1–18. World Scientific (1995)

[10] Anashin, V., Bogdanov, A., Kizhvatov, I.: ABC: A New Fast Flexible Stream Cipher, Version 3. Technical report, eSTREAM (2005),
http://www.ecrypt.eu.org/stream/p2ciphers/abc/abc_p2.pdf

[11] Hong, J., Lee, D.-H., Yeom, Y., Han, D.: A new class of single cycle T-functions. In: Gilbert, H., Handschuh, H. (eds.) FSE 2005. LNCS, vol. 3557, pp. 68–82. Springer, Heidelberg (2005)

[12] Hong, J., Lee, D.H., Yeom, Y., Han, D.: T-function based stream cipher TSC-3. Technical Report 2005/031, eSTREAM (2005),
http://www.ecrypt.eu.org/stream/ciphers/tsc3/tsc3.pdf

[13] Klimov, A., Shamir, A.: Cryptographic applications of T-functions. In: Matsui, M., Zuccherato, R. (eds.) SAC 2003. LNCS, vol. 3006, pp. 248–261. Springer, Heidelberg (2004)

[14] Klimov, A., Shamir, A.: A new class of invertible mappings. In: Kaliski Jr., B.S., Koç, Ç.K., Paar, C. (eds.) CHES 2002. LNCS, vol. 2523, pp. 470–483. Springer, Heidelberg (2003)

[15] Klimov, A., Shamir, A.: New cryptographic primitives based on multiword T-functions. In: Roy, B., Meier, W. (eds.) FSE 2004. LNCS, vol. 3017, pp. 1–15. Springer, Heidelberg (2004)

[16] Klimov, A., Shamir, A.: The TF-i family of stream ciphers. Handout distributed at: The State of the Art of Stream Ciphers - SASC (2004)

[17] Klimov, A.: Applications of T-functions in Cryptography. PhD thesis, Weizmann Institute of Science (2005), http://www.wisdom.weizmann.ac.il/~ask/

[18] Klimov, A.B., Shamir, A.: New applications of T-functions in block ciphers and hash functions. In: Gilbert, H., Handschuh, H. (eds.) FSE 2005. LNCS, vol. 3557, pp. 18–31. Springer, Heidelberg (2005)

[19] Koblitz, N.: p-adic numbers, p-adic analysis, and zeta-functions, 2nd edn. Graduate texts in math., vol. 58. Springer (1984)

[20] Kolokotronis, N.: Cryptographic properties of nonlinear pseudorandom number generators. Designs, Codes and Cryptography 46, 353–363 (2008)

[21] Kotomina, L.: Fast nonlinear congruential generators. Master's thesis, Russian State University for the Humanities, Moscow (1999) (in Russian)

[22] Larin, M.V.: Transitive polynomial transformations of residue class rings. Discrete Mathematics and Applications 12(2), 141–154 (2002)

[23] Synaptic Laboratories Limited. The VEST cryptosystem for semiconductors, http://www.vestciphers.com/en/index.html

[24] Lin, D., Shi, T., Yang, Z.: Ergodic theory over $\mathbb{F}_2[[T]]$. Finite Fields and Appl. (2011) (in press)

[25] Mahler, K.: p-adic numbers and their functions, 2nd edn. Cambridge Univ. Press (1981)

[26] Maximov, A.: A new stream cipher Mir-1. Technical Report 2005/017, eSTREAM (2005), http://www.ecrypt.eu.org/stream

[27] Moon, D., Kwon, D., Han, D., Lee, J., Ryu, G.H., Lee, D.W., Yeom, Y., Chee, S.: T-function based stream cipher TSC-4. Technical Report 2006/024, eSTREAM (2006), http://www.ecrypt.eu.org/stream/papersdir/2006/024.pdf

[28] O'Neil, S., Gittins, B., Landman, H.: VEST. Technical report, eSTREAM (2006), http://www.ecrypt.eu.org/stream/vestp2.html

[29] Schikhof, W.H.: Ultrametric calculus. Cambridge University Press (1984)

[30] Wirt, K.-T.: ASC – A Stream Cipher with Built–In MAC Functionality. Proc. World Acad. Sci. Engineering and Technology 23 (2007)

[31] Zhang, W., Wu, C.-K.: The algebraic normal form, linear complexity and k-error linear complexity of single-cycle T-function. In: Gong, G., Helleseth, T., Song, H.-Y., Yang, K. (eds.) SETA 2006. LNCS, vol. 4086, pp. 391–401. Springer, Heidelberg (2006)

Construction of Resilient and Nonlinear Boolean Functions with Almost Perfect Immunity to Algebraic and Fast Algebraic Attacks*

Tianze Wang[1,2], Meicheng Liu[1,2], and Dongdai Lin[1]

[1] SKLOIS, Institute of Information Engineering, CAS, Beijing 100195, P.R. China
[2] University of Chinese Academy of Sciences, Beijing 100049, P.R. China
meicheng.liu@gmail.com, {wangtianze,ddlin}@iie.ac.cn

Abstract. In this paper, we study a class of Boolean functions with good cryptographic properties. We show that the functions of this class are 1-resilient and have optimal algebraic degree and good nonlinearity. Further, we prove that the functions of this class have at least sub-maximum algebraic immunity. We also check that, at least for small values of the number of variables, the functions of this class have very good nonlinearity, maximum algebraic immunity and almost perfect immunity to fast algebraic attacks.

Keywords: Boolean functions, correlation immunity, resiliency, nonlinearity, algebraic immunity, fast algebraic attacks.

1 Introduction

Boolean functions are frequently used in the design of stream ciphers, block ciphers and hash functions. One of the most vital roles in cryptography of Boolean functions is to be used as filter and combination generators of stream ciphers based on linear feedback shift registers (LFSR), see description e.g. in [3]. Before this century, the Boolean functions used in the combiner and filter models of stream ciphers had mainly to be balanced, to have high algebraic degree, high nonlinearity and, in the case of the filter model, correlation immunity of order 1. In the case of the combiner model, the Boolean functions should have high correlation immunity.

In recent years, algebraic and fast algebraic attacks [1,6,7] have been regarded as the most successful attacks on LFSR-based stream ciphers. These attacks cleverly use over-defined systems of multi-variable nonlinear equations to recover the secret key. Algebraic attacks lower the degree of the equations by multiplying a nonzero function; while fast algebraic attacks obtain equations of small degree by linear combination.

* Supported by the National 973 Program of China under Grant 2011CB302400, the National Natural Science Foundation of China under Grants 10971246, 60970152 and 61173134, and the Strategic Priority Research Program of the Chinese Academy of Sciences under Grant XDA06010701.

M. Kutyłowski and M. Yung (Eds.): Inscrypt 2012, LNCS 7763, pp. 276–293, 2013.

Thus the algebraic immunity ($\mathcal{AI}$), the minimum algebraic degree of anni-hilators of f or $f + 1$, was introduced by W. Meier et al. [21] to measure the ability of Boolean functions to resist algebraic attacks. It was shown by N. Cour-tois and W. Meier [6] that maximum $\mathcal{AI}$ of n-variable Boolean functions is $\lceil \frac{n}{2} \rceil$. Constructions of Boolean functions with maximum $\mathcal{AI}$ were researched in a large number of papers, e.g., [9,16,17,4,28,30]. Also constructions of 1-resilient Boolean functions with (sub-)maximum $\mathcal{AI}$ and good nonlinearity were pro-posed, e.g., [10,26,22,29,14]. However, there are few results referring to construc-tions of Boolean functions with good immunity against fast algebraic attacks.

The resistance against fast algebraic attacks is not covered by algebraic im-munity [8,2,18]. At Eurocrypt 2006, F. Armknecht et al. [2] introduced an ef-fective algorithm for determining the immunity against fast algebraic attacks, and showed that a class of symmetric Boolean functions (the majority functions) have poor resistance against fast algebraic attacks despite their resistance against algebraic attacks. Later M. Liu et al. [18] stated that almost all the symmetric functions including these functions with good algebraic immunity behave badly against fast algebraic attacks. In [23] P. Rizomiliotis introduced three matrices to evaluate the behavior of Boolean functions against fast algebraic attacks us-ing univariate polynomial representation. Recently, M. Liu et al. showed in [19] that even in the case of the univariate polynomial representation one matrix is enough to evaluate the immunity for fast algebraic attacks.

A preprocessing of fast algebraic attacks on LFSR-based stream ciphers, which use a Boolean function $f : GF(2)^n \rightarrow GF(2)$ as the filter or combination gener-ator, is to find a function g of small degree such that the multiple gf has degree not too large. In [7] N. Courtois proved that for any pair of positive integers (e, d) such that $e + d \geq n$, there is a nonzero function g of degree at most e such that gf has degree at most d. This result reveals an upper bound on maximum immunity to fast algebraic attacks. It implies that the function f has maximum possible resistance against fast algebraic attacks, if for any pair of positive in-tegers (e, d) such that $e + d < n$ and $e < n/2$, there is no nonzero function g of degree at most e such that gf has degree at most d. Such functions are said to be perfect algebraic immune ($\mathcal{PAI}$) [19]. Note that one can use the fast general attack by splitting the function into two $f = h + l$ with l being the linear part of f [7]. In this case, e equals 1 and d equals the degree of the function f, where g can be considered as the nonzero constant. Thus $\mathcal{PAI}$ functions have algebraic degree at least $n - 1$. A $\mathcal{PAI}$ function also achieves maximum $\mathcal{AI}$. As a consequence, a $\mathcal{PAI}$ function has perfect immunity against classical and fast algebraic attacks. Besides, it is shown that a perfect algebraic immune function behaves good against probabilistic algebraic attacks as well [19]. Although pre-venting classical and fast algebraic attacks is not sufficient for resisting algebraic attacks on the augmented function [12], the resistance against these attacks de-pends on the update function and tap positions used in a stream cipher and in actual fact it is not a property of the Boolean function. In [19] M. Liu et al. proved that there are n-variable $\mathcal{PAI}$ functions if and only if $n = 2^s$ or $2^s + 1$. More precisely, there exist n-variable $\mathcal{PAI}$ functions with degree $n - 1$ (balanced functions) if and only if $n = 2^s + 1$; there exist n-variable $\mathcal{PAI}$ functions with degree n (unbalanced functions) if and only if $n = 2^s$.

Several classes of Boolean functions, e.g., [4,30,27], are observed through computer experiments by Armknecht's algorithm [2] to have good behavior against fast algebraic attacks. Carlet-Feng functions (see [4]) were proven in [19] to be optimal against fast algebraic attacks, and the functions of D. Tang et al. (see [27]) were proven in [20] to be (almost) optimal against fast algebraic attacks. Both Carlet-Feng functions and the functions of D. Tang et al. have good nonlinearity. Nevertheless, in the previous literature, no single function is shown to be 1-resilient, have good nonlinearity, and behave well against algebraic and fast algebraic attacks.

In this paper, we study a class of $2k$-variable functions which satisfy all the main criteria, including the above properties. The functions of this class are balanced and have correlation immunity of order 1, that is, they are 1-resilient. We show that they have also optimal algebraic degree and we prove a lower bound on their nonlinearities. Besides, we prove that the $\mathcal{AI}$ of these functions is at least sub-maximum. We compute for small values of n the exact values of the nonlinearity, which are very good and behave as $2^{n-1} - n2^{\frac{n}{2}-3}$, and we also check for small values of n that the functions have maximum $\mathcal{AI}$ and are almost $\mathcal{PAI}$. This is the first time a whole class of functions seem able to satisfy all of the main criteria for being used as a filtering function in a stream cipher.

The remainder of this paper is organized as follows. In Section 2 some basic concepts are provided. Section 3 gives the construction of the functions. In section 4, we prove that the functions achieve 1-resiliency and optimal algebraic degree. Besides, we prove a lower bound on their nonlinearity and also give the exact values of the nonlinearity for small values of n. Section 5 studies the algebraic immunity of the functions and presents experimental results of the immunity to fast algebraic attacks. Section 6 concludes the paper.

2   Preliminary

Let $\mathbb{F}_2$ denote the binary field $GF(2)$ and $\mathbb{F}_2^n$ the n-dimensional vector space over $\mathbb{F}_2$. An n-variable Boolean function is a mapping from $\mathbb{F}_2^n$ into $\mathbb{F}_2$. Denote by $\mathbf{B}_n$ the set of all n-variable Boolean functions. An n-variable Boolean function f can be uniquely represented as its truth table, i.e., a binary string of length 2^n,

$$f = [f(0,0,\cdots,0), f(1,0,\cdots,0), \cdots, f(1,1,\cdots,1)].$$

The support of f is given by $\mathrm{supp}(f) = \{x \in \mathbb{F}_2^n \mid f(x) = 1\}$. The Hamming weight of f, denoted by $\mathrm{wt}(f)$, is the number of ones in the truth table of f. An n-variable function f is said to be balanced if its truth table contains equal number of zeros and ones, that is, $\mathrm{wt}(f) = 2^{n-1}$. The Hamming distance between n-variable functions f and g, denoted by $\mathrm{d}(f,g)$, is the number of $x \in \mathbb{F}_2^n$ at which $f(x) \neq g(x)$. It is well known that $\mathrm{d}(f,g) = \mathrm{wt}(f + g)$.

An n-variable Boolean function f can also be uniquely represented as a multivariate polynomial over $\mathbb{F}_2$,

$$f(x_1, \cdots, x_n) = \sum_{c \in \mathbb{F}_2^n} \lambda_c \prod_{i=1}^{n} x_i^{c_i}, \ \lambda_c \in \mathbb{F}_2, c = (c_1, \cdots, c_n),$$

called the algebraic normal form (ANF). The algebraic degree of f, denoted by $\deg(f)$, is defined as $\max\{\text{wt}(c) \mid a_c \neq 0\}$, where $\text{wt}(c)$ is the Hamming weight of c (i.e. the number of ones in the vector c). A Boolean function is affine if it has degree at most 1. The set of all affine functions on n variables is denoted by $\mathbf{A}_n$.

Let $\mathbb{F}_{2^n}$ denote the finite field $GF(2^n)$. The Boolean function f considered as a mapping from $\mathbb{F}_{2^n}$ into $\mathbb{F}_2$ can be uniquely represented as

$$f(x) = \sum_{i=0}^{2^n-1} a_i x^i, \ a_i \in \mathbb{F}_{2^n}, \tag{1}$$

where $f^2(x) \equiv f(x) \pmod{x^{2^n} - x}$. Expression (1) is called the univariate polynomial representation of the function f. It is well known that $f^2(x) \equiv f(x) \pmod{x^{2^n} - x}$ if and only if $a_0, a_{2^n-1} \in \mathbb{F}_2$ and for $1 \leq i \leq 2^n - 2$, $a_{2i \bmod (2^n-1)} = a_i^2$. The algebraic degree of the function f equals $\max_{a_i \neq 0} \text{wt}(i)$, where $i = \sum_{k=1}^{n} i_k 2^{k-1}$ is considered as $(i_1, i_2, \cdots, i_n) \in \mathbb{F}_2^n$.

In this representation, the elements of $\mathbf{A}_n$ are all the functions $\text{Tr}_1^n(ax) + c$, $a \in \mathbb{F}_{2^n}$, $c \in \mathbb{F}_2$, where Tr_1^n is the absolute trace function from $\mathbb{F}_{2^n}$ to $\mathbb{F}_2$: $\text{Tr}_1^n(x) = x + x^2 + x^{2^2} + \cdots + x^{2^{n-1}}$.

Let α be a primitive element of $\mathbb{F}_{2^n}$. The a_i's of Expression (1) are given by $a_0 = f(0), a_{2^n-1} = f(0) + \sum_{j=0}^{2^n-2} f(\alpha^j)$ and

$$a_i = \sum_{j=0}^{2^n-2} f(\alpha^j) \alpha^{-ij}, \ \text{for } 1 \leq i \leq 2^n - 2. \tag{2}$$

Let $n = 2k$. The Boolean function f considered as a mapping from $\mathbb{F}_{2^k} \times \mathbb{F}_{2^k}$ into $\mathbb{F}_2$ can be uniquely represented as

$$f(x, y) = \sum_{i=0}^{2^k-1} \sum_{j=0}^{2^k-1} a_{ij} x^i y^j, \ a_{ij} \in \mathbb{F}_{2^k}, \tag{3}$$

where $f^2(x, y) \equiv f(x, y) \pmod{(x^{2^k} - x, y^{2^k} - y)}$. Expression (3) is called the bivariate polynomial representation of the function f. We can see that $f^2(x, y) \equiv f(x, y) \pmod{(x^{2^k} - x, y^{2^k} - y)}$ if and only if $a_{2^k-1, 2^k-1} \in \mathbb{F}_2$ and for $0 \leq i \leq 2^k - 2$ and $0 \leq j \leq 2^k - 2$,

$$a_{2i,2j} = a_{ij}^2,$$
$$a_{2^k-1,2j} = a_{2^k-1,j}^2, \tag{4}$$
$$a_{2i,2^k-1} = a_{i,2^k-1}^2,$$

where $2i$ and $2j$ are considered as $2i \bmod(2^k-1)$ and $2j \bmod(2^k-1)$ respectively, which implies $a_{0,0}, a_{0,2^k-1}, a_{2^k-1,0} \in \mathbb{F}_2$. The algebraic degree of the function f equals $\max_{a_{ij} \neq 0}\{\mathrm{wt}(i) + \mathrm{wt}(\bar{j})\}$.

In this representation, the elements of $\mathbf{A}_{2k}$ are all the functions $\mathrm{Tr}_1^k(ax) + \mathrm{Tr}_1^k(by) + c$, $a, b \in \mathbb{F}_{2^k}$, $c \in \mathbb{F}_2$.

Many properties of Boolean functions can be described by the Walsh spectra. For $x = (x_1, x_2, \cdots, x_n) \in \mathbb{F}_2^n$ and $w = (w_1, w_2, \cdots, w_n) \in \mathbb{F}_2^n$, let $w \cdot x = w_1 x_1 \oplus w_2 x_2 \oplus \cdots \oplus w_n x_n \in \mathbb{F}_2$. The Walsh transform of the Boolean function f is an integer valued function over $\mathbb{F}_2^n$ which is defined as

$$W_f(w) = \sum_{x \in \mathbb{F}_2^n} (-1)^{f(x) + w \cdot x}.$$

The nonlinearity of f, defined as the minimum Hamming distance between f and the set of affine functions, can be given by

$$\mathcal{NL}(f) = 2^{n-1} - \frac{1}{2} \max_{w \in \mathbb{F}_2^n} |W_f(w)|.$$

A high nonlinearity is surely one of the most important cryptographic criteria.

Correlation immune functions and resilient functions are two important classes of Boolean functions. The function f is m-resilient (resp. m-th order correlation immune) if and only if $W_f(w) = 0$ for $0 \leq \mathrm{wt}(w) \leq m$ (resp. $1 \leq \mathrm{wt}(w) \leq m$).

The algebraic immunity of Boolean functions is defined as follows. Maximum algebraic immunity of n-variable Boolean functions is $\lceil \frac{n}{2} \rceil$ [6].

Definition 1. [21] The algebraic immunity of a function $f \in \mathbf{B}_n$, denoted by $\mathcal{AI}(f)$, is defined as

$$\mathcal{AI}(f) = \min\{\deg(g) \mid gf = 0 \text{ or } g(f+1) = 0, 0 \neq g \in \mathbf{B}_n\}.$$

If there is a nonzero Boolean function g with degree at most e such that the product gf has degree at most d, with e small and d not too large, then the Boolean function f is considered to be weak against fast algebraic attacks. The exact values of e and d for which a fast algebraic attack is feasible depends on several parameters, like the size of the memory and the key size of the stream cipher [13].

Definition 2. [19] Let f be an n-variable Boolean function. The function f is said to be perfect algebraic immune (PAI) if for any positive integers $e < n/2$, the product gf has degree at least $n - e$ for any non-zero function g of degree at most e.

A $\mathcal{PAI}$ function also achieves maximum $\mathcal{AI}$. As a matter of fact, if a function does not achieve maximum $\mathcal{AI}$, then it admits a non-zero function g of degree less than $n/2$ such that $gf = 0$ or $gf = g$, which means that it is not $\mathcal{PAI}$. Therefore $\mathcal{PAI}$ functions are the class of Boolean functions perfectly resistant to algebraic and fast algebraic attacks. However, $\mathcal{PAI}$ functions are quite rare. For a perfect algebraic immune balanced function, the number of input variables is one more than a power of two [19].

Theorem 1. *[19] Let $f \in \mathbf{B}_n$ be a perfect algebraic immune function. Then n is one more than or equal to a power of 2. Further, if the algebraic degree of f is less than n, then n is one more than a power of 2; if the algebraic degree of f is equal to n, then n is a power of 2.*

3   Construction

In this section we present a class of $2k$-variable Boolean functions with $k \geq 3$. The following sections consider their resiliency, algebraic degree, nonlinearity, algebraic immunity and the immunity against fast algebraic attacks.

Construction 1. *Let n, k, s and m be integers such that $n = 2k$, $k \geq 3$, $1 \leq s \leq 2^k - 3$, $\gcd(s(s+1), 2^k - 1) = 1$, $2^{k-1} - 1 \leq m \leq 2^k - 2$. Let $\mathbb{Z}_{2^k-1} = \{0, 1, \ldots, 2^k - 2\}$ and $\Delta_m = \{0, 1, \ldots, 2^{k-1} - 2\} \cup \{m\}$. Let α be a primitive element of $\mathbb{F}_{2^k}$.*

Let f be the Boolean function on $\mathbb{F}_{2^k} \times \mathbb{F}_{2^k}$ whose bivariate polynomial representation is given as follows,

$$f(x, y) = \phi(xy) + (x^{2^k-1} + 1)\psi(y^s) + (y^{2^k-1} + 1)\varphi(x) + ((x+y^s)^{2^k-1} + 1)\lambda(x), \quad (5)$$

where $\phi, \psi, \varphi, \lambda$ are Boolean functions on $\mathbb{F}_{2^k}$ satisfying the following requirements:

- $\mathrm{supp}(\phi) = \{0, 1, \alpha, \ldots, \alpha^{2^{k-1}-2}\}$, *i.e., ϕ is a Carlet-Feng function,*
- $\mathrm{supp}(\psi) = \{\alpha^{\frac{\ell}{t+1}} | \ell \in \mathbb{Z}_{2^k-1} \setminus \Delta_m\}$, *where $t = s^{-1} \bmod (2^k - 1)$,*
- $\mathrm{supp}(\varphi) = \mathrm{supp}(\psi)$,
- $\mathrm{supp}(\lambda) = \mathrm{supp}(\psi) \cup \{0\}$.

Let $A + B$ denote the union of two disjoint sets A and B, and let $A - B$ denote the set difference of A and B for $B \subset A$. Applying to (5) the fact that

$$\mathrm{supp}(f_1 + f_2) = \mathrm{supp}(f_1) \cup \mathrm{supp}(f_2) \setminus (\mathrm{supp}(f_1) \cap \mathrm{supp}(f_2)), \text{ for } f_1, f_2 \in \mathbf{B}_n,$$

it holds for the function f in Construction 1 that

$$\mathrm{supp}(f) = \mathrm{supp}(\phi(xy)) - \{(0, y) | y \in \mathrm{supp}(\psi(y^s))\} - \{(x, 0) | x \in \mathrm{supp}(\psi)\}$$
$$+ \{(x, x^t) | x \in \mathrm{supp}(\psi)\} - \{(0, 0)\}, \quad (6)$$

then the support of f consists of the following four disjoint parts:

- $\bigcup_{\ell=0}^{2^{k-1}-2}\{(x,y)|y=\alpha^\ell x^{-1}, x\in\mathbb{F}_{2^k}^*\}$,
- $\{(0,\alpha^{\frac{\ell t}{t+1}})|\ell\in\Delta_m\}$,
- $\{(\alpha^{\frac{\ell}{t+1}},0)|\ell\in\Delta_m\}$,
- $\{(\alpha^{\frac{\ell}{t+1}},\alpha^{\frac{\ell t}{t+1}})|\ell\in\mathbb{Z}_{2^k-1}\setminus\Delta_m\}$.

Remark 1. The function f is similar to the function of Tu and Deng [29]. The proof methods of the main results of this paper are also similar to those of [29], whereas the details are very different. The nonlinearity of f is a little smaller than the function of Tu and Deng, but the immunity to fast algebraic attacks are much improved. The function of Jin et al. [14], in their case $u=-1$, is closer to our function, but they are still different.

4   Resiliency, Algebraic Degree and Nonlinearity

In Section 4.1, we show that the functions in Construction 1 are 1-resilient. In Section 4.2 we show that they have also optimal algebraic degree, and in Section 4.3 we prove a lower bound on their nonlinearities.

4.1   Resiliency

Theorem 2. *Let f be defined as in Construction 1. Then f is 1-resilient.*

Proof. From the four parts of the support of f, it follows that

$$\text{wt}(f)=(2^k-1)(2^{k-1}-1)+2|\Delta_m|+(2^k-1-|\Delta_m|)=2^{2k-1}-2^{k-1}+|\Delta_m|.$$

Since $|\Delta_m|=2^{k-1}$, we have $\text{wt}(f)=2^{2k-1}$. Thus f is balanced. Then we verify that $W_f(a,b)=0$ for each $(a,b)\in\mathbb{F}_{2^k}\times\mathbb{F}_{2^k}$ with $\text{wt}(a,b)=\text{wt}(a)+\text{wt}(b)=1$. It is sufficient to show $W_f(a,0)=0$ for $a\in\mathbb{F}_{2^k}^*$ and $W_f(0,b)=0$ for $b\in\mathbb{F}_{2^k}^*$. When $(a,b)\neq(0,0)$, we have

$$W_f(a,b)=\sum_{(x,y)\in\mathbb{F}_{2^k}\times\mathbb{F}_{2^k}}(-1)^{f(x,y)+\text{Tr}_1^k(ax+by)}=-2\sum_{(x,y)\in\text{supp}(f)}(-1)^{\text{Tr}_1^k(ax+by)}$$

since $\sum_{(x,y)\in\mathbb{F}_{2^k}\times\mathbb{F}_{2^k}}(-1)^{\text{Tr}_1^k(ax+by)}=0$.
   By the four parts of the support of f, we can see that

$$\sum_{(x,y)\in\text{supp}(f)}(-1)^{\text{Tr}_1^k(ax+by)}$$

$$=\sum_{\ell=0}^{2^{k-1}-2}\sum_{x\in\mathbb{F}_{2^k}^*}(-1)^{\text{Tr}_1^k(ax+b\alpha^\ell x^{-1})}+\sum_{\ell\in\Delta_m}(-1)^{\text{Tr}_1^k(b\alpha^{\frac{\ell t}{t+1}})}$$

$$+\sum_{\ell\in\Delta_m}(-1)^{\text{Tr}_1^k(a\alpha^{\frac{\ell}{t+1}})}+\sum_{\ell\in\mathbb{Z}_{2^k-1}\setminus\Delta_m}(-1)^{\text{Tr}_1^k(a\alpha^{\frac{\ell}{t+1}}+b\alpha^{\frac{\ell t}{t+1}})}.$$

We consider the Walsh spectra for the following two cases.

1. For $a \neq 0, b = 0$, we have

$$\sum_{(x,y)\in \text{supp}(f)} (-1)^{\text{Tr}_1^k(ax+by)}$$

$$= (2^{k-1}-1)(-1)+|\Delta_m|+\sum_{\ell\in\Delta_m} (-1)^{\text{Tr}_1^k(a\alpha^{\frac{\ell}{\ell+1}})} + \sum_{\ell\in\mathbb{Z}_{2^k-1}\setminus\Delta_m} (-1)^{\text{Tr}_1^k(a\alpha^{\frac{\ell}{\ell+1}})}$$

(since $|\Delta_m| = 2^{k-1}$)

$$= 1 + \sum_{\ell\in\mathbb{Z}_{2^k-1}} (-1)^{\text{Tr}_1^k(a\alpha^{\frac{\ell}{\ell+1}})} = 0.$$

2. For $a = 0, b \neq 0$, we have

$$\sum_{(x,y)\in \text{supp}(f)} (-1)^{\text{Tr}_1^k(ax+by)}$$

$$= (2^{k-1}-1)(-1)+|\Delta_m|+\sum_{\ell\in\Delta_m} (-1)^{\text{Tr}_1^k(b\alpha^{\frac{\ell t}{\ell+1}})} + \sum_{\ell\in\mathbb{Z}_{2^k-1}\setminus\Delta_m} (-1)^{\text{Tr}_1^k(b\alpha^{\frac{\ell t}{\ell+1}})}$$

$$= 1 + \sum_{\ell\in\mathbb{Z}_{2^k-1}} (-1)^{\text{Tr}_1^k(b\alpha^{\frac{\ell t}{\ell+1}})} = 0.$$

Now we have proven that $W_f(a, b) = 0$ for $ab = 0$ and hence f is 1-resilient. □

4.2 Bivariate Polynomial Representation and Algebraic Degree

Before giving the bivariate polynomial representation of f, we compute the co-efficients of the four parts of $f(x,y)$, i.e., the coefficients of $\phi(xy), (x^{2^k-1} + 1)\psi(y^s), (y^{2^k-1} + 1)\varphi(x)$ and $((x + y^s)^{2^k-1} + 1)\lambda(x)$.

Let

$$\phi(x) = \sum_{i=0}^{2^k-1} \phi_i x^i, \ \ \psi(x) = \sum_{i=0}^{2^k-1} \psi_i x^i, \ \ \varphi(x) = \sum_{i=0}^{2^k-1} \varphi_i x^i, \ \ \lambda(x) = \sum_{i=0}^{2^k-1} \lambda_i x^i.$$

And denote by $[h(x,y)]_{i,j}$ the coefficient of the monomial $x^i y^j$ in the bivariate polynomial representation of $h(x,y)$.

The coefficients of the bivariate polynomial representation of $\phi(xy)$ are given by

$$[\phi(xy)]_{i,j} = \begin{cases} \phi_i, & i = j, 0 \leq i, j \leq 2^k - 1, \\ 0, & \text{otherwise.} \end{cases}$$

The coefficients of the bivariate polynomial representation of $(x^{2^k-1} + 1)\psi(y^s)$ are given by

$$[(x^{2^k-1} + 1)\psi(y^s)]_{i,j} = \begin{cases} \psi_{2^k-1}, & i \in \{0, 2^k - 1\}, j = 2^k - 1, \\ \psi_{tj}, & i \in \{0, 2^k - 1\}, 0 \leq j \leq 2^k - 2, \\ 0, & \text{otherwise.} \end{cases}$$

The coefficients of the bivariate polynomial representation of $(y^{2^k-1} + 1)\varphi(x)$ are given by

$$[(y^{2^k-1} + 1)\varphi(x)]_{i,j} = \begin{cases} \varphi_i, & 0 \le i \le 2^k - 1, \, j \in \{0, 2^k - 1\}, \\ 0, & \text{otherwise.} \end{cases}$$

The coefficients of the bivariate polynomial representation of $((x + y^s)^{2^k-1} + 1)\lambda(x)$ are given by

$$[((x + y^s)^{2^k-1} + 1)\lambda(x)]_{i,j} = \begin{cases} \lambda_0, & i = 0, j = 0, \\ \lambda_{tj}, & i = 2^k - 1, 0 \le j \le 2^k - 2, \\ \lambda_i, & 0 \le i \le 2^k - 1, j = 2^k - 1, \\ \lambda_0 + \lambda_{2^k-1}, & i + tj \equiv 0 \bmod(2^k - 1) \\ & \text{and } 1 \le i, j \le 2^k - 2, \\ \lambda_{i+tj}, & i + tj \not\equiv 0 \bmod(2^k - 1), \\ & 1 \le i, j \le 2^k - 2, \\ 0, & \text{otherwise.} \end{cases}$$

Thus

$$f_{i,j} = \begin{cases} \phi_0 + \psi_0 + \varphi_0 + \lambda_0, & i = 0, j = 0, \\ \psi_{2^k-1} + \varphi_0 + \lambda_0, & i = 0, j = 2^k - 1, \\ \psi_0 + \varphi_{2^k-1} + \lambda_0, & i = 2^k - 1, j = 0, \\ \phi_{2^k-1} + \psi_{2^k-1} + \varphi_{2^k-1} + \lambda_{2^k-1}, & i = 2^k - 1, j = 2^k - 1, \\ \psi_{tj}, & i = 0, 1 \le j \le 2^k - 2, \\ \psi_{tj} + \lambda_{tj}, & i = 2^k - 1, 1 \le j \le 2^k - 2, \\ \varphi_i, & 1 \le i \le 2^k - 2, j = 0, \\ \varphi_i + \lambda_i, & 1 \le i \le 2^k - 2, j = 2^k - 1, \\ \lambda_0 + \lambda_{2^k-1}, & i + tj \equiv 0 \bmod(2^k - 1) \\ & \text{and } 1 \le i, j \le 2^k - 2, \\ \phi_i + \lambda_{i+tj}, & i = j, 1 \le i, j \le 2^k - 2, \\ \lambda_{i+tj}, & i + tj \not\equiv 0 \bmod(2^k - 1) \\ & \text{and } i \ne j, 1 \le i, j \le 2^k - 2. \end{cases}$$

By (2) and according to the definitions of ϕ, ψ, φ and λ, we can obtain that

$$\phi(x) = 1 + \sum_{i=1}^{2^k-2} \frac{\alpha^{\frac{i}{2}}}{1 + \alpha^{-\frac{i}{2}}} x^i, \tag{7}$$

$$\psi(x) = \varphi(x) = x^{2^k-1} + \sum_{i=1}^{2^k-2} \left(\frac{\alpha^{\frac{i}{2(t+1)}}}{1 + \alpha^{-\frac{i}{2(t+1)}}} + \alpha^{-\frac{im}{t+1}} \right) x^i, \tag{8}$$

$$\lambda(x) = 1 + \sum_{i=1}^{2^k-2} \left(\frac{\alpha^{\frac{i}{2(t+1)}}}{1 + \alpha^{-\frac{i}{2(t+1)}}} + \alpha^{-\frac{im}{t+1}} \right) x^i. \tag{9}$$

Then taking the coefficients of the univariate polynomial representation of ϕ, ψ, φ and λ in the above equality gives the bivariate polynomial representation of the function f,

$$f_{i,j} = \begin{cases} 0, & i = 0 \text{ and } j = 0, \\ 0, & i = 2^k - 1 \text{ or } j = 2^k - 1, \\ 1, & i + tj \equiv 0 \mod(2^k - 1), 1 \le i, j \le 2^k - 2, \\ \psi_{tj}, & i = 0, 1 \le j \le 2^k - 2, \\ \varphi_i, & 1 \le i \le 2^k - 2, j = 0, \\ \phi_i + \lambda_{i+tj}, & i = j, 1 \le i, j \le 2^k - 2, \\ \lambda_{i+tj}, & i + tj \not\equiv 0 \mod(2^k - 1) \text{ and } i \ne j, 1 \le i, j \le 2^k - 2. \end{cases} \tag{10}$$

Theorem 3. *Let f be defined as in Construction 1. Then $\deg(f) = 2k - 2$.*

Proof. From (10), we can see that $f_{2^k-1,j} = f_{i,2^k-1} = 0$ for $0 \le i, j \le 2^k - 1$, and therefore $\deg(f) \le 2k - 2$. Then to prove $\deg(f) = 2k - 2$ we only need to show $f_{2^k-2,2^k-2} \ne 0$. From (10), we can see that

$$f_{2^k-2,2^k-2} = \phi_{2^k-2} + \lambda_{2^k-2-t}$$
$$\text{(combining with Eq. (7) and Eq. (8))}$$

$$= \frac{\alpha^{\frac{2^k-2}{2}}}{1 + \alpha^{-\frac{2^k-2}{2}}} + \frac{\alpha^{\frac{2^k-2-t}{2(t+1)}}}{1 + \alpha^{-\frac{2^k-2-t}{2(t+1)}}} + \alpha^{-\frac{(2^k-2-t)m}{t+1}}$$

$$= \alpha^m \ne 0.$$

Therefore, $\deg(f) = 2k - 2$. $\qquad\square$

Siegenthaler's inequality [25] states that any m-resilient function on n variables $(0 \le m < n - 1)$ has algebraic degree at most $n - m - 1$. Therefore, the function f of Construction 1 has optimal algebraic degree.

4.3   Nonlinearity

Lemma 4. *[27, Theorem 7] Let α be a primitive element of $\mathbb{F}_{2^k}$ and $a \in \mathbb{F}_{2^k}^*$. Then for $0 \le \ell \le 2^k - 2$ and $\gcd(j, 2^k - 1) = 1$,*

$$\left| \sum_{i=\ell}^{2^{k-1}+\ell-1} (-1)^{\mathrm{Tr}_1^k(a\alpha^{ij})} \right| \le \left(\frac{2 + k\ln 2}{\pi} + \frac{\pi}{32} \right) 2^{\frac{k}{2}}.$$

Theorem 5. *Let f be defined as in Construction 1. Then*

$$\mathcal{NL}(f) \ge 2^{2k-1} - \left(\frac{1 + k\ln 2}{\pi} + \frac{\pi + 16}{32} \right) 2^k - \left(\frac{2 + k\ln 2}{\pi} + \frac{\pi}{32} \right) 2^{\frac{k}{2}+1} - 2$$
$$\approx 2^{2k-1} - k2^{k-2}.$$

Proof. From the proof of Theorem 2, we only need to consider

$$-\frac{1}{2} W_f(a, b) = \sum_{(x,y)\in\mathrm{supp}(f)} (-1)^{\mathrm{Tr}_1^k(ax+by)}, \text{ for } a, b \in \mathbb{F}_{2^k}^*.$$

Then by (6) we know that

$$-\frac{1}{2}W_f(a,b) = \sum_{(x,y)\in\mathrm{supp}(\phi(xy))} (-1)^{\mathrm{Tr}_1^k(ax+by)} - \sum_{y\in\mathrm{supp}(\psi(y^s))} (-1)^{\mathrm{Tr}_1^k(by)}$$
$$- \sum_{x\in\mathrm{supp}(\psi)} (-1)^{\mathrm{Tr}_1^k(ax)} + \sum_{x\in\mathrm{supp}(\psi)} (-1)^{\mathrm{Tr}_1^k(ax+bx^t)} - 1.$$

For $a, b \in \mathbb{F}_{2^k}^*$, by Lemma 4, we can see that

$$\left|\sum_{y\in\mathrm{supp}(\psi(y^s))} (-1)^{\mathrm{Tr}_1^k(by)}\right| \leq \left(\frac{2+k\ln 2}{\pi} + \frac{\pi}{32}\right)2^{\frac{k}{2}} + 1$$

and

$$\left|\sum_{x\in\mathrm{supp}(\psi)} (-1)^{\mathrm{Tr}_1^k(ax)}\right| \leq \left(\frac{2+k\ln 2}{\pi} + \frac{\pi}{32}\right)2^{\frac{k}{2}} + 1.$$

For $a, b \in \mathbb{F}_{2^k}^*$, by [27, Theorem 3], it follows that

$$\left|\sum_{(x,y)\in\mathrm{supp}(\phi(xy))} (-1)^{\mathrm{Tr}_1^k(ax+by)}\right| \leq \left(\frac{1+k\ln 2}{\pi} + \frac{\pi}{32}\right)2^k.$$

Therefore, we have

$$\frac{1}{2}|W_f(a,b)| \leq \left(\frac{1+k\ln 2}{\pi} + \frac{\pi}{32}\right)2^k + \left(\frac{2+k\ln 2}{\pi} + \frac{\pi}{32}\right)2^{\frac{k}{2}+1} + 2^{k-1} + 2.$$

Then

$$\mathcal{NL}(f) = 2^{2k-1} - \frac{1}{2}\max_{(a,b)\in\mathbb{F}_{2^k}\times\mathbb{F}_{2^k}} |W_f(a,b)|$$
$$\geq 2^{2k-1} - \left(\frac{1+k\ln 2}{\pi} + \frac{\pi+16}{32}\right)2^k - \left(\frac{2+k\ln 2}{\pi} + \frac{\pi}{32}\right)2^{\frac{k}{2}+1} - 2$$
$$\approx 2^{2k-1} - \frac{k\ln 2}{\pi}2^k \approx 2^{2k-1} - k2^{k-2}. \qquad \square$$

The lower bound given by Theorem 5 shows that the nonlinearity of our function f is good. Moreover, we checked for small values of n that the exact value of $\mathcal{NL}(f)$ behaves as $2^{n-1} - n2^{\frac{n}{2}-3}$. We give in Table 1 below, for even n ranging from 6 to 18, the values of the nonlinearity of f compared with the functions of [26,29,27] and with the value $2^{n-1} - n2^{\frac{n}{2}-3}$. The nonlinearity of the function of Construction 1 listed in Table 1 is for $(s,m) = (1, 2^{k-1} - 1)$. For other values of (s,m) the functions could have higher nonlinearity. For example, when $n = 12$, a large number of functions (e.g. $(s,m) = (10, 31)$) have the nonlinearity 1976, which is better than the nonlinearity 1964 as shown in Table 1. Besides, the values of $\mathcal{NL}(f)$ are related to the primitive element we choose in $\mathbb{F}_{2^k}$.

All the functions listed in this table are balanced. The functions of [26,29] are also 1-resilient. From this table, we have seen that the nonlinearity of our function f is very close to that of [27], much better than that of [26], and a little smaller than that of [29].

Table 1. The values of the nonlinearity of f compared with previous constructions and the values of $2^{n-1} - n2^{\frac{n}{2}-3}$

n	6	8	10	12	14	16	18
Construction of [26]	-	-	388	1600	6552	26628	107828
Construction 3.1 of [29]	24	112	484	1996	8100	32588	130760
Construction 2 of [27]	22	108	476	1982	8028	32508	130504
Construction 1	20	108	472	1964	7976	32372	130228
$2^{n-1} - n2^{\frac{n}{2}-3}$	26	112	472	1952	7968	32256	129920

5   Immunity against Algebraic and Fast Algebraic Attack

5.1   Algebraic immunity

Lemma 6. *[5,14,20] Let $k \geq 3$ be an integer. For any $0 \leq u \leq 2^k - 2$, we have*

$$\#\{(i,j)|0 \leq i,j \leq 2^k - 2, i-j \equiv u \ (\mathrm{mod} \ 2^k - 1), \mathrm{wt}(i) + \mathrm{wt}(j) \leq k - 1\} \leq 2^{k-1}.$$

Lemma 7. *[14,20] Let $k \geq 3$ be an integer. For any $1 \leq u \leq 2^k - 2$, we have*

$$\#\{(i,j)|0 \leq i,j \leq 2^k - 2, i-j \equiv u \ (\mathrm{mod} \ 2^k - 1), \mathrm{wt}(i) + \mathrm{wt}(j) \leq k - 1\} \leq 2^{k-1} - 1.$$

Theorem 8. *Let f be defined as in Construction 1. Then f has no annihilator with algebraic degree less than k and $f + 1$ has no annihilator with algebraic degree less than $k - 1$. Thus $\mathcal{AI}(f) \geq k - 1$.*

Proof. Let $g : \mathbb{F}_{2^k} \times \mathbb{F}_{2^k} \to \mathbb{F}_2$ be a Boolean function with $\deg(g) < k$ and $f \cdot g = 0$. We will prove $g = 0$.

Since $\deg(g) < k$, we can write g as

$$g(x,y) = \sum_{i=0}^{2^k-2} \sum_{j=0}^{2^k-2} g_{i,j} x^i y^j,$$

where $g_{i,j} \in \mathbb{F}_{2^k}$. For any $(a,b) \in \mathrm{supp}(f)$, we have $g(a,b) = 0$. Then by

$$\bigcup_{\ell=0}^{2^{k-1}-2} \{(x, \alpha^\ell x^{-1})|x \in \mathbb{F}_{2^k}^*\} \subset \mathrm{supp}(f),$$

it follows that for $0 \le \ell \le 2^{k-1} - 2$,

$$0 = g(x, \alpha^\ell x^{-1}) = \sum_{i=0}^{2^k-2} \sum_{j=0}^{2^k-2} g_{i,j} \alpha^{\ell j} x^{i-j} = \sum_{u=0}^{2^k-2} g_u(\alpha) x^u, \qquad (11)$$

where

$$g_u(\alpha) = \sum_{\substack{0 \le i,j \le 2^k-2 \\ i-j \equiv u \bmod 2^k-1}} g_{i,j} \alpha^{\ell j}, \quad \text{for } 0 \le u \le 2^k - 2.$$

Let x run through $\mathbb{F}_{2^k}^*$. Then from Eq. (11) we get the equation

$$(g_0(\alpha), g_1(\alpha), \dots, g_{2^k-2}(\alpha)) \begin{pmatrix} 1 & 1 & \cdots & 1 \\ 1 & \alpha & \cdots & \alpha^{2^k-2} \\ 1 & \alpha^2 & \cdots & (\alpha^{2^k-2})^2 \\ \vdots & \vdots & \ddots & \vdots \\ 1 & \alpha^{2^k-2} & \cdots & (\alpha^{2^k-2})^{2^k-2} \end{pmatrix} = (0,0,\dots,0).$$

By the invertibility of Vandermonde matrix, it is obvious that $g_u(\alpha) = 0$, i.e. for $0 \le u \le 2^{k-1} - 2$

$$\sum_{\substack{0 \le i,j \le 2^k-2 \\ i-j \equiv u \bmod 2^k-1}} g_{i,j} \alpha^{\ell j} = 0, \quad 0 \le \ell \le 2^k - 2. \qquad (12)$$

When $1 \le u \le 2^k - 2$, by Lemma 7 the number of $g_{i,j}$ in Eq. (12) is at most $2^{k-1} - 1$. Without loss of generality, we suppose the $2^{k-1} - 1$ different $g_{i,j}$'s are $\{g_{i_1,j_1}, \dots, g_{i_{2^{k-1}-1}, j_{2^{k-1}-1}}\}$. Since Eq. (12) holds for $0 \le \ell \le 2^{k-1} - 2$, we have that

$$\begin{pmatrix} 1 & 1 & \cdots & 1 \\ \alpha^{j_1} & \alpha^{j_2} & \cdots & \alpha^{j_{2^{k-1}-1}} \\ (\alpha^{j_1})^2 & (\alpha^{j_2})^2 & \cdots & (\alpha^{j_{2^{k-1}-1}})^2 \\ \vdots & \vdots & \ddots & \vdots \\ (\alpha^{j_1})^{2^{k-1}-2} & (\alpha^{j_2})^{2^{k-1}-2} & \cdots & (\alpha^{j_{2^{k-1}-1}})^{2^{k-1}-2} \end{pmatrix} \begin{pmatrix} g_{i_1,j_1} \\ g_{i_2,j_2} \\ \vdots \\ g_{i_{2^{k-1}-1}, j_{2^{k-1}-1}} \end{pmatrix} = \begin{pmatrix} 0 \\ 0 \\ \vdots \\ 0 \end{pmatrix}.$$

By the invertibility of Vandermonde matrix we have

$$g_{i_1,j_1} = \cdots = g_{i_{2^{k-1}-1}, j_{2^{k-1}-1}} = 0,$$

which implies that for $0 \le i,j \le 2^k - 2$ and $1 \le u \le 2^k - 2$, it holds that $g_{i,j} = 0$ if $i - j \equiv u \bmod (2^k - 1)$.

Thus $g_{0,j} = 0$ for $1 \le j \le 2^k - 2$. Since $(0,1) \in \text{supp}(f)$, we have $\sum_{j=0}^{2^k-2} g_{0,j} = g(0,1) = 0$, which implies that $g_{0,0} = 0$. By Lemma 6, Eq. (12) have at most $2^{k-1} - 1$ different $g_{i,j}$'s when $i = j$. By the similar argument we can prove $g_{i,i} = 0$

for $1 \leq i \leq 2^k - 2$. Therefore $g = 0$, i.e. f has no annihilator of degree less than k.

To prove $f + 1$ has no annihilator of degree less than $k - 1$, we first give the support of $f + 1$. One can check that $\mathrm{supp}(f+1)$ is equal to the following disjoint part:

- $\bigcup_{\ell=2^{k-1}-1}^{2^k-2}\{(x,y)|y = \alpha^\ell x^{-1}, x \in \mathbb{F}_{2^k}^* \setminus \{\alpha^{\frac{\ell}{i+1}}\}\}$,
- $\{(0, \alpha^{\frac{\ell t}{i+1}})|\ell \in \mathbb{Z}_{2^k-1} \setminus \Delta_m\}$,
- $\{(\alpha^{\frac{\ell}{i+1}}, 0)|\ell \in \mathbb{Z}_{2^k-1} \setminus \Delta_m\}$,
- $\{(0,0)\} \cup \{(\alpha^{\frac{m}{i+1}}, \alpha^{\frac{mt}{i+1}})\}$.

Let $g : \mathbb{F}_{2^k} \times \mathbb{F}_{2^k} \to \mathbb{F}_2$ be a Boolean function with $\deg(g) < k-1$ and $g(f+1) = 0$. We will prove $g = 0$.

We suppose $g(x,y) = \sum_{i=0}^{2^k-1} \sum_{j=0}^{2^k-1} g_{i,j} x^i y^j$, where $g_{i,j} \in \mathbb{F}_{2^k}$. Since $\deg(g) < k - 1$, we have that $g_{i,2^k-1} = g_{i,2^k-2} = g_{2^k-1,i} = g_{2^k-2,i} = 0$ for $0 \leq i \leq 2^k - 1$. Thus we can write g as

$$g(x,y) = \sum_{i=0}^{2^k-3} \sum_{j=0}^{2^k-3} g_{i,j} x^i y^j.$$

For any $(a,b) \in \mathrm{supp}(f + 1)$, we have $g(a,b) = 0$. Then by

$$\bigcup_{\ell=2^{k-1}-1}^{2^k-2} \{(x, \alpha^\ell x^{-1})|x \in \mathbb{F}_{2^k}^* \setminus \{\alpha^{\frac{\ell}{i+1}}\}\} \subset \mathrm{supp}(f+1),$$

it follows that for $2^{k-1} - 1 \leq \ell \leq 2^k - 2$,

$$0 = g(x, \alpha^\ell x^{-1}) = \sum_{i=0}^{2^k-3} \sum_{j=0}^{2^k-3} g_{i,j} \alpha^{\ell j} x^{i-j} = \sum_{u=0}^{2^k-3} g_u(\alpha) x^u, \qquad (13)$$

where

$$g_u(\alpha) = \sum_{\substack{0 \leq i,j \leq 2^k-3 \\ i-j \equiv u \bmod 2^k-1}} g_{i,j} \alpha^{\ell j}, \quad \text{for } 0 \leq u \leq 2^k - 3.$$

Let x run through $\mathbb{F}_{2^k}^* \setminus \{\alpha^{\frac{\ell}{i+1}}\}$ and by the invertibility of Vandermonde matrix from Eq. (13) we get $g_u(\alpha) = 0$, i.e. for $0 \leq u \leq 2^k - 3$

$$\sum_{\substack{0 \leq i,j \leq 2^k-3, i-j \equiv u \bmod 2^k-1}} g_{i,j} \alpha^{\ell j} = 0, \quad 2^{k-1} - 1 \leq \ell \leq 2^k - 2. \qquad (14)$$

For each u, Eq. (14) has at most 2^{k-1} different $g_{i,j}$'s by Lemma 6 and Lemma 7. Since ℓ has 2^{k-1} different values. Then by the invertibility of Vandermonde matrix we have that $g_{i,j} = 0$. This implies that $g = 0$. Thus, $f + 1$ has no annihilator of degree less than $k - 1$.

Therefore, we have $\mathcal{AI}(f) \geq k - 1$. □

Remark 2. For the Boolean function f in Construction 1, experimental results show that $f + 1$ neither has no annihilator with algebraic degree less than k. We check for $3 \leq k \leq 6$ that $AI(f) = k$, i.e., f has maximum algebraic immunity. For the function with $(s, m) = (1, 2^{\frac{n}{2}-1} - 1)$, we also check for $k = 7$.

5.2   Immunity against Fast Algebraic Attacks

Thanks to the results of [20], the immunity of a Boolean function on $\mathbb{F}_{2^k} \times \mathbb{F}_{2^k}$ against fast algebraic attacks is related to a matrix $B(f; e, d)$ whose entries are represented by the coefficients of its bivariate polynomial representation.

Theorem 9. *[20] Let* $f \in B_{2k}$, $e < k$ *and* $e \leq d$. *Let* $\sum_{i=0}^{2^k-1} \sum_{j=0}^{2^k-1} f_{i,j} x^i y^j$ *($f_{ij} \in \mathbb{F}_{2^k}$) be the bivariate polynomial representation of* f. *Let* $B(f; e, d)$ *be the* $\sum_{i=d+1}^{2k} \binom{2k}{i} \times \sum_{i=0}^{e} \binom{2k}{i}$ *matrix whose* $((a, b), (u, v))$*-th entry, where* $wt(a, b) \geq d + 1$ *and* $wt(u, v) \leq e$ *($0 \leq a, b, u, v \leq 2^k - 1$), is equal to*

$$
B_{(a,b),(u,v)} = \begin{cases} 0, & \text{if } a = 0, u \neq 0 \text{ or } b = 0, v \neq 0, \\ f_{0,b-v} + f_{2^k-1,b-v}, & \text{if } a = u \neq 0, b \neq 0, b \neq v, \\ f_{a-u,0} + f_{a-u,2^k-1}, & \text{if } a \neq 0, a \neq u, b = v \neq 0, \\ f_{a-u,b-v}, & \text{otherwise}, \end{cases} \tag{15}
$$

where $x - y$ *is considered as* $x - y \bmod (2^k - 1)$ *when* $x - y < 0$.
    Then there exists no nonzero function g *of degree at most* e *such that the product* gf *has degree at most* d *if and only if the matrix* $B(f; e, d)$ *has full column rank.*

By Eq. (10) we can get the following result.

Proposition 10. *Let* f *be defined as in Construction 1. Then the entries of matrix* $B(f; e, d)$ *are given as*

$$
B_{(a,b),(u,v)} = \begin{cases} 0, & \text{if } a = 0, u \neq 0 \text{ or } b = 0, v \neq 0, \\ f_{a-u,b-v}, & \text{otherwise}, \end{cases}
$$

where $f_{i,j}$ *is described in* (10).

Then we can investigate the immunity of f against fast algebraic attack by computing the column rank of its corresponding matrix $B(f; e, d)$. Experimental results suggest the following properties of the class of functions of Construction 1:

-   For $n = 6$ and any pair of integers (s, m), no nonzero function g of degree at most e and no function h of degree at most d exist such that $fg = h$, when $(e, d) = (2, 2)$; and for $n = 6$ and any pair of integers (s, m) with $s = 1, 2, 4$, no nonzero function g of degree at most e and no function h of degree at most d exist such that $fg = h$, when $(e, d) = (1, 3)$.

– For $n = 8, 10, 12$ and any pair of integers (s, m), no nonzero function g of degree at most e and no function h of degree at most d exist such that $fg = h$, when $e + d < n - 1$ and $e < \frac{n}{2}$. We conjecture it for every even $n \geq 8$. For each function of Construction 1, we also check for $n = 14$ and $e < 4$. For the function with $(s, m) = (1, 2^{\frac{n}{2}-1} - 1)$, we further check for $n = 14$ and $e < \frac{n}{2}$, for $n = 16$ and $e < 4$, and for $n = 18$ and $e < 3$.

To the best of our knowledge, this is the first time where a whole class of 1-resilient and nonlinear functions with almost perfect immunity against fast algebraic attacks can be observed.

6   Conclusion

The functions of Construction 1 seem to gather all the cryptographic criteria, including 1-resiliency, high nonlinearity, high degree, high algebraic immunity and good behavior against fast algebraic attacks, which are needed for allowing the stream ciphers using them as filtering functions to resist all the main attacks, including the Berlekamp-Massey attacks, (fast) correlation attacks, and (fast) algebraic attacks. To the best of our knowledge, they are the only functions of this kind found so far.

References

1. Armknecht, F.: Improving fast algebraic attacks. In: Roy, B., Meier, W. (eds.) FSE 2004. LNCS, vol. 3017, pp. 65–82. Springer, Heidelberg (2004)
2. Armknecht, F., Carlet, C., Gaborit, P., Künzli, S., Meier, W., Ruatta, O.: Efficient computation of algebraic immunity for algebraic and fast algebraic attacks. In: Vaudenay, S. (ed.) EUROCRYPT 2006. LNCS, vol. 4004, pp. 147–164. Springer, Heidelberg (2006)
3. Carlet, C.: Boolean functions for cryptography and error correcting codes. In: Crama, Y., Hammer, P. (eds.) Boolean Methods and Models in Mathematics, Computer Science, and Engineering, pp. 257–397. Cambridge University Press, Cambridge (2010)
4. Carlet, C., Feng, K.: An infinite class of balanced functions with optimal algebraic immunity, good immunity to fast algebraic attacks and good nonlinearity. In: Pieprzyk, J. (ed.) ASIACRYPT 2008. LNCS, vol. 5350, pp. 425–440. Springer, Heidelberg (2008)
5. Cohen, G., Flori, J.P.: On a generalized combinatorial conjecture involving addition $\bmod 2^k - 1$. Cryptology ePrint Archive, Report 2011/400, http://eprint.iacr.org/
6. Courtois, N.T., Meier, W.: Algebraic attacks on stream ciphers with linear feedback. In: Biham, E. (ed.) EUROCRYPT 2003. LNCS, vol. 2656, pp. 345–359. Springer, Heidelberg (2003)
7. Courtois, N.T.: Fast algebraic attacks on stream ciphers with linear feedback. In: Boneh, D. (ed.) CRYPTO 2003. LNCS, vol. 2729, pp. 176–194. Springer, Heidelberg (2003)
8. Courtois, N.T.: Cryptanalysis of sfinks. In: Won, D.H., Kim, S. (eds.) ICISC 2005. LNCS, vol. 3935, pp. 261–269. Springer, Heidelberg (2006)

9. Dalai, D.K., Maitra, S., Sarkar, S.: Basic theory in construction of Boolean functions with maximum possible annihilator immunity. Designs, Codes and Cryptography 40(1), 41–58 (2006)

10. Du, Y., Zhang, F.: A class of 1-resilient functions in odd variables with high nonlinearity and suboptimal algebraic immunity. IEICE Transactions (IEICET) 95-A(1), 417–420 (2012)

11. Feng, K., Liao, Q., Yang, J.: Maximal values of generalized algebraic immunity. Designs, Codes and Cryptography 50(2), 243–252 (2009)

12. Fischer, S., Meier, W.: Algebraic immunity of S-boxes and augmented functions. In: Biryukov, A. (ed.) FSE 2007. LNCS, vol. 4593, pp. 366–381. Springer, Heidelberg (2007)

13. Hawkes, P., Rose, G.G.: Rewriting variables: The complexity of fast algebraic attacks on stream ciphers. In: Franklin, M. (ed.) CRYPTO 2004. LNCS, vol. 3152, pp. 390–406. Springer, Heidelberg (2004)

14. Jin, Q., Liu, Z., Wu, B.: 1-Resilient Boolean function with optimal algebraic immunity. Cryptology ePrint Archive, Report 2011/549, http://eprint.iacr.org/

15. Jin, Q., Liu, Z., Wu, B., et al.: A general conjecture similar to T-D conjecture and its applications in constructing Boolean functions with optimal algebraic immunity. Cryptology ePrint Archive, Report 2011/515, http://eprint.iacr.org/

16. Li, N., Qu, L., Qi, W., et al.: On the construction of Boolean Functions with optimal algebraic immunity. IEEE Transactions on Information Theory 54(3), 1330–1334 (2008)

17. Li, N., Qi, W.-F.: Construction and analysis of Boolean functions of $2t+1$ variables with maximum algebraic immunity. In: Lai, X., Chen, K. (eds.) ASIACRYPT 2006. LNCS, vol. 4284, pp. 84–98. Springer, Heidelberg (2006)

18. Liu, M., Lin, D., Pei, D.: Fast algebraic attacks and decomposition of symmetric Boolean functions. IEEE Transactions on Information Theory 57(7), 4817–4821 (2011)

19. Liu, M., Zhang, Y., Lin, D.: Perfect algebraic immune functions. In: Wang, X., Sako, K. (eds.) ASIACRYPT 2012. LNCS, vol. 7658, pp. 172–189. Springer, Heidelberg (2012)

20. Liu, M., Zhang, Y., Lin, D.: On the immunity of Boolean functions against fast algebraic attacks using bivariate polynomial representation (extended abstract). In: The Third International Conference on Symbolic Computation and Cryptography, SCC 2012 (2012), A full version is available at http://eprint.iacr.org/2012/498/

21. Meier, W., Pasalic, E., Carlet, C.: Algebraic attacks and decomposition of Boolean functions. In: Cachin, C., Camenisch, J. (eds.) EUROCRYPT 2004. LNCS, vol. 3027, pp. 474–491. Springer, Heidelberg (2004)

22. Pan, S., Fu, X., Zhang, W.: Construction of 1-resilient Boolean functions with optimal algebraic immunity and good nonlinearity. J. Comput. Sci. Technol. (JCST) 26(2), 269–275 (2011)

23. Rizomiliotis, P.: On the resistance of Boolean functions against algebraic attacks using univariate polynomial representation. IEEE Transactions on Information Theory 56(8), 4014–4024 (2010)

24. Rizomiliotis, P.: On the security of the Feng-Liao-Yang Boolean functions with optimal algebraic immunity against fast algebraic attacks. Designs, Codes and Cryptography 57(3), 283–292 (2010)

25. Siegenthaler, T.: Correlation-immunity of nonlinear combining functions for cryptographic applications. IEEE Transactions on Information Theory 30(5), 776–780 (1984)

26. Su, W., Zeng, X., Hu, L.: Construction of 1-resilient Boolean functions with optimum algebraic immunity. Int. J. Comput. Math. (IJCM) 88(2), 222–238 (2011)
27. Tang, D., Carlet, C., Tang, X.: Highly nonlinear Boolean functions with optimal algebraic immunity and good behavior against fast algebraic attacks. IEEE Transactions on Information Theory (2012),
http://dx.doi.org/10.1109/TIT.2012.2217476, 10.1109/TIT.2012.2217476
28. Tu, Z., Deng, Y.: A conjecture about binary strings and its applications on constructing Boolean functions with optimal algebraic immunity. Designs, Codes and Cryptography 60(1), 1–14 (2011)
29. Tu, Z., Deng, Y.: Boolean functions optimizing most of the cryptographic criteria. Discrete Applied Mathematics 160(4-5), 427–435 (2012)
30. Zeng, X., Carlet, C., Shan, J., Hu, L.: More balanced Boolean functions with optimal algebraic immunity and good nonlinearity and resistance to fast algebraic attacks. IEEE Transactions on Information Theory 57(9), 6310–6320 (2011)
31. Zhang, Y., Liu, M., Lin, D.: On the immunity of rotation symmetric Boolean functions against fast algebraic attacks. Cryptology ePrint Archive, Report 2012/111, http://eprint.iacr.org/

An Improved Time-Memory-Data Trade-Off Attack against Irregularly Clocked and Filtered Keystream Generators

Lin Jiao[1,2], Mingsheng Wang[3], Bin Zhang[3], and Yongqiang Li[3]

[1] Institute of Software, Chinese Academy of Sciences, Beijing 100190, P.R. China
[2] Graduate University of Chinese Academy of Sciences, Beijing 100049, P.R. China
[3] State Key Laboratory of Information Security, Institute of Information Engineering, Chinese Academy of Sciences, Beijing 100093, P.R. China
jiaolin@is.iscas.ac.cn

Abstract. In this paper, we propose a new key recovery attack against irregularly clocked keystream generators, using the approach of time-memory-data trade-offs. The main idea behind our attack is creating several look-up tables and finally recovering the initial states of $LFSR_d$ and $LFSR_c$ synchronously, by alternatively deriving the initial states of $LFSR_d$ and $LFSR_c$ along the chains. We show that our attack is more efficient, and improves the previous attacks on the cipher model. Especially, we prove that our attack almost always needs less complexity than that of the normal time-memory-data trade-off attack [3] on the cipher model. We test our attack on LILI-128, and find out that it can successfully break the cipher with $2^{56.6}$ bit-comparison operations, 2^{49} pairs of 89-bit words memory and 2^{59} keystream bits. This result is better than those in [15,6], which possess the complexity of 2^{62} parity checks and 2^{63} bit operations respectively. Moreover, our attack can be divided and computed in parallel, and the actual runtime of the attack can be reduced depending on the number of computers we access.

Keywords: Time-Memory-Data Trade-Off Attack, Stream Cipher, Irregularly Clocked Shift Registers, LILI-128.

1 Introduction

In this paper, we present a new key recovery time-memory-data trade-off attack against ciphers based on an irregularly clocked linear feedback shift register (LFSR) filtered by a Boolean function. The cipher model we attack is composed of two components, the clock control generator and the data generator, which is shown in Fig 1.

1. The data generator subsystem consists of $LFSR_d$ of length l_d and a nonlinear filter function f_d, which outputs the bit stream v.
2. The clock control subsystem consists of $LFSR_c$ of length l_c and a clock function f_c, whose output is the clock control sequence of integers c.

M. Kutyłowski and M. Yung (Eds.): Inscrypt 2012, LNCS 7763, pp. 294–310, 2013.
© Springer-Verlag Berlin Heidelberg 2013

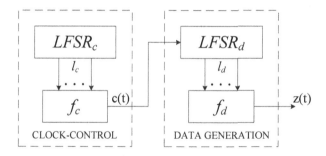

Fig. 1. The general cipher model we attack in this paper

The effect of the irregularly clocking is that v is irregularly decimated and the positions of the bits in the stream are altered. The result from this decimation is the keystream z. The secret key in this cipher is the $(l_c + l_d)$ initialization bits for $LFSR_c$ and $LFSR_d$ (I_c, I_d). If the matching states of $LFSR_c$ and $LFSR_d$ at certain clock are obtained, it is equivalent that the key of the initialization is recovered.

The previous effective algorithms are not specially designed to attack irregularly clocked and filtered generators. In 1980, Hellman introduced a technique of time-memory trade-offs for breaking block ciphers [8]. An analogous technique for stream ciphers was proposed by Babbage in 1995 [2]. More recently, Biryukov and Shamir combined these approaches in work when the adversary has more data to deal with, which can lessen the memory and the precomputation complexity [3]. Khoo et. al. presented a time-memory-data trade-off attack against stream ciphers whose filter or combiner generators are based on Maiorana-McFarland functions [11].

Although nearly all the attacks against irregularly clocked and filtered keystream generators are correlation attacks in the past [10,14,15], we propose a time-memory-data trade-off attack on the cipher model in this paper. Our attack is not designed to attack only the data generator or the control subsystem, but especially aims at clock controlled keystream generators as one system. In most irregularly clocked cryptosystems, the length of $LFSR_c$ is usually much smaller than that of $LFSR_d$. Then by means of comparing the keystream and the output sequence which is regularly clocked by $LFSR_d$, the state of $LFSR_c$ can be determined within a complexity not too large. The attack consists of two stages. In the offline stage, several look-up tables are obtained. First, a fixed string is chosen to be a segment of keystream whose length is big enough to derive the initial state of $LFSR_c$ by comparison. Next, we create several matrices of chains with the points which are l_d-bit words formed by the possible initial states of $LFSR_d$. They are generated by alternatively determining the initial states of $LFSR_d$ and $LFSR_c$, in the way of guessing the startpoint of the chain to be the initial state of $LFSR_d$ and deriving the initial state of $LFSR_c$ by comparing the fixed string and the regularly clocked output sequence of $LFSR_d$, then running the whole system to obtain the following l_d bits in the keystream which form the next point in the chain and updating the initial state of $LFSR_d$ with this point, repeatedly. We store the startpoints and endpoints of these chains in several tables corresponding to the matrices. In the online stage, we search the tables and recover the key. We observe the keystream to find the fixed string, and the following l_d bits in the keystream indeed form a point in the chains. Then we search for a match among the endpoints in the way beforehand along the chains and determine the initial states synchronously. Actually, we propose a general framework to attack the cipher model, and all the effective attacks against the subsystems [4,13,9,5,16,17] can be applied depending on the specific ciphers.

The complexity of our attack is analyzed. We prove that the runtime of our attack is less than that of the original time-memory-data trade-off attack proposed by Biryukov and Shamir on the cipher model in case of the same memory requirement. Especially, to attack the LILI-128 cipher, our method needs $2^{56.6}$ bit-comparison operations, with 2^{49} pairs of 89-bit words memory and 2^{59} keystream bits, whose success probability is more than 98%. There is also a time-memory trade-off attack against LILI-128 proposed by Saarinen [18] using the period of $LFSR_c$, which needs approximately 2^{45} 89-bit words of computer memory and 2^{46} keystream bits, with the success probability of 90%. The runtime complexity is claimed to be 2^{48} DES operations, which is not easy to be compared with the general runtime complexity. The algebraic attack proposed by Courtois and Meier [6] aims at the data generator subsystem of LILI-128, and calls for 2^{63} bit operations, with 2^{42} bit memory and 2^{57} keystream bits to break the whole cipher. The success probability of algebraic attacks is hard and scarcely analyzed in literatures so far. A correlation attack proposed by Molland and Helleseth was presented in [15], which just determines the initial state of $LFSR_c$. The attack is in the runtime of 2^{62} parity checks, with 2^{46} bit memory and 2^{29} keystream bits. In fact, the efficiency of our attack depends on the memory size. Besides, if there are 2^{10} or more(at most 2^{20}) computers to parallel compute the algorithm, the runtime of the attack can be reduced below $2^{46.6}$(accordingly $2^{36.6}$) bit-comparison operations.

The rest of this paper is organized as follows. In Section 2, we give the general model we attack. In Section 3, we present the attack in details. In Section 4, we apply the attack to LILI-128. Conclusion is given in Section 5.

2   General Model

Here we present some details of the general model for irregularly clocked and filtered stream ciphers we attack in this paper.

Let $g_d(x)$ and $g_c(x)$ be the feedback polynomials for the shift registers $LFSR_d$ of length l_d and $LFSR_c$ of length l_c. The initialization states (I_c, I_d) define the secret key for the given cipher system. From $g_c(x)$ we can calculate a clock control sequence c in the following way. Let $c(t) = f_c(L_c^t(I_c)) \in \{a_1, a_2, \ldots, a_A\}, a_j \geq 0$, be a function where the input $L_c^t(I_c)$ is the inner state of $LFSR_c$ after t feedback shifts and A is the number of values that $c(t)$ can take. $LFSR_d$ produces the stream which is filtered by f_d. The output from f_d is $v_k = f_d(L_d^t(I_d))$. The clock

$c(t)$ decides how many times $LFSR_d$ is clocked before the output bit v_k is taken as keystream bit $z(t)$. Thus the keystream $z(t)$ is produced by $z(t) = v_{k(t)}$, where $k(t)$ is the total sum of the clock at time t, that is $k(t) \leftarrow k(t-1) + c(t)$.

The f_c function described above can be those in the shrinking generator, the step-1/step-2 generator, the stop and go generator and so on, in this model.

3   Attack

3.1   Cryptanalytic Time-Memory-Data Trade-Offs for Stream Ciphers

At first, we give an introduction to the approach of time-memory-data trade-offs by briefly citing contents of [3]. There are five key parameters:

- N represents the size of the search space.
- P represents the time required by the preprocessing phase of the attack.
- M represents the amount of random access memory available to the attacker.
- T represents the time required by the realtime phase of the attack.
- D represents the amount of realtime data available to the attacker.

The origin of the attack against stream ciphers is Hellman's time-memory trade-off attack against block ciphers, which considers the random function f that maps the key x to the ciphertext block y for some fixed chosen plaintext, where f is easy to evaluate but hard to invert. Hellman uses a preprocessing stage which tries to cover all the N points of the preimage space with an $m \times t$ matrix whose rows are the chains obtained by iterating the function f t times on m randomly chosen startpoints. The pairs of startpoints and endpoints are stored. During the actual attack, we are given a value y and asked to find its predecessor x under f. Since x is covered by one of the precomputed chains, the algorithm repeatedly applies f to y until it reaches the stored endpoint, then jumps to its associated startpoint, and repeatedly applies f to the startpoint until it reaches y again. The previous point it visits is the desired x. The matrix in Hellman's attack is shown in Fig 2.

A single matrix cannot efficiently cover all the N points, thus we add more rows to the matrix. Assume that the first m chains are all disjoint, and the additional path contains t distinct points, where t is less than $\sqrt{N}$. By the birthday paradox, the two sets are likely to be disjoint as long as $t \times mt \leq N$, and thus we choose m and t that satisfy the relationship $mt^2 = N$, which we call the matrix stopping rule. Thus, the waste of repetitive coverage can be reduced. A single $m \times t$ matrix covers only a fraction of $mt/N = 1/t$ of the space according to the matrix stopping rule, and thus we need at least t unrelated matrices to cover the whole space. Hellman's method is using variants f_is of the original f defined by $f_i(x) = h_i(f(x))$, where h_i is some simple output modification. The total precomputation requires $P \approx N$ time, since we have to cover the space with the precomputed chains. The total memory requires to store mt pairs of startpoints and endpoints of the chains in the t matrices. We

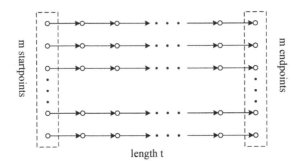

Fig. 2. Hellman's Matrix

have to perform t inversion attempts according to every matrix, each requiring at most t evaluations of some f_i to recover x. Thus the total time complexity of the attack is t^2.

Differently, in the stream ciphers all the given output vectors can be inverted with respect to the same function by using the same precomputed table. The attack is successful if any of the D given output vectors is found, since under such condition the generator can be run forward to find the initial state. Thus, Biryukov and Shamir use a large value of D to speed up the attack. Same basic approaches are used in this attack as those in Hellman's. We reduce the total number of points to be covered from N to N/D, and still get a collision between the stored and actual states. The attack reduces the number of matrices r from t to t/D in order to decrease the total coverage by a factor of D and keep each matrix as large as possible, which is allowed by the matrix stopping rule $mt^2 = N$. Then the total memory is reduced from $M = mt$ to $M = mt/D$. The total preprocessing time is similarly reduced from $P = N$ to $P = N/D$. The attack time T is the product of the number of matrices, the length of each chain, and the number of available data points. This product is $T = (t/D) \cdot t \cdot D = t^2$, which is the same as in Hellman's original attack. We can use the matrix stopping rule to find the time-memory-data trade-off in this attack, which satisfies the invariant relationship:

$$TM^2D^2 = t^2 \cdot (mt/D)^2 \cdot D^2 = (mt^2)^2 = N^2.$$

This relationship is valid for any $t \geq D$, i.e., $D^2 \leq T \leq N$.

3.2   Our Attack against Irregularly Clocked and Filtered Keystream Generators

Our time-memory-data trade-off attack is based on the aforementioned cryptanalysis, but specially designed to analyze irregularly clocked and filtered keystream generators described in Section 2. We usually see $l_c < l_d$ in most clock controlled cryptosystems. The initial state of $LFSR_c$ can be determined within a short runtime by comparing the keystream z and the regular output sequence

v. The attack has two phases: During the preprocessing phase, we explore the general structure of the cryptosystem, and summarize the findings in a large table, which are not tied to particular keys. During the realtime phase, we are given actual data produced from a particular unknown key, and our goal is to use the precomputed table to find the key as quickly as possible.

Procedures in details are as follows. The representations are defined the same as in the previous subsection.

- Preprocessing Phase:
    1. Choose a fixed string $s \in GF(2)^l$ (as a segment of keystream for determining the initial state of $LFSR_c$).
    2. Randomly seed an l_d-bit maximum LFSR and generate a sequence of distinct l_d-bit vectors $X_1, X_2, \ldots, X_r$, which is similar to that described in (Khoo et. al.,2007) for reducing the cross points of the chains as h_is in Hellman's method.
    3. Form r number of $m \times t$ matrices that try to cover $1/d$ of the whole search space which is composed of all the possible initial states of $LFSR_d$ as follows. For matrix i, $i = 1, 2, \ldots, r$:

        (a) Randomly choose m startpoints of the chains, each point formed by a vector of length of l_d which is to be an injection into $LFSR_d$ as initialization $\widehat{I_d}$.
        (b) Regularly clock $LFSR_d$ and obtain the output string v. Compare v with s, through the method of matching a fixed bit of s with consecutive A bits of v, to filter out the impossible values of the control sequence c and determine the correspondingly initial state of $LFSR_c$. By further cutting down the possible initial states of $LFSR_c$ through the check of several more keystream bits in s, the unique solution of the initial state of $LFSR_c$ $\widehat{I_c}$ can be derived. Thus, the overall system is obtained. Operate the system and generate the following l_d keystream bits from this moment on. Exclusive-OR the l_d-bit vector with X_i and make it the next point in the chain. Update the initial state of $LFSR_d$ with this point. Suppose that the runtime of this step is about t_0.
        (c) Iterate Step (b) t times on each startpoint respectively.
        (d) Store the pairs of startpoints and endpoints $(SP_j, EP_j), j = 1, \ldots, m$ in table i.
        The relationship among the integers t, m, d, r is $mtr \geq 2^{l_d}/d$, and $mt^2 = 2^{l_d}$ according to the matrix stopping rule.
- Realtime Phase:
    1. Observe the keystream and find d number of l-bit strings matching with string s. For one such string, let the following l_d bits in the keystream be y.
    2. For each y, search among the endpoints in overall tables in this way. For table i, check if there is EP_j, $j = 1, \ldots, m$ matching with $y \oplus X_i$ first. If not, iterate Step (b) w times on $y \oplus X_i$ until it matches with one

of EP_j, $j = 1,\ldots,m$, where $w = 1,\ldots,t$. When there is a match, jump to the corresponding startpoint, and repeatedly apply Step (b) to the startpoint until the l_d-bit keystream vector reaches y again. Then the previous point visited is the initial state of $LFSR_d$ I_d, and the state $\widehat{I_c}$ just figured out in Step (b) is the initial state of $LFSR_c$ I_c.

Firstly, we consider the complexity of the attack. Analogously to the last subsection, the whole search space is composed of all the possible initial states of $LFSR_d$, whose cardinality is 2^{l_d}. Our tables only need to cover $1/d$ of the space because we just need to break the cipher for one out of the d strings in the keystream. The memory is $M = m \cdot r$, since we only store the startpoints and endpoints of all the chains in the matrices. For each of the d data, we need to compute for r tables and calculate Step (b) at most t times for each table. The time taken is $T = t \cdot r \cdot d \cdot t_0$. Moreover, we need to sample $D = d \cdot 2^l$ consecutive keystream bits to collect the required d strings, because the string s of length l occurs on average once in 2^l keystream bits . The preprocessing time for building the tables is $P = m \cdot t \cdot r \cdot t_0$.

Secondly, we compare our attack with the normal time-memory-data trade-off attack proposed by Biryukov and Shamir, which is introduced in the last subsection. Based on the same irregularly clocked and filtered keystream generator, the whole search space of the normal attack is made up of all the combinations of the possible initial states of $LFSR_d$ and $LFSR_c$. We prove that our attack outperforms the normal one on the cipher model at runtime, with regard to the same success probability and available memory which is in consideration of feasibility.

Theorem 1. *Let the representations for variables be the same as stated above, and mark the normal attack and ours with subscript 1 and subscript 2 respectively. We have $m_1 t_1 r_1 = 2^{l_d + l_c}/d_1$, $M_1 = m_1 r_1$, $T_1 = t_1 r_1 d_1$, and $m_2 t_2 r_2 = 2^{l_d}/d_2$, $M_2 = m_2 r_2$, $T_2 = t_2 r_2 d_2 t_0$. Then we derive that*

$$T_2 < T_1 \text{ if and only if } t_0 < 2^{l_c}$$

when $M_1 = M_2$ and $r_1 = r_2$.

Proof. We easily have that

$$\frac{t_1}{t_2} = 2^{l_c} \frac{d_2}{d_1}$$

from the conditions. Then

$$\frac{T_1}{T_2} = \frac{t_1 d_1}{t_2 d_2} \frac{r_1}{r_2 t_0} = 2^{l_c} \frac{r_1}{r_2 t_0}.$$

We have $\frac{T_1}{T_2} > 1$ if and only if

$$t_0 < 2^{l_c} \frac{r_1}{r_2}.$$

When $r_1 = r_2$, it is equivalent to $t_0 < 2^{l_c}$, which means that our attack takes less runtime if and only if Step (b) is better than exhaustive search. □

Moreover, we have $D_1 = d_1$, $D_2 = d_2 d_0$ where d_0 denotes the extra data for matching with string s, and $m_1 t_1^2 = 2^{l_d + l_c}$, $m_2 t_2^2 = 2^{l_d}$ according to the matrix stopping rule. Then we derive

$$\frac{m_1}{m_2} \frac{t_1}{t_2}^2 = 2^{l_c}.$$

Substitute $\frac{t_1}{t_2} = 2^{l_c} \frac{d_2}{d_1}$ and $\frac{m_1}{m_2} = \frac{r_2}{r_1}$ into the equation, and have

$$d_2 = 2^{-l_c/2} d_1 \sqrt{\frac{r_1}{r_2}}.$$

We may as well let $d_0 = 2^{l_c}$ like the example of LILI-128, and derive

$$D_2 = D1 \cdot 2^{l_c/2} \sqrt{\frac{r_1}{r_2}},$$

which is more than D_1. It seems that we use data to exchange for time, whereas the runtime of the normal attack is always too long to make the attack practical. We calculate

$$\triangle T = \frac{T_1}{T_2} = \frac{2^{l_c}}{t_0} \quad \text{and} \quad \triangle D = \frac{D_2}{D_1} = 2^{l_c/2}$$

when $r_1 = r_2$, and find out $\triangle T > \triangle D$ if $t_0 < 2^{l_c/2}$. In our attack against LILI-128, we see $\triangle T$ is much more than $\triangle D$. In general, our attack no more treats the clock controlled cipher as a black box, and creates the chains only consisting the possible states of the data LFSR as the corresponding states of the clock control LFSR are implicitly tackled based on the internal structure of the cipher. Moreover, the choice of d is more flexible, since there is not restriction of $d < t$ like that in the normal attack.

Thirdly, we compare our attack with other attacks. Unlike those attacks which just can be computed as a whole and cannot be divided and conquered, such as correlation attacks and algebraic attacks, our attack can be parallel computed by at most d computers, each using one of the d strings. Then the actual runtime can be reduced to $t \cdot r \cdot t_0 \cdot d/u$, where u is the number of computers we can use. Actually, this is a general framework to analyze irregularly clocked and filtered keystream generators, and all the previous effective attacks against the subsystems can be applied, such as in Step (b), depending on the specific ciphers. Moreover, for certain ciphers conforming to the model, if there is an attack against the data generator subsystem with a short runtime and a small data requirement, the whole search space can change into the set of all the possible initial states of $LFSR_c$ instead and our attack can be still valid. That is to say, our attack may improve the previous attacks on the cipher model.

Finally, we analyze the success probability of our attack. The fundamental problem is that points can appear within more than one chain. Therefore, estimating the probability of success is equivalent to estimating the probability of such duplication. We use the classic occupancy problem to estimate the success probability, which is described nicely by Feller [7]. We apply the model of throwing mtr balls into $2^{l_d}/d$ urns, where balls and urns correspond to the points in the matrices and the keys to be covered in the search space respectively. The ratio of the expected number of urns that have at least one ball and the number of the urns is the success probability. Then, approximately,

$$Pr(success) = 1 - e^{-\frac{mtrd}{2^{l_d}}}.$$

The probabilities for various choices of $mtrd$ are given in Table 1. Although the attack is only probabilistic, the probability of success is high.

Table 1. Approximate success probability

$mtrd$	0	2^{l_d-5}	2^{l_d-4}	2^{l_d-3}	2^{l_d-2}	2^{l_d-1}	2^{l_d}	2^{l_d+1}	2^{l_d+2}	2^{l_d+3}	∞
$Pr(success)$	0	0.03	0.06	0.12	0.22	0.39	0.63	0.86	0.98	0.99	1.00

4   Application

The LILI-128 cipher [19] is based on the general model we attack in this paper. To explain our new attack, we have exemplified it on this cipher.

4.1   The LILI-128 Cipher

LILI-128 is a stream cipher proposed by Simpson et al. for NESSIE. It is comprised of a 39-bit linear feedback shift register $LFSR_c$ responsible for clock control and an 89-bit $LFSR_d$ to generate the keystream. The 128-bit secret key is substituted into $LFSR_c$ and $LFSR_d$ respectively as the initial states. The feedback polynomial of $LFSR_c$ which is a primitive polynomial is

$$g_c(x) = x^{39} + x^{35} + x^{33} + x^{31} + x^{17} + x^{15} + x^{14} + x^2 + 1.$$

After clocking $LFSR_c$ once, 2 bits from $LFSR_c$ are input to

$$f_c(x_{12}, x_{20}) = 2x_{12} + x_{20} + 1$$

to output $c(t) \in \{1, 2, 3, 4\}$. The feedback polynomial of $LFSR_d$ which is a primitive polynomial is

$$g_d(x) = x^{89} + x^{83} + x^{80} + x^{55} + x^{53} + x^{42} + x^{39} + x + 1.$$

After clocking $LFSR_d$ $c(t)$ times, 10 bits from $LFSR_d$ are input to
$f_d(x_0, x_1, x_3, x_7, x_{12}, x_{20}, x_{30}, x_{44}, x_{65}, x_{80}) = x_{13} + x_8 + x_4 + x_2 + x_{81}x_{21} + x_{81}x_8 + x_{66}x_4 + x_{66}x_1 + x_{45}x_2 + x_{45}x_1 + x_{31}x_{21} + x_{81}x_{66}x_{13} + x_{81}x_{66}x_8 + x_{81}x_{66}x_4 + x_{81}x_{66}x_2 + x_{81}x_{45}x_8 + x_{81}x_{45}x_4 + x_{81}x_{31}x_{21} + x_{81}x_{31}x_{13} + x_{81}x_{31}x_8 + x_{66}x_{45}x_{21} + x_{66}x_{45}x_4 + x_{66}x_{31}x_{21} + x_{66}x_{31}x_8 + x_{66}x_{31}x_4 + x_{81}x_{66}x_{45}x_{21} + x_{81}x_{66}x_{45}x_8 +$

$x_{81}x_{66}x_{45}x_4 + x_{81}x_{66}x_{45}x_1 + x_{81}x_{66}x_{31}x_{21} + x_{81}x_{66}x_{31}x_8 + x_{81}x_{66}x_{31}x_2 + x_{81}x_{45}x_{31}$
$x_{13} + x_{81}x_{45}x_{31}x_4 + x_{66}x_{45}x_{31}x_8 + x_{66}x_{45}x_{31}x_2 + x_{66}x_{31}x_{21}x_{13} + x_{66}x_{31}x_{21}x_8 +$
$x_{81}x_{66}x_{45}x_{31}x_8 + x_{81}x_{66}x_{45}x_{31}x_4 + x_{81}x_{66}x_{31}x_{21}x_{13} + x_{81}x_{66}x_{31}x_{21}x_8 + x_{66}x_{45}x_{31}$
$x_{21}x_{13} + x_{66}x_{45}x_{31}x_{21}x_8 + x_{81}x_{66}x_{45}x_{31}x_{21}x_{13} + x_{81}x_{66}x_{45}x_{31}x_{21}x_8,$
which is balanced and with the nonlinearity of 480, to output binary data $z(t)$ used as the keystream.

4.2   Our Attack against LILI-128

4.2.1 Step (b) In Our Attack against LILI-128

At first, we present the detailed process in Step (b) in our attack against LILI-128. Assume that we have obtained 39 keystream bits $z(t), t = 1, \ldots, 39$ and the initial state of $LFSR_d$ right now. Our goal is to derive the unique solution of the initial state of $LFSR_c$. The method is the same as that mentioned in [20].
(b.1) Narrow down the output sequence that $c(t), t = 1, \ldots, 8$ can take, by comparing the keystream $z(t), t = 1, \ldots, 8$ with the output sequence $v(t)$ regularly clocked by $LFSR_d$. For example, let $z(t) = \{1, 0, 0, 1, 1, 0, 1, 0, \ldots\}$ and $v(t) = \{1, 0, 1, 0, 0, 0, 1, 1, \ldots\}$. First, we check all the four values of $c(1)$ to see if $z(1) = v(c(1))$ holds, and find

$$z(1) = v(1), \text{ when } c(1) = 1$$
$$z(1) \neq v(2), \text{ when } c(1) = 2$$
$$z(1) = v(3), \text{ when } c(1) = 3$$
$$z(1) \neq v(4), \text{ when } c(1) = 4.$$

Thus, 1 or 3 is the possible value of $c(1)$. Next, we check that what value $c(2)$ takes can make $z(2) = v(c(1) + c(2))$ tenable for either of these two possible values of $c(1)$, 1 or 3. Repeat until $t = 8$. Compute 16 bits of $(x_{12}(t), x_{20}(t))$ in the state of $LFSR_c$ where $t = 1, \ldots, 8$, using the bijective function f_c, i.e,

$$(x_{12}(1), x_{20}(1)) = (0, 0), \text{ when } c(1) = 1$$
$$(x_{12}(1), x_{20}(1)) = (0, 1), \text{ when } c(1) = 2$$
$$(x_{12}(1), x_{20}(1)) = (1, 0), \text{ when } c(1) = 3$$
$$(x_{12}(1), x_{20}(1)) = (1, 1), \text{ when } c(1) = 4$$

and the sequences of $c(t), t = 1, \ldots, 8$ narrowed down above. The sketch is given in Fig 3.
(b.2) Narrow down the output sequence candidates of $c(t), t = 9, \ldots, 31$ to compute the remaining indeterminate 23 bits in the state of $LFSR_c$. It is done in the same way as that described in the preceding step. Since $x_{12}(t), t = 9, \ldots, 31$ is already known for $x_{12}(t) = x_{20}(t - 8), t = 9, \ldots, 31$, only one bit $x_{20}(t)$ of $(x_{12}(t), x_{20}(t))$ can be determined per clock, for

$t = 9, \ldots, 31$. Repeat this series of computation until t becomes 31, then consecutive 39 state bits of $LFSR_c$ are determined, and the initial state of $LFSR_c$ is obtained by running forward.

(b.3) Compare the output sequence of the whole system based on those 39-bit candidates for the initial state of $LFSR_c$ narrowed down in Step (b.2) with the keystream $z(t), t = 31, \ldots, 39$ to see if the candidates are correct. Whenever a comparison of 1 bit is made, those candidates are reduced by one half in number . When $t = 39$, only one candidate remains, and it is just the unique solution of the initial state of $LFSR_c$. (Specific illustrates are given in the following analysis of the complexity of Step (b)).

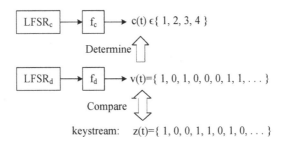

Fig. 3. Sketch for comparing and determining

Next, we discuss the amount of computation needed for Step (b). The basic operation is bit comparison. Assume that the keystream behaves as random numbers, since the keystream is filtered by a balanced Boolean function from an LFSR based on a primitive polynomial, and the values of 0 and 1 are equally output in the sequence of $LFSR_d$ and the keystream of the whole system.

It is thought that comparing one bit of the obtained keystream with the output sequence regularly clocked by $LFSR_d$ allows narrowing down the possible values of $c(t)$ by an average of one half. Concretely, when $t = 1$, we check the four candidate values of $c(1)$ and narrow down them to two. The number of trails is four, and the number of remaining candidates of $c(1)$ is two. When $t = 2$, we check the four candidate values of $c(2)$, for either of these two possible values of $c(1)$. The number of trials totals 2×4, and the number of remaining candidates for $(c(1), c(2))$ is 2^2. The number of trials and the number of remaining candidates for $(c(1), c(2), \ldots, c(t))$ are analyzed in this way until $t = 8$ in Step (b.1). The amount of computation at t-th clock is $4\times$ (the number of remaining candidates of $(c(1), c(2), \ldots, c(t-1))$ at $(t-1)$-th clock), and the number of remaining candidates of $(c(1), c(2), \ldots, c(t))$ is one half of the computation above, for $t = 1, \ldots, 8$. Consequently, the total number of trials for $c(t), t = 1, \ldots, 8$ in Step (b.1) is obtained as follows.

$$4 + 2 \times 4 + 2^2 \times 4 + \cdots + 2^7 \times 4 \approx 2^{10.0}$$

And the number of remaining candidates of $(c(1), c(2), \ldots, c(8))$ at 8th clock is about 2^8.

In Step (b.2), when $t = 9$, only the value of $x_{20}(9)$ remains indeterminate since $x_{12}(9)$ is fixed. For f_c is invertible, there are two possible values of $c(9)$. They are narrowed down by one half through one bit comparison of $z(9)$ and $v(c(1) + ... + c(9))$. The number of trials made in this fragment is $2^8 \times 2$, and the number of possible values of $(c(1), c(2), \ldots, c(9))$ stays 2^8. The number of trials and the number of remaining candidates for $(c(1), c(2), \ldots, c(t))$ are analyzed in the same way until $t = 31$. The amount of computation at t-th clock keeps $2^8 \times 2$, and the number of remaining candidates for $(c(1), c(2), \ldots, c(t))$ is 2^8 all along for $t = 9, \ldots, 31$. Thus, the total number of trials for $c(t), t = 9, \ldots, 31$ in Step (b.2) is as follows.

$$2^8 \times 2 \times (31 - 9 + 1) \approx 2^{13.6}$$

And the number of remaining candidate sequences of $(c(1), c(2), \ldots, c(31))$ at 31st clock stays about 2^8.

Since there is a one-to-one correspondence between $c(t)$ and $(x_{12}(t), x_{20}(t))$, by the analysis of Step (b.1) and (b.2), there are 2^8 candidates for the initial state of $LFSR_c$ narrowed down. We check to find a match of 8 bits in the following output sequences from the overall system based on those candidates with the remaining 8 bits of the obtained keystream. As far as one of the 8 bits is concerned, the candidates are narrowed down by one half. Thus, the total number of trials made in Step (b.3) is

$$2^8 + 2^7 + \cdots + 2 \approx 2^{9.0}.$$

At 39-th clock, only one candidate stays. Thus the overall system is obtained. Operate the cipher and generate the following 89 keystream bits. Exclusive-OR them with X_i and let the sum form the next point in the chain.

Consequently, the total amount of computation in Step (b) becomes

$$t_0 = 2^{10.0} + 2^{13.6} + 2^{9.0} \approx 2^{13.8}.$$

4.2.2 The Complete Attack against LILI-128

Given Step (b) stated above, we present our complete attack against LILI-128. In the preprocessing phase, we choose a fixed string $s \in GF(2)^{39}$ as the obtained keystream segment, and generate a sequence of distinct 89-bit vectors $X_1, X_2, \ldots, X_d$ as stated in Step 2. Next, we form r number of $m \times t$ matrices to cover the whole search space of $\mathbb{F}_2^{89}$. For every matrix, we randomly choose m startpoints, each formed by a possible initial state of $LFSR_d$ $\widehat{I}_d$. Then regularly clock the $LFSR_d$ and execute Step (b) in part 4.2.1. Hereto, only one solution of the initial state of $LFSR_c$ $\widehat{I}_c$ remains. Thus the overall system is obtained. We generate 89 more keystream bits and X-or them with X_i corresponding to the matrix to form the next point in the chain. It is iterated t times on each startpoint. Store the pairs of startpoints and endpoints (SP_j, EP_j). The integers t, m, d, r satisfy the relationship $mtr \geq 2^{89}/d$, and $mt^2 = 2^{89}$ according to the matrix stopping rule,.

In the realtime phase, we observe the keystream to find d number of 39-bit strings matching with s, and let the following 89 bits in the keystream be y. Check a match of $y \oplus X_i$ and a match of the result of impacting Step (b) on $y \oplus X_i$ at most t times, with the endpoints in the tables. When there is a match, we jump to the associated startpoint, and repeatedly apply Step (b) to the startpoint until it reaches $y \oplus X_i$ again. Then the previous point it has visited is the initial state I_d of $LFSR_d$, and the corresponding initial state of $LFSR_c$ just figured out in Step (b) is I_c. Thereby, the key of LILI-128 is recovered.

4.2.3 Techniques to Improve Our Attack against LILI-128

Many techniques can be employed to enhance our attack, since what we provide is a general framework on clock controlled keystream generators. For example, the skills to analyze the filter generator which is a subsystem of the cipher model can be used to improve our attack according to specific cryptosystems. Besides, our attack is a method based on time-memory-data trade-offs. Then the skills to reduce the cross points can be used to increase the success probability of our attack as well. There are a great many literatures for reference, such as "false alarms" provided in [1], "rainbow chains" provided in [12], and "special point" provided in [3]. In addition, we can exploit hash functions on the pairs of startpoints and endpoints in order to reduce the memory complexity.

Especially, for our attack against LILI-128, we still use the method of time-memory trade-offs to reduce the amount of computation in Step (b). The basic computation in Step (b) is the comparison of $v(t)$ and $z(t)$ at every clock which is for narrowing down the candidates for $LFSR_c$ data. If the steps for such comparison are computed and stored as a table, we can look it up to determine the candidates for $LFSR_c$ data directly in the online stage (The specific way is mentioned in [20] which is similar to the discussion on the amount of computation given in part 4.2.1). Table 2 shows the frequency of clocks versus the memory size required to hold the computed tables and the frequency of table-lookups that is needed in Step (b.1) and Step (b.2). The frequency of table-lookups is nothing but the runtime in Step (b.1) and Step (b.2). However, the amount of computation in Step (b.3) cannot be reduced by means of providing tables to look up. The complexity of our attack that can be reduced depends on the size of extra memory M'. In this paper, we estimate the amount of computation in Step (b) when the memory size is 2^{42} bits or less. We will see that the extra memory can hardly affect the order of the memory size of the whole attack against LILI-128 in the next part. Thus Step (b) takes

$$t_0 = 2^{4.6} + 2^{10.0} + 2^{9.0} \approx 2^{10.6}.$$

4.2.4 Complexity and Success Probability of Our Attack against LILI-128

In this part, the complexity of our attack is considered. We discuss the relationship among the memory size, the amount of computation and the data required for our attack. Different parameters for the complexity and success probability

Table 2. Diminished computation of Step (b.1) and Step (b.2)

Frequency of clocks	Memory	Step (b.1)	Frequency of clocks	Memory	Step (b.2)
-	0	$2^{10.0}$	-	0	$2^{13.6}$
1	2^7	$2^{8.0}$	1	2^7	$2^{12.6}$
2	2^{14}	$2^{6.4}$	2	2^{14}	$2^{11.6}$
4	2^{27}	$2^{4.6}$	3	2^{21}	$2^{11.0}$
8	2^{52}	1	4	2^{28}	$2^{10.6}$
			6	2^{42}	$2^{10.0}$
			8	2^{56}	$2^{9.6}$

are presented. We also give a comparison of our time-memory-data trade-off attack and the normal one proposed by Biryukov and Shamir, and a comparison of our attack and the previous attacks against LILI-128.

The whole search space of our attack is composed of all the possible initial states of $LFSR_d$, whose cardinality is 2^{89}. Our tables need to cover $1/d$ of the space. The memory is $M = mr + M'$. For each of the d data, we need to look up r tables and compute Step (b) at most t times. The time taken is $T = trdt_0$, where t_0 is $2^{10.6}$. The number of consecutive keystream bits needed to collect the required d strings is $D = d \cdot 2^{39}$. The preprocessing time for building the tables is $P = mtrt_0$. As stated above, we know the success probability of our attack which is approximately

$$Pr(success) = 1 - e^{-\frac{mtrd}{2^{89}}}.$$

As shown in Table 3, we have calculated some versions of the parameters of m, t, r, d versus the success probability, which satisfy the relationship

$$mt^2 = 2^{89}, \ mtr \geq 2^{89}/d.$$

From the table, we see that the extra memory M' required as stated in part 4.2.3 can hardly affect the memory size of the whole attack.

We compare our attack with the normal time-memory-data trade-off attack against LILI-128. For clarification, we only list the case with the same success probability. Moreover, for the sake of hardware requirement, we set the memory of these two attacks in the same size. For the normal attack against LILI-128, the whole search space is formed by all the 2^{128} combinations of the possible initial states of $LFSR_d$ and $LFSR_c$. For the success probability of 63%, the time, memory and data complexity of the normal attack should satisfy the relationship below

$$TM^2D^2 = 2^{2 \cdot 128} \ \text{for} \ D^2 \leq T \leq N$$

Table 3. Different versions of parameters of our attack with the corresponding complexity and success probability

t	r	m	d	T	M	D	P	$Pr(success)$
2^{20}	1	2^{49}	2^{20}	$2^{50.6}$	2^{49}	2^{59}	$2^{79.6}$	0.63
2^{22}	2^3	2^{45}	2^{20}	$2^{55.6}$	2^{48}	2^{59}	$2^{80.6}$	0.86
2^{22}	2^4	2^{45}	2^{20}	$2^{56.6}$	2^{49}	2^{59}	$2^{81.6}$	0.98
2^{23}	2^6	2^{43}	2^{20}	$2^{59.6}$	2^{49}	2^{59}	$2^{82.6}$	0.99

according to the matrix stopping rule. A comparison of parameters of these two attacks are presented in Table 4, where the parameters in the normal attack is calculated as follows

$$M = mt/D, T = t^2, P = N/D, t \geq D.$$

From the table, we find out that the ratio $\Delta D = \frac{D_2}{D_1} = 2^{19}$ is much smaller than $\Delta T = \frac{T_1}{T_2} = 2^{27.4}$, which conforms to the statement in the last section. We also see that the runtime of the normal attack is too long for feasibility.

Table 4. Complexity comparison with the normal time-memory-data trade-off attack against LILI-128

	t	r	m	d	T	M	D	P
normal	2^{39}	1	2^{50}	–	2^{78}	2^{50}	2^{39}	2^{89}
improved	2^{20}	2	2^{49}	2^{19}	$2^{50.6}$	2^{50}	2^{58}	$2^{80.6}$

We also compare our attack with the previous attacks against LILI-128. The amount of memory, computation, keystream needed, and the according success probability are shown in Table 5. The total amount of computation in our attack against LILI-128 is

$$T = 2^{22} \times 2^4 \times 2^{20} \times 2^{10.6} = 2^{56.6}.$$

The memory calls for 2^{49} pairs of 89-bit words. The data requires 2^{59} keystream bits. The success probability of our attack is more than 0.98. Our attack can easily be parallelized and distributed among processors, since there is no need for communication between the processors, unlike those attacks which just can be computed as a whole.

Table 5. Complexity comparison with the previous attacks against LILI-128

	Time (T)	Data (D)	Memory (M)	Success probability (Pr(success))
Our method	$2^{56.6}$ bit-comparisons	2^{59} bits	2^{49} pairs of 89-bit words	0.98
Algebraic Attack [6]	2^{63} bit operations	2^{57} bits	2^{42} bits	hard to estimate
TMTO [18]	2^{48} DES operations	2^{46} bits	2^{45} 89-bit words	0.90
Correlation Attack [15]	2^{62} bit parity checks	2^{29} bits	2^{46} bits	0.99

5 Conclusion

A new key recovery time-memory-data trade-off attack against irregularly clocked keystream generators is proposed in this paper. It is a method of low runtime, which is feasible to compute in parallel. Moreover, we attack LILI-128 for example to illustrate our attack. Since the attack is a frame, it can be combined with other efficient approaches to analyze this kind of ciphers, such as Grain, and we believe that it can improve the previous attacks on the cipher model.

Acknowledgements. We would like to thank anonymous referees for their helpful comments and suggestions. The research presented in this paper is supported by the National Natural Science Foundation of China (Grant No. 60833008, No.60603018, No.60970134), the "Strategic Priority Research Program" of the Chinese Academy of Sciences (Grant No. XDA06010701) and the IIE's Cryptography Research Project (Grant No. Y2Z0011102).

References

1. Avoine, G., Junod, P., Oechslin, P.: Time-memory trade-offs: False alarm detection using checkpoints. In: Maitra, S., Veni Madhavan, C.E., Venkatesan, R. (eds.) INDOCRYPT 2005. LNCS, vol. 3797, pp. 183–196. Springer, Heidelberg (2005)
2. Babbage, S.: Improved exhaustive search attacks on stream ciphers. In: European Convention on Security and Detection 1995, IEE Conference Publication, pp. 161–166 (1995)
3. Biryukov, A., Shamir, A.: Cryptanalytic time/memory/data tradeoffs for stream ciphers. In: Okamoto, T. (ed.) ASIACRYPT 2000. LNCS, vol. 1976, pp. 1–13. Springer, Heidelberg (2000)
4. Chepyzhov, V.V., Johansson, T., Smeets, B.: A simple algorithm for fast correlation attacks on stream ciphers. In: Schneier, B. (ed.) FSE 2000. LNCS, vol. 1978, pp. 181–195. Springer, Heidelberg (2001)

5. Courtois, N.T.: Fast algebraic attacks on stream ciphers with linear feedback. In: Boneh, D. (ed.) CRYPTO 2003. LNCS, vol. 2729, pp. 176–194. Springer, Heidelberg (2003)

6. Courtois, N.T., Meier, W.: Algebraic attacks on stream ciphers with linear feedback. In: Biham, E. (ed.) EUROCRYPT 2003. LNCS, vol. 2656, pp. 345–359. Springer, Heidelberg (2003)

7. Grubbs, F.E.: An introduction to probability theory and its applications. Technometrics 9(2), 342 (1967)

8. Hellman, M.: A cryptanalytic time-memory trade-off. IEEE Transactions on Information Theory 26, 401–406 (1980)

9. Johansson, T., Jonsson, F.: Theoretical analysis of a correlation attack based on convolutional codes. IEEE Transactions on Information Theory 48, 2173–2181 (2002)

10. Jonsson, F., Johansson, T.: A fast correlation attack on LILI-128. Information Processing Letters 81(3), 127–132 (2002)

11. Khoo, K., Chew, G., Gong, G., Lee, H.K.: Time-memory-data trade-off attack on stream ciphers based on Maiorana-McFarland functions. IEICE Transactions 92A(1), 11–21 (2009)

12. Khoo, K., Gong, G., Lee, H.-K.: The rainbow attack on stream ciphers based on Maiorana-McFarland functions. In: Zhou, J., Yung, M., Bao, F. (eds.) ACNS 2006. LNCS, vol. 3989, pp. 194–209. Springer, Heidelberg (2006)

13. Meier, W., Staffelbach, O.: Fast correlation attacks on stream ciphers. In: Günther, C.G. (ed.) EUROCRYPT 1988. LNCS, vol. 330, pp. 301–314. Springer, Heidelberg (1988)

14. Molland, H.: Improved linear consistency attack on irregular clocked keystream generators. In: Roy, B., Meier, W. (eds.) FSE 2004. LNCS, vol. 3017, pp. 109–126. Springer, Heidelberg (2004)

15. Molland, H., Helleseth, T.: An improved correlation attack against irregular clocked and filtered keystream generators. In: Franklin, M. (ed.) CRYPTO 2004. LNCS, vol. 3152, pp. 373–389. Springer, Heidelberg (2004)

16. Oechslin, P.: Making a faster cryptanalytic time-memory trade-off. In: Boneh, D. (ed.) CRYPTO 2003. LNCS, vol. 2729, pp. 617–630. Springer, Heidelberg (2003)

17. Pasalic, E.: On guess and determine cryptanalysis of LFSR-based stream ciphers. IEEE Transactions on Information Theory 55, 3398–3406 (2009)

18. Saarinen, M.-J.O.: A time-memory tradeoff attack against LILI-128. In: Daemen, J., Rijmen, V. (eds.) FSE 2002. LNCS, vol. 2365, pp. 231–236. Springer, Heidelberg (2002)

19. Simpson, L.R., Dawson, E., Golić, J.D., Millan, W.L.: LILI keystream generator. In: Stinson, D.R., Tavares, S. (eds.) SAC 2000. LNCS, vol. 2012, pp. 248–261. Springer, Heidelberg (2001)

20. Tsunoo, Y., Saito, T., Shigeri, M., Kubo, H., Minematsu, K.: Shorter bit sequence is enough to break stream cipher LILI-128. IEEE Transactions on Information Theory 51, 4312–4319 (2005)

New Sequences of Period p^n and $p^n + 1$ via Projective Linear Groups

Lin Wang[1] and Zhi Hu[2]

[1] Science and Technology on Communication Security Laboratory
Chengdu 610041, Sichuan, P.R. China
linwang@math.pku.edu.cn
[2] Beijing International Center for Mathematical Research, Peking University
Beijing 100871, P.R. China
huzhi@math.pku.edu.cn

Abstract. Two pseudorandom number generators are devised based on the projective linear group over $\mathbb{F}_{p^n}$, outputting balanced sequences on $\mathbb{F}_p$ meeting some statistical randomness properties. Sequences generated by the first generator have least period $p^n + 1$ if $p^n \geq 7$, and linear complexity at least $p^n - p^{n-1}$. Furthermore, autocorrelation of such sequences oscillates within a low amplitude except for the trivial peaks. If $p^n \notin \{2, 4, 8, 16\}$, sequences generated by the second generator have least period p^n, linear complexity at least $p^{n-1} + 1$, and good k-error linear complexity when $p = 2$. If $p = 2$ and 2^n is large enough, then for a binary sequence generated by either generator, a randomly chosen 2-tuple is almost uniformly distributed in $\{00, 01, 10, 11\}$, the probability that a randomly chosen 3-tuple is a run of length one is approximately $1/4$. For such a binary sequence s and integers $0 < i_1 < i_2 < \cdots < i_k \leq m$, $s(t) + s(t + i_1) + s(t + i_2) + \cdots + s(t + i_k)$ is equal to 0 or 1 at almost the same probability when m is far less than $2^{n/2}$.

Keywords: Pseudorandom number generator, Sequence, Projective linear group, Autocorrelation, Linear complexity.

1 Introduction

Pseudorandom sequences of desirable properties are utilized abroad in impulse response detection, ranging systems, digital communication systems, coding and cryptography. A well designed pseudorandom number generator(PRNG) is expected to produce a huge number of sequences of satisfactory randomness and unpredictability. To assess cryptographic randomness of a pseudorandom sequence, one usually considers its period, balancedness, autocorrelation, run property, n-tuple distribution and linear complexity.

In cryptography it is a new trend to generate pseudorandom sequences directly by nonlinear means, e.g. Trivium[4], a finalist of eSTREAM. In Monte Carlo methods, pseudorandom numbers in the unit interval generated via inversion of finite fields have acceptable discrepancy and also perform well in the lattice test and the serial test [10,11,12,14,15,16,17,18,19,23].

M. Kutyłowski and M. Yung (Eds.): Inscrypt 2012, LNCS 7763, pp. 311–330, 2013.
© Springer-Verlag Berlin Heidelberg 2013

Contribution. Following the "good plus bad = good" philosophy[7] and extending the inversive generators, in this paper we propose two pseudorandom number generators based on projective linear groups over finite fields. Sequences on finite fields generated by them can have guaranteed long periods and guaranteed large linear complexity. In such a binary sequence of large period, a randomly chosen 2-tuple is almost uniformly distributed in $\{00, 01, 10, 11\}$, approximately a quarter of 3-tuples are a run of length one, and a nontrivial linear combination of randomly chosen consecutive m bits is almost uniformly distributed when m is far less than $2^{n/2}$. While inversive Monte Carlo methods use a one-to-one correspondence between PRNG states and pseudorandom numbers, in our PRNGs only one finite field element is contracted by trace functions from each state. Compared to [21] where the PRNG state ranges over $\mathbb{F}_p^*$, our PRNG state essentially traverses the quotient group $\mathbb{F}_{p^2}^*/\mathbb{F}_p^*$.

The rest of this paper is organized as follows: Section 2 is mathematical preparation. In Section 3, we characterize two pseudorandom number generators outputting sequences on finite fields. In Section 4, the outputted sequences of the pseudorandom number generators are proved to be balanced and we also describe a distribution feature of linear combination of consecutive bits of those sequences. In Section 5, we compute autocorrelation of outputted sequences and thereby characterize 2-tuple distribution and the number of runs of length one. In Section 6, we give least periods of sequences generated by our pseudorandom number generators. In Section 7, linear complexity of the outputted sequences is computed. In Section 8, we discuss implementation of proposed pseudorandom number generators. In the last section, we give a summary and leave two questions.

Notations. Throughout let p be a prime integer and let $\mathbb{F}_q$ be an extension of the finite field $\mathbb{F}_p$ with $q = p^n$. We always denote the algebraic closure of $\mathbb{F}_q$ by $\overline{\mathbb{F}_q}$, and $\mathbb{F}_q^* = \mathbb{F}_q \backslash \{0\}$. Let $\mathbb{Z}$ be the set of integers. A *sequence* s on $\mathbb{F}_p$ is a mapping $s : \mathbb{Z} \to \mathbb{F}_p$. A sequence on $\mathbb{F}_2$ is called a *binary sequence*. An integer $t \in \mathbb{Z}$ satisfying $s(i) = s(i + t)$ for any $i \in \mathbb{Z}$ is called a *period* of s, and the minimal positive integer which is a period of s is called the *least period* of s. Denote the Euler totient function by φ. For convenience, a 2×2 matrix

$$\begin{pmatrix} a & b \\ c & d \end{pmatrix}$$

is denoted by $[a, b; c, d]$. Denote the residue class ring modulo m by $\mathbb{Z}/m\mathbb{Z}$, the cardinality of a set S by $|S|$, and the greatest integer less than or equal to $r \in \mathbb{R}$ by $[r]$.

2   Preliminaries

In this section we prepare necessary mathematical tools for constructing our pseudorandom number generators, including the trace function of finite fields, estimation of exponential sums, and the projective linear group over finite fields.

2.1 Trace Function

The trace function from $\mathbb{F}_q$ to $\mathbb{F}_p$ is defined to be

$$\mathrm{Tr}\,(x) = x + x^p + x^{p^2} + \cdots + x^{p^{n-1}}, \ x \in \mathbb{F}_q.$$

The trace function of finite fields is known to be surjective. Hence,

Lemma 1. *For any $a \in \mathbb{F}_p$, $|\{x \in \mathbb{F}_q : \mathrm{Tr}\,(x) = a\}| = q/p$.*

2.2 Exponential Sum

Define an additive character on $\mathbb{F}_q$ as

$$e_p(x) = \exp(2\pi i \mathrm{Tr}\,(x)\,/p), \ x \in \mathbb{F}_q.$$

To use exponential sums on the projective line, we need the following lemma directly derived from [3, Theorem 5].

Lemma 2 (Bombieri). *Let C be a complete nonsingular curve of genus g defined on $\mathbb{F}_q$. Let R be a rational function on C with the divisor of poles $(R)_\infty = \sum_{i=1}^t n_i(x_i)$, $x_i \in C$. Denote by $\overline{\mathbb{F}_q}(C)$ the function field of C as a curve defined over $\overline{\mathbb{F}_q}$. If R satisfies*

$$R \neq h^p - h \text{ for any } h \in \overline{\mathbb{F}_q}(C),$$

then

$$\left| \sum_{x \in C \setminus \{x_1, \ldots, x_t\}} e_p\,(R(x)) \right| \leq \left(2g - 2 + t + \sum_{i=1}^t n_i \right) \sqrt{q}.$$

Particularly, the Kloosterman sum on $\mathbb{F}_q$, defined by

$$K_q^*(a) = \sum_{x \in \mathbb{F}_q^*} e_p\,(ax + x^{-1}),$$

is an exponential sum in extensive use, and the Weil's bound[22] gives

$$\left| K_q^*(a) \right| \leq 2\sqrt{q}, \ a \in \mathbb{F}_q.$$

For simplicity we write $K_q(a) = 1 + K_q^*(a)$ and hence $|K_q(a)| \leq 2\sqrt{q} + 1$.

2.3 Projective Linear Groups of the Projective Line

Let f be a permutation on a set S. For $x \in S$, denote $f^0(x) = x$ and $f^n(x) = f(f^{n-1}(x))$. We also denote the inverse of f by f^{-1}. If $x \in S$ satisfies $f(x) = x$, then x is called a *fixed point* of f. If $S = \{f^i(x) : i \in \mathbb{Z}\}$ for some(any) $x \in S$, then f is said to be *transitive* on S.

Let $\mathbb{P}^1(\mathbb{F}_q)$ be the projective line over $\mathbb{F}_q$. The homogeneous coordinate of a point in $\mathbb{P}^1(\mathbb{F}_q)$ is written as $[x_0, x_1]$, where at least one $x_i \in \mathbb{F}_q$ is nonzero; and $[cx_0, cx_1]$, $c \in \mathbb{F}_q^*$, represent the same point. Conventionally, the point $[x_0, x_1]$ is identified as x_0/x_1 if $x_1 \neq 0$, and $[1,0]$ is identified as the infinity point ∞.

Let $\mathrm{GL}_2(\mathbb{F}_q)$ be the group of invertible 2×2 matrices over $\mathbb{F}_q$. Denote the identity matrix in $\mathrm{GL}_2(\mathbb{F}_q)$ by I. A matrix $[a, b; c, d] \in \mathrm{GL}_2(\mathbb{F}_q)$ induces a projective linear transformation σ on $\mathbb{P}^1(\mathbb{F}_q)$ as

$$\sigma(x) = (ax + b)/(cx + d), \text{ for } x \in \mathbb{P}^1(\mathbb{F}_q),$$

where $0 = 1/\infty$ and $1/0 = \infty$. The set of projective linear transformations forms a group under composition, i.e. the *projective linear group* over $\mathbb{F}_q$, denoted by $\mathrm{PGL}_2(\mathbb{F}_q)$. One sees that $A, B \in \mathrm{GL}_2(\mathbb{F}_q)$ induce the same projective linear transformation if and only if $A = cB$ for some $c \in \mathbb{F}_q^*$. In fact, $\mathrm{PGL}_2(\mathbb{F}_q)$ is isomorphic to the quotient group $\mathrm{GL}_2(\mathbb{F}_q)/\mathbb{F}_q^* I$.

Let G be a finite group. The *order* of $x \in G$, denoted by $o(x)$, is the least positive integer m such that $x^m = 1_G$, where 1_G is the unit of G. Denote

$$V_q = \{\sigma \in \mathrm{PGL}_2(\mathbb{F}_q) : o(\sigma) = q + 1\}.$$

Now we need to characterize V_q. Let ζ be a primitive element of $\mathbb{F}_{q^2}$ and

$$U_q = \{\zeta^i : 1 \leq i < (q+1)/2, \gcd(i, q+1) = 1\}.$$

Denote by P_q the set of minimal polynomials over $\mathbb{F}_q$ of all elements of U_q. Each polynomial in P_q is irreducible over $\mathbb{F}_q$ since $U_q \cap \mathbb{F}_q = \emptyset$.

Lemma 3. *If $X^2 - \tau X + \delta$ is a polynomial in P_q, then $\tau \neq 0$, and $X^2 - c\tau X + c^2\delta \notin P_q$ for $1 \neq c \in \mathbb{F}_q$. Furthermore,*

$$|P_q| = |U_q| = \varphi(q+1)/2.$$

Proof. Suppose α to be a root of $X^2 - \tau X + \delta$ such that $\alpha \in U_q$. Then $\alpha^m \notin \mathbb{F}_q$ if $(q+1) \nmid m$. If $\tau = 0$, then $\alpha^2 \in \mathbb{F}_q$, which is absurd. Let $1 \neq c \in \mathbb{F}_q$. Since ζ^{q+1} is a generator of $\mathbb{F}_q^*$, neither $c\alpha$ nor $c\alpha^q$ is in U_q. Thus, $X^2 - c\tau X + c^2\delta = (X - c\alpha)(X - c\alpha^q) \notin P_q$.

Since ζ^i and ζ^j share the same minimal polynomial over $\mathbb{F}_q$ if and only if $j \equiv \pm i \mod q+1$. It does not occur when $1 \leq i, j < (q+1)/2$. Hence, $|P_q| = |U_q|$. Finally, we count $|U_q| = \varphi(q+1)/2$. $\square$

Lemma 4. *Let $\sigma \in \mathrm{PGL}_2(\mathbb{F}_q)$ be induced by $A \in \mathrm{GL}_2(\mathbb{F}_q)$. Then σ has at most two fixed points. Denote the characteristic polynomial of A by f_A. If f_A is reducible over $\mathbb{F}_q$, then $o(\sigma) = p$ or $o(\sigma)|q - 1$. Let α be a root of f_A and and let k be the order of α in the quotient group $\mathbb{F}_{q^2}^*/\mathbb{F}_q^*$. If f_A is irreducible over $\mathbb{F}_q$, then $o(\sigma) = k$, $o(\sigma)|(q+1)$, and σ has no fixed point in $\mathbb{P}^1(\mathbb{F}_q)$.*

Proof. If $[a, b; c, d]$ induces σ, then potential fixed points are the solutions of $cx^2 + (cy + d - a)x + dy - b = 0$. Thus, σ has at most two fixed points.

Assume the Jordan form of $\boldsymbol{A}$ to be $\boldsymbol{J} = [\alpha, \gamma; 0, \beta]$.

Suppose that $f_{\boldsymbol{A}}$ is reducible over $\mathbb{F}_q$. Then $\boldsymbol{A}$ has its eigenvalues $\alpha, \beta \in \mathbb{F}_q$. Hence, if $\gamma \neq 0$ then $\alpha = \beta$ and $\boldsymbol{J}^p \in \mathbb{F}_q^*\boldsymbol{I}$, i.e. $\boldsymbol{A}^p \in \mathbb{F}_q^*\boldsymbol{I}$; if $\gamma = 0$ then $\boldsymbol{J}^{q-1} \in \mathbb{F}_q^*\boldsymbol{I}$, i.e. $\boldsymbol{A}^{q-1} \in \mathbb{F}_q^*\boldsymbol{I}$.

Suppose that $f_{\boldsymbol{A}}$ is irreducible over $\mathbb{F}_q$. Then $\gamma = 0$, $\alpha \in \mathbb{F}_{q^2} \backslash \mathbb{F}_q$, and $\beta = \alpha^q$. Since $\boldsymbol{A}^m$ is a constant matrix if and only if $\boldsymbol{J}^m$ is a constant matrix, i.e., $\alpha^m \in \mathbb{F}_q$, we have $o(\sigma) = k$. Since $\alpha^{(q+1)(q-1)} = 1$, we have $k|(q+1)$.

Suppose that σ has a fixed point $x \in \mathbb{P}^1(\mathbb{F}_q)$. Notice that $(x, 1)^T$ is an eigenvector of $\boldsymbol{A}$, where $(x, 1)^T$ is the transpose of the vector $(x, 1)$. Thus, the eigenvalue of $\boldsymbol{A}$ with respect to $(x, 1)^T$ belongs to $\mathbb{F}_q$ and $f_{\boldsymbol{A}}$ is therefore reducible over $\mathbb{F}_q$. $\qquad\square$

From now on we denote

$$M(u, w, \tau, \delta) = [u, (u(\tau - u) - \delta)/w; w, \tau - u], \text{ for } u \in \mathbb{F}_q, \, w, \tau, \delta \in \mathbb{F}_q^*;$$

$$M(\tau, \delta) = \left\{ M(u, w, \tau, \delta) : u \in \mathbb{F}_q, w \in \mathbb{F}_q^* \right\};$$

$$M_q = \bigcup_{X^2 - \tau X + \delta \in P_q} M(\tau, \delta).$$

Theorem 1. *Use notations above. Then (1) M_q is the disjoint union of $M(\tau, \delta)$, where $X^2 - \tau X + \delta$ runs over polynomials in P_q; and (2) V_q are exactly the set of projective linear transformations induced by matrices in M_q, with no distinct matrices in M_q inducing the same projective linear transformation. Furthermore,*

$$|M(\tau, \delta)| = q(q - 1) \text{ and } |V_q| = |M_q| = q(q - 1)\varphi(q + 1)/2.$$

Proof. Clearly, $|M(\tau, \delta)| = q(q - 1)$. Since $M(\tau, \delta)$ is the set of matrices on $\mathbb{F}_q$ whose characteristic polynomial is $X^2 - \tau X + \delta$, we have $M(\tau_1, \delta_1) \cap M(\tau_2, \delta_2) = \emptyset$ when $(\tau_1, \delta_1) \neq (\tau_2, \delta_2)$. Thus, M_q is the disjoint union of $M(\tau, \delta)$, $X^2 - \tau X + \delta \in P_q$. Therefore, by Lemma 3, $|M_q| = q(q - 1)|P_q| = q(q - 1)\varphi(q + 1)/2$.

On one hand, we show that any $\sigma \in V_q$ is induced by some matrix in M_q. Assume that $\boldsymbol{A} \in \mathrm{GL}_2(\mathbb{F}_q)$ induces σ and the characteristic polynomial of $\boldsymbol{A}$ is $f_{\boldsymbol{A}}$. Let α be a root of $f_{\boldsymbol{A}}$. Since $o(\sigma) = q + 1$, by Lemma 4, $f_{\boldsymbol{A}}$ is irreducible over $\mathbb{F}_q$ and $\alpha^i \in \mathbb{F}_q$ implies $(q + 1)|i$. Since $\mathbb{F}_{q^2}^*$ is a cyclic group of order $q^2 - 1$ generated by ζ, there exists $1 \leq j < q + 1$ such that $\zeta^j \alpha^{-1} \in \mathbb{F}_q^*$ and $\gcd(j, q + 1) = 1$. Take

$$\beta = \begin{cases} \zeta^j \alpha^{-1}, & \text{if } 1 \leq j < (q+1)/2, \\ \zeta^{q+1-j} \alpha^{-q}, & \text{if } (q+1)/2 < j \leq q. \end{cases}$$

Then $\beta \in \mathbb{F}_q$ and the minimal polynomial of $\beta\alpha$ over $\mathbb{F}_q$ is in P_q. Hence $\beta\boldsymbol{A} \in M_q$ also induces σ.

On the other hand, we prove that distinct matrices in M_q induce distinct projective linear transformations. Let $\boldsymbol{A}, \boldsymbol{B} \in M_q$ and $\boldsymbol{A} \neq \boldsymbol{B}$. By Lemma 3, there exists no $c \in \mathbb{F}_q$ such that $\boldsymbol{A} = c\boldsymbol{B}$. Hence, $\boldsymbol{A}$ and $\boldsymbol{B}$ induce different projective linear transformations.

Therefore, $|V_q| = |M_q|$. $\qquad\square$

For $\sigma \in \mathrm{PGL}_2(\mathbb{F}_q)$ induced by $\boldsymbol{A} = [a, b; c, d] \in \mathrm{GL}_2(\mathbb{F}_q)$, where $c \neq 0$, the polynomial

$$f_\sigma(x) = -(ad - bc)(c^2 x + cd)^{q-2} + a/c$$

characterizes a permutation on $\mathbb{F}_q$, and we call f_σ to be the *permutation associated to* σ (also the *permutation induced by* $\boldsymbol{A}$). Clearly,

$$f_\sigma(x) = \begin{cases} \sigma(x), & \text{if } x \neq -d/c, \\ a/c, & \text{if } x = -d/c. \end{cases} \tag{2}$$

Now define

$$H_q = \{f_\sigma : \sigma \in V_q\}.$$

Theorem 2. *Each projective linear transformation in V_q is a transitive permutation on $\mathbb{P}^1(\mathbb{F}_q)$, and each permutation in H_q is transitive on $\mathbb{F}_q$.*

Proof. Let $\sigma \in V_q$ be induced by $\boldsymbol{A} \in M_q$, and let α be a root of the characteristic polynomial of $\boldsymbol{A}$ such that $\alpha \in U_q$. Since $\alpha^m \in \mathbb{F}_q$ only if $(q+1)|m$, the characteristic polynomials of $\boldsymbol{A}^i$, $i = 1, 2, \ldots, q$, are all irreducible over $\mathbb{F}_q$. Thus, by Lemma 4, σ^i, $i = 1, 2, \ldots, q$, have no fixed point in $\mathbb{P}^1(\mathbb{F}_q)$. For $z \in \mathbb{P}^1(\mathbb{F}_q)$, we have $\{\sigma^i(z) : i = 0, 1, 2, \ldots, q\} = \mathbb{P}^1(\mathbb{F}_q)$, i.e., σ is transitive on $\mathbb{P}^1(\mathbb{F}_q)$. Besides, by Eq.(2), f_σ is transitive on $\mathbb{F}_q$ if and only if σ is transitive on $\mathbb{P}^1(\mathbb{F}_q)$. $\square$

Theorem 3. *Let $q \geq 5$. If $\sigma_1, \sigma_2 \in V_q$ and $\sigma_1 \neq \sigma_2$, then $f_{\sigma_1} \neq f_{\sigma_2}$. Besides,*

$$|H_q| = q(q-1)\varphi(q+1)/2.$$

Proof. Suppose $f_{\sigma_1} = f_{\sigma_2}$. By Eq.(2), if $q \geq 5$, there exist at least three distinct elements x_1, x_2, x_3 in $\mathbb{F}_q$ such that

$$\sigma_1(x_i) = f_{\sigma_1}(x_i) = f_{\sigma_2}(x_i) = \sigma_2(x_i), \ i = 1, 2, 3.$$

A projective linear transformation is determined by the images of any three distinct points, and hence $\sigma_1 = \sigma_2$. Since distinct permutations are associated to distinct projective linear transformations, we have $|H_q| = |V_q|$, where $|V_q|$ is given by Theorem 1. $\square$

If $q \leq 4$, different invertible matrices may induce the same permutation on $\mathbb{F}_q$.

Example 1. Let w be a root of the polynomial $X^2 + X + 1$ over $\mathbb{F}_2$. The permutation on $\mathbb{F}_4$

$$w \to 1 \to w + 1 \to 0 \to w$$

is induced both by $[0, 1; 1, w + 1]$ and by $[w, 1; 1, 0]$.

3   Sequence Generators

In this section we propose two pseudorandom number generators outputting sequences on $\mathbb{F}_p$. Main properties of sequences generated by them are discussed in later sections. The mode of such nonlinear generators comprises a finite state automaton and a shrinking function. The state transition transformation updates phases of the finite state automaton, and the shrinking function extracts a bit from each phase of the finite state automaton.

A sequence s_1 is said to be *equivalent* to a sequence s_2 if there exists $t \in \mathbb{Z}$ such that $s_1(i + t) = s_2(i)$ for all $i \in \mathbb{Z}$. Actually, this equivalence relation describes shifting of sequences. The *equivalence class* of a sequence s is the set of all sequences equivalent to s. We only concentrate on equivalence classes of sequences because main properties of sequences are independent of shifting, such as period, autocorrelation, tuple distribution and linear complexity.

PRNG 1. Pseudorandom number generator I

Choose a projective linear transformation $\sigma \in V_q$.
Choose $\lambda \in \mathbb{F}_q^*$, determining a linear function $x \mapsto \mathrm{Tr}\,(\lambda x)$ on $\mathbb{F}_q$. Extend the linear function to $\mathbb{P}^1(\mathbb{F}_q)$ by enforcing $\mathrm{Tr}\,(\infty) = 0$.
Choose an initial state $z := z_0 \in \mathbb{P}^1(\mathbb{F}_q)$.
loop
   Output $\mathrm{Tr}\,(\lambda z)$.{Data extraction}
   $z := \sigma(z)$.{State transition}
end loop

PRNG1 generates a sequence s described as

$$s(i) = \mathrm{Tr}\left(\lambda \sigma^i(z_0)\right),$$

with its equivalence class denoted by $S(\lambda, \sigma)$.

PRNG 2. Pseudorandom number generator II

Choose a permutation $\psi \in H_q$.
Choose $\lambda \in \mathbb{F}_q^*$, determining a linear function $x \mapsto \mathrm{Tr}\,(\lambda x)$ on $\mathbb{F}_q$.
Choose an initial state $z := z_0 \in \mathbb{F}_q$.
loop
   Output $\mathrm{Tr}\,(\lambda z)$.{Data extraction}
   $z := \psi(z)$.{State transition}
end loop

PRNG2 generates a sequence s described as

$$s(i) = \mathrm{Tr}\left(\lambda \psi^i(z_0)\right),$$

with its equivalence class denoted by $S(\lambda, \psi)$.

Remark 1. By Theorem 2, we conclude that $q + 1$ is a period of sequences generated by PRNG1, and q is a period of sequences generated by PRNG2.

Remark 2. Let $\sigma \in V_q$, $\psi \in H_q$ the permutation associated to σ, and $\lambda \in \mathbb{F}_q^*$. By Theorem 2 and Eq.(2), a sequence in $S(\lambda, \psi)$ can be obtained by deleting a bit in each consecutive $q + 1$ bits of some sequence in $S(\lambda, \sigma)$.

Remark 3. Suppose $q \geq 5$. By Theorem 1 and Theorem 3, the number of parameter settings for both PRNG1 and PRNG2 is $q(q-1)^2 \varphi(q+1)/2$ if we do not count in initial states, which only cause shifting of outputted sequences.

4   Balancedness and Linear Combination

In this section we consider balancedness of sequences generated by PRNG1 and PRNG2, and also balancedness of linear combination of their consecutive shifts.

A sequence $\boldsymbol{s}$ on $\mathbb{F}_p$ of period ν is said to be *balanced* if

$$[\nu/p] \leq |1 \leq i \leq \nu : s(i) = a| \leq [\nu/p] + 1 \text{ for any } a \in \mathbb{F}_p.$$

Theorem 4. *A sequence generated by PRNG1 or by PRNG2 is balanced.*

Proof. By Theorem 2, $\psi \in H_q$ (resp. $\sigma \in V_q$) is a transitive permutation of $\mathbb{F}_q$(resp. $\mathbb{P}^1(\mathbb{F}_q)$), we have

$$\{\psi^i(z_0) : i = 1, 2, \ldots, q\} = \mathbb{F}_q;$$
$$\{\sigma^i(z_0) : i = 1, 2, \ldots, q+1\} = \mathbb{P}^1(\mathbb{F}_q).$$

Suppose $\lambda \in \mathbb{F}_q^*$, $s_1(i) = \mathrm{Tr}\left(\lambda \sigma^i(z_0)\right)$ and $s_2(i) = \mathrm{Tr}\left(\lambda \psi^i(z_0)\right)$. By Lemma 1, for $a \in \mathbb{F}_p$, we have further $|\{1 \leq i \leq q : s_2(i) = a\}| = q/p$ and

$$|\{1 \leq i \leq q+1 : s_1(i) = a\}| = \begin{cases} q/p, & \text{if } a \neq 0, \\ q/p + 1, & \text{if } a = 0. \end{cases} \qquad \square$$

Given a sequence $\boldsymbol{s}$ on $\mathbb{F}_p$ of period ν and $b_0, b_1, \ldots, b_{k-1} \in \mathbb{F}_p$,

$$\hat{s}(i) = b_0 s(i) + b_1 s(i+1) + \cdots + b_{k-1} s(i+k-1)$$

characterizes a sequence $\hat{\boldsymbol{s}}$ of period ν.

Theorem 5. *Let $\sigma \in V_q$, $\psi \in H_q$, $\lambda \in \mathbb{F}_q^*$, $s_1 \in S(\lambda, \sigma)$ and $s_2 \in S(\lambda, \psi)$. Let $1 \leq k \leq q$ and $b_0, b_1, \ldots, b_{k-1} \in \mathbb{F}_p$ with at least one nonzero. Then*

$$\left| \sum_{i=1}^{q+1} e_p \left(\sum_{j=0}^{k-1} b_j s_1(i+j) \right) \right| \leq (k-1)(2\sqrt{q}+1) + 1; \tag{3}$$

$$\left| \sum_{i=1}^{q} e_p \left(\sum_{j=0}^{k-1} b_j s_2(i+j) \right) \right| \leq (k-1)(2\sqrt{q}+1). \tag{4}$$

Proof. Consider the projective line over $\mathbb{F}_q$ and the rational function $R(x) = b_0 x + b_1 \sigma(x) + \cdots + b_{k-1} \sigma^{k-1}(x)$ on $\mathbb{P}^1(\mathbb{F}_q)$. Denote $S = \{\infty, \sigma^{-1}(\infty), \ldots, \sigma^{1-k}(\infty)\}$. Since σ is a projective linear transformation of order $q + 1$ and b_js are not all zeros, the divisor of poles $(R)_\infty \leq (\infty) + (\sigma^{-1}(\infty)) + \cdots + (\sigma^{1-k}(\infty))$, i.e., the multiplicity of a pole is one and furthermore $R(x) = \infty$ only if $x \in S$. Hence, $R \neq h^p - h$ for any rational function on $\mathbb{P}^1(\overline{\mathbb{F}_q})$, because no pole of R has multiplicity divisible by p. Since $\mathbb{P}^1(\mathbb{F}_q)$ has genus 0, Lemma 2 gives

$$\left| \sum_{x \notin S} e_p\left(\lambda R(x)\right) \right| \leq (2k - 2)\sqrt{q}.$$

Then the inequality (3) follows from

$$\sum_{i=1}^{q+1} e_p\left(\sum_{j=0}^{k-1} b_j s_1(i+j)\right) = \sum_{x \notin S} e_p\left(\lambda R(x)\right) + \sum_{i=0}^{k-1} e_p\left(\lambda \sum_{j=0}^{k-1} b_j \sigma^{j-i}(\infty)\right).$$

Since $\psi(x) = \sigma(x)$ if $x \notin S$, the inequality (4) follows from

$$\sum_{i=1}^{q} e_p\left(\sum_{j=0}^{k-1} b_j s_2(i+j)\right) = \sum_{x \notin S} e_p\left(\lambda R(x)\right) + \sum_{i=1}^{k-1} e_p\left(\lambda \sum_{j=0}^{k-1} b_j \psi^j(\sigma^{-i}(\infty))\right). \quad \square$$

Remark 4. Let $\hat{s}$ be a nontrivial sequence derived from linear combination of k consecutive shifts of a binary sequences generated by PRNG1 or PRNG2. If k is far less than $2^{n/2}$, then Theorem 5 implies that a randomly chosen bit in $\hat{s}$ is almost uniformly distributed in $\{0, 1\}$ with a negligible probability error less than $2k/2^{n/2}$.

5   Autocorrelation and Distribution

In this section we consider autocorrelation, 2-tuple distribution and the number of runs of length one for sequences generated by PRNG1 and PRNG2.

The *autocorrelation* function of a sequence s on $\mathbb{F}_p$ of period ν is defined to be

$$C_s(t) = \frac{1}{\nu} \sum_{i=0}^{\nu-1} \exp((s(i+t) - s(i))2\pi\mathbf{i}/p).$$

Clearly, $C_s(t) = 1$ are trivial peaks if $\nu | t$.

Theorem 6. *Let $\sigma \in V_q$ be induced by $M(u, w, \tau, \delta) \in M_q$ and let $\psi \in H_q$ be associated to σ. Suppose $\lambda \in \mathbb{F}_q^*$, $s_1 \in S(\lambda, \sigma)$ and $s_2 \in S(\lambda, \psi)$. For $m \in \mathbb{Z}$, denote $\lfloor m \rceil = \min\{|m - qi| : i \in \mathbb{Z}\}$. Then*

$$|C_{s_1}(t)| \leq 2\left(1 + \sqrt{q}\right)/(q + 1), \quad (q + 1) \nmid t;$$

$$C_{s_2}(1) = e_p\left(\lambda \tau / c\right) K_q(\delta \lambda^2 / w^2)/q;$$

$$|C_{s_2}(t)| \leq (2\lfloor t \rceil + 2\sqrt{q} - 1)/q, \quad q \nmid t. \tag{5}$$

Proof. For $a, b, d \in \mathbb{F}_q$ and $c \in \mathbb{F}_q^*$ satisfying $ad - bc \neq 0$, we have

$$\sum_{-d/c \neq x \in \mathbb{F}_q} e_p\left(\lambda\left((ax+b)/(cx+d) - x\right)\right)$$

$$= \sum_{-d/c \neq x \in \mathbb{F}_q} e_p\left(\lambda\left(a/c - (ad-bc)/(c(cx+d)) - x\right)\right)$$

$$= \sum_{y \in \mathbb{F}_q^*} e_p\left(\lambda(a+d)/c - \lambda(ad-bc)y/c^2 - \lambda/y\right)$$

$$= e_p\left(\lambda(a+d)/c\right) \sum_{z \in \mathbb{F}_q^*} e_p\left(\lambda^2(ad-bc)z/c^2 + 1/z\right)$$

$$= e_p\left(\lambda(a+d)/c\right) K_q^*(\lambda^2(ad-bc)/c^2).$$

Supposing $(q+1) \nmid t$ and $\sigma^t(x) = (ax+b)/(cx+d)$, we compute

$$C_{s_1}(t) = \frac{1}{q+1} \sum_{x \in \mathbb{P}^1(\mathbb{F}_q)} e_p\left(\lambda\left((ax+b)/(cx+d) - x\right)\right)$$

$$= \frac{1}{q+1}\left(e_p(\lambda a/c) + e_p(\lambda d/c) + \sum_{-d/c \neq x \in \mathbb{F}_q} e_p\left(\lambda\left((ax+b)/(cx+d) - x\right)\right)\right)$$

$$= \frac{1}{q+1}\left(e_p(\lambda a/c) + e_p(\lambda d/c) + e_p(\lambda(a+d)/c) K_q^*((ad-bc)/c^2)\right),$$

yielding

$$|C_{s_1}(t)| \leq \left(2 + \left|K_q^*(\lambda^2(ad-bc)/c^2)\right|\right)/(q+1) \leq 2\left(1 + \sqrt{q}\right)/(q+1).$$

Similarly,

$$C_{s_2}(1) = \frac{1}{q} \sum_{x \in \mathbb{F}_q} e_p\left(\lambda\left((ux + (u(\tau-u) - \delta)/w)(wx + \tau - u)^{q-2} - x\right)\right)$$

$$= \frac{1}{q} \sum_{x \in \mathbb{F}_q} e_p\left(\lambda\left(u/w - \delta(wx + \tau - u)^{q-2}/w - x\right)\right)$$

$$= \frac{1}{q}\left(e_p(\lambda\tau/w) + \sum_{(u-\tau)/w \neq x \in \mathbb{F}_q} e_p\left(\lambda\left(u/w - \delta(wx + \tau - u)^{q-2}/w - x\right)\right)\right)$$

$$= e_p(\lambda\tau/w)\left(1 + K_q^*(\delta\lambda^2/w^2)\right)/q$$

$$= e_p(\lambda\tau/w) K_q(\delta\lambda^2/w^2)/q.$$

Now assume $x_1 = u/w$ and $x_i = \psi(x_{i-1})$, $i = 2, 3, \ldots, q$. Let $\sigma^t(x) = (ax+b)/(cx+d)$ and let g be the associated permutation of σ^t. Then $x_{q-t+1} = -d/c$ and $x_t = a/c$. Suppose $0 < t < q$. Observing

$$\psi^t(x_i) = \begin{cases} \sigma^t(x_i) = g(x_i), & 1 \leq i \leq q-t, \\ \sigma^{t+1}(x_i), & q-t < t \leq q, \end{cases}$$

we compute

$$C_{s_2}(t) = \frac{1}{q} \sum_{i=1}^{q} e_p \left(\lambda(\psi^t(x_i) - x_i) \right)$$

$$= \frac{1}{q} \sum_{i=1}^{q-t} e_p \left(\lambda(g(x_i) - x_i) \right) + \frac{1}{q} \sum_{i=q-t+1}^{q} e_p \left(\lambda(\sigma^{t+1}(x_i) - x_i) \right)$$

$$= \frac{1}{q} \sum_{-d/c \neq x \in \mathbb{F}_q} e_p \left(\lambda(g(x) - x) \right) - \frac{1}{q} \sum_{i=q-t+2}^{q} e_p \left(\lambda(g(x_i) - x_i) \right)$$

$$+ \frac{1}{q} \sum_{i=q-t+1}^{q} e_p \left(\lambda(\sigma^{t+1}(x_i) - x_i) \right)$$

$$= \frac{1}{q} e_p \left(\lambda(a+d)/c \right) K_q^*(\lambda^2(ad - bc)/c^2) - \frac{1}{q} \sum_{i=q-t+2}^{q} e_p \left(\lambda(g(x_i) - x_i) \right)$$

$$+ \frac{1}{q} \sum_{i=q-t+1}^{q} e_p \left(\lambda(\sigma^{t+1}(x_i) - x_i) \right),$$

implying

$$|C_{s_2}(t)| \leq \left(\left| K_q^*(\lambda^2(ad - bc)/c^2) \right| + 2t - 1 \right) / q \leq (2\sqrt{q} + 2t - 1)/q.$$

Since $|C_s(t)| = |C_s(q - t)|$, we conclude

$$|C_{s_2}(t)| \leq (2 \min\{t, q - t\} + 2\sqrt{q} - 1)/q, \ 0 \leq t < q. \square$$

Remark 5. As q tends to infinity, autocorrelation values of sequences generated by PRNG1 asymptotically decrease to zero except the trivial peaks. As $t \bmod q$ approaches to $q/2$, some numerical experiments show that $|C_{s_2}(t)|$ is much less than our bound Eq.(5), and hence it is expected to give a sharper bound of $C_{s_2}(t)$.

For a sequence s, a vector $(s(i), s(i+1), \ldots, s(i+m-1))$ is called an *m-tuple* of s. A vector $(s(i), s(i+1), \ldots, s(i+m-1))$ is a called an *a-run* of length m of s if $s(i-1) \neq a$, $s(i+m) \neq a$ and $s(i) = s(i+1) = \cdots = s(i+m-1) = a$. In this part now we only consider tuple distribution of binary sequences, i.e. $p = 2$.

Lemma 5. *Let s be a binary sequence of period ν. For $b_0, b_1, b_2 \in \mathbb{F}_2$, denote*

$$N_{b_0 b_1}^{\tau} = |\{1 \leq i \leq \nu : s(i) = b_0, s(i+\tau) = b_1\}|,$$

$$N_{b_0 b_1 b_2}^{\tau_1, \tau_2} = |\{1 \leq i \leq \nu : s(i) = b_0, s(i+\tau_1) = b_1, s(i+\tau_2) = b_2\}|.$$

If $\sum_{i=1}^{\nu}(-1)^{s(i)} = \epsilon$, $\nu \nmid \tau$, $\nu \nmid \tau_1$ and $\nu \nmid \tau_2$, then

$$N_{01}^{\tau} = N_{10}^{\tau} = (1 - C_s(\tau))\nu/4,$$

$$N_{00}^{\tau} = (\nu + 2\epsilon + \nu C_s(\tau))/4,$$

$$N_{11}^{\tau} = (\nu - 2\epsilon + \nu C_s(\tau))/4,$$

$$N_{010}^{\tau_1, \tau_2} + N_{101}^{\tau_1, \tau_2} = (1 + C_s(\tau_2) - 2C_s(\tau_1))\nu/4 - \epsilon.$$

Proof. By the definition of autocorrelation,

$$\nu C_s(\tau) = N_{00}^\tau + N_{11}^\tau - N_{01}^\tau - N_{10}^\tau.$$

Moreover, counting zeros or ones in 2-tuples yields

$$N_{00}^\tau + N_{01}^\tau = N_{00}^\tau + N_{10}^\tau = (\nu + \epsilon)/2,$$
$$N_{01}^\tau + N_{11}^\tau = N_{10}^\tau + N_{11}^\tau = (\nu - \epsilon)/2.$$

Solving equations above gives N_{00}^τ, N_{01}^τ, N_{10}^τ and N_{11}^τ.

Furthermore, we count the number of 2-tuples in 3-tuples and get

$$N_{000}^{\tau_1,\tau_2} + N_{001}^{\tau_1,\tau_2} = N_{000}^{\tau_1,\tau_2} + N_{100}^{\tau_1,\tau_2} = N_{00}^{\tau_1} = (\nu + 2\epsilon + \nu C_s(\tau_1))/4,$$
$$N_{010}^{\tau_1,\tau_2} + N_{011}^{\tau_1,\tau_2} = N_{001}^{\tau_1,\tau_2} + N_{101}^{\tau_1,\tau_2} = N_{01}^{\tau_1} = (1 - C_s(\tau_1))\nu/4,$$
$$N_{100}^{\tau_1,\tau_2} + N_{101}^{\tau_1,\tau_2} = N_{010}^{\tau_1,\tau_2} + N_{110}^{\tau_1,\tau_2} = N_{10}^{\tau_1} = (1 - C_s(\tau_1))\nu/4,$$
$$N_{110}^{\tau_1,\tau_2} + N_{111}^{\tau_1,\tau_2} = N_{011}^{\tau_1,\tau_2} + N_{111}^{\tau_1,\tau_2} = N_{11}^{\tau_1} = (\nu - 2\epsilon + \nu C_s(\tau_1))/4,$$
$$N_{000}^{\tau_1,\tau_2} + N_{010}^{\tau_1,\tau_2} = N_{101}^{\tau_1,\tau_2} + N_{111}^{\tau_1,\tau_2} = N_{11}^{\tau_2} = (\nu - 2\epsilon + \nu C_s(\tau_2))/4,$$
$$N_{100}^{\tau_1,\tau_2} + N_{110}^{\tau_1,\tau_2} = N_{001}^{\tau_1,\tau_2} + N_{011}^{\tau_1,\tau_2} = N_{01}^{\tau_2} = (1 - C_s(\tau_2))\nu/4.$$

One also obtains $N_{010}^{\tau_1,\tau_2} + N_{101}^{\tau_1,\tau_2}$ from equations above.   □

Part of Lemma 5 is similar to [13, Proposition 2], and we reinterpret it here for readability.

Applying Theorem 6 and Lemma 5, we immediately have the following two theorems on tuple distribution of sequences generated by PRNG1 and PRNG2.

Theorem 7. *Let* $\sigma \in V_{2^n}$, $\lambda \in \mathbb{F}_{2^n}^*$ *and* $s \in S(\lambda, \sigma)$. *Use notations as in Lemma 5. If* $(2^n + 1) \nmid \tau$, $(2^n + 1) \nmid \tau'$ *and* $(2^n + 1) \nmid (\tau - \tau')$, *then*

$$\left| N_{b_0 b_1}^\tau - 2^{n-2} \right| \le 2^{n/2-1} + 5/4;$$
$$\left| N_{010}^{\tau,\tau'} + N_{101}^{\tau,\tau'} - 2^{n-2} \right| \le 3 \cdot 2^{n/2-1} + 9/4.$$

Theorem 8. *Let* $\psi \in H_{2^n}$ *be induced by* $M(u, w, \tau, \delta)$, $\lambda \in \mathbb{F}_{2^n}^*$ *and* $s \in S(\lambda, \psi)$. *Use notations as in Lemma 5. Then*

$$\left| N_{b_0 b_1}^1 - 2^{n-2} \right| \le 2^{n/2-1} + 1/4;$$
$$\left| N_{010}^{1,2} + N_{101}^{1,2} - 2^{n-2} \right| \le 3 \cdot 2^{n/2-1} + 5/4.$$

Particularly, $N_{00}^1 = N_{01}^1 = N_{10}^1 = N_{11}^1 = 2^{n-2}$ *if and only if* $K_{2^n}(\delta\lambda^2/w^2) = 0$.

Remark 6. Actually, $N_{b_0 b_1}^1$ describes the number of the 2-tuple $b_0 b_1$ in a period, and $N_{010}^{1,2} + N_{101}^{1,2}$ describes the the number of runs of length one in a period. By Theorem 7 and Theorem 8, if 2^n grows large enough, in a binary sequence generated by PRNG1 or PRNG2, a randomly chosen 2-tuple is almost uniformly distributed in $\{00, 01, 10, 11\}$ with negligible probability errors; and a randomly chosen 3-tuple is in $\{010, 101\}$ at a probability approximately close to $1/4$. Particularly, if parameters are chosen to satisfy $K_{2^n}(\delta\lambda^2/w^2) = 0$, then sequences in $S(\lambda, \psi)$ have uniform 2-tuple distribution.

6   Least Period

In this section we determine the least periods of sequences generated by PRNG1 and PRNG2.

Theorem 9. *If $q \geq 7$, then the least period of sequences generated by PRNG1 is $q + 1$.*

Proof. Note that $q + 1$ is the the least period of s if and only if $C_s(t) = 1$ holds only when $(q + 1)|t$. By Theorem 6, $C_s(t) < 1$ if $(q + 1) \nmid t$ and $q \geq 7$.   □

Theorem 10. *Let p be an odd prime. Then the least period of sequences generated by PRNG2 is q.*

Proof. Let $\sigma \in V_q$ be induced by $[a, b; c, d]$ and let $\psi \in H_q$ be associated to σ. Suppose $\lambda \in \mathbb{F}_q^*$ and $s \in S(\lambda, \psi)$. Denote $x_1 = a/c$ and $x_i = \psi^{i-1}(x_1)$, $i \in \mathbb{Z}$. Without loss of generality, suppose $s(i) = \text{Tr}(\lambda x_i)$, $i \in \mathbb{Z}$. As in Remark 1, the least period of s is a divisor of q. Note that $\psi(x) = \sigma(x)$ for $x \neq -d/c$. Thus,

$$\psi^{q/p}(x_i) = \begin{cases} \sigma^{q/p}(x_i), & 1 \leq i \leq q - q/p; \\ \sigma^{q/p+1}(x_i), & q - q/p < i \leq q. \end{cases}$$

Denote

$$A_1 = \left\{ x_i : \text{Tr}\left(\lambda\left(\sigma^{q/p}(x_i) - x_i\right)\right) = 0, 1 \leq i \leq q - q/p \right\},$$

$$A_2 = \left\{ x_i : \text{Tr}\left(\lambda\left(\sigma^{q/p+1}(x_i) - x_i\right)\right) = 0, q - q/p < i \leq q \right\},$$

and $A = A_1 \cup A_2$. One sees that q/p is a period of s if and only if $|A| = q$. Let $A_1' = \{x \in \mathbb{F}_q : \text{Tr}(\lambda(\sigma^{q/p}(x) - x)) = 0\}$. Clearly, $A_1 \subset A_1'$.

Denote $B_y = \{x \in \mathbb{F}_q : \sigma^{q/p}(x) - x = y\}$. Since $o(\sigma) = q + 1$ and $\gcd(q/p, q + 1) = 1$, we have $o(\sigma^{q/p}) = q + 1$, and hence $\sigma^{q/p}$ has no fixed point in $\mathbb{F}_q$ by Lemma 4. Then

$$A_1' \subset \bigcup_{y \in \mathbb{F}_q^*, \text{Tr}(\lambda y) = 0} B_y.$$

Moreover, letting $[a', b'; c', d']$ induce $\sigma^{q/p}$, one sees that $B_y = \{x \in \mathbb{F}_q : c'x^2 + (c'y + d' - a')x + d'y - b' = 0\}$ and hence $|B_y| \leq 2$. Since $\{y \in \mathbb{F}_q : \text{Tr}(\lambda y) = 0\}$ is a subspace over $\mathbb{F}_p$, we have

$$|A| \leq |A_1| + |A_2| \leq |A_1'| + |A_2|$$

$$\leq \sum_{y \in \mathbb{F}_q^*, \text{Tr}(\lambda y) = 0} |B_y| + |A_2|$$

$$\leq 2(q/p - 1) + q/p < q.$$

Therefore, q/p is not a period of s and hence q is the least period.   □

Now we consider the least period of binary sequences generated by PRNG2.

Theorem 11. *Let $\psi \in H_{2^n}$ and $s \in S(\lambda, \psi)$, where $\lambda \in \mathbb{F}_q^*$. If $n \geq 6$, then the least period of s is 2^n.*

Proof. Denote $N = |\{1 \leq i \leq 2^{n-1} : s(i + 2^{n-1}) \neq s(i)\}|$. The least period of s is 2^n if and only if $N \geq 1$.

Suppose ψ is induced by $[a, b; c, d]$. Denote $x_1 = a/c$ and $x_i = \psi(x_{i-1})$, $i = 2, 3, \ldots, 2^n$. Without loss of generality, suppose $s(i) = \mathrm{Tr}\,(\lambda x_i)$. Then ψ permutates $\mathbb{F}_q$ as

$$x_1 \to x_2 \to \cdots \to x_{2^{n-1}} \to x_{2^{n-1}+1} \to \cdots \to x_{2^n} \to x_1.$$

Assume ψ is associated to $\sigma \in V_q$ and let $g(x) = (a_0 x + a_1)^{2^n - 2} + a_2$ be the associated permutation of $\sigma^{2^{n-1}}$. Then g permutates $\mathbb{F}_q$ as

$$x_{2^{n-1}} \to x_{2^n} \to x_{2^{n-1}-1} \to x_{2^n-1} \to \cdots \to x_1 \to x_{2^{n-1}+1} \to x_{2^{n-1}}.$$

Explicitly, by Eq.(2),

$$g(x_i) = \begin{cases} x_{i+2^{n-1}}, & 1 \leq i \leq 2^{n-1}, \\ x_{i-2^{n-1}-1}, & 2^{n-1} + 2 \leq i \leq 2^n, \\ x_{2^{n-1}}, & i = 2^{n-1} + 1. \end{cases}$$

Denote $y_1 = x_{2^{n-1}}$ and $y_i = g(y_{i-1})$, $i \in \mathbb{Z}$. Suppose $s'(i) = \mathrm{Tr}\,(\lambda y_i)$. In fact, $s' \in S(\lambda, g)$. Then

$$s'(i) = \begin{cases} s(2^{n-1} - (i-1)/2), & i = 1, 3, 5, \ldots, 2^n - 1; \\ s(2^n - i/2 + 1), & i = 2, 4, 6, \ldots, 2^n. \end{cases}$$

Let N' be the number of runs of length one in a period of s', i.e.,

$$N' = |\{1 \leq i \leq 2^n : s'(i) \neq s'(i+1), s'(i+1) \neq s'(i+2)\}|.$$

Observe that in each run of length one of s' there exists a 2-tuple $(s(i), s(i + 2^{n-1}))$ for some $i \in \mathbb{Z}$. Thus, $N \geq N'/2$. By Theorem 8, $N \geq 2^{n-3} - 3 \cdot 2^{n/2-2} - 5/8$. We have $N \geq 1$ if $n \geq 6$. Hence, 2^n is the least period of s. □

Claim. Through computer programming we find out that the least period of binary sequences generated by PRNG2 is 32 if $q = 32$.

When $p = 2$ and $n \leq 4$, the least period of sequences generated by PRNG2 is not necessarily 2^n. Below is such an example.

Example 2. Let w be a root of the polynomial $X^4 + X + 1$ over $\mathbb{F}_2$, ψ the permutation induced by $[1, w^6; w^{10}, w^4]$. The finite state automaton runs with 16 consecutive states as follows:

$$\ldots, 0, w^2, w^{12}, w, w^{13}, w^{10}, w^{14}, w^9, w^5, w^8, w^7, 1, w^{11}, w^4, w^3, w^6, \ldots$$

Take $\lambda = 1$, and PRNG2 outputs a sequence of period 8 as below:

$$\ldots, 0, 0, 1, 0, 1, 0, 1, 1, 0, 0, 1, 0, 1, 0, 1, 1, \ldots$$

7   Linear Complexity

The linear complexity of a sequence s is the length of the shortest linear feedback shift register which generates s [7, 2.3.1]. Specifically, the *linear complexity* of a sequence s on $\mathbb{F}_p$ is defined to be

$$L(s) = \min\{m : \text{there exist } a_0, a_1, \ldots, a_{m-1} \in \mathbb{F}_p, \text{ such that}$$
$$a_0 s(i) + a_1 s(i-1) + a_2 s(i-2) + \cdots + a_{m-1} s(i-m+1) = 0, i \in \mathbb{Z}\}.$$

To ensure cryptographic randomness, the linear complexity of a sequence of period ν should be at least $[\nu/2]$. For a sequence s of least period ν, the *k-error linear complexity* of s [8,9] is defined to be

$$EC_k(s) = \min\{L(s') : |\{1 \le i \le \nu : s'(i) \neq s(i)\}| \le k; s'(i+\nu) = s'(i), i \in \mathbb{Z}\}.$$

The k-error linear complexity quantifies stability of linear complexity.

First, we estimate the linear complexity of sequences generated by PRNG2.

It immediately follows from Theorem 4, Theorem 10, Theorem 11, [1, Proposition 2] and [20, Corollary 2.6] that

Theorem 12. *If (1) $p = 2$ and $q \ge 32$ or (2) $p \ge 3$, then a sequence s generated by PRNG2 satisfies*

$$q/p + 1 \le L(s) < q.$$

Furthermore, the k-error linear complexity of binary sequences generated by PRNG2 is estimated as below.

Theorem 13. *Let $n \ge 6$ and $k = [2^{n-3} - 3 \cdot 2^{n/2-2} - 13/8]$. Then any binary sequence generated by PRNG2 satisfies*

$$2^{n-1} + 1 \le EC_k(s) \le 2^n.$$

Proof. As in the proof of Theorem 11,

$$\left|\{1 \le i \le 2^{n-1} : s(i + 2^{n-1}) \neq s(i)\}\right| \ge 2^{n-3} - 3 \cdot 2^{n/2-2} - 5/8 \ge k + 1.$$

Thus, for any binary sequence s' of period 2^n satisfying $|\{1 \le i \le 2^n : s'(i) \neq s(i)\}| \le k$, the least period of s' is also 2^n, implying $2^{n-1} + 1 \le L(s') \le 2^n$ by [1, Proposition 2]. Therefore, $2^{n-1} + 1 \le EC_k(s) \le 2^n$.   □

Example 3. Linear complexities of some binary sequences generated by PRNG2 are listed in Table1.

Now we estimate the linear complexity of sequences generated by PRNG1.

Theorem 14. *Let $\sigma \in V_q$, $\lambda \in \mathbb{F}_q^*$, $s \in S(\lambda, \sigma)$ and β be a fixed point of σ in $\mathbb{F}_{q^2}$. Then*

$$L(s) \ge q - q/p.$$

Particularly, if (1) β is normal over $\mathbb{F}_p$, or (2) $p = 2$ and $\mathrm{Tr}_p^{q^2}(\beta) \neq 0$, where $\mathrm{Tr}_p^{q^2}$ is the trace function of $\mathbb{F}_{q^2}$ over $\mathbb{F}_p$, then $L(s) = q$.

Table 1. Linear complexity of sequences by PRNG2

q	linear complexity
16	{7, 9, 11, 13, 15}
32	{21, 23, 25, 27, 29, 31}
64	{47, 49, 51, 53, 55, 57, 59, 61, 63}
128	{101, 103, 111, 113, 115, 117, 119, 121, 123, 125, 127}
256	{215, 227, 229, 233, 235, 237, 239, 241, 243, 245, 247, 249, 251, 253, 255}

To prove Theorem 14 we need the following lemmas.

Lemma 6. *[7, Lemma 8.2.1]Let s be a sequence of period ν and define a polynomial*

$$S(X) = s(0) + s(1)X + s(2)X^2 + \cdots + s(\nu - 1)X^{\nu-1}.$$

Then the linear complexity of s is given by

$$\nu - \deg \gcd(X^\nu - 1, S(X)).$$

Let ξ be a primitive $(q + 1)$-th root of unity in $\mathbb{F}_{q^2}$. Then

$$\sum_{i=1}^{q} \xi^{ki} = \begin{cases} -1, & \text{if } (q + 1) \nmid k, \\ 0, & \text{if } (q + 1) | k. \end{cases} \tag{6}$$

For $k \in \mathbb{Z}$, define

$$J(k) = \sum_{i=1}^{q} \xi^{ki}/(\xi^i - 1).$$

Lemma 7. *Assume $q > 2$. Then for $k \in \mathbb{Z}$,*

$$J(k) = [(k - 1)/(q + 1)] - (k - 1).$$

Proof. See that $J(k)$ depends on $k \mod q + 1$.

Notice that $\{\xi^i : i = 1, 2, \ldots, q\}$ are exactly roots of the polynomial

$$(X^{q+1} - 1)/(X - 1) = X^q + X^{q-1} + \cdots + X + 1.$$

Thus, $\{(\xi^i - 1)^{-1} : i = 1, 2, \ldots, q\}$ are exactly roots of the polynomial

$$Y^q \sum_{i=0}^{q} (Y^{-1} + 1)^i = \sum_{i=0}^{q} \sum_{j=i}^{q} \binom{j}{i} Y^{q-i}.$$

We compute the coefficient of Y^{q-1} and get

$$\sum_{i=1}^{q} (\xi^i - 1)^{-1} = -\sum_{j=1}^{q} \binom{j}{1} = \begin{cases} 0, & \text{if } q \neq 2, \\ 1, & \text{if } q = 2. \end{cases}$$

Hence, $J(k) = 0$ if $(q+1)|k$. Suppose $k = d + a(q+1)$ and $0 < d < q+1$, where $a, d \in \mathbb{Z}$. If $q > 2$, then $J(k) = J(d)$ and by Eq.(6) we have

$$J(d) = \sum_{i=1}^{q} \left(\xi^{i(d-1)} + \xi^{i(d-2)} + \cdots + \xi^i + 1 + (\xi^i - 1)^{-1} \right)$$

$$= -(d-1) + \sum_{i=1}^{q} (\xi^i - 1)^{-1}$$

$$= -(d-1).$$

Besides, $[(k-1)/(q+1)] - (k-1) = 1 - d - aq \equiv 1 - d \mod p$. Therefore, $J(k) = [(k-1)/(q+1)] - (k-1) \in \mathbb{F}_p$. □

Lemma 8. *Let the mapping* $\chi : \mathbb{Z}/(q+1)\mathbb{Z} \to \mathbb{F}_p^n$ *be defined as*

$$\chi(x) = (J(x), J(xp), \ldots, J(xp^{n-1})).$$

Then the restriction of χ *on* $(\mathbb{Z}/(q+1)\mathbb{Z})\setminus\{0\}$ *is injective, i.e.,* $\chi(x) \neq \chi(y)$ *if* $x, y \in \{1, 2, \ldots, q\}$ *and* $x \neq y$.

Proof. Suppose $0 < k < p^n = q$ and $k = k_0 + k_1 p + k_2 p^2 + \cdots + k_{n-1}p^{n-1}$, where $k_0, k_1, k_2, \ldots, k_{n-1} \in \{0, 1, \ldots, p-1\}$. Then for $m = 1, 2, \ldots, n-1$,

$$kp^m \equiv \sum_{j=1}^{m} (-k_{n-j})p^{m-j} + \sum_{j=0}^{n-m-1} k_j p^{m+j} \mod q+1.$$

Suppose $k_0 = k_1 = \cdots = k_{t-1} = 0$ and $k_t \neq 0$. By Lemma 7,

$$J(p^m k) = \begin{cases} 1 - k_0, & \text{if } m = 0, \\ 1 + k_{n-m}, & \text{if } 1 \leq m \leq n-1-t, \\ k_{n-m}, & \text{if } n-t \leq m \leq n-1. \end{cases}$$

Thus, χ is injective except for $\chi(0) = (0, 0, \ldots, 0) = \chi(q - p + 1)$. □

Proof (of Theorem 14.). Without loss of generality, suppose that $s(i) = \mathrm{Tr}\,(\lambda\sigma^i(\infty))$. Assume σ is induced by $\mathbf{A} \in M_q$ and the Jordan form of $\mathbf{A}$ is $\mathbf{T}^{-1}\mathbf{AT} = [\alpha, 0; 0, \alpha^q]$, where $\mathbf{T} = [t_1, t_2; t_3, t_4] \in \mathrm{GL}_2(\mathbb{F}_{q^2})$. Let $\xi_0 = \alpha^{1-q}$. By Lemma 4, ξ_0 is a primitive $(q+1)$-th root of unity. Assign $\beta = t_1/t_3$. Then β is a fixed point of σ in $\mathbb{P}^1(\mathbb{F}_{q^2})$, because $(t_1, t_3)^T$ (resp. $(t_2, t_4)^T$) is an eigenvector with respect to the eigenvalue α(resp. α^q). Take

$$x_i = \sigma^i(\infty) = \frac{\xi_0^i t_1/t_3 - t_2/t_4}{\xi_0^i - 1} = \frac{\xi_0^i \beta - \beta^q}{\xi_0^i - 1} = \beta + \frac{\beta - \beta^q}{\xi_0^i - 1}.$$

Below we compute $I(k) = \sum_{i=1}^{q} \mathrm{Tr}\,(\lambda x_i)\,\xi_0^{ki}$. By Lemma 6, $L(s) = |\{0 \leq k \leq q : I(k) \neq 0\}|$ since $X^{q+1} - 1$ has no multiple roots in $\overline{\mathbb{F}_q}$. By Theorem 2, $\{x_i : i = 1, 2, \ldots, q\} = \mathbb{F}_q$, and hence $I(k) = 0$ if $(q+1)|k$ by Lemma 1. Now consider $(q + 1) \nmid k$. Since $\xi_0^{p^j}$ is a primitive $(q + 1)$-th root of unity, by Eq.(6) and Lemma 7, we have

$$
\begin{aligned}
I(k) &= \sum_{i=1}^{q} \left(\sum_{j=1}^{n} x_i^{p^j} \right) \xi_0^{ki} = \sum_{j=1}^{n} \sum_{i=1}^{q} x_i^{p^j} \xi_0^{ki} \\
&= \sum_{j=1}^{n} \sum_{i=1}^{q} \left(\beta + (\beta - \beta^q)(\xi_0^i - 1)^{-1} \right)^{p^j} \xi_0^{ki} \\
&= \sum_{j=1}^{n} \beta^{p^j} \sum_{i=1}^{q} \xi_0^{ki} + \sum_{j=1}^{n} (\beta - \beta^q)^{p^j} \sum_{i=1}^{q} \xi_0^{ki}/(\xi_0^{ip^j} - 1) \\
&= - \sum_{j=1}^{n} \beta^{p^j} + \sum_{j=1}^{n} (\beta - \beta^q)^{p^j} J(-p^{n-j}k).
\end{aligned}
$$

Take $(\beta - \beta^q)^p, (\beta - \beta^q)^{p^2}, \ldots, (\beta - \beta^q)^{p^n}$ as a family of vectors over $\mathbb{F}_p$, of rank at least one. Thus, there exist at most p^{n-1} vectors $(x_1, x_2, \ldots, x_n) \in \mathbb{F}_p^n$ such that

$$
\sum_{j=1}^{n} (\beta - \beta^q)^{p^j} x_j - \sum_{j=1}^{n} \beta^{p^j} = 0,
$$

that is, $|\{1 \le k \le q : I(k) = 0\}| \le p^{n-1}$. Therefore, $L(s) \ge q - q/p$.

Furthermore, if β is normal over $\mathbb{F}_p$, then $I(k) \ne 0$ for $1 \le k \le q$, implying $L(s) = q$.

Assume $p = 2$ and $\mathrm{Tr}_p^{q^2}(\beta) \ne 0$. See

$$
I(k)^q - I(k) = \sum_{j=1}^{n} (\beta + \beta^q)^{p^j} (1 - 2J(-p^{n-j}k)) = \mathrm{Tr}_p^{q^2}(\beta) \ne 0.
$$

Thus, $I(k) \ne 0$ for $1 \le k \le q$, yielding $L(s) = q$.   □

Remark 7. If one takes $\mathrm{Tr}(\infty) = a \ne 0$, the lower bound $q - q/p$ of linear complexity by Theorem 14 also holds.

8   Implementation and Applications

Parameter Setting. To implement PRNG1 and PRNG2, parameters can be chosen in an easy manner, since in Section 2.3 we choose a primitive element of $\mathbb{F}_{q^2}$ and thereby characterize the set of matrices M_q which exactly induce V_q. To obtain uniform 2-tuple distribution of sequences from PRNG2, one can choose parameters such that $K_q((ad - bc)\lambda^2/c^2) = 0$, where $[a, b; c, d]$ induces the permutation. To obtain sequences of large linear complexity by PRNG1, $\sigma \in V_q$ is chosen to have a fixed point which is normal over $\mathbb{F}_p$.

Computation cost. Main computation of PRNG1 and PRNG2 is respectively a projective linear transformation and a permutation polynomial over $\mathbb{F}_q$, wherein majority computational resources are taken by a finite field inversion or division. Based on contemporary technology, the pseudorandom number generators proposed here are still far from being efficient compared with practical stream ciphers, say Trivium. It is comparatively more convenient to apply our pseudorandom number generators in public key infrastructure where finite field inversion is available. However, we refer to [6, Chapter 11] for many speeding-up techniques. Particularly, in most applications q is a power of 2, and for such a case efficient implementation of finite field inversion is available in [12].

9   Summary and Future Work

We have presented two pseudorandom number generators through projective linear transformations on $\mathbb{F}_q$. Sequences generated by PRNG1 have least period $q+1$ if $q \geq 7$ and large linear complexity at least $q-q/p$, and their autocorrelation functions oscillate within a low amplitude except the trivial peaks. Sequences generated by PRNG2 have least period q if $q \notin \{2, 4, 8, 16\}$ and large linear complexity at least $q/p + 1$. For binary sequences generated by PRNG1 and PRNG2, a randomly chosen 2-tuple is almost uniformly distributed, a randomly chosen 3-tuple is a run of length one at probability approximately $1/4$, and nontrivial linear combination of bits of a randomly chosen tuple of short length is equal to 0 or 1 at almost the same probability.

Finally, we leave two questions for future work.

Question 1. Do pseudorandom number generators proposed in Section 3 with different parameter settings produce different equivalence classes of sequences? Specifically, let $\sigma_1, \sigma_2 \in V_q$, $\psi_1, \psi_2 \in H_q$, $\lambda_1, \lambda_2 \in \mathbb{F}_q^*$, and suppose (1)$p \geq 3$, $q \geq 7$; or (2)$p = 2$, $q \geq 32$. If $\sigma_1 \neq \sigma_2$ or $\lambda_1 \neq \lambda_2$, can one conclude $S(\lambda_1, \sigma_1) \cap S(\lambda_2, \sigma_2) = \emptyset$? If $\psi_1 \neq \psi_2$ or $\lambda_1 \neq \lambda_2$, can one conclude $S(\lambda_1, \psi_1) \cap S(\lambda_2, \psi_2) = \emptyset$? Given Remark 3, the answer to this question is useful in determining the number of equivalence classes of sequences generated by PRNG1 and PRNG2.

Question 2. A span m *de Bruijn sequence* on $\mathbb{F}_p$ is a sequence of period p^m which is generated by a feedback shift register in Fibonacci configuration. Under what condition can a sequence generated by PRNG2 be a span n de Bruijn sequence?

Acknowledgments. The authors would like to express their sincere gratitude to the anonymous referees who made a number of valuable comments to improve the manuscript. The first author is supported by the Applied Basic Research Program (Grant No. 2011JY0143) of the Sichuan Province, P.R.China.

References

1. Blackburn, S.R., Etzion, T.: Permutation polynomials, de Bruijn sequences, and linear complexity. J. Combin. Theory Ser. A 76, 55–82 (1996)
2. Blackburn, S.R., Gomez-Perez, D., Gutierrez, J., Shparlinski, I.E.: Predicting nonlinear pseudorandom number generators. Math. Comp. 74, 1471–1494 (2005)

3. Bombieri, E.: On exponential sums in finite fields. Amer. J. of Math. 88, 11–32 (1966)
4. De Cannière, C., Preneel, B.: TRIVIUM. In: Robshaw, M., Billet, O. (eds.) New Stream Cipher Designs. LNCS, vol. 4986, pp. 244–266. Springer, Heidelberg (2008)
5. Chou, W.S.: On inversive maximal period polynomials over finite fields. Appl. Algebra Engrg. Comm. Comput. 6, 245–250 (1995)
6. Cohen, H., Frey, G., et al.: Handbook of Elliptic and Hyperelliptic Curve Cryptography. Chapman & Hall/CRC Taylor & Francis Group, Boca Raton (2006)
7. Cusick, T.W., Ding, C., Renvall, A.: Stream Ciphers and Number Theory. North-Holland Mathematical Library, vol. 55. Elsevier, North-Holland (1998)
8. Ding, C.: Lower bounds on the weight complexities of cascaded binary sequences. In: Seberry, J., Pieprzyk, J.P. (eds.) AUSCRYPT 1990. LNCS, vol. 453, pp. 39–43. Springer, Heidelberg (1990)
9. Ding, C., Xiao, G., Shan, W.: The Stability Theory of Stream Ciphers. LNCS, vol. 561. Springer, Heidelberg (1991)
10. Eichenauer, J., Lehn, J.: A nonlinear congruential pseudorandom number generator. Statist. Hefte 27(4), 315–326 (1986)
11. Eichenauer-Herrmann, J., Grothe, H.: A new inversive congruential pseudorandom number generator with power of two modulus. ACM Transactions on Modeling and Computer Simulation (TOMACS) 2(1), 1–11 (1992)
12. Eichenauer-Herrmann, J., Niederreiter, H.: Digital Inversive Pseudorandom Numbers. ACM Trans. Model. Comput. Simul. 4(4), 339–349 (1994)
13. Gong, G., Youssef, A.M.: Cryptographic properties of the Welsh-Gong transformation sequence generators. IEEE Transactions on Information Theory 48(11), 2837–2846 (2002)
14. Niederreiter, H.: Random number generation and quasi-Monte Carlo methods. SIAM, Philadelphia (1992)
15. Niederreiter, H., Rivat, J.: On the correlation of pseudorandom numbers generated by inversive methods. Monatshefte für Mathematik 153(3), 251–264 (2008)
16. Niederreiter, H., Shparlinski, I.E.: Recent advances in the theory of nonlinear pseudorandom number generators. In: Proc. Conf. Monte Carlo and Quasi-Monte Carlo Methods 2000, pp. 86–102. Springer, Berlin (2002)
17. Niederreiter, H., Shparlinski, I.E.: Dynamical systems generated by rational functions. In: Fossorier, M., Høholdt, T., Poli, A. (eds.) AAECC 2003. LNCS, vol. 2643, pp. 6–17. Springer, Heidelberg (2003)
18. Niederreiter, H., Winterhof, A.: Lattice structure and linear complexity of nonlinear pseudorandom numbers. Appl. Algebra Eng. Commun. Comput. 13(4), 319–326 (2002)
19. Niederreiter, H., Winterhof, A.: Incomplete exponential sums over finite fields and their applications to new inversive pseudorandom number. Acta Arith. 93, 387–399 (2000)
20. Paterson, K.G.: Perfect factors in the de Bruijn graph. Designs, Codes and Cryptography 5, 115–138 (1995)
21. Si, W., Ding, C.: A simple stream cipher with proven properties. Cryptography and Communications 4, 79–104 (2012)
22. Weil, A.: On some exponential sums. Mathematics, Proc. Natl. Acad. Sci. USA 34, 204–207 (1948)
23. Winterhof, A.: Recent results on recursive nonlinear pseudorandom number generators. In: Carlet, C., Pott, A. (eds.) SETA 2010. LNCS, vol. 6338, pp. 113–124. Springer, Heidelberg (2010)

Touch Gestures Based Biometric Authentication Scheme for Touchscreen Mobile Phones

Yuxin Meng, Duncan S. Wong, Roman Schlegel, and Lam-for Kwok

Department of Computer Science,
College of Science and Engineering,
City University of Hong Kong,
Hong Kong, China
ymeng8@student.cityu.edu.hk

Abstract. Nowadays, touchscreen mobile phones make up a larger and larger share in the mobile market. Users also often use their mobile phones (e.g., Android phones) to store personal and sensitive data. It is therefore important to safeguard mobile phones by authenticating legitimate users and detecting impostors. In this paper, we propose a novel user authentication scheme based on touch dynamics that uses a set of behavioral features related to touch dynamics for accurate user authentication. In particular, we construct and select 21 features that can be used for user authentication. To evaluate the performance of our scheme, we collect and analyze touch gesture data of 20 Android phone users by comparing several known machine learning classifiers. The experimental results show that a neural network classifier is well-suited to authenticate different users with an average error rate of about 7.8% for our selected features. Finally, we optimize the neural network classifier by using Particle Swarm Optimization (PSO) to deal with variations in users' usage patterns. Experimental results show that the average error rate of our optimized scheme is only about 3%, achieved solely by analyzing the touch behavior of users on an Android phone.

Keywords: Behavioral Biometrics, Touch Dynamics, User Authentication, Access Control, Mobile Security and Usability.

1 Introduction

Mobile phones using touchscreens (such as smartphones based on the Android OS[1] or iPhones using iOS[2]) have been pervasively integrated into our daily work and everyday lives. In the current smartphone market, Android OS and iOS make up the largest share with a combined 80% of smartphones powered by either the Android OS or iOS, according to the *Mobile Mix report* [28]. Furthermore, *touchscreens* are the leading input method on the mobile platform, with 65% of all phones using a touch screen [28], and this percentage seems to be increasing.

Thanks to the increasingly diverse capabilities of current touchscreen mobile phones, users store more and more sensitive information (e.g., credit card numbers, passwords,

---

[1] http://www.android.com/
[2] http://www.apple.com/ios/

M. Kutyłowski and M. Yung (Eds.): Inscrypt 2012, LNCS 7763, pp. 331–350, 2013.
© Springer-Verlag Berlin Heidelberg 2013

personal photos) on their phones [16] and use them for sensitive applications such as mobile banking, online shopping or as electronic wallets. This kind of stored sensitive information can more easily be exploited for financial gain (compared to phone numbers or text messages) and as a consequence, mobile phones (and smartphones in particular) are becoming an attractive target for hackers and for malware [26,46]. Stolen mobile phones and particularly smartphones often contain a lot of personal and sensitive information which can be exploited for malicious use, and users are in fact concerned about the stored sensitive information when losing their mobile phones [29].

To mitigate this problem, it is very crucial to develop intelligent user authentication schemes for touchscreen mobile phones. Currently, user authentication systems for mobile phones are mainly based on three techniques: *passwords, physiological biometrics* and *behavioral biometrics*. Password authentication usually uses a Personal Identification Number (PIN) [5] or password patterns [13,50] to verify a legitimate user. Passwords and patterns are the most commonly used methods to date for user authentication. But password authentication has well-known drawbacks [21], for instance, passwords can often easily be stolen through "shoulder surfing" [47].[3]

To overcome the drawbacks of password authentication, research is being done into biometric methods for user authentication on mobile phones. *Biometrics* are defined as an automated method of authentication by using measurable human physiological or behavioral characteristics to model and represent a user's identity [25]. *Physiological biometrics* usually uses measurements from the human body such as fingerprints [23], iris scans [45], hand scans [8], retina scans [19] and facial scans [49]. These kind of biometrics can achieve a consistent performance, but the common drawback is that these authentication systems perform a one-time authentication at the beginning of a session and afterwards allow access for the duration of the session without re-authentication. In addition, physiological biometrics usually requires special hardware which is not typically available in mobile phones. *Behavioral biometric methods*, which are a kind of continuous authentication [9], use measurements from human actions such as keystroke dynamics [2,31] or mouse dynamics [38]. Both of these dynamics have been actively studied in the context of desktop computers, but only keystroke dynamics has been explored on mobile phones [6,15,52]. Authentication based on keystroke dynamics on mobile phones learns legitimate users' behavior and verifies a user periodically or continuously, which overcomes the drawback of physiological biometrics which only authenticates the user at the beginning of a session. A major limitation of behavioral biometric methods is that they are unsuitable for instantaneous authentication [9].

Motivation. With the increased popularity of touchscreen mobile phones, touch behavior is becoming more and more important compared to keystroke behavior, as many smartphones now feature touchscreens as the main input method [28]. Our motivation is therefore to develop a user authentication scheme based on touch gestures on mobile phones.

In this paper, we employ behavioral biometric methods and mainly focus on a novel user behavioral biometric, namely *touch dynamics*, which refers to collecting detailed information about individual touches, such as touch duration and touch direction. The goal is to use touch dynamics on touchscreen mobile phones to enhance user

---

[3] Shoulder surfing refers to using direct observation techniques.

authentication. First, we illustrate the relationship between touch dynamics, keystroke dynamics and mouse dynamics. We reveal that touch dynamics is different from keystroke dynamics and mouse dynamics but that there are still some similarities. We then propose a biometric authentication scheme based on touch dynamics for touch-screen mobile phones. Similar to keystroke dynamics and mouse dynamics, our scheme also does not require any special hardware device for data collection. In particular, our scheme extracts and constructs 21 features related to the touch dynamics of a user as an *authentication signature* by adapting behavioral features from keystroke dynamics and mouse dynamics. We also consider *multi-touch* (i.e., the process of touching a touch-screen with multiple fingers at the same time) as one of the extracted features in our work, which we believe also clearly distinguishes our work from other schemes such as keystroke dynamics and mouse dynamics.

To validate the performance of our scheme, we conducted an initial experiment with 20 users using Android touchscreen phones. To classify users we then use several known machine learning algorithms (e.g., Naive Bayes, decision tree). Initial experimental results show that our scheme can perform well when using neural network classifiers such as Radial Basis Function Network (RBFN) and Back Propagation Neural Network (BPNN). Finally, we implement a classifier that combines a Particle Swarm Optimization (PSO) algorithm with RBFN for our scheme to deal with variations in users' touch behavior, favoring RBFN over BPNN because of its faster training speed and higher accuracy. In additional experiments, we explore the performance of our hybrid PSO-RBFN classifier on the collected touch gesture data. The results show that our proposed classifier achieves an average error rate of approximately 3%.

The rest of the paper is organized as follows: In Section 2, we briefly introduce the architecture of the Android OS to better illustrate how our feature collection works, and we describe some related work. We then describe touch dynamics, extracted features and the architecture of our authentication system on Android phones in Section 3. In Section 4, we investigate the feasibility and performance of our scheme by using several existing classification schemes. We also analyze the performance of our proposed PSO-RBFN algorithm and present the results in Section 5. The limitations of our current work and our future directions are discussed in Section 6 and we conclude our paper in Section 7.

2   Background

As our prototype was built on the basis of the Android platform, we briefly introduce the architecture of the Android operating system to illustrate how the feature collection works in our system and to justify our design choices. We then briefly describe some related work concerning behavioral biometrics, including keystroke dynamics, mouse dynamics and touch behavior.

2.1   Android Operating System

The Android OS is an open source, Linux-based operating system for mobile devices such as mobile phones or tablets. Fig. 1 shows the major components of the Android

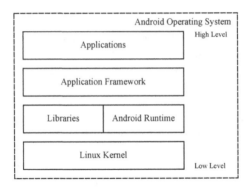

Fig. 1. This figure shows the architecture of the Android operating system and its different layers

operating system. There are five major components in the architecture: the *Linux kernel*, *libraries*, the *Android runtime*, the *application framework* and *applications*.

- *Linux kernel.* Android relies on Linux version 2.6 for core system services such as security, memory management and drivers. This layer contains drivers for devices such as USB, display, camera, Bluetooth chip and flash memory. The kernel also acts as an abstraction layer between the hardware and the rest of the software stack.
- *Libraries.* Android includes a set of C/C++ libraries such as the System C library, media libraries and 3D libraries, which are all used by various components of the Android system. Developers can make use of these libraries through the *Application framework*.
- *Android runtime.* Android includes a runtime which contains a set of core libraries that provide different functionalities. In addition, every Android application runs in its own process, with its own virtual machine instance.
- *Application framework.* The Android application framework is a high-level layer to provide the developer with a development platform for creating new Android applications. Developers can access location information, run background services, add notifications to the status bar, and access lots of other information and functionality.
- *Applications.* This is the highest level of the Android operating system architecture. Android ships with a set of core applications and widgets including an email client, messaging application, calendar, maps, browser, contacts and others. Users can also easily add more applications.

Understanding the structure of the Android OS allows us to determine how to best integrate a system such as touch-dynamics-based user authentication into the OS. In our case, modifying the *application framework layer* allows us to implement the desired functionality without the need to modify any applications or to delve into any other parts of the OS. The details of how we collected data are described in Section 3.3.

2.2 Related Work

The idea of using touch dynamics for user authentication is not completely new, but most of the previous research focuses on desktop machines or on finger identification.

Numabe et al. [35], for example, presented a finger identification method which works on touch panels. According to their research, when tapping a touch panel, the exact coordinates of a tap depend on the finger used, so that different fingers generate slightly different coordinates. They called this phenomenon *tapping fluctuation* and mainly used it to make touch input more versatile, by varying the function executed depending on which finger was used to tap the touchscreen.

A peculiar characteristics of touch-screen input is the possibility to use several fingers, which is often called *multi-touch* input. Kim et al. [18] exploited the features of multi-touch interaction to inhibit shoulder surfing, with the goal of enhancing PIN input (e.g., at an ATM-Automated Teller Machine). Fiorella et al. [12] provide a preliminary study about multi-touch input for 3D object manipulation on mobile devices, compared to a traditional button GUI.

De Luca et al. [9] proposed using touch dynamics to assist the password pattern based authentication mechanism on a touchscreen phone with the purpose of defending against shoulder surfing attack during the mobile phone logon process. But it is the instantaneous authentication approach which is very different from the continuous authentication approach that we are studying in this paper. In their studies, various characteristics associated with touch-movement are studied, while characteristics regarding multi-touch gesture and single-touch are not covered, and touch dynamics for continuous authentication are not addressed.

To the best of our knowledge, touch dynamics for continuous authentication on mobile phones has not been explored in the research literature with regard to its suitability for continuously authenticating users on mobile phones. In this paper, we therefore make an effort in further exploring it, especially by providing a comprehensive studies on single-touch, touch-movement and specific multi-touch gestures in touch dynamics. To better illustrate the relation between touch dynamics, keystroke dynamics and mouse dynamics in Section 3.1, we briefly summarize some of the most prominent research on keystroke dynamics and mouse dynamics in the remaining part of this section.

Keystroke dynamics has been studied for authenticating users for mobile phones. Clarke et al. [6] presented a study which demonstrated the ability of neural network classifiers to authenticate users based on their key hold-time and inter-key latency on keypads of mobile handsets. In their work, they found that neural network classifiers were able to perform classification with an average equal error rate of 12.8%. Karatzouni et al. [15] investigated the performance of keystroke analysis on thumb-based keyboard deployed on mobile devices by using the same features of key hold-time and inter-key latency. Their approach achieved an average equal error rate of 12.2% when using the inter-keystroke latency. Zahid et al. [52] analyzed keystroke dynamics of smart phone users with six features (e.g., key hold-time, digraph time[4], error rate, etc.). They collected and analyzed keystroke data of 25 smartphone users and showed that a fuzzy classifier is suitable for clustering and classifying users. They finally used an optimized classifier based on Particle Swarm Optimizers and Genetic Algorithms together with a PIN-based verification mechanism and achieved an average error rate of 2%. Maiorana et al. [24] proposed a statistical approach based on keystroke dynamics for mobile phones that achieves good verification rates even when the number of

---

[4] The time difference between releasing one key and pressing the next one.

enrollment acquisitions is low. The results show that their approach can be employed effectively as a password hardening mechanism in operational contexts where there are a low number of stored acquisitions. Nauman et al. [34] pointed out that current keystroke-based authentication scheme cannot be applied to services outside of the mobile phone and proposed a protocol for keystroke dynamics analysis which allows web-based applications to authenticate users. There are also several other, earlier studies related to keystroke dynamics (e.g., [4,20,30,32,44]).

Mouse dynamics is mainly suitable for authenticating users on a desktop machine which uses a mouse as an input device. Pusara and Brodley [38] described an approach for user re-authentication based on mouse movements. They collected raw cursor movement data and extracted features such as distance, angle and speed between data points. Their results from experiments with 11 users show that their method achieved a false positive rate of 0.43% and a false negative rate of 1.75%. Ahmed and Traore [1] introduced a new biometric system based on mouse dynamics. Specifically, they used a set of features (e.g., mouse movement speed, mouse movement direction) to model the normal behavior of a user by means of artificial neural networks. The results of their main experiment showed that their approach achieved a false acceptance rate of 2.4649% and a false rejection rate of 2.4614%, respectively. Some recent work on authenticating users by using mouse dynamics can be found in [33,53] and several limitations regarding to mouse dynamics were discussed in [14].

3   User Authentication Based on Touch Dynamics

In this section, we first introduce the notion of touch dynamics and analyze how it is related to keystroke dynamics and mouse dynamics. We then give an overview of the architecture of our touch-dynamics-based authentication system and describe the method for collecting data on Android phones. Lastly, we give an in-depth description of the feature selection and feature extraction used in our scheme.

3.1   Touch Dynamics

Compared to other behavioral dynamics [1,52], *touch dynamics* can be described as the characteristics of the inputs received from a touchscreen when a user is interacting with a device (e.g., a touchscreen mobile phone). The characteristics of touch dynamics can be described by a set of features generated by analyzing touchscreen inputs. In this paper, we classify inputs as captured by the touchscreen on a mobile phone into one of the following categories:

- Single-Touch (ST): the input starts with a touch press down, followed by a touch press up without any movement in-between.
- Touch-Movement (TM): the input starts with a touch press down, movement (also called *drag*), followed by a touch press up.
- Multi-Touch (MT): an input with two or more simultaneous, distinct touch press down events at different coordinates of the touch screen (i.e., two fingers press down on the touchscreen simultaneously), either with or without any movement before a touch press up event.
- No input: there is no input on the touchscreen.

Comparing the above inputs to the inputs in keystroke dynamics and mouse dynamics, we can see that they are different and each category has their own, particular inputs. *Keystroke dynamics* usually has two input types: press button down and press button up with characteristics such as key hold-time and digraph time. The typical inputs of *mouse dynamics* are mouse-move, drag-drop and move-click with characteristics such as movement speed, movement direction and movement distance.

Differences between Touch, Keystroke Dynamics and Mouse Dynamics. Intuitively, touch dynamics is different from keystroke dynamics in that touch dynamics has more input types such as multi-touch and touch-movement. Touch dynamics is also different from mouse dynamics in that touch dynamics has a possibility of multi-touch input. Keystroke dynamics only has buttons as input devices, which do not have a movement feature, while touch dynamics has movement and can therefore provide more behavioral characteristics. Looking at mouse dynamics, the trace in mouse dynamics is continuous (i.e., mouse inputs start from the last point where the last mouse input was terminated) while the trace in touch dynamics can be non-continuous (i.e., a touch input can start at a different point than the point where the last touch input ended).

Similarities between Touch, Keystroke and Mouse Dynamics. Although these three types of behavioral dynamics have their own input types and special characteristics, touch dynamics is still similar in some aspects to the other two. The inputs of press button up and press button down in keystroke dynamics are similar to the actions of touch press up and touch press down (e.g., single touch) in touch dynamics. Compared to mouse dynamics, touch dynamics has similar movement input types (i.e., mouse movement versus touch movement). In addition, a single touch input can be considered to be similar to a click action in mouse dynamics. Touch dynamics can therefore be considered as a combination of keystroke dynamics and mouse dynamics with respect to the main input types. This allows to use some behavioral features in touch dynamics that are also used in keystroke dynamics and mouse dynamics.

3.2 Architecture of Touch-Dynamics-Based Authentication System on Mobile Phones

To realize a touch-dynamics-based user authentication system, which collects touch-based behavioral data to authenticate whether a user is legitimate, a system is needed which continuously collects raw data from the touchscreen and translates them into features and performs verification of the user. A high-level architecture of our touch-dynamics-based authentication system is shown in Fig. 2.

The system consists of three main components: *data collection component, behavior modeling component* and *behavior comparison component*. The data collection component is responsible for collecting raw data from the touchscreen (i.e., recording and storing all touch gesture data into a database) and converting the raw data into meaningful information (i.e., identifying sessions for users, distinguishing a single touch or multi-touch action and filtering out noise data). The behavior modeling component is responsible for analyzing collected data, extracting features to generate an *authentication signature* for a legitimate user and modeling a user's touch behavior by training the authentication system with several generated authentication signatures during the *train-*

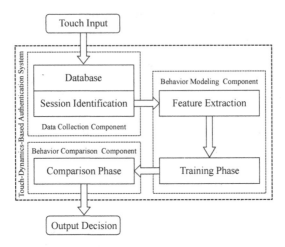

Fig. 2. This figure shows the architecture of the touch-dynamics-based authentication system

ing phase. Lastly, the behavior comparison component is responsible for comparing the current user's behavior with the relevant generated authentication signatures during the *comparison phase* and determining whether the current user is a legitimate user or an impostor.

3.3   Data Collection Component

In this section, we describe the main tasks performed by the data collection component.

Data Collection. For this paper we used a Google/HTC *Nexus One* Android phone with a capacitive touchscreen (resolution 480×800 px) to perform the experiments. The advantage of this particular phone is that the stock Android operating system installed on it can be replaced with a modified custom version of the Android OS. In particular, we updated the phone with a modified Android OS version 2.2 based on *CyanogenMod*[5]. The modification consists of changes to the application framework layer to record raw input data from the touchscreen, such as the timing of touch inputs, the coordinates x and y, and the type of the input (e.g., single-touch, multi-touch or movement). In addition, we installed a separate application, which allowed us to easily extract the recorded data from the phone.

A sample of raw data collected from the touchscreen and recorded by the phone is shown in Table 1. Each record consists of at least the following four fields: *input type*, *x-coordinate*, *y-coordinate*, and *system time (S-time)*. The system time in Table 1 is relative to the last start-up of the phone. The duration of each touch input can then be calculated by taking the difference in system-time. These four fields allow us to precisely determine the type of touch inputs, their coordinates and their duration.

This description of the data collection also shows that no special hardware is required for our touch-dynamics-based authentication system, the information can be collected

---

[5] http://www.cyanogenmod.com/

Table 1. This table shows a sample of raw data collected from touchscreen inputs

Input Type	X-Coordinate	Y-Coordinate	Time (ms)
Press Down	475.46866	659.6717	1770785
Press Move	472.56793	660.3004	1770807
Press Move	470.2978	660.9292	1770814
Press Move	466.76645	662.0609	1770852
Press Move	470.55002	659.9232	1770898
Press Move	472.56793	658.6658	1770910
Press Up	471.6851	658.9172	1770933

by updating certain parts of the Android application framework. Also, our system could easily be adopted for passive user monitoring which would be useful for intrusion detection [10,27].

Session Identification. The purpose of the session identification module is to determine when a new session starts, and when an existing session ends. During the authentication, our scheme has to extract the *authentication signature* which consists of 21 touch gesture features. By means of comparing different extracted *authentication signatures* across sessions, our scheme can determine whether the current user is a legitimate user.

Session identification is therefore critical for extracting an *authentication signature*. The specific length of a session can be configured, for example 10 minutes per session. Beginning and end of a session are determined as follows:

- A new session starts when a touch input is recorded and the last session has ended.
- A session ends if the duration of the current session has reached or exceeded the maximum session duration time. For instance, if we choose a session duration time of 10 minutes, then our scheme will terminate a session and start a new session when the duration time of the current session reaches or exceeds 10 minutes.

The *session start* and *session end* events can easily be determined by looking at the timing information in the raw data log. In the evaluation part, we selected the length of a session to be 10 minutes because longer sessions provide more information to better model a user's behavior. We leave it as an open problem for our future work to study the performance of shorter sessions (e.g., 5 minutes).

3.4 Feature Extraction

The main task of the *behavior modeling component* is to extract touch dynamic features from the collected raw data. As mentioned earlier, we extract 21 different features to construct an *authentication signature* for user authentication. The features are the following: *average touch movement speed per direction* (8 directions), *fraction of touch movements per direction* (8 directions), *average single-touch time*, *average multi-touch time*, *number of touch movements per session*, *number of single-touch events per session*, and *number of multi-touch events per session*. In the remainder of this section, we give an in-depth description and analysis of each feature extracted from the collected raw data.

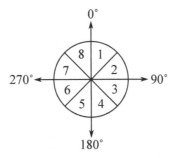

Fig. 3. This figure shows the 8 different directions of a touch movement

Average Touch Movement Speed Per Direction. Here we use 8 different directions to divide a touch movement input into different features. The 8 different directions are defined as shown in Fig. 3.

After categorizing the touch movements according to their direction, we then calculate the *average touch movement speed* (denoted *ATMS*) for each of the 8 directions, represented by *ATMSi* (e.g., *ATMS1* represents the *ATMS* in direction 1, *ATMS3* represents the *ATMS* in direction 3).

Suppose that there are two points $(x1, y1)$ and $(x2, y2)$ in a touch movement with $S1$ and $S2$ (suppose $S1 < S2$) as their event system time. The *touch movement speed* (TMS) and *touch movement angle* between these two points can be calculated as follows:

$$TMS = \frac{\sqrt{(x2 - x1)^2 + (y2 - y1)^2}}{S2 - S1}$$

Touch movement angle: $\theta = \arctan \dfrac{y2 - y1}{x2 - x1}, \theta \in [0, 360^\circ]$

Fig. 4 shows the distribution of the *average touch movement speed* against the direction of the touch movement for two different users (User1 and User2) in their first session. It is clearly visible that the distributions for these two users are different: the touch movements of User1 in direction 1 and 8 are performed with a higher speed than other directions, while the touch movements of User2 have a higher speed in direction 2, 3, 6, and 7. This illustrates nicely that the feature *ATMS* per direction (total of 8 features) can be used to model the characteristics of a user's touch behavior.

Fraction of Touch Movements Per Direction. We observe that there are usually certain directions that contain more touch movements than other directions and that for different users the fraction per direction varies. Fig. 5 shows the distribution of the *fractions of touch movements* (denoted *FTM*) versus the direction of a touch movement for User1 and User2.

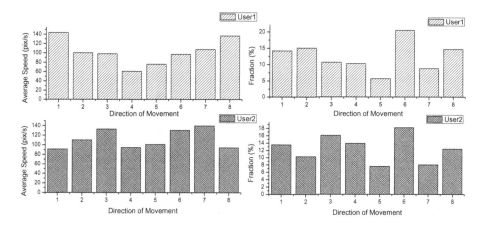

Fig. 4. This figure shows the average touch movement speed versus the direction of movement for 2 different users

Fig. 5. This figure shows the fraction of touch movements versus the direction of movement for 2 different users

In Fig. 5, User1 performed relatively more touch movements in direction 1, 2, 6 and 8, while User2 performed more touch movements in direction 1, 3, 4, 6, and 8. The *FTM* in 8 directions (total of 8 features) can therefore also be used to characterize the touch behavior of a user.

Average Single-touch/Multi-touch Time. In addition to touch movements, single-touch and multi-touch are also two important types of touch inputs. We observe that the average duration time of a single-touch or multi-touch is different for different users. Fig. 6 shows the histogram for these two features, *Average Single-touch time* (denoted *AST*) and *Average Multi-touch time* (denoted *MTT*) again for the two users User1 and User2.

In this example, User1 on average spent a longer time for *AST* and *MTT* compared to User2, showing that these two features can also be used to characterize and hence distinguish the touch behavior of different users.

Number of Touch Action Events. Single-touch, touch movement and multi-touch events are three major input types on a touchscreen, and we observe that the total number of these three touch events over one session varies for different users. We therefore distinguish the three features *number of touch movements per session* (denoted *NTM*), *number of single-touch events per session* (denoted *NSTE*), and *number of multi-touch events per session* (denoted *NMTE*). Fig. 7 shows the histogram for these three features for the two users User1 and User2.

We can see from Fig. 7 that User1 performed more touch movements and multi-touches than User2, while User2 performed more single-touches than User1. It is also clearly visible that the numbers differ significantly between the users, making this also a suitable feature to distinguish between users' touch behavior.

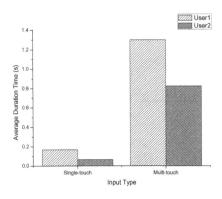 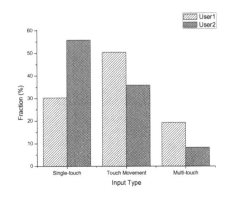

Fig. 6. This figure shows the average single-touch time and the average multi-touch time for 2 different users

Fig. 7. This figure shows the number of single-touch events, touch movements and multi-touch events per session for 2 different users

3.5   Training and Comparison Phase

As mentioned earlier, our system generates authentication signatures for each session, where each session has a determined length (e.g., 10 minutes). Each authentication signature comprises the 21 features explained above, which are extracted from the collected raw data input from the touchscreen. These 21 features (e.g., *ATMS1, ATMS2, ATMS3, ATMS4, ATMS5, ATMS6, ATMS7, ATMS8, FTM1, FTM2, FTM3, FTM4, FTM5, FTM6, FTM7, FTM8, AST, MTT, NTM, NSTE* and *NMTE*) together then characterize and authenticate a user's touch behavior.

In the *training phase* of the *behavior modeling component*, our scheme uses a classifier to recognize a user's profile by training with the user's authentication signatures. The training itself can be further divided into two types: *initial training* and *dynamic training*. A training phase starts with the initial training by collecting and utilizing several initial sessions from a user (i.e., several authentication signatures) to model a user's profile. Then it moves to dynamic training, which continuously trains the authentication system to integrate changes in the user's behavior.

In the *comparison phase* of the *behavior comparison component*, the system extracts the authentication signature from the current user's touch behavior and compares it with the profile of a legitimate user.

4   Evaluation of Classification Classifiers

In this section, we investigate the performance of 5 existing classification schemes when applied to our system: Decision tree (J48), Naive Bayes, Kstar, Radial Basis Function Network (RBFN) and Back Propagation Neural Network (BPNN).

J48 [40,41] is a decision tree classifier that classifies data items by generating decision trees from training data. Naive Bayes [42,43] is a probabilistic classifier based on the assumption that the presence (or absence) of a particular feature of a class is unrelated to the presence (or absence) of any other feature. Kstar [7] is a statistical classifier based on the assumption that similar instances will have similar classes. Thus, it uses similarity functions to create instance-based classifications. RBFN [3,36] and BPNN [11,37] are neural network classifiers. RBFN is an artificial neural network that uses radial basis functions as activation functions. Its approximation capabilities are used to model complex mappings. The BPNN classifier has two main steps: (1) to present input and propagate it forward through the network to compute the output values for each output unit; (2) to perform backward passes through the network and calculate appropriate weights.

To remove any implementation related bias, we performed our evaluation using WEKA [48] (using default settings), which is an open-source machine learning software that provides a collection of machine learning algorithms.

For the evaluation in this paper, we ran the classification algorithms on a desktop machine. In a real-world setting, however, the classification itself would be run on the smartphone itself. Current smartphones are becoming comparable in terms of computation power to desktop machines, but it could also be envisaged to off-load the heaviest part of the computation to the cloud. This is already commonly done for example when transcribing speech as an input method, or enabling voice commands.[6] We leave running the classifier also on the smartphone for future work.

4.1 User Data Collection

Methodology. For this paper we had 20 Android phone users (12 female and 8 male) participate in our experiments and among the participants were students (85%) as well as professionals (15%). All participants were regular mobile phone users and ranged in age from 20 to 48 years. For the data collection we provided participants with an Android phone (a Google/HTC Nexus One) equipped with a modified version of the Android OS. All participants used the same phone to ensure that all data was collected using the same device. Before starting the collection, we described our objective to all participants and showed what kind of data would be collected. We asked participants to use the Android phones the same way they would use their own phones during the data collection period. Participants were asked to do the actual data collection outside of the lab, allowing them to get familiar with the phone first. They could also decide by themselves when to start the collection process (allowing them enough time to get familiar). Participants were asked to complete the collection of 6 sessions (with each session lasting 10 minutes) within 3 days, and they could use the phone freely as their own phones (e.g., using it to browse the web, install new software, etc.) during the entire collection period.

We collected raw data for altogether 120 sessions of 10 minutes each, with an average of 6 sessions per user. If the duration of a session from a participant was shorter than 10 minutes, we discarded the data and asked the participants to record a new session. During the collection, only one invalid dataset was found and it was due to a transmission error. After collecting the raw data for a particular user, the phone was restored to its original state, to ensure that all participants had the same conditions for

---

[6] http://www.apple.com/iphone/features/siri.html

Table 2. Evaluation results for the tested classifiers

Measure	J48	NBayes	Kstar	RBFN	BPNN
FAR (%)	22.43	22.45	14.11	7.08	8.85
FRR (%)	25.01	18.36	16.69	8.34	14.3
Avg. err. rate	23.72	20.41	15.4	7.71	11.58
SD in FAR	16.46	18.1	12.3	6.4	7.72
SD in FRR	21.33	7.63	13.73	6.83	10.6

their experiment. Completing the data collection (i.e., collecting 120 sessions in total from 20 users) took altogether two months. The collected data was then analyzed and the selected features were extracted from the raw data.

4.2   Evaluation Measures

Ideally, a machine learning classifier would be able to classify whether a phone user is a legitimate user or an impostor with 100% accuracy. However, this is not realistic in real world systems. The following two measures are used to measure the accuracy of touch dynamics authentication:

- False Acceptance Rate (FAR): indicates the probability that an impostor is classified as a legitimate user.
- False Rejection Rate (FRR): indicates the probability that a legitimate user is classified as an impostor.

In practice, a trade-off is usually made between the false acceptance rate (security) and the false rejection rate (usability). In general, a false rejection is less costly than a false acceptance, since a higher false acceptance rate will lower the security level of the authentication system, while a higher false rejection rate will frustrate a legitimate user, which is still unfortunate but arguably less problematic than a lower security level. In terms of security and usability, both lower FAR and FRR are desirable.

4.3   Evaluation Results

For the evaluation of the system, we used the WEKA framework to test each classifier and get the FAR and FRR for each user, and we also calculate an average error rate over all users for each classifier. The results of the evaluation are shown in Table 2.

The evaluation results show that for the data collected from our participants, the two neural network classifiers (RBFN and BPNN) have the best performance with an average error rate of 7.71% and 11.58%, respectively, compared to the other classifiers, which have average error rates of between 15% and 24%.

Although these experimental results are encouraging for the feasibility of our scheme, an average error rate of about 7.8% is still very high for real world systems. The reason for an error rate of around 7.8% is that the performance of the classifiers decreases as the variance of the feature datasets increases. Table 2 shows the standard deviation of the FAR and FRR for each classifiers, ranging from 7% to 22%.

A more ideal classifier suitable for our system should therefore meet the following requirements:

- The classifier should provide a relatively small FAR and FRR (less than 5% each) [52].
- The classifier should be economical in terms of computational power required, considering that it will be run on mobile devices with limited resources.
- The classifier should be able to deal with the sometimes significant variations in the feature dataset.

5   PSO-RBFN Classifier

The variation in the datasets is a major challenge for a regular RBFN classifier [22]. To improve the performance of the classification when working on data with significant variations in a user's behavior, we applied an algorithm that combines Particle Swarm Optimization (PSO) and an RBFN classifier. In our work, the RBFN classifier was selected for two reasons: (1) RBFN has the lowest FAR and FRR compared to the other classifiers, as shown in Table 2; and (2) comparing the two neural network classifiers (RBFN and BPNN), RBFN has better accuracy and is faster when authenticating a user (e.g., to analyze 120 sessions, RBFN only requires about 1 second for building the model while BPNN requires about 3 seconds), which is a desirable property for applications that are run on resource-limited devices such as mobile phones. PSO, on the other hand, was selected for the following two reasons: (1) PSO [17] is one of the most commonly used evolutionary algorithms used to optimize the structure of neural networks (e.g., RBFN) [51]; and (2) PSO can achieve faster convergence speed and requires fewer optimized parameters compared to other evolutionary algorithms such as Genetic algorithms [22], which benefits the implementation on a mobile phone. The principle of the PSO-RBFN classifier is described below.

RBFN is a three-layer feedback network which consists of an *input layer*, a *hidden layer* and an *output layer*. The input layer contains a set of source nodes that connect the network to the environment. In the hidden layer, each hidden unit employs a radial activation function that carries out a nonlinear transformation from the input space to the hidden space, while in the output layer, each output unit implements a weighted sum of hidden unit outputs. In hybrid PSO-RBFN, PSO can be used to enhance the RBFN training by optimizing the radial activation function and weighted sum of RBFN with a population-based iterative search procedure, so that PSO-RBFN can better deal with variations in a user's touch behavior compared to regular RBFN. Hybrid PSO-RBFN has also been tested in the field of artificial intelligence and implementation details can be found in [39]. In our work, we implemented the PSO-RBFN classifier using the WEKA platform [48].

We applied this combined classifier on the data collected in our experiments, and the results of PSO-RBFN compared to regular RBFN are shown in Table 3. The numbers clearly show that using a combination of PSO and RBFN significantly improves the accuracy, reducing the average error rate from 7.71% for RBFN to 2.92% for PSO-RBFN. An FAR of 2.5% and FRR of 3.34% mean that the possibility of identifying an impostor as a legitimate user and the possibility of identifying a legitimate user as an

Table 3. This table shows the experimental results of comparing the PSO-RBFN classifier against the regular RBFN classifier

Measure	RBFN	PSO-RBFN
FAR (%)	7.08	2.5
FRR (%)	8.34	3.34
Average error rate	7.71	2.92
SD in FAR	6.4	1.22
SD in FRR	6.83	1.89

impostor are low. Furthermore, both the FAR and the FRR are below 5% when using the PSO-RBFN classifier and the standard deviation is also significantly lower compared to RBFN.

6   Limitations and Future Work

In this section, we discuss some open problems of our touch-dynamics-based user authentication system and propose some possible future work.

- *Multi-touch Gestures.* In this work, we define a multi-touch action as an input with two or more simultaneous, distinct touch press down events at different coordinates of the touch screen. That is, our scheme only identifies a multi-touch action either without specifying the specific multi-touch gestures (e.g., pinch to zoom, scroll, spread, etc.) or without distinguishing two or more fingers on the touch screen. We leave it as an open problem for future work to collect such data and analyze these specific multi-touch gestures for user authentication.
- *Other Platforms.* Our current user authentication scheme is effective on an Android operating system. Other mobile phone operating systems, however, might incur different touch gestures and user behavior. We plan to explore the feasability of our scheme on other mobile operating systems such as Windows Mobile, Symbian and others.
- *Complexity.* A user authentication scheme on a mobile phone should have a small computational complexity to not impact the performance of the mobile phone adversely. Possible future work could be to evaluate the resource consumption of our scheme and to explore the relationship between the number of features analyzed and the computational complexity incurred, and the relationship between the collection of training profiles and the computational complexity.
- *Consistency.* The scheme presented in this paper can achieve an FAR of 2.5% and an FRR of 3.34% respectively, when evaluated with 20 users and data from 120 sessions. Nevertheless, involving more participants and collecting more touch gesture data would help us to get an even better understanding of the performance of our scheme. In addition, future work could also include evaluating the consistency of our scheme, such as how having several profiles on a phone impacts the accuracy of our system, and the impact of the session duration on the accuracy of our system.

7 Concluding Remarks

In this paper, we studied and proposed a behavioral biometric authentication approach which is based on touch gestures on a touchscreen mobile phone. Through this approach we obtained encouraging results on authenticating individuals through the collection of features extracted from raw touchscreen inputs. We showed that touch dynamics is similar yet different from keystroke dynamics and mouse dynamics. We also described an authentication signature which consists of 21 touch-related features that can be used for user authentication. To evaluate the performance of our scheme, we performed a comparison of 5 existing classifiers, applying them to touch gesture data collected from 20 Android phone users. The experimental results show that regular neural network classifiers can achieve an average error rate of about 7.8% for our collected experimental data. To further improve this result, we implemented a hybrid classifier called PSO-RBFN. Applied on the same experimental data, the results show that our optimized PSO-RBFN classifier significantly reduces the average error rate down to 2.92% (FAR of 2.5% and FRR of 3.34%).

To the best of our knowledge, our work represents an early work in the aspect of continuously authenticating users by means of touch dynamics on touchscreen mobile phones. We reported positive results and discussed some open problems. As part of our future work we plan to include more specific multi-touch gestures. We also plan to evaluate our solution with a larger set of participants. In addition, future work could also include further development of our solution in terms of scalability, complexity and consistency.

Acknowledgments. We would like to thank the participants for their hard work in the data collection and the anonymous reviewers for their helpful comments.

References

1. Ahmed, A.A.E., Traore, I.: A New Biometric Technology based on Mouse Dynamics. IEEE Transactions on Dependable and Secure Computing 4(3), 165–179 (2007)
2. Bergadano, F., Gunetti, D., Picardi, C.: User Authentication through Keystroke Dynamics. ACM Transactions on Information and System Security 5(4), 367–397 (2002)
3. Bishop, C.: Improving the Generalization Properties of Radial Basis Function Neural Networks. Neural Computation 3(4), 579–588 (1991)
4. Bleha, S., Slivinsky, C., Hussien, B.: Computer-access Security Systems Using Keystroke Dynamics. IEEE Transactions on Pattern Analysis and Machine Intelligence 12(12), 1217–1222 (1990)
5. Clarke, N.L., Furnell, S.M.: Telephones -A Survey of Attitudes and Practices. Computers & Security 24(7), 519–527 (2005)
6. Clarke, N.L., Furnell, S.M.: Authenticating Mobile Phone Users Using Keystroke Analysis. International Journal of Information Security 6(1), 1–14 (2007)
7. Cleary, J.G., Trigg, L.E.: K*: An Instance-based Learner Using an Entropic Distance Measure. In: Proceedings of the 12th International Conference on Machine Learning, pp. 108–114. Morgan Kaufmann (1995)
8. Dai, J., Zhou, J.: Multifeature-based high-Resolution Palmprint Recognition. IEEE Transactions on Pattern Analysis and Machine Intelligence 33(5), 945–957 (2011)

9. De Luca, A., Hang, A., Brudy, F., Lindner, C., Hussmann, H.: Touch Me Once and I Know It's You!: Implicit Authentication based on Touch Screen Patterns. In: Proceedings of the 2012 ACM Annual Conference on Human Factors in Computing Systems (CHI), pp. 987–996. ACM, New York (2012)
10. Denning, D.E.: An Intrusion-Detection Model. IEEE Transactions on Software Engineering 13(2), 222–232 (1987)
11. Fahlman, S.E.: An Empirical Study of Learning Speed in Back-propagation Networks. Technical Report CMU-CS-88-162, Carnegie Mellon University, Pittsburgh, PA 15213 (1988)
12. Fiorella, D., Sanna, A., Lamberti, F.: Multi-touch User Interface Evaluation for 3D Object Manipulation on Mobile Devices. Journal on Multimodal User Interfaces 4(1), 3–10 (2010)
13. Jermyn, I., Mayer, A., Monrose, F., Reiter, M.K., Rubin, A.D.: The Design and Analysis of Graphical Passwords. In: Proceedings of the 8th USENIX Security Symposium, pp. 1–15. USENIX Association (1999)
14. Jorgensen, Z., Yu, T.: On Mouse Dynamics as a Behavioral Biometric for Authentication. In: Proceedings of the 6th ACM Symposium on Information, Computer and Communications Security (ASIACCS), New York, USA, pp. 476–482 (2011)
15. Karatzouni, S., Clarke, N.: Keystroke Analysis for Thumb-based Keyboards on Mobile Devices. In: Venter, H., Eloff, M., Labuschagne, L., Eloff, J., von Solms, R. (eds.) New Approaches for Security, Privacy and Trust in Complex Environments. IFIP, vol. 232, pp. 253–263. Springer, Boston (2007)
16. Karlson, A.K., Brush, A.B., Schechter, S.: Can I Borrow Your Phone?: Understanding Concerns When Sharing Mobile Phones. In: Proceedings of the 27th International Conference on Human Factors in Computing Systems (CHI), pp. 1647–1650. ACM, New York (2009)
17. Kennedy, J., Eberhart, R.: Particle Swarm Optimization. In: Proceedings of the 1995 IEEE International Conference on Neural Networks, pp. 1942–1948 (1995)
18. Kim, D., Dunphy, P., Briggs, P., Hook, J., Nicholson, J.W., Nicholson, J., Olivier, P.: Multi-Touch Authentication on Tabletops. In: Proceedings of the 28th International Conference on Human Factors in Computing Systems (CHI), pp. 1093–1102. ACM, New York (2010)
19. Köse, C., İkibaş, C.: A Personal Identification System using Retinal Vasculature in Retinal Fundus Images. Expert Systems with Applications 38(11), 13670–13681 (2011)
20. Leggett, J., Williams, G., Usnick, M., Longnecker, M.: Dynamic Identity Verification via Keystroke Characteristics. International Journal of Man-Machine Studies 35(6), 859–870 (1991)
21. Lemos, R.: Passwords: the Weakest Link? Hackers can Crack most in less than a Minute (May 2002), http://news.com/2009-1001-916719.html
22. Liu, Y., Zheng, Q., Shi, Z., Chen, J.: Training Radial Basis Function Networks with Particle Swarms. In: Yin, F.-L., Wang, J., Guo, C. (eds.) ISNN 2004. LNCS, vol. 3173, pp. 317–322. Springer, Heidelberg (2004)
23. Maio, D., Maltoni, D., Wayman, J.L., Jain, A.K.: Fvc2000: Fingerprint Verification Competition. IEEE Transactions on Pattern Analysis and Machine Intelligence 24(3), 402–412 (2002)
24. Maiorana, E., Campisi, P., González-Carballo, N., Neri, A.: Keystroke Dynamics Authentication for Mobile Phones. In: Proceedings of the 2011 ACM Symposium on Applied Computing (SAC), pp. 21–26. ACM, New York (2011)
25. Matyás Jr., V., Riha, Z.: Toward Reliable User Authentication through Biometrics. IEEE Security and Privacy 1(3), 45–49 (2003)
26. McAfee and Carnegie Mellon University. Mobility and Security: Dazzling Opportunities, profound challenges (May 2011),
    http://www.mcafee.com/mobilesecurityreport
27. McHugh, J.: Intrusion and Intrusion Detection. International Journal of Information Security 1(1), 14–35 (2001)

28. Millennial Media. Mobile mix: The mobile device index (2011),
    `http://www.millennialmedia.com/research`
29. N. Mobile and NCSA. Report on Consumer Behaviors and Perceptions of Mobile Security
    (January 2012),
    `http://docs.nq.com/NQ_Mobile_Security_Survey_Jan2012.pdf`
30. Monrose, F., Reiter, M.K., Wetzel, S.: Password Hardening based on Keystroke Dynamics.
    International Journal of Information Security 1(2), 69–83 (2002)
31. Monrose, F., Rubin, A.: Authentication via Keystroke Dynamics. In: Proceedings of the 4th
    ACM Conference on Computer and Communications Security (CCS), pp. 48–56. ACM, New
    York (1997)
32. Monrose, F., Rubin, A.: Keystroke Dynamics as a Biometric for Authentication. Future Gen-
    eration Computer Systems 16(4), 351–359 (2000)
33. Nakkabi, Y., Traoré, I., Ahmed, A.A.E.: Improving Mouse Dynamics Biometric Performance
    using Variance Reduction via Extractors with Separate Features. IEEE Transactions on Sys-
    tems, Man, and Cybernetics, Part A 40(6), 1345–1353 (2010)
34. Nauman, M., Ali, T., Rauf, A.: Using Trusted Computing for Privacy Preserving Keystroke-
    based Authentication in Smartphones. Telecommunication Systems, 1–13 (2011)
35. Numabe, Y., Nonaka, H., Yoshikawa, T.: Finger Identification for Touch Panel Operation
    using Tapping Fluctuation. In: Proceedings of the IEEE 13th International Symposium on
    Consumer Electronics, pp. 899–902 (May 2009)
36. Orr, M.J.L.: Introduction to Radial Basis Function Networks (1996)
37. Paola, J.D., Schowengerdt, R.A.: A Detailed Comparison of Backpropagation Neural Net-
    work and Maximum-likelihood Classifiers for Urban Land Use Classification. IEEE Trans-
    actions on Geoscience and Remote Sensing 33(4), 981–996 (1995)
38. Pusara, M., Brodley, C.E.: User Re-Authentication via Mouse Movements. In: Proceed-
    ings of the 2004 ACM Workshop on Visualization and Data Mining for Computer Security
    (VizSEC/DMSEC), pp. 1–8. ACM, New York (2004)
39. Qasem, S.N., Shamsuddin, S.M.: Hybrid Learning Enhancement of RBF Network based on
    Particle Swarm Optimization. In: Yu, W., He, H., Zhang, N. (eds.) ISNN 2009, Part III.
    LNCS, vol. 5553, pp. 19–29. Springer, Heidelberg (2009)
40. Quinlan, J.R.: C4.5: Programs for Machine Learning. Morgan Kaufmann Publishers Inc.,
    San Francisco (1993)
41. Quinlan, J.R.: Improved Use of Continuous Attributes in C4.5. Journal of Artificial Intelli-
    gence Research 4(1), 77–90 (1996)
42. Rennie, J.D.M., Shih, L., Teevan, J., Karger, D.R.: Tackling the Poor Assumptions of Naive
    Bayes Text Classifiers. In: Proceedings of the 20th International Conference on Machine
    Learning, pp. 616–623 (2003)
43. Rish, I.: An Empirical Study of the Naive Bayes Classifier. In: Proceedings of IJCAI 2001
    Workshop on Empirical Methods in AI, pp. 41–46 (2001)
44. Robinson, J.A., Liang, V.W., Chambers, J.A.M., MacKenzie, C.L.: Computer User Verifi-
    cation using Login String Keystroke Dynamics. IEEE Transactions on Systems, Man, and
    Cybernetics, Part A 28(2), 236–241 (1998)
45. Schmid, N.A., Ketkar, M.V., Singh, H., Cukic, B.: Performance Analysis of Iris-based Iden-
    tification System at the Matching Score Level. IEEE Transactions on Information Forensics
    and Security 1(2), 154–168 (2006)
46. Shabtai, A., Fledel, Y., Kanonov, U., Elovici, Y., Dolev, S., Glezer, C.: Google Android: A
    Comprehensive Security Assessment. IEEE Security Privacy 8(2), 35–44 (2010)
47. Tari, F., Ozok, A.A., Holden, S.H.: A Comparison of Perceived and Real Shoulder-Surfing
    Risks between Alphanumeric and Graphical Passwords. In: Proceedings of the 2nd Sympo-
    sium on Usable Privacy and Security (SOUPS), pp. 56–66. ACM, New York (2006)

48. The University of Waikato. WEKA-Waikato Environment for Knowledge Analysis, `http://www.cs.waikato.ac.nz/ml/weka/`
49. Wallace, R., McLaren, M., McCool, C., Marcel, S.: Cross-pollination of Normalisation Techniques from Speaker to Face Authentication using Gaussian Mixture Models. IEEE Transactions on Information Forensics and Security 7(2), 553–562 (2012)
50. Weiss, R., De Luca, A.: Passshapes: Utilizing Stroke based Authentication to Increase Password Memorability. In: Proceedings of the 5th Nordic Conference on Human-Computer Interaction: Building Bridges (NordiCHI), pp. 383–392. ACM, New York (2008)
51. Yao, X.: Evolving Artificial Neural Networks. Proceedings of the IEEE 87(9), 1423–1447 (1999)
52. Zahid, S., Shahzad, M., Khayam, S.A., Farooq, M.: Keystroke-Based User Identification on Smart Phones. In: Kirda, E., Jha, S., Balzarotti, D. (eds.) RAID 2009. LNCS, vol. 5758, pp. 224–243. Springer, Heidelberg (2009)
53. Zheng, N., Paloski, A., Wang, H.: An Efficient User Verification System via Mouse Movements. In: Proceedings of the 18th ACM Conference on Computer and Communications Security (CCS), pp. 139–150. ACM, New York (2011)

Secure Product Tracking in Supply Chain

Mehdi Khalfaoui[1], Refik Molva[2], and Laurent Gomez[1]

[1] SAP Labs France, Mougins 06254 France
{mehdi.khalfaoui,laurent.gomez}@sap.com
[2] Eurecom Institut, Biot 06410 France
refik.molva@eurecom.fr

Abstract. In this paper, we propose a secure and efficient product tracking mechanism implemented using wireless sensor nodes. This mechanism aims at tracking goods, and actions performed by each actor of the supply chain, while preserving the actors' privacy. Our solution is based on generating identifiers of the actors and their activities using AND Anti collusion codes. The identifiers are encrypted using homomorphic encryption to ensure security against adversaries, and to be able to compress the collected identifiers. In this work, wireless sensor nodes are not required to perform complex computation, which makes our solution feasible.

Keywords: Supply chain, Sensor networks, Tracking, Privacy, AND-ACC, Homomorphic Encryption.

1 Introduction

This paper aims at introducing a secure and privacy preserving product tracking solution using wireless sensor networks into supply chains. To this effect, we use sensors as secure storage tokens to store the steps of the path. More precisely, the memory capacity of the sensor nodes that are attached to the product store the identities of the involved steps. At each step, the sensor updates its memory to add the current step identity. The set of steps collected by a sensor is the path trace that the product went through. Each step has a secure identity, in order to be identified and to prevent impersonation attacks. At the end of the supply chain, a verifier extracts the steps and verifies their validity. The verifier is often a supply chain manager. He wants to have a global overview of its supply chain in order to mitigate any potential threat.

In order to preserve the actors privacy, the steps' identities should be kept secret. Encryption appears to be a straightforward solution preventing eavesdroppers from stealing identities and impersonating any legitimate supply chain actor. However, any technical solution that addresses secure and privacy preserving product tracking should take into account the limitations of sensor nodes. These are constrained devices in terms of computation power, memory, and energy. Due to the limited memory featured by sensors, straightforward storage of the collected steps cannot be afforded. Thus, a compression mechanism to

M. Kutyłowski and M. Yung (Eds.): Inscrypt 2012, LNCS 7763, pp. 351–370, 2013.

reduce the size of the path traces is a mandatory requirement in order to over-come the memory limitation of sensors. Also, the limited power computing and the energy of the sensor nodes, make the implementation of complex functions such as public key encryption algorithms difficult. Therefore, any operations that have to be performed by the sensors should be compatible with such constraint environment.

This paper introduces a mechanism to track products in supply chain while protecting sensitive information of supply chain actors and products. The main idea is to store on the sensor node an encrypted and compressed path trace for tracing the product. For that purpose, we propose to generate identities for the different steps using AND-Anti Collusion Code (AND-ACC) [19]. This code can be easily compressed by construction. Furthermore, to assure privacy, steps' IDs should be protected using an encryption mechanism that is compatible with the compression technique. Therefore, homomorphic encryption seems to be a natural choice. In addition, to ensure the legitimacy of the involved actors, sensors use Rabin scheme to authenticate them. The main features of the suggested product tracking scheme are as follows:

- It allows the supply chain manager to verify the legitimacy of the path taken by a product. More precisely, it allows the supply chain manager to verify which set of steps, a product has visited.
- It guarantees the privacy of products and therewith partners in the supply chain. Only the supply chain manager is able to verify the path taken by a product.
- It allows the restriction of information available to each supply chain actor, such as the origin of the product and the final destination.

Moreover the scheme is suitable for low capacity sensors. It only requires a few Kbytes storage. The protocol execution for each supply chain step requires only two modular multiplication.

2   Related Work

The idea of our use case that WSN can be used for tracking the goods in the supply chain was first suggested in [1]. However, research focuses mainly on Tag RFIDs to achieve a secure supply chain. Ouafi and Vaudenay [11] address coun-terfeiting of products using strong cryptography on RFID tags. Elkhiyaoui et al. [1] presented a tracker, a new mechanism to protect against malicious state update of tags in each step of the supply chain. Secure tracking of specific target using WSAN was also addressed in [5]. It describes a mechanism of tracking a moving target based on relaxation algorithms [13]. However, passive RFID tags have limited resources, which make security hard to achieve. As a matter of fact, any public key cryptosystem cannot be used with this type of RFID tag. Only hash functions can be implemented and used in passive RFID tag environment. Chawla et al. [2] check whether covert channels exist in a supply chain that leak information about a supply chains internal details to an adversary using secu-rity mechanism implemented in RFID tag. Therefore, a tag's state is frequently synchronized with a backend database. If a tag's state contains data that is not in the database, the tag is rejected. Our mechanism's focus, however, is on the secure, privacy-preserving detection of which path a tag has taken. Shuihua and Chu [15] detect malicious tampering of a tags state in a supply chain using watermarks. However, there is neither a way to identify a tag's path, nor to protect its privacy in the supply chain. Kerschbaum and Oertel [9] detect counterfeits in the supply chain using pattern matching for anomaly detection. When a tag is read, this information is stored in a central database along with the ID of the tag. Unlike our mechanism, the focus of this paper is on the privacy-preservation of readers participating in the supply chain. There is no privacy for the tags in the supply chain. Regarding simple product genuineness verification, solutions exist that rely on physical properties of a "tag". For example, TAGSYS produces holographic "tags" that are expensive to clone [18]. Verayo produces tags with Physically no clonable Functions (PUF) [20]. While these approaches solve product genuineness verification, they neither support identification of tags paths nor any kind of privacy properties. Our construction based on anti collusion code can be similar to collusion detection in multimedia files using fingerprints [19]. It allows a privacy preserving and the anonymity of the supply chain actors. Furthermore, a sensor node has more resources , which enables the use of more advanced cryptographic tools.

3   Background

Supply Chain is the movement of materials as they flow from their source to the end customer. Supply Chain includes purchasing, manufacturing, warehousing, transportation, customer service, demand planning , supply planning and supply chain management. It is made up of people, activities, information and resources involved in moving a product from its supplier to customer.

Formally, a supply chain is represented by a digraph $G = (V, E)$ whereby each vertex v represents one step in the supply chain. A step v in the supply chain is uniquely associated with an entity.

Each directed edge e, which links vertex v_i to vertex v_j , express that v_j is a possible next step to step v_i in the supply chain. This simply means that according to the organization of the supply chain, a product might proceed to step v_j after the completion of step v_i. Note that a supply chain can include loops and reflexive edges, but for the sake of simplicity, we assume that in our system there are no loops or reflexive edges. Whenever a product in the supply chain proceeds to step v_i , the entity interacts first with the sensor. A path P is defined as finite sequence of steps $P = v_0, ..., v_l$, where l is the length of the path P. A Path P is deemed valid if it is part of a legitimate supply chain networks.

3.1   Entities

A Secure Product Tracking (SPT) system consists of the following components:

- **Sensor** S: each product in the supply chain is equipped with a sensor. A sensor S is a re-writeable memory that stores the sensor state $s_{(S,v_j)}$, where v_j represents the current step that is being visited by S.
- **Supply chain manager** M: M is in charge of the the initial setup of sensors and of the verification of the path taken by each sensor. In order to verify the path of sensor S, M reads the current state $s_{(S,v_j)}$ of S, and decides whether the sequence visited by S is legitimate in the supply chain. We assume that M can enumerate all the valid paths in the supply chain.
- **actor** a: each actor is a legitimate single entity of the supply chain. When a product visits a step, the actor associated with that step interacts with the sensor S attached to the product.
- **trace** T: T is a digest of the path taken by a product and stored in the sensor attached to it.

Thus, a SPT system is:

- a Supply Chain $G = (V, A)$
- a Sensor S
- a set of possible traces $\mathcal{T}$
- a set of different actors $\dashv$
- a supply chain manager M
- a set of valid paths $\mathcal{P}$

4   Adversary Model

In our protocol, we assume that actors are semi-honest. That is, actors generate well formed protocol messages but they potentially can forge paths, impersonate other actors, or try to retrieve the identity of the steps encoded in a path trace. Any adversary can read the sensor's memory, since sensors are not tamper-resistant. However, a sensor can only update its trace after a successful authentication. Therefore, only the legitimate supply actors can make sensor updates to its path trace. The security and the privacy of the protocol will be evaluated based on a formal adversary model inspired by Valbuany et al. [11].

The adversary $\mathcal{A}$ that aims at violating the security and privacy properties, relies on the following oracles:

- $\mathcal{O}_{Choose}$: picks a sensor from the supply chain.
- $\mathcal{O}_{Read}$: takes a sensor S as input, and reads its trace.
- $\mathcal{O}_{Send}$: takes a sensor S as input, and sends a trace to it.
- $\mathcal{O}_{Check}$: returns $TRUE$ if the sensor S went through a valid path, otherwise it returns $FALSE$.
- $\mathcal{O}_{Inject}$: injects a sensor S in the supply chain.

We describe the security and privacy properties of our protocol as follows:

4.1   Security

Our protocol aims at preventing path forgery by an adversary by assuming the following property: if the verification of a sensor's trace T by the supply chain manager M returns a valid path P_v, then S must have visited all the steps of the path P_v.

In the rest of this section, we introduce two phases, Learning phase when $\mathcal{A}$ can query the oracle $\mathcal{O}_{Choose}$, that randomly selects a sensor within the supply chain and gives it to $\mathcal{A}$. During this phase, $\mathcal{A}$ is allowed to read traces stated in S and sends traces to S using the oracles $\mathcal{O}_{Read}$ and $\mathcal{O}_{Send}$ respectively. Then, $\mathcal{A}$ checks the validity of the trace in the sensor S, by querying the oracle $\mathcal{O}_{Check}$.

In the challenge phase, $\mathcal{A}$ randomly chooses a sensor S that has been already deployed in the supply chain, and authenticates itself to it. Then, $\mathcal{A}$ sends some value to S using $\mathcal{O}_{Send}$. Therefore, $\mathcal{A}$ has to successfully bypass the authentication process, to make S update its path trace. Finally, $\mathcal{A}$ injects the sensor in the supply chain using $\mathcal{O}_{Inject}$. If M accepts the sensor as a valid one, $\mathcal{A}$ wins.

For Cloning attacks, We use the same mitigation technique presented by Elkhiyaoui et al. [1]. M has a database DB_c of the sensors that went through valid path of supply chain, and were verified correctly by M. Therefore, $\mathcal{A}$ cannot clone a sensor more than once, thus, the cloning cannot be performed in large scale.

4.2   Privacy

An adversary $\mathcal{A}$ in our protocol, beside his ability to eavesdrop the sensor's communications with the actors' systems, she is able to tamper with the sensor's memory as well. Thus, we identify privacy requirement as step unlinkability. Step unlinkability prevents $\mathcal{A}$ from telling that two different sensors interacted with a common step.

To have a formal definition, we introduce the following oracles into our adversary model:

- $\mathcal{O}_{distinguish}$: takes as input two states $s_{(S_i, v_k)}$ and $s_{(S_j, v_k)}$, and returns $TRUE$ if the S_i, and S_j refer to the same sensor.
- $\mathcal{O}_{step}$: takes as input a sensor S and step v, and returns $TRUE$ if the S went through step v, and false otherwise.

the privacy game has two phases, learning phase and challenge phase. In the learning phase, $\mathcal{O}_{choose}$ provides to $\mathcal{A}$ a list of sensors. $\mathcal{A}$ can then observe the numerous protocol exchanges and collect sequences of valid paths. In the challenge phase, after several additional interactions, a random sensor Sc, that is already provided to $\mathcal{A}$ in the learning phase, is chosen. If $\mathcal{A}$ is able to distinguish with high probability which sensor from its list corresponds to the sensor challenger, $\mathcal{A}$ wins.

5 Protocol Description

5.1 Approach

In this section, we introduce our approach, and the different requirements that our solution has to fulfill.

The main idea of this work is to use the sensors as secure storage tokens for the path traces. More precisely, sensor node S is attached to the goods along the supply chain. At each step, S collects the current step's identity. S keeps track of which step interacted with the goods and which activity has been performed. The activity can be any process that the actor is supposed to perform, such as transportation or delivery.

There are three phases in our solution: *Initialization, Collection,* and *Verification*.

- *Initialization*: M generates the steps' IDs. Then, M distributes each step's ID to the corresponding supply chain actor.
- *Collection*: IDs are kept secret by the actors. During the course of regular supply chain operations, when a product is handled by a supply chain actor, the sensor S that is attached to the product and the actor interact through this phase of the protocol. As part of this phase, S verifies the legitimacy of the supply chain actor. If the actor is legitimate, S includes the current step's ID in the path trace.
- *Verification*: At the end of the supply chain, M retrieves the path trace from S and extracts the steps' IDs from the trace and verifies their legitimacy.

In addition to the security and privacy properties introduced in section 4, this approach requires the actors' IDs to be kept secret. Furthermore, the solution has to take into account the limitations of sensors in terms of computational power and memory. Therefore, straightforward storage of actors IDs and complex cryptographic operations such as asymmetric encryption cannot be afforded by sensors.

The first objective of the solution thus is to come up with a data compression technique that allows to store a digest of the path in the sensors. This technique should also allow the retrieval of actors IDs form the trace by M. The second requirement is for the confidentiality of the content of the path namely, the actor ID's included therein. Encryption that appears to be the most suitable solution to meet that requirement has to comply with the compression technique. Moreover, to allow the integration of encrypted actor ID's into the path digest without decrypting the former, homomorphic encryption seems to be an appropriate solution to this question.

To build a scheme that satisfies the aforementioned requirements, we leverage on a number of well established primitives. As for the compression technique, our solution relies on Anti-Collusion Code (ACC). We leverage on Paillier encryption to enable S to aggregate the encrypted IDs without decrypting them. Finally, we use polynomial conversion in order to convert a ACC code vector to a polynomial evaluation of a specific value. This conversion allow to encrypt a value instead of a vector without information loss.

5.2   Preliminaries

Anti Collusion Code

Definition. A binary code $C = \{c_1, c_2, \ldots, c_n\}$ such that the logical AND of any subset of k or fewer code vectors is non-zero and distinct from the logical AND of any other subset of k or fewer code vectors is a k-resilient AND anti-collusion code, or an AND-ACC code. [19]

Such code is often used in digital fingerprinting to prevent collusion attacks against traditional watermarking techniques [10]. It allows the identification of groups of K or less colluders. This is similar to our case, since the supply chain actors could be considered as colluders that collaborate to perform specific actions on the product. Therefore, each supply chain actor can be associated to a code vector. The result of the bitwise AND operation between the code vectors marks the path of the product. The bitwise AND operation does not increase the size of the path, therefore, the path size can stay manageable by the sensor all along the supply chain. Also, encoding and decoding operations does not require a lot of resources.

Encoding. To encode up k code vectors in a single code vector c_{enc}, we perform bitwise AND operations on the input code vectors.

$$c_{enc} = c_1 \text{ AND } c_2 \ldots \text{ AND } c_l \tag{1}$$

Decoding. To decode c_{enc}, we extract the positions of c_{enc} coefficients that equal to 1. All the code vectors c_i that have their coefficients at the extracted positions equal to 1 are the ones encoded in the c_{enc}.

Example. The columns of the following matrix form a 2-resilient AND-ACC code

$$\begin{pmatrix} 0 & 0 & 0 & 1 & 1 & 1 & 1 \\ 0 & 1 & 1 & 0 & 0 & 1 & 1 \\ 1 & 0 & 1 & 0 & 1 & 0 & 1 \\ 0 & 1 & 1 & 1 & 1 & 0 & 0 \\ 1 & 1 & 0 & 0 & 1 & 1 & 0 \\ 1 & 1 & 0 & 1 & 0 & 0 & 1 \end{pmatrix}$$

This code requires 7 bits for 7 users and provides 2-resiliency since any two column vectors share a unique pair of 1 bits. The encoding result of c_1 and c_7 is $c_{enc} = c_1 \text{ AND } c_7 = \{0,0,1,0,0,1\}$.

Based on the decoding technique c_{enc} has 1's at positions 3 and 7. Thus, the decoding of c_{enc} yields c_1 and c_7 since these are the only two code vectors with 1's at these positions.

Paillier Cryptosystem. Paillier cryptosystem [12] that we use in order to encrypt the steps' IDs, has an interesting property:

Additive Homomorphic property. This property allows us to compute the encrypted sum of two or several encrypted values as follows:

$$\mathcal{E}(m_1, r_1) * \mathcal{E}(m_2, r_2) = \mathcal{E}(m_1 + m_2, r_1 r_2) \tag{2}$$

Rabin Scheme. Rabin cryptosystem [14] is used to achieve authentication of the supply chain actors. Rabin encryption is single square modular encryption, which makes it feasible for low capacity devices such as sensor nodes. Rabin's public key $n_R = p_R q_R$ is stored in the sensor to perform the authentication with the visited supply chain actors. The public key is necessary for later encoding and can be published, while the private key must be possessed only by the recipient of the message.

The key-generation process can be summarized as follows:

– Choose two large distinct primes p and q.
– Let $n_R = p \cdot q$. Then n is the public key. The pair (p, q) is the private key.

Encryption. using the public key n_R, the plaintext is encrypted as follows:

$$\mathcal{R}(m) = m^2 \bmod n_R \tag{3}$$

Decryption. Using the private key (p,q), the decryption operation requires the solution of

$$x^2 = \mathcal{R}(m) \bmod N \tag{4}$$

which is "easy" if the factors of n_R are known. This equation has four roots in $\mathbb{Z}^*_{N_R}$. The solution is the one that fulfills the following additional requirement:

$$x \bmod 2 = 0 \ and \ ((x \bmod p) + (x \bmod q)) \bmod 2 = 0 \ [14] \tag{5}$$

Put It All Together. AND-ACC allows to encode the path, which is done by assigning to each supply chain actor a code vector as identifier. The collected identifiers are encoded into a single value using bitwise AND operation. However, as the actors' identities have to be kept secret, thus to be encrypted before getting collected. Therefore, an encryption mechanism that is homomorphic with bitwise AND is required to ensure the confidentiality of the actors' IDs.

Definition. $\mathcal{E}$ is homomorphic with respect to bitwise AND operation, if and only if there is an operation *op*, which verifies the following: for any pair of messages m_1 and m_2, we have:

$$\mathcal{E}(m_1 AND m_2) = \mathcal{E}(m_1) \ op \ \mathcal{E}(m_2) \tag{6}$$

Unfortunately, there is no such encryption mechanism that is homomorphic with respect to bitwise AND operation. The only homomorphic encryption that we know, are homomorphic with respect to the multiplication such as the RSA cryptosystem

$$m_1{}^e \cdot m_2{}^e = (m_1 \cdot m_2)^e$$

or homomorphic with respect to the addition such as Paillier cryptosystem

$$g^{m_1} \cdot g^{m_2} = g^{(m_1 + m_2)}$$

So ideally, we need a way to associate bitwise AND operation with arithmetic addition or multiplication, in order to be able to use one of the existing homomorphic encryption algorithms.

AND-SUM Conversion. We decided to apt for a conversion between bitwise AND operation and arithmetic addition is based on the following property:

Property 1. Let's $x_1, \ldots, x_n$ be n binary values, we have the following equivalences of Table 1:

$$x_1 + \ldots + x_1 = n \iff x_1 = \ldots = x_n = 1 \iff x_1 \wedge \ldots \wedge x_n = 1 \qquad (7)$$

Table 1. AND-SUM conversion

addition $+$	AND $\wedge$
$\sum_{i=0}^{n} x_i = n$	$\wedge_{i=0}^{n} x_i = 1$
$\sum_{i=0}^{n} x_i < n$	$\wedge_{i=0}^{n} x_i = 0$

By interpreting binary code vectors as arithmetic ones, we can sum them as follows:

$$c_{sum}[j] = \sum_{i=0}^{n} c_i[j] \qquad (8)$$

Thanks to Property 1, the expected result of the AND bitwise operation $c_{enc} = \wedge_{i=0}^{n} c_i$, can be retrieved on simple reasoning. Indeed, the $\max_{i=0}^{length(c_{sum})} c_{sum}[i]$ corresponds to the number of the input code vectors. Thus,

$$if\, c_{sum}[j] = \max_{j=0}^{length(c_{sum})} c_{sum}[j]\, then\, c_{and}[j] = 1 \qquad (9)$$

$$if\, c_{sum}[j] < \max_{j=0}^{length(c_{sum})} c_{sum}[j]\, then\, c_{and}[j] = 0 \qquad (10)$$

AND-ACC Operations on Encrypted Code Vectors. Now that the basic encoding of actors' IDs can be represented based on the sum of code vectors in AND-ACC code, the additively homomorphic Paillier encryption seems to be a suitable solution to assure the privacy of steps' IDs as part of the scheme. Thus, each code vector c_i is encrypted using Paillier cryptosystem $\mathcal{E}$

$$\mathcal{E}(c_i) = \begin{pmatrix} \mathcal{E}(c_i[0]) \\ \mathcal{E}(c_i[1]) \\ \dots \\ \mathcal{E}(c_i[len]) \end{pmatrix} \tag{11}$$

The encrypted path can then be computed using the additively homomorphic property of Paillier, as follows:

$$\mathcal{E}(Path_{sum}) = \prod_{i=0}^{len} \begin{pmatrix} \mathcal{E}(c_i[0]) \\ \mathcal{E}(c_i[1]) \\ \dots \\ \mathcal{E}(c_i[len]) \end{pmatrix} \tag{12}$$

$$\mathcal{E}(Path_{sum}) = \begin{pmatrix} \mathcal{E}(\sum_{i=0}^{len} c_i[0]) \\ \mathcal{E}(\sum_{i=0}^{len} c_i[1]) \\ \dots \\ \mathcal{E}(\sum_{i=0}^{len} c_i[len]) \end{pmatrix} \tag{13}$$

An encrypted path is decrypted as follows:

$$Path_{sum} = \mathcal{D}(\mathcal{E}(Path_{sum})) = \begin{pmatrix} \sum_{i=0}^{len} c_i[0] \\ \sum_{i=0}^{len} c_i[1] \\ \dots \sum_{i=0}^{len} c_i[len] \end{pmatrix} \tag{14}$$

Finally, the actual cleartext value of the path encoding is derived from $Path_{sum}$ using the reverse conversion as described in 5.2.

Due to separate encryption of each coefficient in the code vectors, the path encoding scheme still would require large memory space to store a single path trace. The path encoding scheme, thus, involves an additional technique that allows us to represent code vectors as simple integers.

Vector-Integer Conversion.   In order to convert a vector $v = (v_0, \dots, v_l)$ to an integer, we consider the coordinates of v as coefficient of polynomial P. We choose a value x bigger than $k + 1$ (k is the parameter such as AND-ACC is K-resilient), and we compute $\text{Poly}(v)(x) = \sum_{i=0}^{len} v_i x^i$. where len is the length of v.

The inverse conversion is easily achieved by means of subsequent divisions to extract the coefficients of the polynomial, which are the coefficients of the vector by construction.

It should be noted that the sum of polynomial evaluation representing two code vectors is identical to the polynomial representation of the sum of the two code vectors.

5.3   SPT Protocol

Based on the aforementioned building blocks, the operations of the SPT are depicted in three phases.

Initialization. SPT's setup is as follows:

- Supply chain manager M shares with the supply chain actors a Rabin's private key (p_R, q_R). Then, M stores the public key n_R in the sensor.
- M generates a Paillier cryptosystem public and private keys. M publishes the Paillier's public key to all the supply chain actors.
- M generates randomly a list of ACC codes v using Generate algorithm. Then, M converts each code vector v to a value $Poly(v)(x)$, which corresponds to an identity of the supply chain step.
- M encrypts each value $Poly(v_i)$ to get $\mathcal{E}(a_i)$, using Paillier's public key. Then, M sends the encrypted value to the corresponding a_i through a secure channel.
- M generates an s_{id} for each sensor S, and key k for keyed-HMAC computation. Then, M computes the *encrypted hash* $\mathcal{E}(HMAC_k(s_{id}))$. M keeps a database $DB_s ensor$ of sensor identities s_{id}, and their hashes $HMAC_k(s_{id})$.
- M stores in the sensor S, Rabin's public key n_R, the keyed-HMAC $HMAC_k(s_{id})$, and the initial value $\mathcal{E}(HMAC_k(s_{id}))$. $\mathcal{E}(HMAC_k(s_{id}))$ corresponds to the initial trace stored on the sensor.

  Now, for each sensor entering the supply chain, M has already stored on it the initial value $s_{(T_0)} = E(HMAC_k(s_{id}))$.

Collection. This phase starts when S arrives to the supply chain actor. Here, we assume that the sensor S has visited the steps $step_0, \ldots, step_l$. When, S visits the step $step_{l+1}$, it has already stored the trace of the path $\mathcal{P}_l = \overrightarrow{step_0 step_1 ... step_l}$. Therefore, the current path trace that is stored in the sensor is $\mathcal{E}(T_l)$, which corresponds to the state of the sensor after visiting l steps.

There are two sub-phases, authentication sub-phase to check the legitimacy of the actor, and the trace collection sub-phase to update the path trace.

In the authentication sub-phase, S chooses a random value $r \in \mathcal{F}_{n_R}$ and sends $Rabin(r) = r^2 mod\, n_R$ to the current actor. This latter decrypts $Rabin(r)$ using its private key, and returns $hash(r)$. S considers the authentication as successful, if the received value matched the hash value of the generated one. Then, S can proceed to trace collection phase.

In the collection sub-phase, S sends its $HMAC_k(s_{id}) \oplus r$ to the current actor. This latter computes $\mathcal{E}(Poly(v_{l+1}(x)))^{HMAC_k(s_{id})} = \mathcal{E}(Poly(v_{l+1}(x)) * HMAC_k(s_i d))$, and he sends to S, the value $\mathcal{E}(Poly(v_{l+1}(x)) * HMAC_k(s_{id})) \oplus r$. S retrieves $\mathcal{E}(Poly(v_{l+1}(x)) * HMAC_k(s_i d))$, and updates the path trace $\mathcal{E}(T_{l+1})$ as follows:

$$\mathcal{E}(T_{l+1}) = \mathcal{E}(T_l) * \mathcal{E}(Poly(v_{l+1}(x)) * HMAC_k(s_{id})) \, mod\, N^2 \qquad (15)$$

$$\mathcal{E}(T_{l+1}) = \mathcal{E}(T_l + Poly(v_{l+1}(x)) * HMAC_k(s_{id})) \, mod\, N^2 \qquad (16)$$

$$\mathcal{E}(T_{l+1}) = \mathcal{E}((\sum_{j=0}^{len-1} (\sum_{i=0}^{l+1} v_i[j])x^j) * HMAC_k(s_{id})) \; mod \; N^2 \qquad (17)$$

Table 2 illustrates the exchanged messages between S and the current actor $a_{current}$.

Table 2. Authentication phase

S picks randomly a number r
$S \longrightarrow a_{current} : r^2 mod N_R$
$a_{current} \longrightarrow S : hash(r)$
$a_{current} \longrightarrow S : \mathcal{E}(Poly(v_{l+1}(x))) \oplus r$

Verification. Using the authentication protocol presented in the collection phase, · M authenticates the sensor S. Then, M verifies if $HMAC_k(s_{id})$ is in DB_{sensor} to check the legitimacy of the sensor and to prevent massive cloning attacks. If $HMAC_k(s_{id})$ exists in DB_{sensor}, M accepts the path trace T_m from S, otherwise it rejects it. M decrypts the path trace using the secret key of Paillier cryptosystem. the decryption result is $T_m = HMAC_k(s_{id}) * \sum_{1 \leq i \leq n} Poly(v_i)(x)$.

M checks if T_m is well formed by verifying $T_m \; mod \; HMAC_k(s_{id}) = 0$. If it is the case, M extracts the coefficients of the polynomial, using simple euclidean division operations to have the vector c_{vec} which is the sum of the coordinates of the different actors' identifiers.

Table 3 shows the algorithm to extract the value of the vector c_{vec}.

Table 3. c_{vec} extraction algorithm

Let $qot(a,b)$ the quotient of the division of a by b
$qot(T_m, HMAC_k(s_id)) = \sum_{0 \leq i \leq l} Poly(v_i)(x)$
$qot(T_m, HMAC_k(s_id) = \sum_{0 \leq i \leq l} \sum_{0 \leq j \leq len-1} v_i[j]x^j$
$c_{vec}[i] = \sum_{0 \leq j \leq len-1} v_i[j]$

Using the mechanism explained in section 5.2, we convert c_{vec} to its corresponding binary vector c_{enc}.

c_{enc} represents AND bitwise operation result for the different vectors v_i. M decodes c_{enc}, and extracts the involved steps. Then, M checks if the path is a valid one or not.

In this section, we presented our solution in detail. We demonstrated that only a two modular multiplication operations are executed in the sensor node per step. Furthermore, our solution can be used for path enforcement by a supply chain manager, or by a high authority to trace back the actors that interacted with the product. In Section 6, we present a provable security to our approach. We describe our simulator to show that any adversary who is able to break our system, she can solve the hard problem of the quadratic residue problem [12].

6   Security Analysis

In this section we prove the security of SPT system. The proof was inspired from [1] [11].

6.1 $\mathcal{A}$ Is Not a Legitimate Actor

if $\mathcal{A}$ authenticates successfully itself to S, she breaks the Rabin scheme security by definition. Therefore, only the legitimate supply actors can try to update the path trace maliciously.

6.2 $\mathcal{A}$ Is a Legitimate Actor

If $\mathcal{A}$ is legitimate actor, the authentication process will succeed, and S accepts the received value from $\mathcal{A}$. In this case, we use the security of keyed-HMAC and the decisional composite residuosity assumption to prove the security of SPT protocol against forgery by a legitimate actor.

Security of keyed-HMAC. For our proof sketch, we are using the property indistinguishability of keyed hash function.

Indistinguishability property. Let $\mathcal{O}_{distinguish}$ be an oracle that when $\mathcal{A}$ provides it with a message m, $\mathcal{O}^{distinguish}$ returns with the same probability a random number, or $HMAC_k(m)$. $\mathcal{A}$ cannot guess with no-negligible probability if the returned value is a random number, or $HMAC_k(m)$.

Lemma. Producing a new valid trace contradicts the indistinguishiability property of $HMAC_k$. Proof (Sketch). From $\mathcal{A}$, we can build an adversary $\mathcal{A}'$ that uses $\mathcal{A}$ to break the indistinguishability property of keyed-HMAC. we provide $\mathcal{A}$, with a sensor S and its s_{id}. $\mathcal{A}$ produces a new valid trace $\mathcal{E}(T_m)$ that corresponds to the sensor s_{id}. $\mathcal{A}$ provides s_{id} to $\mathcal{O}_{distinguish}$. $\mathcal{O}_{distinguish}$ returns value H to be tested. $\mathcal{A}$ decrypts $\mathcal{E}(T_m)$. She gets T_m, and computes $T_m \bmod H$. If $T_m \bmod H = 0$, H is the $HMAC_k(s_id)$, otherwise H is a random number.

The decisional composite residuosity assumption (DCRA). The DCRA states that given a composite n and an integer z, it is hard to decide whether z is a n-residue mod n^2 or not. In other words, whether there exists y such that $z = y^n mod\, n^2$. This assumption is mainly used to proof the semantic security of Paillier cryptosystem [12].

Definition 1. *A cryptographic protocol is semantically secure if its indistinguishability against chosen plaintext attacks (IND-CPA) holds.*

Theorem 1. *SPT is semantically secure if and only if DCRA and the indistinguishibilty of keyed-HMAC hold.*

Proof. The main idea of this proof is to build an attacker $\mathcal{A}\prime$ from $\mathcal{A}$ whose advantage ϵ to forge a valid path, that is able to break DCRA. As shown in the previous *Lemma*, $\mathcal{A}$ cannot provide a new valid path trace from scratch. Now, Let's assume that $\mathcal{A}$ can update a valid path trace that she got from the learning phase to a new valid path trace. For the sake of simplicity, we consider that the SPT system has only one valid path.

Let $\mathcal{O}_{DCRA}$ be an oracle that, when it is queried with a parameter n, it flips a coin $b \in 0,1$. If $b = 1$ it takes a $y \in Z$ and returns $y^n mod\ n^2$ otherwise, it returns a random number C.

$\mathcal{A}\prime$ creates SPT system with a valid path, $(step_0, \ldots, step_m)$. Then, she generates the AND-ACC identifier corresponds to each step.

Let $\mathcal{E}(T_{m-1})$ be the encrypted path trace until the $step_{m-1}$. First, $\mathcal{A}'$ sends a query to $\mathcal{O}_{DCRA}$ with N (Paillier modular) as parameter, and gets a challenge C. $\mathcal{A}'$ computes $\mathcal{E}(T_{m-1})*C$ mod N^2, and writes the result in a sensor S.

If in the challenge phase, $\mathcal{A}$ is able to update the trace to a valid path trace $\mathcal{E}(T_m)$, then $\mathcal{E}(T_{m-1})$. C mod N^2 is a valid ciphertext of T_{m-1} (i.e $\mathcal{E}(T_{m-1})$. C mod N^2 is re-encryption to $\mathcal{E}(T_{m-1})$). Therefore, C is N-residue mod N^2, and $\mathcal{A}'$ breaks the DCRA assumption, with advantage of $1/2*\epsilon$, since she is wrong half of the time because of oracle's coin flip.

Table 4 illustrates the messages exchanged between the involved entities during the challenge game.

Table 4. Forgery challenge game

$\mathcal{O}_{DCRA}$	$\mathcal{A}'$	$\mathcal{A}$
receive N $\longleftarrow$	send N	
pick C $\longrightarrow$	receive C	
	compute $\mathcal{E}(T_{m-1}).C mod\ N^2$ $\longrightarrow$	receive $\mathcal{E}(T_{m-1}).C mod\ N^2$
	receive $\mathcal{E}(T_m)$ $\longleftarrow$	update trace $\mathcal{E}(T_m)$
receive 1 or 0 $\longleftarrow$	if $\mathcal{E}(T_m)$ is valid, send 1 else send 0	

7   Privacy Analysis

In this section we prove the privacy requirement of step unlinkability of SPT system.

Theorem 2. *SPT provides step unlinkability under DCRA.*

Proof. Assume there is an adversary A whose advantage ϵ to break the step unlinkability experiment is non-negligible. We now construct a new adversary $\mathcal{A}'$ that executes $\mathcal{A}$ and breaks the semantic security of Paillier.

Let $\mathcal{O}_{DCRA}$ be an oracle that, when it is queried with a parameter n, it flips a coin $b \in 0, 1$. If $b = 1$ it takes a $y \in Z$ and returns $y^n \bmod n^2$ otherwise, it returns a random number C.

$\mathcal{A}\prime$ creates SPT system with multiple valid paths. Then, She generates the AND-ACC identifiers correspond to each step. First, $\mathcal{A}'$ sends a query to $\mathcal{O}_{DCRA}$ with N (Paillier modular) as parameter, and gets a challenge C. Then, $\mathcal{A}'$ builds two traces for two different path, with one step in common. Let $\mathcal{E}(T_m)$ the path trace for the path $(step_0, \ldots, step_m)$, and $\mathcal{E}(T'_m)$ the path trace for the path $(step'_0, \ldots, step'_m)$ with $step_i$ and $step'_i$ are the common step. However, the identifier is $\mathcal{E}(v_i)$ for $step_i$ and $\mathcal{E}(v_i)*C \bmod N^2$ for $step'_i$. $\mathcal{A}'$ provides the two traces to $\mathcal{A}$ in the challenge phase.

If in the challenge phase, $\mathcal{A}$ is able to decide if both traces has a common step with an advantage ϵ, then $\mathcal{E}(v_i)$. $C \bmod N^2$ is a valid ciphertext of v_i). Therefore, C is N-residue mod N^2, and $\mathcal{A}'$ breaks DCRA, with advantage of $1/2*\epsilon$, since She is wrong the half of the time because of oracle's coin flip.

Table 5 illustrates the messages exchanged during the challenge game.

Table 5. Step unlinkability challenge game

$\mathcal{O}_{DCRA}$		$\mathcal{A}'$	$\mathcal{A}$
receive N	$\longleftarrow$	send N	
pick C	$\longrightarrow$	receive C	
		compute $\mathcal{E}(T_m)$ and $\mathcal{E}(T'_m)$	$\longrightarrow$ receive $\mathcal{E}(T_m)$ and $\mathcal{E}(T'_m)$
		receive 1 or 0	$\longleftarrow$ check if $\mathcal{E}(T_m)$ and $\mathcal{E}(T'_m)$ have a common step
receive 1 or 0 $\longleftarrow$ if 1 is received, send 1 otherwise send 0			

8   Performance Analysis

This section is allotted to present the analytical performance evaluation of the proposed scheme. First, we evaluate the AND-ACC code reduction performance, then the performances related to the sensor itself. The performance evaluation criteria of the sensor, are the storage cost, the computation cost and the communication cost.

In this paper, a Rabin's public key has a size of 1024 bits. The hash function used is SHA1, which has an output's size of 160 bits. Paillier encryption has an output's size of 2048 bits. For sensor identity, a size of 160 bits is chosen. Rabin's encryption is a single modular square which is considered equivalent to a single modular multiplication in this paper. It requires roughly $100\mu J$ using ATmel128 microprocessor [7] based on the result of Gaubatz et al. [4]. In our scheme, we use TinyRNG [3] to generate random numbers. TinyRNG consumes around $58\mu J$ at each random number generation. Hash function consumes roughly $1\mu J$ [6]. The communication cost are set to $e_s = 0.209\mu J$ and $e_r = 0.226\mu J$ from the characteristics of the CC2420 transceiver used in the Xbows MICA-Z and Telos B sensor nodes [8].

8.1 AND-ACC Reduction Cost

For the sake of simplicity, we consider that our supply chain has only one valid path. Let l be the number of steps in our supply chain. Let (C) consist of all l-bit binary vectors that have only a single 0 bit. For example, when $l = 4$, $(C) = \{1110; 1101; 1011; 0111\}$. It is easy to see when $k \leq l-1$ of these vectors are combined under AND, that this combination is unique. This code has cardinality d, and can produce at most d vectors.

The encrypted path trace $\mathcal{E}(T)$ is valid only if the size of T is less than 1024 bits. Therefore, the trace $T = \sum_{i=0}^{l} v_i x^i$ of the path $\{step_0, ..., step_{l-1}\}$ has to have a size less than 1024 bits. As mentioned in section 5.2, $x \geq l$, thus:

$$T \leq \sum_{i=0}^{l} v_i l^i \leq \sum_{i=0}^{l})l * (l+1)^i \leq (l+1)^{l+1} \leq 2^{1024} \tag{18}$$

The biggest value of l that satisfies (18) is 193. This technique can trace the product in supply chain contains up to 193 steps.

8.2 Storage Cost

The storage cost is computed as the number of bytes that the sensor node has to store. Generally, this storage cost is introduced by the storage of different parameters and keys necessary to the function of our scheme. The proposed privacy preserving product tracking scheme does not require much memory overhead.

- Initialization phase: in this phase, the sensor stores Rabin's public key of size $sizeof(N_R)$, the path trace initialization of size $sizeof(\mathcal{E}(T))$, paillier modular N^2 of size $2 * sizeof(N) = sizeof(\mathcal{E}(T))$ and a sensor ID of size $sizeof(S_{id})$. Therefore, the total storage needed by S at this phase is $2 * sizeof(\mathcal{E}(T))$, $+ sizeof(S_{id}) + sizeof(N_R)$.
- Collection phase: in this phase, S has to generate random number to start the authentication with the actor's system. The generated nonce has a size of $sizeof(N_R)$. Hash value of the generated nonce of size $sizeof(hash)$ has to be stored as well. Therefore, the total storage needed by S at this phase is $sizeof(N_R) + sizeof(hash)$. The update path process does not increase the size of the path trace, thus, no more memory capacity is required.
- Verification phase: in this phase, no storage by the sensor is required.

The total storage cost needed by S in our scheme is:

$$storageCost = 2 * sizeof(\mathcal{E}(T)) + sizeof(S_{id})$$
$$+ 2 * sizeof(N_R) + sizeof(hash) \tag{19}$$

Table 6 illustrates the storage cost for our scheme.

Table 6. Storage cost of SPT scheme

Parameter	value
sizeof(S_{id})	160 bits
sizeof(N_R)	1024 bits
sizeof($hash$)	160 bits
sizeof($\mathcal{E}(T)$)	2048 bits
The storage cost	6378 bits

8.3   Computation Cost

The computation cost can be measured in terms of time, use of CPU or energy dissipation. In fact, these parameters are related and each one can be deduced from the other. For instance, the energy dissipation can be deduced from the time as follows: Energy=Power*Time, where Power represents the CPU power when it is in its active state and Time represents the computing time. In the present analysis, the term cost is used in its general form without specifying the unit. The computation cost of our scheme during each phase can be computed as the sum of the computation cost of the main operations executed during this phase.

- Initialization phase: in this phase, the main operations are performed by M himself. Therefore, no computation required by the sensor S.
- Collection phase: in this phase, S generates a random number $rand$ at each step, which gets encrypted using Rabin scheme. Then, S computes a hash function of $rand$ in order to check the validity of the actor's response. If the validation is succeeded, S updates the path trace by modular multiplying the received step's ID with the current trace. In total, S consumes $cost(rabin)$ + $cost(rand)$ + $c(hash)$ + $cost(modular multiplication)$ for each step.
- Verification phase: in this phase, S has to authenticate the supply chain manager M, which is similar to authenticate a supply chain actor. Therefore, S consumes in this phase, $cost(rabin)$ + $cost(rand)$ + $cost(hash)$.

The total computation cost needed by S in our scheme is:

$$compCost = (cost(rabin) + costrand + costhash) * (l + 1)$$
$$+ cost(modular multiplication) * l \tag{20}$$

Table 7. Computation cost of SPT scheme

Parameter	value
$cost(rabin)$	$100\mu J$
$cost(rand)$	$58\mu J$
$cost(hash)$	$1\mu J$
$cost(modularmultiplication)$	$100\mu J$
The computation cost	$160, 59mJ$ for supply chain with 100 steps

where l is the number of the supply chain steps that the product has visited. Table 7 illustrates the computation cost for our scheme.

8.4 Communication Cost

The main factor of the communication cost is the energy dissipation. The communication cost is computed using the same approach as TKH [16]. Actually, the communication cost in terms of energy dissipation is computed as the size of sent/received messages multiplied by the energy dissipated for the sent/receive of one bit. We denote e_r the energy consumed by S, when it receives one bit, and e_s when S sends one bit.

- Initialization phase: in this phase, S does not send any messages, however, it receives the initialization parameters. Therefore, S consumes (sizeof(N_R)+ sizeof(S_{id})+2*sizeof($\mathcal{E}(T)$)))*e_r.
- Collection phase: in this phase, S sends encrypted rabin value, which has the same size as the Rabin's public key, and it receives a hashed value. Then, S receives the current encrypted step's ID from the actor's site. Therefore, for each step S consumes (sizeof(N_R)*e_s+ (sizeof($hash$) +sizeof($\mathcal{E}(T)$)))* e_r.
- Verification phase: in this phase, S authenticates M, then, sends the path trace to him. Therefore, S consumes (sizeof(N_R)+ sizeof(S_{id}+ sizeof($\mathcal{E}(T)$)))*e_s+ (sizeof($hash$))* e_r

The total communication cost needed by S in our scheme is:

$$\begin{aligned} commCost =&(sizeof(N_R) + sizeof(hash) * (l + 1) \\ &+ sizeof(S_{id}) + sizeof(\mathcal{E}(T)) * (l + 2)) * e_r \qquad (21) \\ &+ (sizeof(N_R) * (l + 1) + sizeof(\mathcal{E}(T))) * e_s \end{aligned}$$

where l is the number of the supply chain actors that interact with the product. Table 8 illustrates the communication cost for our scheme.

It is worth to mention that the storage cost, computation cost, and the communication cost can have a different result depending on the size of the security keys, and the algorithms that M may choose.

Table 8. Communication cost of SPT scheme

Parameter	value
sizeof(S_{id}	160 bits
sizeof(N_R)	1024 bits
sizeof($hash$)	160 bits
sizeof($\mathcal{E}(T)$)	2048 bits
e_r	$0,209\mu J$
e_s	$0.226\mu J$
The communication cost	$12,34mJ$ for supply chain with 100 steps

9   Conclusion

In this paper, we presented a cryptographic protocol to address security and privacy challenges in tracking the goods within supply chain management. Our main idea is to use AND-ACC code as identifiers of the different actors in the supply chain. Then, use a mathematical transformation to convert their AND property to additive property. Finally, an additive homomorphic encryption is used to ensure both the confidentiality of the identities, and the compression in the sensors.

Sensors collect the identities of the visited steps , and update their path traces. This allows supply chain manager to trace back all the steps that a product went through. The security of our protocol against adversaries relies on the semantic security of Paillier and the indistiguishibility property of keyed HMAC. Rabin's scheme used to check the legitimacy of the supply chain actors, however, other techniques can be used such as the one presented by Sorniotti et al. [17].

In our supply chain scenario, we assume that we have a global supply chain manager. There is no notion of multiple managers. However in real world that might not be true. Supply chain can have a quality, security, and recall mangers. Delivering the right information to the right manager is an issue, especially in big scale supply chains. However, this is left to future work.[1]

References

1. Blass, E., Elkhiyaoui, K., Molva, R.: Tracker: security and privacy for RFID-based supply chains. In: 18th Annual Network and Distributed System Security Symposium, NDSS 2011, San Diego, California, USA, February 6-9 (2011) ISBN: 1-891562-32-0
2. Chawla, K., Robins, G., Weimer, W.: On Mitigating Covert Channels in RFID-Enabled Supply Chains. In: RFIDSec Asia, Singapore (2010)

---

[1] Research was partially funded by the German Federal Ministry of Education and Research under the promotional reference 01ISO7009 and by the French Ministry of Research within the RESCUE-IT project. The authors take the responsibility for the content.

3. Francillon, A., Castelluccia, C.: Tinyrng: A cryptographic random number generator for wireless sensors network nodes. In: 5th International Symposium on Modeling and Optimization in Mobile, Ad Hoc and Wireless Networks and Workshops, WiOpt 2007, pp. 1–7. IEEE (2007)

4. Gaubatz, G., Kaps, J.-P., Sunar, B.: Public key cryptography in sensor networks—revisited. In: Castelluccia, C., Hartenstein, H., Paar, C., Westhoff, D. (eds.) ESAS 2004. LNCS, vol. 3313, pp. 2–18. Springer, Heidelberg (2005)

5. Gupta, R., Das, S.R.: Tracking moving targets in a smart sensor network. In: 2003 IEEE 58th Vehicular Technology Conference, VTC 2003-Fall, pp. 3035–3039. IEEE (2003)

6. Hempstead, M., Lyons, M.J., Brooks, D., Wei, G.Y.: Survey of hardware systems for wireless sensor networks. Journal of Low Power Electronics, 11–20 (2008)

7. http://www.atmel.com/Images/doc2467.pdf (last access: June 01, 2012)

8. http://www.xbow.com/ (last access: June 01, 2012)

9. Kerschbaum, F., Deitos, R.J.: Security against the business partner. In: Proceedings of the 2008 ACM Workshop on Secure Web Services, pp. 1–10. ACM (2008)

10. Lee, S.J., Jung, S.H.: A survey of watermarking techniques applied to multimedia. In: Proceedings of the IEEE International Symposium on Industrial Electronics, ISIE 2001, vol. 1, pp. 272–277. IEEE (2001)

11. Ouafi, K., Vaudenay, S.: Pathchecker: An RFID Application for Tracing Products in Supply-Chains. In: International Conference on RFID Security. Citeseer (2009)

12. Paillier, P.: Public-key cryptosystems based on composite degree residuosity classes. In: Stern, J. (ed.) EUROCRYPT 1999. LNCS, vol. 1592, pp. 223–238. Springer, Heidelberg (1999)

13. Pattipati, K.R., Deb, S., Bar-Shalom, Y., Washburn Jr., R.B.: A new relaxation algorithm and passive sensor data association. IEEE Transactions on Automatic Control, 198–213 (1992)

14. Rabin, M.O.: Digitalized signatures and public-key functions as intractable as factorization (1979)

15. ShuiHua, H., Chu, C.H.: Tamper Detection in RFID-Enabled Supply Chains Using Fragile Watermarking. In: 2008 IEEE International Conference on RFID, pp. 111–117. IEEE (2008)

16. Son, J.-H., Lee, J.-S., Seo, S.-W.: Topological key hierarchy for energy-efficient group key management in wireless sensor networks. Wirel. Pers. Commun. 52(2), 359–382 (2010)

17. Sorniotti, A., Molva, R., Gomez, L.: Efficient access control for wireless sensor data. Ad Hoc & Sensor Wireless Networks, 325–336 (2009)

18. TAGSYS. RFID luxury goods solutions (2012)

19. Trappe, W., Wu, M., Wang, Z.J., Liu, K.J.R.: Anti-collusion fingerprinting for multimedia. IEEE Transactions on Signal Processing 51(4), 1069–1087 (2003)

20. VERAYO. Unclonable-RFIDs (2012)

The Bussard-Bagga and Other Distance-Bounding Protocols under Attacks

Aslı Bay, Ioana Boureanu, Aikaterini Mitrokotsa,
Iosif Spulber, and Serge Vaudenay

EPFL, Lausanne, Switzerland
http://lasec.epfl.ch

Abstract. The communication between an honest prover and an honest verifier can be intercepted by a malicious man-in-the-middle (MiM), without the legitimate interlocutors noticing the intrusion. The attacker can simply relay messages from one party to another, eventually impersonating the prover to the verifier and possibly gaining the privileges of the former. This sort of simple relay attacks are prevalent in wireless communications (e.g., RFID-based protocols) and can affect several infrastructures from contactless payments to remote car-locking systems and access-control verification in high-security areas. As the RFID/NFC technology prevails, a practical and increasingly popular countermeasure to these attacks is given by distance-bounding protocols. Yet, the security of these protocols is still not mature. Importantly, the implications of the return channel (i.e., knowing whether the protocol finished successfully or not) in the security of some distance-bounding protocols have not been fully assessed. In this paper, we demonstrate this by a series of theoretical and practical attacks.

We first show that the Bussard-Bagga protocol DBPK-Log does not fulfill its goal: *it offers no protection against distance fraud and terrorist fraud*. Then, we show how to mount several concrete MiM attacks against several follow-up variants, including the protocol by Reid et al.

1 Introduction

Relay attacks are man-in-the-middle (MiM) attacks that enable an adversary to impersonate a prover to a verifier by acting as a carrier for their legitimate messages. *Distance-bounding* (DB) protocols are lightweight authentication protocols considered as a main countermeasure against relay attacks. As their name suggests, distance-bounding protocols enable a verifier to establish an *upper bound* on the physical distance to an un-authenticated prover. This is achieved by measuring the round trip time-of-flights during several challenge-response bit-exchanges. Such DB protocols were first introduced in 1993 by Brands and Chaum [7] in order to preclude MiM attacks against ATMs, whilst the idea of measuring times-of-flight to protect against MiM goes back to Beth and Desmedt [4]. A broad range of distance-bounding protocols followed, being proposed for RFID communications [21, 24, 25, 30, 33, 39], ultra-wideband (UWB) devices [18, 26, 27], wireless ad-hoc networks [11, 14, 38], sensor networks [29], etc.

M. Kutyłowski and M. Yung (Eds.): Inscrypt 2012, LNCS 7763, pp. 371–391, 2013.
© Springer-Verlag Berlin Heidelberg 2013

The importance of distance-bounding protocols in preventing relay attacks can be easily assessed if we simply look at nowadays ubiquitous applications such as access-control to high-security areas and contactless payments. Indeed, relay attacks have also been launched against bankcards [16] and the demonstrated countermeasure against this type of attacks was again based on an implementation of a distance-bounding protocol [16]. Another aspect to consider is that of car manufacturers, who are now using RFID protocols to lock/unlock cars remotely, even if these protocols are themselves susceptible to relay attacks [17]. Thus, there is a stringent need for secure distance-bounding protocols in order to safeguard the growingly spread use of, e.g., RFID-based security-sensitive protocols.

Some MiM attacks also assume that the adversary has access to a side channel showing whether the protocol completed successfully or not. In the case of, e.g., car-locking systems, this would just consist in looking at whether the car opens. We call this the *return channel*. In the RFID community, it was not immediate to realize that the return channel strongly influences the security of the protocols therein invoked. For instance, the HB+ protocol [23] was proposed to resist MiM attacks, but—as soon as the adversary is given access to the return channel [19]— the protocol was found in fact vulnerable to MiM attacks. In the formalism by Vaudenay [40], adversaries with *no* access to the return channel are called *narrow adversaries*. Again, addressing *non-narrow adversaries* in RFID proved challenging. In this paper, we show how non-narrow adversaries can successfully mount a series of attacks on several DB protocols.

Distance-bounding protocols should resist to *distance fraud*. I.e., a malicious prover who is far away from a verifier should not succeed to pass the protocol. Another well established threat model against distance-bounding is the so-called notion of *terrorist fraud* [15]. In this model, a malicious prover who is far away from a verifier tries to mount a distance fraud with the help of an adversary, but without giving him any credential or an advantage that he may later abuse. To defeat terrorist fraud, Bussard and Bagga [8–10] proposed a protocol in which passing the distance-bounding phase would require the knowledge of a key. Many follow-up protocols were inspired from [8–10].

Contribution & Structure. In this paper, we first look at the Bussard-Bagga DBPK-Log protocols [8–10]. We show that its main goals, namely, resistance to distance fraud and terrorist fraud, are not fulfilled. Then, we consider variants and successors. We provide a non-narrow MiM adversary who tries to learn the credential (i.e., the distance-bounding secret key) from an honest prover. This will enable the MiM to impersonate the prover during the distance-bounding phase at a later stage. Consequently, a distance-bounding protocol susceptible to these attacks would not be compliant with its very *raison d'être*. Namely, we show concrete forms of this MiM attack mounted onto variants/successors of the Bussard-Bagga protocols [9, 10] e.g., instances of the Reid *et al.* protocol [34]. Whilst the main pattern of the attacks follows a simple idea [25] and our extension on it, these frauds become possible via pretty intricate statistical and general theoretical analyses that we detail herein.

This paper is organized as follows. In Section 2, we remind the structure of numerous [34, 39] distance-bounding protocols, and we explain the idea behind a basic MiM attack-scenario [25] that can be launched against this family of distance-bounding protocols. We conclude this section by showing how to extend this simple attack, potentially rendering it more dangerous. In Section 4, we describe several MiM attacks, concrete instantiations of the scenario presented in Section 2. In Section 3 we describe the Bussard and Bagga [8–10] or the so-called DBPK-Log (distance-bounding proof of knowledge based on the discrete logarithm) protocols. We mount a distance fraud and a terrorist fraud against DBPK-Log and motivate to consider variants and successors of DBPK. In Section 4 we consider several proposed encryption functions to be used inside the DBPK distance-bounding protocols and variants, and we expose their failures. In Section 4.4, we present the implementation and evolution of the most elaborate of these attacks, mounted onto the most involved successor of the DBPK distance-bounding protocol proposed in [8,9]. In Section 5, we briefly discuss about the possible fixes to the DB protocols exposed to our kind of threat. Finally, Section 6 concludes the paper.

2   Distance-Bounding and MiM Attacks

We first describe a family of distance-bounding protocols [34,39] that use similar methods to generate the responses to be employed in the challenge/response phase. Figure 1 depicts a general view of this family of protocols.

More precisely, in all the protocols that belong in this family, the following steps are executed.

- **Initialization Phase:** Let the prover P and the verifier V share a secret key x. This initialization phase is not time critical and is executed as follows. The verifier V chooses a random number N_V and transmits it to the prover P. After receiving N_V, the prover P also chooses a random number N_P and computes a session key a such that $a = f_x(C, N_V, N_P)$, where f denotes a pseudorandom function (PRF) and C represents any additional parameters that may be required, e.g., the identifiers of the prover P and the verifier V. We should note here that the computation of the session key a varies. In particular, in the protocol in [39] the session key a depends on both random nonces N_V and N_P.

- **Distance-Bounding Phase:** This time-sensitive phase starts right after the initialization phase and involves the exchange of challenges-responses at maximum bit-rate over a period of time. It is repeated m times (rounds), with i varying from 1 to m. The actual number of rounds m is normally dictated by a security parameter. At each round i, the challenge-response delay Δt_i is measured. V starts by choosing a random bit c_i, initializing the clock with zero and transmitting c_i to P. The values received by P are denoted by c_i. Next, P answers by sending

$$r_i := \begin{cases} a_i, & if \ c_i = 0, \\ a_i \oplus x_i, & if \ c_i = 1. \end{cases}$$

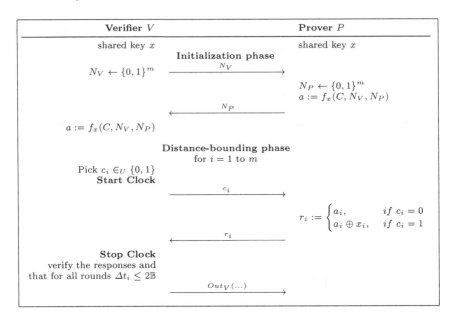

Fig. 1. The General Structure of Numerous Distance-Bounding Protocols (present in [34, 39])

Assuming noiseless communication, we can denote the values received by V also by r_i. Upon receiving r_i, V stops the clock and stores the received answer and the delay time Δt_i.

After the end of the distance-bounding phase, a final *verification* phase is performed. The verifier V checks the correctness of the received responses and if the response-times Δt_i are bellow the maximum allowed response-time $2\mathbb{B}$. At the end of this phase the verifier V indicates if the prover P is authenticated or not ($Out_V = 1$ or $Out_V = 0$, respectively).

On noisy/noiseless channels. On the one hand, some of the DB provers used in distance-bounding are cheap and, whilst having time constraints also, do not usually cater for error correction. On the other hand, adversaries can be equipped with powerful devices which are less error-prone and/or are also able to correct all the errors/noise of the channels. For simplicity, we will mainly consider noiseless channels in our MiM attacks to follow. However, we note here that noise can be considered easily [21]. I.e., we can augment the model, requiring that the verifier allows at most $m - \tau$ incorrect answers (answers with errors or delayed). Consider the probability p of one response being correct (non-erroneous and not delayed). Then, the probability that at least τ responses out of m are of the correct kind is given by

$$B(m, \tau, p) = \sum_{i=\tau}^{m} \binom{m}{i} p^i (1-p)^{m-i}.$$

This could then be easily factored into the success probability of our attacks.

On (the feasibility of) MiM attacks. The MiM attacks to be described in here are mounted along the following intuitive pattern. In a *learning phase*, the MiM adversary $\mathcal{A}$ can "play" with a prover P, which could be close to V, and "play" with a verifier V. The subsequent *attack phase* allows interaction several times with a far-away prover and one time with the verifier.

We should note here that if the legitimate prover is located far-away from the legitimate verifier then the MiM attack can be easily deployed. But, we believe that MiM attacks with a prover and his neighboring verifier are also easy to mount when the adversary can initiate protocols with both of them, using a different channel with each. For instance, an attacker could interfere with the initial frequency-synchronization phase so that each of the participants (prover and verifier) would end up communicating with the adversary through two different channels (i.e., frequency bands). Then, the prover does not even realize that another concurrent conversation is taking place (as such a prover and the verifier cannot confer, i.e., two users cannot communicate with each other as long as they "occupy" different frequency bands).

Non-Narrow MiM Attack by Flipping One Challenge [25]: A Case in Point for DB Insecurity. Linear, active MiM attacks can be launched against any protocol from the family in Figure 1. The generic sketch of these attacks was briefly described[1] in [25] against [39]. In this attack, a powerful, non-narrow adversary $\mathcal{A}$ acts as an active MiM during the distance-bounding phase. We consider a scenario where a legitimate verifier and a prover run successfully the initialization phase of the distance-bounding protocol and both of them compute the session key a (see Figure 1). We further assume that the prover and the verifier are close to each other. During the distance-bounding phase, the adversary injects a modified version c'_j of a challenge c_j (for some fixed $j \in \{1, \ldots, n\}$). Let r'_i be the response that the attacker sends to V for c_i and r_i be the response that the prover sends to $\mathcal{A}$. In fact, the attacker will act such that $r'_i = r_i$ for $i \neq j$ and will let r'_j be a random bit. In noiseless condition, it is the case that by looking at the output of the verifier and knowing what choice he made for r'_j, this non-narrow attacker can make a simple calculation to find the jth bit of the key x, i.e., :

$$x_j = r'_j \oplus r_j \oplus \overline{Out_V}$$

By repeating this strategy for $j = 1, \ldots, m$, the adversary is able to deduce all the bits of the secret key x. In noiseless conditions, the success probability of the attack is 1.

We now extend this attack in [25] to flipping more than one challenge in one distance-bounding session. We will use both flavors of this scenario in what follows.

---

[1] And, to this end, the *Swiss-Knife* protocol [25] was designed to defeat this attack by introducing a MAC in the protocol exchanges.

An Extended Variant of Non-Narrow MiM Attacks: Flipping a Batch of Challenges. As a variant of this attack, the attacker can select a "small size" batch of challenges, i.e., $J \subseteq \{1, \ldots, m\}$, and do $c'_j = \bar{c}_j$ for all $j \in J$ and $c'_i = c_i$ for all $i \notin J$. Let the responses r'_js by the attacker for all $j \in J$ be as he pleases and let $r'_i = r_i$ for all $i \notin J$. If $Out_V = 1$, the attacker deduces $x_j = r_j \oplus r'_j$, for all $j \in J$. This happens with probability $2^{-|J|}$ in a single protocol version, but may allow the finding of a batch of the bits of the key at once.

3   The Bussard-Bagga Protocols and Terrorist Fraud

3.1   The Bussard-Bagga Protocols

Bussard and Bagga have proposed in [8–10] a distance-bounding protocol relying on public key cryptography, e.g., commitments and proofs of knowledge. It is also called DBPK (distance-bounding proof of knowledge). The protocol uses a proof of knowledge in order to protect against terrorist frauds.

In the generic DBPK protocol, the prover P has a secret key x and a published certificate on its public key $y = \Gamma(x)$. The protocol is composed of four phases: the *initialization* phase, the *distance-bounding* phase, the phase for the *opening of commitments* therein used, and the *proof of knowledge* phase.

– **Initialization Phase:** In the initialization phase, the prover generates a random secret session key $k \in_R \{0,1\}^m$ and uses this session key in order to encrypt his private key x. The encryption of x is done using a publicly known symmetric key encryption method $\mathcal{E} : \{0,1\}^m \times \{0,1\}^m \to \{0,1\}^m$. Thus, we have $e = \mathcal{E}_k(x)$. Of course, the knowledge of both e and k reveals the private key x, i.e., $x = \mathcal{D}_k(e)$, where $\mathcal{D}_k$ is the decryption function inverting, under k, the encryption $\mathcal{E}_k$. After encrypting x and computing e, the prover P uses a secure bit commitment scheme to commit to each bit of k and e using randomnesses v and v' respectively. More precisely, if we let i be a bit-index ($i \in 1, \ldots, m$), then the commitments to the ith bit of the session key k and of the key e are respectively denoted as

$$z_{k,i} = commit(k_i, v_i) \text{ and } z_{e,i} = commit(e_i, v'_i).$$

– **Distance-Bounding Phase:** In the distance-bounding phase, a number of m single-bit challenge-response exchanges take place at maximum bit rate. At each round i, the challenge-response delay Δt_i is measured. The verifier V selects a random bit as the challenge c_i and the prover responds with a response r_i such that

$$r_i := \begin{cases} k_i, & if \ c_i = 0, \\ e_i, & if \ c_i = 1. \end{cases}$$

– **Commitments' Opening Phase:** In this phase, the prover P opens some commitments on the bits of k and e corresponding to his answers in the distance-bounding phase. I.e., to vouch for his DB responses, the prover

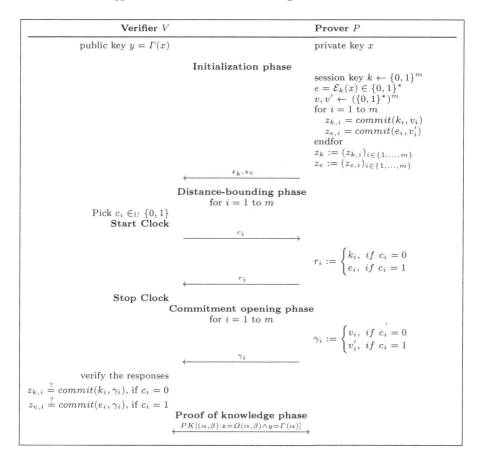

Fig. 2. The DBPK Protocol proposed by Bussard and Bagga [8–10]

sends the randomness v_i to open $z_{k,i}$ if challenge i was 0, and he sends v'_i otherwise. This is denoted in Figure 2 through sending the value γ_i. In case that the openings of $z_{k,i}$ and $z_{e,i}$ do not pass, the verifier V sends an error notification message to the prover P.

– **Proof of Knowledge Phase:** In this phase, the prover P convinces the verifier V with a zero-knowledge interaction that he has generated the commitments which correspond to a unique private key x and this private key corresponds to the public key y that is used by the verifier to authenticate the prover. The proof of knowledge is denoted as

$$PK[(\alpha, \beta) : z = \Omega(\alpha, \beta) \wedge y = \Gamma(\alpha)],$$

where the knowledge of α, β is being proven, while z, y are as per the protocol, known to the verifier. In the protocol, we have $y = \Gamma(x)$ and $z = \Omega(x, (v, v'))$. The value of z can be computed from the $z_{k,i}$ and $z_{e,i}$.

The number m of DB rounds and the size m of the key is dictated by a security parameter. Typically, m varies between 128 and 1024.

3.2   Commitments and the Proof of Knowledge in DBPK-Log

The only instances of DBPK providing concrete commitments and proofs of knowledge are based on the discrete logarithm in $\mathbf{Z}_p^*$ and are called DBPK-Log. We now describe these commitments and proofs of knowledge.

We use a strong prime p, two generators g, h of $\mathbf{Z}_p^*$, an element x of $\mathbf{Z}_{p-1}^*$, and $y = g^x \bmod p$.[2]

We have $commit(b, v) = g^b h^v \bmod p$. The main property of this commitment is that given all $z_{k,i}$, $z_{e,i}$, v_i, v_i', we can form $z = \prod_i (z_{k,i} z_{e,i})^{2^{i-1}}$, $v = \sum_i (v_i + v_i')2^{i-1}$, and obtain that

$$z = commit((k + e) \bmod (p - 1), v).$$

The proposed encryption methods use $e = (ux - k) \bmod (p - 1)$ with either $u = 1$ [10] or u random and publicly revealed [8,9]. So, the proof of knowledge consists of proving knowledge of x and v such that $y = g^x$ and $z = g^{ux} h^v$ in $\mathbf{Z}_p$.

The proof of knowledge [9] is repeating t times what follows: the prover sends $w_1 = g^{u\rho_1} h^{\rho_2} \bmod p$ for some random $\rho_1, \rho_2 \in \mathbf{Z}_{p-1}$; the verifier sends some challenge $c \in \{0, 1\}$; the prover responds by $s_1 = \rho_1 - cx \bmod (p - 1)$ and $x_2 = \rho_2 - cv \bmod (p - 1)$; the verifier checks $w_1 = z^c g^{us_1} h^{s_2} \bmod p$ and $w_2 = y^c g^{s_1} \bmod p$.

3.3   Terrorist Fraud and Distance Fraud against DBPK-Log

We now show that the public-key techniques which are used in the DBPK-Log protocol are ineffective to defeat terrorist fraud. For this, we consider a malicious prover who is far away from an honest verifier. There is an adversary close to the verifier who will get some help from the prover to pass the protocol without getting any advantage to further impersonate the prover. The attack is sketched in Fig. 3.

First, the malicious prover selects u and $v \in \mathbf{Z}_{p-1}$ (with either $u = 1$ or a random u, as specified in DBPK-Log), then computes $z = g^{ux} h^v \bmod p$ and sends z to the adversary. The adversary selects some random k_i, e_i, v_i, v_i', $i = 1, \ldots, m$, and a random bit c_1. Then, he computes $z_{k,i} = commit(k_i, v_i)$ and $z_{e,i} = commit(e_i, v_i')$ for $i = 2, \ldots, m$. If $c_1 = 0$, he sets $z_{k,1} = commit(k_1, v_1)$ and $z_{e,1}$ remains free. If $c_1 = 1$, he sets $z_{e,1} = commit(e_1, v_1')$ and $z_{k,1}$ remains free. Then, he can solve the equation $z = \prod_i (z_{k,i} z_{e,i})^{2^{i-1}} \bmod p$ in the remaining free variable. Next, the adversary runs the DBPK-Log initialization phase, distance-bounding phase, and opening phase using these values. Note that if the value of the challenge c_1 received from the verifier differs from the value of the

---

[2] In [8–10], h is not necessarily a generator and $x \in \mathbf{Z}_{p-1} \setminus \{q\}$ with $q = \frac{p-1}{2}$.

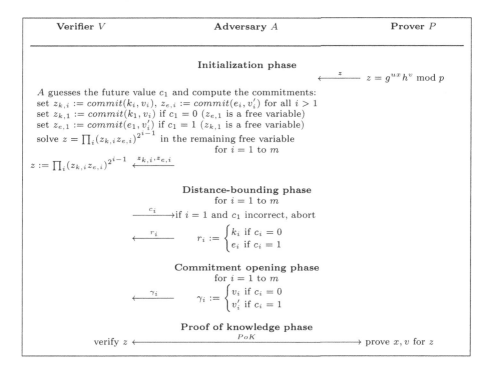

Fig. 3. Terrorist Fraud against DBPK-Log

bit c_1 which were selected, the attack aborts.[3] Otherwise, it is straightforward to see that the adversary can answer all challenges and open all commitments. Then, the verifier will compute z which matches the one selected by the malicious prover. Finally, the adversary relays the proof of knowledge for x and v (such that $z = g^{ux}h^v \bmod p$).

Clearly, this attack succeeds with probability $\frac{1}{2}$ (or even 1 if the verifier allows an error in the first round). It is also clear that since the proof-of-knowledge is zero-knowledge and that x is not used anywhere else, that the adversary learns no information about x. So, it is a valid terrorist fraud.

Distance Fraud. In distance-fraud settings, the malicious prover could simulate the adversary in the above attack and select $k_i = e_i$, $i = 2, \ldots, m$. This way, the prover could answer to c_i by $r_i = k_i = e_i$ before receiving the challenge c_i and therefore making the correct response to arrive on time to the verifier.

Equivalently, a malicious prover could just simulate the honest prover selecting $k \approx \frac{x}{2}$ and $u = 1$ and answering to the challenges by anticipation. Concretely, if x is even, the malicious prover can select $k = e = \frac{x}{2}$ and $u = 1$ and we have $r_i = k_i = e_i$ for every i. If x is odd, he could select $k = \frac{x-1}{2}$, $e = \frac{x+1}{2}$, and

---

[3] The attack could also go on with the adversary taking c_1 as the value he selected, and counting on that the verifier will accept this error as due to noise.

$u = 1$ so that $r_i = k_i = e_i$ for $i \geq 2$. The $i = 1$ case can be counted in the error tolerance.

4 Non-narrow MiM Attacks against DBENC

We now consider the protocol by Reid *et al.* [34] which is a variant of DBPK no longer based on public-key cryptography. Indeed, the prover and the verifier now share the secret x. In addition to this, k and e are derived from PRF computations (done at both sides) based on x and some nonces. (See Fig. 4.) This protocol, that we call DBENC, has no longer any commitment or proof of knowledge phase.

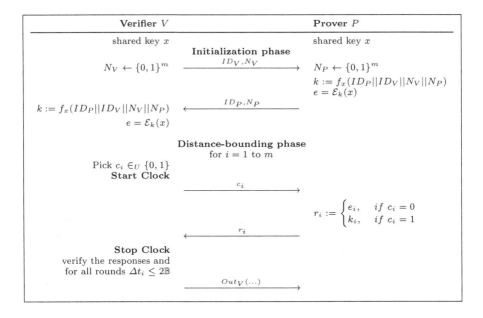

Fig. 4. Protocol proposed by Reid *et al.* [34]

Clearly, the attack scenario in Section 2 lends itself to concrete attacks against the DBENC protocol. First consider that a non-narrow MiM adversary specializes in the batch-version of the attack on the DB phase. Namely, let first $|J| \geq 2$. This attacker selects indexes $J \subseteq \{1, \ldots, m\}$ for flipped challenges. Then, for this protocol, with probability $2^{-|J|}$, he obtains the following: 1. the bits e_j and k_j, for all $j \in J$; 2. either the bit e_i or the bit k_i, when $j \notin J$. Secondly, for the case that $|J| = 1$, the success probability of the attacker is 1, as per Section 2. In any case, depending the encryption algorithm, this can help in recovering some piece of information about x.

The designers of DBPK and DBENC suggest [8–10, 34] several possible encryption methods ($\mathcal{E}$) to be used therein. In the next subsections, we consider them in a case-by-case fashion (see Sections 4.1, 4.2, 4.3), showing the concrete MiM attack that would break the corresponding instance of the DBENC protocol. In DBPK-Log, the encryption is based on the modulo $p - 1$ arithmetic. We fully describe attacks in these cases (Sections 4.2 and 4.3).

4.1   MiM Attack on the "One-Time-Pad DBENC"

We consider here that $\mathcal{E}_k(x) = x \oplus k$ is to be used as the encryption inside the DBENC protocol, with $x \in \{0, 1\}^m$ and $k \in_U \{0, 1\}^m$. We denote it simply by $e = x \oplus k$. Of course, for any bit position $i \in \{1, \ldots, m\}$, we then have $e_i = x_i \oplus k_i$. Hence, the attack-schema in Section 2, recovers $x_j = e_j \oplus k_j$ (for $j \in J$) by using a single session with a flipped challenge c_j. By iterating at most m times (in the single-flip case), he fully recovers x.

Reid *et al.* [34] suggested to use a "semantically secure encryption function" and proposed one-time pad: $\mathcal{E}_k(x) = x \oplus k$. Clearly, instances of DBENC based on one-time pad fall under the attack in Section 2.

4.2   MiM Attack on the "Addition Modulo n DBENC"

We consider here that $\mathcal{E}_k(x) = x - k \bmod n$ is to be used as the encryption inside the DBENC protocol, with $x \in \mathbf{Z}_n$, $k \in_U \mathbf{Z}_n$, and some fixed n of m bits.[4] We denote this encryption simply by $e = x - k \bmod n$. Clearly, we have

$$e = x - k + cn, \tag{1}$$

where $c = 1_{k>x}$. For $e_1 = \mathsf{lsb}(e)$, we have

$$e_1 = \begin{cases} x_1 \oplus k_1, & if \ x \geq k, \\ x_1 \oplus k_1 \oplus n_1, & if \ x < k. \end{cases}$$

This can be written as $e_1 = x_1 \oplus k_1 \oplus c \times n_1$.

The actual tactics of the attack will be separated into subcases, upon the characteristic of n, e.g., considering whether n is odd or even. Some of these sub-cases contain cross-references to one another.

The n even case.
• **The subcase where $n = 2^m$.** For $n = 2^m$, of course, $n_1 = 0$. Then, based on (1), we reduce to $e_1 = x_1 \oplus k_1$. Hence, our attacker recovers $x_1 = e_1 \oplus k_1$ by using a single session. Then, once he learned x_1, he can recover x_2 by employing the fact that $e_2 = x_2 \oplus k_2 \oplus \bar{x}_1 k_1$. To see this, first note that if the query to the prover reveals e_1, the adversary can infer $k_1 = e_1 \oplus x_1$. Otherwise, the query reveals k_1 anyway. Hence, we can take for granted that k_1 is known to the attacker.

---

[4] In [10], it is proposed for DBPK-Log with $n = p - 1$ and a strong prime p.

Since a second iteration of our attack recovers e_2 and k_2, he can clearly deduce $x_2 = e_2 \oplus k_2 \oplus \bar{x}_1 k_1$. He can continue further to uncover all bits of x using m iterations.

• **The subcase where** $n = 2^{m'} n'$ **with** n' **odd.** Let $n = 2^{m'} n'$ with n' odd. Again, we are in the case where $e = (x - k) \bmod 2^{m'} n'$. So, we have $e \equiv x - k \pmod{2^{m'}}$. Thus, using the previous attack, the attacker can first recover $x_1, \ldots, x_{m'}$ using m' iterations. Then, he will have to employ the attack-scenario for the case for a modulus which is odd, here for n'; this case is stated below. Combining the two results will give the attacker the bits $x_1, \ldots, x_{m'}$ of x.

The n odd case.
• **Calculating the least significant bit in the** n **odd case.** For n odd, we have $n_1 = 1$. Then, based on (1), we have $e_1 = x_1 \oplus k_1 \oplus c$ where $c = 1_{k > x}$. Let $p = \mathbb{P}[c = 1]$, then it holds that

$$p = \mathbb{P}[c = 1] = \mathbb{P}[k > x] = 1 - \frac{(x + 1)}{n}.$$

Hence, when x is far from $n/2$, c is strongly biased. On the one hand, if $x > n/2$, most of c's are 0, so x_1 is the majority of the obtained $e_1 \oplus k_1$. On the other hand, if $x < n/2$, x_1 is the complement of the majority of the obtained $e_1 \oplus k_1$.

Assuming that the adversary first guesses whether $x > n/2$, then he deduces x_1 by mounting a statistical attack. In more detail, assume that the adversary tries N sessions, i.e.,:

$$\mathsf{Bit}_i = e_1 \oplus k_1 = x_1 \oplus c_i, \ \forall i \in \{1, \ldots, N\},$$

where c_i depends on the session i since k is refreshed in every session. The adversary uses a majority function to find x_1 such as

$$\mathsf{Majority}(\mathsf{Bit}_1, \ldots, \mathsf{Bit}_N) \approx \begin{cases} x_1, & if \ x > \frac{n}{2}, \\ x_1 \oplus 1, & if \ x < \frac{n}{2}. \end{cases}$$

More precisely, $\mathbb{P}[\mathsf{Bit}_i = x_1 \oplus 1_{x < n/2}] = 1/2 + |p - 1/2|$. Thus, thanks to the Chernoff bound (*Lemma 2*, in the Appendix),

$$\mathbb{P}\left[\mathsf{Majority}(\mathsf{Bit}_1, \ldots, \mathsf{Bit}_N) = x_1 \oplus 1_{x < n/2}\right] \geq 1 - e^{-2N(p - 1/2)^2}.$$

We can just take $N \approx (1/2 - (x + 1)/n)^{-2}$ to deduce x_1 by the guess $1_{x < n/2}$.

• **Calculating the** i**-th least significant bit in the** n **odd case.** Assuming that $x_1, \ldots, x_{i-1}$ have been recovered (possibly from a guess on the sign of $x - n/2$), similarly as before, the queries to the prover leak $k_1, \ldots, k_{i-1}$. Thus, based on (1), we have

$$e_i = x_i \oplus k_i \oplus B(c, k_1, \ldots, k_{i-1}, x_1, \ldots, x_{i-1}) , \tag{2}$$

where $c = 1_{k>x}$ and B is a Boolean function computing the carry on the ith bit in $x - k + cn$. To express the dependence of B on the overall value of c, we write

$$B(c, k_1, \ldots, k_{i-1}, x_1, \ldots, x_{i-1}) =$$
$$c\alpha(k_1, \ldots, k_{i-1}, x_1, \ldots, x_{i-1}) \oplus \beta(k_1, \ldots, k_{i-1}, x_1, \ldots, x_{i-1}).$$

There are many cases where $\alpha(k_1, \ldots, k_{i-1}, x_1, \ldots, x_{i-1}) = 0$ (i.e., B does not depend on c and can be computed by the attacker using just the information on the bits 0 to $i - 1$ of the known parts). So, by Equation (2), the attacker can recover x_i in one session. There are rare cases in which we have $\alpha(k_1, \ldots, k_{i-1}, x_1, \ldots, x_{i-1}) = 1$, whatever $k_1, \ldots, k_{i-1}$. Such a case is given by $i = 0$, as shown in the last paragraph. So, in these corner cases, a statistical attack is needed in order to recover x_i.

• **Calculating several most significant bits and the least significant one bit in the n odd case.** Going back to the attack on the least significant bit, we realize that the statistics on the estimate of $\mathbb{P}[c = 1] = \mathbb{P}[k > x]$ reveals several most significant bits of x.

Let $B = (1/N)\sum_{i=1}^{N} \text{Bit}_i$, the average of Bit_i's. Note that $\mathbb{E}[\text{Bit}_i] = \mathbb{E}[c_i]$ or $\mathbb{E}[\text{Bit}_i] = 1 - \mathbb{E}[c_i]$. Hence, we get either $\mathbb{E}[B] = \mathbb{E}[c_i] = 1 - (x + 1)/n$ or $\mathbb{E}[B] = 1 - \mathbb{E}[c_i] = (x + 1)/n$. It holds that

$$\left| \frac{1}{2} - \mathbb{E}[B] \right| = \left| \frac{(x + 1)}{n} - \frac{1}{2} \right| \tag{3}$$

and we can recover the ℓ most significant bits of x by using Hoeffding's Bound (*Lemma 1*, in the Appendix), i.e., $\mathbb{P}\left[|B - \mathbb{E}[B]| \leq \varepsilon\right] > 1 - 2e^{-2N\varepsilon^2}$. To recover the ℓ most significant bits, we set $\varepsilon = 2^{-\ell}$ and $N = 2^{2\ell}$. Notice that this attack is similar to the statistical attack described before, hence, the attacker can get x_1, as well.

• **Calculating the least significant bit in the n odd case, revisited.** Assuming that the adversary guesses the most significant bit x_m of x, then he pays attention to (x_m, c_m, r_m). In many cases, c can be deduced non-ambiguously from this. For instance, if $c_m = 0$ (so $r_m = k_m$) and $x_m \neq r_m$, then $c = k_m$ for sure. In the case where $x_m = 0$, if $c_m = 1$ (so $r_m = e_m$) and $r_m = 1$, then $c = 1$ for sure. If c cannot be deduced, the adversary waits for another session. Hence, with $J = \{1\}$, he directly deduces

$$x_1 = e_1 \oplus k_1 \oplus c.$$

He can proceed to recover all other bits by ruling out sessions in which c cannot be deduced. This way, he can always compute c and deduce

$$x_i = e_i \oplus k_i \oplus B(c, k_1, \ldots, k_{i-1}, x_1, \ldots, x_{i-1}).$$

This can be used as follows to recover all bits based on the guess of x_m: assuming $x_m, x_1, \ldots, x_{j-1}$ are known, the attack with $J = \{j\}$ will reveal the response to either k_i or e_i for $i = 1, \ldots, j-1$ (while x_i is known), and the response to both k_j and e_j. So, for each $i \leq j$ we know two out of the three values x_i, k_i, e_i. The above relation allows to compute the third one iteratively for each $i \leq j$, so deduce x_j. The expected number of sessions to recover all bits is here less than $4m$. Indeed, the key has length m and the probability of deducing c is larger than the probability that $c_0 = 0$ and $x_m \neq k_m$, which is $1/4$.

4.3   MiM Attack on the "Modular Addition with Random Factor DBENC"

We consider here $\mathcal{E}_k(x) = (u, ux - k \bmod n)$ with $x \in \mathbf{Z}_n$, $k \in_U \mathbf{Z}_n$, $u \in_U \mathbf{Z}_n^*$ freshly selected for each encryption, and some number prime n of m bits.[5] We denote $e = ux - k \bmod n$.

We have

$$e = (ux \bmod n) - k + cn,$$

where $c = 1_{k > ux \bmod n}$.

By looking at the least significant bit (i.e., $J = \{1\}$), we note that

$$\mathsf{lsb}(ux \bmod n) = e_1 \oplus k_1 \oplus c.$$

For simplicity reasons, we assume that $x \in \mathbf{Z}_n^*$. Therefore, $(ux \bmod n) \in_U \mathbf{Z}_n^*$. In sessions where k_m and k_{m-1} are revealed and happen to be both 1 (i.e., $c_m = c_{m-1} = 0$ and $r_m = r_{m-1} = 1$), the probability that $c = 1$ is

$$\mathbb{E}\left[\left.\frac{k-1}{n-1}\right| k \geq 2^{m-1} + 2^{m-2}\right] \geq \frac{3}{4}.$$

Hence, we can rule out other sessions (we need 16 sessions to have one unruled), and consider that c is a biased bit with $\mathbb{P}[c = 1] \geq 3/4$.

Next, by writing $u = 2u' \bmod n$, we observe that

$$\mathsf{lsb}(ux \bmod n) = \mathsf{lsb}\left(2(u'x \bmod n) - n 1_{u'x \bmod n \geq \frac{n}{2}}\right) = 1_{u'x \bmod n \geq \frac{n}{2}}.$$

The function $1_{u'x \bmod n \geq \frac{n}{2}}$ is sometimes called the most significant bit of $u'x \bmod n$ in the literature, although it is not always the most significant bit in the binary representation. For this reason, we write it $M_1(u'x \bmod n)$. Hence, our attack recovers some $(u', M_1(u'x \bmod n) \oplus c)$ pairs. The problem of finding x is then called the *Hidden Number with Noise Problem (HNNP)* [5].

More generally, we have $\mathsf{lsb}_\ell(ux \bmod n) = e + k - cn \bmod 2^\ell$. By setting $J = \{1, \ldots, \ell\}$, we recover $\mathsf{lsb}_\ell(ux \bmod n)$ with probability $2^{-\ell}$. We filter sessions for which $k_m, \ldots, k_{m-\ell'+1}$ are revealed and are all 1 so that $\mathbb{P}[c = 1] \geq 1 - 2^{-\ell'}$. We need $2^{\ell + 2\ell'}$ sessions to get one sample. We have that

$$\mathsf{lsb}_\ell(ux \bmod n) = \mathsf{lsb}_\ell\left(2^\ell(u'x \bmod n) - n\left\lfloor\frac{u'x \bmod n}{n/2^\ell}\right\rfloor\right), \text{ for } u = 2^\ell u' \bmod n.$$

This is an one-to-one mapping of $M_\ell(u'x \bmod n) = \left\lfloor\frac{u'x \bmod n}{n/2^\ell}\right\rfloor$.

---

[5] In [9], the value $u = 0$ is authorized. However, since it does not make decryption possible, we omit it in this section. Our results are not affected by this choice.

The *Hidden Number Problem (HNP)* was introduced by Boneh and Venkatesan [5] to prove the hardness of the most significant bits of the secret keys in Diffie-Hellman schemes. In HNP, for a given prime n and a given generator g of $\mathbf{Z}_n^*$, the aim is to find a hidden number $\alpha \in \mathbf{Z}_n^*$ by querying an oracle which has access to a function $L_{n,\ell,\alpha}$ such that

$$L_{n,\ell,\alpha}(x) \triangleq M_\ell(\alpha \times g^x \bmod n).$$

This leads to two versions of the problem called *randomized* or *sampling* HNP. In our case, x is chosen uniformly and independently at random in $\mathbf{Z}_n^*$. Boneh-Venkatesan [5] solved this problem by providing an algorithm which works for any $\ell \geq \varepsilon\sqrt{\log n}$ in running time polynomial in $\log n$ for all $\epsilon > 0$. Hence, it can work in practice with a very low ℓ. It also works with noise provided that $2^{\ell'} \geq \log n$.

It requires D samples to recover x according to [32] (where, in [5], D is equal to $2\sqrt{\log n}$). The complexity is $n^{\mathcal{O}(1/\log\log n)}$ for $\ell = \log\log n$ (or even $\ell = 2$ but with an oracle to find the L_∞-closest vector in a lattice). Therefore, we have a practical attack (even though not polynomial) using $2^{2\ell'} \times 2^\ell \times D$ sessions.

The attack runs as follows:

1: **for** each session **do**
2:    **if** it leaks $k_m, \ldots, k_{m-\ell'+1}$, and all bits are 1 **then**
3:       **if** the attack with $J = \{1, \ldots, \ell\}$ reveals $\mathsf{lsb}_\ell(e)$ and $\mathsf{lsb}_\ell(k)$ **then**
4:          deduce u' and $M_\ell(u'x \bmod n)$ (except with probability $\leq 2^{-\ell'}$)
5:          stop when D such pairs are deduced
6:       **end if**
7:    **end if**
8: **end for**.

With the D pairs, run the hidden problem solver algorithm.

The HPN solving algorithm works roughly as follows. Given u'_i and $v_i = M_\ell(u'_i x \bmod n)$ for $i = 1, \ldots, D$, we define the lattice of dimension $D+1$ spanned by the vector $(u'_1, \ldots, u'_D, 1/n)$ and the D vectors $(0, \ldots, 0, n, 0, \ldots, 0, 0)$. In these last vectors, the value n appears iteratively from position 1 to position D, up to the exhaustion of the set. Then, the lattice vector closest to $(v_1, \ldots, v_D, 0)$ is likely to be $(u'_1 x \bmod n, \ldots, u'_D x \bmod n, x/n)$. Indeed, the Euclidean distance between them is about $(n/2^\ell)\sqrt{D}$ and the volume of the lattice is n^{D-1}. Since such a short distance is quite unusual in a volume of this size, this is likely to be indeed the closest vector. If it is found, then x can be deduced.

4.4 Feasibility of the Latter Attack

The latter attack is the most intricate and demanding of all the attacks in this section. Thus, we endeavored in studying its practical feasibility. We hereby report our findings.

Implementation Details. In our implementation, we used a modified version of the lattice reduction of HNP in [5]: the basis reduction is done with the BKZ

(Block Korkin-Zolotarev) [36] algorithm[6], and the closest vector is found using Babai's *closest plane* algorithm [3]. These algorithms are implemented in NTL [37] and, in our coding of the attack, we use these implementations.

Implementation Results. In our implementation, we are mainly interested in the number of protocol sessions needed to perform the attack, for a given length of the modulus. Table 1 reports the above aim, together with the variation of several key parameters presented in the previous section. When we called the BKZ algorithm with its default NTL parameters, we obtained the respective number of protocol sessions reported in the table. When we manually tuned some of BKZ's parameters through extensive experiments, we succeeded in a slight reduction in this number of sessions. This improvement is reported with underlined figures in our table of results (i.e., in line 3, we show a drop from 2^{16} to 2^{15} in number of sessions, through adjusting BKZ's calling-parameters).

Note that—up to some point—we can achieve a time/accuracy trade-off (and implicitly lower ℓ). Namely, one can β-*block reduce*[7] the basis of a lattice to get much better closest vector solutions [36], where β is at most the size of the lattice (in our case, we have $\beta = D + 1$, with $D \in \mathcal{O}(\sqrt{\log n})$ as in the table). If the size of the modulus is small, β will increase, but we can always increase D to lower ℓ (and require less sessions), and choose a sensible value for β. This trade-off can reduce the number of sessions by a few, but it can dramatically increase the running time. These facts were also confirmed experimentally. In the implemented attack, we took $\ell' = 3$. Below, we report values that yield efficient attacks.

Table 1. Number of Sessions per Modulus Size

Prime size	ℓ	D	β	# sessions	Time (s)
8	3	$\lfloor 6\sqrt{\log n} \rfloor = 12$	13	2^{12}	0.002
16	4	$\lfloor 6\sqrt{\log n} \rfloor = 24$	25	2^{14}	0.005
32	4	$\lfloor 6\sqrt{\log n} \rfloor = 30$	31	2^{14}	0.357
64	5	$\lfloor 3\sqrt{\log n} \rfloor = 24$	25	$2^{16}, \underline{2^{15}}$	0.18
128	5	$\lfloor 6\sqrt{\log n} \rfloor = 66$	31	2^{17}	71
256	7	$\lfloor 6\sqrt{\log n} \rfloor = 96$	25	$2^{20}, \underline{2^{19}}$	267
512	9	$\lfloor 5\sqrt{\log n} \rfloor = 110$	20	$2^{26}, \underline{2^{21}}$	1920
1024	15	$\lfloor 3\sqrt{\log n} \rfloor = 96$	23	$2^{32}, \underline{2^{27}}$	1616

In the above table, we present the results for the attack working with a probability greater than or equal to 7/8 (i.e., we took $\ell' = 3$). The last column indicates the running time it took to find the secret on a 2GHz Dual Core processor with

---

[6] This algorithm is a generalization of the famous LLL algorithm [28], from blocks of size 2 to blocks of larger sizes.

[7] Vaguely speaking, a lattice basis is block reduced with block size β if for every β consecutive vectors, the orthogonal projections of them in the span of some previous vectors are reduced in the sense of Hermite and Korkin-Zolotarev [35].

4GB of RAM, given the ℓ most significant bits of the key (with ℓ respectively reported in the table).

There may be further optimization to perform onto our implementation. For instance, there is the new BKZ 2.0 [12] that could be implemented separately (i.e., it is not available in NTL). This could yield faster, more accurate solutions for the CVP, which in itself could allow β to go higher. With such a reduced basis, for a higher β, one could replace NTL's versions of Babai's Nearest Plane algorithm (found in NTL) with more efficient algorithms for the CVP such as Enum [1]. We feel however that this is a project in its own right, concerning optimizations of lattice-based implementations, which is out of our scope. Through this section, we desired to show that our computationally most expensive attack could still be deployed in practice, with a significant yet not impossible effort.

5   On Strengthening/Fixing DBENC (and DB in General)

As we showed, the DBENC protocols (e.g., variants of Reid *et al.* [34]) are vulnerable to reasonable MiM attacks. In this section, we assess the possible (existent or to-be-found) alternative.

DBPK appeared with the aim of protecting against terrorist-fraud [15]. Some other protocols followed its path in more recent years. We briefly discuss now such descendants and their countermeasures to attacks. On the one hand, the Swiss-Knife protocol [25] can counter terrorist fraud, and—by using a MAC and a secret sharing scheme—it eliminates the pattern of insecurity by Kim [25] that we extend to full statistical attacks in here. On the other hand, the Tu and Piramuthu protocol [39] is fully susceptible to the type of attacks described in here (see [31] for more on the insecurity of Tu and Piramuthu's protocol). As per the actual DBPK protocol itself, we also consider that a first way in which it could improve its insecurity status consists of changing the proof of knowledge into the authentication of the protocol exchanges. Another way is that of employing different encryption functions or other cryptographic primitives to those proposed by the authors.

Unfortunately, changing the encryption to some more involved scheme leads to other vulnerabilities against terrorist fraud, as shown by Hancke [20].

Most importantly, the sad aspect in DB is that most arguments of security (and insecurity for that matter) are heuristic. And, other, completely different patterns of attacks have been exposed recently [6] for a large class of DB protocols. That attack pattern demolished the PRF assumption, which has been voidly invoked in some security arguments for DB protocols. In that sense, even in the Bussard-Bagga protocol, it should not be sufficient to replace the encryption by a PRF in a vacuous manner, i.e., with no further conditions/proofs.

We personally consider that the solution of basing the responses on pre-established sub-secrets and on secrets by using a secret sharing scheme [2] (along with other assessed modifications) is viable.

Nevertheless, this brief encounter into the status of DBPK-Log and DBPK's descendants goes to show that the threats exhibited are real and should carefully be considered, especially in implementations of (these terrorist-fraud protecting) DB.

Consequently, we emphasize that what is really missing is a clear, sound security model for DB, where resistance to terrorist-fraud and resistance to MiM can *provably* co-exist.

6   Conclusions

In this paper, we raise the signal that distance fraud, terrorist fraud, and MiM attacks can be launched against allegedly secure existing distance-bounding protocols. We show intricate applications of this attack-scenario, using statistical and theoretical analyses. These concrete frauds are respectively performed against the different proposed instantiations and successors of the DBPK distance-bounding protocols [8–10]. We present a distance fraud and a terrorist fraud against DBPK-Log, thus disproving its very purpose. Our non-narrow MiM adversaries can therein retrieve all or several bits of the secret key, depending on the used encryption scheme in the respective instantiation of DBENC, i.e. variants of Reid *et al.* [34]. We present an implementation and short evaluation of the most demanding of these attacks. Our results show that a bad choice of the encryption function inside concrete instantiations of proposed protocol-schemas can lead to MiM attacks. This vouches for our feeling that this serious attack-strategy possibly finds applications in many other DB protocols. Simple fixes (replacing the encryption with a PRF) may not be the way forward either [6], since the core issue is the absence of necessary and sufficient conditions to describe DB security. Further, this dwells within the lack of sound, clear security models for DB with accompanying provably secure protocols. We herein provide some cases in point.

Acknowledgements. This work was partially supported by

- the National Competence Center in Research on Mobile Information and Communication Systems (NCCR-MICS), under the Swiss National Science Foundation;
- the European Commission through the ICT program under contract ICT-2007-216646 ECRYPT II;
- the Marie Curie IEF Project "PPIDR: Privacy-Preserving Intrusion Detection and Response in Wireless Communications", Grant No. 252323.

References

1. Hanrot, G., Pujol, X., Stehlé, D.: Algorithms for the shortest and closest lattice vector problems. In: Chee, Y.M., Guo, Z., Ling, S., Shao, F., Tang, Y., Wang, H., Xing, C. (eds.) IWCC 2011. LNCS, vol. 6639, pp. 159–190. Springer, Heidelberg (2011)
2. Avoine, G., Lauradoux, C., Martin, B.: How Secret-sharing can Defeat Terrorist Fraud. In: Proceedings of the 4th ACM Conference on Wireless Network Security – WiSec 2011, Hamburg, Germany. ACM Press (June 2011)

3. Babai, L.: On Lovász' lattice reduction and the nearest lattice point problem. Combinatorica 6(1), 1–13 (1986)

4. Beth, T., Desmedt, Y.: Identification tokens – or: Solving the chess grandmaster problem. In: Menezes, A., Vanstone, S.A. (eds.) CRYPTO 1990. LNCS, vol. 537, pp. 169–176. Springer, Heidelberg (1991)

5. Boneh, D., Venkatesan, R.: Hardness of Computing the Most Significant Bits of Secret Keys in Diffie-Hellman and Related Schemes. In: Koblitz, N. (ed.) CRYPTO 1996. LNCS, vol. 1109, pp. 129–142. Springer, Heidelberg (1996)

6. Boureanu, I., Mitrokotsa, A., Vaudenay, S.: On the Pseudorandom Function Assumption in (Secure) Distance-Bounding Protocols. In: Hevia, A., Neven, G. (eds.) LATINCRYPT 2012. LNCS, vol. 7533, pp. 100–120. Springer, Heidelberg (2012)

7. Brands, S., Chaum, D.: Distance-Bounding Protocols (Extended Abstract). In: Helleseth, T. (ed.) EUROCRYPT 1993. LNCS, vol. 765, pp. 344–359. Springer, Heidelberg (1994)

8. Bussard, L.: Trust Establishment Protocols for Communicating Devices. PhD thesis, Ecole Nationale Supérieure des Télécommunications, Institut Eurécom, Télécom Paris (2004)

9. Bussard, L., Bagga, W.: Distance-Bounding Proof of Knowledge Protocols to Avoid Terrorist Fraud Attacks. Technical Report RR-04-109, Institute EURECOM (May 2004)

10. Bussard, L., Bagga, W.: Distance-bounding proof of knowledge to avoid real-time attacks. In: Sasaki, R., Qing, S., Okamoto, E., Yoshiura, H. (eds.) Security and Privacy in the Age of Ubiquitous Computing. IFIP, vol. 181, pp. 223–238. Springer, Boston (2005)

11. Čapkun, S., Buttyán, L., Hubaux, J.-P.: SECTOR: Secure Tracking of Node Encounters in Multi-hop Wireless Networks. In: ACM Workshop on Security of Ad Hoc and Sensor Networks - SASN, pp. 21–32 (2003)

12. Chen, Y., Nguyen, P.Q.: BKZ 2.0: Better lattice security estimates. In: Lee, D.H., Wang, X. (eds.) ASIACRYPT 2011. LNCS, vol. 7073, pp. 1–20. Springer, Heidelberg (2011)

13. Chernoff, H.: A measure of asymptotic efficiency for tests of a hypothesis based on the sum of observations. Statistics 23(4), 493–507 (1952)

14. Clulow, J., Hancke, G.P., Kuhn, M.G., Moore, T.: So Near and Yet So Far: Distance-Bounding Attacks in Wireless Networks. In: Buttyán, L., Gligor, V., Westhoff, D. (eds.) ESAS 2006. LNCS, vol. 4357, pp. 83–97. Springer, Heidelberg (2006)

15. Desmedt, Y.: Major Security Problems with the "Unforgeable" (Feige)-Fiat-Shamir Proofs of Identity and How to Overcome Them, Paris, France, March 15-17, pp. 147–159. SEDEP (1988)

16. Drimer, S., Murdoch, S.J.: Keep your enemies close: distance bounding against smartcard relay attacks. In: Proceedings of 16th USENIX Security Symposium, pp. 7:1–7:16. USENIX Association, Berkeley (2007)

17. Francillon, A., Danev, B., Čapkun, S.: Relay attacks on passive keyless entry and start systems in modern cars. Cryptology ePrint Archive, Report 2010/332 (2010), http://eprint.iacr.org/

18. Gezici, S., Tian, Z., Biannakis, G.B., Kobayashi, H., Molisch, A.F., Poor, V., Sahinoglu, Z.: Localization via ultra-wideband radius: a look at positioning aspects for future sensor networks. IEEE Signal Processing Magazine 22(4), 70–84 (2005)

19. Gilbert, H., Robshaw, M., Sibert, H.: An Active Attack Against HB+ - A Provably Secure Lightweight Authentication Protocol. Technical report, IACR Cryptology ePrint Archive 237 (2005)

20. Hancke, G.: Distance-bounding for RFID: Effectiveness of 'terrorist fraud' in the presence of bit errors. In: IEEE International Conference on RFID-Technology and Applications – IEEE RFID TA 2012. IEEE Press, Nice (2012)
21. Hancke, G.P., Kuhn, M.G.: An RFID Distance Bounding Protocol. In: SECURECOMM, pp. 67–73 (2005)
22. Hoeffding, W.: Probability Inequalities for Sums of Bounded Random Variables. Journal of the American Statistical Association 58(301), 13–30 (1963)
23. Juels, A., Weis, S.A.: Authenticating Pervasive Devices with Human Protocols. In: Shoup, V. (ed.) CRYPTO 2005. LNCS, vol. 3621, pp. 293–308. Springer, Heidelberg (2005)
24. Kim, C.H., Avoine, G.: RFID Distance Bounding Protocol with Mixed Challenges to Prevent Relay Attacks. In: Garay, J.A., Miyaji, A., Otsuka, A. (eds.) CANS 2009. LNCS, vol. 5888, pp. 119–133. Springer, Heidelberg (2009)
25. Kim, C.H., Avoine, G., Koeune, F., Standaert, F.-X., Pereira, O.: The Swiss-Knife RFID Distance Bounding Protocol. In: Lee, P.J., Cheon, J.H. (eds.) ICISC 2008. LNCS, vol. 5461, pp. 98–115. Springer, Heidelberg (2009)
26. Kuhn, M., Luecken, H., Tippenhauer, N.O.: UWB Impulse Radio Based Distance Bounding. In: Proceedings of the 7th Workshop on Positioning, Navigation and Communication 2010, WPNC 2010 (2010)
27. Lee, J.-Y., Scholtz, R.A.: Ranging in a Dense Multipath Environment using an UWB Radio Link. IEEE Journal on Selected Areas in Communications 20(9) (2002)
28. Lenstra, A.K., Lenstra, H.W., Lovász, L.: Factoring Polynomials with Rational Coefficients. Mathematische Annalen 261, 515–534 (1982), 10.1007/BF01457454
29. Meadows, C., Syverson, P., Chang, L.: Towards More Efficient Distance Bounding Protocols for Use in Sensor Networks. In: Proceedings of the International Conference on Security and Privacy in Communication Networks (SECURECOMM 2006), pp. 1–5 (2006)
30. Munilla, J., Peinado, A.: Distance Bounding Protocols for RFID Enhanced by Using Void-challenges and Analysis in Noisy Channels. Wireless Communications and Mobile Computing 8, 1227–1232 (2008)
31. Munilla, J., Peinado, A.: Security Analysis of Tu and Piramuthu's Protocol. In: New Technologies, Mobility and Security – NTMS 2008, Tangier, Morocco, pp. 1–5. IEEE Computer Society (November 2008)
32. Nguyen, P.Q., Shparlinski, I.: The Insecurity of the Digital Signature Algorithm with Partially Known Nonces. J. Cryptology 15(3), 151–176 (2002)
33. Nikov, V., Vauclair, M.: Yet Another Secure Distance-Bounding Protocol. In: Proceedings of the Conference on Security and Cryptography (SECRYPT 2008), pp. 218–221 (July 2008)
34. Reid, J., Gonzalez Nieto, J.M., Tang, T., Senadji, B.: Detecting Relay Attacks with Timing-based Protocols. In: ASIACCS 2007: Proceedings of the 2nd ACM Symposium on Information, Computer and Communications Security, pp. 204–213. ACM (2007)
35. Schnorr, C.P.: Block Reduced Lattice Bases and Successive Minima. Combinatorics, Probability and Computing 3(04), 507–522 (1994)
36. Schnorr, C.P., Euchner, M.: Lattice Basis Reduction: Improved Practical Algorithms and Solving Subset Sum Problems. Math. Programming, 181–191 (1993)
37. Shoup, V.: NTL: A Library for Doing Number Theory, http://shoup.net/ntl
38. Singelée, D., Preneel, B.: Location Verification Using Secure Distance Bounding Protocols. In: Proceedings of the IEEE International Conference on Mobile Adhoc and Sensor Systems (MASS 2005), pp. 834–840 (2005)

39. Tu, Y.-J., Piramuthu, S.: RFID Distance Bounding Protocols. In: First International EURASIP Workshop on RFID Technology (2007)
40. Vaudenay, S.: On Privacy Models for RFID. In: Kurosawa, K. (ed.) ASIACRYPT 2007. LNCS, vol. 4833, pp. 68–87. Springer, Heidelberg (2007)

A   Appendix

If $X_1, \ldots, X_n$ are independent Bernoulli random variables with $X_k \in \{0, 1\}$ and $\mathbb{P}[X_k = 1] = \mu$ for all k, then

$$\mathbb{P}\left[\sum_{k=1}^n X_k \geq u\right] = \sum_{k=0}^u \binom{n}{k} \mu^k (1-\mu)^{n-k}. \tag{4}$$

This probability can be bounded via *Hoeffding's inequality* [22], i.e.,:

Lemma 1 (Hoeffding Bound). *For independent random variables $X_1, \ldots, X_n$ such that $X_i \in [a_i, b_i]$, with $\mu_i \triangleq \mathbb{E}\,X_i$ and $t > 0$,*

$$\mathbb{P}\left[\sum_{i=1}^n X_i \geq \sum_{i=1}^n \mu_i + nt\right] = \mathbb{P}\left(\sum_{i=1}^n X_i \leq \sum_{i=1}^n \mu_i - nt\right) \leq \exp\left(-\frac{2n^2 t^2}{\sum_{i=1}^n (b_i - a_i)^2}\right).$$

Lemma 2 (Chernoff Bound [13]). *For independent Bernoulli random variables $X_1, \ldots, X_n$ with $\mathbb{P}[X_i = 1] = \mu > 1/2$, then the probability of simultaneous occurrence of more that $n/2$ of the events $\{X_k = 1\}$ has a lower bound, namely*

$$P \geq 1 - \exp(-2n(\mu - 1/2)^2).$$

Author Index